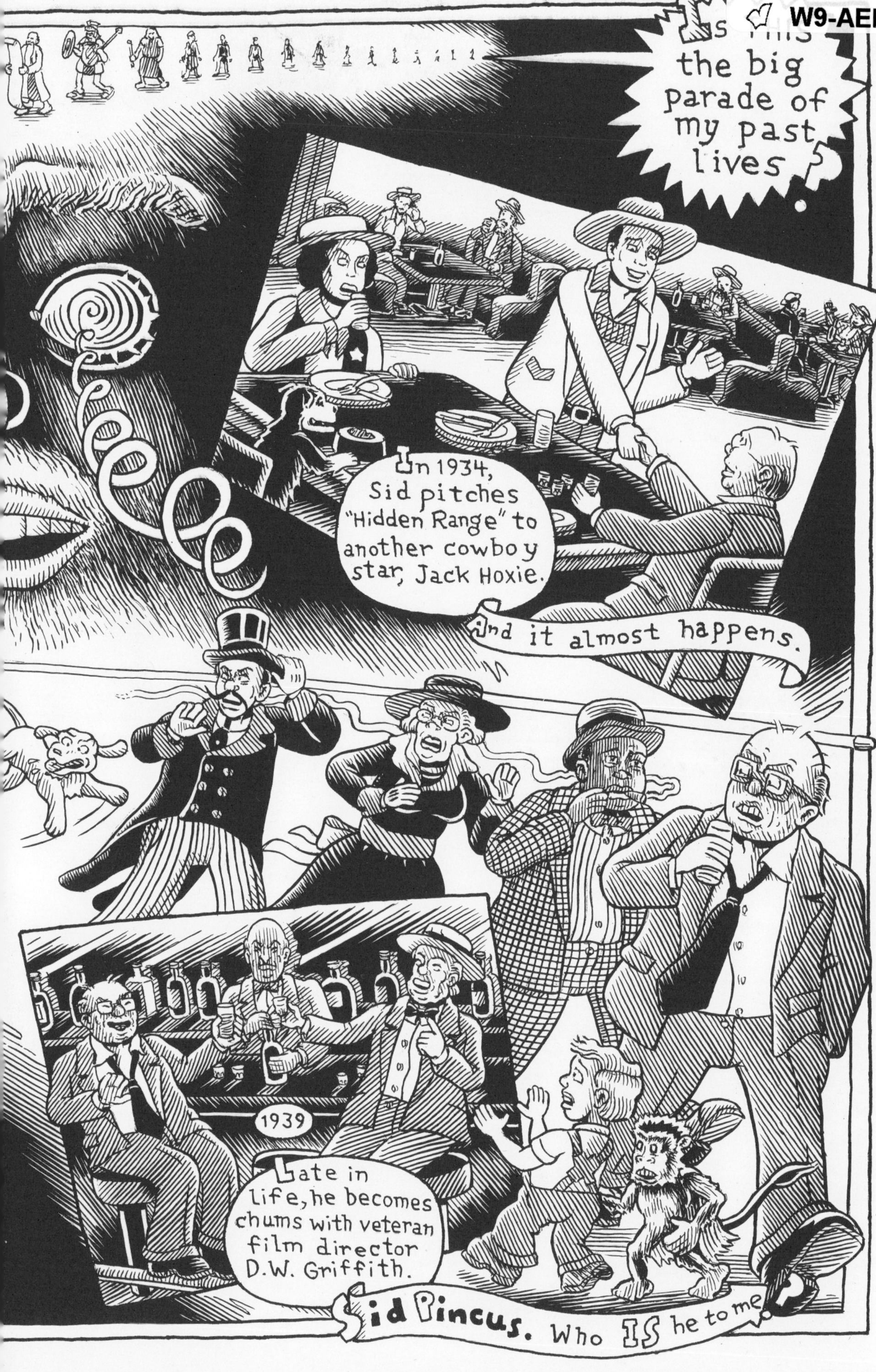
Is this the big parade of my past lives?
In 1934, Sid pitches "Hidden Range" to another cowboy star, Jack Hoxie.
And it almost happens.
1939
Late in life, he becomes chums with veteran film director D.W. Griffith.
Sid Pincus. Who IS he to me?

Reincarnation Stories

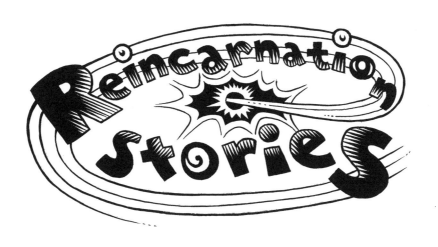

This book is dedicated to my wonderful wife Pam. Special thanks to everyone at Fantagraphics for doing such a great job and in particular, Keeli McCarthy.

Editor: Gary Groth
Editorial Assistance: Conrad Groth
Design: Kim Deitch and Keeli McCarthy
Production: Preston White
Associate Publisher: Eric Reynolds
Publisher: Gary Groth

Fantagraphics Books, Inc.
7563 Lake City Way NE
Seattle, WA 98115

ISBN: 978-1-68396-261-8
Library of Congress Control Number: 2019933495
First Fantagraphics Books edition: August 2019
Printed in Korea

Reincarnation Stories

BY Kim Deitch

FANTAGRAPHICS BOOKS

Table of Contents

What does it all Mean? ———— page 6

Shrine of the Monkey God! ———— page 24

PLOT ROBOT (Part 1.) ———— page 48

(Part 2.) Hidden Range by Sidney Pincus — page 60

THE JACK HOXIE SHOW ———— page 86

"If It's Weird It Works" ———— page 124

Young Avatar! ———— page 134

What it all means! ———— page 176

Appendix

Kitten on the **Keys!** ———— page 212

WHO WAS SPAIN? ———— page 224

Who was Buck Jones? ———— page 235

Who was Jack Hoxie? ———— page 243
Who **IS Pam Butler?** —— page 246
His eye is on the Pigeon. —— page 250
What is the **Plot Robot?** — page 253
Um tut …. ———— page 256
In the Works ……… ———— page 258

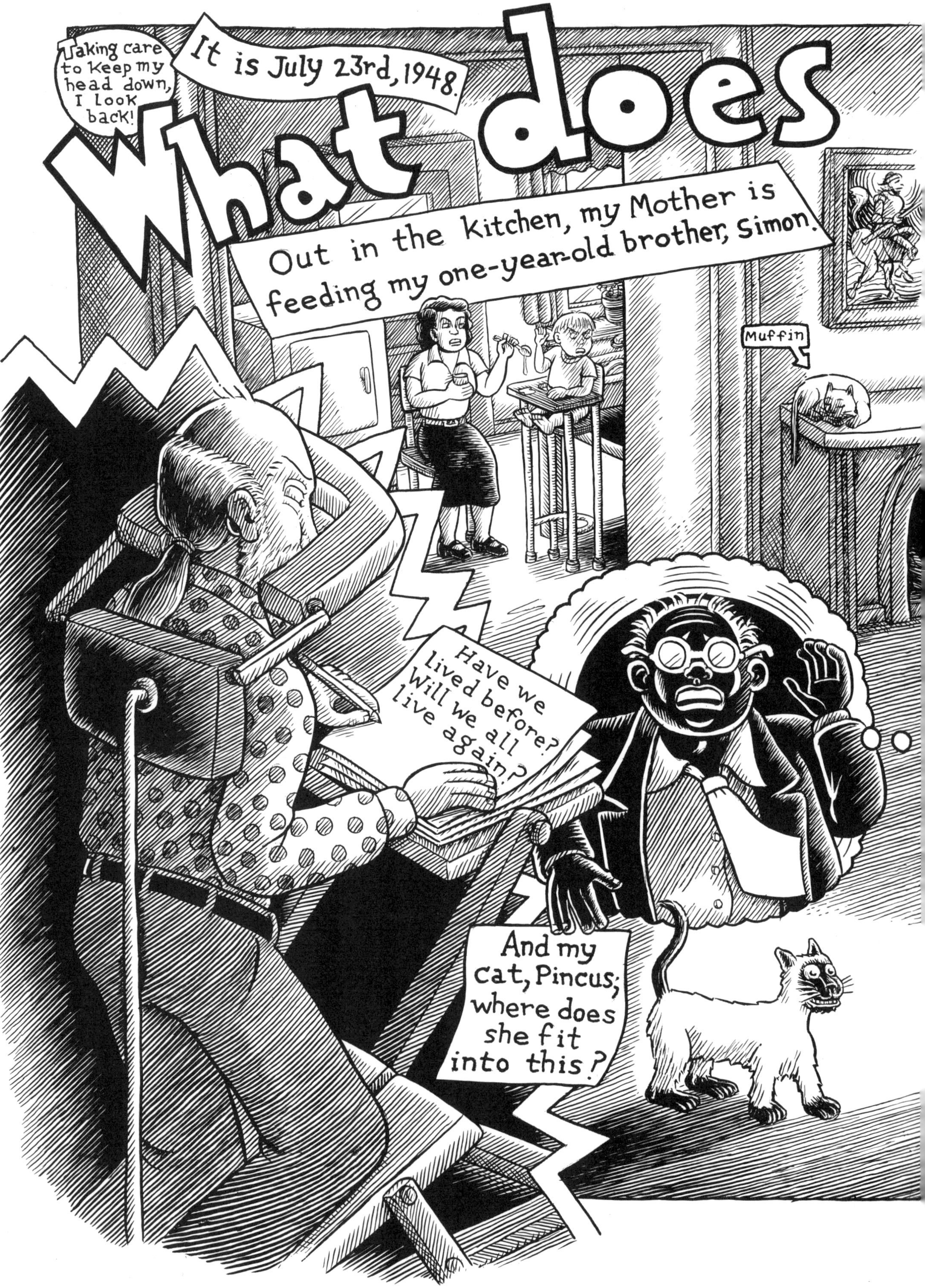

Taking care to keep my head down, I look back!
It is July 23rd, 1948.
What does
Out in the kitchen, my Mother is feeding my one-year-old brother, Simon.
Muffin
Have we lived before? Will we all live again?
And my cat, Pincus; where does she fit into this?

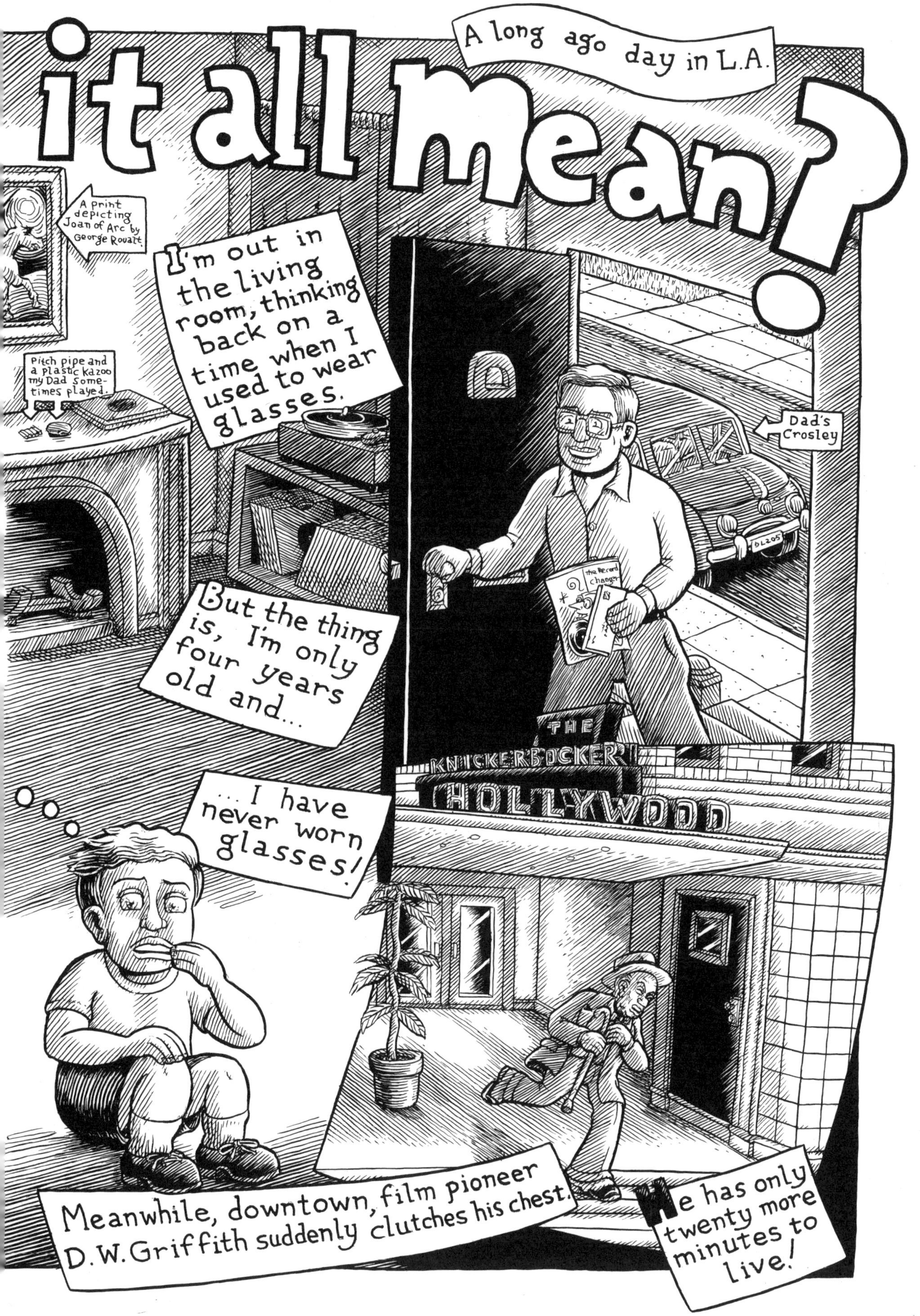
it all mean?
A long ago day in L.A.
A print depicting Joan of Arc by George Rouault
Pitch pipe and a plastic kazoo my Dad sometimes played.
I'm out in the living room, thinking back on a time when I used to wear glasses.
Dad's Crosley
DL205
the Record Changer
But the thing is, I'm only four years old and...
...I have never worn glasses!
THE KNICKERBOCKER HOLLYWOOD
Meanwhile, downtown, film pioneer D.W. Griffith suddenly clutches his chest.
He has only twenty more minutes to live!

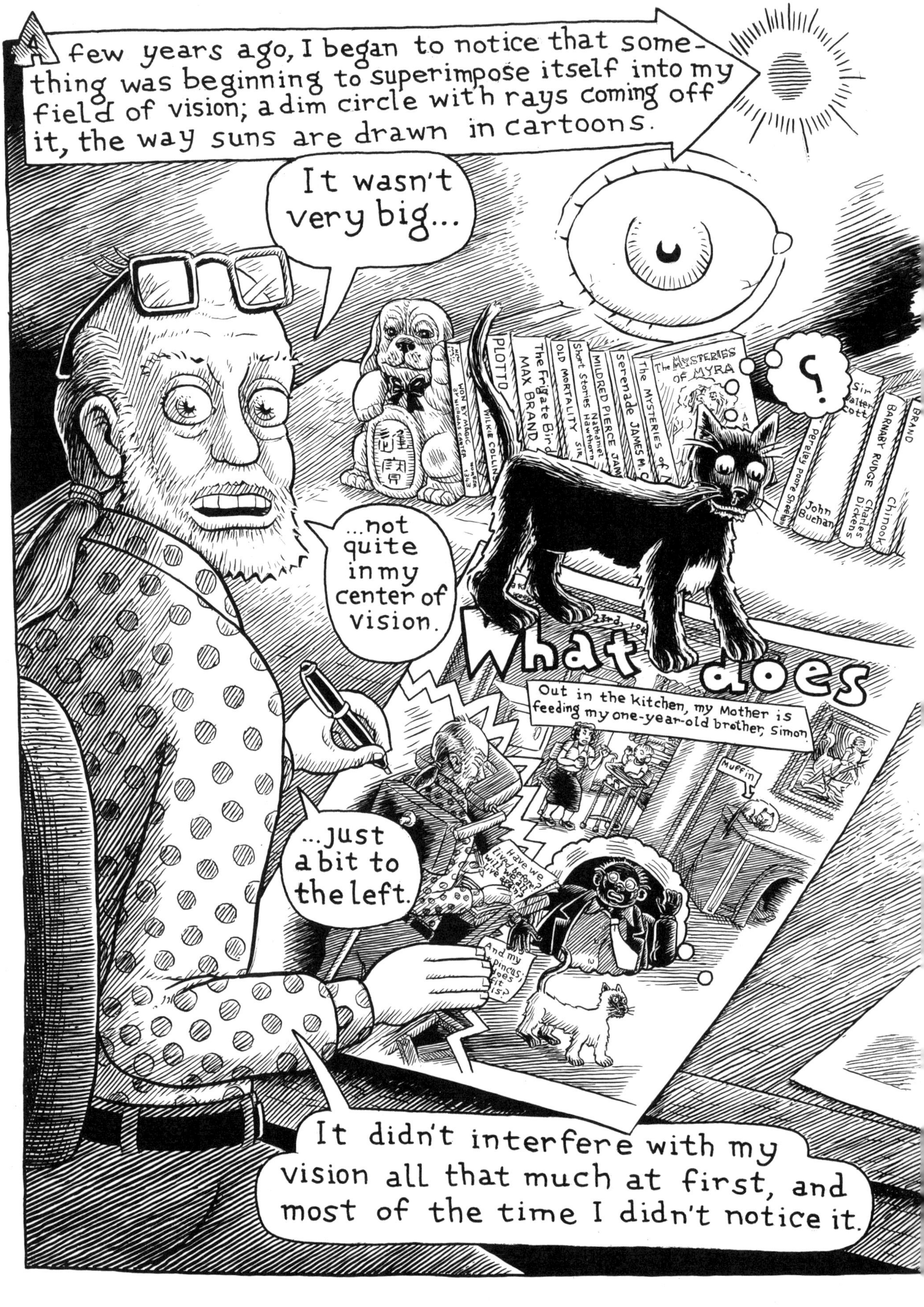
A few years ago, I began to notice that something was beginning to superimpose itself into my field of vision; a dim circle with rays coming off it, the way suns are drawn in cartoons.
It wasn't very big...
...not quite in my center of vision.
...just a bit to the left.
What does
Out in the kitchen, my Mother is feeding my one-year-old brother, Simon
Muffin
It didn't interfere with my vision all that much at first, and most of the time I didn't notice it.

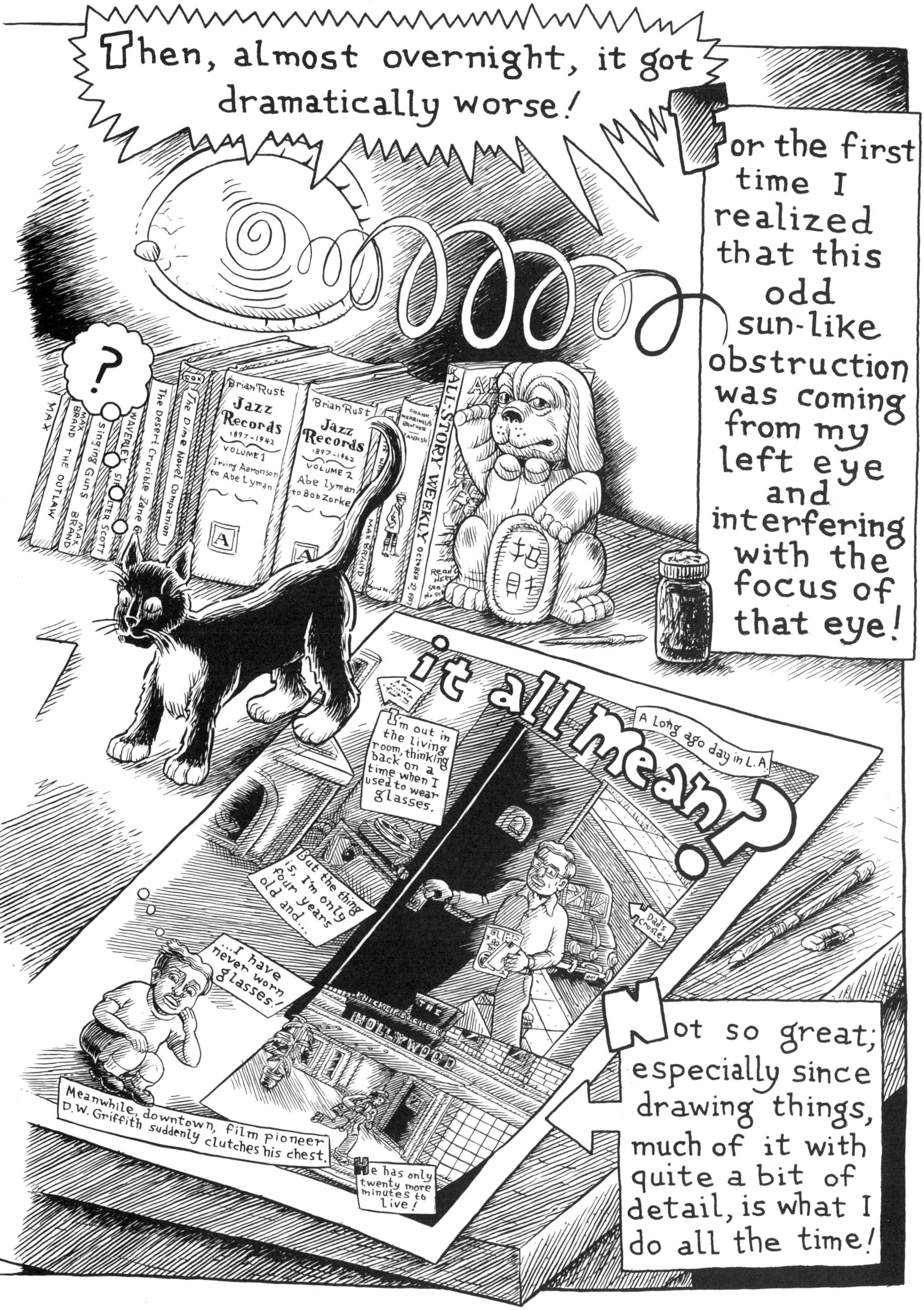
Then, almost overnight, it got dramatically worse!
For the first time I realized that this odd sun-like obstruction was coming from my left eye and interfering with the focus of that eye!
?
Brian Rust Jazz Records 1897-1942 Volume 1 Irving Aaronson to Abe Lyman
Brian Rust Jazz Records 1897-1942 Volume 2 Abe Lyman to Bob Zorke
The Dime Novel Companion
The Desert Crucible Zane G
Waverley
Walter Scott
Singing Guns Max Brand
Max Brand The Outlaw
All-Story Weekly
it all mean?
A long ago day in L.A.
I'm out in the living room, thinking back on a time when I used to wear glasses.
But the thing is, I'm only four years old and...
...I have never worn glasses!
Dad's Crosley
Hollywood
Meanwhile, downtown, film pioneer D.W. Griffith suddenly clutches his chest.
He has only twenty more minutes to live!
Not so great; especially since drawing things, much of it with quite a bit of detail, is what I do all the time!

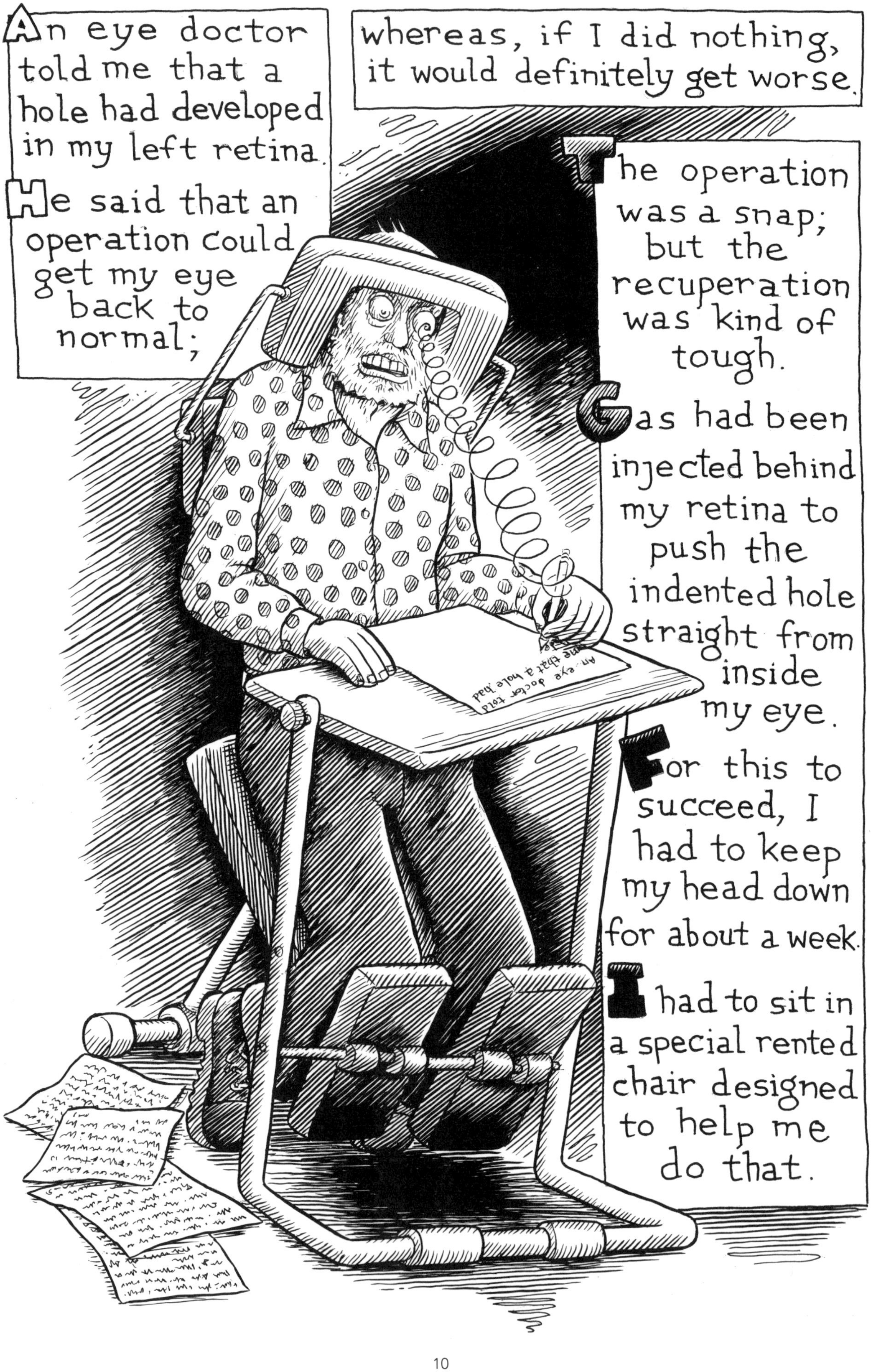
An eye doctor told me that a hole had developed in my left retina.
He said that an operation could get my eye back to normal;
whereas, if I did nothing, it would definitely get worse.
The operation was a snap; but the recuperation was kind of tough.
Gas had been injected behind my retina to push the indented hole straight from inside my eye.
For this to succeed, I had to keep my head down for about a week.
I had to sit in a special rented chair designed to help me do that.

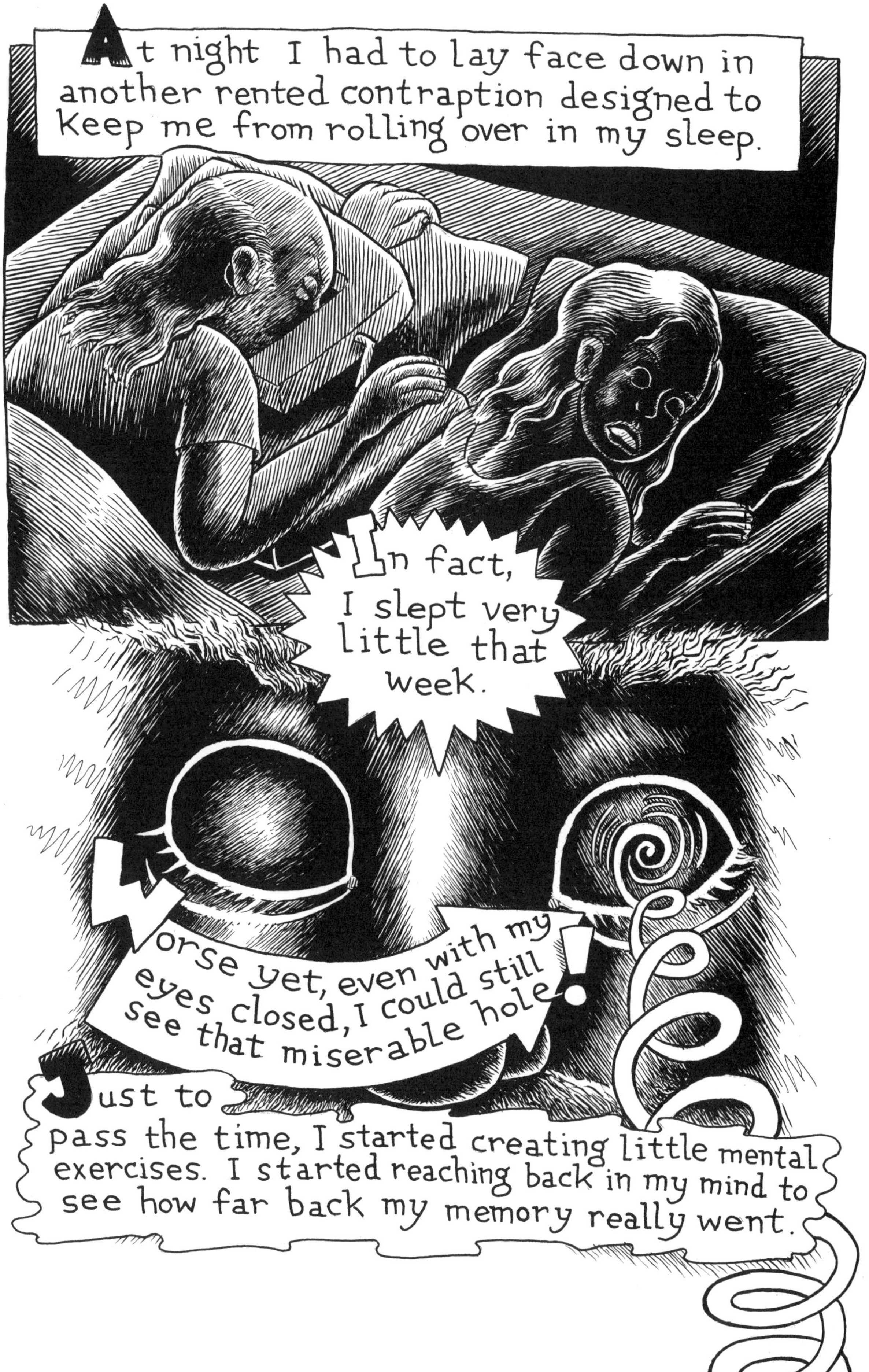
At night I had to lay face down in another rented contraption designed to keep me from rolling over in my sleep.
In fact, I slept very little that week.
Worse yet, even with my eyes closed, I could still see that miserable hole!
Just to pass the time, I started creating little mental exercises. I started reaching back in my mind to see how far back my memory really went.

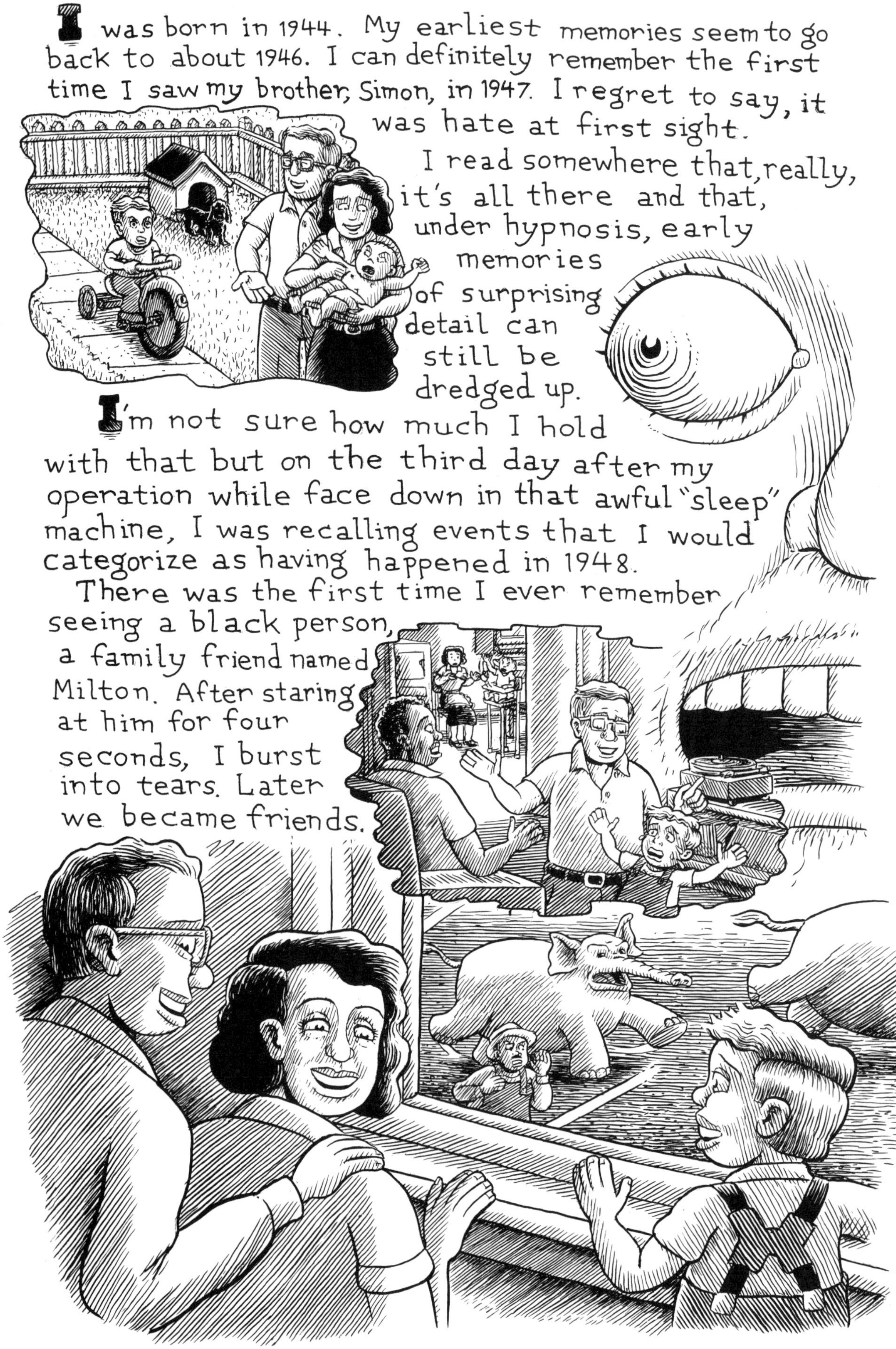
I was born in 1944. My earliest memories seem to go back to about 1946. I can definitely remember the first time I saw my brother, Simon, in 1947. I regret to say, it was hate at first sight.
I read somewhere that, really, it's all there and that, under hypnosis, early memories of surprising detail can still be dredged up.
I'm not sure how much I hold with that but on the third day after my operation while face down in that awful "sleep" machine, I was recalling events that I would categorize as having happened in 1948.
There was the first time I ever remember seeing a black person, a family friend named Milton. After staring at him for four seconds, I burst into tears. Later we became friends.

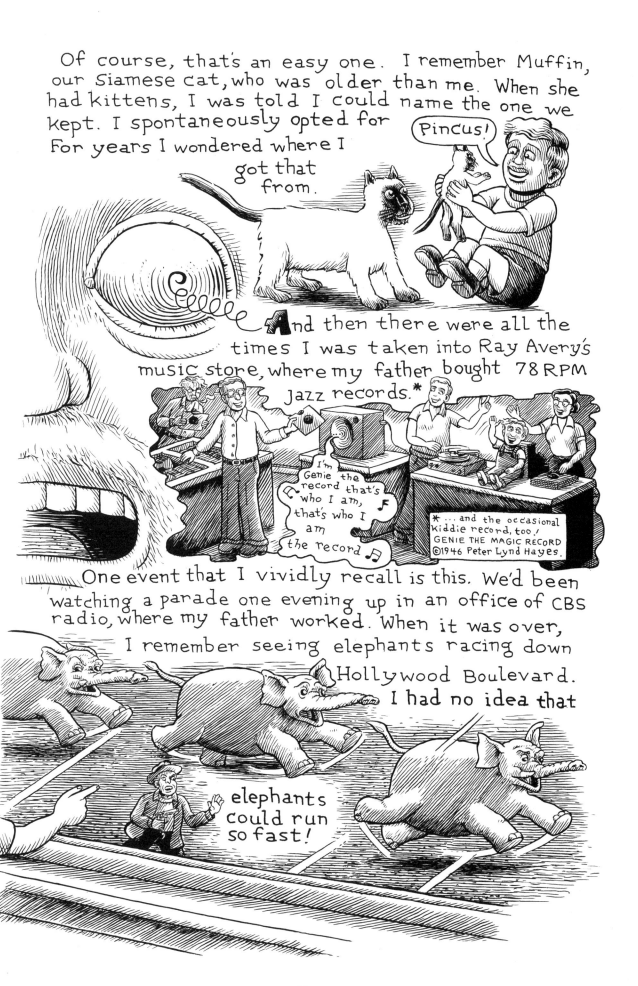

Of course, that's an easy one. I remember Muffin, our Siamese cat, who was older than me. When she had kittens, I was told I could name the one we kept. I spontaneously opted for For years I wondered where I got that from.

Pincus!

And then there were all the times I was taken into Ray Avery's music store, where my father bought 78 RPM jazz records.*

♪ I'm Genie the record that's who I am, that's who I am the record ♪

* ...and the occasional kiddie record, too! GENIE THE MAGIC RECORD ©1946 Peter Lynd Hayes.

One event that I vividly recall is this. We'd been watching a parade one evening up in an office of CBS radio, where my father worked. When it was over, I remember seeing elephants racing down Hollywood Boulevard. I had no idea that

elephants could run so fast!

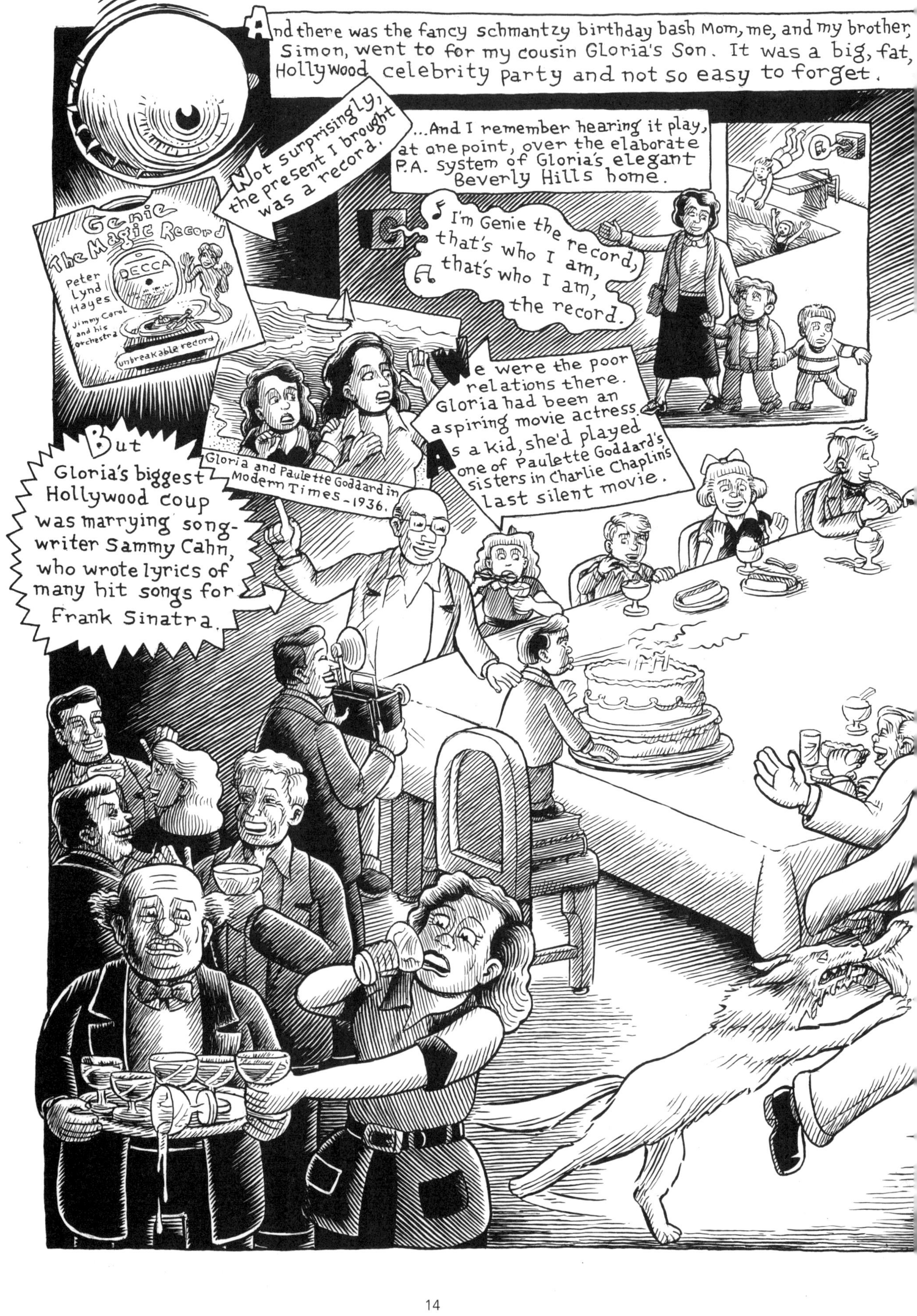
And there was the fancy schmantzy birthday bash Mom, me, and my brother, Simon, went to for my cousin Gloria's Son. It was a big, fat, Hollywood celebrity party and not so easy to forget.
Not surprisingly, the present I brought was a record.
Genie The Magic Record
Peter Lynd Hayes
DECCA
Jimmy Carol and his orchestra
unbreakable record
...And I remember hearing it play, at one point, over the elaborate P.A. system of Gloria's elegant Beverly Hills home.
I'm Genie the record, that's who I am, that's who I am, the record.
We were the poor relations there. Gloria had been an aspiring movie actress. As a kid, she'd played one of Paulette Goddard's sisters in Charlie Chaplin's last silent movie.
Gloria and Paulette Goddard in Modern Times-1936.
But Gloria's biggest Hollywood coup was marrying songwriter Sammy Cahn, who wrote lyrics of many hit songs for Frank Sinatra.

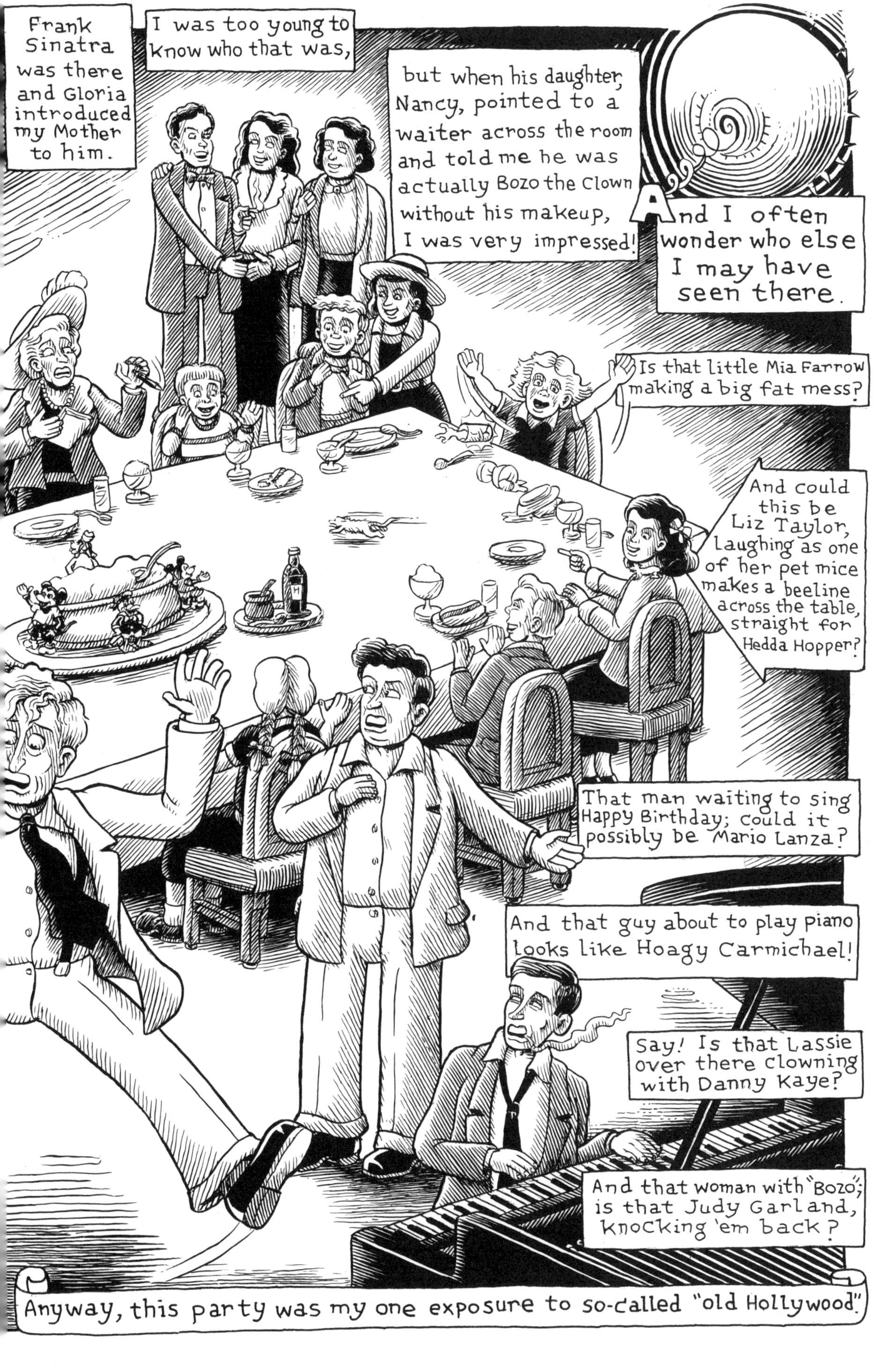

Frank Sinatra was there and Gloria introduced my Mother to him.
I was too young to know who that was,
but when his daughter, Nancy, pointed to a waiter across the room and told me he was actually Bozo the Clown without his makeup, I was very impressed!
And I often wonder who else I may have seen there.
Is that little Mia Farrow making a big fat mess?
And could this be Liz Taylor, laughing as one of her pet mice makes a beeline across the table, straight for Hedda Hopper?
H
That man waiting to sing Happy Birthday; could it possibly be Mario Lanza?
And that guy about to play piano looks like Hoagy Carmichael!
Say! Is that Lassie over there clowning with Danny Kaye?
And that woman with "Bozo," is that Judy Garland, knocking 'em back?
Anyway, this party was my one exposure to so-called "old Hollywood."

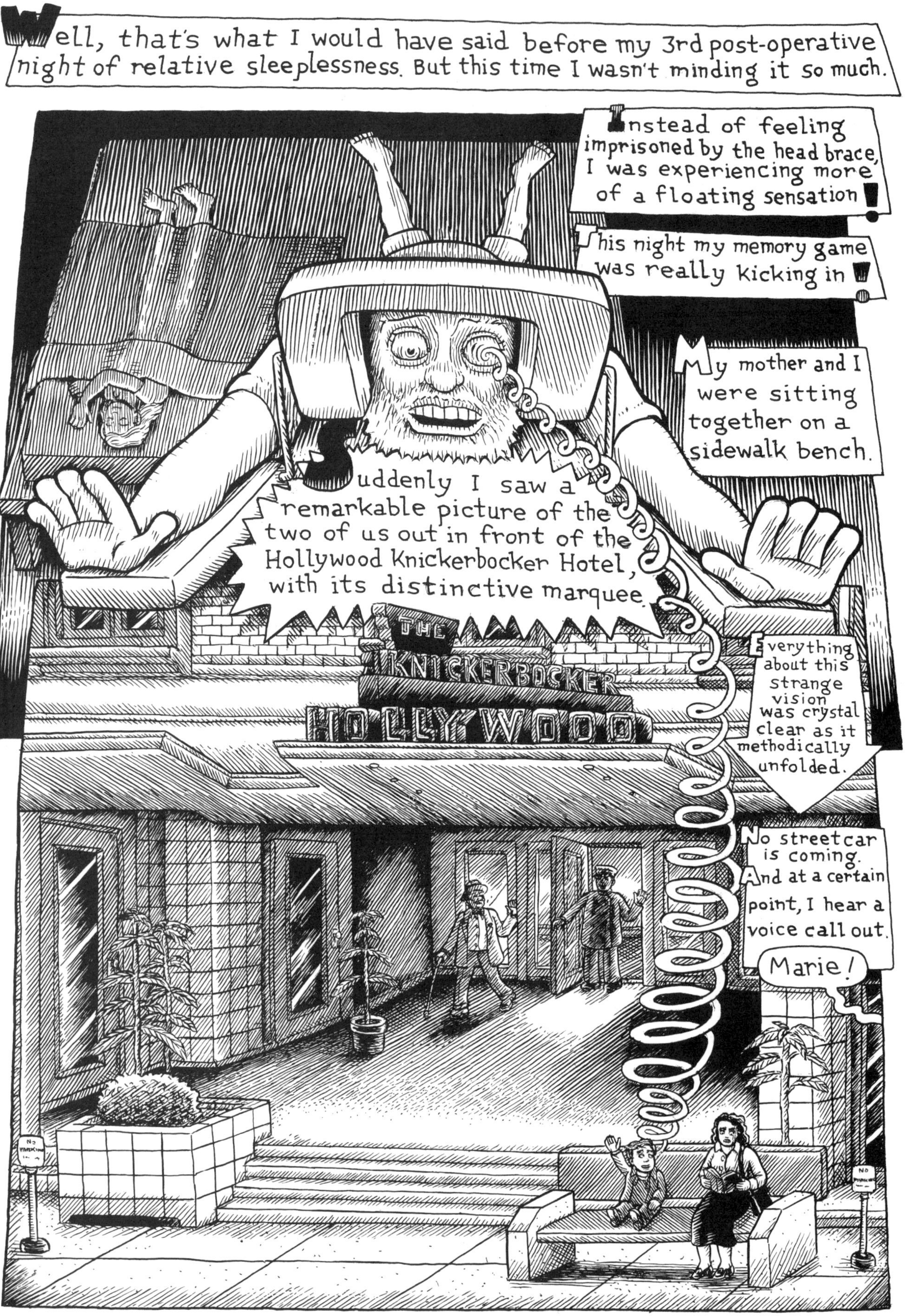
Well, that's what I would have said before my 3rd post-operative night of relative sleeplessness. But this time I wasn't minding it so much.
Instead of feeling imprisoned by the head brace, I was experiencing more of a floating sensation!
This night my memory game was really kicking in!
My mother and I were sitting together on a sidewalk bench.
Suddenly I saw a remarkable picture of the two of us out in front of the Hollywood Knickerbocker Hotel, with its distinctive marquee.
THE KNICKERBOCKER HOLLYWOOD
Everything about this strange vision was crystal clear as it methodically unfolded.
No streetcar is coming. And at a certain point, I hear a voice call out.
Marie!

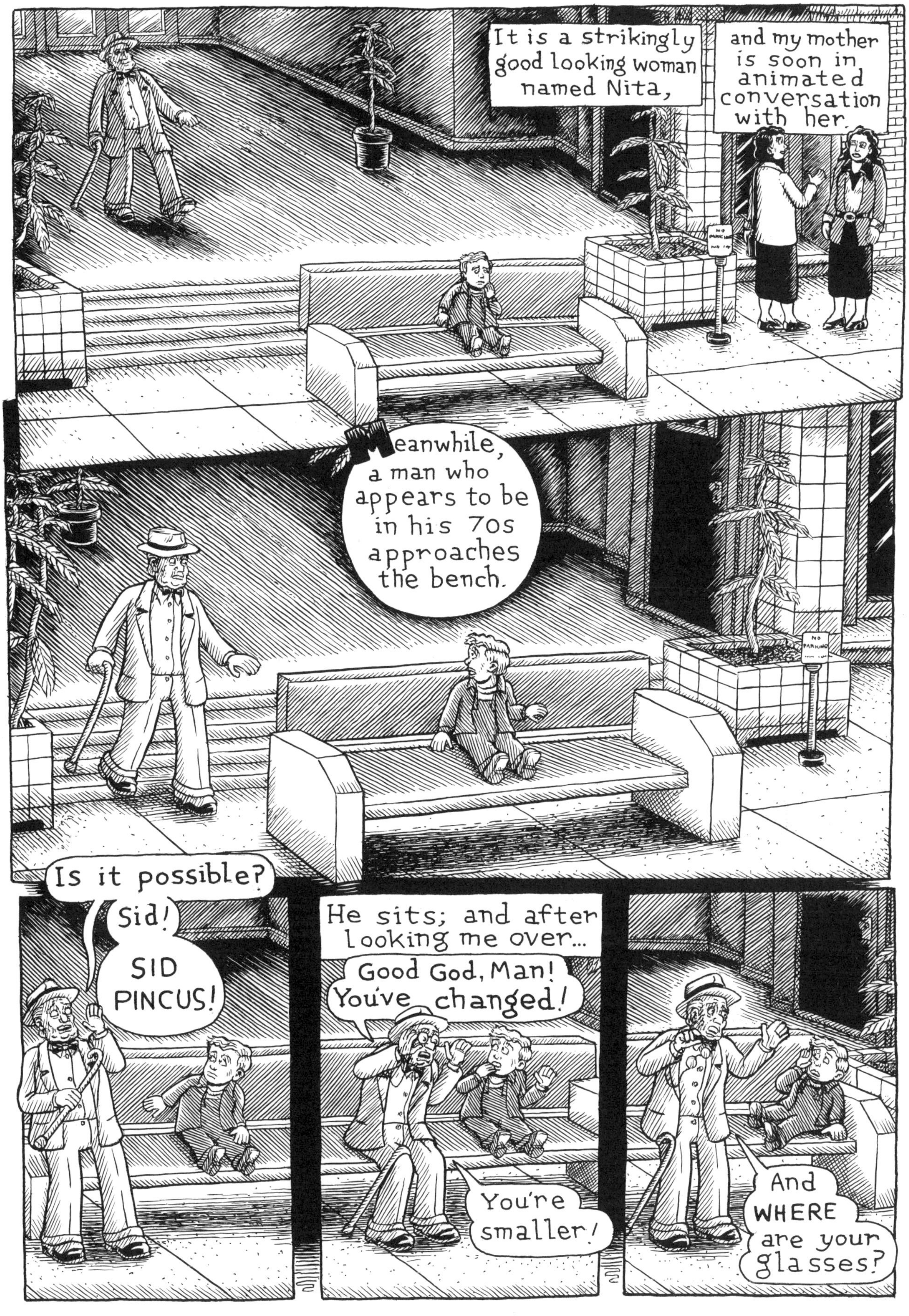
It is a strikingly good looking woman named Nita,
and my mother is soon in animated conversation with her.
Meanwhile, a man who appears to be in his 70s approaches the bench.
Is it possible?
Sid!
SID PINCUS!
He sits; and after looking me over...
Good God, Man! You've changed!
You're smaller!
And WHERE are your glasses?

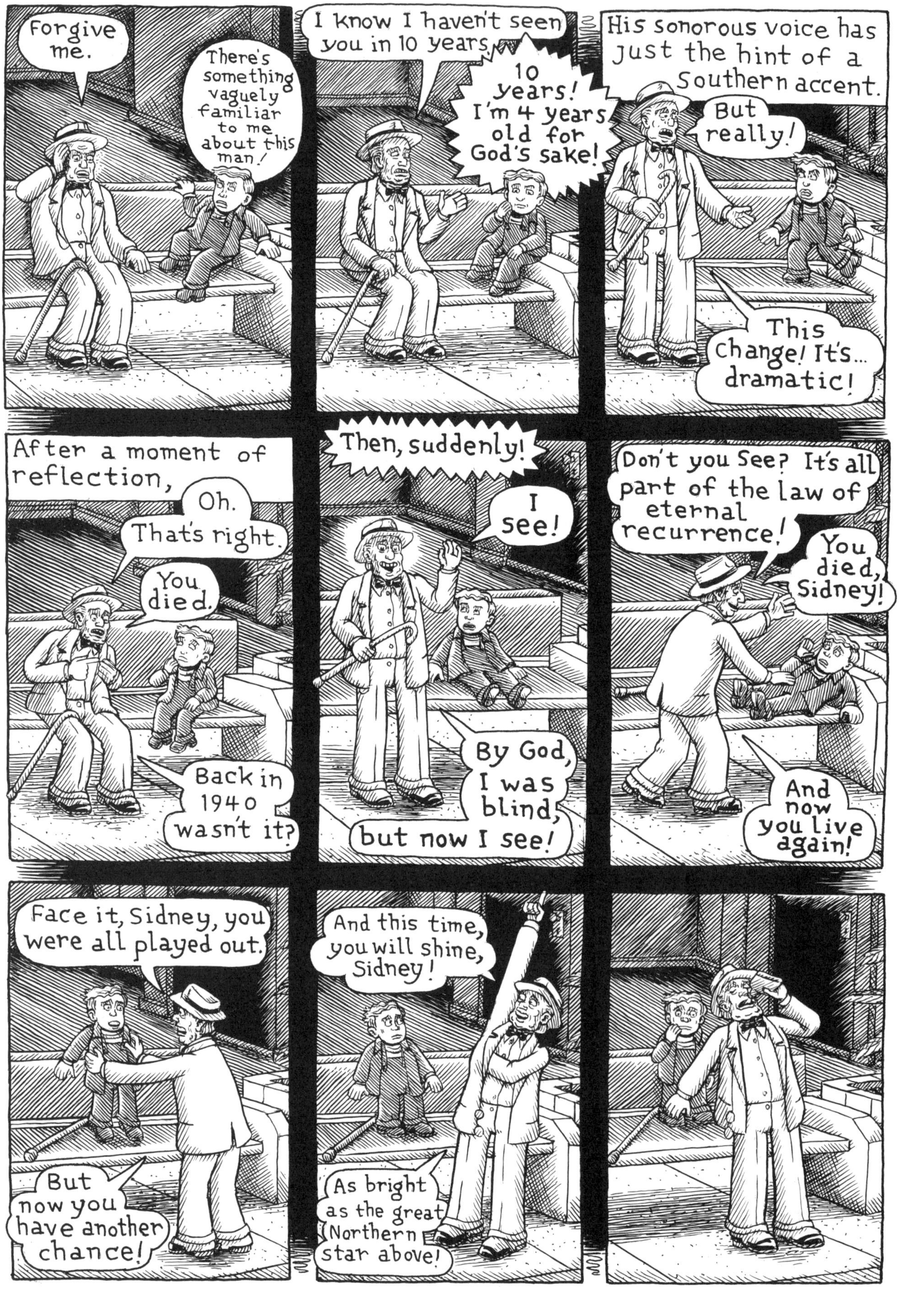

Forgive me.
There's something vaguely familiar to me about this man!
I know I haven't seen you in 10 years,
10 years! I'm 4 years old for God's sake!
His sonorous voice has just the hint of a Southern accent.
But really!
This change! It's... dramatic!
After a moment of reflection,
Oh. That's right.
You died.
Back in 1940 wasn't it?
Then, suddenly!
I see!
By God, I was blind,
but now I see!
Don't you see? It's all part of the law of eternal recurrence!
You died, Sidney!
And now you live again!
Face it, Sidney, you were all played out.
But now you have another chance!
And this time, you will shine, Sidney!
As bright as the great Northern star above!

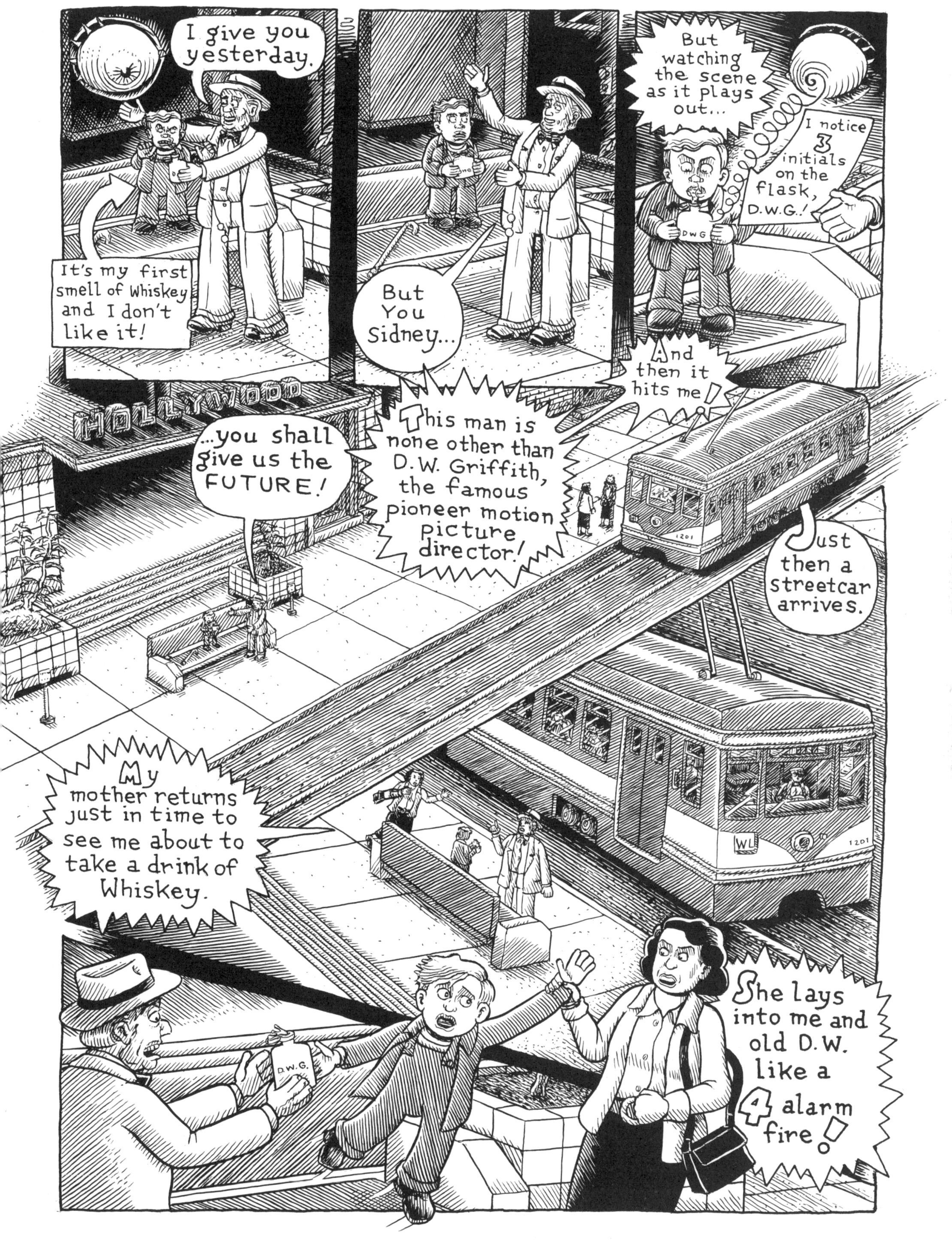
I give you yesterday.
It's my first smell of Whiskey and I don't like it!
But You Sidney...
...you shall give us the FUTURE!
But watching the scene as it plays out...
I notice 3 initials on the flask, D.W.G.!
DWG
And then it hits me!
This man is none other than D.W. Griffith, the famous pioneer motion picture director!
HOLLYWOOD
Just then a streetcar arrives.
1201
WL
My mother returns just in time to see me about to take a drink of Whiskey.
D.W.G.
She lays into me and old D.W. like a 4 alarm fire!

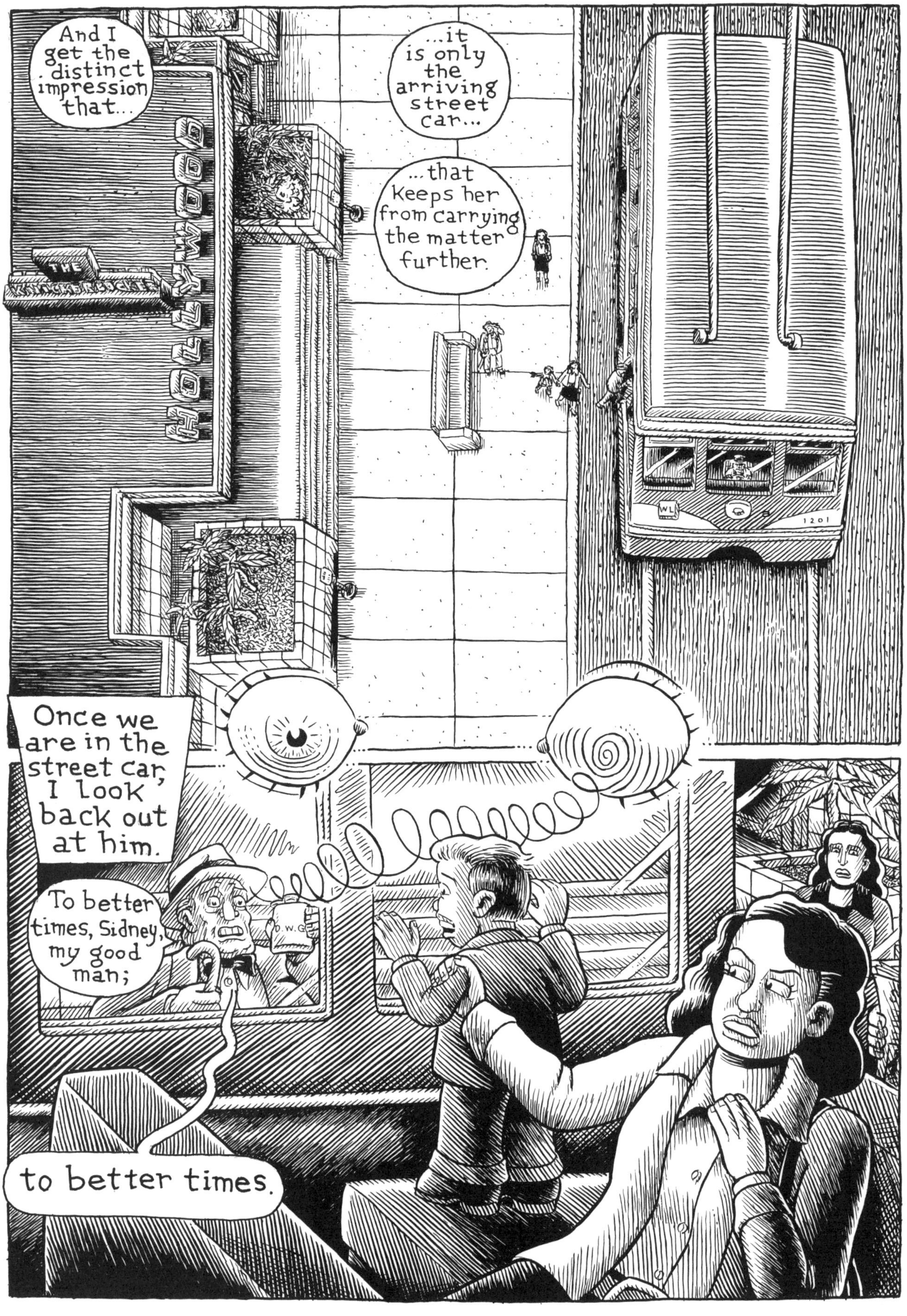
And I get the distinct impression that...
...it is only the arriving street car...
...that keeps her from carrying the matter further.
HOLLYWOOD
Once we are in the street car, I look back out at him.
To better times, Sidney, my good man;
to better times.

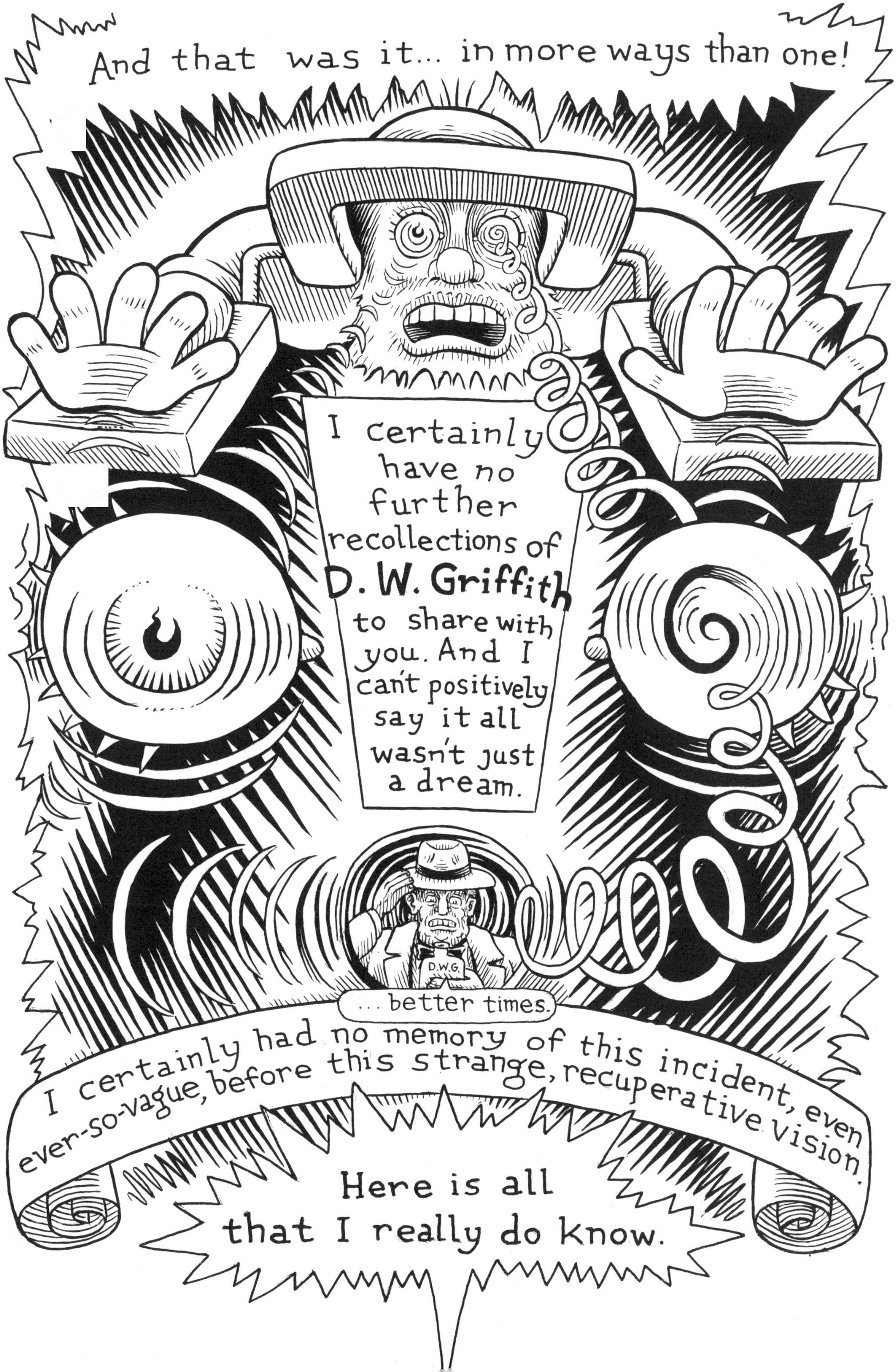
And that was it... in more ways than one!
I certainly have no further recollections of D. W. Griffith to share with you. And I can't positively say it all wasn't just a dream.
D.W.G.
... better times.
I certainly had no memory of this incident, even ever-so-vague, before this strange, recuperative vision.
Here is all that I really do know.

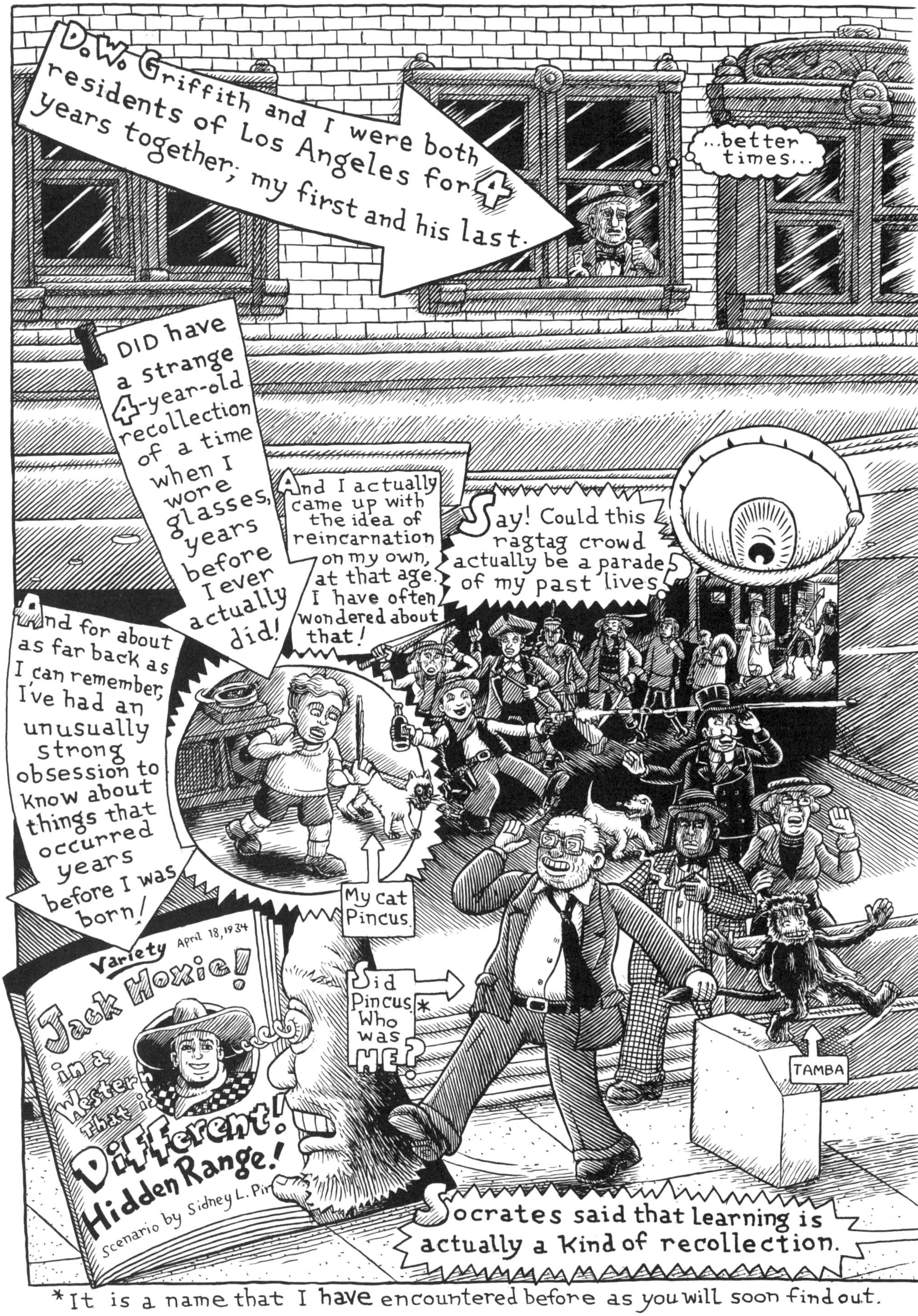
D.W. Griffith and I were both residents of Los Angeles for 4 years together; my first and his last.
...better times...
I DID have a strange 4-year-old recollection of a time when I wore glasses, years before I ever actually did!
And I actually came up with the idea of reincarnation on my own, at that age. I have often wondered about that!
Say! Could this ragtag crowd actually be a parade of my past lives?
And for about as far back as I can remember, I've had an unusually strong obsession to know about things that occurred years before I was born!
My cat Pincus.
Variety April 18, 1934
Jack Hoxie! in a Western that is Different! Hidden Range!
Scenario by Sidney L. Pi
Sid Pincus* Who was HE?
TAMBA
Socrates said that learning is actually a kind of recollection.

*It is a name that I have encountered before as you will soon find out.

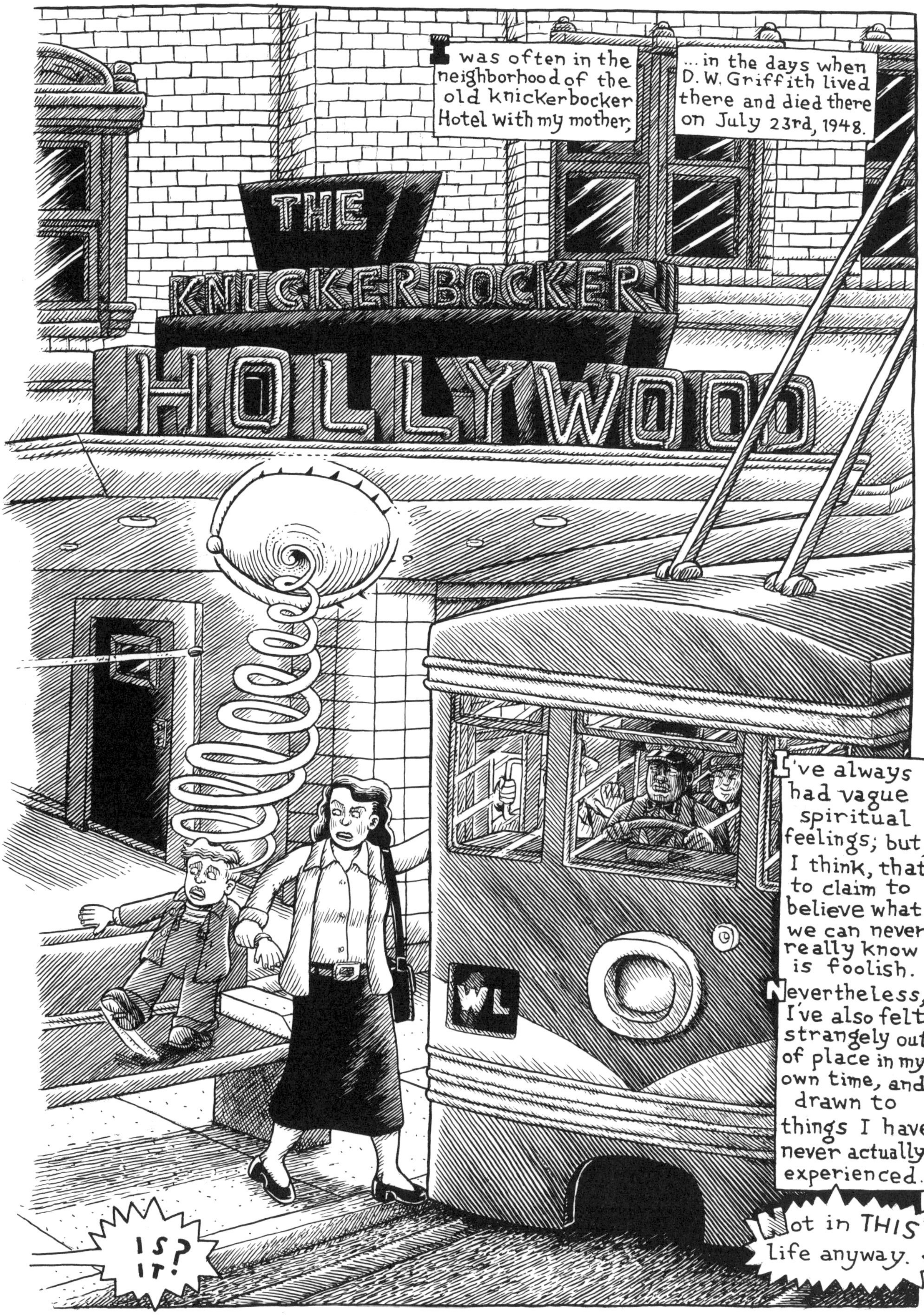
I was often in the neighborhood of the old knickerbocker Hotel with my mother,
...in the days when D. W. Griffith lived there and died there on July 23rd, 1948.
THE KNICKERBOCKER HOLLYWOOD
I've always had vague spiritual feelings; but, I think, that to claim to believe what we can never really know is foolish.
Nevertheless, I've also felt strangely out of place in my own time, and drawn to things I have never actually experienced.
Not in THIS life anyway.
IS? IT!
WL

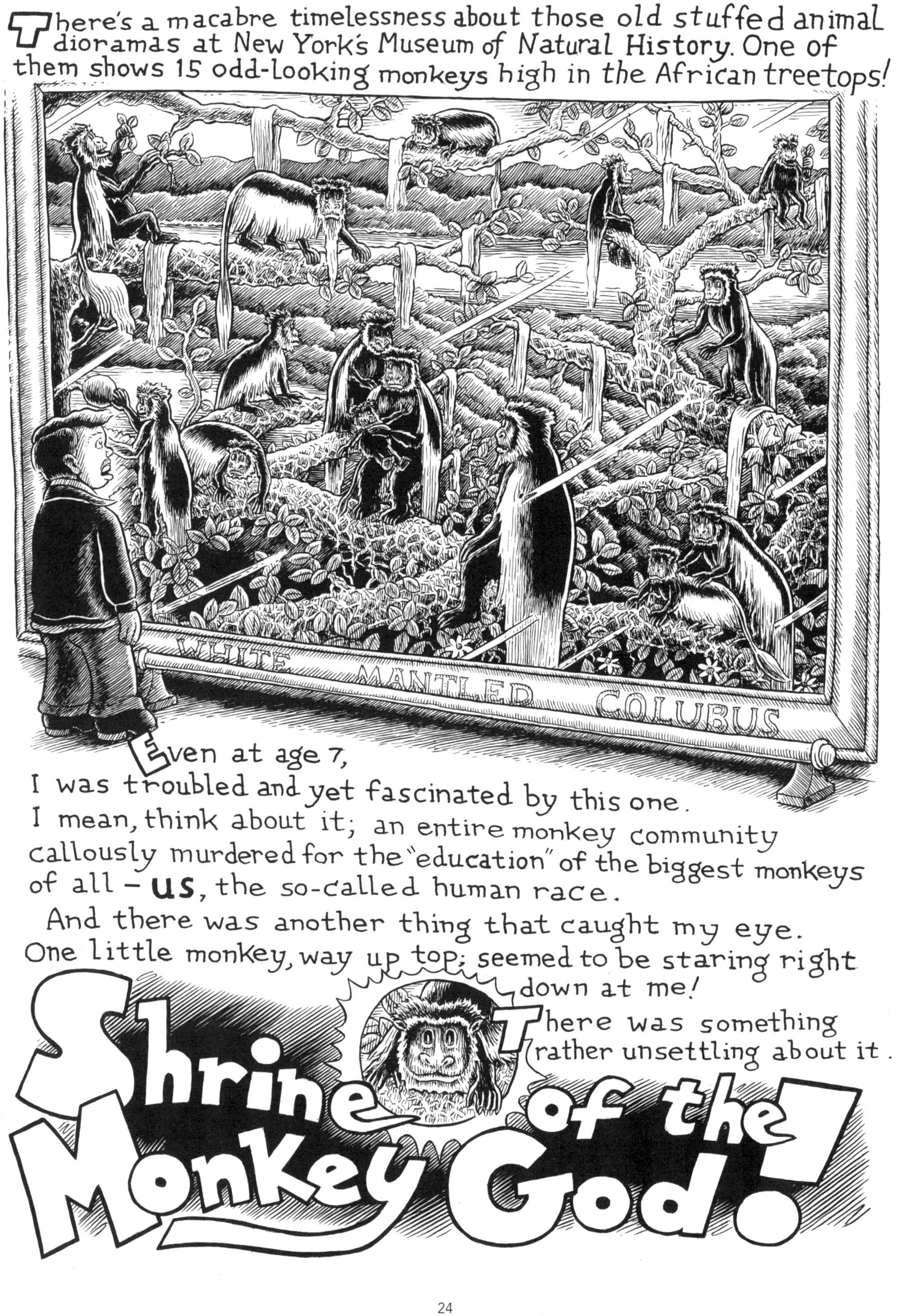
There's a macabre timelessness about those old stuffed animal dioramas at New York's Museum of Natural History. One of them shows 15 odd-looking monkeys high in the African treetops!
WHITE MANTLED COLUBUS
Even at age 7,
I was troubled and yet fascinated by this one.
I mean, think about it; an entire monkey community callously murdered for the "education" of the biggest monkeys of all – US, the so-called human race.
And there was another thing that caught my eye.
One little monkey, way up top, seemed to be staring right down at me!
There was something rather unsettling about it.
Shrine of the Monkey God!

The time-locked quality of those dioramas was really brought home to me recently when my wife and I visited the old museum.

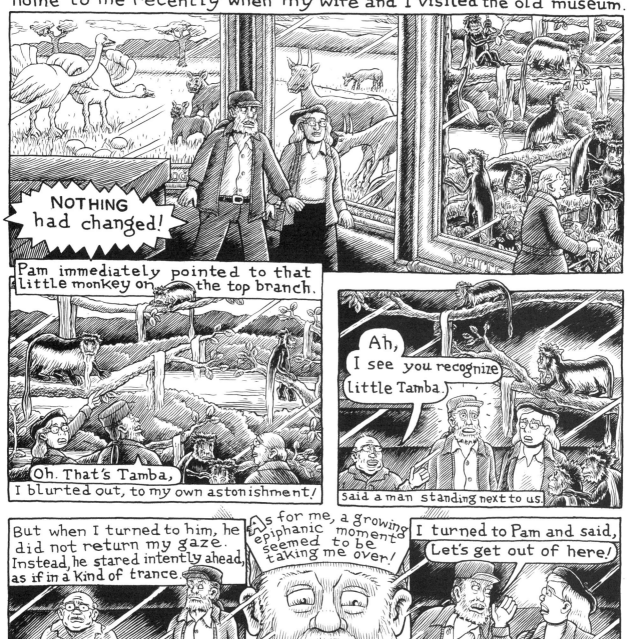

NOTHING had changed!

Pam immediately pointed to that little monkey on the top branch.

Oh. That's Tamba, I blurted out, to my own astonishment!

Ah, I see you recognize little Tamba.

said a man standing next to us.

But when I turned to him, he did not return my gaze. Instead, he stared intently ahead, as if in a kind of trance.

As for me, a growing epiphanic moment seemed to be taking me over!

I turned to Pam and said, Let's get out of here!

Out on the museum steps, Pam said,

Do you know that old man?

Well, ...uh, not really, but I think we've met before!

However, even as I hemmed and hawed...

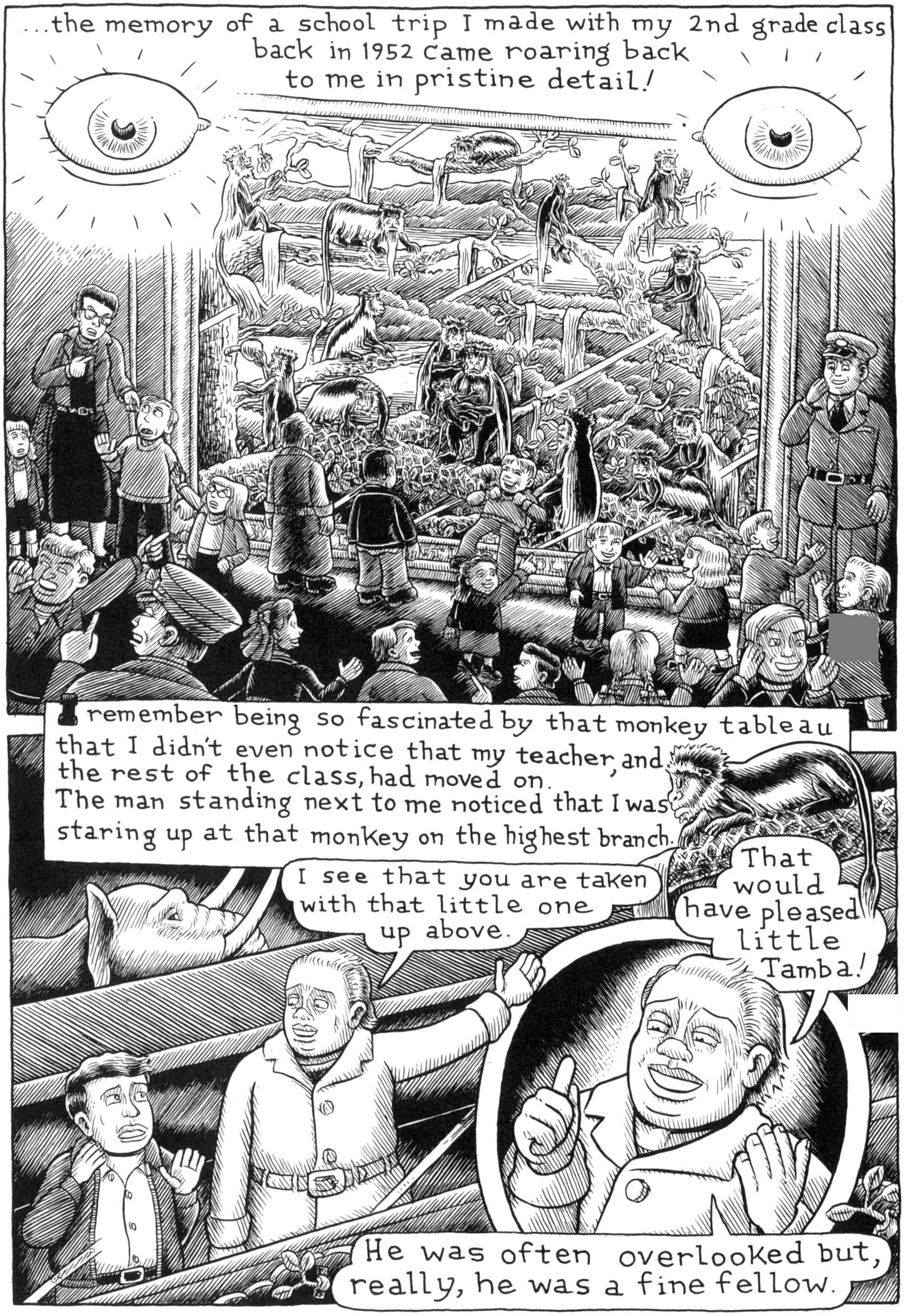
...the memory of a school trip I made with my 2nd grade class back in 1952 came roaring back to me in pristine detail!
I remember being so fascinated by that monkey tableau that I didn't even notice that my teacher, and the rest of the class, had moved on. The man standing next to me noticed that I was staring up at that monkey on the highest branch.
I see that you are taken with that little one up above.
That would have pleased little Tamba!
He was often overlooked but, really, he was a fine fellow.

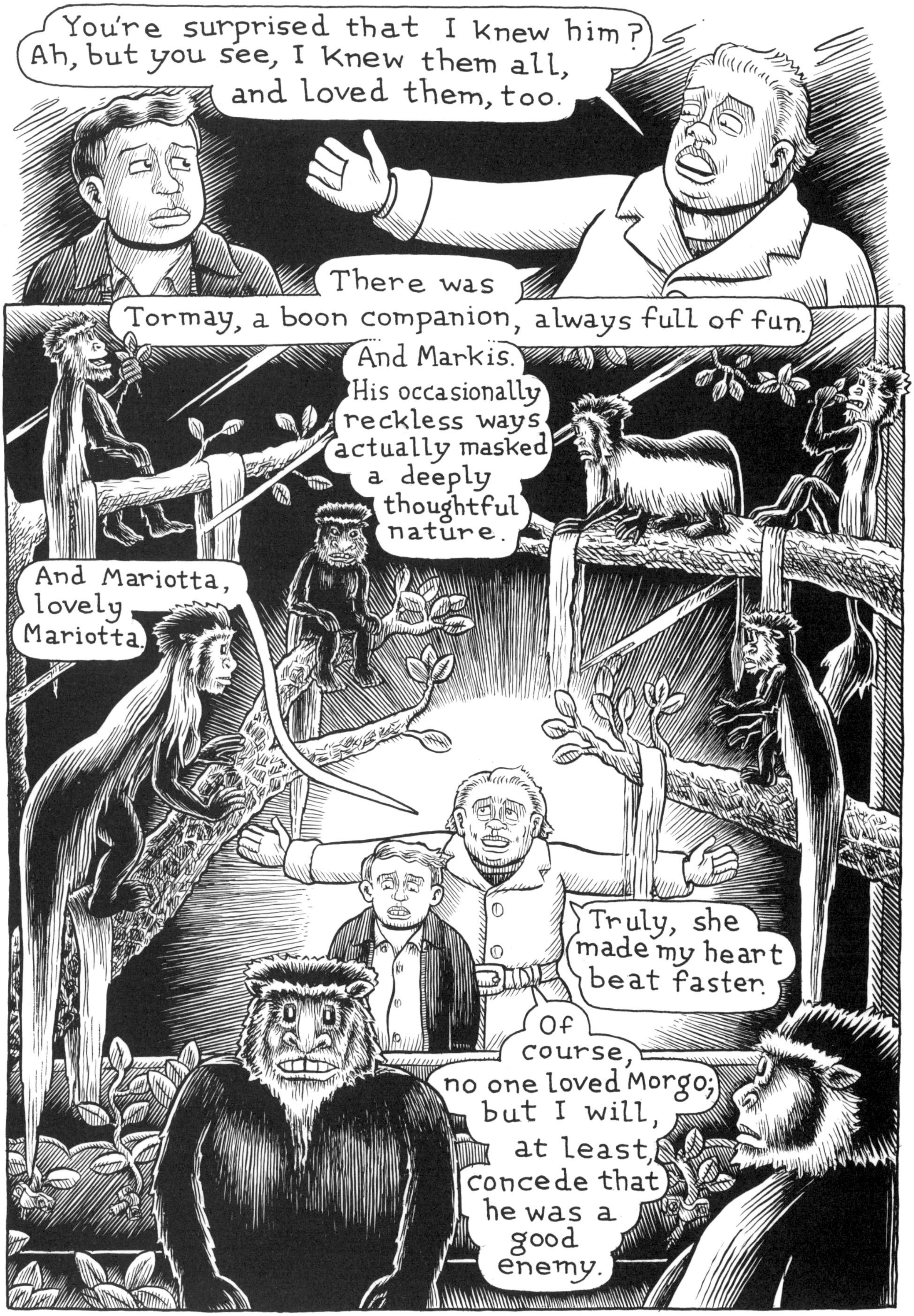
You're surprised that I knew him? Ah, but you see, I knew them all, and loved them, too.
There was Tormay, a boon companion, always full of fun.
And Markis. His occasionally reckless ways actually masked a deeply thoughtful nature.
And Mariotta, lovely Mariotta.
Truly, she made my heart beat faster.
Of course, no one loved Morgo; but I will, at least, concede that he was a good enemy.

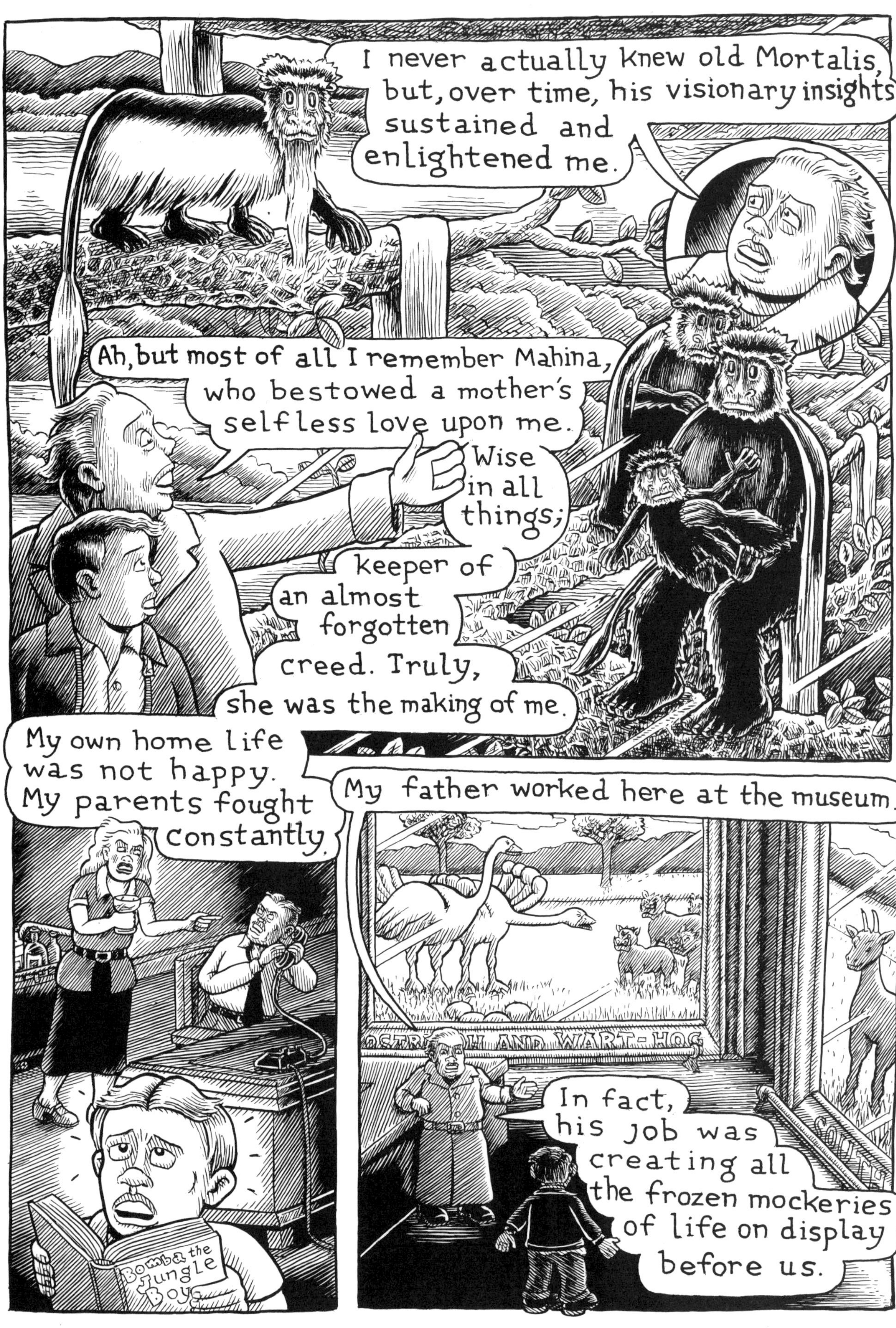

I never actually knew old Mortalis, but, over time, his visionary insights sustained and enlightened me.
Ah, but most of all I remember Mahina, who bestowed a mother's selfless love upon me.
Wise in all things;
keeper of an almost forgotten creed. Truly, she was the making of me.
My own home life was not happy. My parents fought constantly.
Bomba the Jungle Boy
My father worked here at the museum.
OSTRICH AND WART-HOG
In fact, his job was creating all the frozen mockeries of life on display before us.

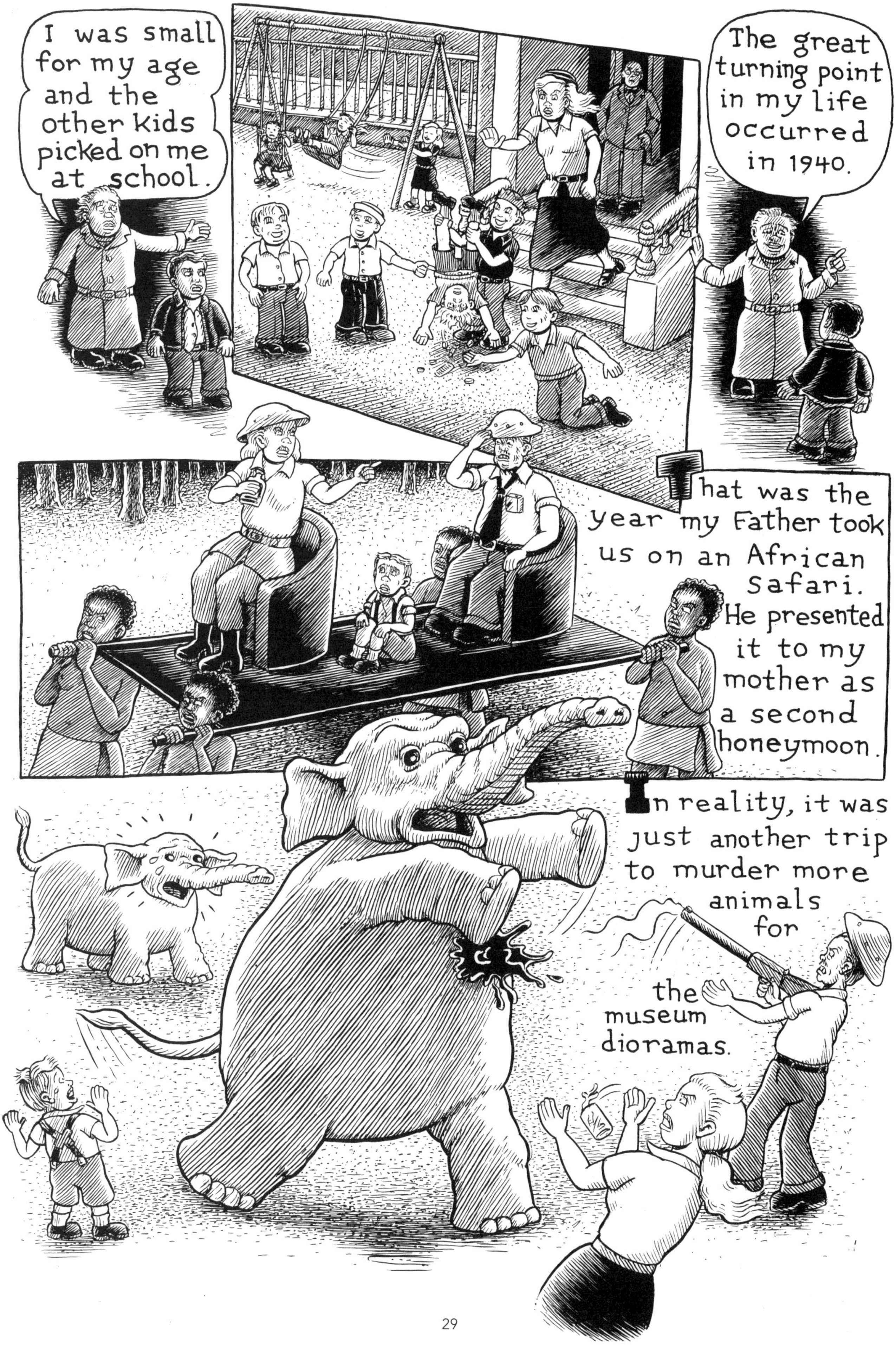
I was small for my age and the other kids picked on me at school.
The great turning point in my life occurred in 1940.
That was the year my Father took us on an African safari. He presented it to my mother as a second honeymoon.
In reality, it was just another trip to murder more animals for the museum dioramas.

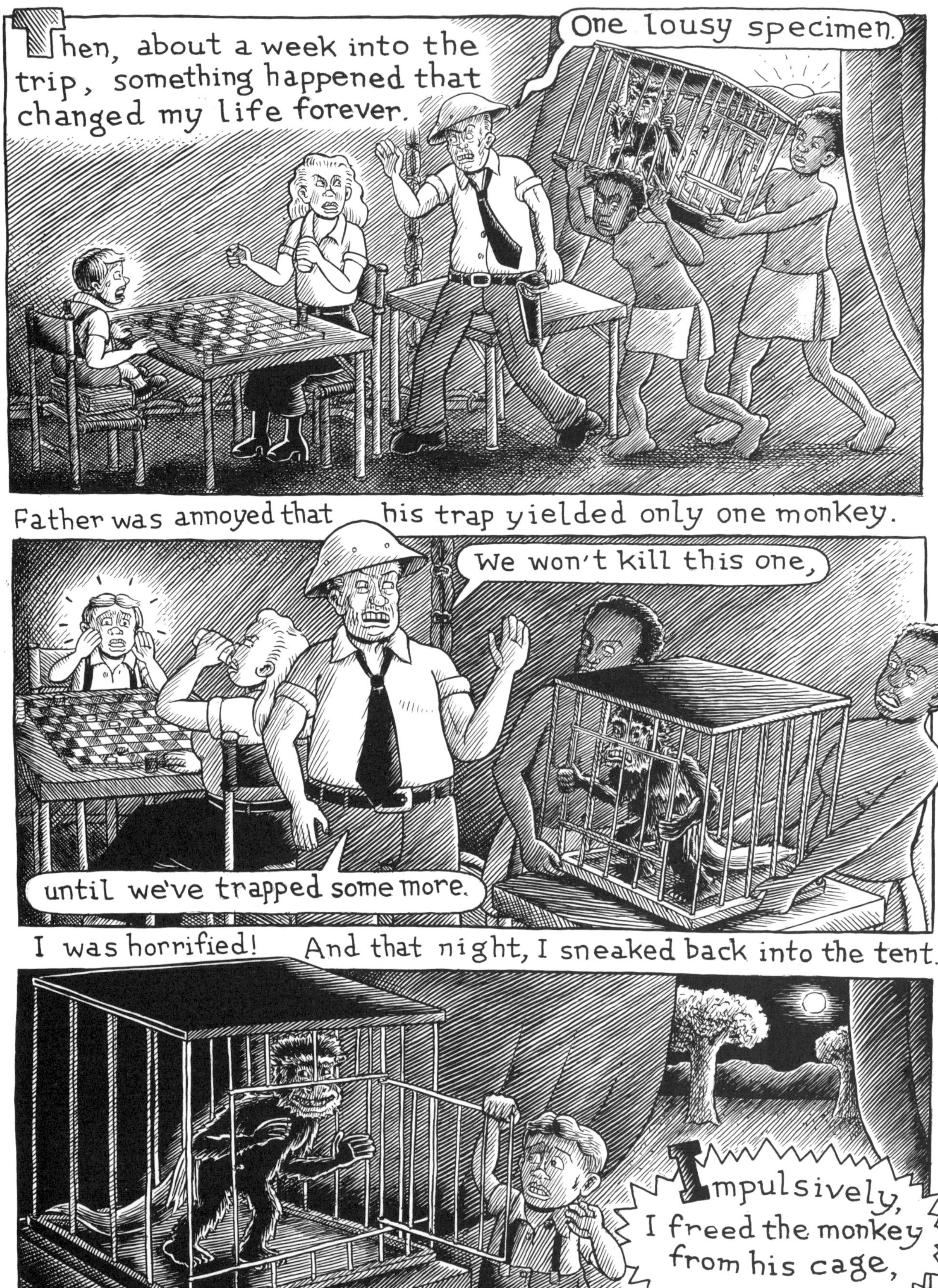
Then, about a week into the trip, something happened that changed my life forever.
One lousy specimen.
Father was annoyed that his trap yielded only one monkey.
We won't kill this one,
until we've trapped some more.
I was horrified! And that night, I sneaked back into the tent.
Impulsively, I freed the monkey from his cage,

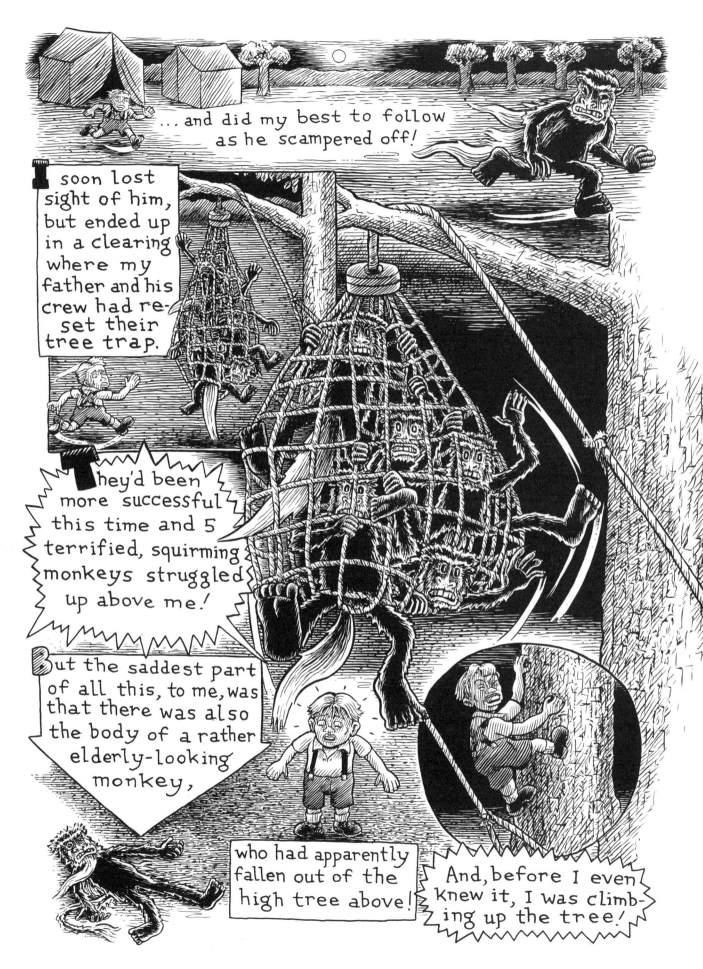

...and did my best to follow as he scampered off!

I soon lost sight of him, but ended up in a clearing where my father and his crew had re-set their tree trap.

They'd been more successful this time and 5 terrified, squirming monkeys struggled up above me!

But the saddest part of all this, to me, was that there was also the body of a rather elderly-looking monkey,

who had apparently fallen out of the high tree above!

And, before I even knew it, I was climbing up the tree!

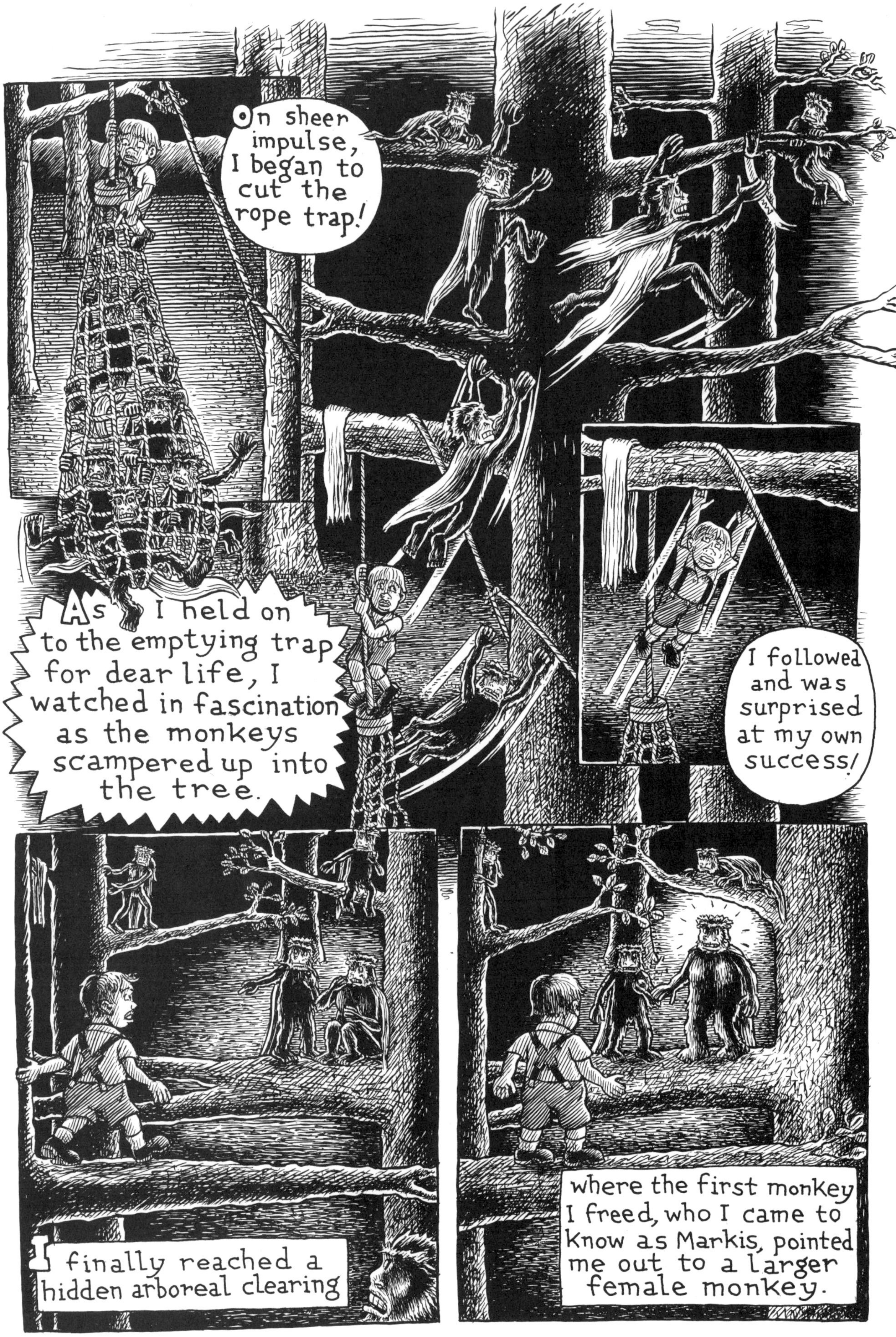
On sheer impulse, I began to cut the rope trap!
As I held on to the emptying trap for dear life, I watched in fascination as the monkeys scampered up into the tree.
I followed and was surprised at my own success!
I finally reached a hidden arboreal clearing
where the first monkey I freed, who I came to know as Markis, pointed me out to a larger female monkey.

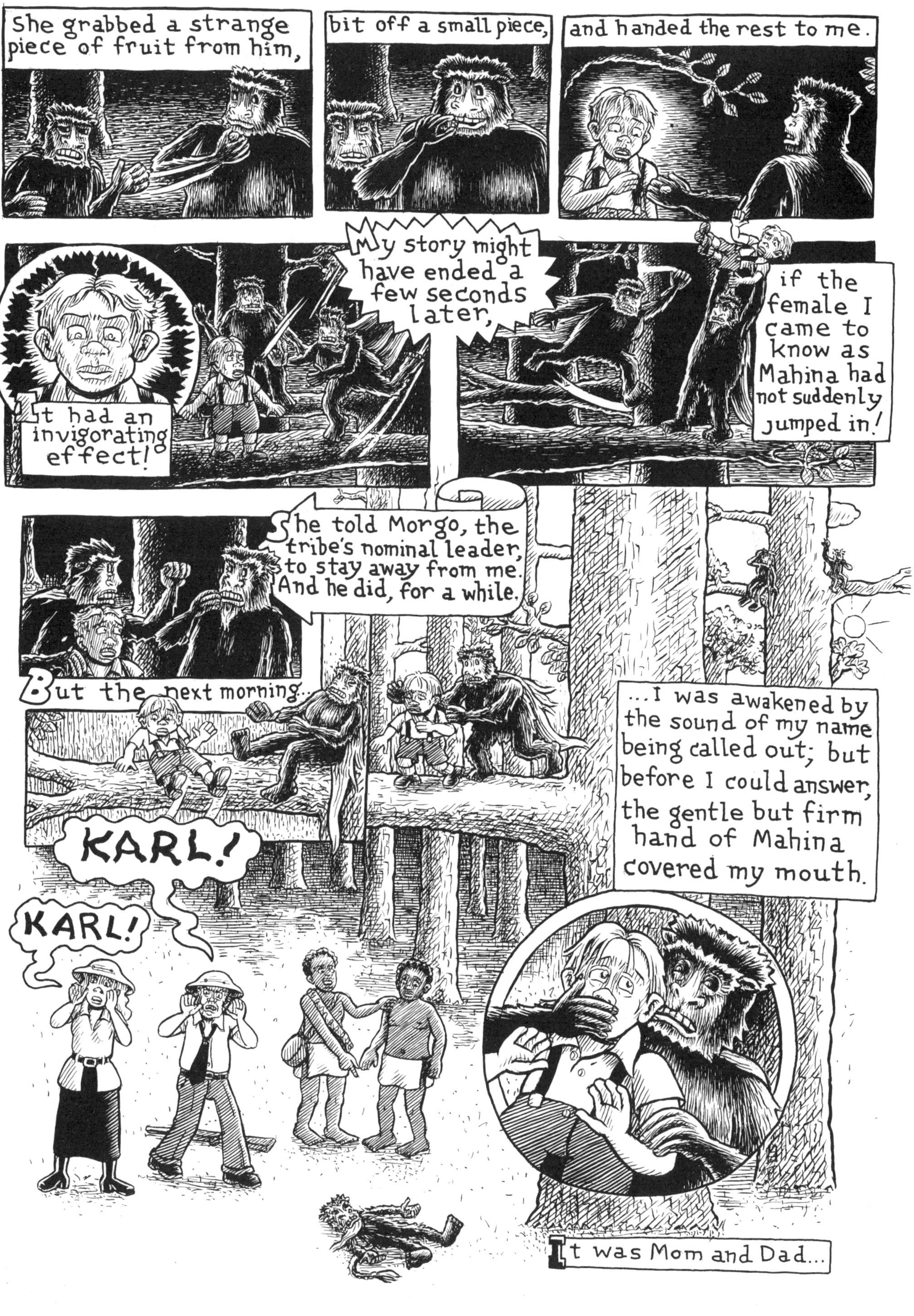

She grabbed a strange piece of fruit from him,
bit off a small piece,
and handed the rest to me.
It had an invigorating effect!
My story might have ended a few seconds later,
if the female I came to know as Mahina had not suddenly jumped in!
She told Morgo, the tribe's nominal leader, to stay away from me. And he did, for a while.
But the next morning...
...I was awakened by the sound of my name being called out; but before I could answer, the gentle but firm hand of Mahina covered my mouth.
KARL!
KARL!
It was Mom and Dad...

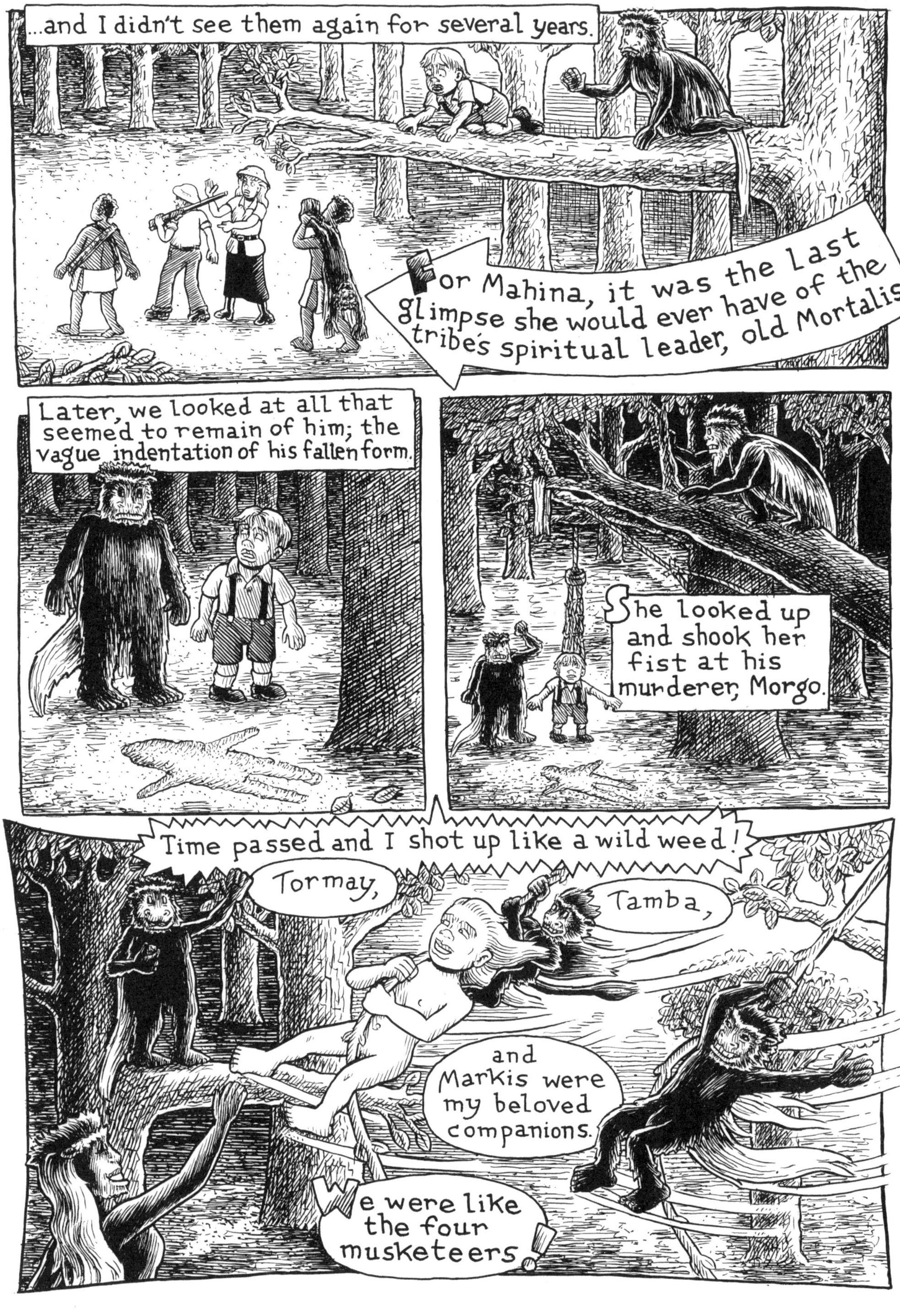
...and I didn't see them again for several years.
For Mahina, it was the last glimpse she would ever have of the tribe's spiritual leader, old Mortalis.
Later, we looked at all that seemed to remain of him; the vague indentation of his fallen form.
She looked up and shook her fist at his murderer, Morgo.
Time passed and I shot up like a wild weed!
Tormay,
Tamba,
and Markis were my beloved companions.
We were like the four musketeers!

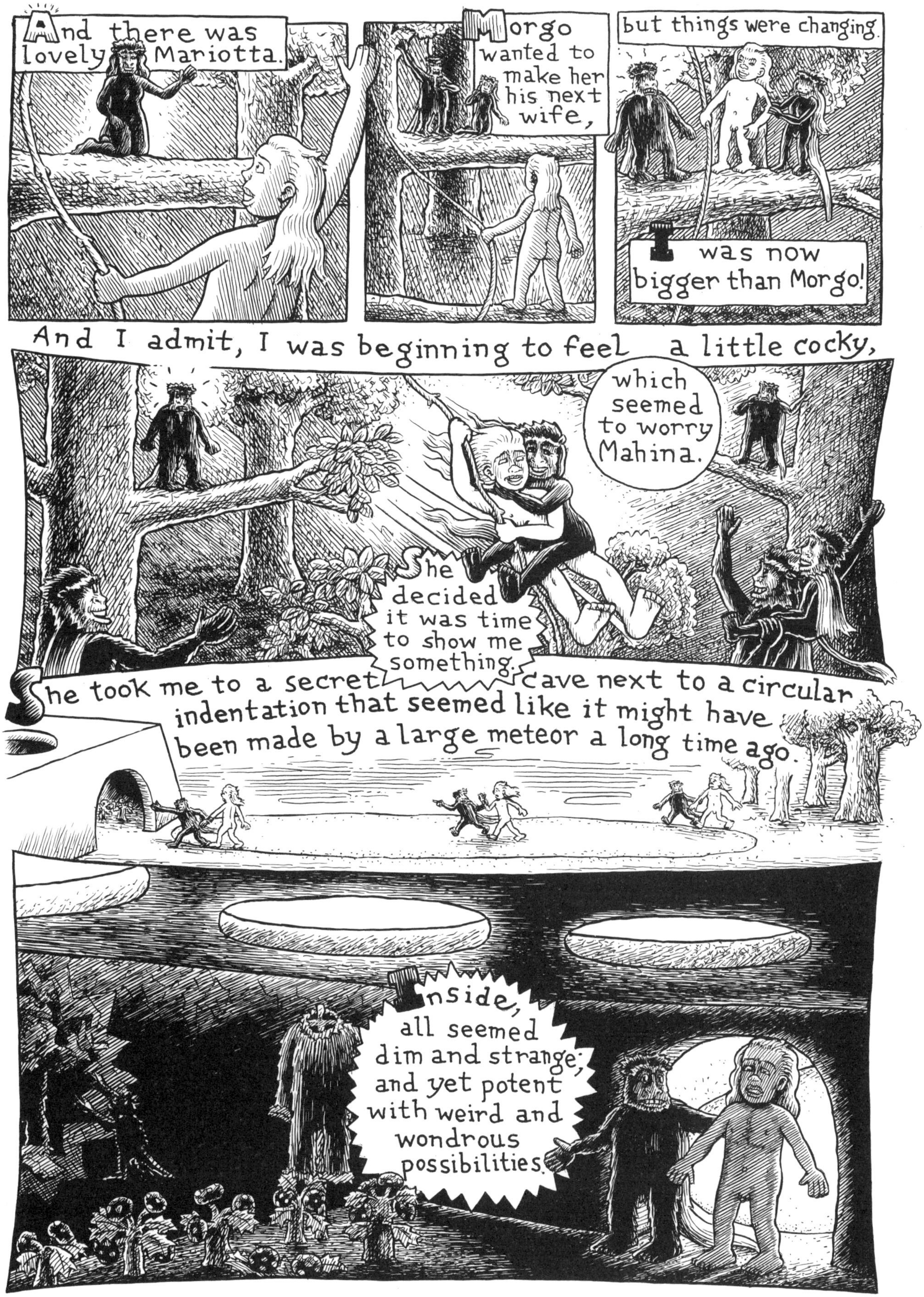
And there was lovely Mariotta.
Morgo wanted to make her his next wife,
but things were changing.
I was now bigger than Morgo!
And I admit, I was beginning to feel a little cocky,
which seemed to worry Mahina.
She decided it was time to show me something.
She took me to a secret cave next to a circular indentation that seemed like it might have been made by a large meteor a long time ago.
Inside, all seemed dim and strange; and yet potent with weird and wondrous possibilities.

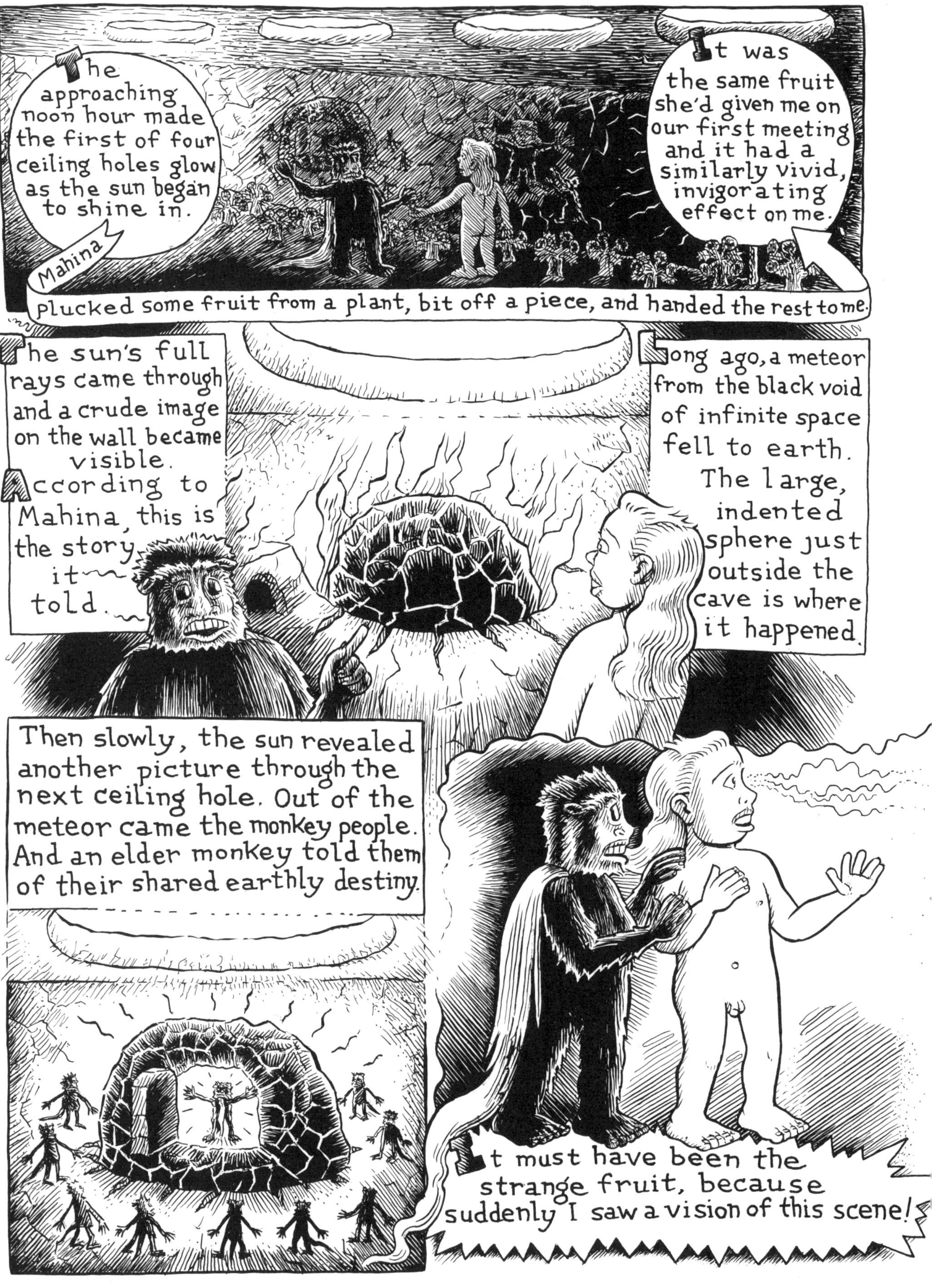
The approaching noon hour made the first of four ceiling holes glow as the sun began to shine in.
Mahina
plucked some fruit from a plant, bit off a piece, and handed the rest to me.
It was the same fruit she'd given me on our first meeting and it had a similarly vivid, invigorating effect on me.
The sun's full rays came through and a crude image on the wall became visible. According to Mahina, this is the story it told.
Long ago, a meteor from the black void of infinite space fell to earth. The large, indented sphere just outside the cave is where it happened.
Then slowly, the sun revealed another picture through the next ceiling hole. Out of the meteor came the monkey people. And an elder monkey told them of their shared earthly destiny.
It must have been the strange fruit, because suddenly I saw a vision of this scene!

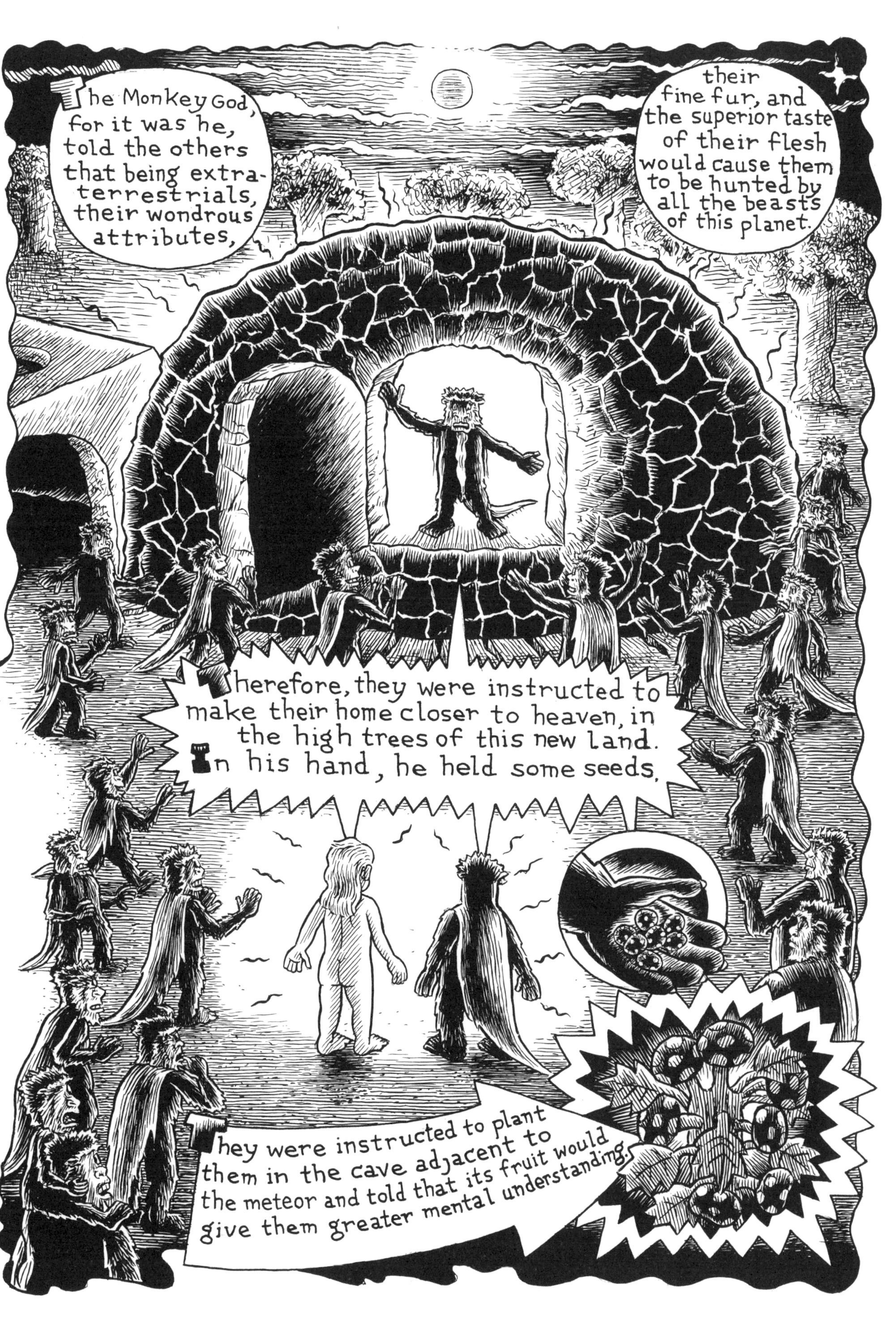
The Monkey God, for it was he, told the others that being extra-terrestrials, their wondrous attributes,
their fine fur, and the superior taste of their flesh would cause them to be hunted by all the beasts of this planet.
Therefore, they were instructed to make their home closer to heaven, in the high trees of this new land. In his hand, he held some seeds.
They were instructed to plant them in the cave adjacent to the meteor and told that its fruit would give them greater mental understanding.

The moving sun hit the 3rd hole and the story shifted to things yet to come.

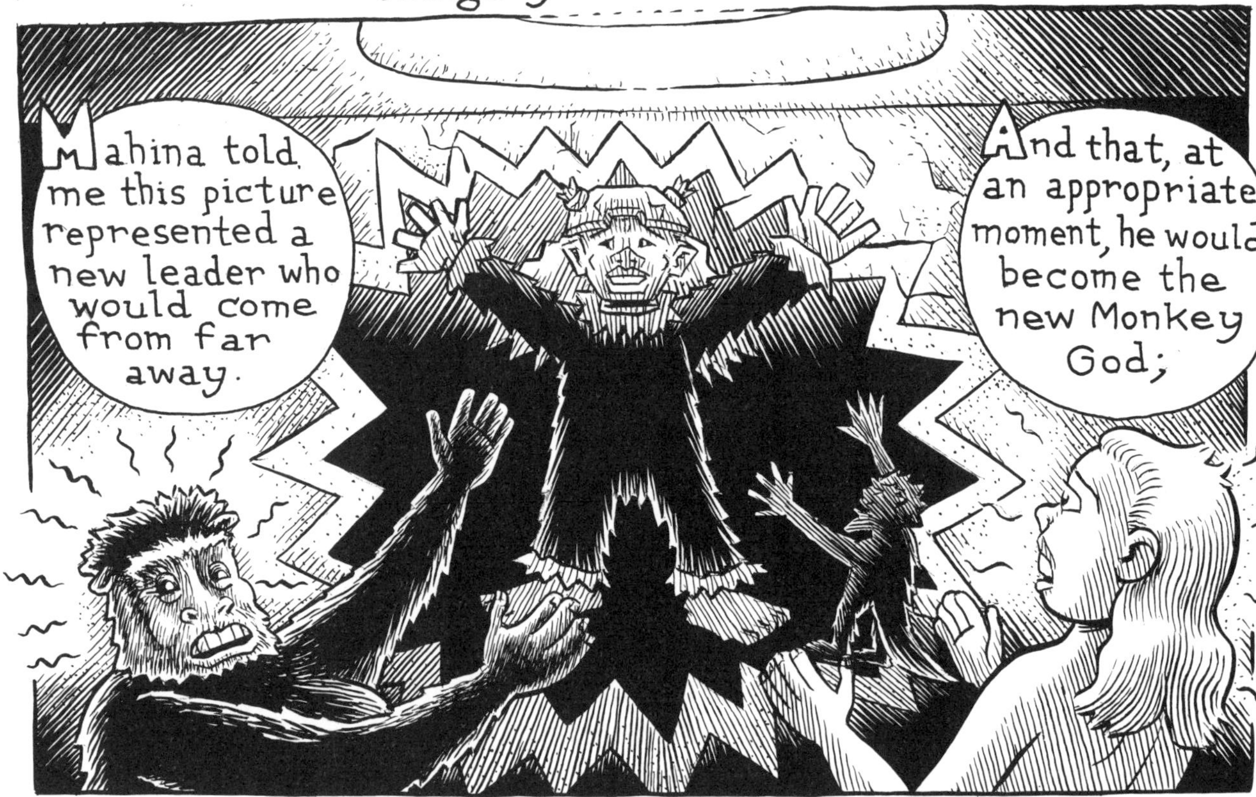
Mahina told me this picture represented a new leader who would come from far away.
And that, at an appropriate moment, he would become the new Monkey God;

that the new God would cause them to be transported to a new place, where they would be together always.

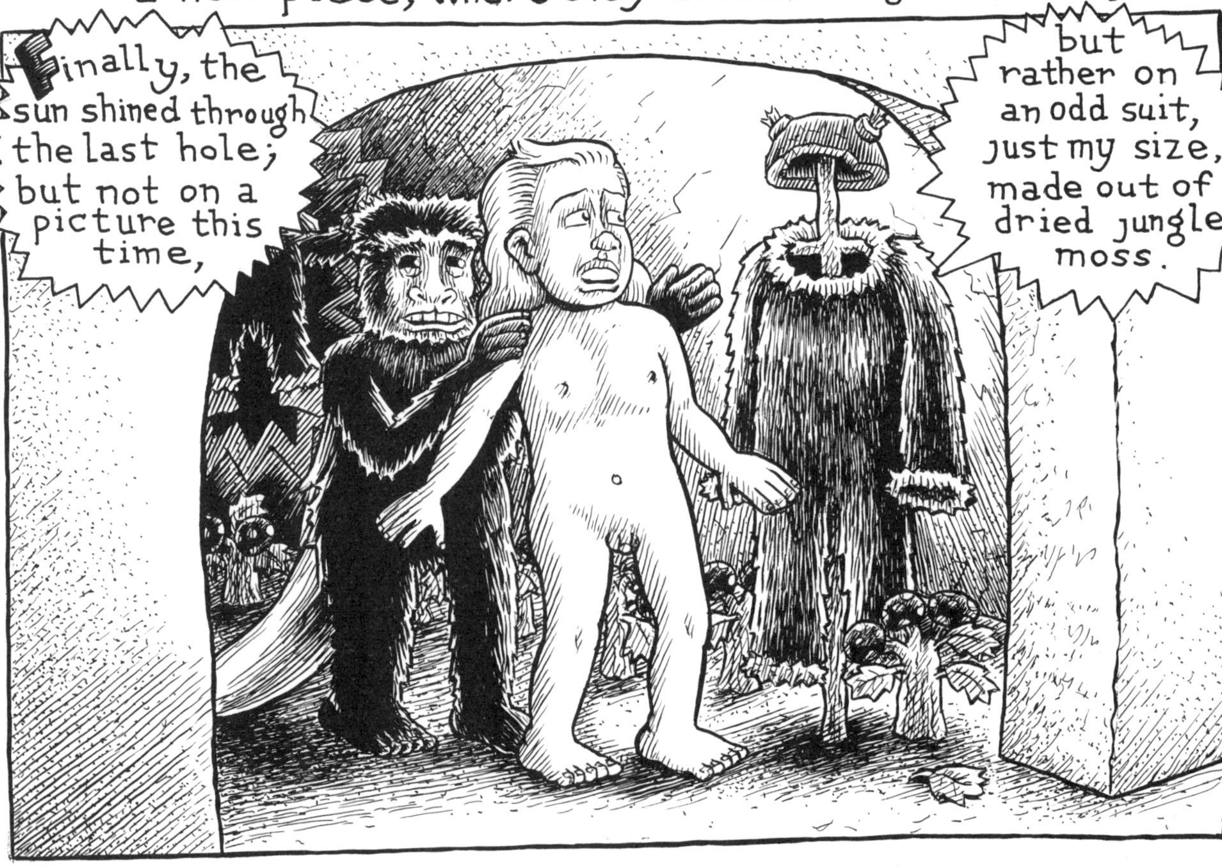
Finally, the sun shined through the last hole; but not on a picture this time,
but rather on an odd suit, just my size, made out of dried jungle moss.

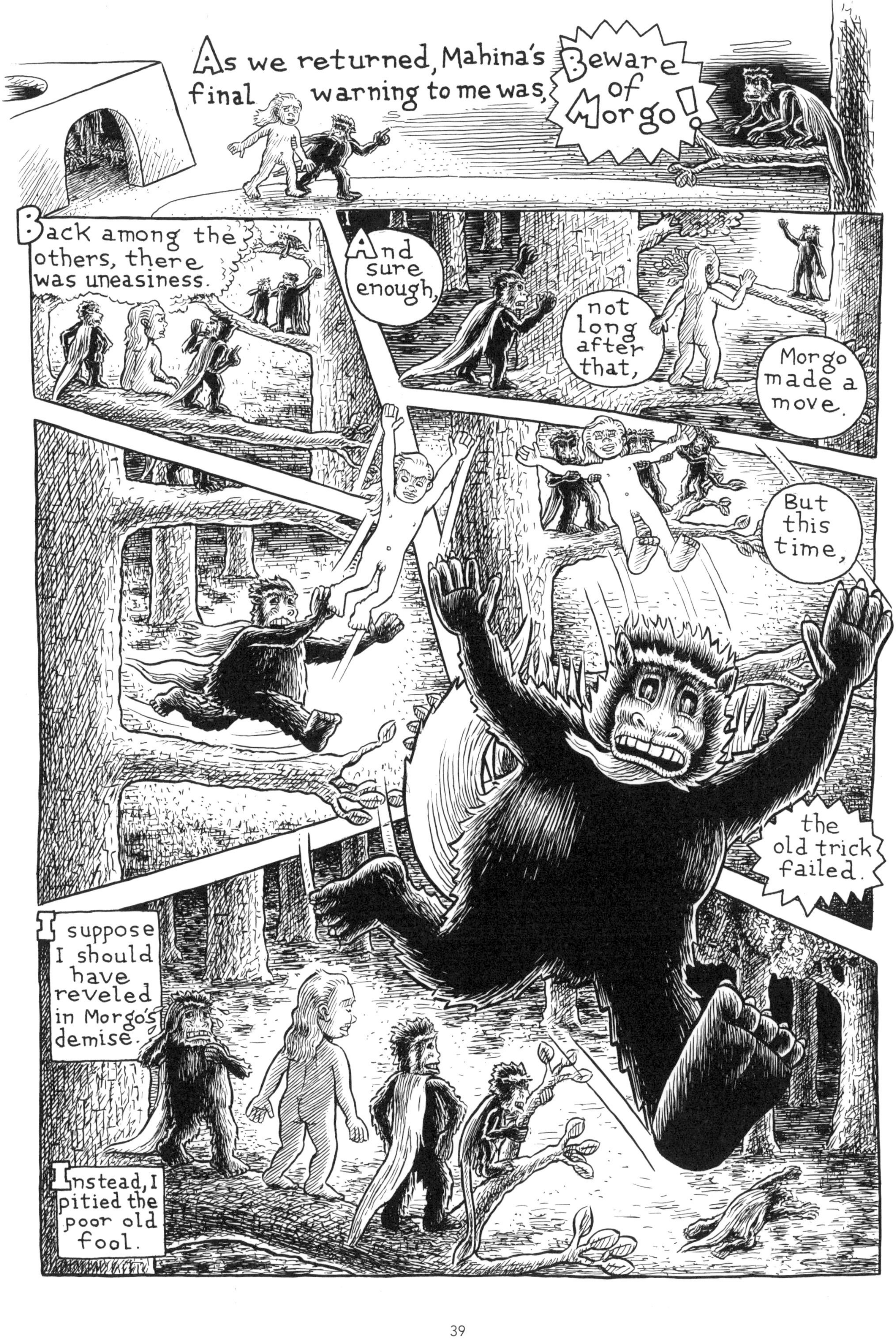
As we returned, Mahina's final warning to me was,
Beware of Morgo!
Back among the others, there was uneasiness.
And sure enough,
not long after that,
Morgo made a move.
But this time,
the old trick failed.
I suppose I should have reveled in Morgo's demise.
Instead, I pitied the poor old fool.

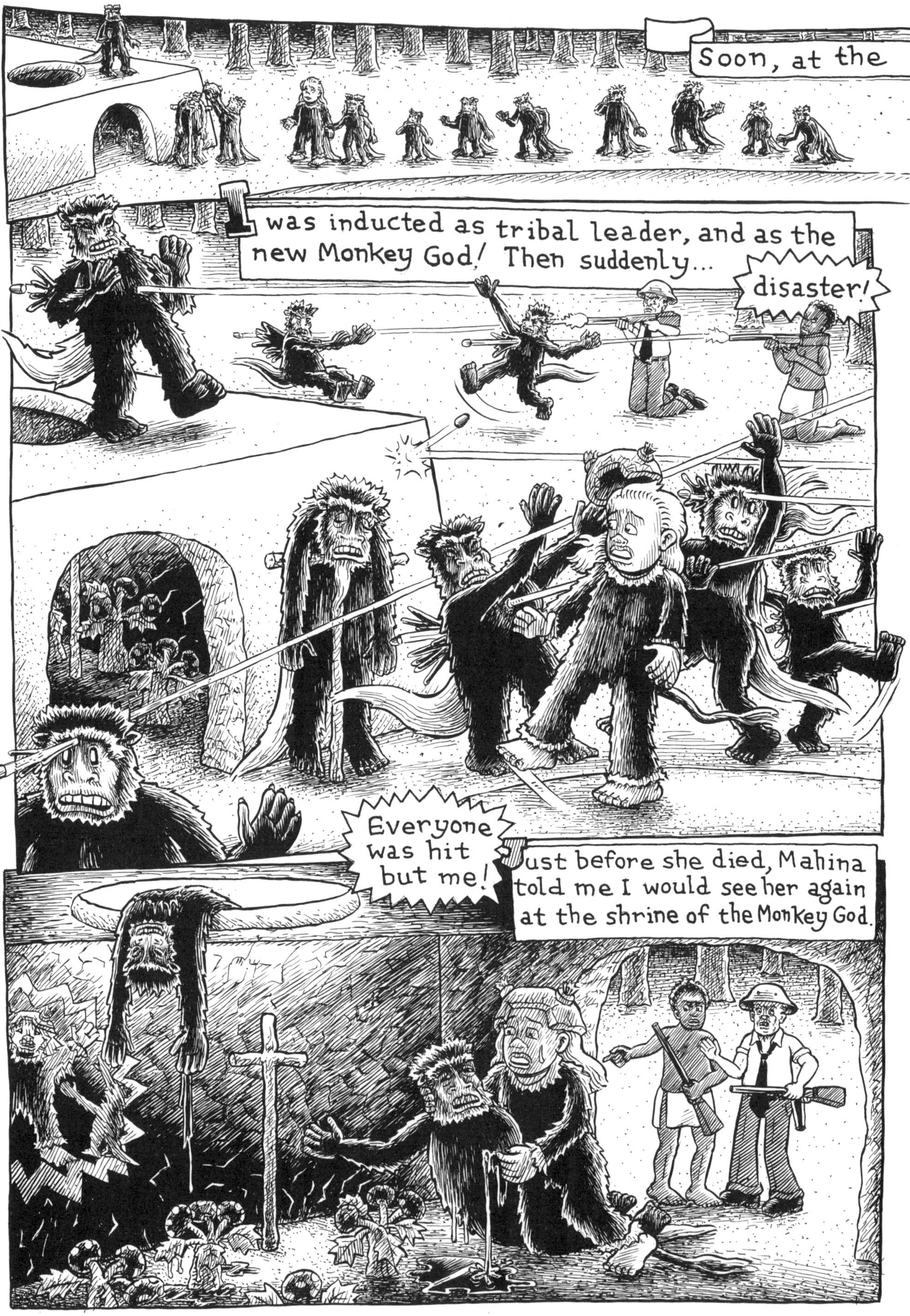

Soon, at the
I was inducted as tribal leader, and as the new Monkey God! Then suddenly...
disaster!
Everyone was hit but me!
Just before she died, Mahina told me I would see her again at the shrine of the Monkey God.

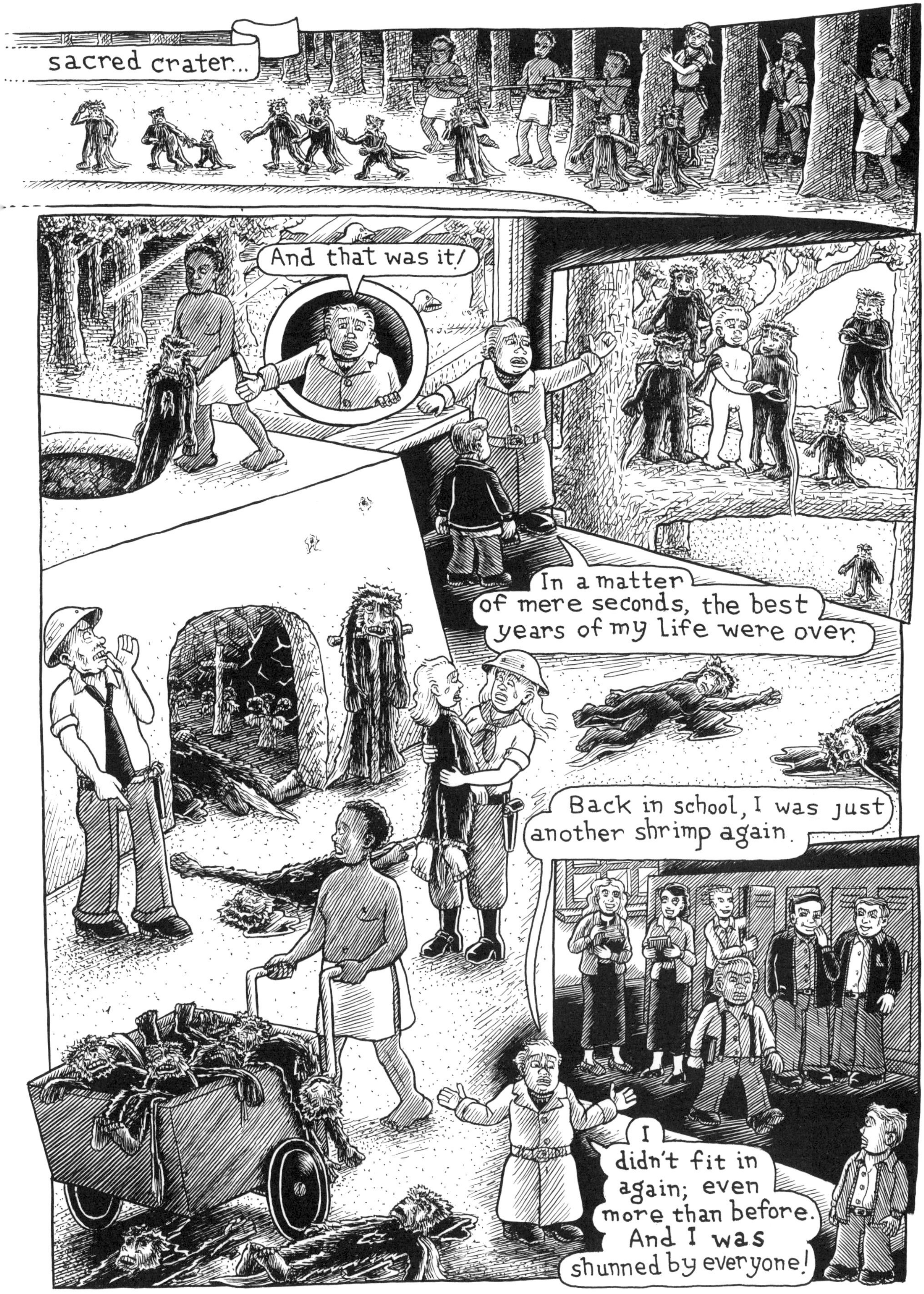

sacred crater...
And that was it!
In a matter of mere seconds, the best years of my life were over.
Back in school, I was just another shrimp again.
I didn't fit in again; even more than before. And I was shunned by everyone!

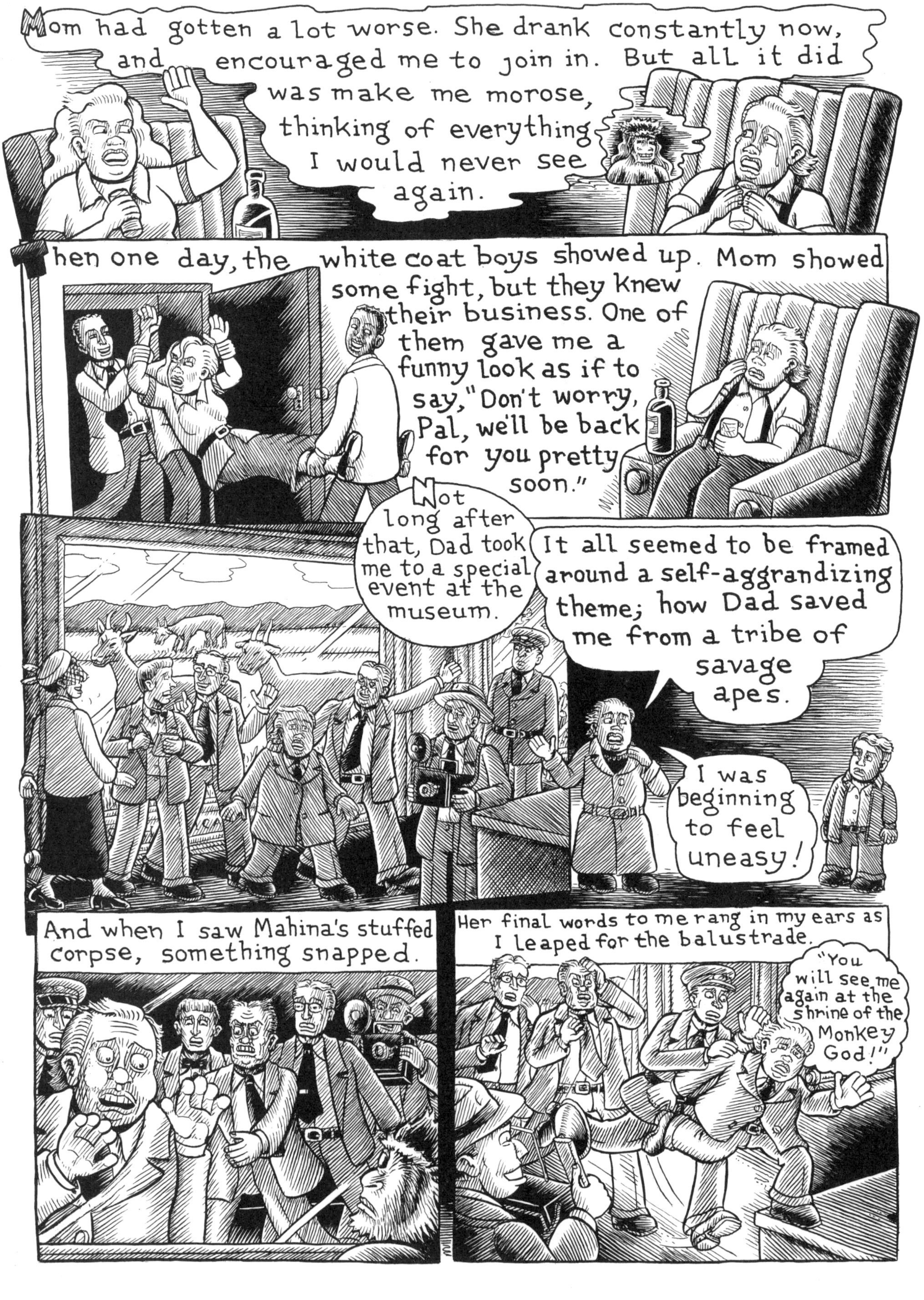
Mom had gotten a lot worse. She drank constantly now, and encouraged me to join in. But all it did was make me morose, thinking of everything I would never see again.
Then one day, the white coat boys showed up. Mom showed some fight, but they knew their business. One of them gave me a funny look as if to say, "Don't worry, Pal, we'll be back for you pretty soon."
Not long after that, Dad took me to a special event at the museum.
It all seemed to be framed around a self-aggrandizing theme; how Dad saved me from a tribe of savage apes.
I was beginning to feel uneasy!
And when I saw Mahina's stuffed corpse, something snapped.
Her final words to me rang in my ears as I leaped for the balustrade.
"You will see me again at the shrine of the Monkey God!"

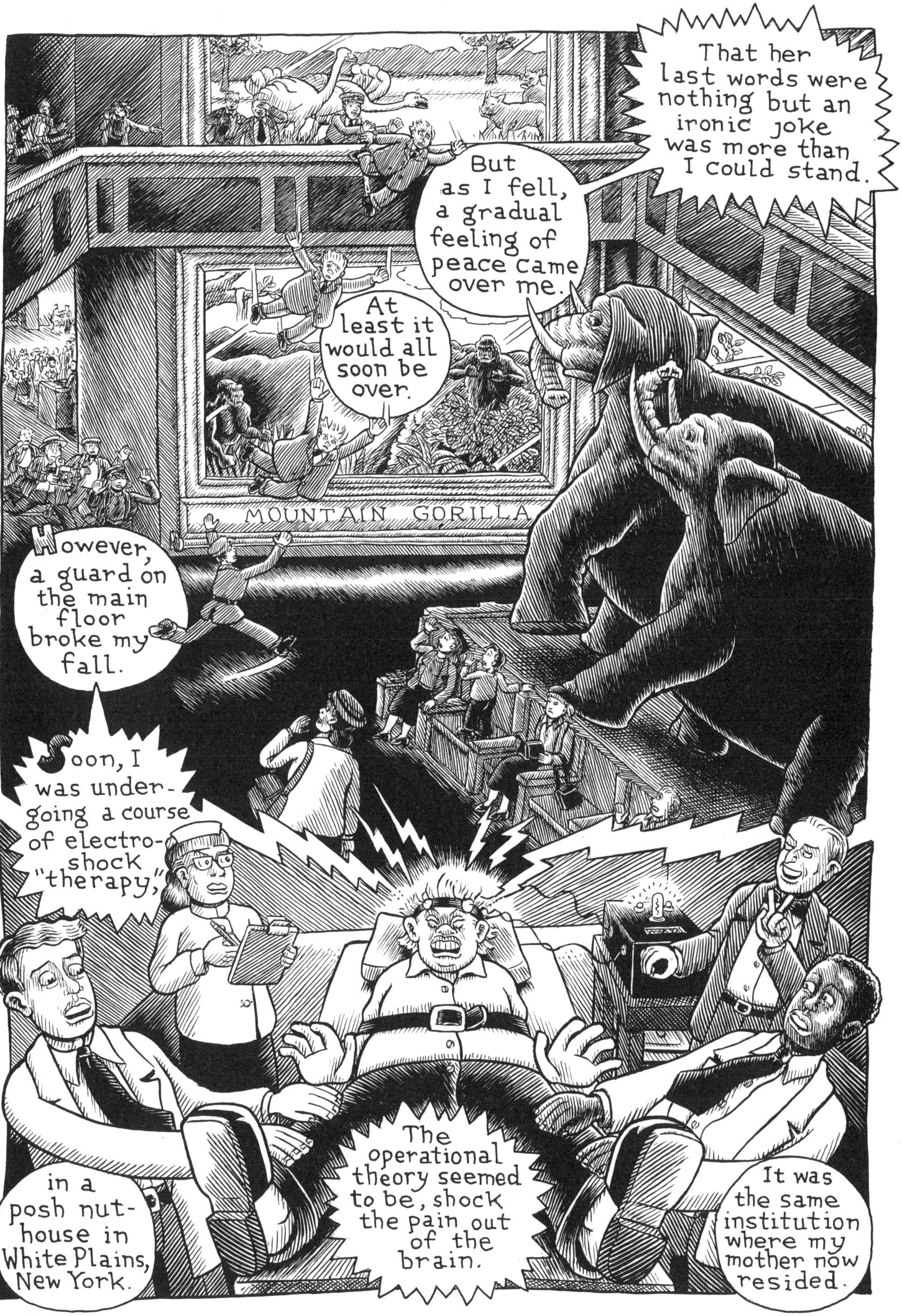
That her last words were nothing but an ironic joke was more than I could stand.
But as I fell, a gradual feeling of peace came over me.
At least it would all soon be over.
MOUNTAIN GORILLA
However, a guard on the main floor broke my fall.
Soon, I was undergoing a course of electro-shock "therapy,"
in a posh nut-house in White Plains, New York.
The operational theory seemed to be, shock the pain out of the brain.
It was the same institution where my mother now resided.

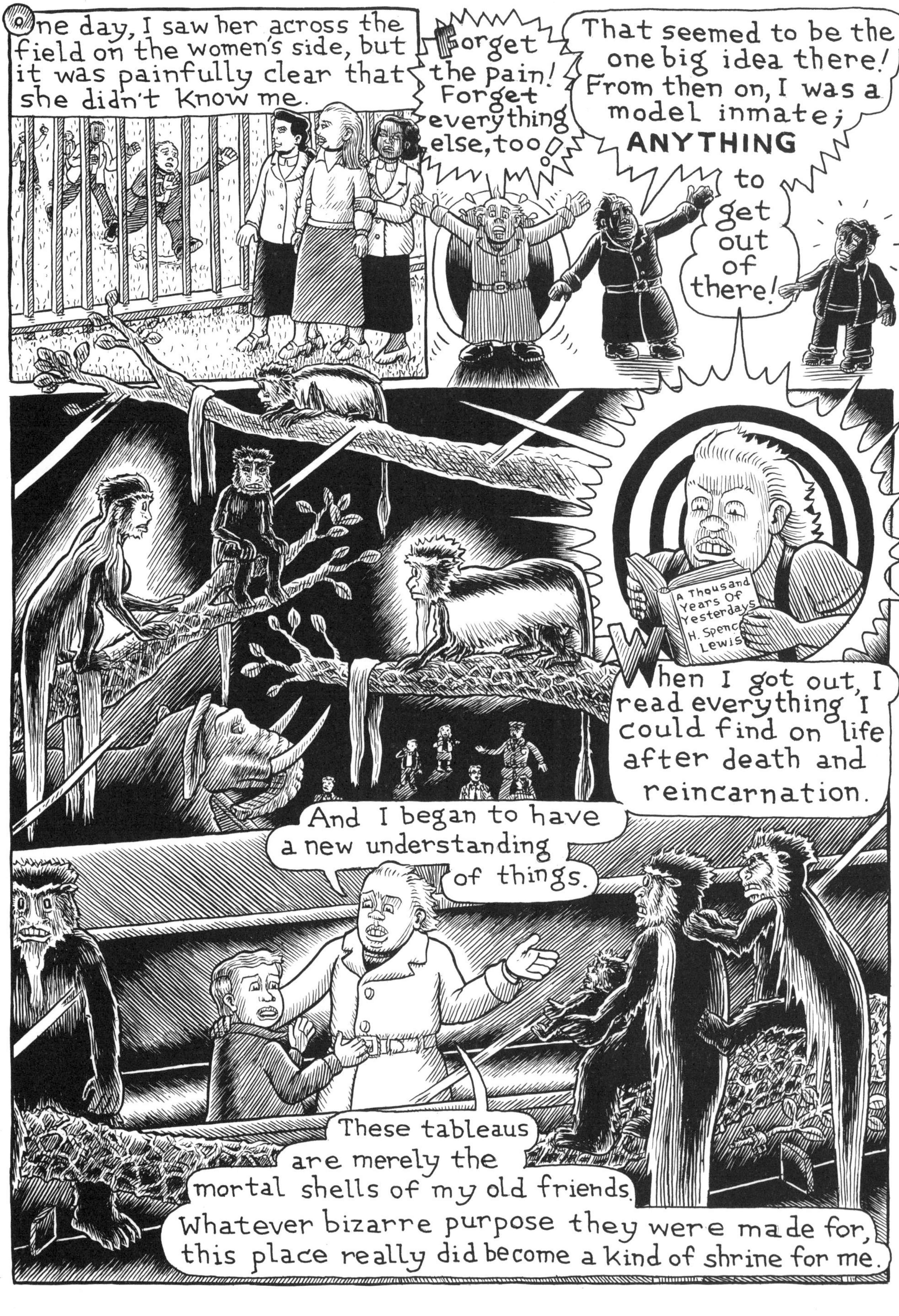
One day, I saw her across the field on the women's side, but it was painfully clear that she didn't know me.
Forget the pain! Forget everything else, too!
That seemed to be the one big idea there! From then on, I was a model inmate; ANYTHING to get out of there!
A Thousand Years Of Yesterdays H. Spenc Lewis
When I got out, I read everything I could find on life after death and reincarnation.
And I began to have a new understanding of things.
These tableaus are merely the mortal shells of my old friends.
Whatever bizarre purpose they were made for, this place really did become a kind of shrine for me.

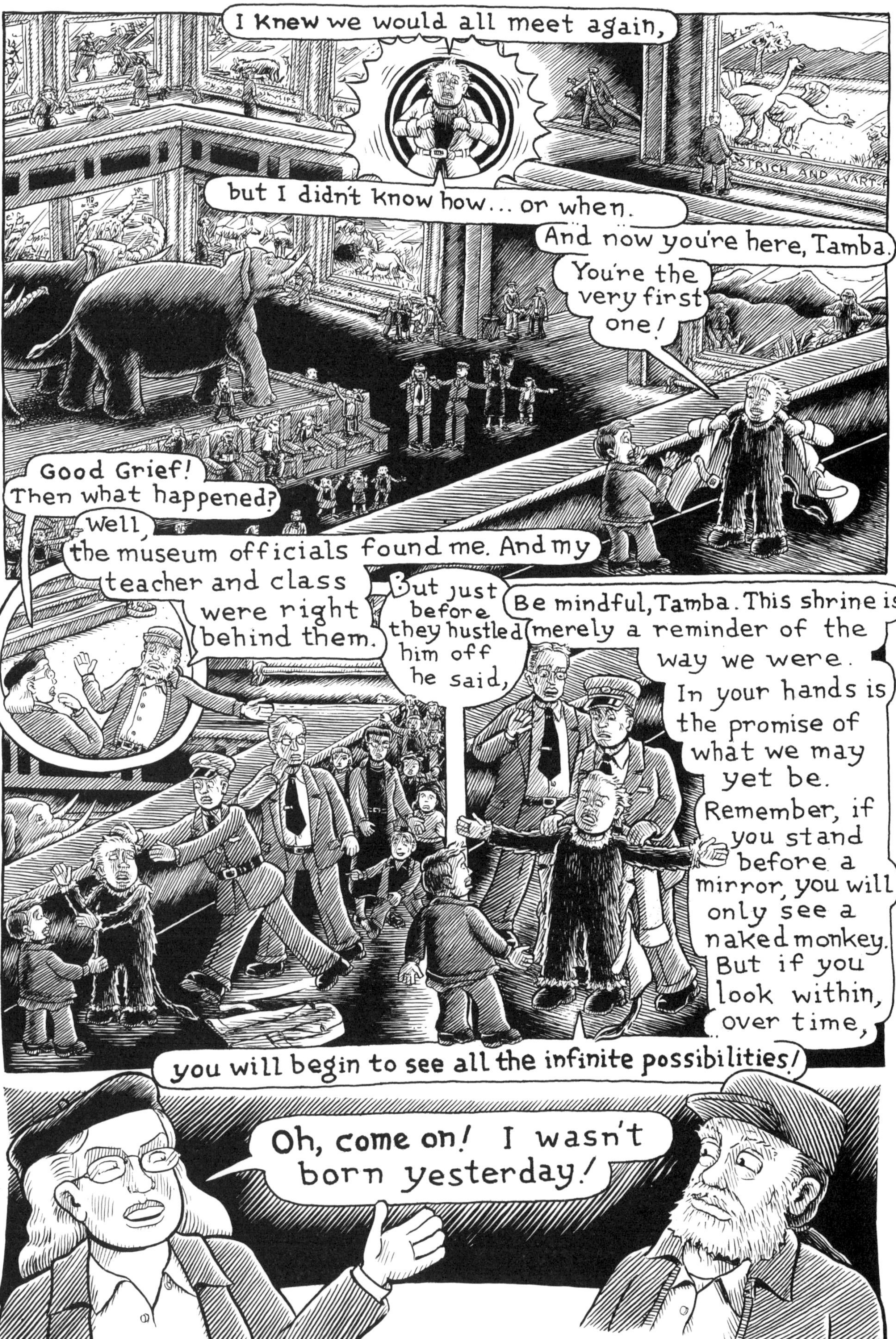
I knew we would all meet again,
but I didn't know how... or when.
And now you're here, Tamba.
You're the very first one!
Good Grief! Then what happened?
Well, the museum officials found me. And my teacher and class were right behind them.
But just before they hustled him off he said,
Be mindful, Tamba. This shrine is merely a reminder of the way we were.
In your hands is the promise of what we may yet be.
Remember, if you stand before a mirror, you will only see a naked monkey.
But if you look within, over time,
you will begin to see all the infinite possibilities!
Oh, come on! I wasn't born yesterday!

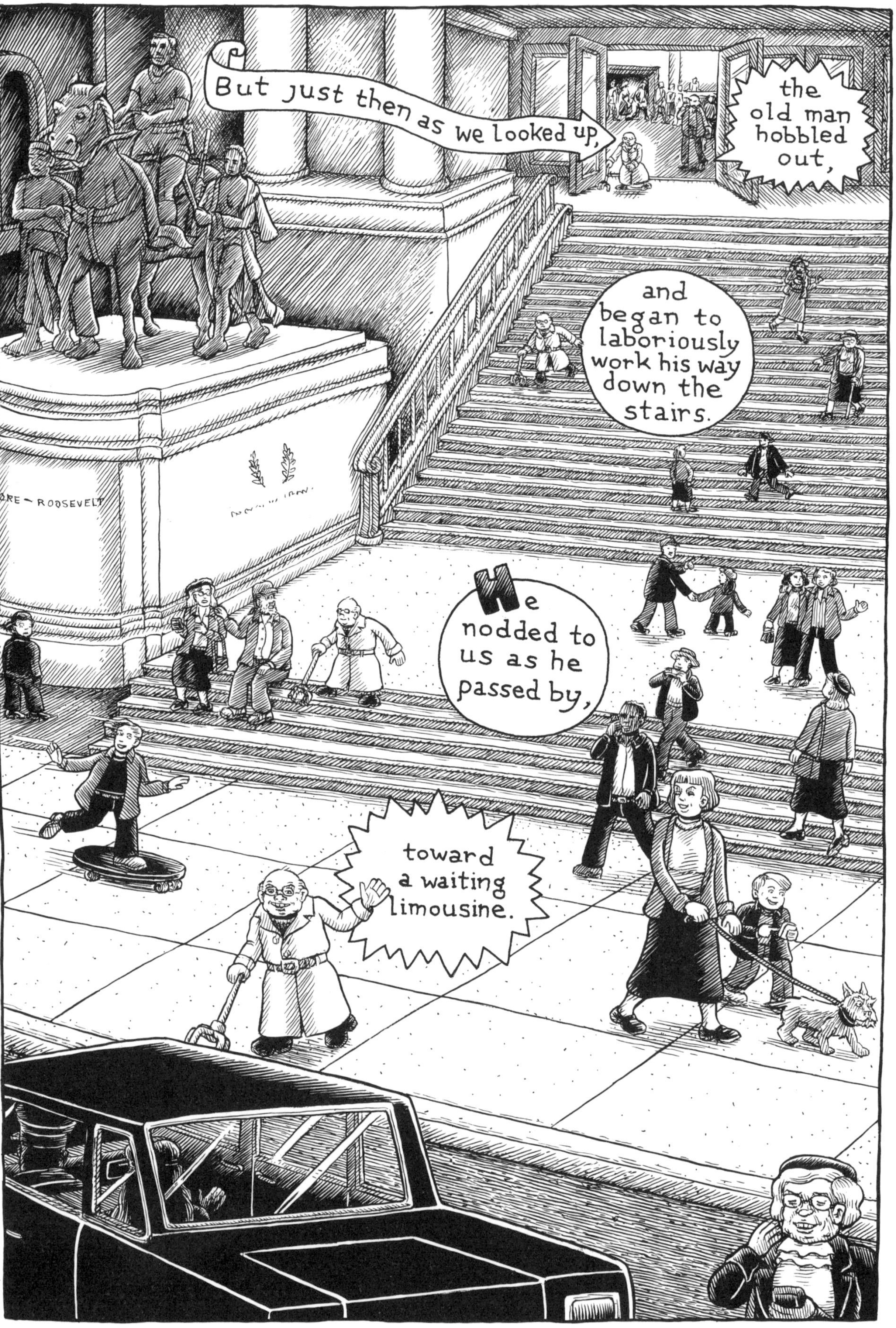
But just then as we looked up,
the old man hobbled out,
and began to laboriously work his way down the stairs.
ORE – ROOSEVELT
He nodded to us as he passed by,
toward a waiting limousine.

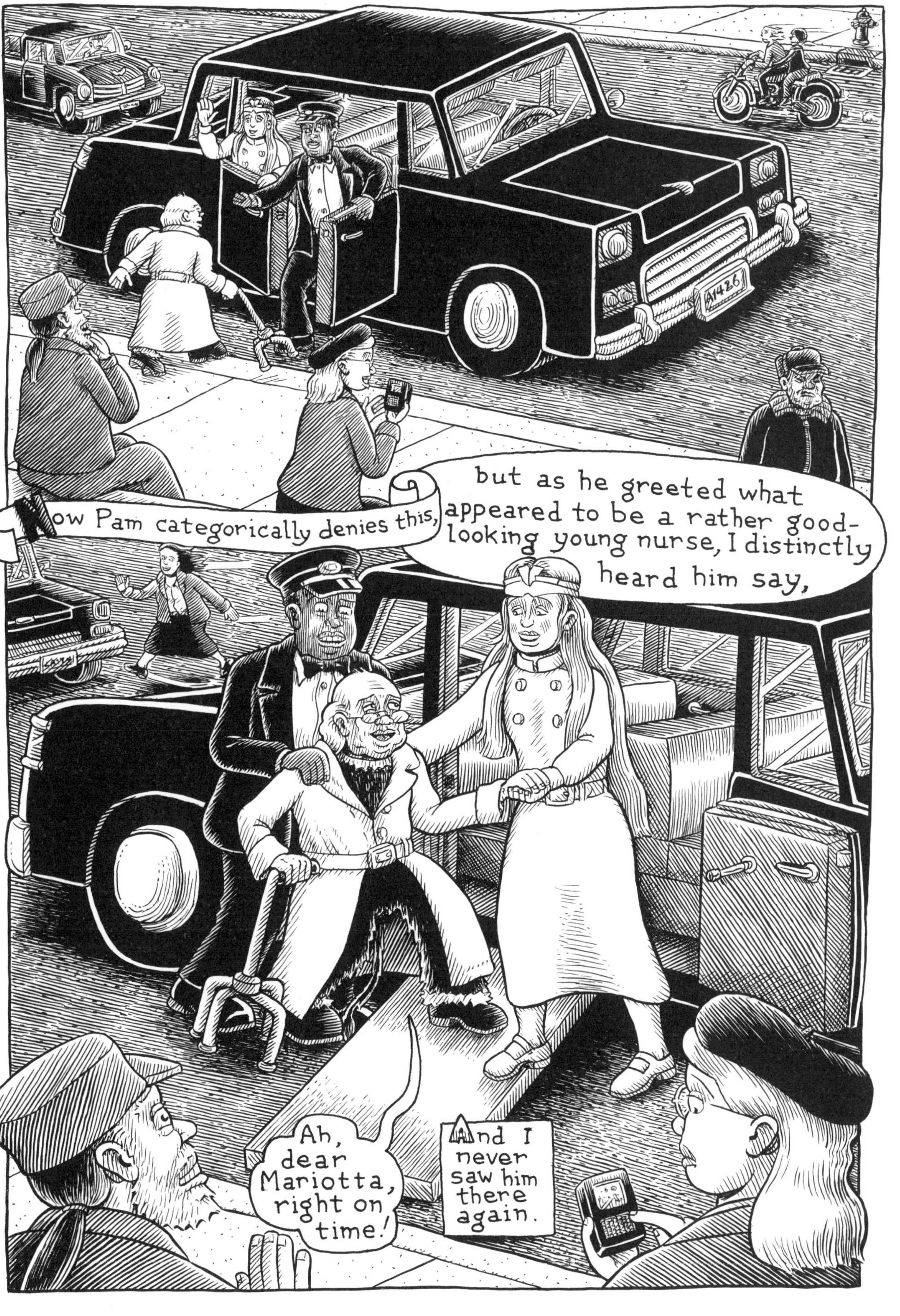
Now Pam categorically denies this,
but as he greeted what appeared to be a rather good-looking young nurse, I distinctly heard him say,
Ah, dear Mariotta, right on time!
And I never saw him there again.

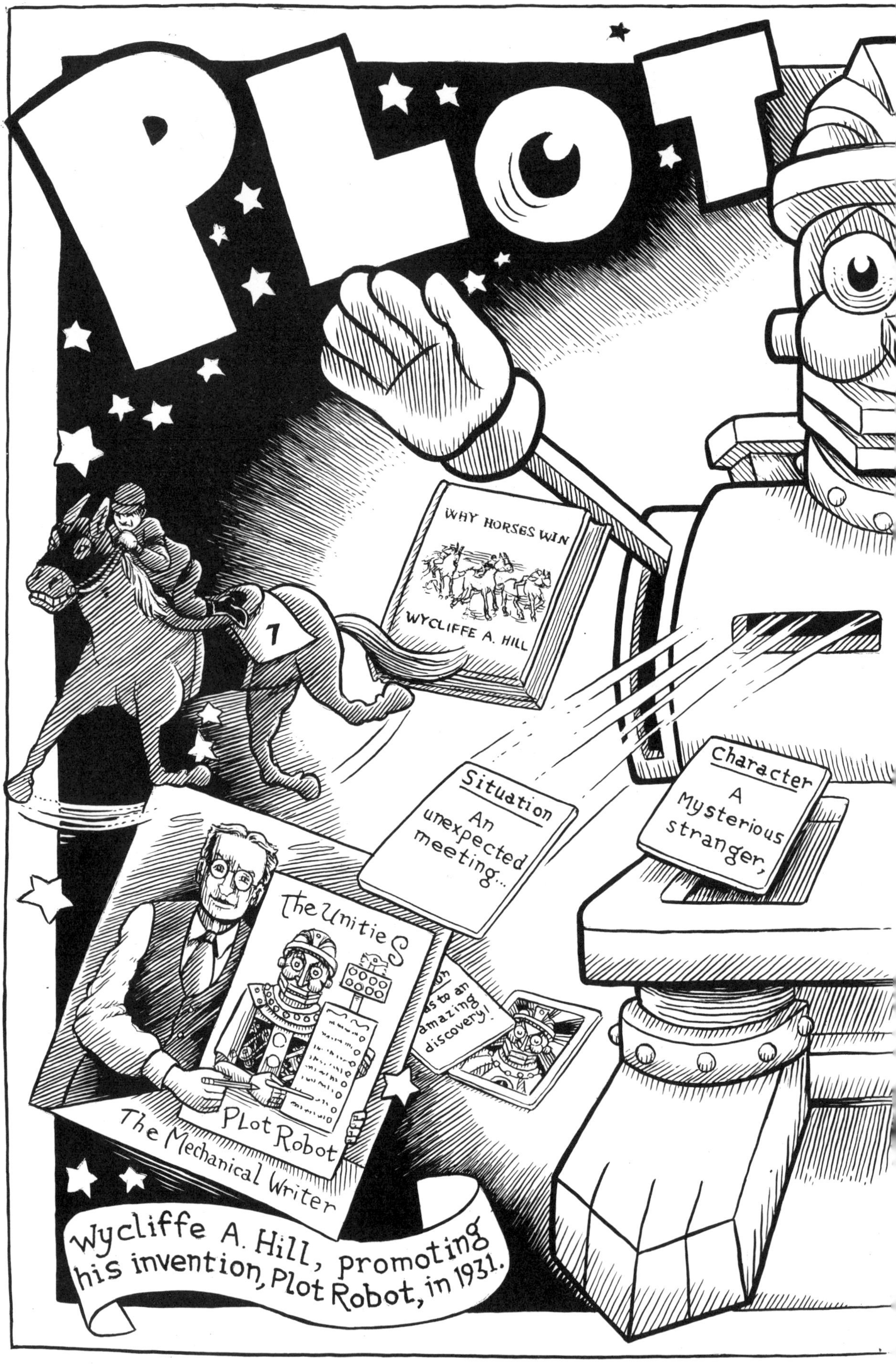
PLOT
WHY HORSES WIN
WYCLIFFE A. HILL
7
Situation
An unexpected meeting...
Character
A Mysterious stranger,
The Unities
Plot Robot
The Mechanical Writer
amazing discovery!
Wycliffe A. Hill, promoting his invention, Plot Robot, in 1931.

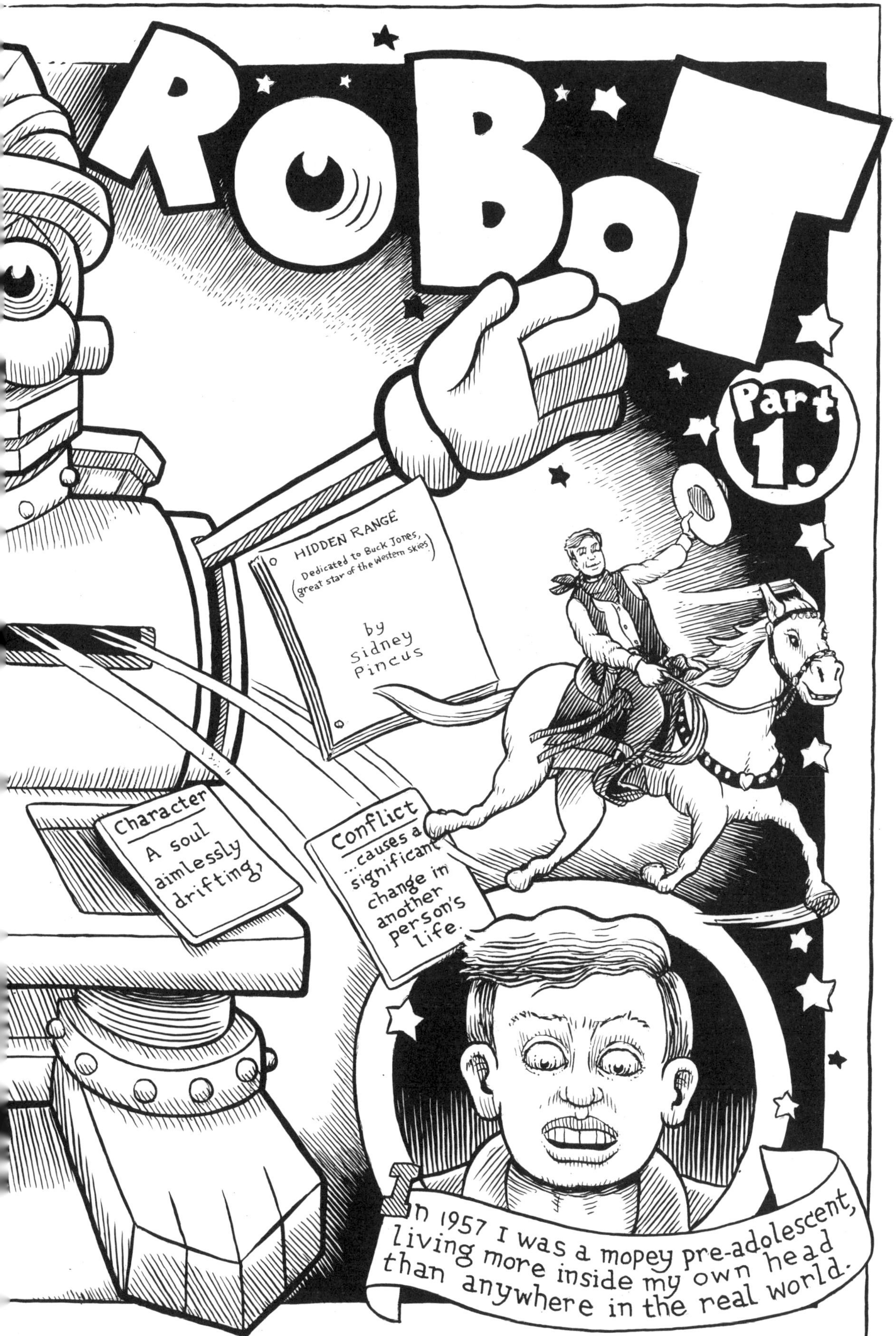
ROBOT
Part 1.
HIDDEN RANGE
Dedicated to Buck Jones, (great star of the Western skies)
by Sidney Pincus
Character
A soul aimlessly drifting,
Conflict
...causes a significant change in another person's life.
In 1957 I was a mopey pre-adolescent, living more inside my own head than anywhere in the real world.

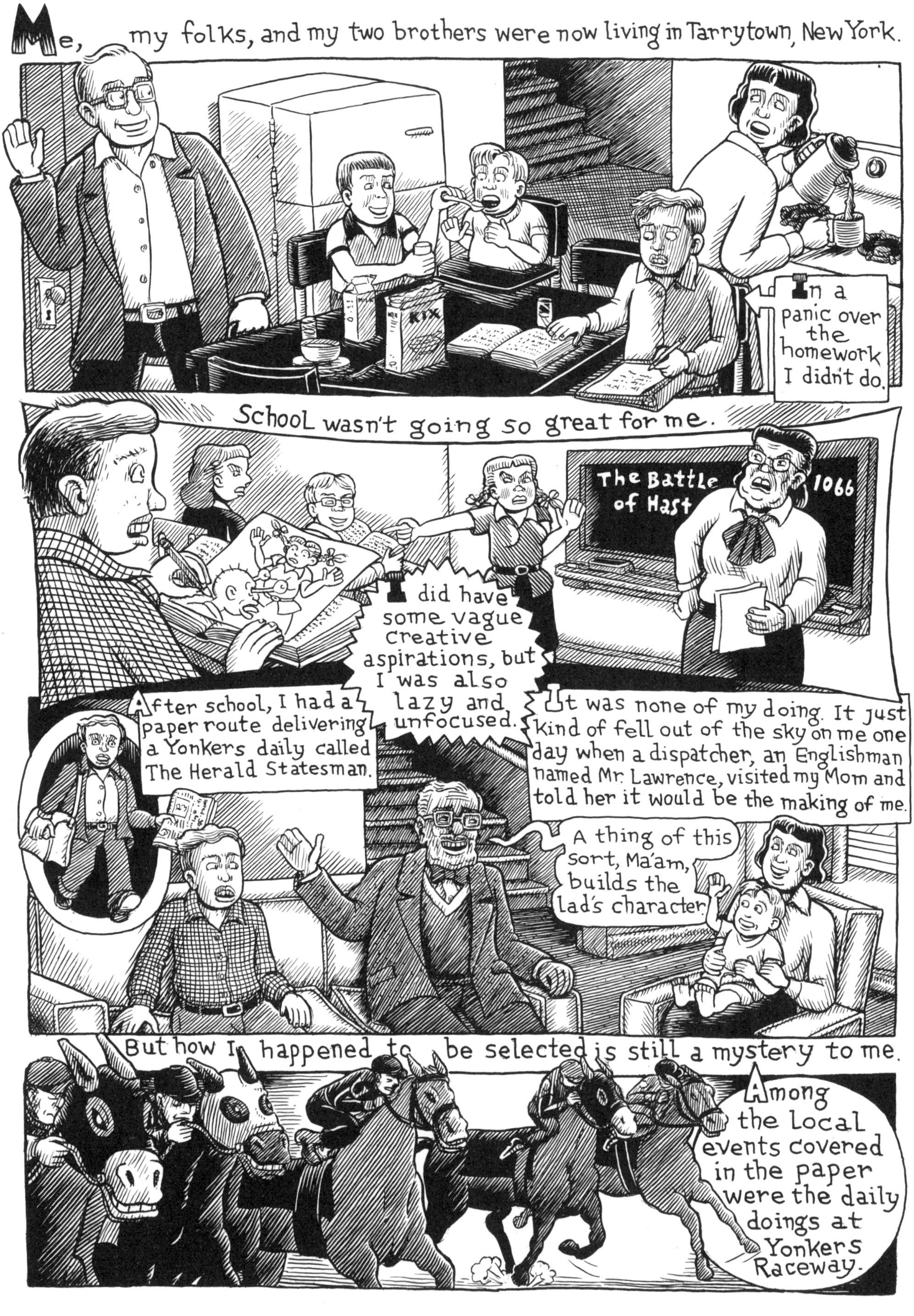
Me, my folks, and my two brothers were now living in Tarrytown, New York.
KIX
In a panic over the homework I didn't do.
School wasn't going so great for me.
The Battle of Hast 1066
I did have some vague creative aspirations, but I was also lazy and unfocused.
After school, I had a paper route delivering a Yonkers daily called The Herald Statesman.
It was none of my doing. It just kind of fell out of the sky on me one day when a dispatcher, an Englishman named Mr. Lawrence, visited my Mom and told her it would be the making of me.
A thing of this sort, Ma'am, builds the lad's character.
But how I happened to be selected is still a mystery to me.
Among the local events covered in the paper were the daily doings at Yonkers Raceway.

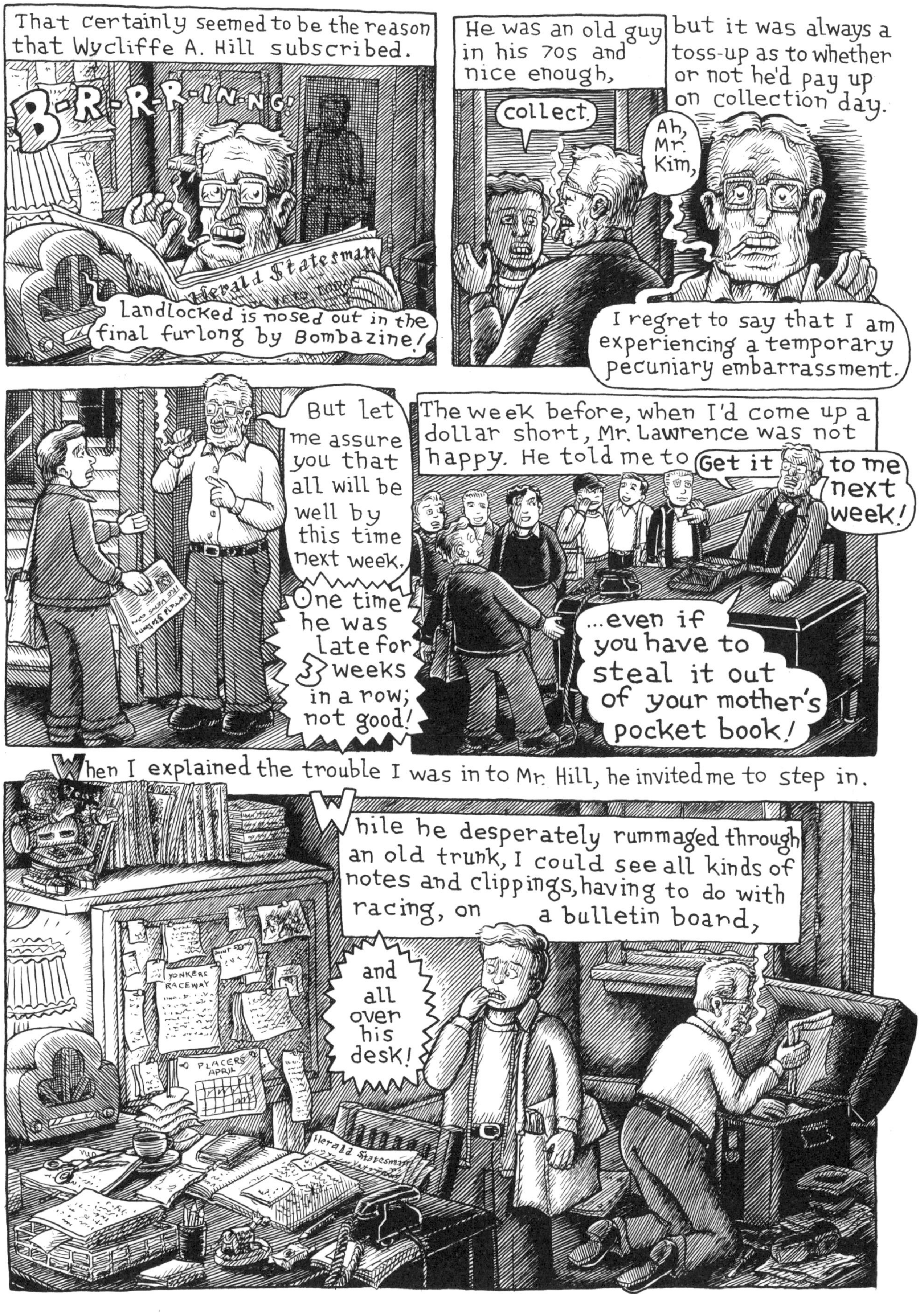
That certainly seemed to be the reason that Wycliffe A. Hill subscribed.
B-R-R-R-IN-NG!
Herald Statesman
Landlocked is nosed out in the final furlong by Bombazine!
He was an old guy in his 70s and nice enough,
collect.
but it was always a toss-up as to whether or not he'd pay up on collection day.
Ah, Mr. Kim,
I regret to say that I am experiencing a temporary pecuniary embarrassment.
But let me assure you that all will be well by this time next week.
One time he was late for 3 weeks in a row; not good!
The week before, when I'd come up a dollar short, Mr. Lawrence was not happy. He told me to
Get it to me next week!
...even if you have to steal it out of your mother's pocket book!
When I explained the trouble I was in to Mr. Hill, he invited me to step in.
While he desperately rummaged through an old trunk, I could see all kinds of notes and clippings, having to do with racing, on a bulletin board,
and all over his desk!
YONKERS RACEWAY
PLACERS APRIL
Herald Statesman

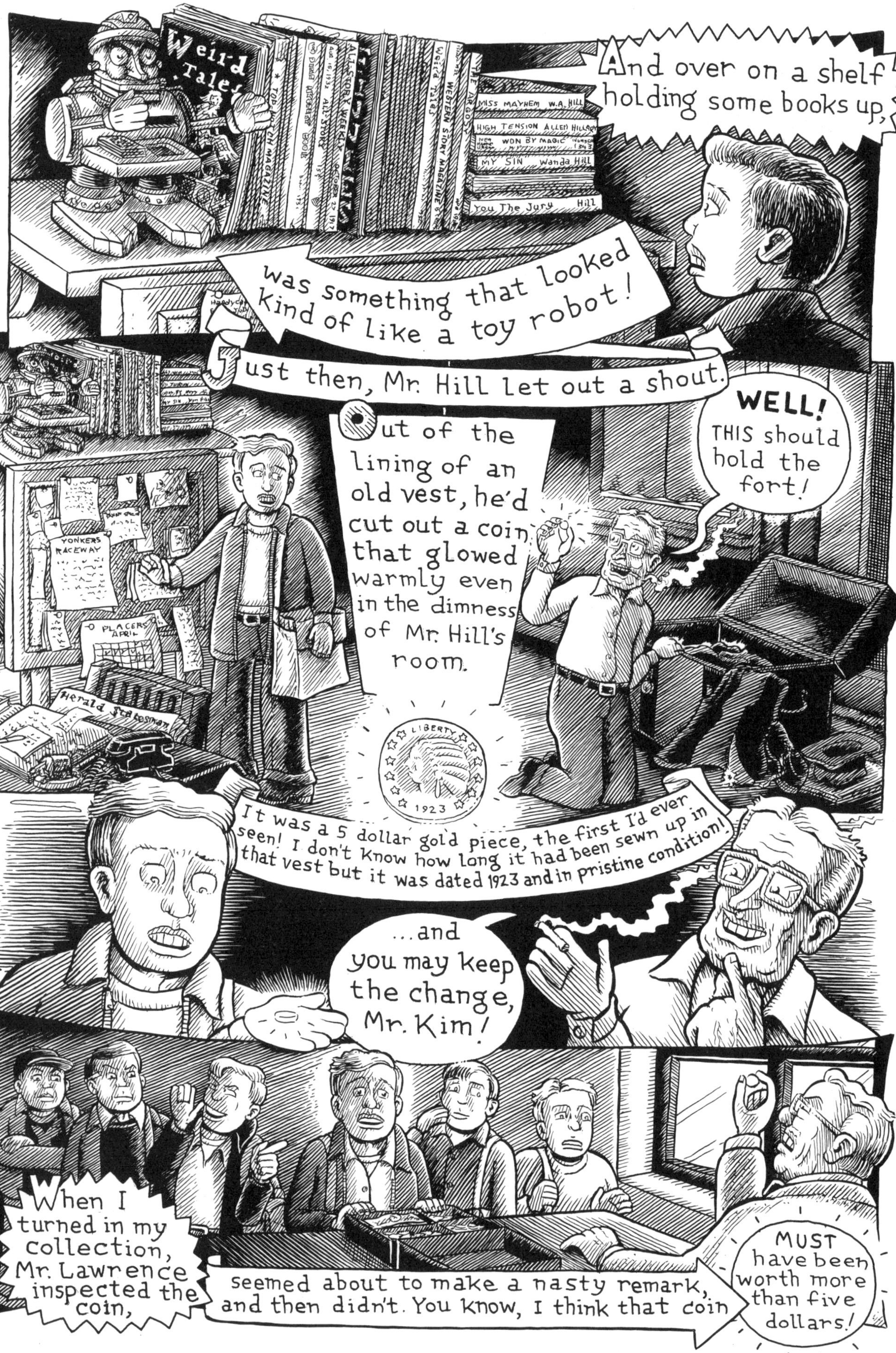
And over on a shelf holding some books up,
was something that looked kind of like a toy robot!
Just then, Mr. Hill let out a shout.
Out of the lining of an old vest, he'd cut out a coin that glowed warmly even in the dimness of Mr. Hill's room.
WELL! THIS should hold the fort!
It was a 5 dollar gold piece, the first I'd ever seen! I don't know how long it had been sewn up in that vest but it was dated 1923 and in pristine condition!
...and you may keep the change, Mr. Kim!
When I turned in my collection, Mr. Lawrence inspected the coin,
seemed about to make a nasty remark, and then didn't. You know, I think that coin
MUST have been worth more than five dollars!

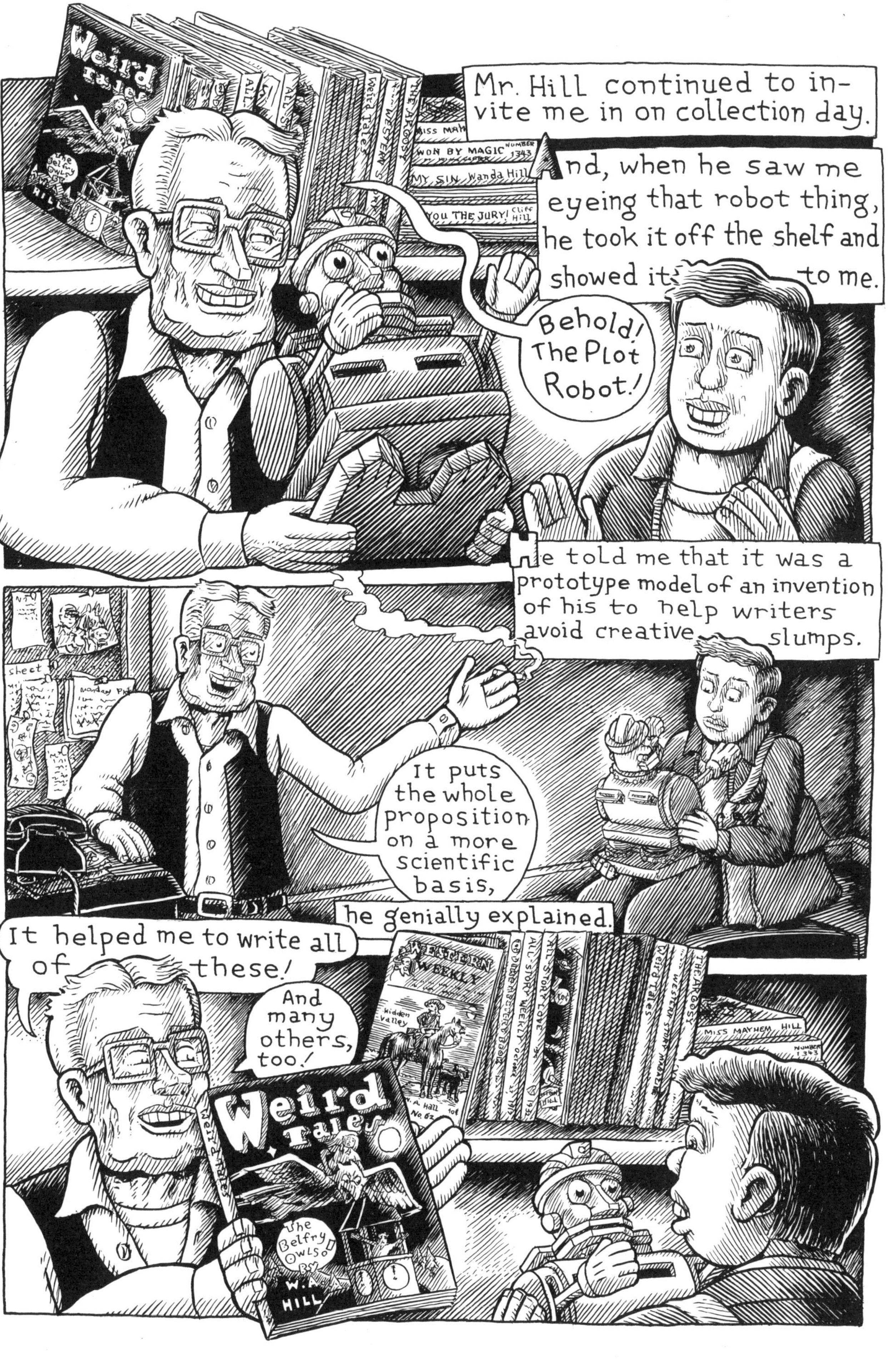
Mr. Hill continued to invite me in on collection day.
And, when he saw me eyeing that robot thing, he took it off the shelf and showed it to me.
Behold! The Plot Robot!
He told me that it was a prototype model of an invention of his to help writers avoid creative slumps.
It puts the whole proposition on a more scientific basis,
he genially explained.
It helped me to write all of these!
And many others, too!
Weird Tales
The Belfry Owls
W. A. Hill
Western Weekly
The Argosy
Miss Mayhem Hill

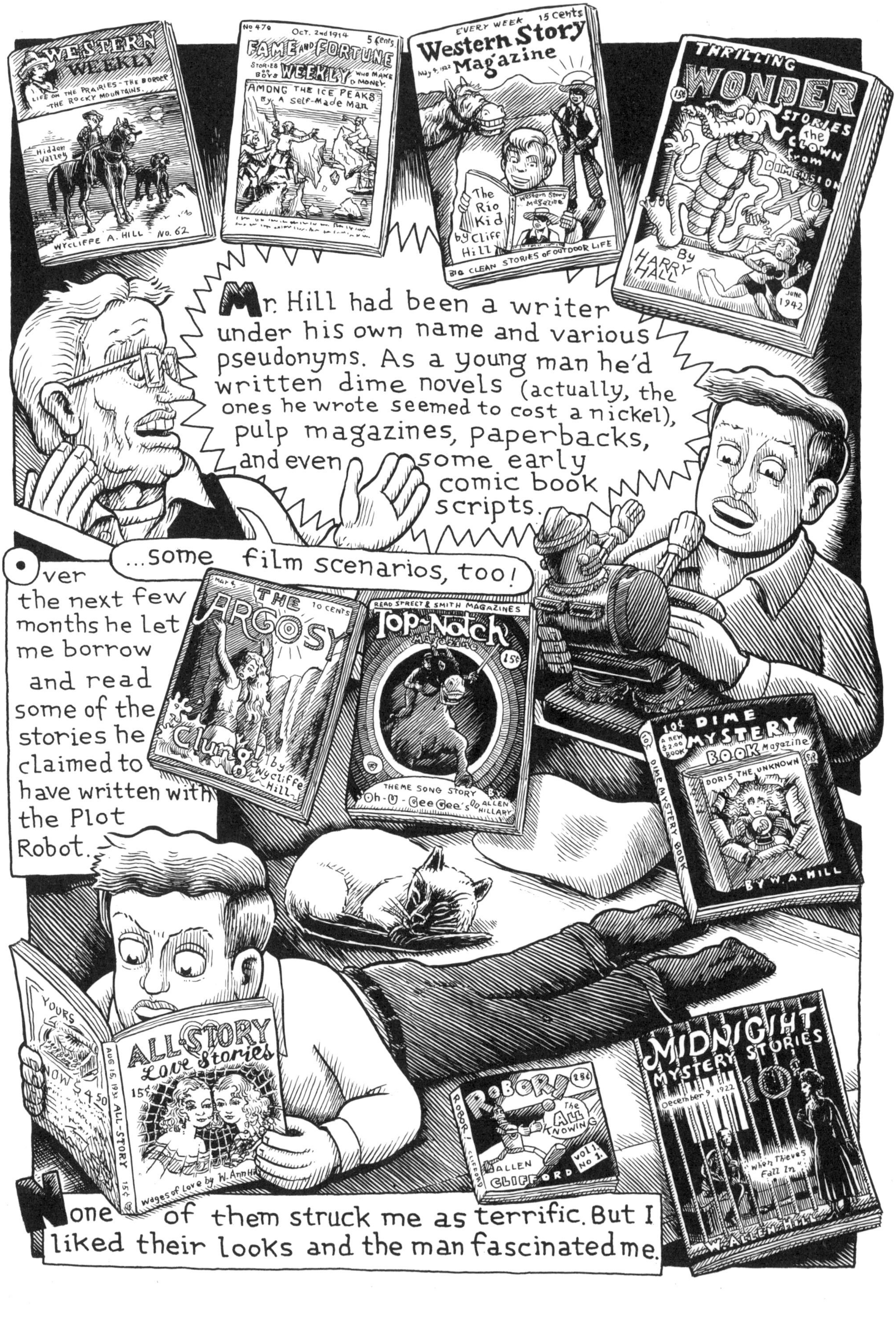
Western Weekly
Life on the Prairies - The Border - The Rocky Mountains.
Hidden Valley
Wycliffe A. Hill No. 62
No 470 Oct. 2nd 1914 5 cents
Fame and Fortune Weekly
Stories of Boys who make money.
Among the Ice Peaks
By A Self-Made Man
Every Week 15 cents
Western Story Magazine
May 4, 1922
The Rio Kid by Cliff Hill
Big Clean Stories of Outdoor Life
Thrilling Wonder Stories
The Clown from Dimension X
By Harry Hall
June 1942
Mr. Hill had been a writer under his own name and various pseudonyms. As a young man he'd written dime novels (actually, the ones he wrote seemed to cost a nickel), pulp magazines, paperbacks, and even some early comic book scripts.
...some film scenarios, too!
Over the next few months he let me borrow and read some of the stories he claimed to have written with the Plot Robot.
The Argosy 10 cents
Clung! by Wycliffe Hill
Read Street & Smith Magazines
Top-Notch Magazine 15¢
Theme Song Story
Oh-U-Gee Gee's
By Allen Hillary
10¢ Dime Mystery Book Magazine
A new $2.00 book
Doris the Unknown
By W. A. Hill
All-Story Love Stories
Aug 15 1932 15¢
Wages of Love by W. Ann Hill
Robor! The All Knowing
Vol 1, No 1
Allen Clifford
Midnight Mystery Stories 10¢
December 9, 1922
When Thieves Fall In
None of them struck me as terrific. But I liked their looks and the man fascinated me.

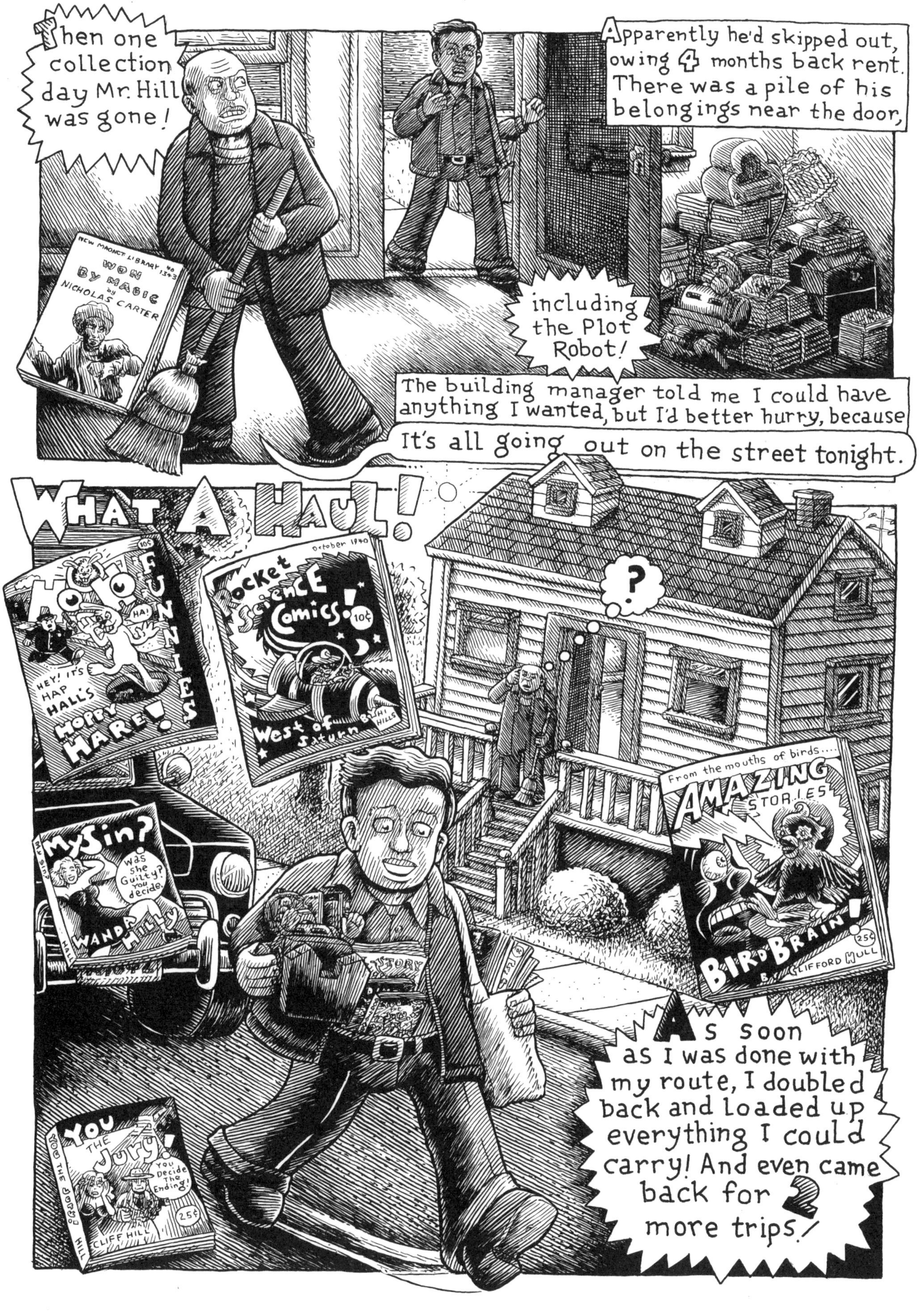
Then one collection day Mr. Hill was gone!
Apparently he'd skipped out, owing 4 months back rent. There was a pile of his belongings near the door,
NEW MAGNET LIBRARY No. 1343 WON BY MAGIC by NICHOLAS CARTER
including the Plot Robot!
The building manager told me I could have anything I wanted, but I'd better hurry, because
It's all going out on the street tonight.
WHAT A HAUL!
10¢ FUNNIES HA! HEY! IT'S HAP HALL'S HOPPY HARE!
October 1940 Rocket Science Comics! 10¢ West of Saturn
?
My Sin? Was she Guilty? You decide. WANDA HILL
From the mouths of birds.... AMAZING STORIES BIRD BRAIN! 25¢ By CLIFFORD HULL
YOU THE JURY! You Decide The Ending! 25¢ CLIFF HILL
As soon as I was done with my route, I doubled back and loaded up everything I could carry! And even came back for 2 more trips!

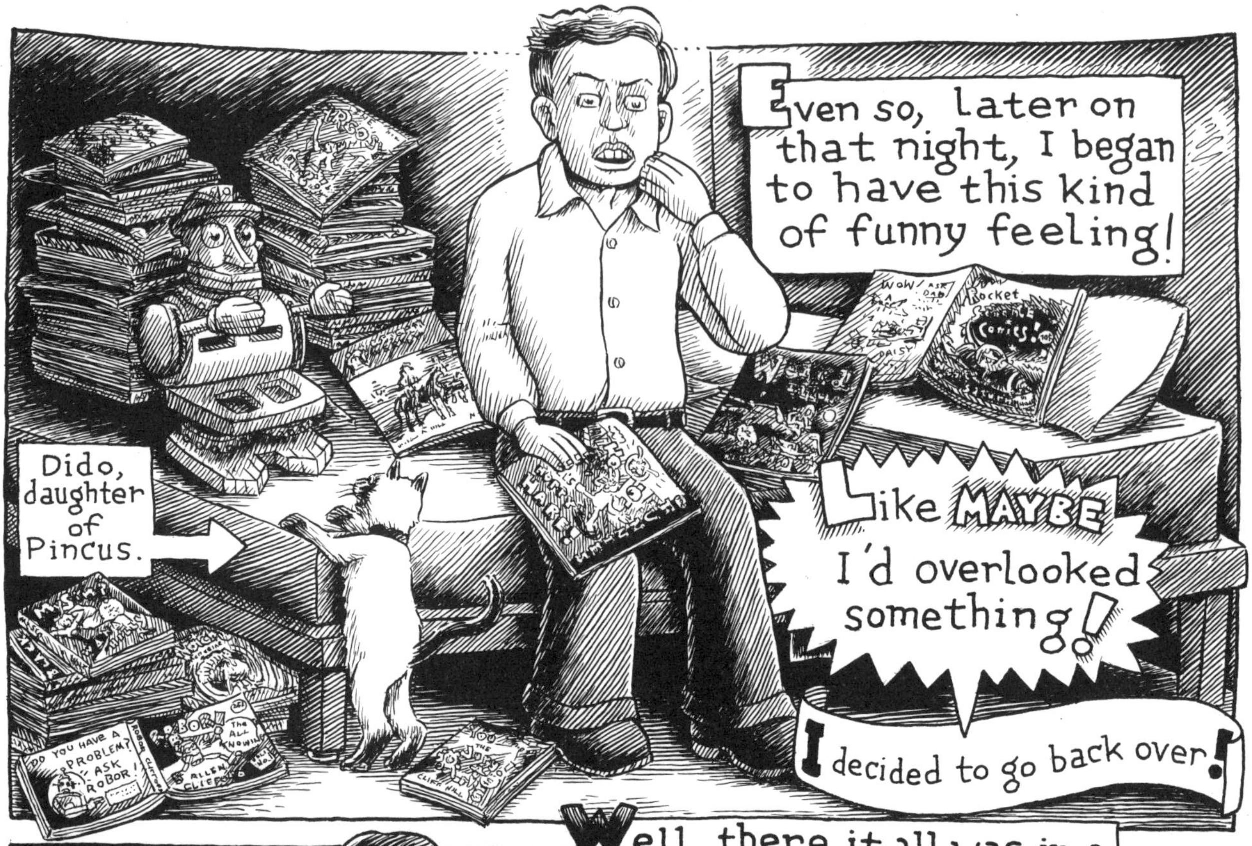
Even so, later on that night, I began to have this kind of funny feeling!
Dido, daughter of Pincus.
Like MAYBE I'd overlooked something!
I decided to go back over!
DO YOU HAVE A PROBLEM? ASK ROBOR!

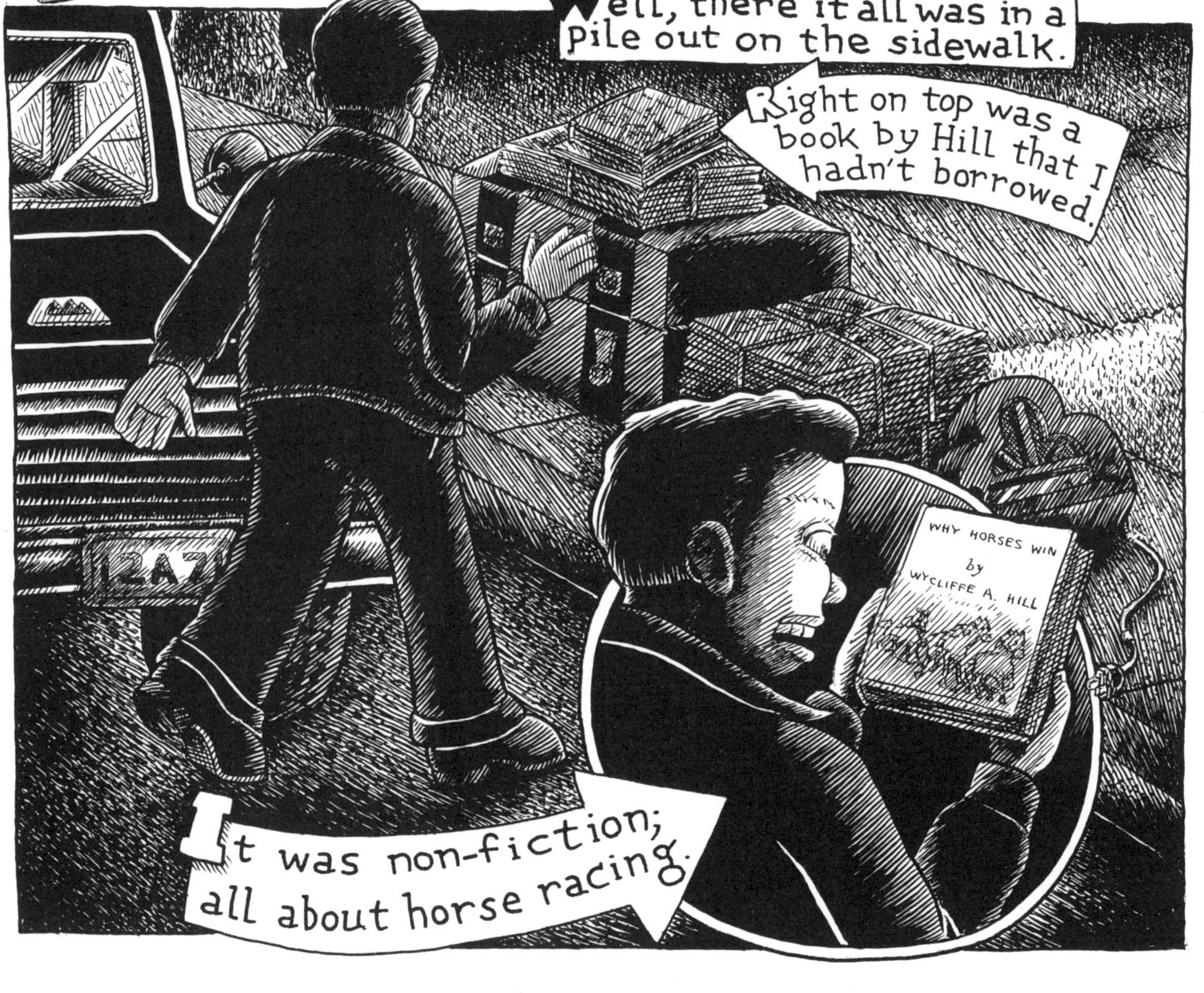
Well, there it all was in a pile out on the sidewalk.
Right on top was a book by Hill that I hadn't borrowed.
WHY HORSES WIN by WYCLIFFE A. HILL
It was non-fiction; all about horse racing.

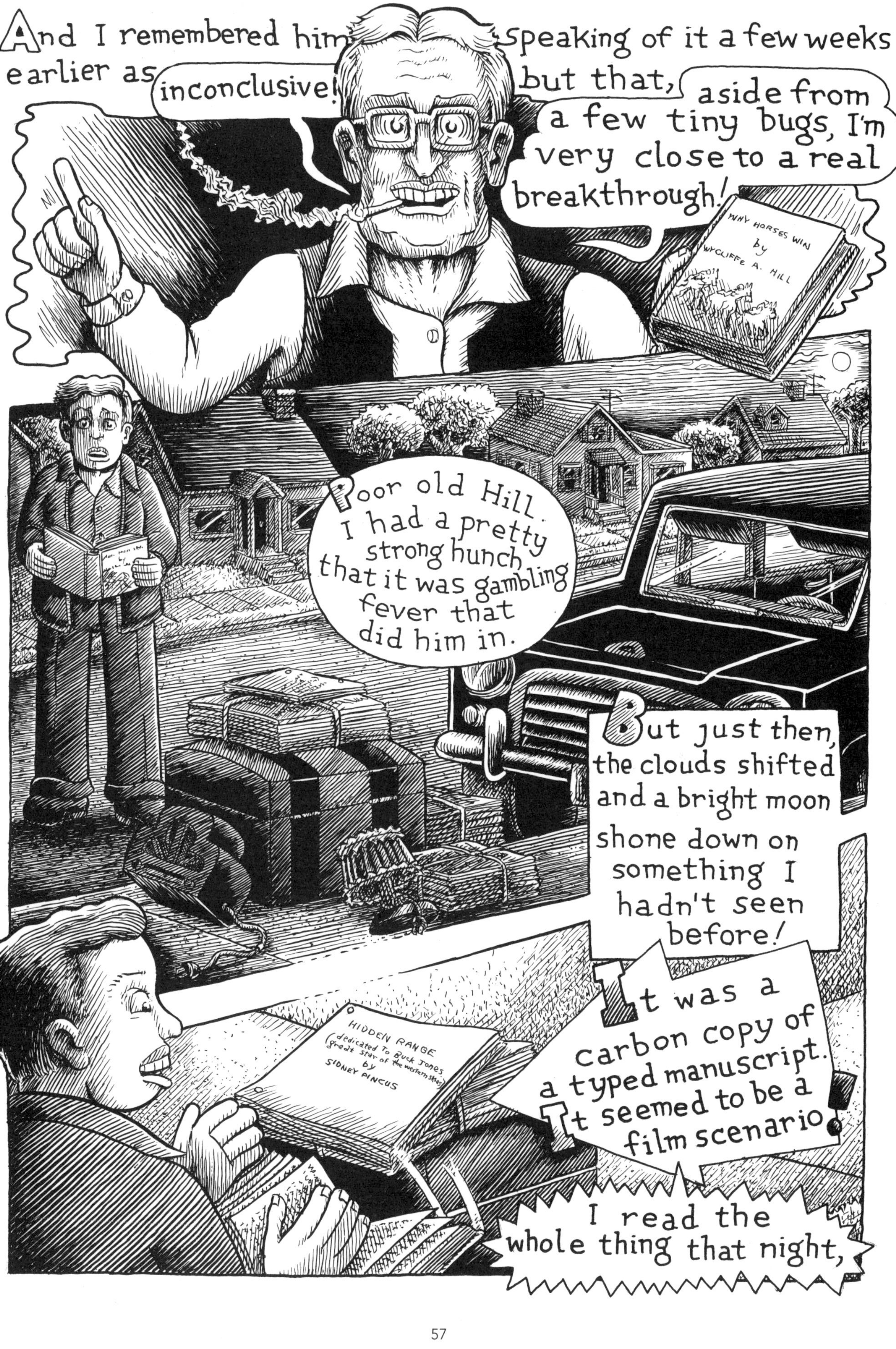
And I remembered him speaking of it a few weeks earlier as
inconclusive!
but that,
aside from a few tiny bugs, I'm very close to a real breakthrough!
WHY HORSES WIN by WYCLIFFE A. HILL
Poor old Hill. I had a pretty strong hunch that it was gambling fever that did him in.
But just then, the clouds shifted and a bright moon
shone down on something I hadn't seen before!
It was a carbon copy of a typed manuscript. It seemed to be a film scenario!
HIDDEN RANGE
(dedicated To Buck Jones great star of the western skies)
by
SIDNEY PINCUS
I read the whole thing that night,

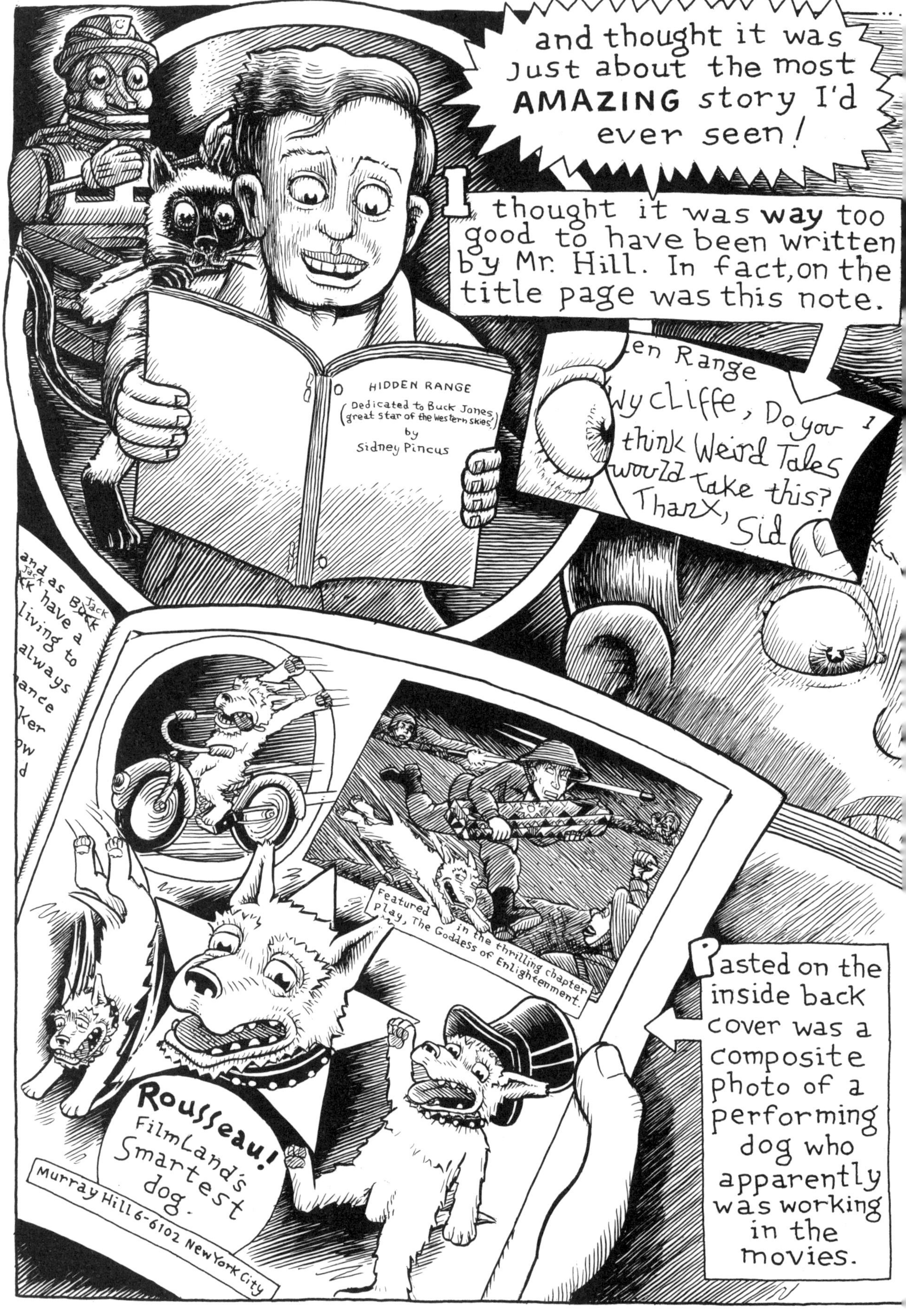
and thought it was just about the most AMAZING story I'd ever seen!
I thought it was way too good to have been written by Mr. Hill. In fact, on the title page was this note.
HIDDEN RANGE
(Dedicated to Buck Jones, great star of the western skies)
by
Sidney Pincus
en Range
Wycliffe, Do you think Weird Tales would take this? Thanx, Sid
Pasted on the inside back cover was a composite photo of a performing dog who apparently was working in the movies.
Featured in the thrilling chapter play, The Goddess of Enlightenment.
Rousseau! FilmLand's Smartest dog.
Murray Hill 6-6102 New York City

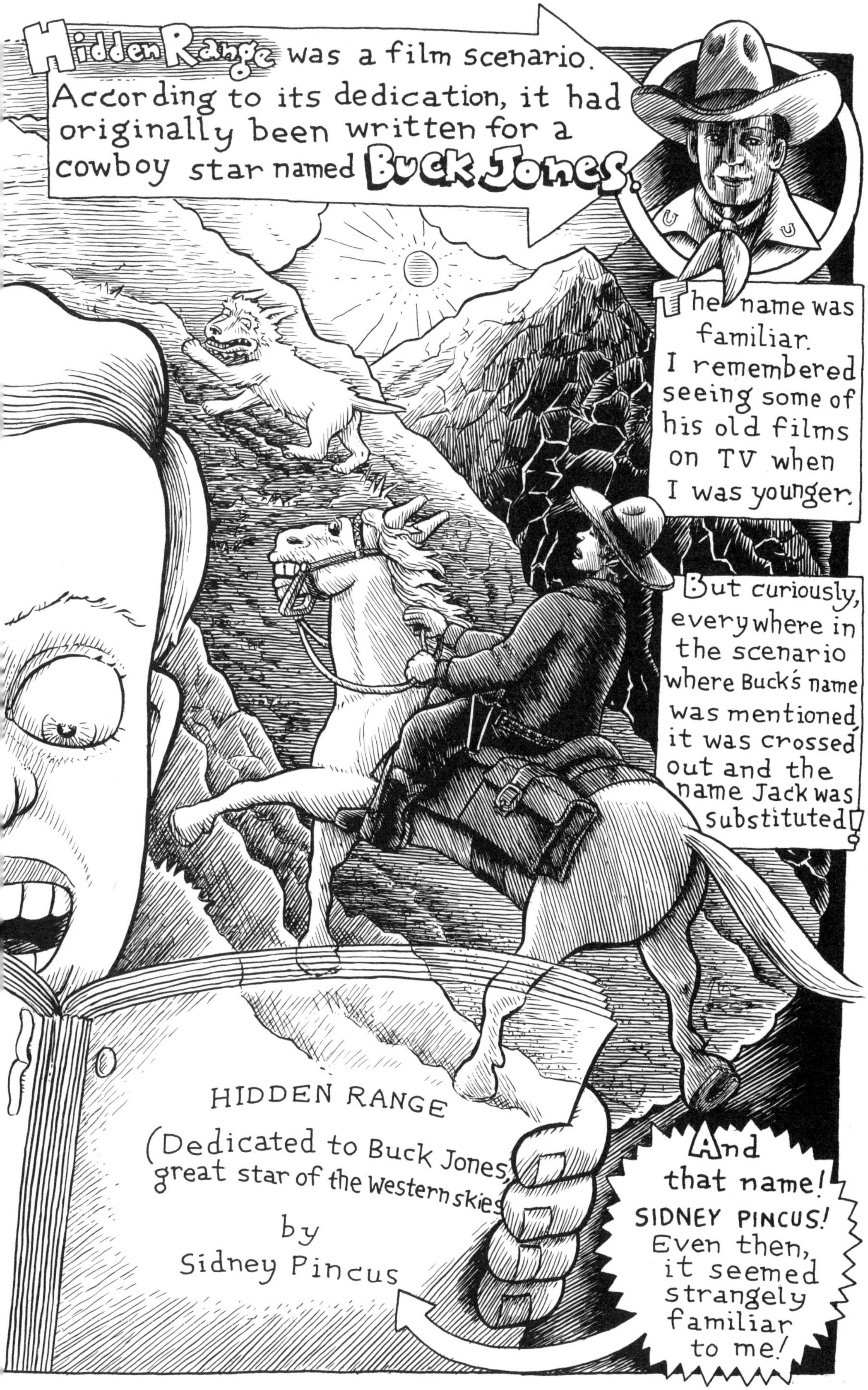
Hidden Range was a film scenario. According to its dedication, it had originally been written for a cowboy star named Buck Jones.
The name was familiar. I remembered seeing some of his old films on TV when I was younger.
But curiously, everywhere in the scenario where Buck's name was mentioned, it was crossed out and the name Jack was substituted!
HIDDEN RANGE
(Dedicated to Buck Jones, great star of the Western skies)
by
Sidney Pincus
And that name! SIDNEY PINCUS! Even then, it seemed strangely familiar to me!

Part 2.

Hidden Range

Here, visualized, is the original screenplay of **Hidden Range**. When you read it, you'll quickly see WHY it never really stood a chance of being a vehicle for Buck Jones. But times change and it is my distinct pleasure to present it to you as originally conceived by Sidney Pincus in 1927. What is perhaps more remarkable is that it came pretty close to being produced as a talking picture in the 1930s. But that is another story.

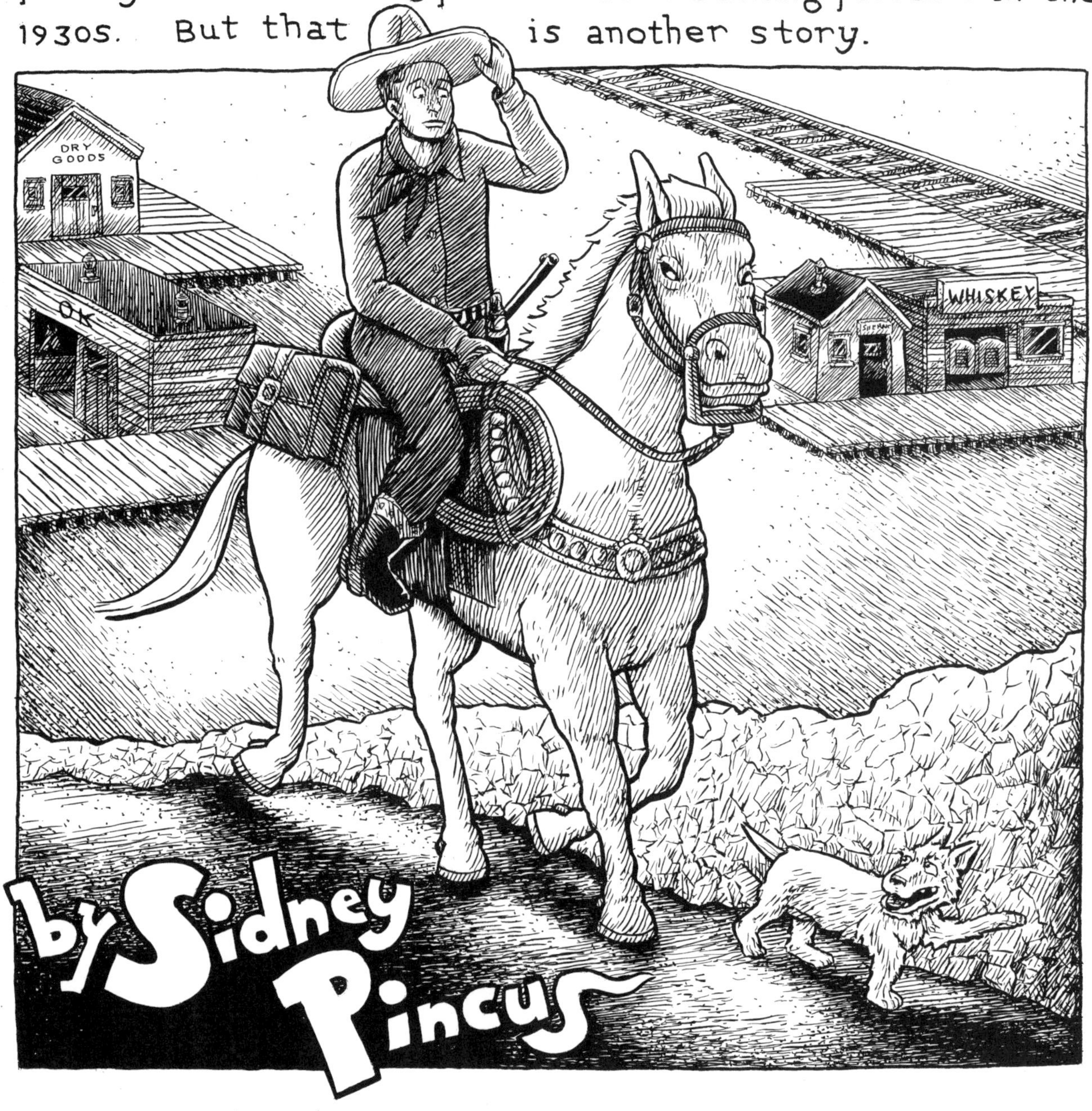

DRY GOODS
OK
WHISKEY
by Sidney Pincus

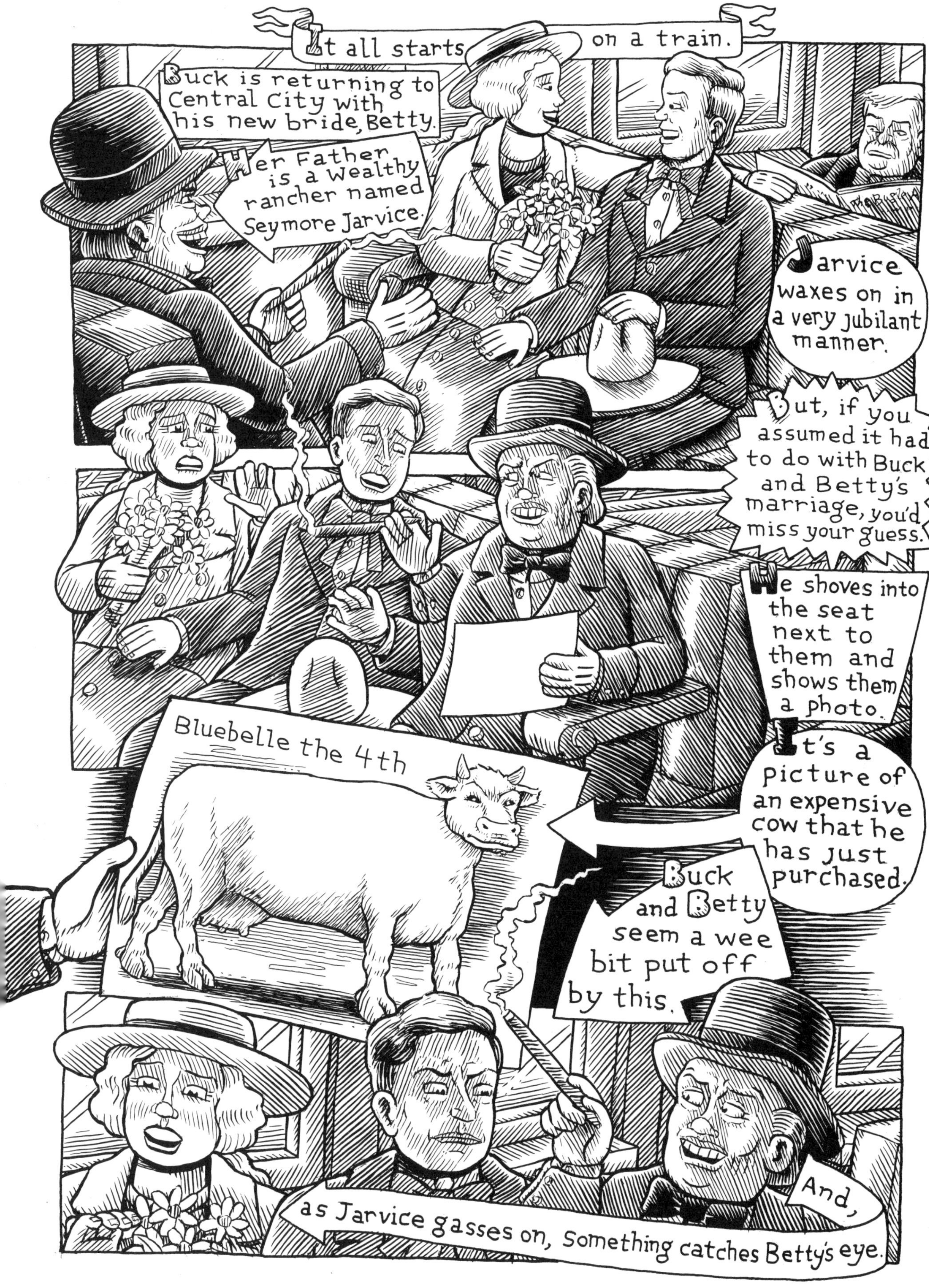

It all starts on a train.
Buck is returning to Central City with his new bride, Betty.
Her Father is a Wealthy rancher named Seymore Jarvice.
Jarvice waxes on in a very jubilant manner.
But, if you assumed it had to do with Buck and Betty's marriage, you'd miss your guess.
He shoves into the seat next to them and shows them a photo.
Bluebelle the 4th
It's a picture of an expensive cow that he has just purchased.
Buck and Betty seem a wee bit put off by this.
And, as Jarvice gasses on, something catches Betty's eye.

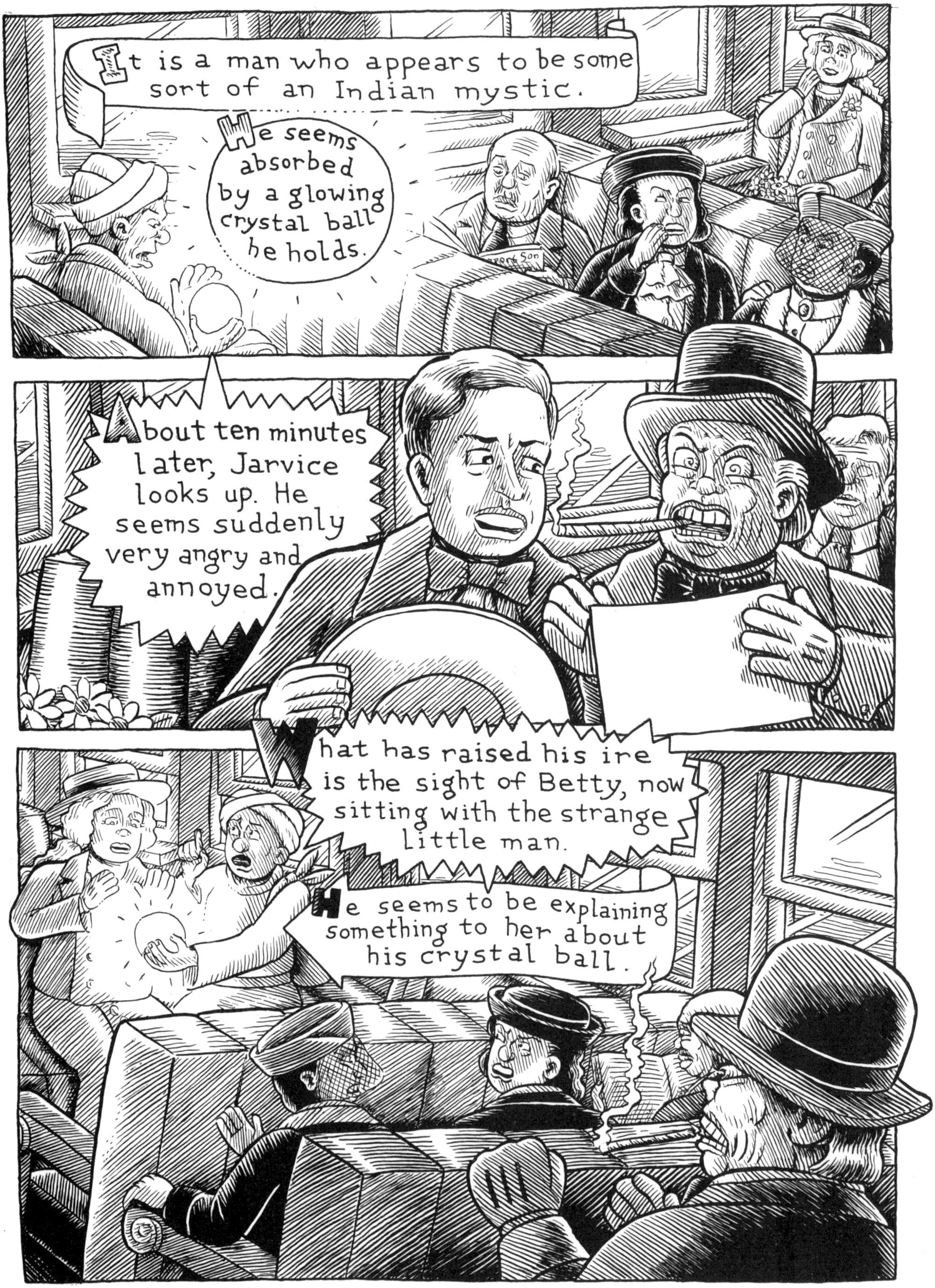
It is a man who appears to be some sort of an Indian mystic.
He seems absorbed by a glowing crystal ball he holds.
About ten minutes later, Jarvice looks up. He seems suddenly very angry and annoyed.
What has raised his ire is the sight of Betty, now sitting with the strange little man.
He seems to be explaining something to her about his crystal ball.

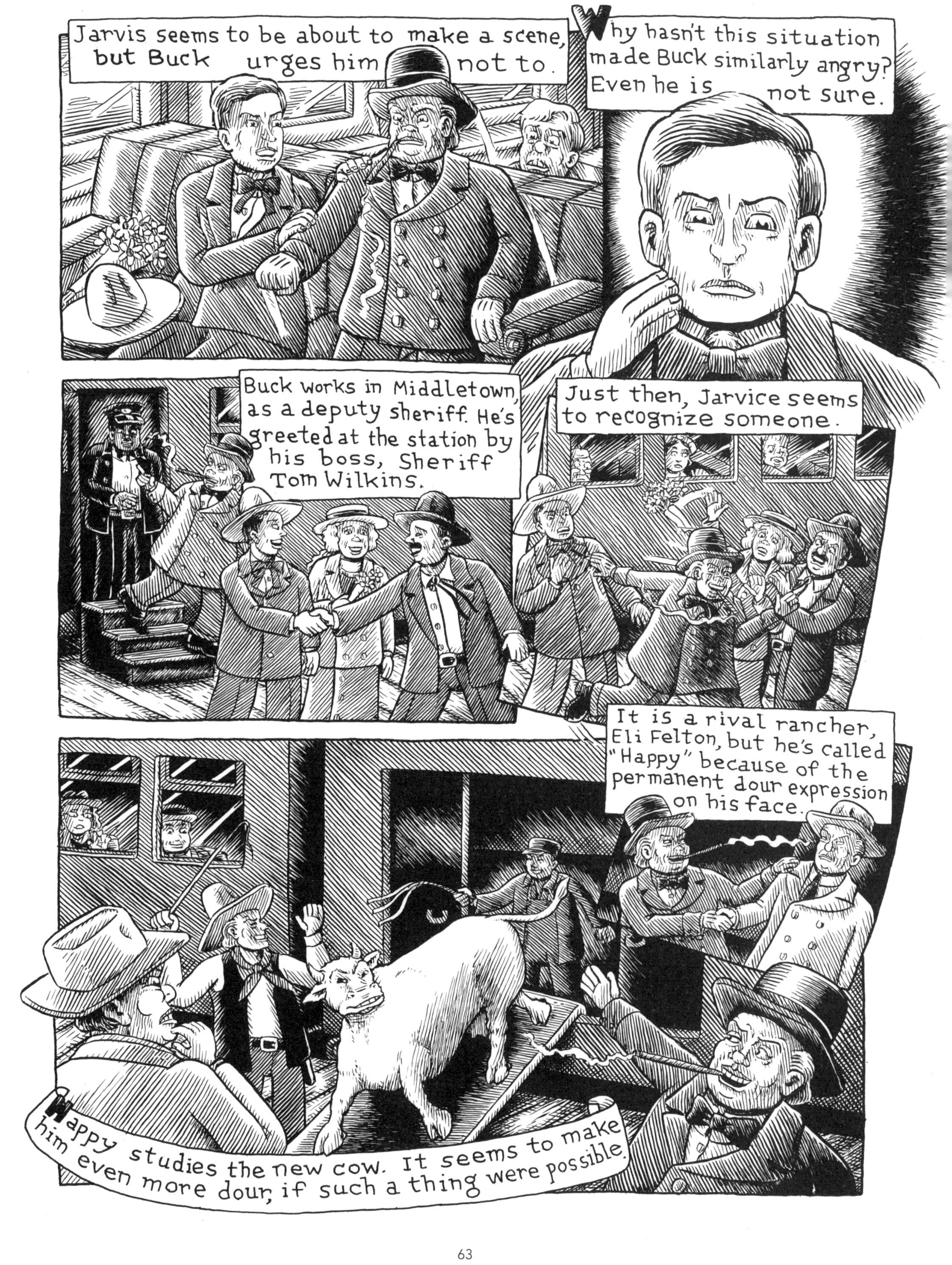
Jarvis seems to be about to make a scene, but Buck urges him not to.
Why hasn't this situation made Buck similarly angry? Even he is not sure.
Buck works in Middletown, as a deputy sheriff. He's greeted at the station by his boss, Sheriff Tom Wilkins.
Just then, Jarvice seems to recognize someone.
It is a rival rancher, Eli Felton, but he's called "Happy" because of the permanent dour expression on his face.
Happy studies the new cow. It seems to make him even more dour, if such a thing were possible.

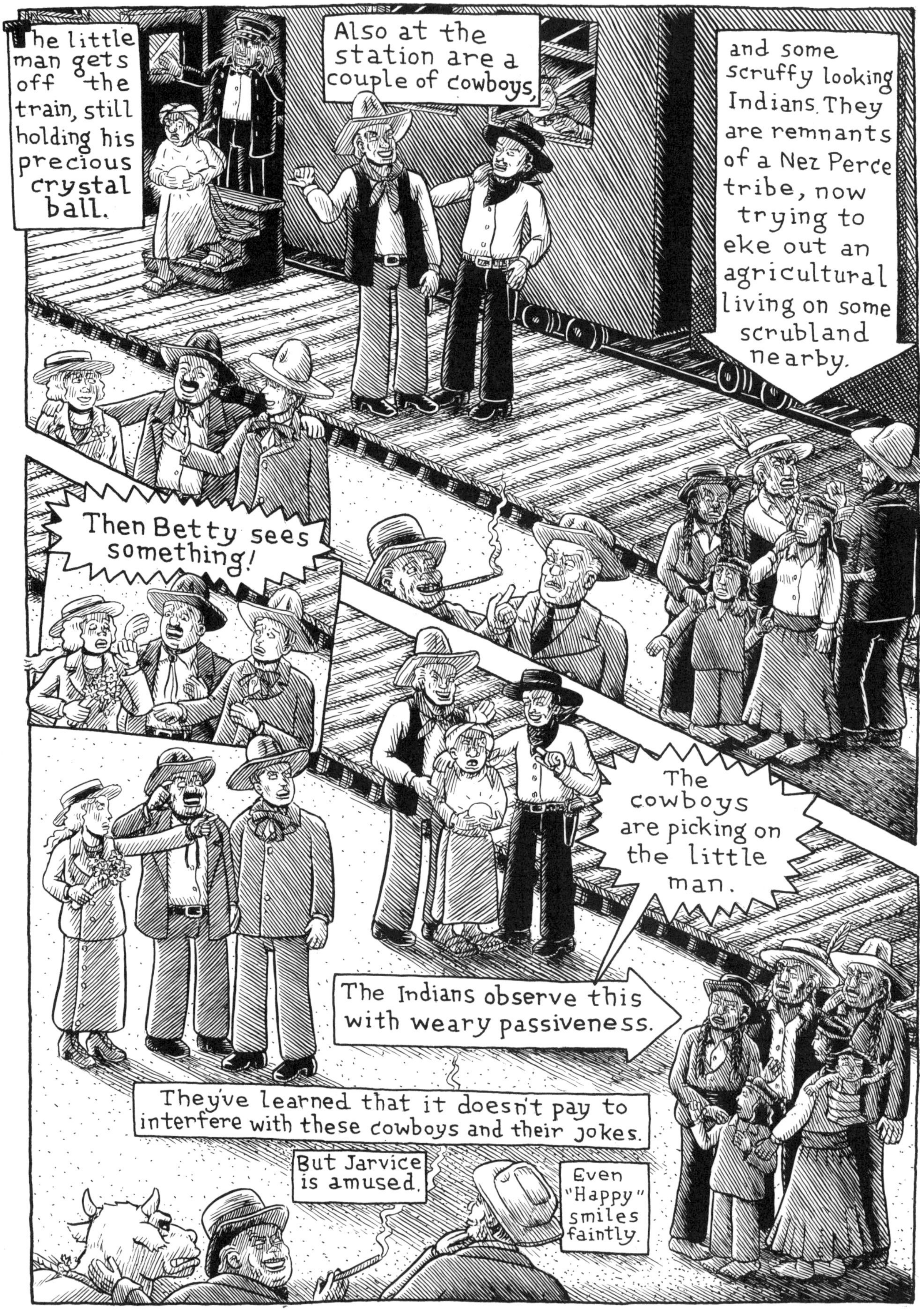
The little man gets off the train, still holding his precious crystal ball.
Also at the station are a couple of cowboys,
and some scruffy looking Indians. They are remnants of a Nez Perce tribe, now trying to eke out an agricultural living on some scrubland nearby.
Then Betty sees something!
The cowboys are picking on the little man.
The Indians observe this with weary passiveness.
They've learned that it doesn't pay to interfere with these cowboys and their jokes.
But Jarvice is amused.
Even "Happy" smiles faintly.

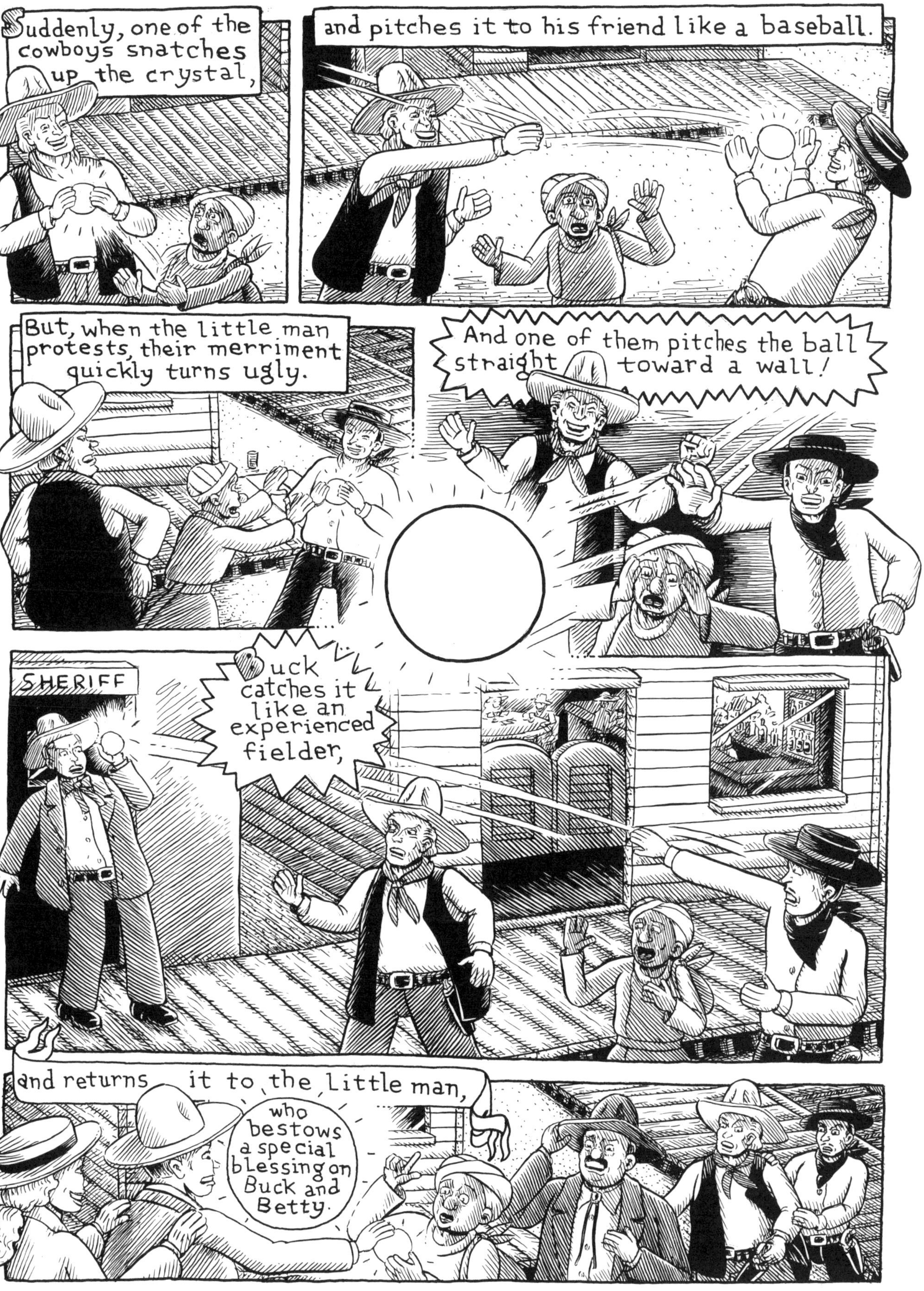
Suddenly, one of the cowboys snatches up the crystal,
and pitches it to his friend like a baseball.
But, when the little man protests, their merriment quickly turns ugly.
And one of them pitches the ball straight toward a wall!
SHERIFF
Buck catches it like an experienced fielder,
and returns it to the little man,
who bestows a special blessing on Buck and Betty.

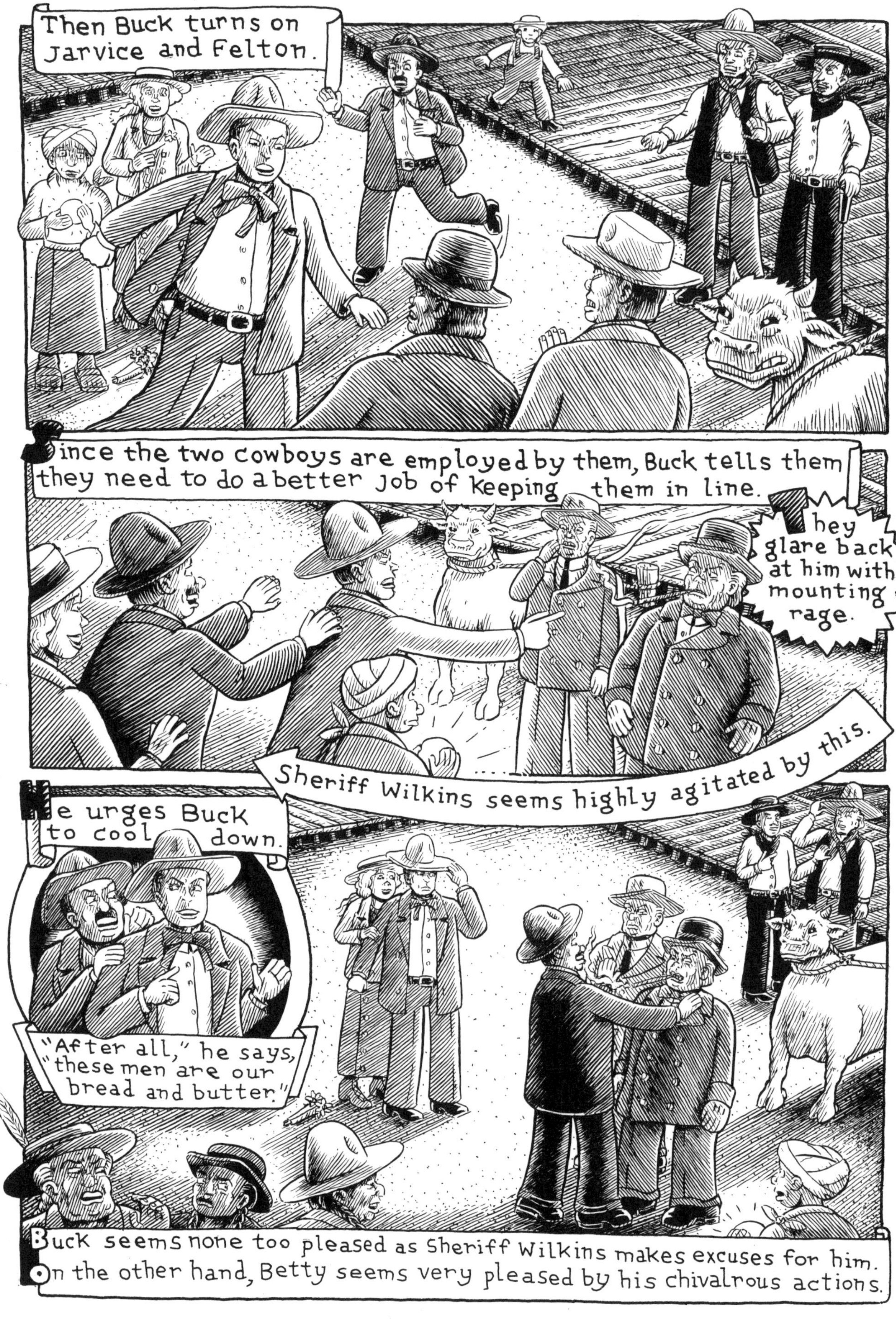
Then Buck turns on Jarvice and Felton.
Since the two cowboys are employed by them, Buck tells them they need to do a better job of keeping them in line.
They glare back at him with mounting rage.
Sheriff Wilkins seems highly agitated by this.
He urges Buck to cool down.
"After all," he says, "these men are our bread and butter."
Buck seems none too pleased as Sheriff Wilkins makes excuses for him.
On the other hand, Betty seems very pleased by his chivalrous actions.

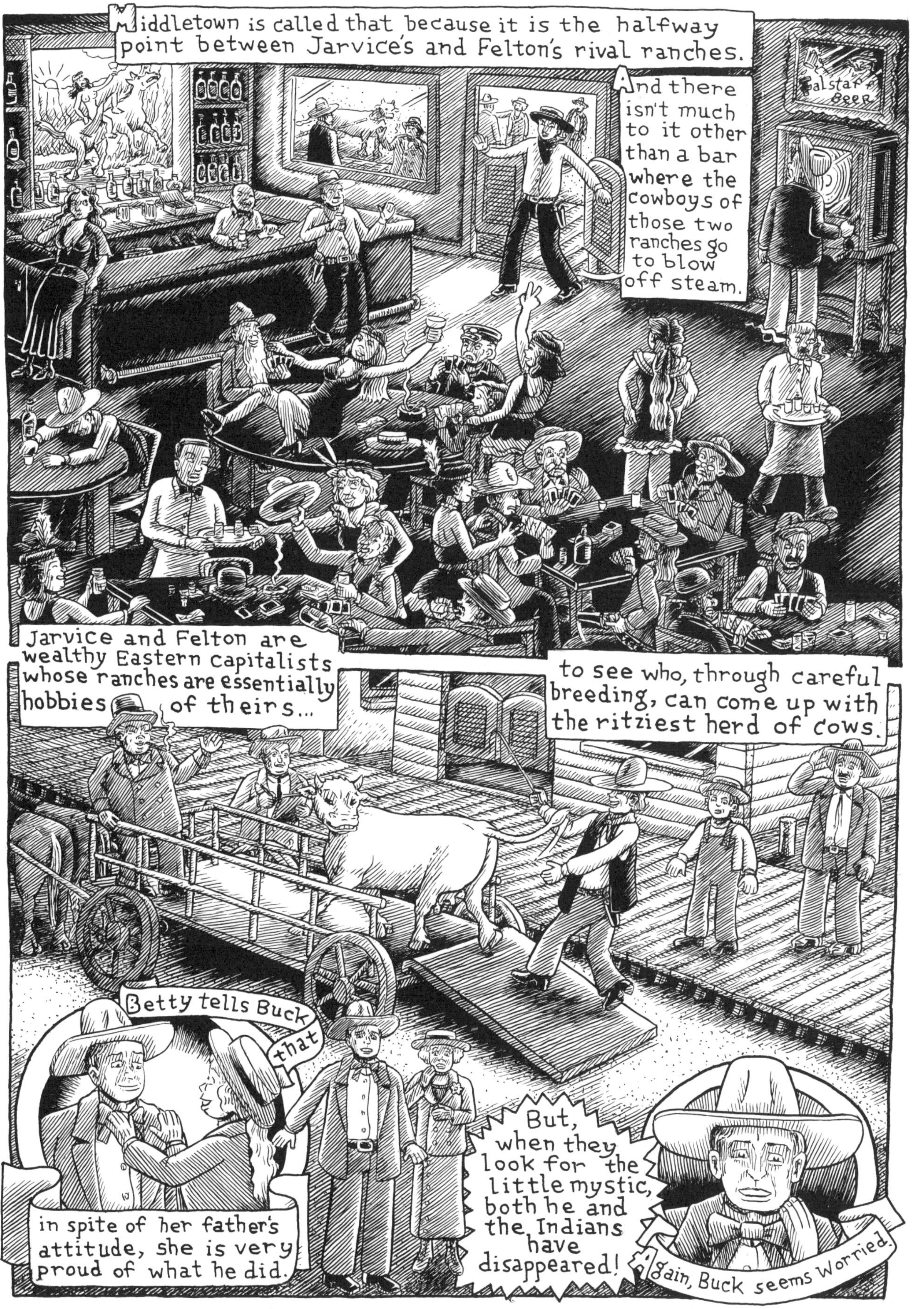
Middletown is called that because it is the halfway point between Jarvice's and Felton's rival ranches.
And there isn't much to it other than a bar where the cowboys of those two ranches go to blow off steam.
Jarvice and Felton are wealthy Eastern capitalists whose ranches are essentially hobbies of theirs...
to see who, through careful breeding, can come up with the ritziest herd of cows.
Betty tells Buck that
in spite of her father's attitude, she is very proud of what he did.
But, when they look for the little mystic, both he and the Indians have disappeared!
Again, Buck seems worried.

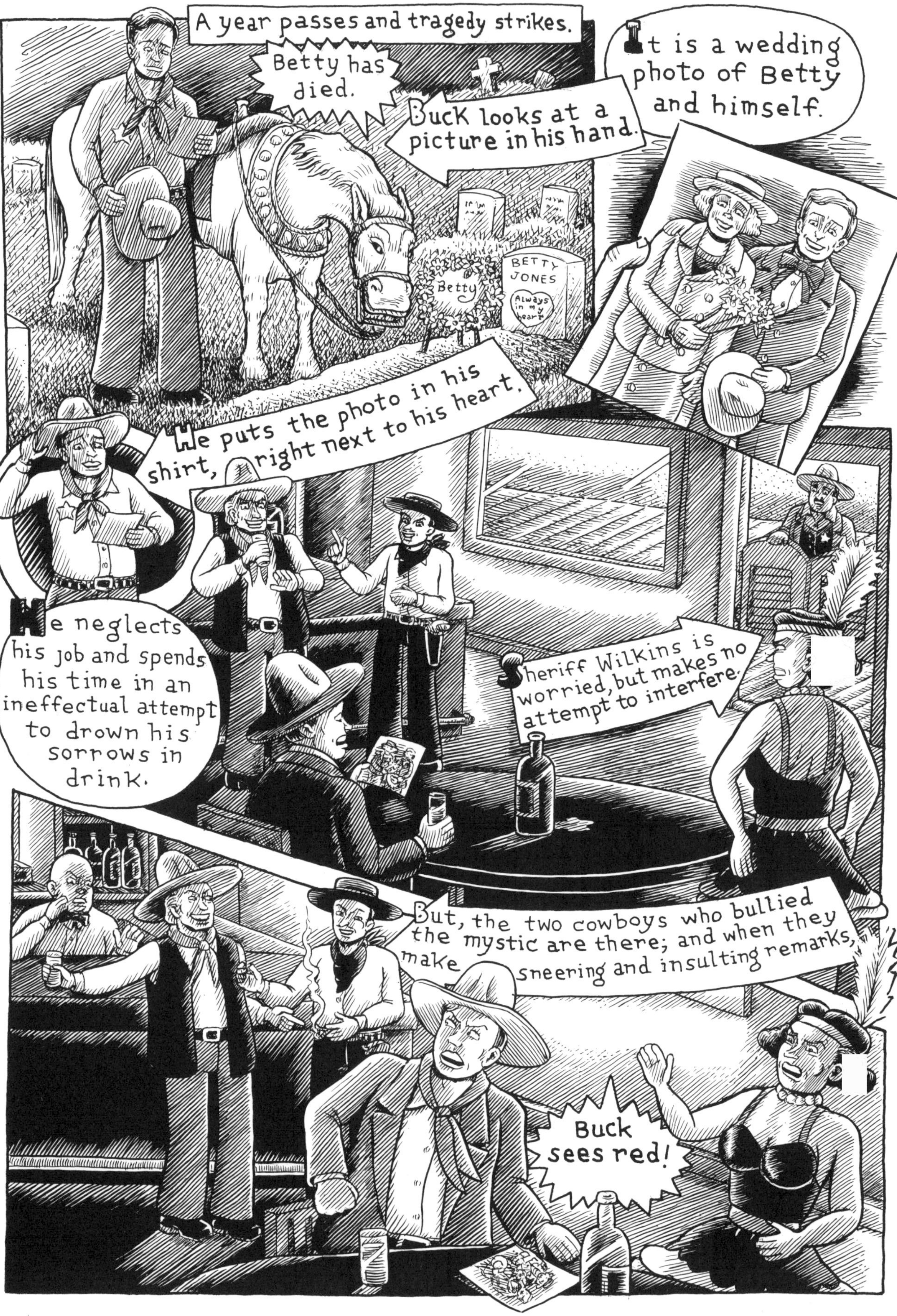

A year passes and tragedy strikes.
Betty has died.
Buck looks at a picture in his hand.
Betty
BETTY JONES
Always in my heart
It is a wedding photo of Betty and himself.
He puts the photo in his shirt, right next to his heart.
He neglects his job and spends his time in an ineffectual attempt to drown his sorrows in drink.
Sheriff Wilkins is worried, but makes no attempt to interfere.
But, the two cowboys who bullied the mystic are there; and when they make sneering and insulting remarks,
Buck sees red!

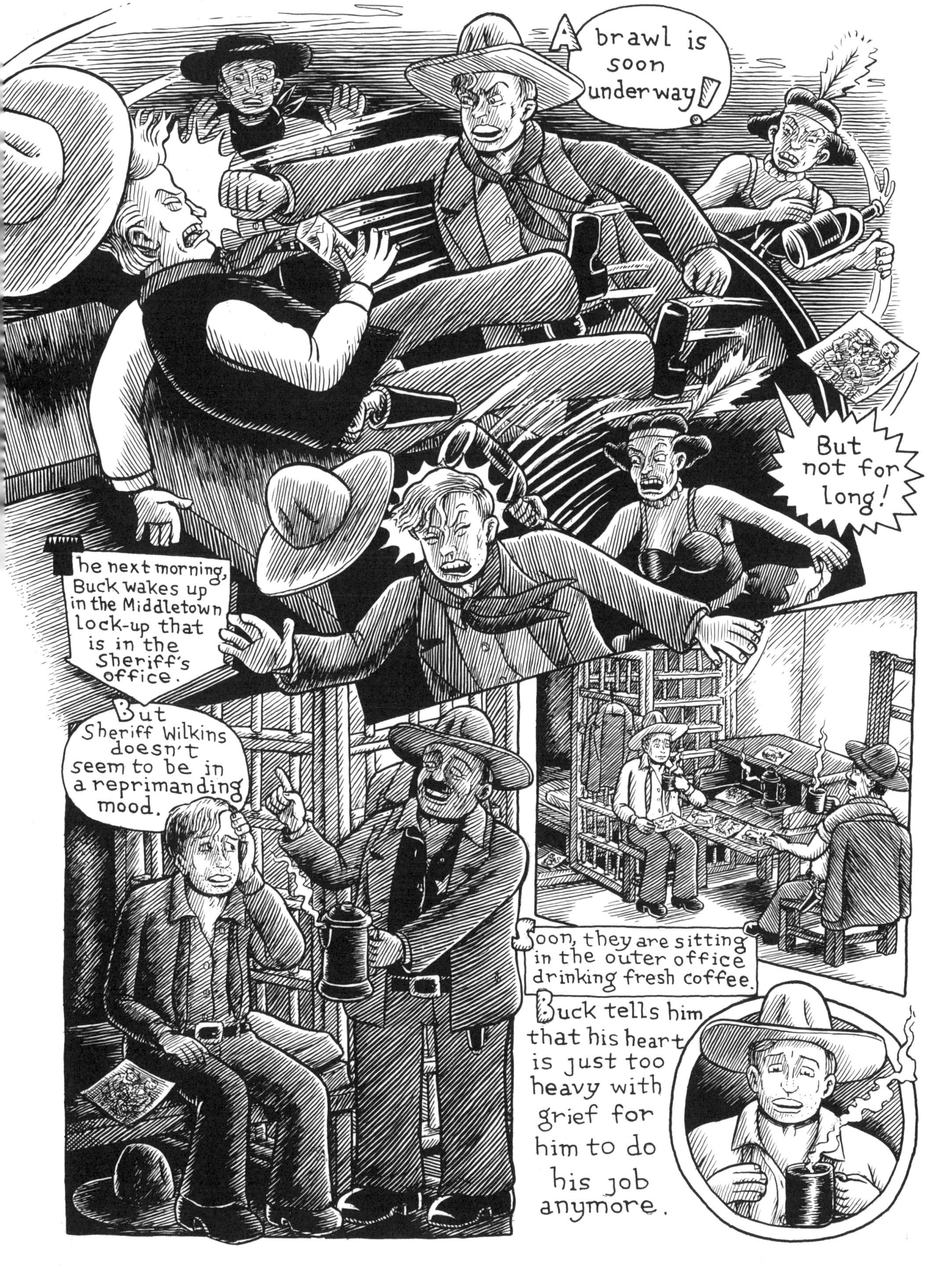
A brawl is soon underway!
But not for long!
The next morning, Buck wakes up in the Middletown lock-up that is in the Sheriff's office.
But Sheriff Wilkins doesn't seem to be in a reprimanding mood.
Soon, they are sitting in the outer office drinking fresh coffee.
Buck tells him that his heart is just too heavy with grief for him to do his job anymore.

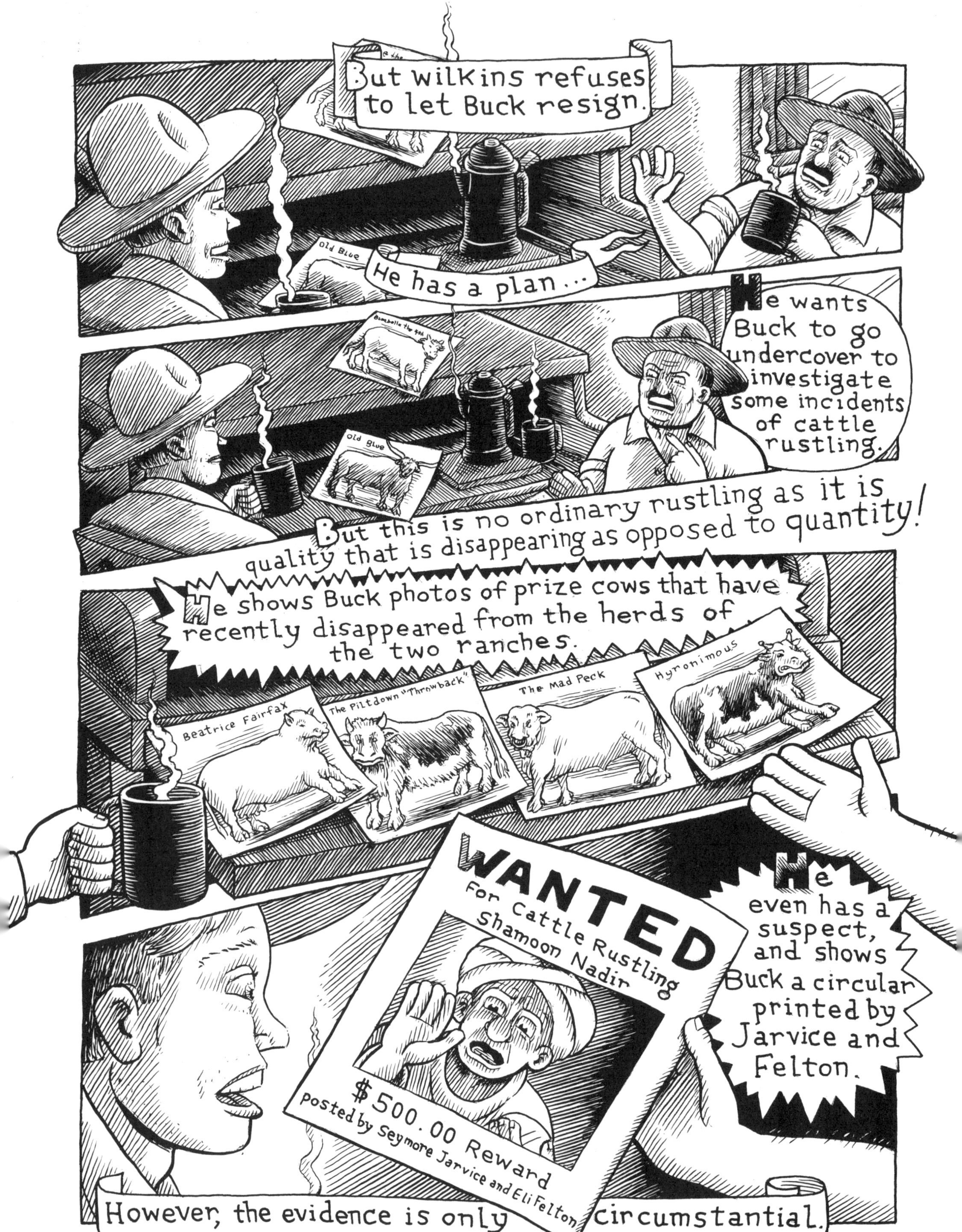
But wilkins refuses to let Buck resign.
Old Blue
He has a plan...
He wants Buck to go undercover to investigate some incidents of cattle rustling.
Old Blue
But this is no ordinary rustling as it is quality that is disappearing as opposed to quantity!
He shows Buck photos of prize cows that have recently disappeared from the herds of the two ranches.
Beatrice Fairfax
The Piltdown "Throwback"
The Mad Peck
Hyronimous
WANTED
For Cattle Rustling
Shamoon Nadir
$500.00 Reward
posted by Seymore Jarvice and Eli Felton
He even has a suspect, and shows Buck a circular printed by Jarvice and Felton.
However, the evidence is only circumstantial.

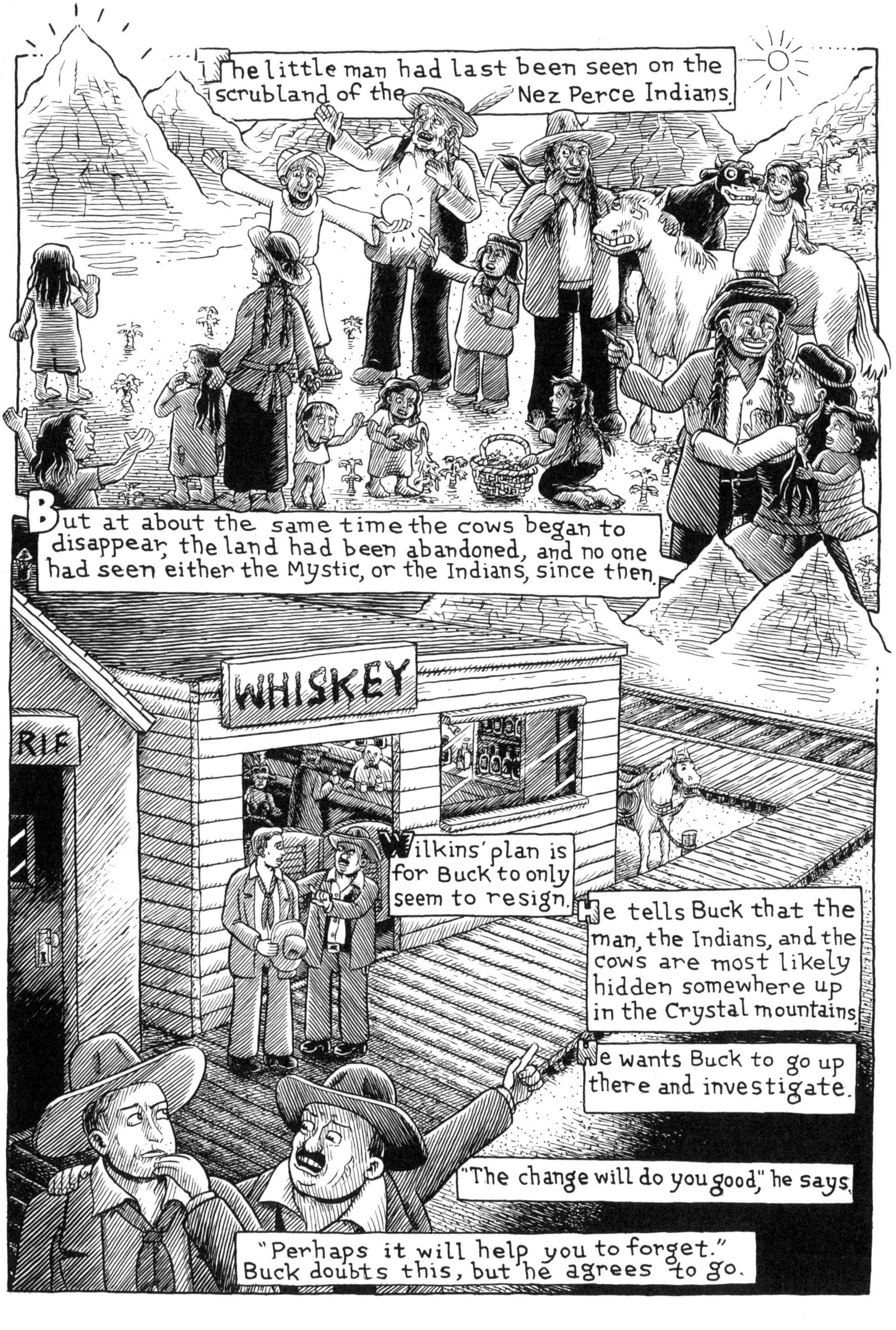
The little man had last been seen on the scrubland of the Nez Perce Indians.
But at about the same time the cows began to disappear, the land had been abandoned, and no one had seen either the Mystic, or the Indians, since then.
WHISKEY
RIF
Wilkins' plan is for Buck to only seem to resign.
He tells Buck that the man, the Indians, and the cows are most likely hidden somewhere up in the Crystal mountains.
He wants Buck to go up there and investigate.
"The change will do you good," he says.
"Perhaps it will help you to forget."
Buck doubts this, but he agrees to go.

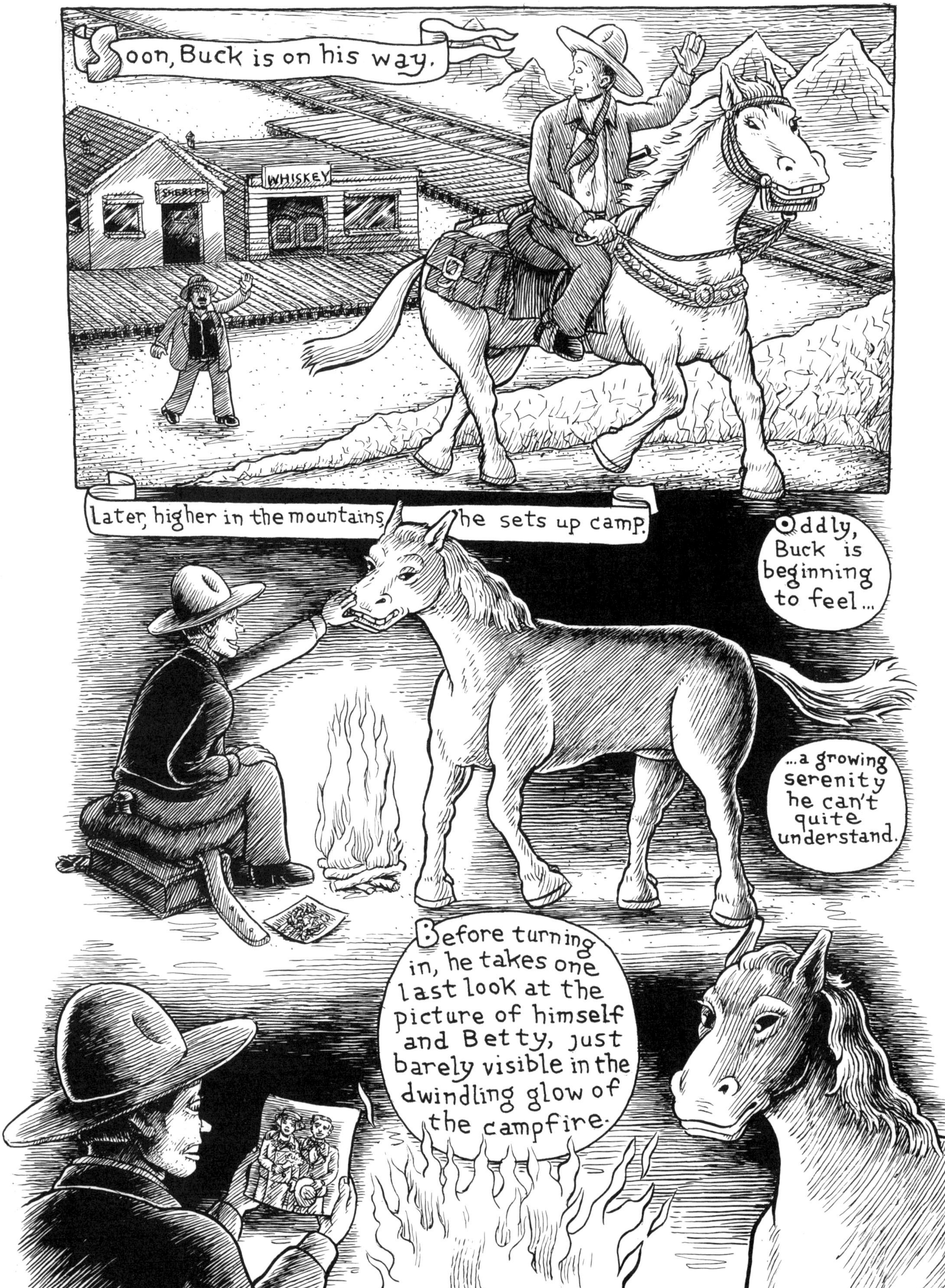
Soon, Buck is on his way.
SHERIFF
WHISKEY
Later, higher in the mountains, he sets up camp.
Oddly, Buck is beginning to feel...
...a growing serenity he can't quite understand.
Before turning in, he takes one last look at the picture of himself and Betty, just barely visible in the dwindling glow of the campfire.

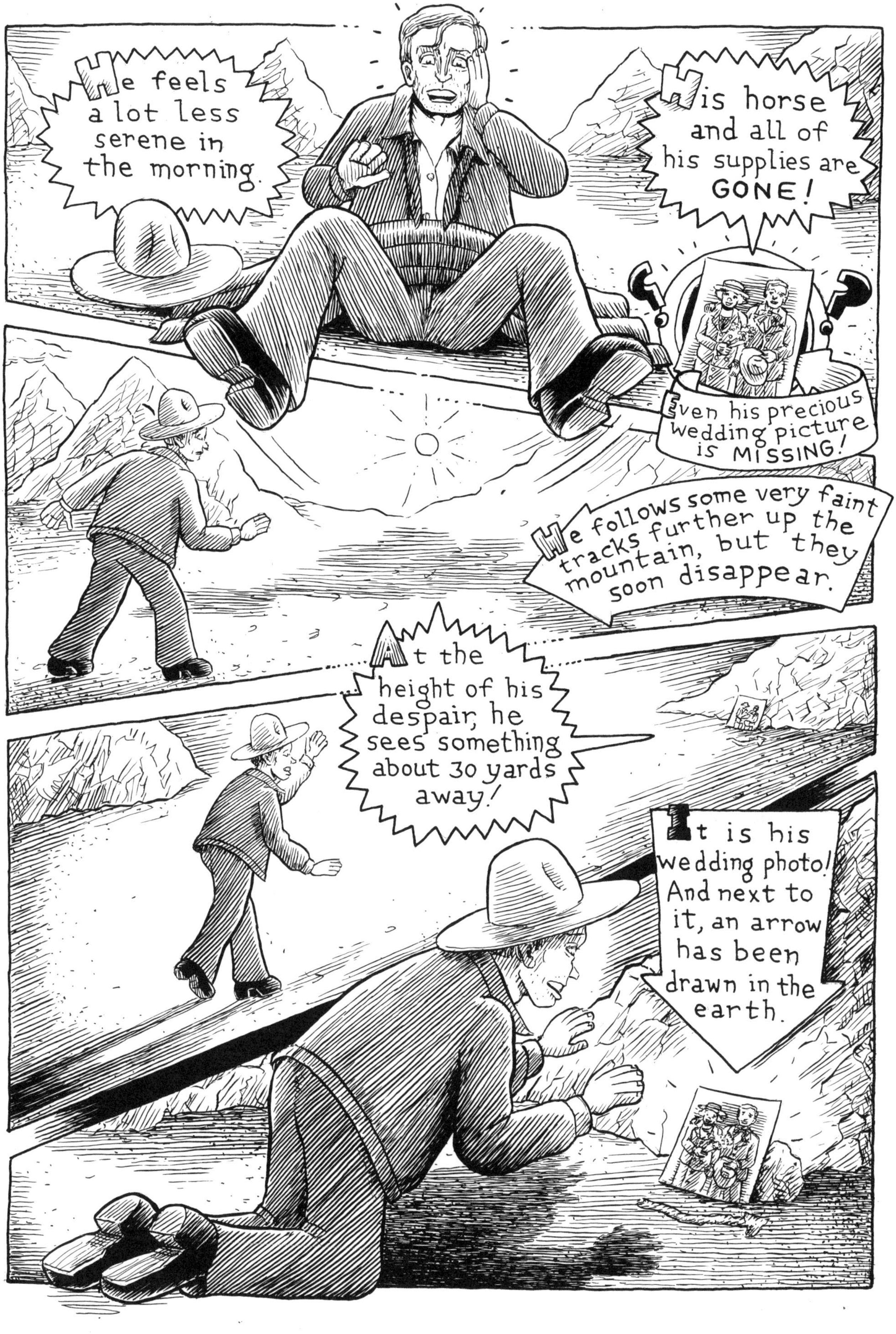
He feels a lot less serene in the morning.
His horse and all of his supplies are GONE!
Even his precious wedding picture is MISSING!
He follows some very faint tracks further up the mountain, but they soon disappear.
At the height of his despair, he sees something about 30 yards away!
It is his wedding photo! And next to it, an arrow has been drawn in the earth.

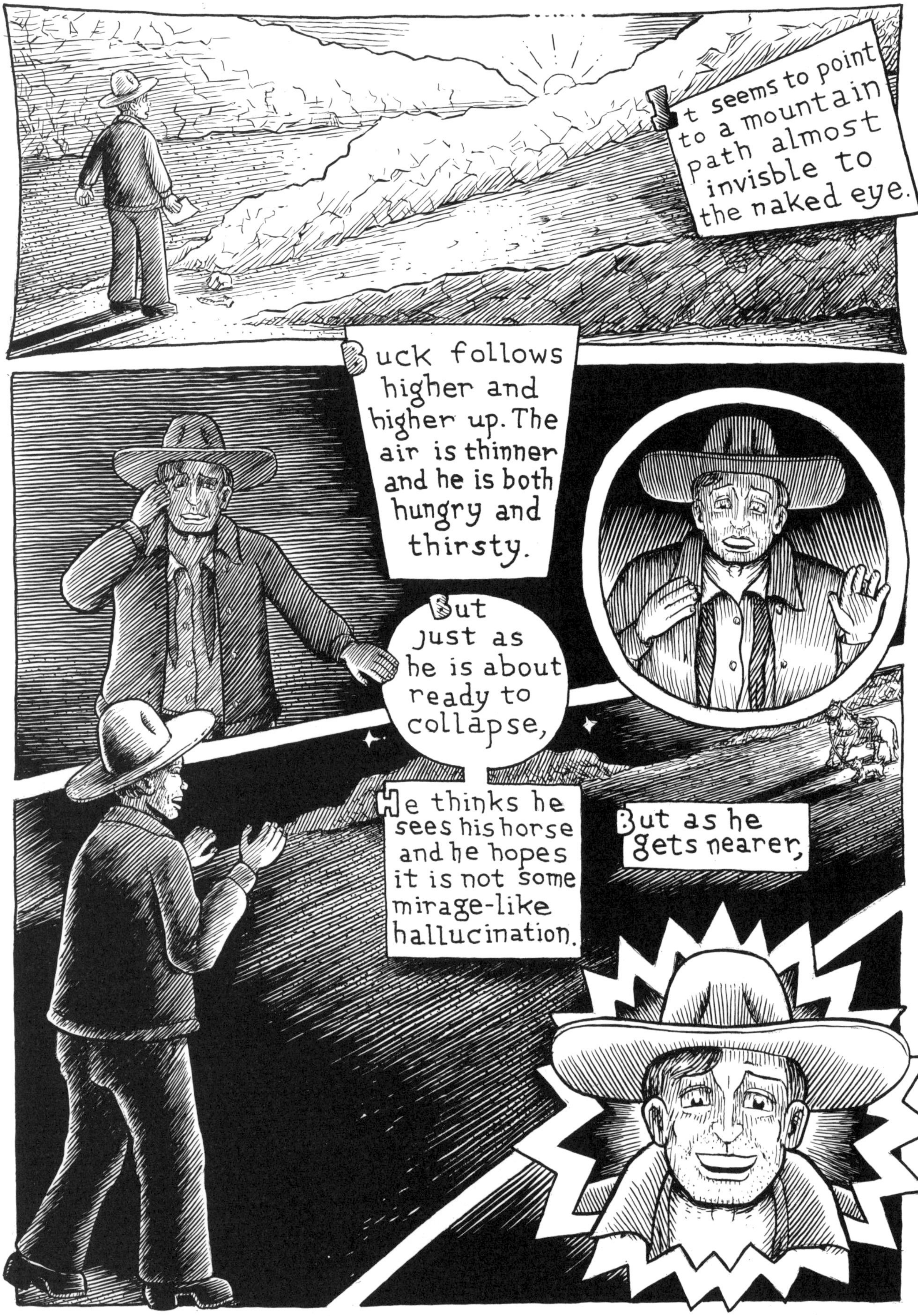
It seems to point to a mountain path almost invisble to the naked eye.
Buck follows higher and higher up. The air is thinner and he is both hungry and thirsty.
But just as he is about ready to collapse,
He thinks he sees his horse and he hopes it is not some mirage-like hallucination.
But as he gets nearer,

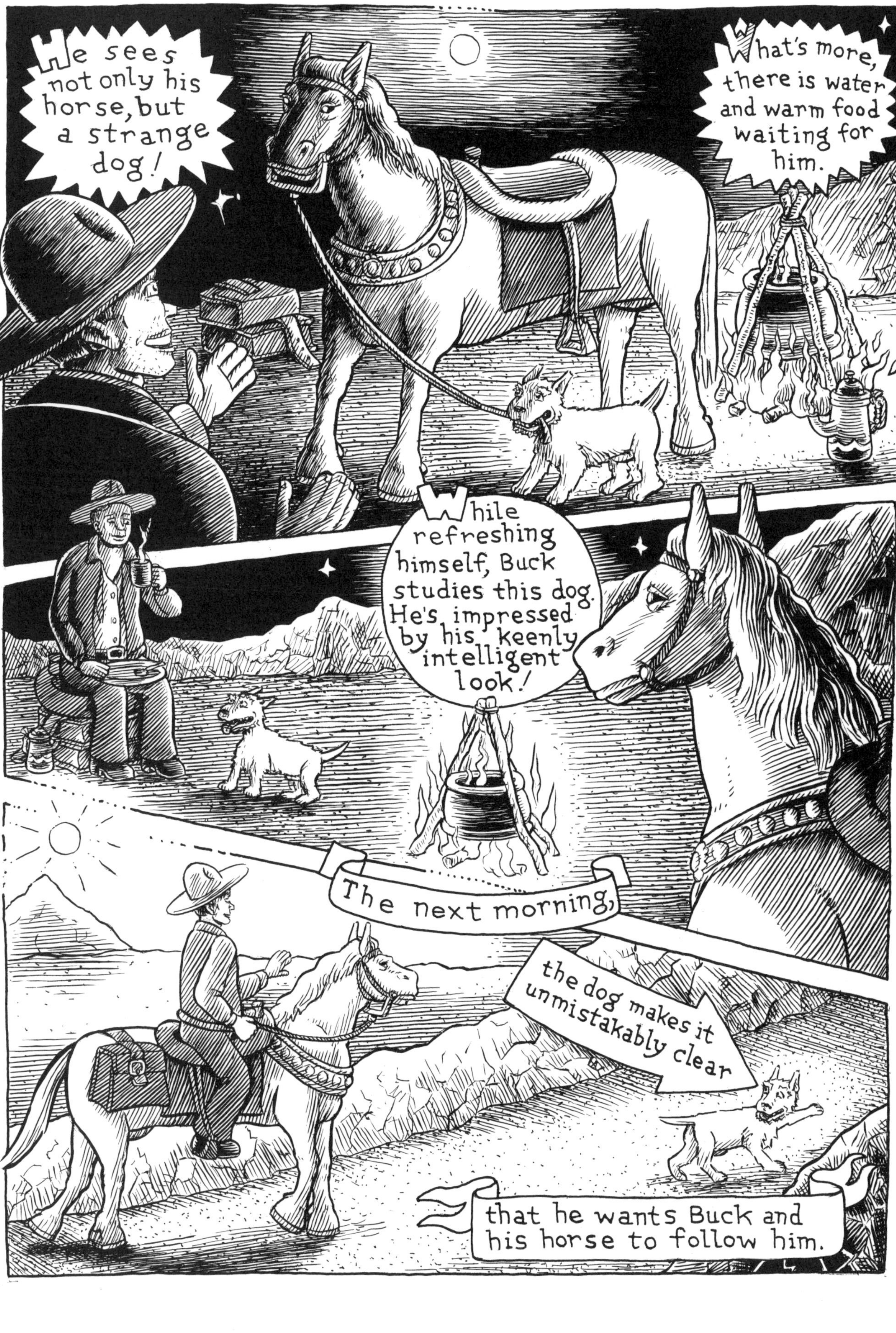
He sees not only his horse, but a strange dog!
What's more, there is water and warm food waiting for him.
While refreshing himself, Buck studies this dog. He's impressed by his keenly intelligent look!
The next morning,
the dog makes it unmistakably clear
that he wants Buck and his horse to follow him.

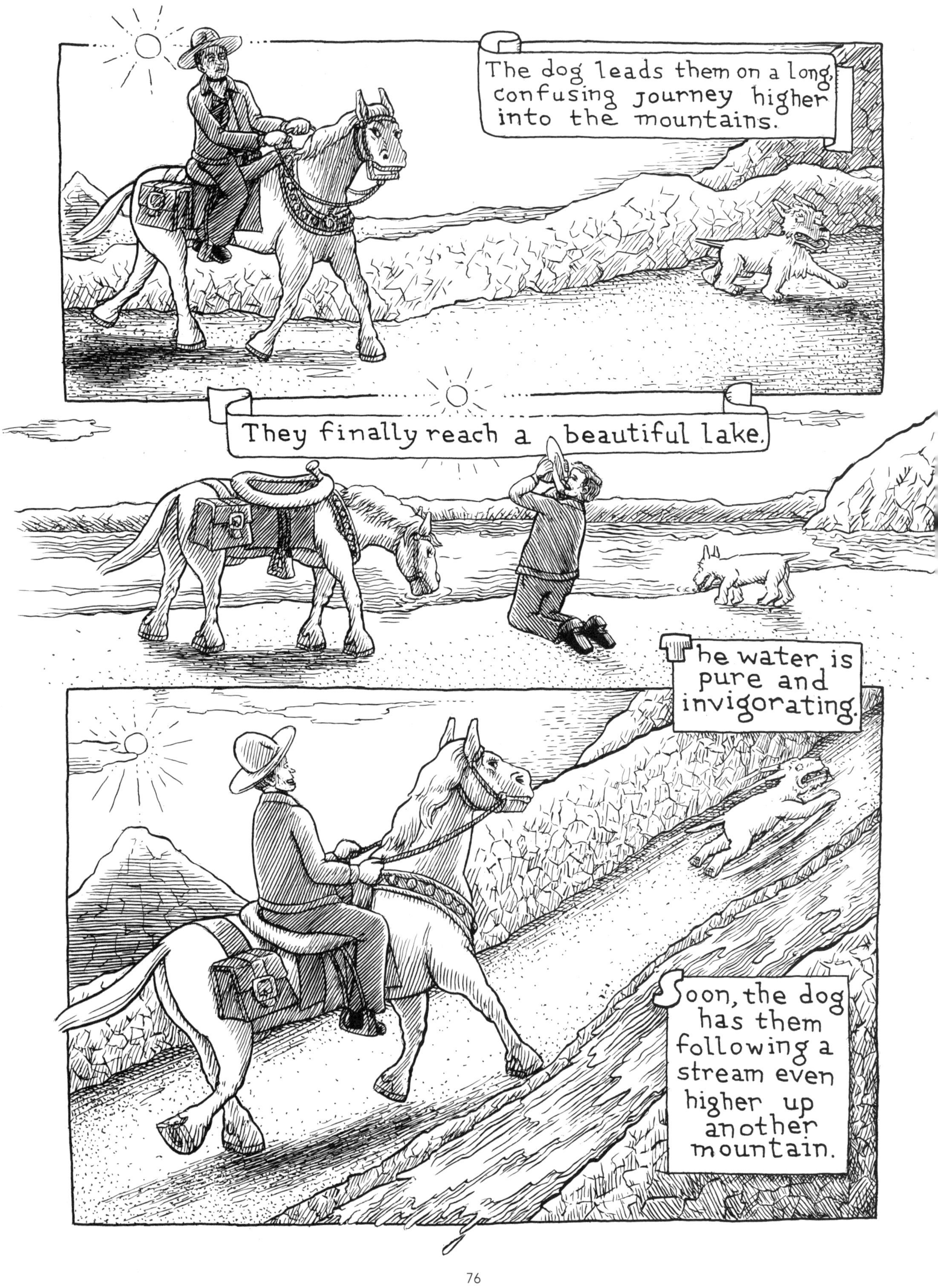
The dog leads them on a long, confusing journey higher into the mountains.
They finally reach a beautiful lake.
The water is pure and invigorating.
Soon, the dog has them following a stream even higher up another mountain.

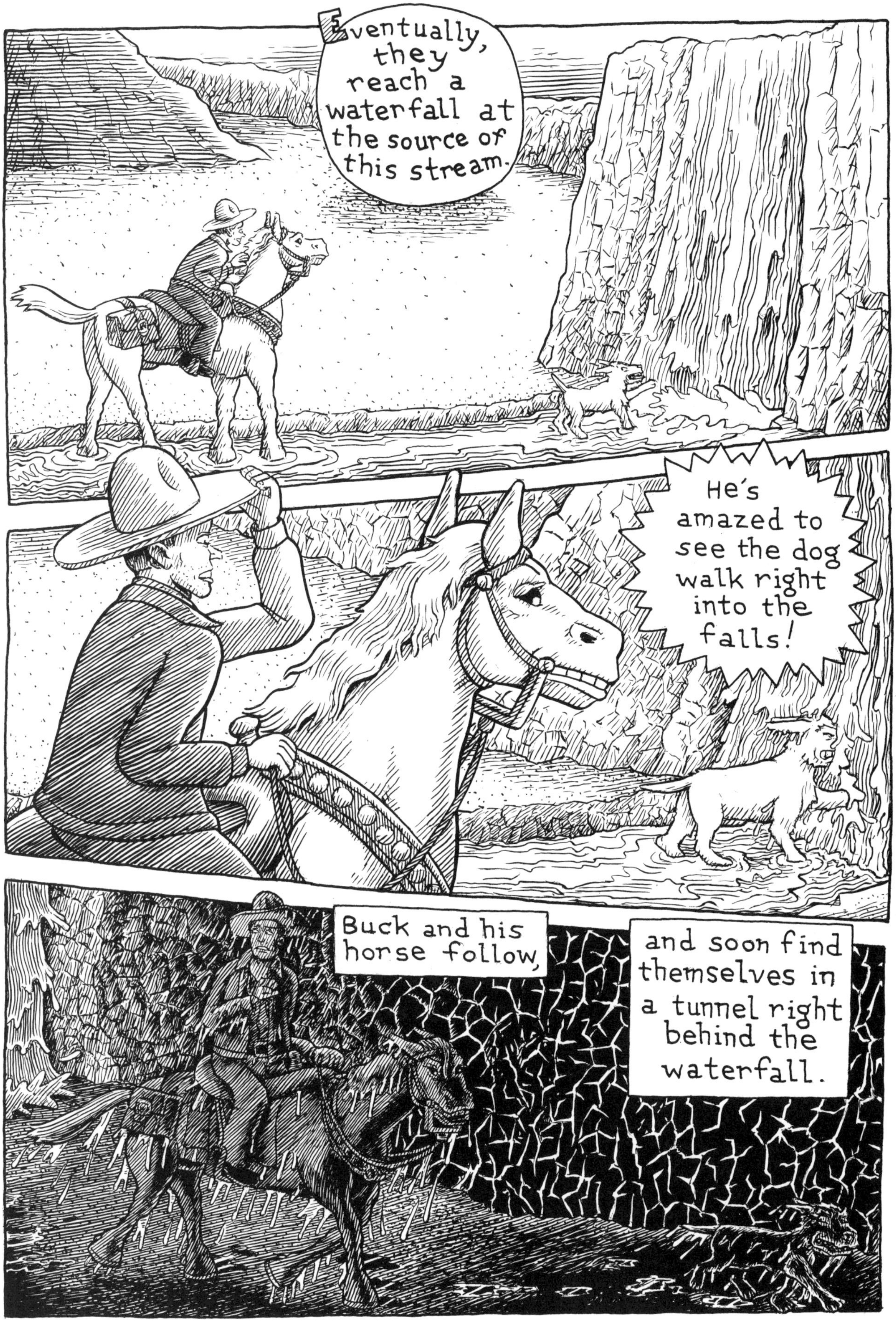
Eventually, they reach a waterfall at the source of this stream.
He's amazed to see the dog walk right into the falls!
Buck and his horse follow,
and soon find themselves in a tunnel right behind the waterfall.

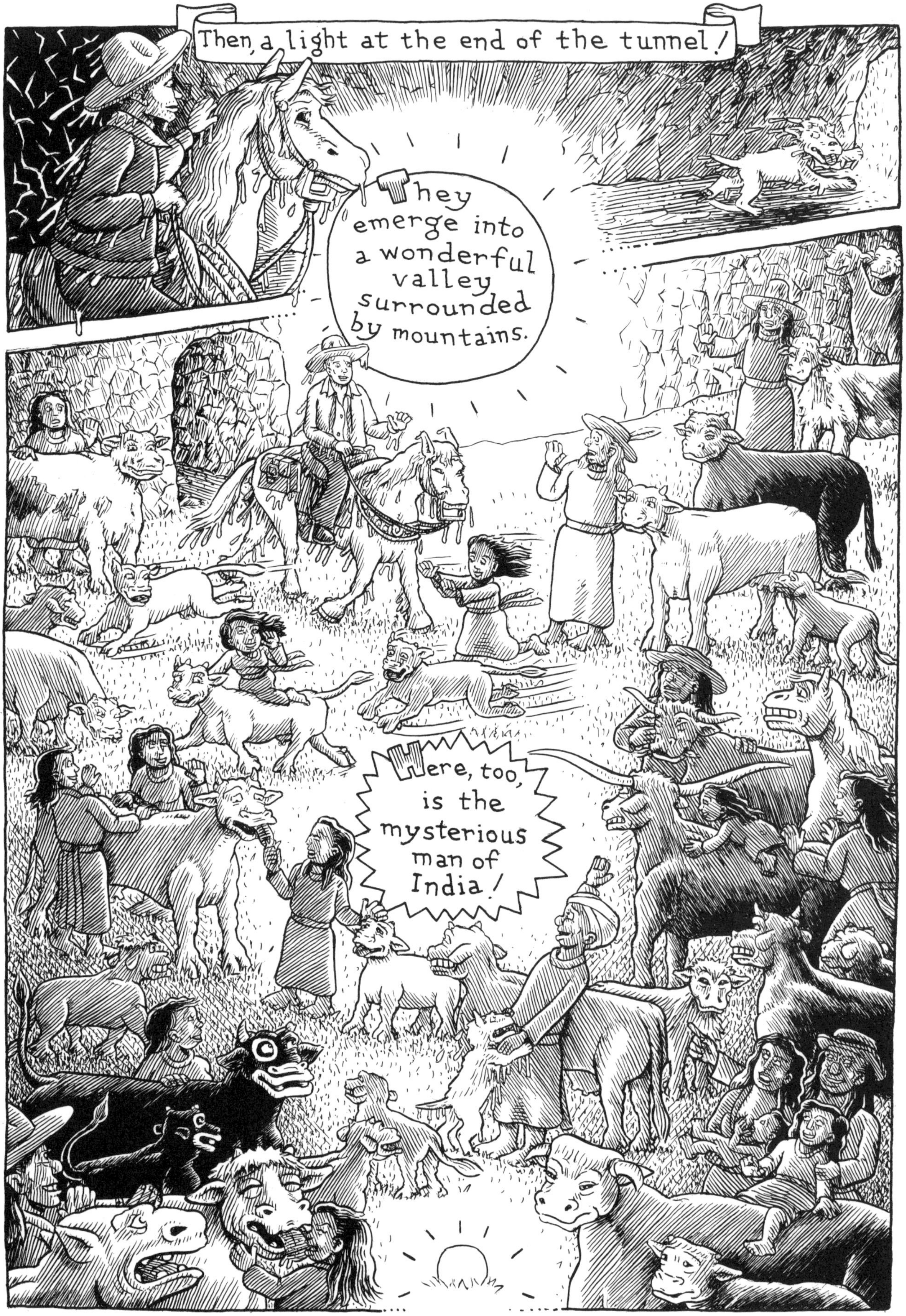
Then, a light at the end of the tunnel!
They emerge into a wonderful valley surrounded by mountains.
Here, too, is the mysterious man of India!

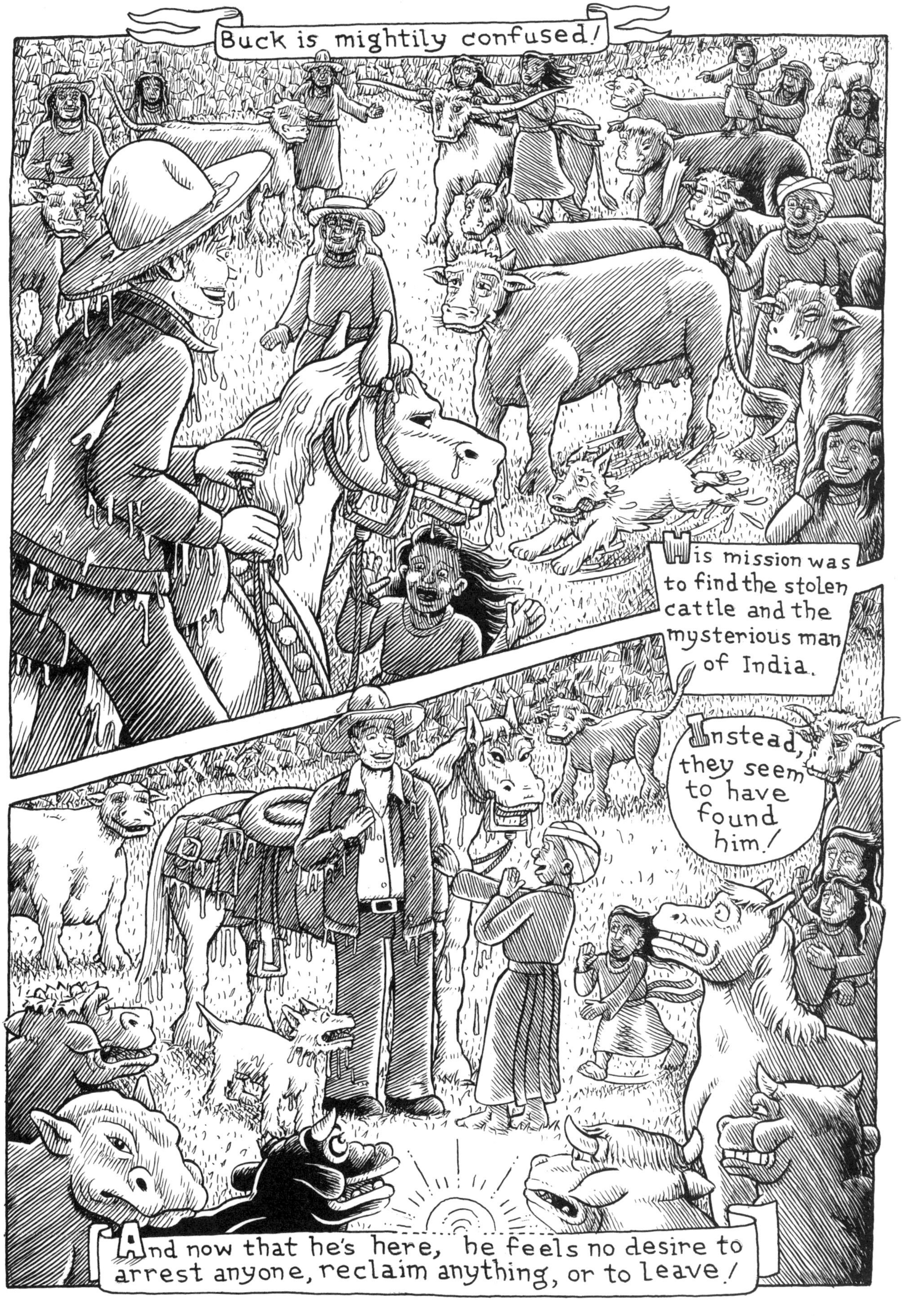
Buck is mightily confused!
His mission was to find the stolen cattle and the mysterious man of India.
Instead, they seem to have found him!
And now that he's here, he feels no desire to arrest anyone, reclaim anything, or to leave!

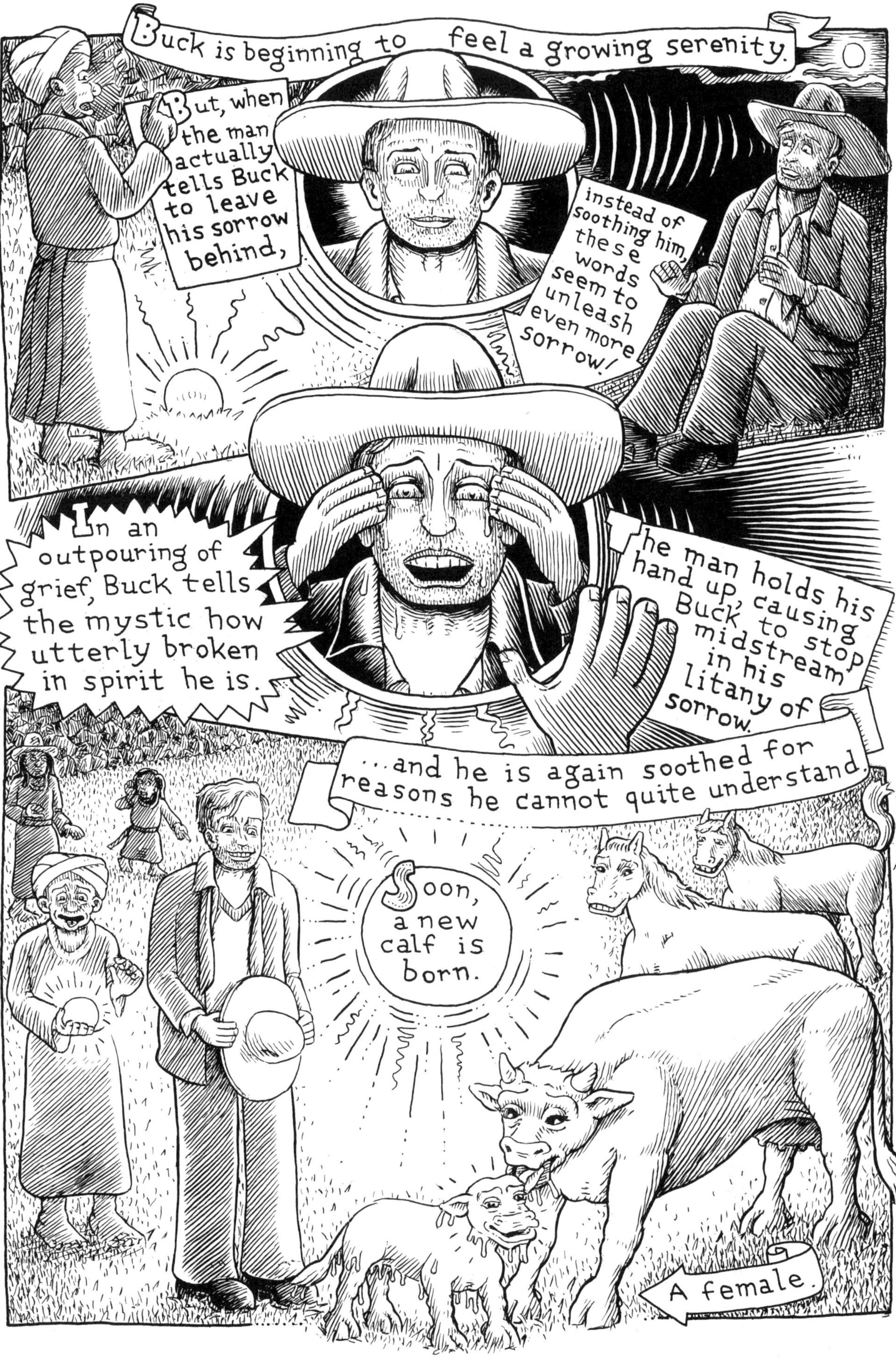
Buck is beginning to feel a growing serenity.
But, when the man actually tells Buck to leave his sorrow behind,
instead of soothing him, these words seem to unleash even more sorrow!
In an outpouring of grief, Buck tells the mystic how utterly broken in spirit he is.
The man holds his hand up, causing Buck to stop midstream in his litany of sorrow.
...and he is again soothed for reasons he cannot quite understand.
Soon, a new calf is born.
A female.

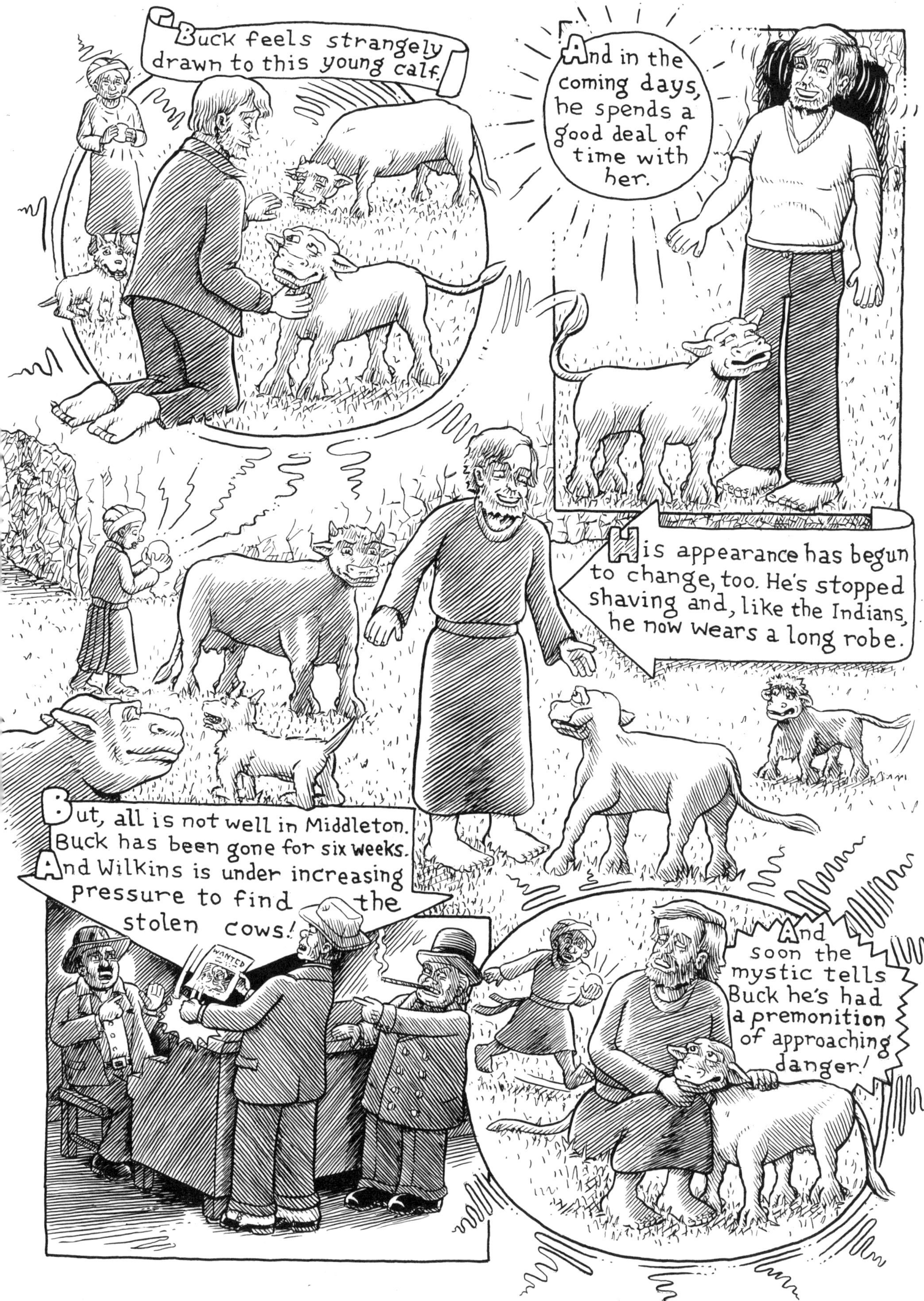

Buck feels strangely drawn to this young calf.
And in the coming days, he spends a good deal of time with her.
His appearance has begun to change, too. He's stopped shaving and, like the Indians, he now wears a long robe.
But, all is not well in Middleton. Buck has been gone for six weeks. And Wilkins is under increasing pressure to find the stolen cows!
WANTED
And soon the mystic tells Buck he's had a premonition of approaching danger!

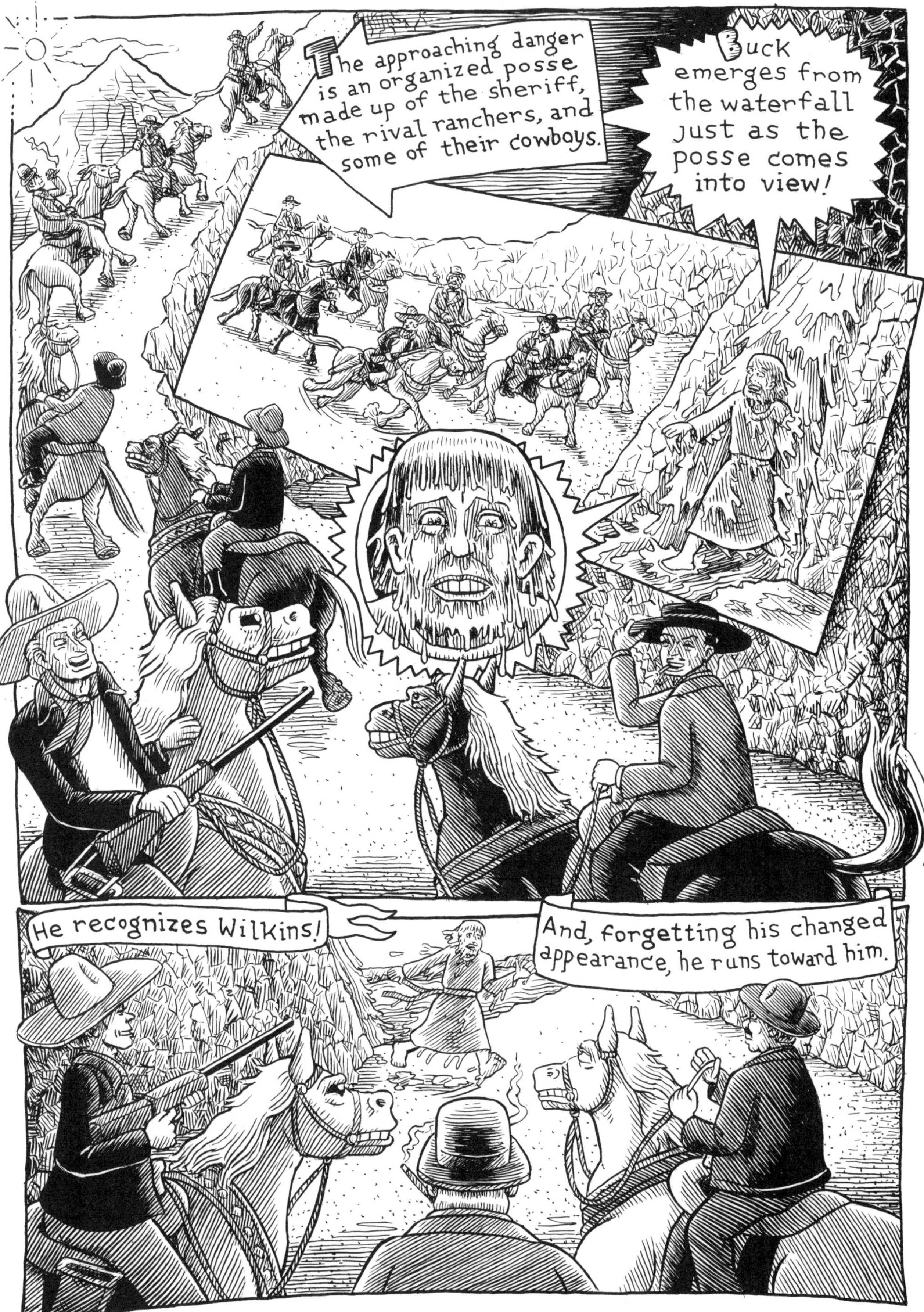
The approaching danger is an organized posse made up of the sheriff, the rival ranchers, and some of their cowboys.
Buck emerges from the waterfall just as the posse comes into view!
He recognizes Wilkins!
And, forgetting his changed appearance, he runs toward him.

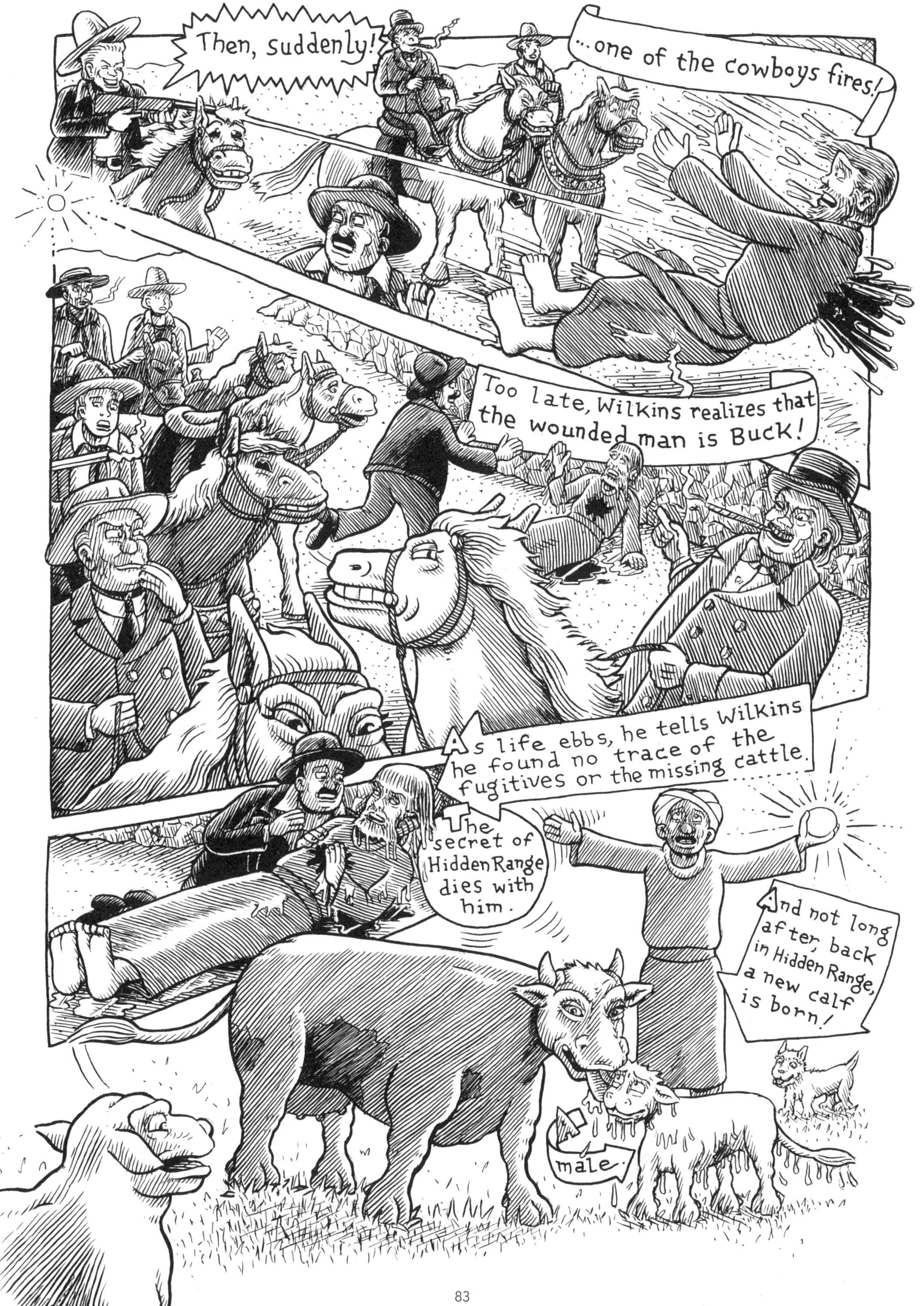

Then, suddenly!
...one of the cowboys fires!
Too late, Wilkins realizes that the wounded man is Buck!
As life ebbs, he tells Wilkins he found no trace of the fugitives or the missing cattle.
The secret of Hidden Range dies with him.
And not long after, back in Hidden Range, a new calf is born!
male.

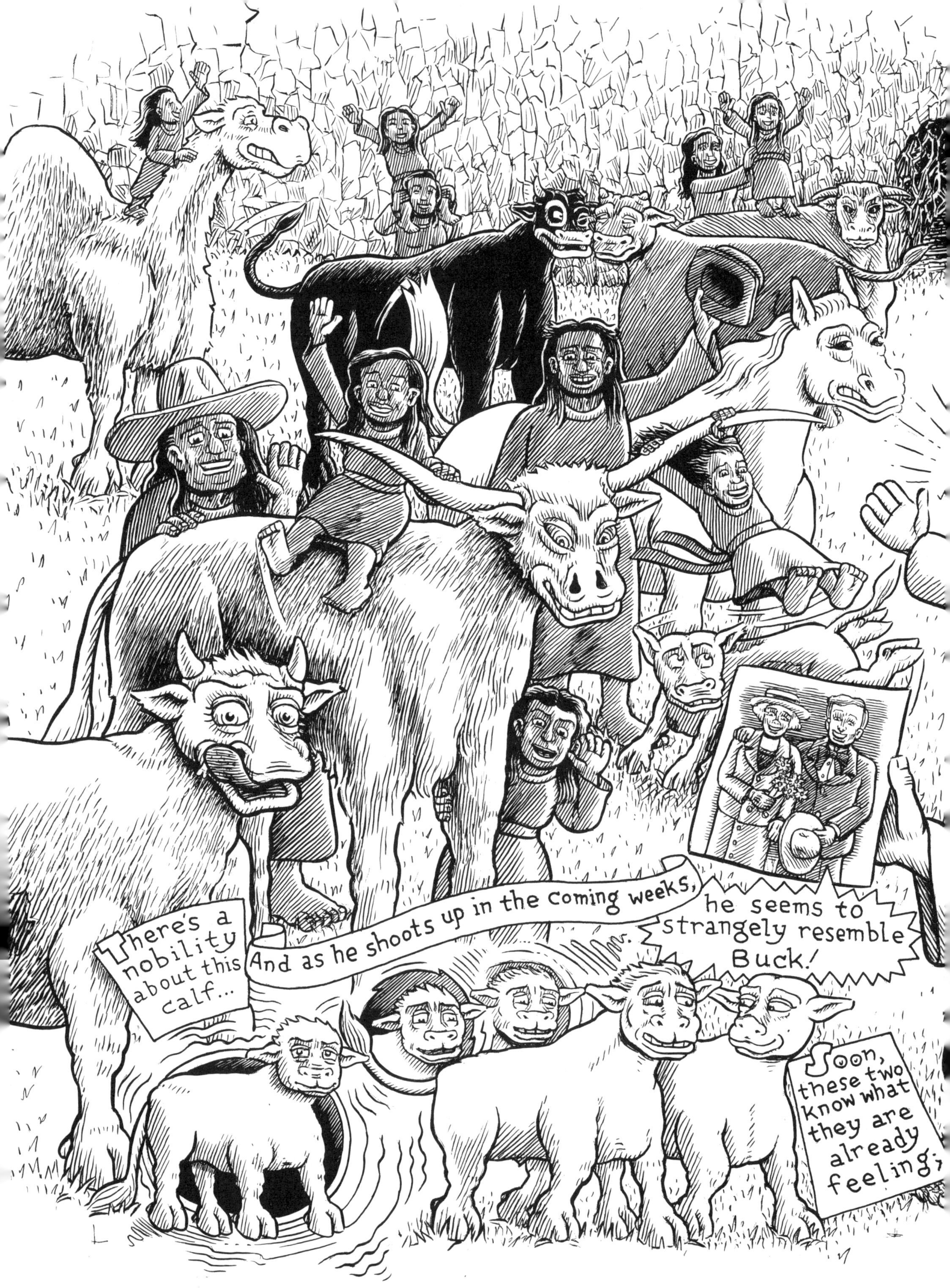
There's a nobility about this calf...
And as he shoots up in the coming weeks,
he seems to strangely resemble Buck!
Soon, these two know what they are already feeling;

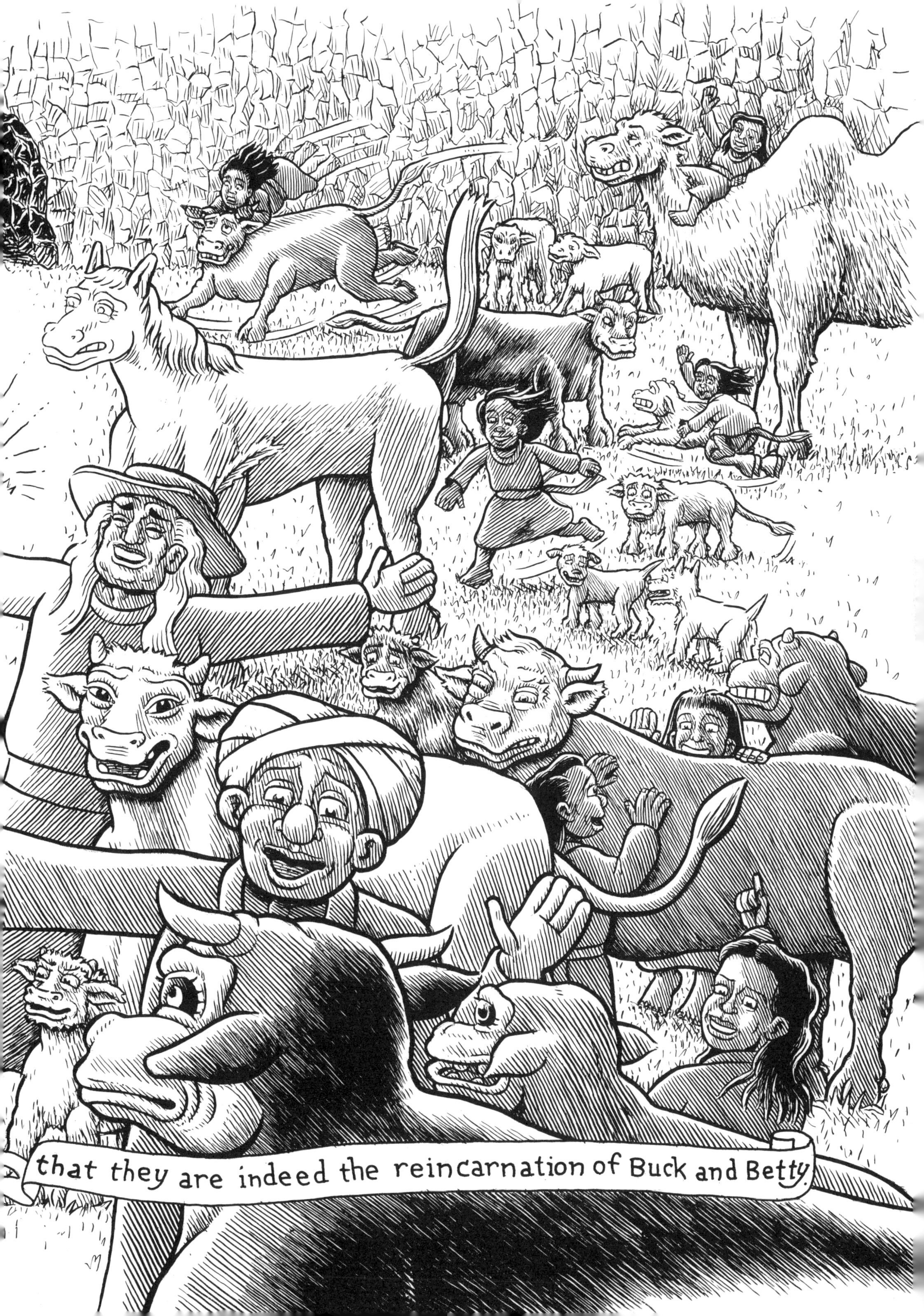
that they are indeed the reincarnation of Buck and Betty.

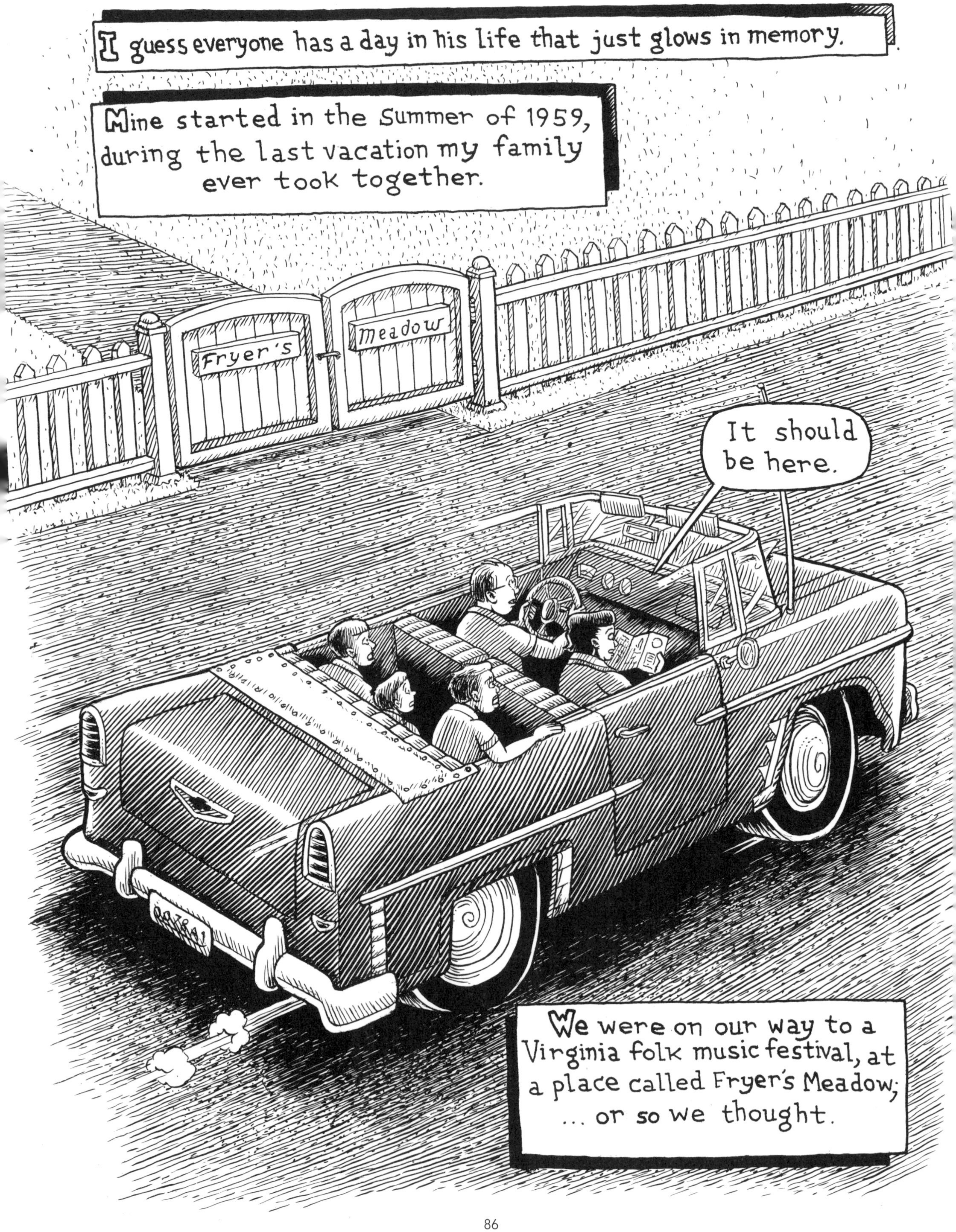
I guess everyone has a day in his life that just glows in memory.
Mine started in the summer of 1959, during the last vacation my family ever took together.
Fryer's
Meadow
It should be here.
We were on our way to a Virginia folk music festival, at a place called Fryer's Meadow; ... or so we thought.

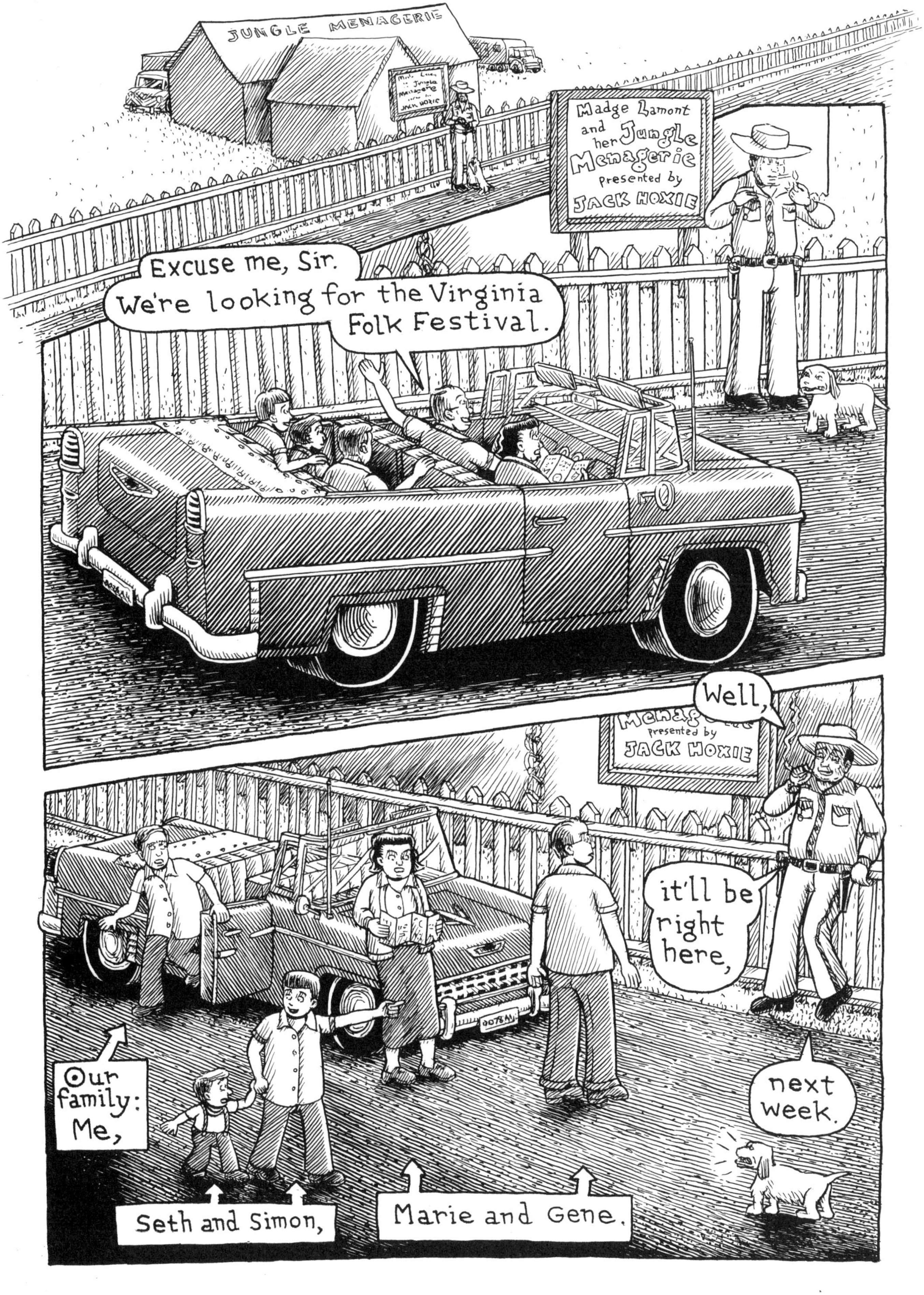
JUNGLE MENAGERIE
Madge Lamont and her Jungle Menagerie presented by JACK HOXIE
Excuse me, Sir. We're looking for the Virginia Folk Festival.
presented by JACK HOXIE
Well,
it'll be right here,
next week.
Our family: Me,
Seth and Simon,
Marie and Gene.

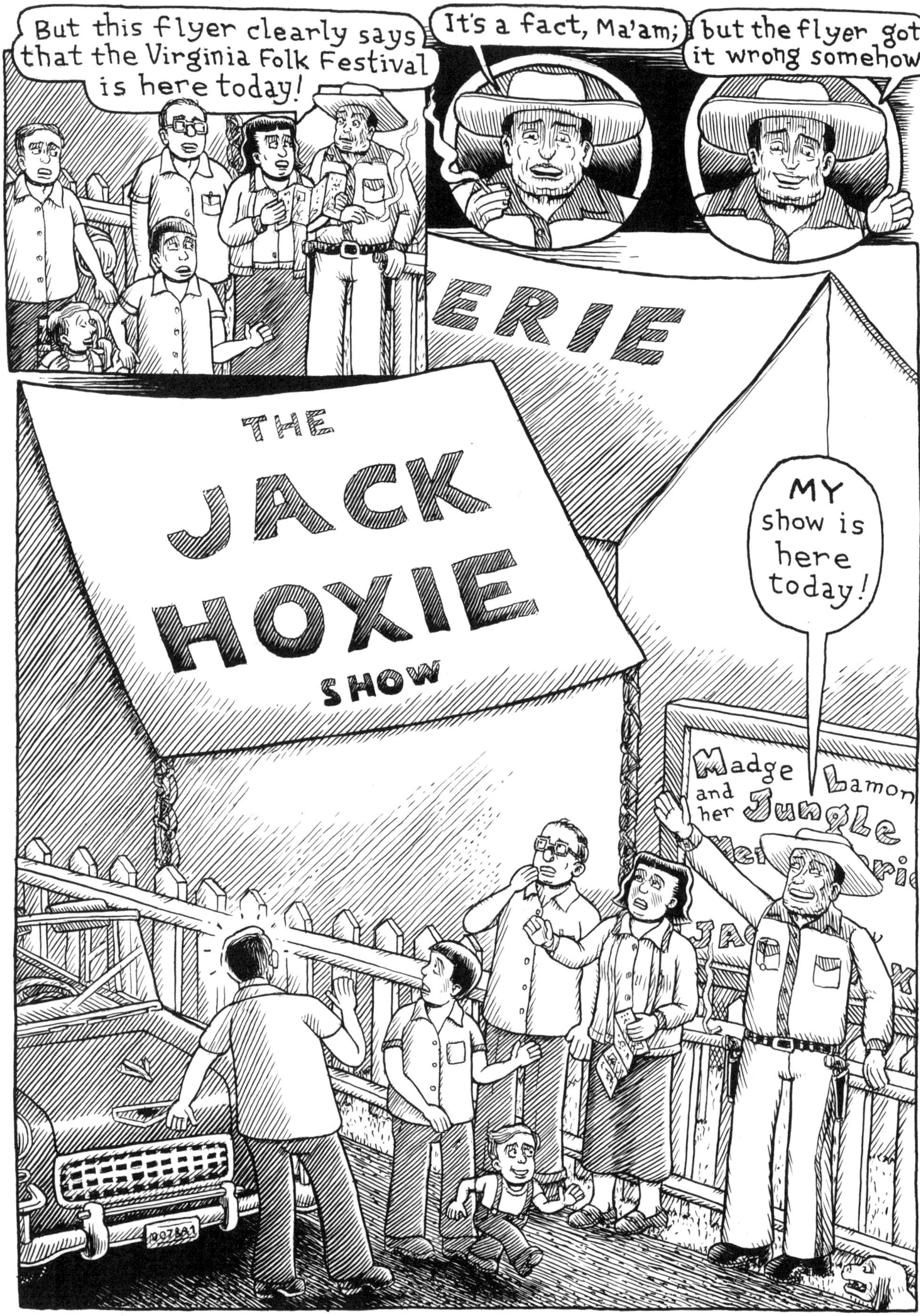
But this flyer clearly says that the Virginia Folk Festival is here today!
It's a fact, Ma'am;
but the flyer got it wrong somehow.
ERIE
THE JACK HOXIE SHOW
MY show is here today!
Madge Lamon and her Jungle

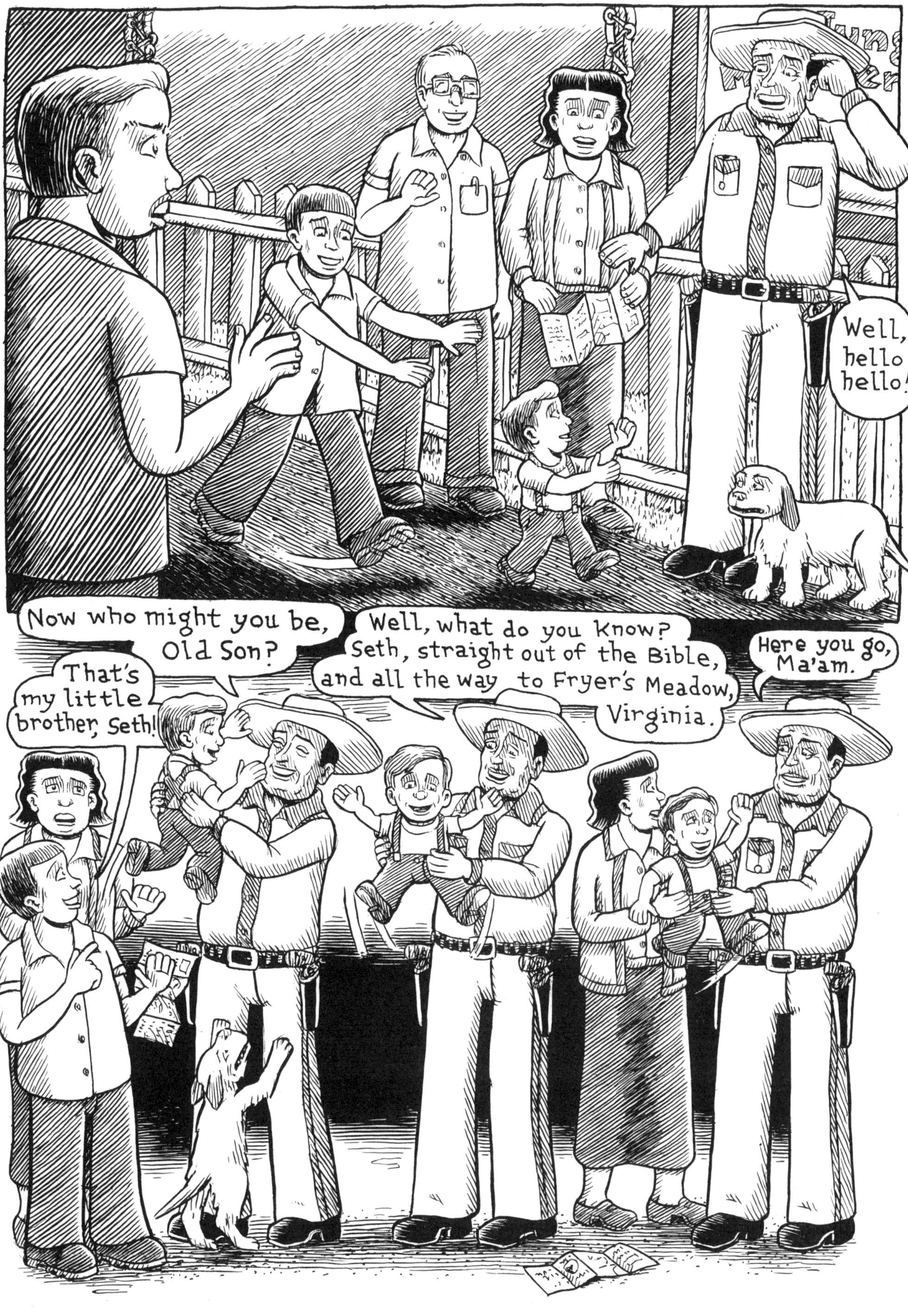
Well, hello hello!
Now who might you be, Old Son?
That's my little brother, Seth!
Well, what do you know? Seth, straight out of the Bible, and all the way to Fryer's Meadow, Virginia.
Here you go, Ma'am.

Jack was fascinating and we all warmed up to him right away.

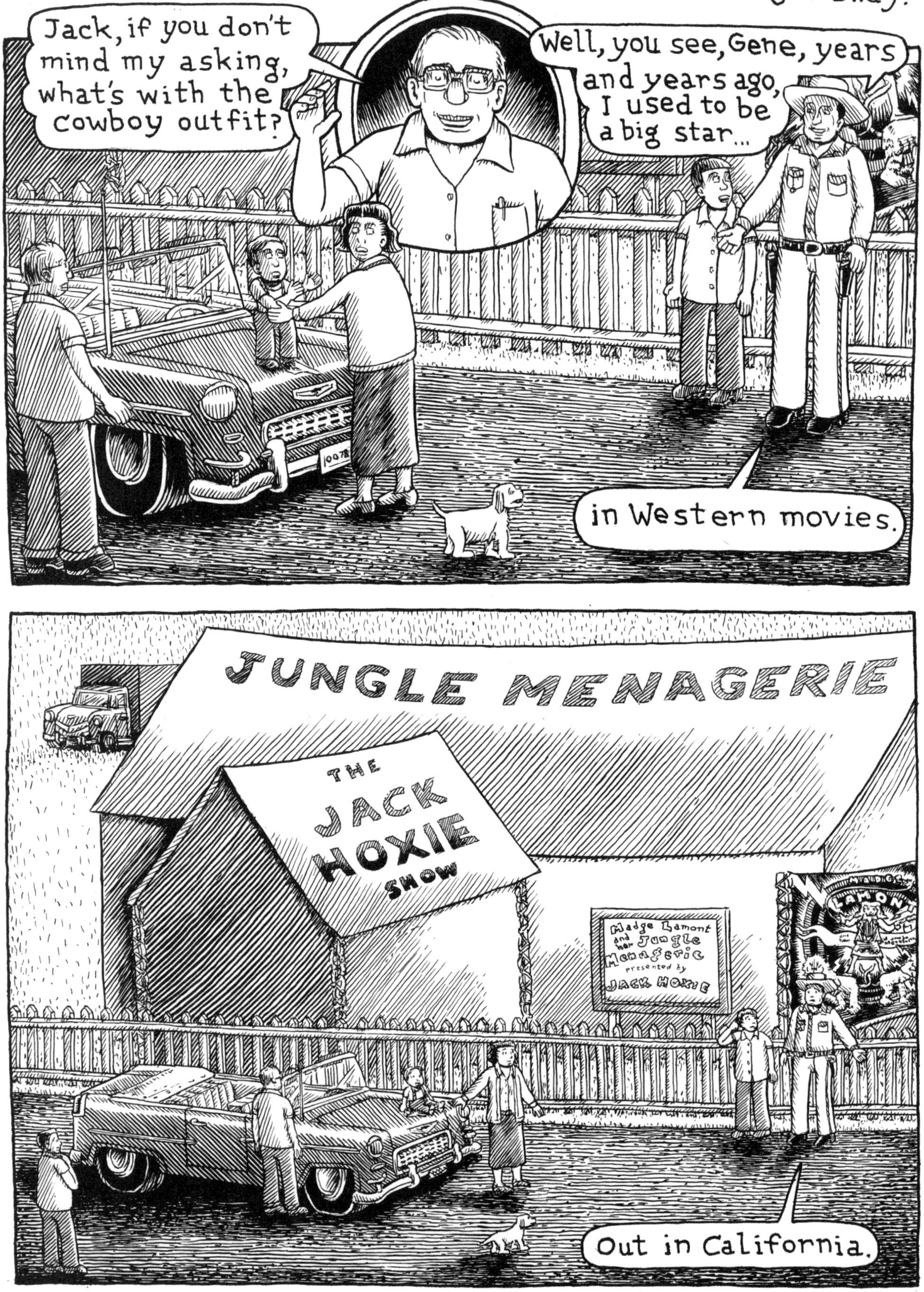
Jack, if you don't mind my asking, what's with the cowboy outfit?
Well, you see, Gene, years and years ago, I used to be a big star...
in Western movies.
JUNGLE MENAGERIE
THE JACK HOXIE SHOW
Madge Lamont and her Jungle Menagerie presented by JACK HOXIE
Out in California.

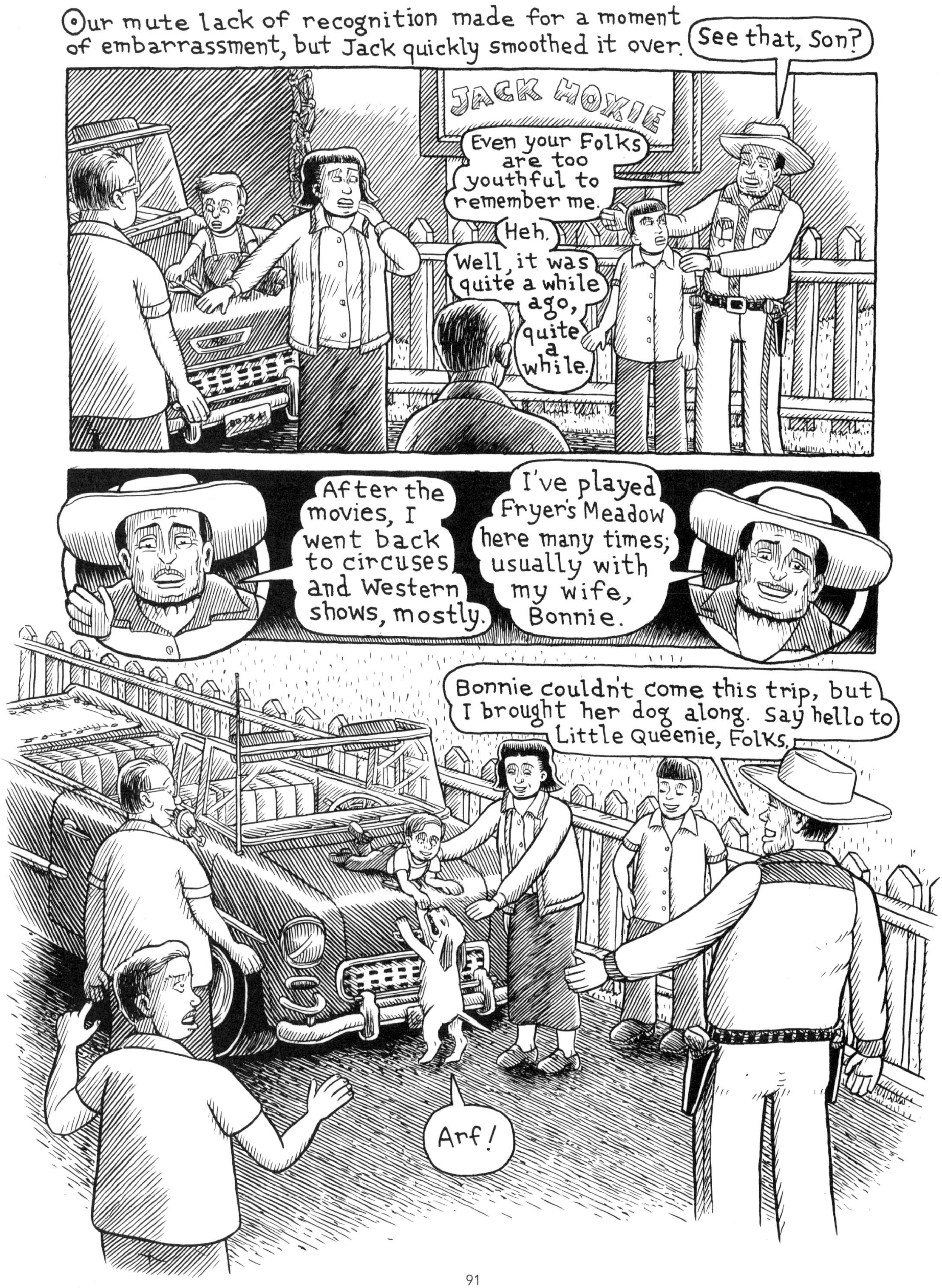
Our mute lack of recognition made for a moment of embarrassment, but Jack quickly smoothed it over.
See that, Son?
JACK HOXIE
Even your Folks are too youthful to remember me.
Heh.
Well, it was quite a while ago, quite a while.
After the movies, I went back to circuses and Western shows, mostly.
I've played Fryer's Meadow here many times; usually with my wife, Bonnie.
Bonnie couldn't come this trip, but I brought her dog along. Say hello to Little Queenie, Folks.
Arf!

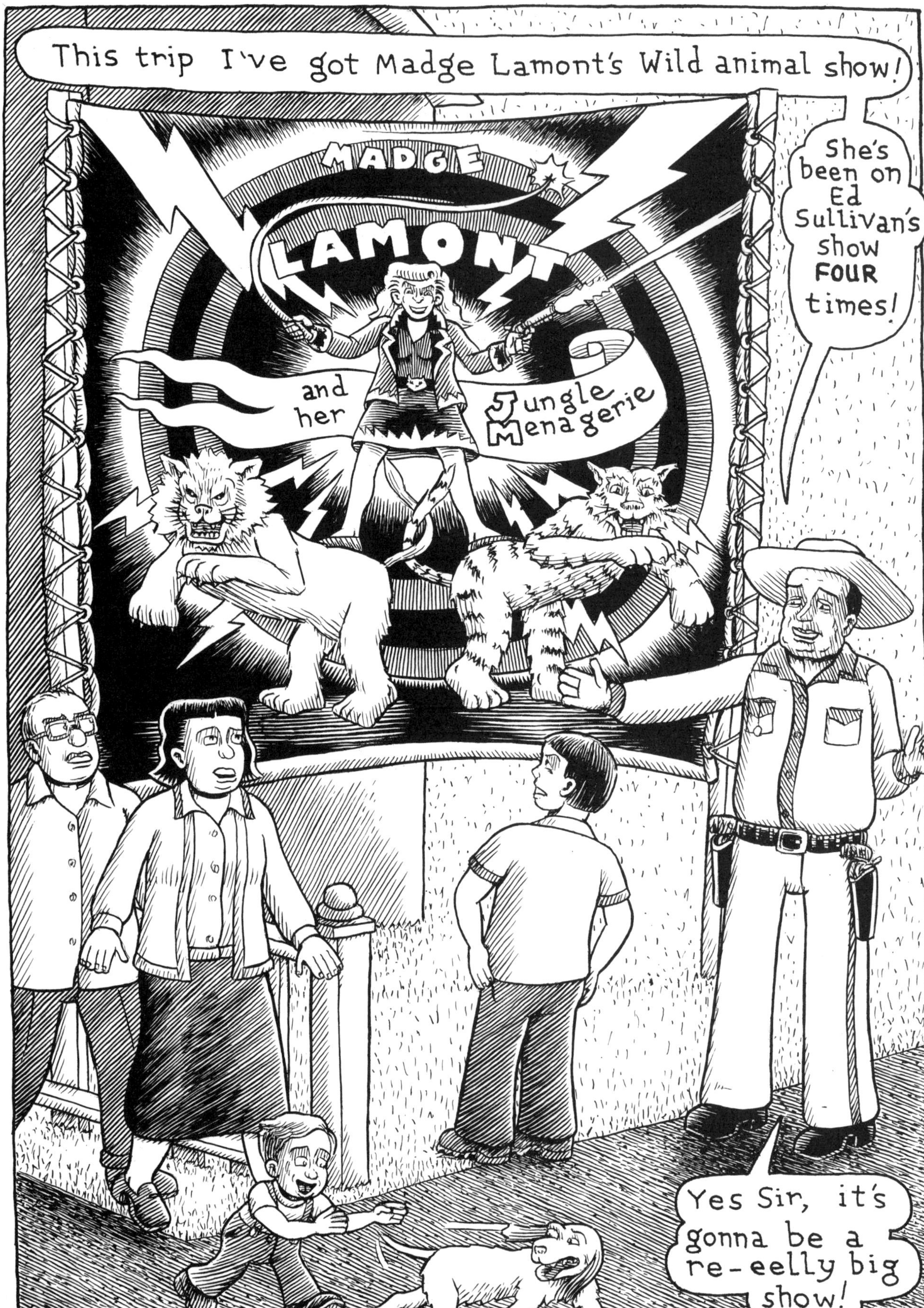

This trip I've got Madge Lamont's Wild animal show!
She's been on Ed Sullivan's show FOUR times!
MADGE LAMONT and her Jungle Menagerie
Yes Sir, it's gonna be a re-eelly big show!

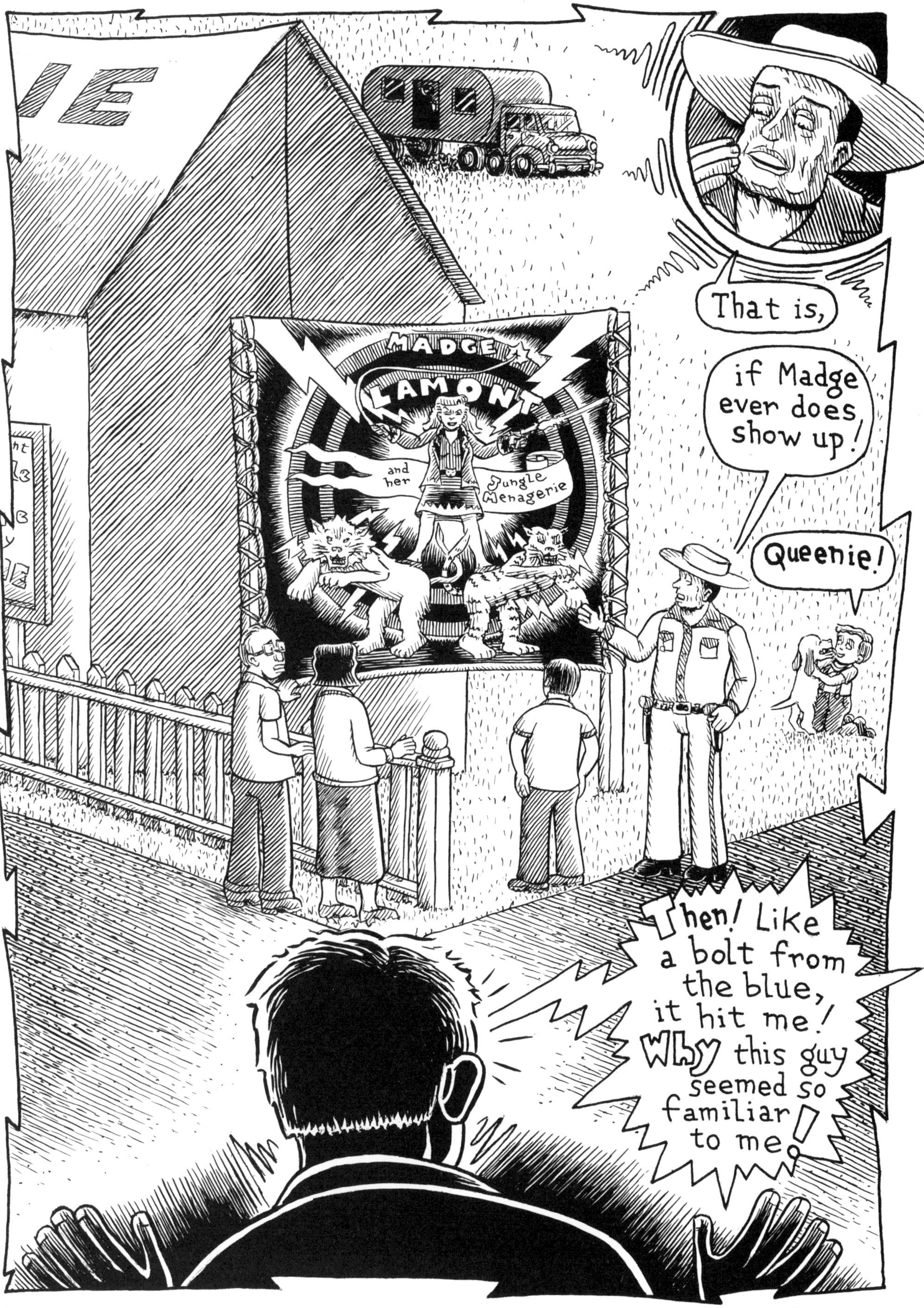
MADGE LAMONT and her Jungle Menagerie
That is,
if Madge ever does show up!
Queenie!
Then! Like a bolt from the blue, it hit me! Why this guy seemed so familiar to me!

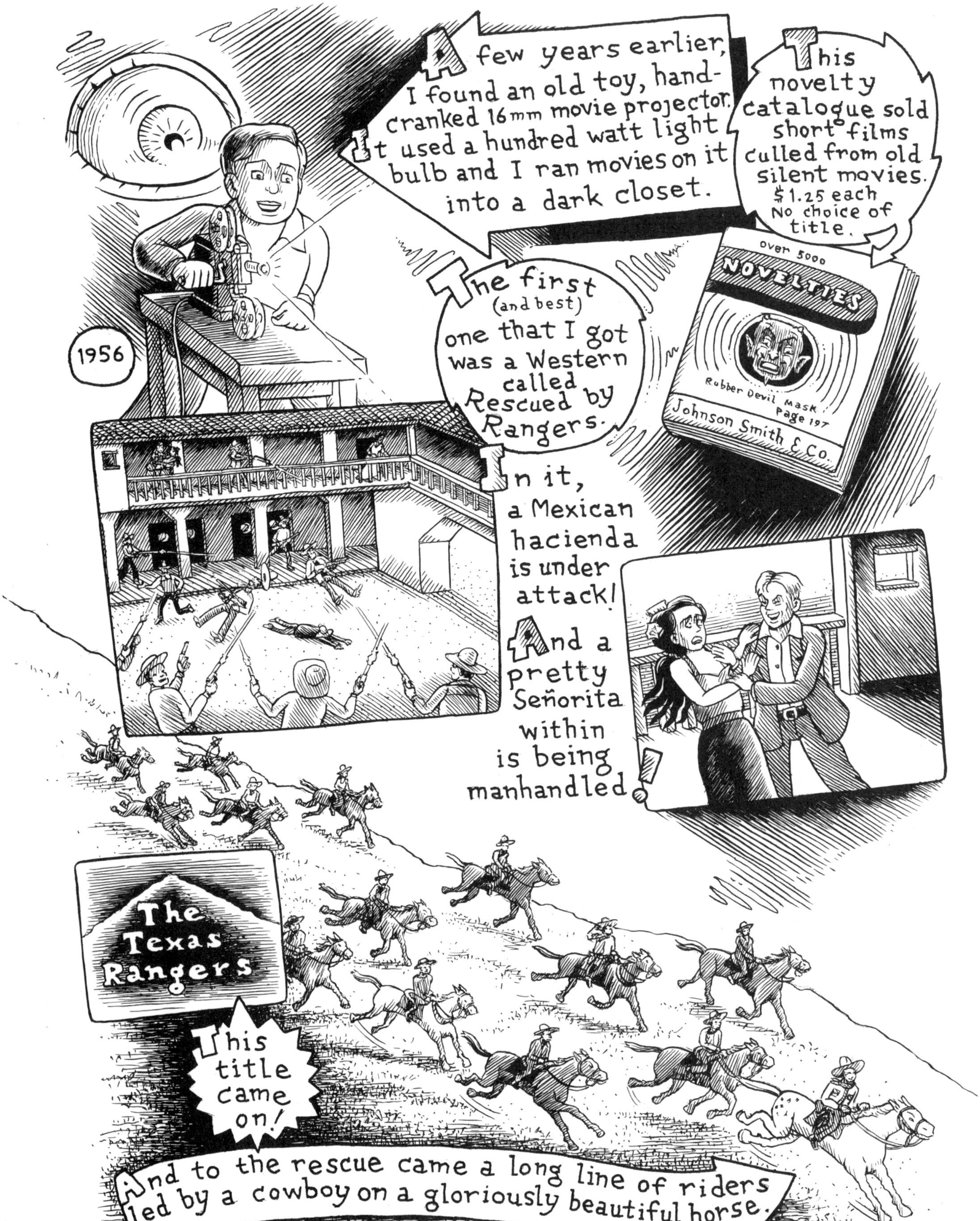
1956
A few years earlier, I found an old toy, hand-cranked 16mm movie projector. It used a hundred watt light bulb and I ran movies on it into a dark closet.
This novelty catalogue sold short films culled from old silent movies. $1.25 each No choice of title.
over 5000 NOVELTIES
Rubber Devil Mask page 197
Johnson Smith & Co.
The first (and best) one that I got was a Western called Rescued by Rangers.
In it, a Mexican hacienda is under attack!
And a pretty Señorita within is being manhandled!
The Texas Rangers
This title came on!
And to the rescue came a long line of riders led by a cowboy on a gloriously beautiful horse.

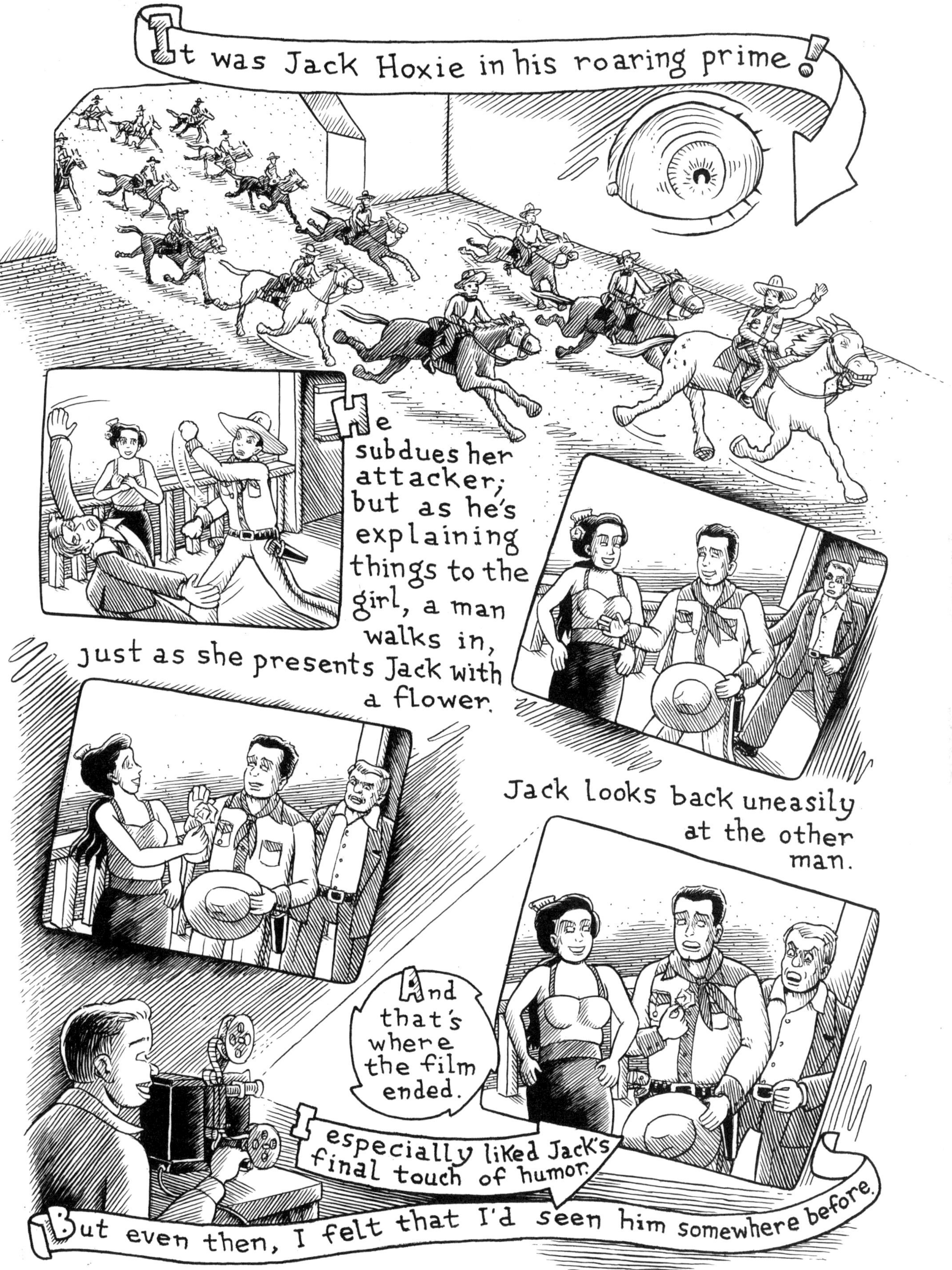
It was Jack Hoxie in his roaring prime!
He subdues her attacker; but as he's explaining things to the girl, a man walks in, just as she presents Jack with a flower.
Jack looks back uneasily at the other man.
And that's where the film ended.
I especially liked Jack's final touch of humor.
But even then, I felt that I'd seen him somewhere before.

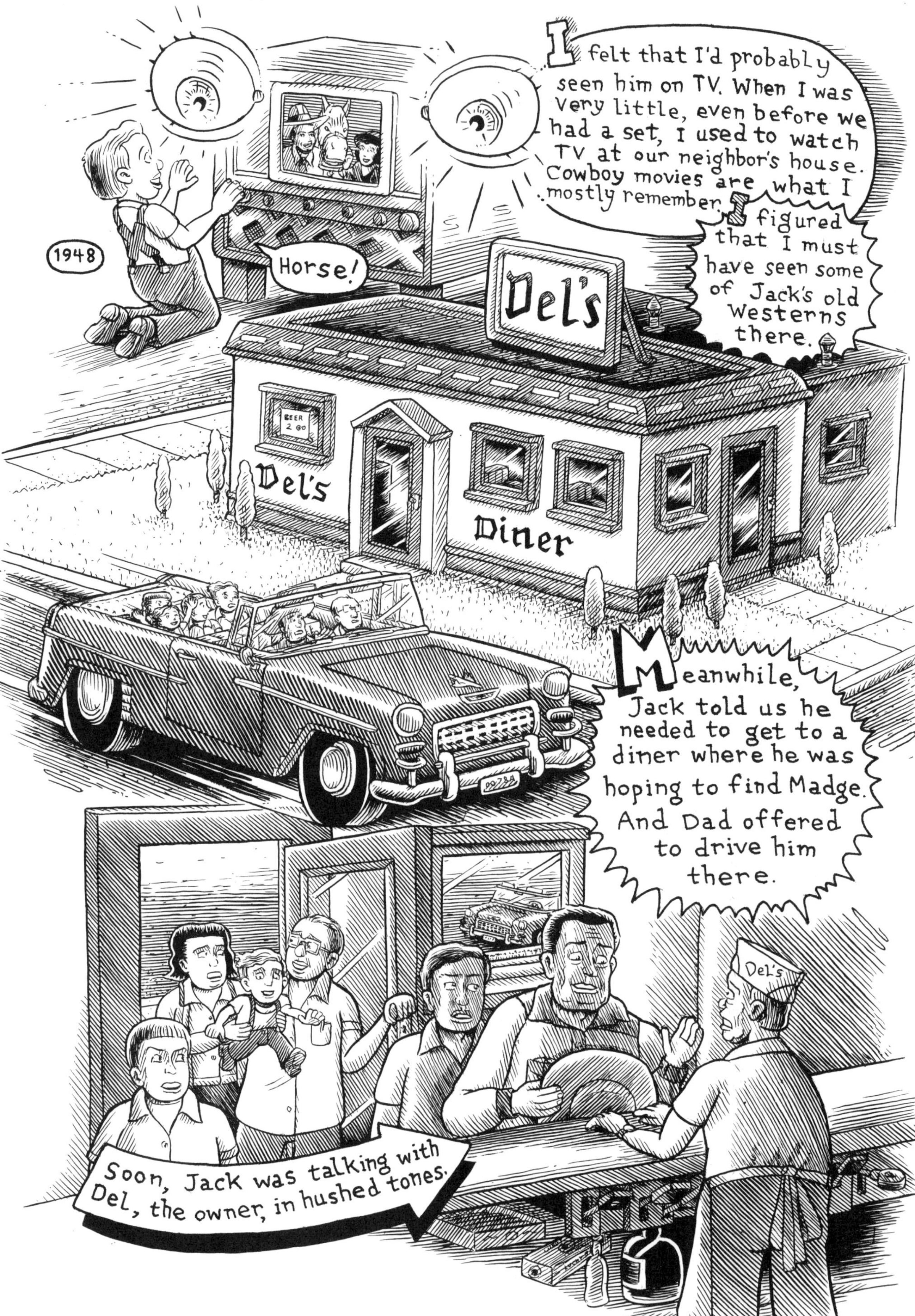
I felt that I'd probably seen him on TV. When I was very little, even before we had a set, I used to watch TV at our neighbor's house. Cowboy movies are what I mostly remember.
1948
Horse!
I figured that I must have seen some of Jack's old Westerns there.
Del's
BEER 2 GO
Del's Diner
Meanwhile, Jack told us he needed to get to a diner where he was hoping to find Madge. And Dad offered to drive him there.
Del's
Soon, Jack was talking with Del, the owner, in hushed tones.

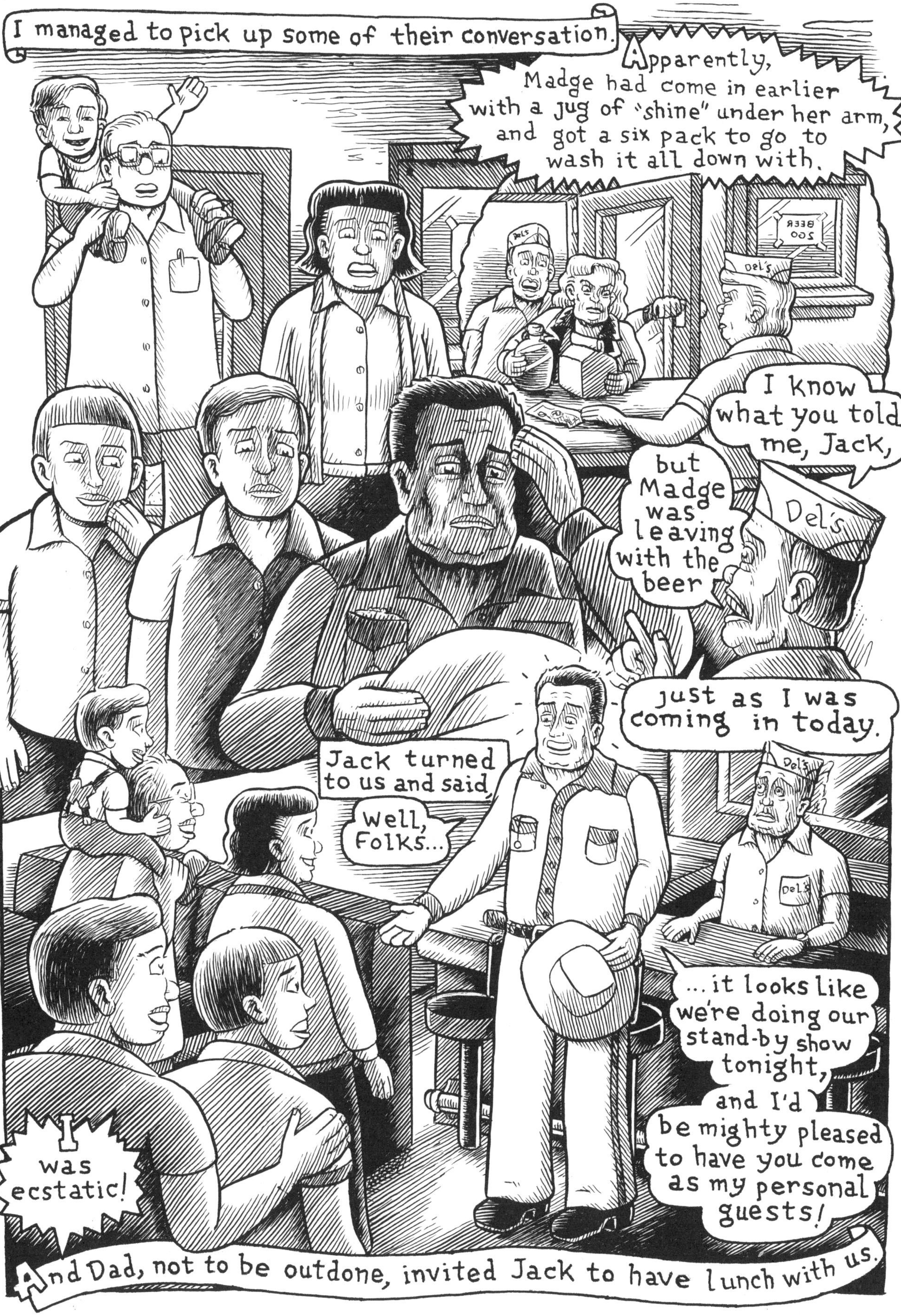
I managed to pick up some of their conversation.
Apparently, Madge had come in earlier with a jug of "shine" under her arm, and got a six pack to go to wash it all down with.
BEER 200
Del's
I know what you told me, Jack,
but Madge was leaving with the beer
just as I was coming in today.
Jack turned to us and said
Well, Folks...
...it looks like we're doing our stand-by show tonight,
and I'd be mighty pleased to have you come as my personal guests!
I was ecstatic!
And Dad, not to be outdone, invited Jack to have lunch with us.

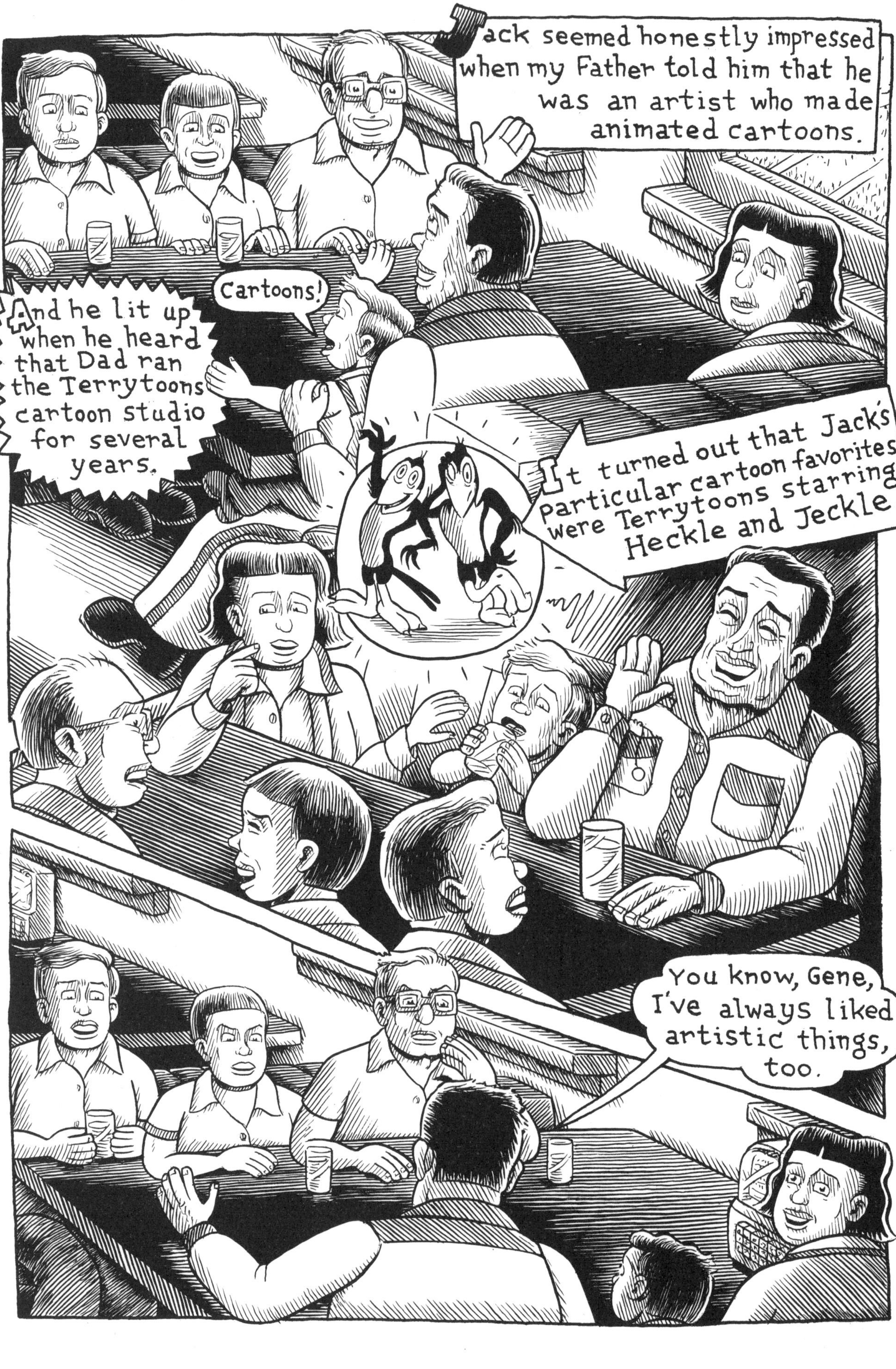
Jack seemed honestly impressed when my Father told him that he was an artist who made animated cartoons.
Cartoons!
And he lit up when he heard that Dad ran the Terrytoons cartoon studio for several years.
It turned out that Jack's particular cartoon favorites were Terrytoons starring Heckle and Jeckle.
You know, Gene, I've always liked artistic things, too.

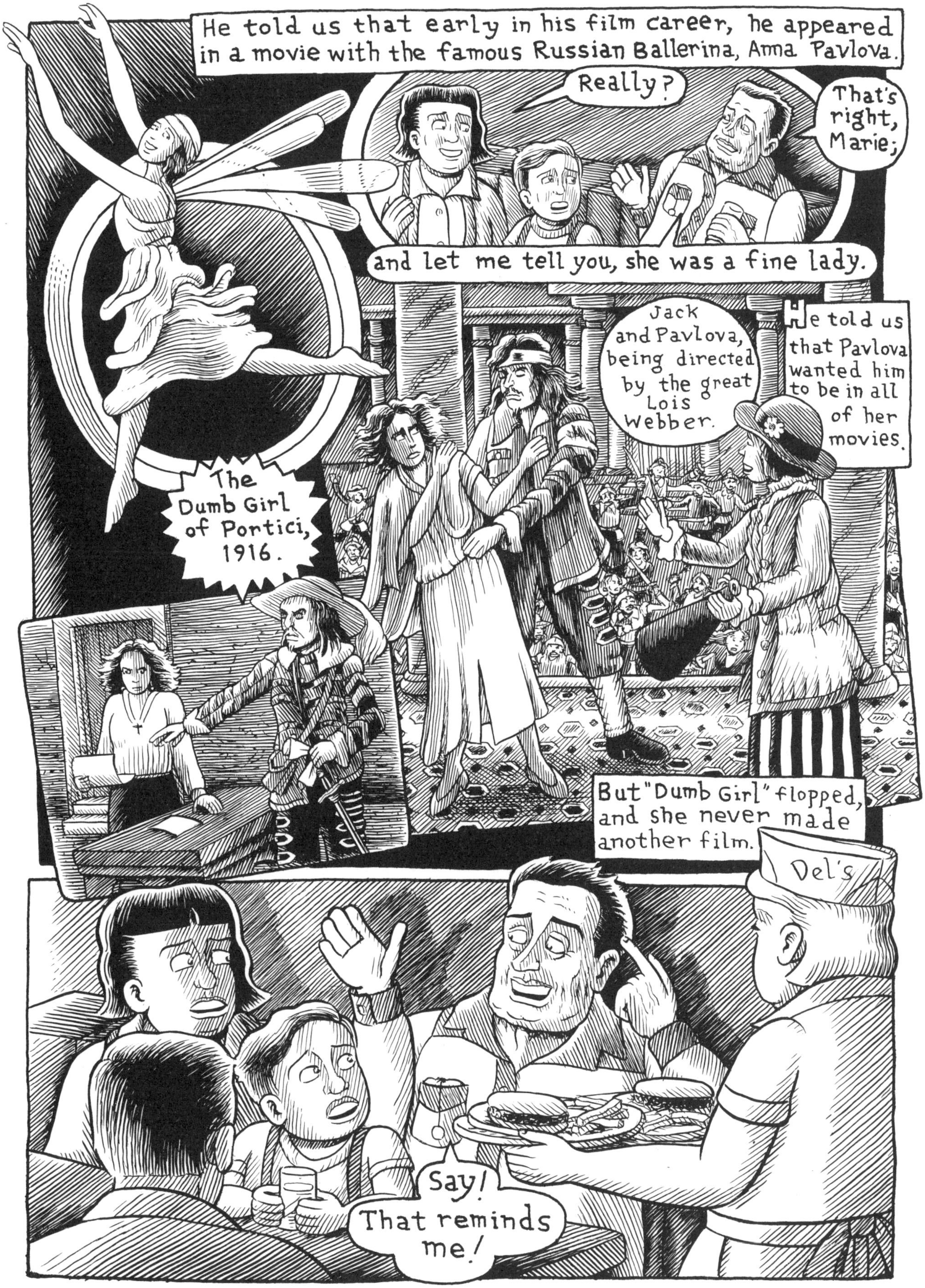
He told us that early in his film career, he appeared in a movie with the famous Russian Ballerina, Anna Pavlova.
Really?
That's right, Marie;
and let me tell you, she was a fine lady.
The Dumb Girl of Portici, 1916.
Jack and Pavlova, being directed by the great Lois Webber.
He told us that Pavlova wanted him to be in all of her movies.
But "Dumb Girl" flopped, and she never made another film.
Del's
Say! That reminds me!

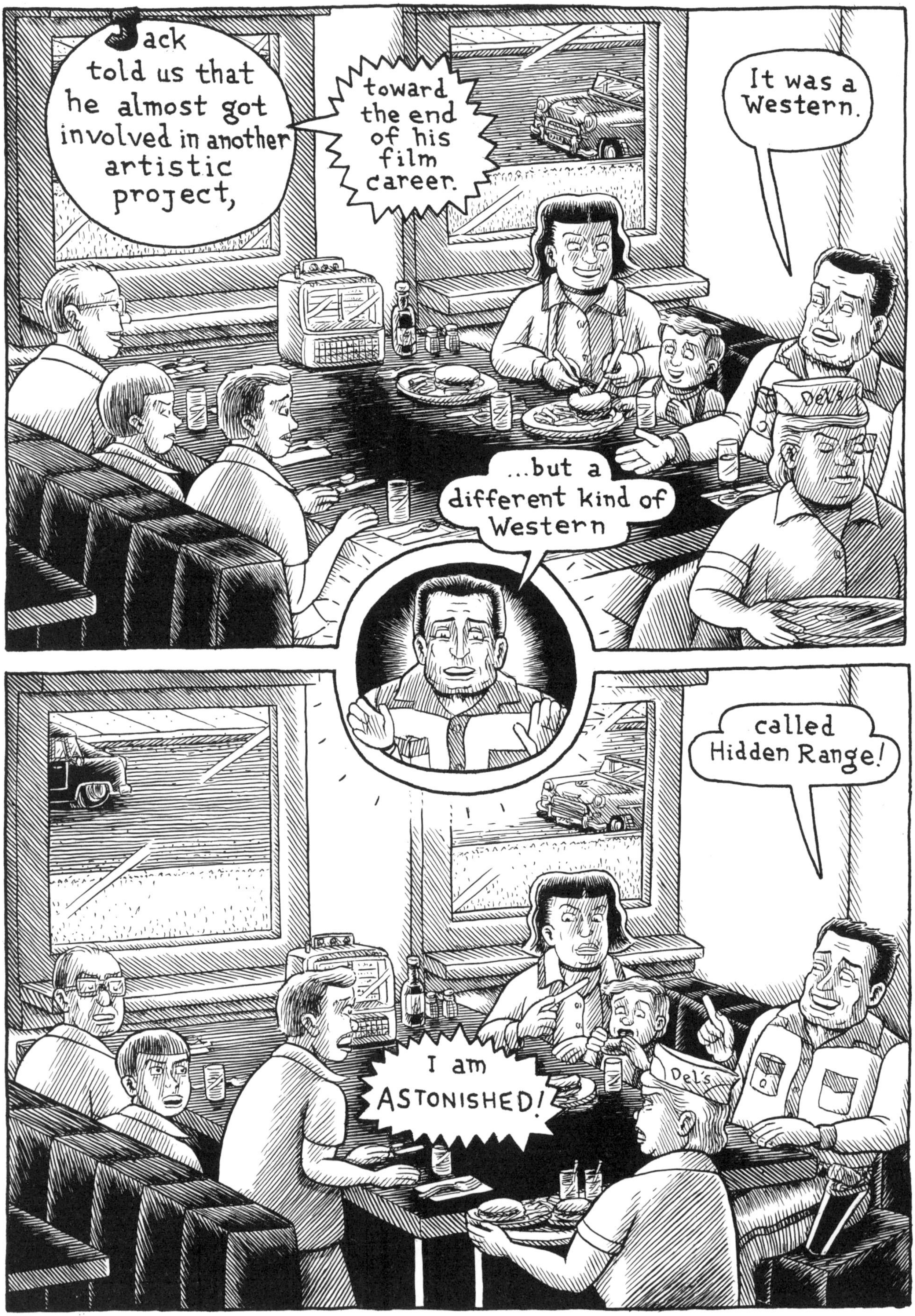

Jack told us that he almost got involved in another artistic project,
toward the end of his film career.
It was a Western.
...but a different kind of Western
called Hidden Range!
I am ASTONISHED!

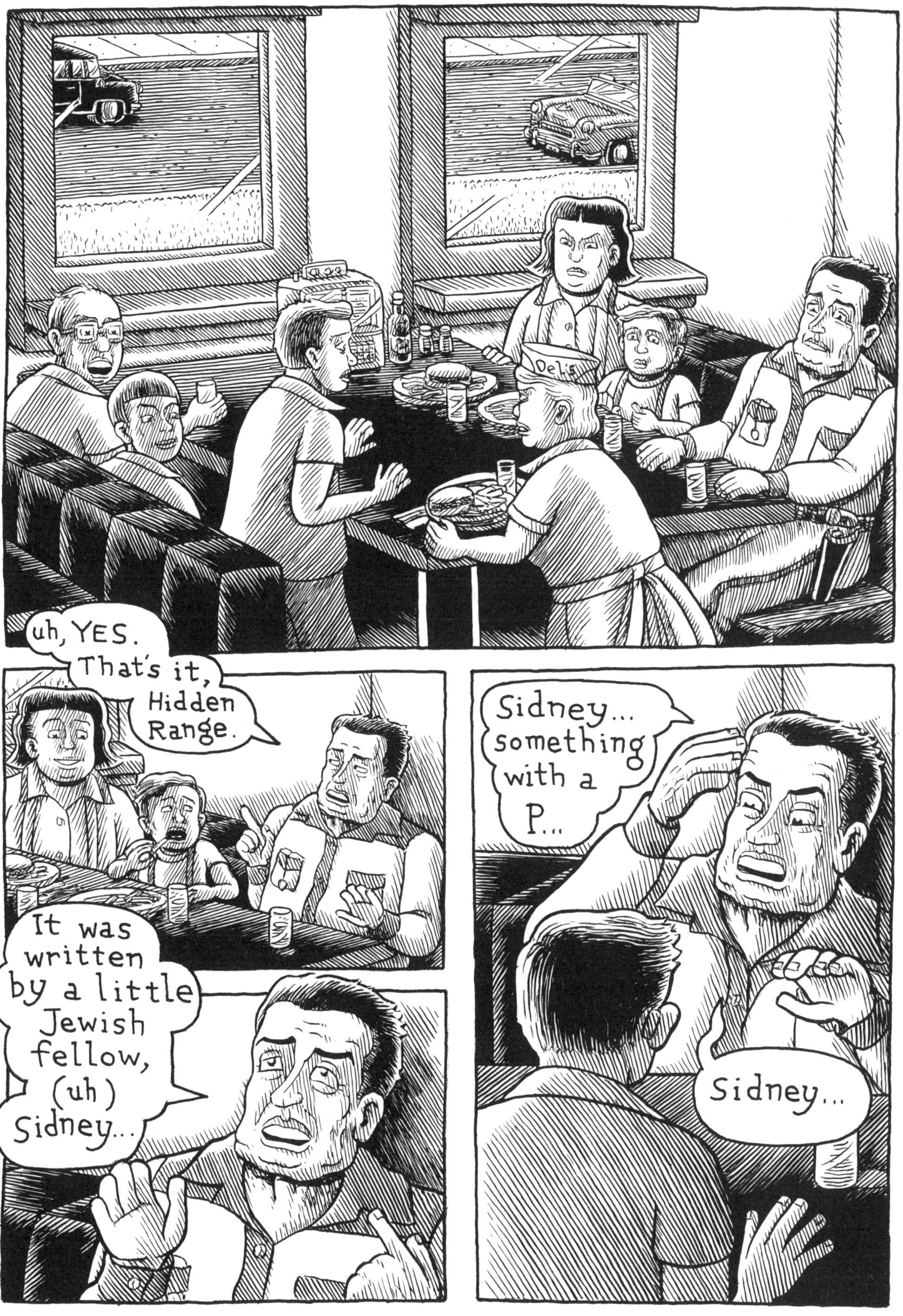
Del's
uh, YES. That's it, Hidden Range.
It was written by a little Jewish fellow, (uh) Sidney...
Sidney... something with a P...
Sidney...

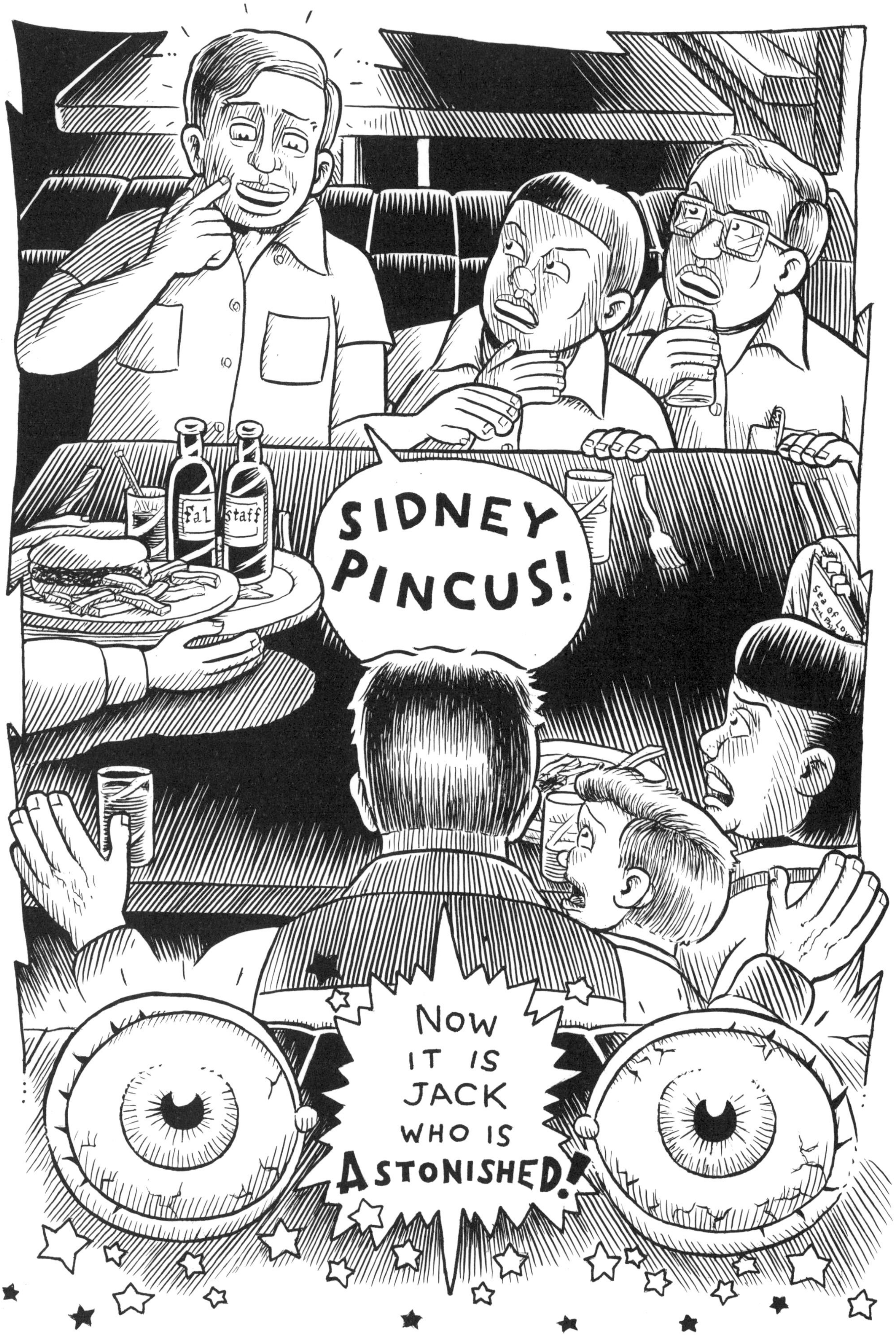
fal
staff
SIDNEY PINCUS!
NOW IT IS JACK WHO IS ASTONISHED!

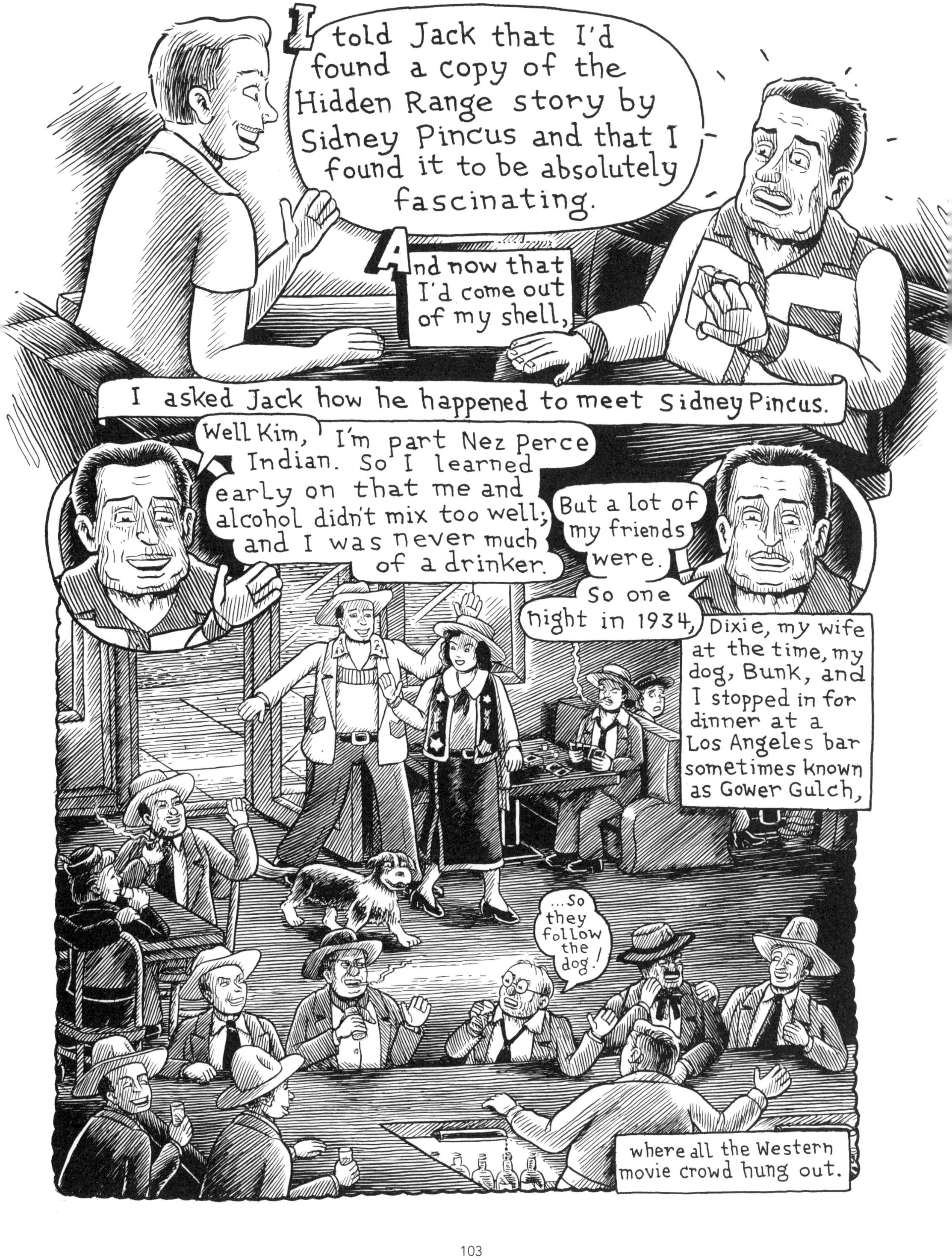

I told Jack that I'd found a copy of the Hidden Range story by Sidney Pincus and that I found it to be absolutely fascinating.
And now that I'd come out of my shell,
I asked Jack how he happened to meet Sidney Pincus.
Well Kim, I'm part Nez Perce Indian. So I learned early on that me and alcohol didn't mix too well; and I was never much of a drinker.
But a lot of my friends were.
So one night in 1934,
Dixie, my wife at the time, my dog, Bunk, and I stopped in for dinner at a Los Angeles bar sometimes known as Gower Gulch,
...So they follow the dog!
where all the Western movie crowd hung out.

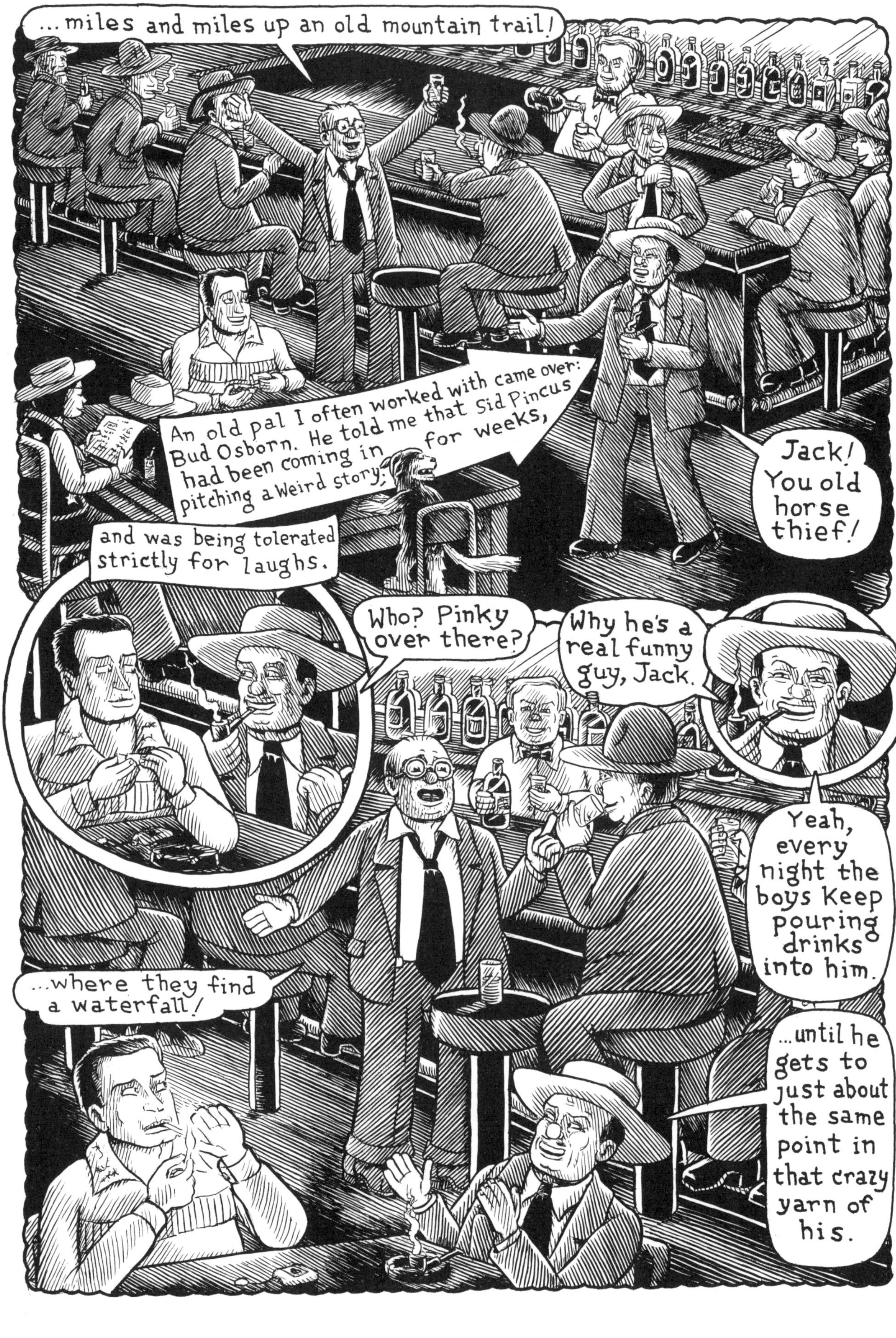
...miles and miles up an old mountain trail!
An old pal I often worked with came over: Bud Osborn. He told me that Sid Pincus had been coming in for weeks, pitching a weird story,
Jack! You old horse thief!
and was being tolerated strictly for laughs.
Who? Pinky over there?
Why he's a real funny guy, Jack.
Yeah, every night the boys keep pouring drinks into him.
...where they find a waterfall!
...until he gets to just about the same point in that crazy yarn of his.

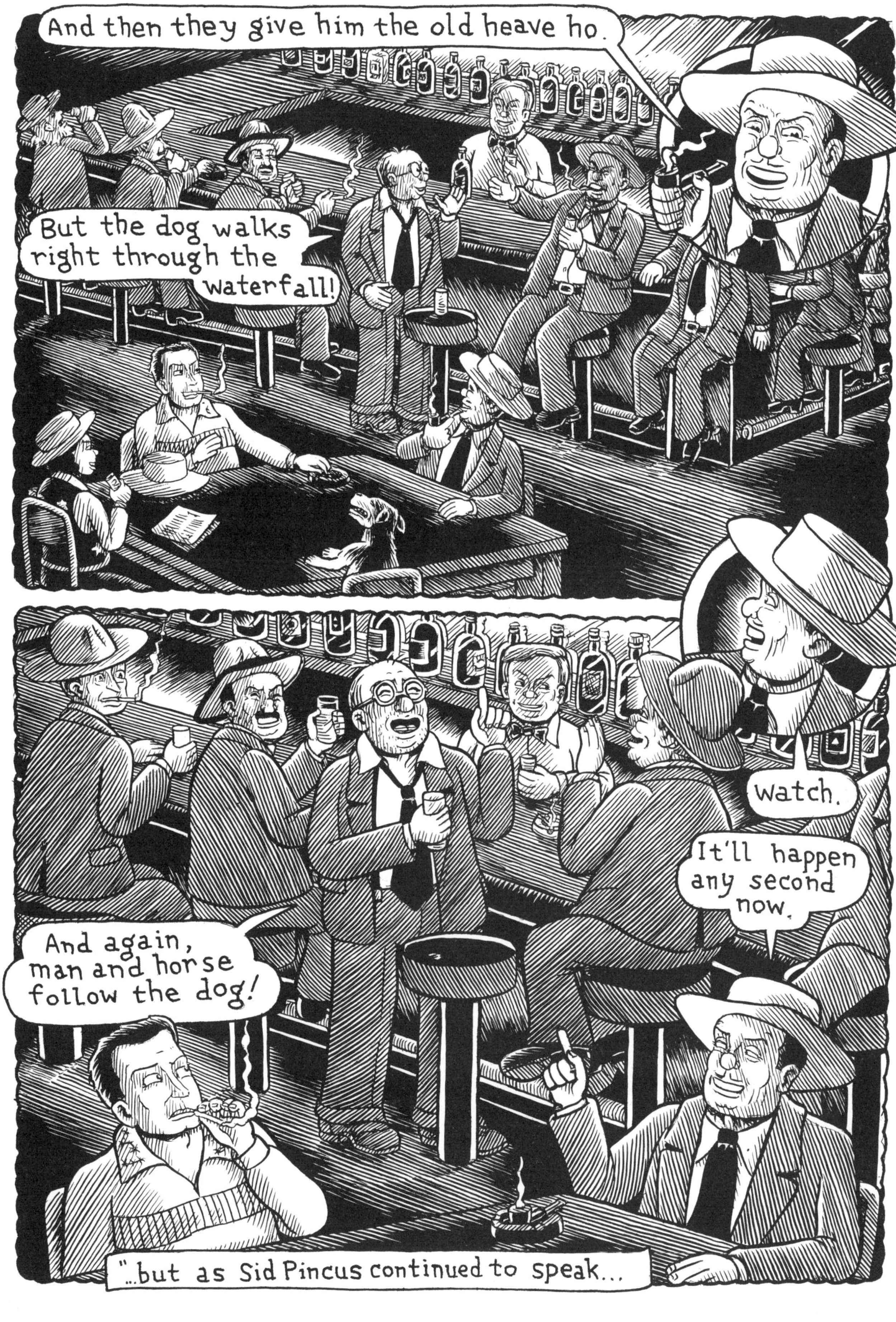
And then they give him the old heave ho.
But the dog walks right through the waterfall!
Watch.
It'll happen any second now.
And again, man and horse follow the dog!
"...but as Sid Pincus continued to speak...

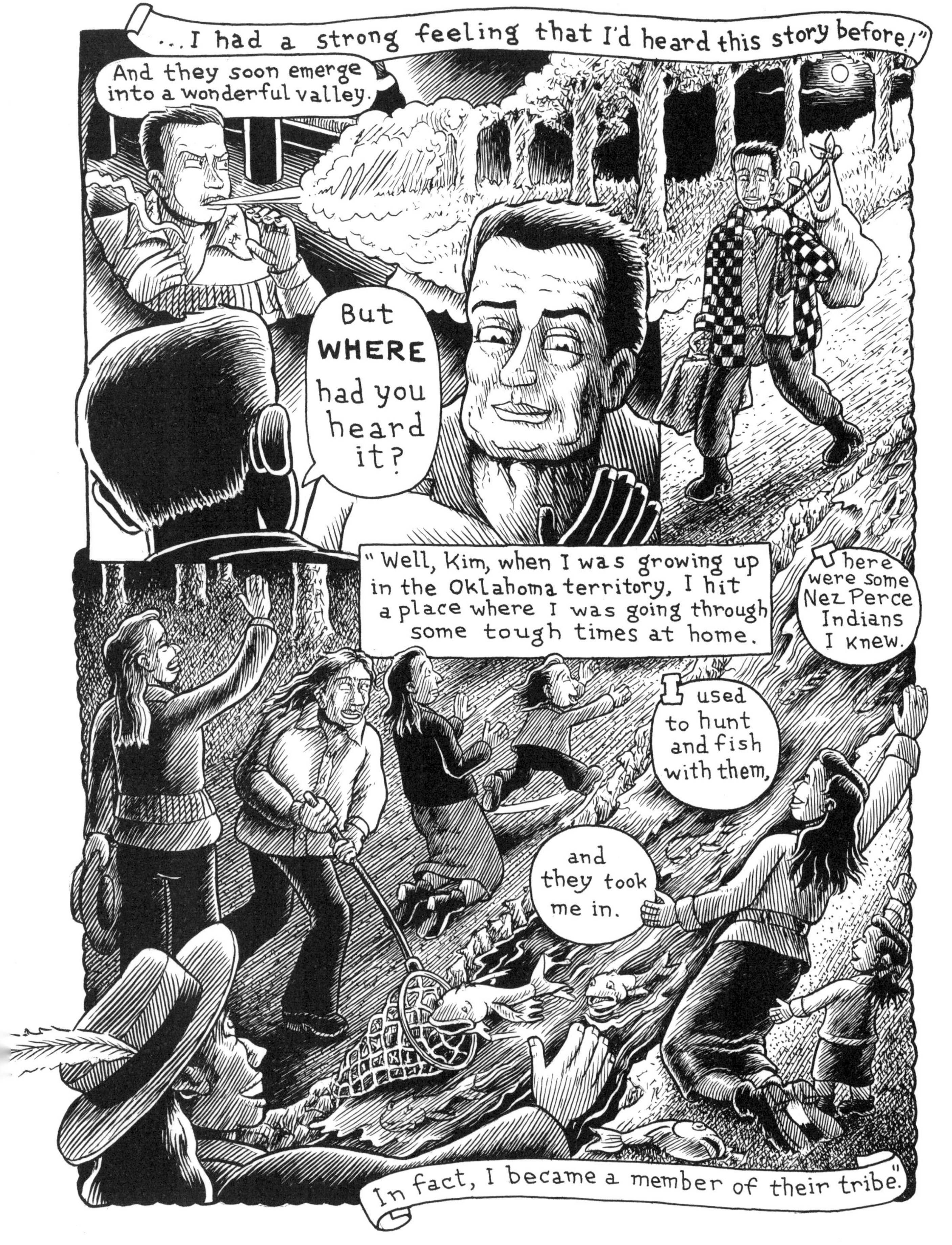
...I had a strong feeling that I'd heard this story before!"
And they soon emerge into a wonderful valley.
But WHERE had you heard it?
"Well, Kim, when I was growing up in the Oklahoma territory, I hit a place where I was going through some tough times at home.
There were some Nez Perce Indians I knew.
I used to hunt and fish with them,
and they took me in.
In fact, I became a member of their tribe."

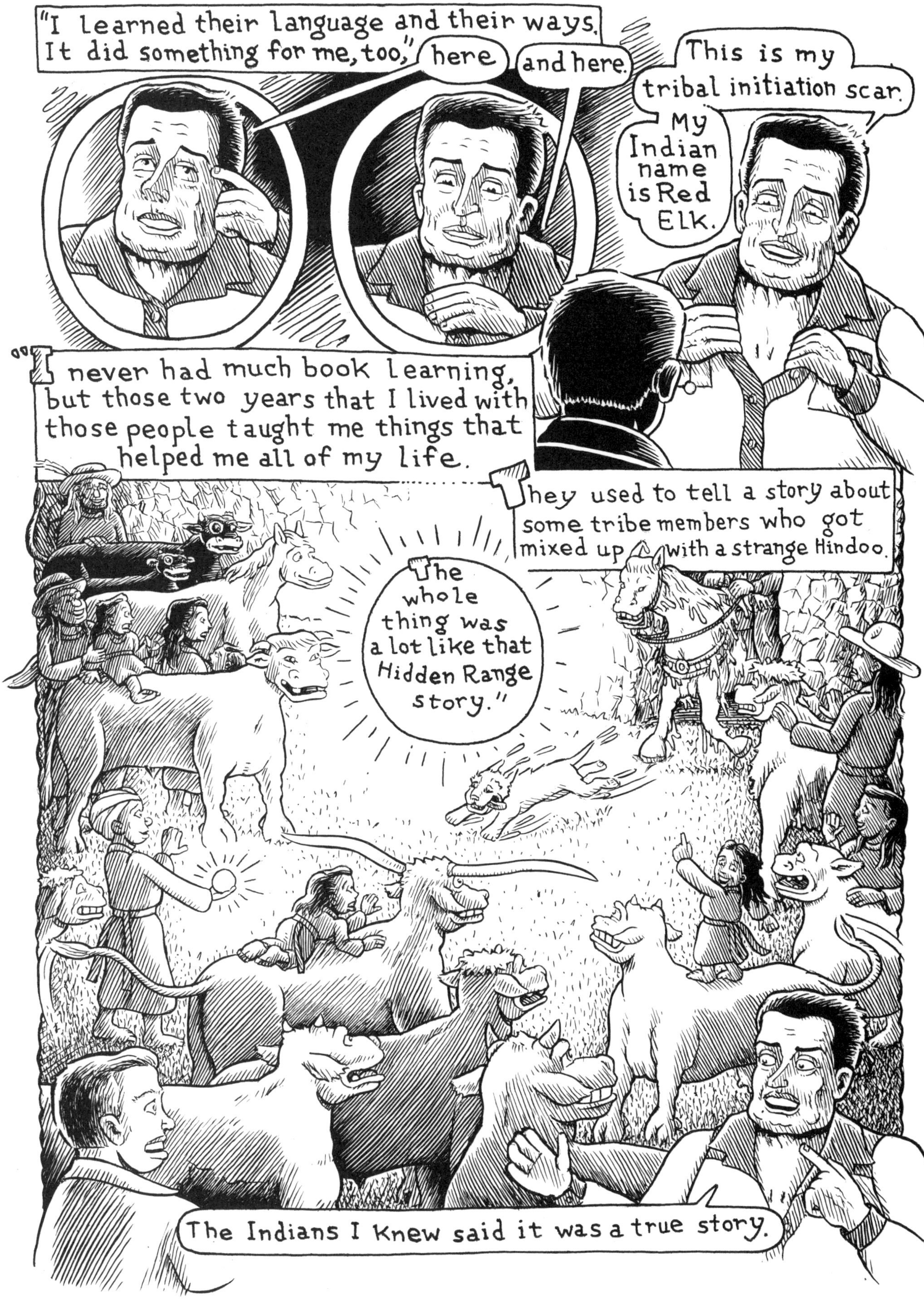
"I learned their language and their ways. It did something for me, too,"
here
and here.
This is my tribal initiation scar.
My Indian name is Red Elk.
"I never had much book learning, but those two years that I lived with those people taught me things that helped me all of my life.
They used to tell a story about some tribe members who got mixed up with a strange Hindoo.
The whole thing was a lot like that Hidden Range story."
The Indians I knew said it was a true story.

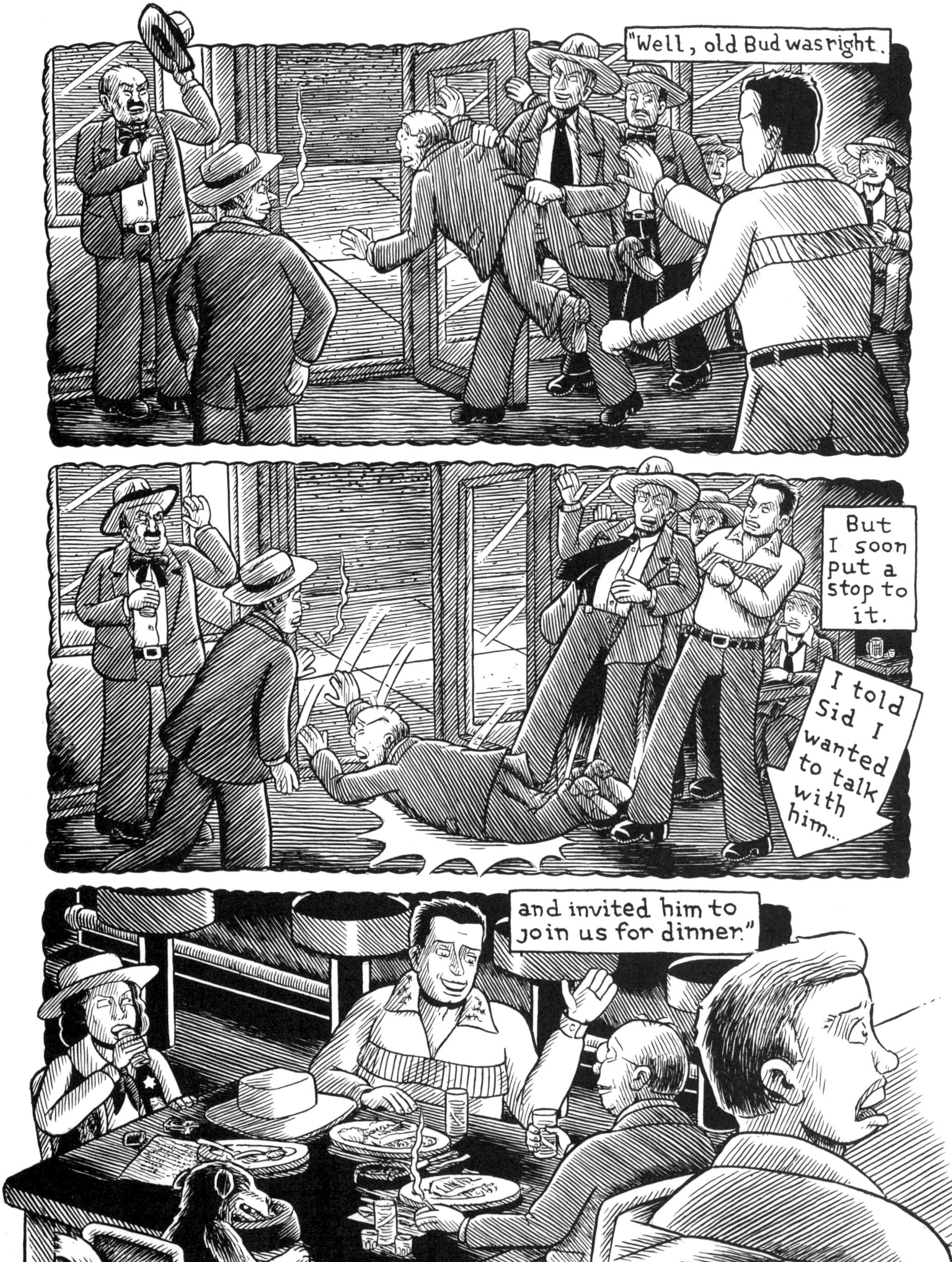
"Well, old Bud was right.
But I soon put a stop to it.
I told Sid I wanted to talk with him...
and invited him to join us for dinner."

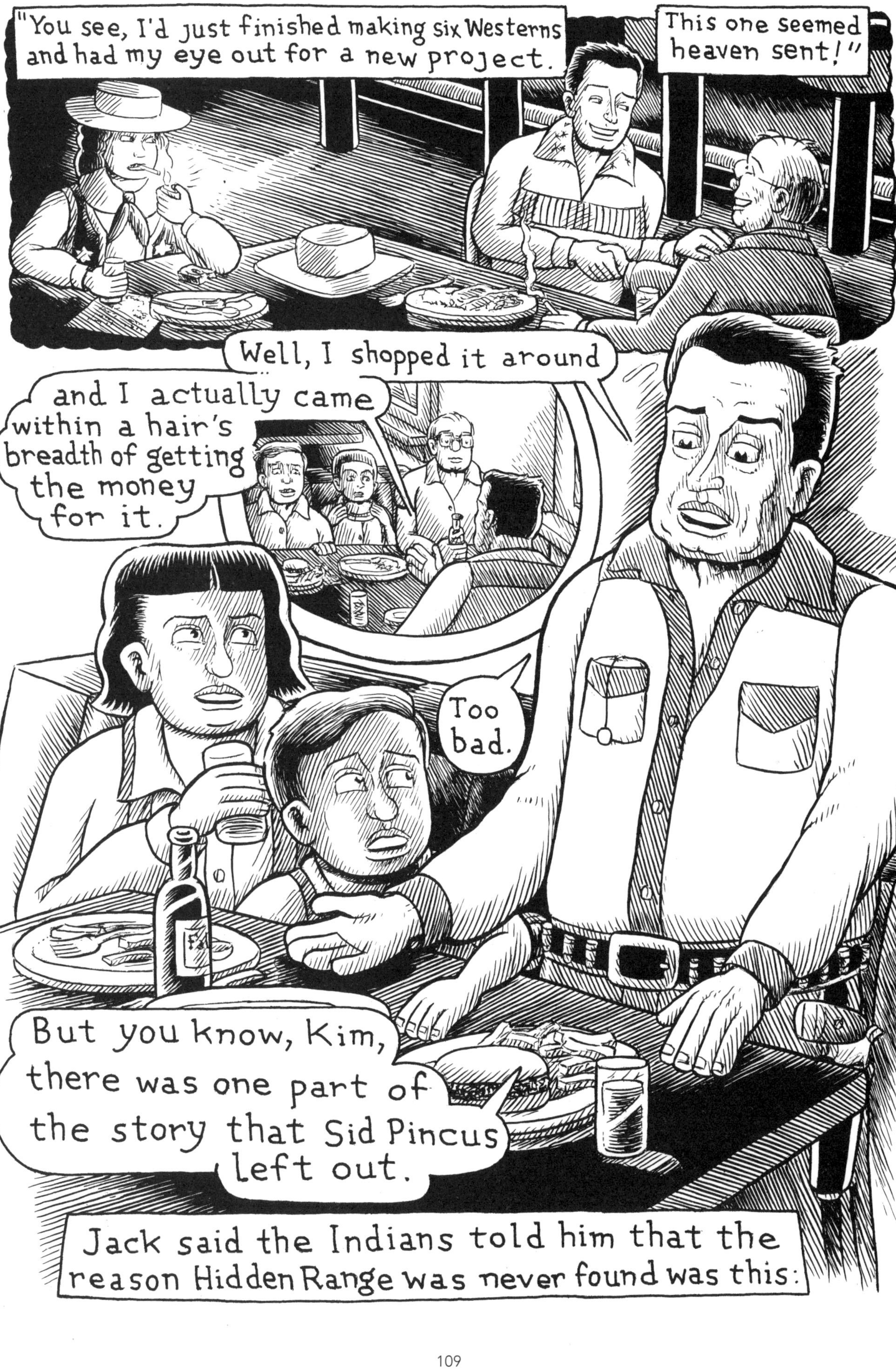
"You see, I'd just finished making six Westerns and had my eye out for a new project.
This one seemed heaven sent!"
Well, I shopped it around
and I actually came within a hair's breadth of getting the money for it.
Too bad.
But you know, Kim, there was one part of the story that Sid Pincus left out.
Jack said the Indians told him that the reason Hidden Range was never found was this:

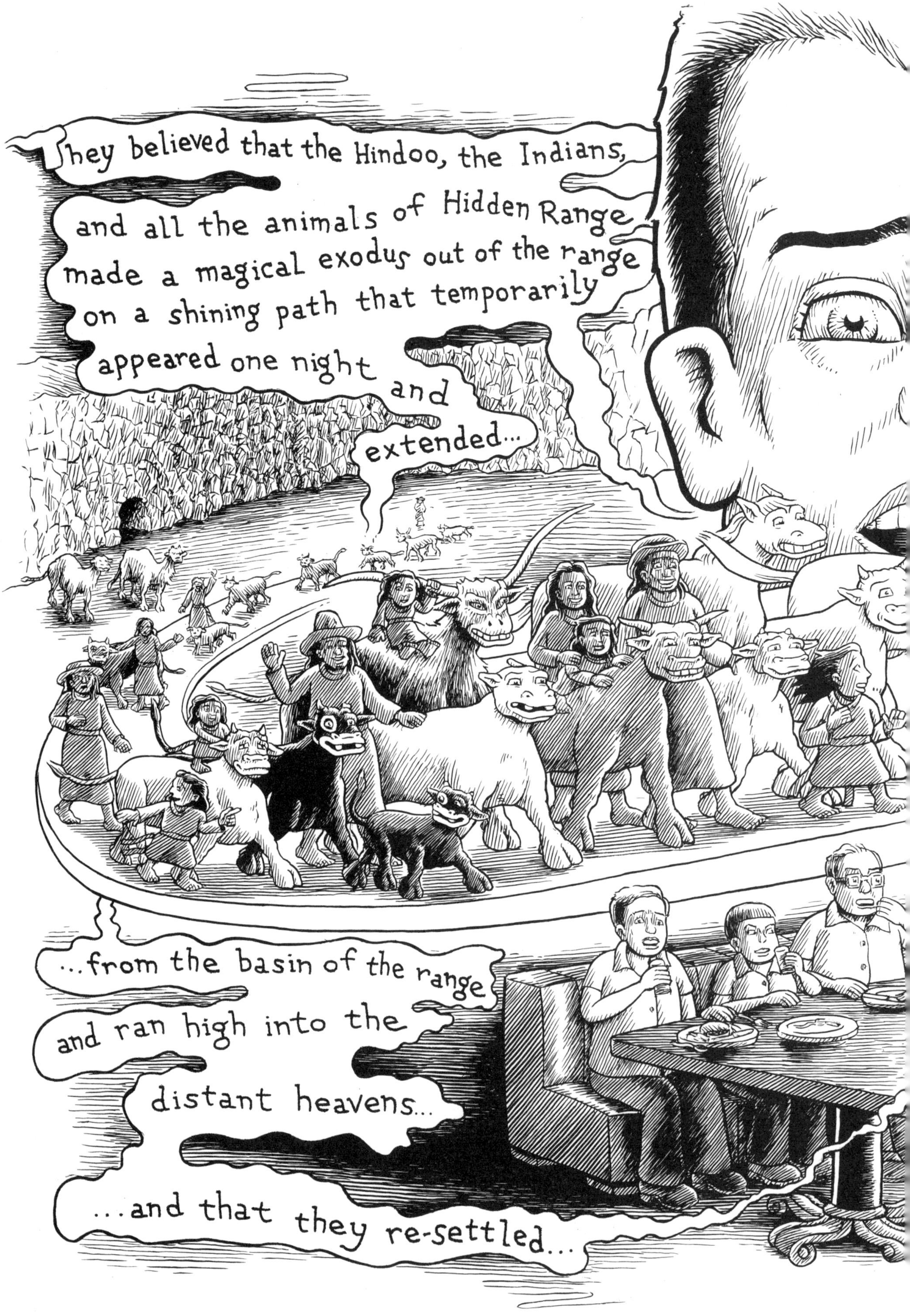
They believed that the Hindoo, the Indians,
and all the animals of Hidden Range made a magical exodus out of the range on a shining path that temporarily appeared one night and extended...
...from the basin of the range
and ran high into the distant heavens...
...and that they re-settled...

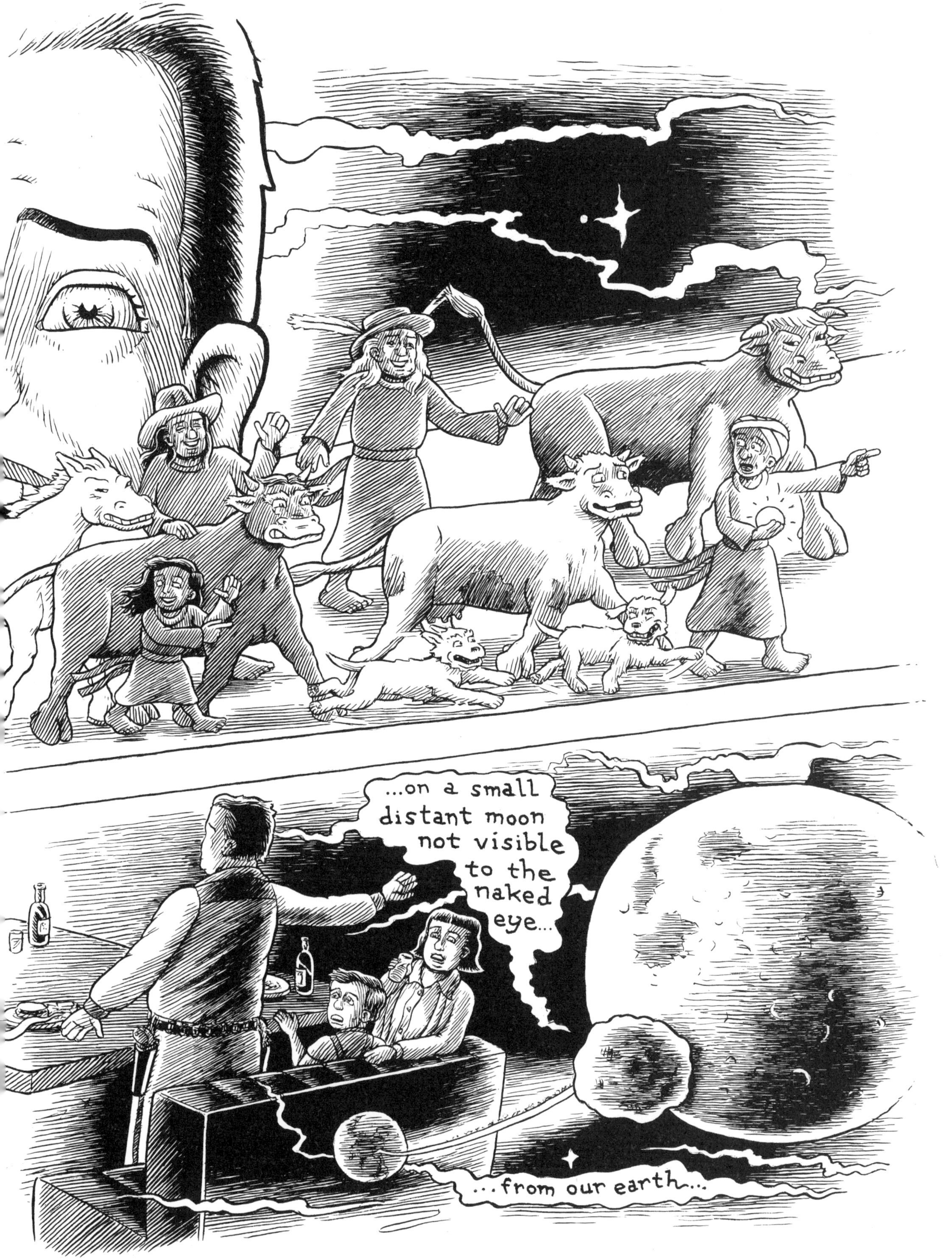
...on a small distant moon not visible to the naked eye...
...from our earth...

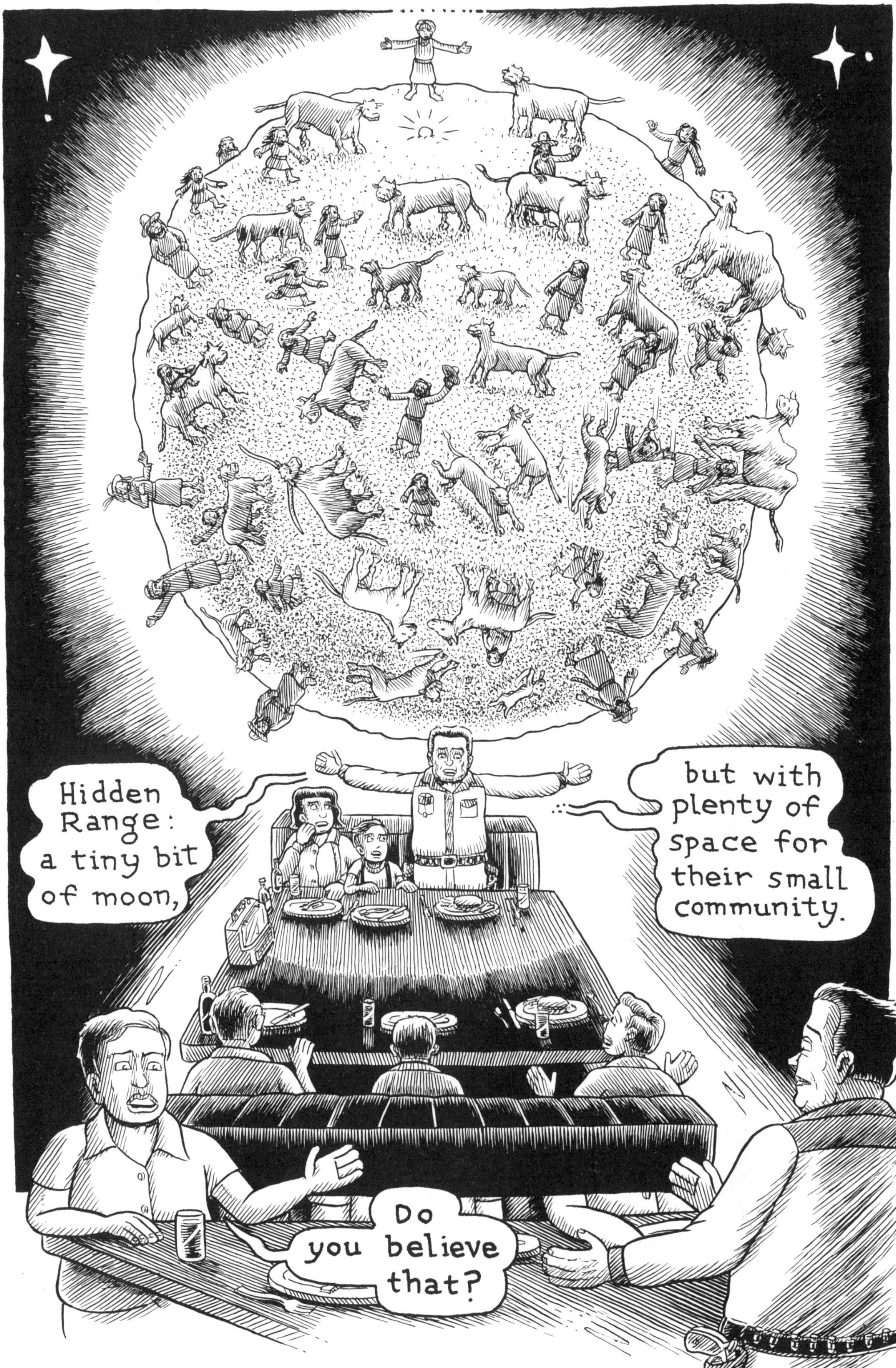
Hidden Range: a tiny bit of moon,
but with plenty of space for their small community.
Do you believe that?

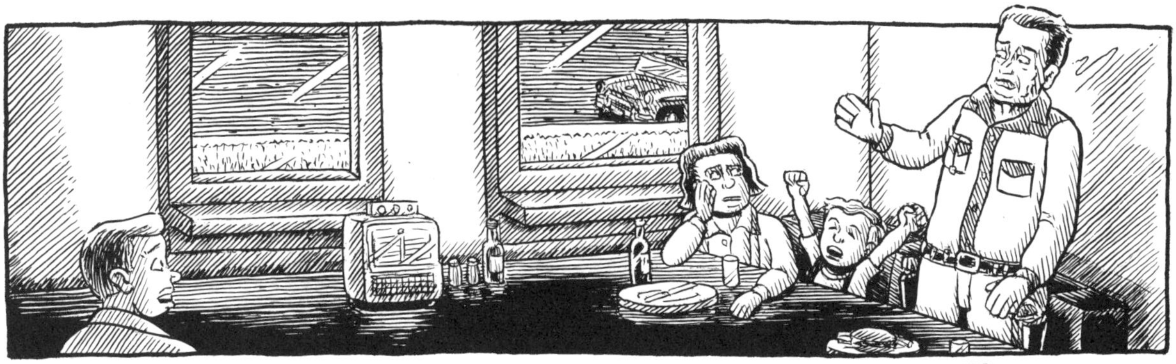

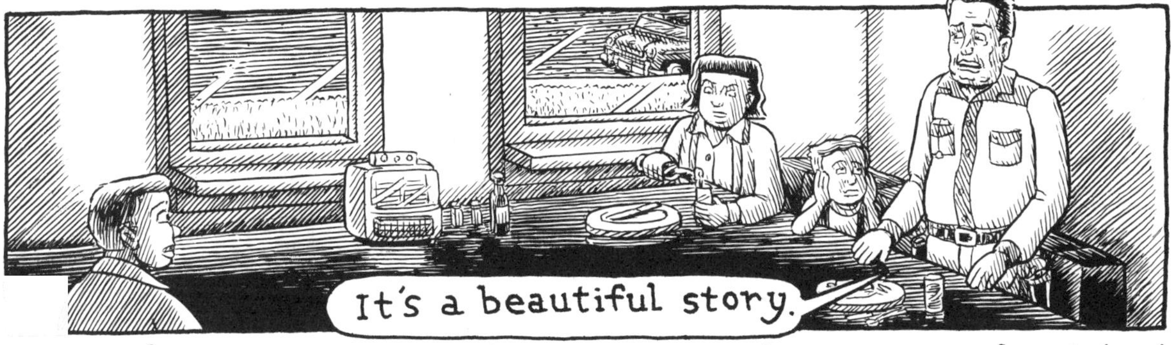
It's a beautiful story.

That night, Jack commandeered Simon and me as special assistants.

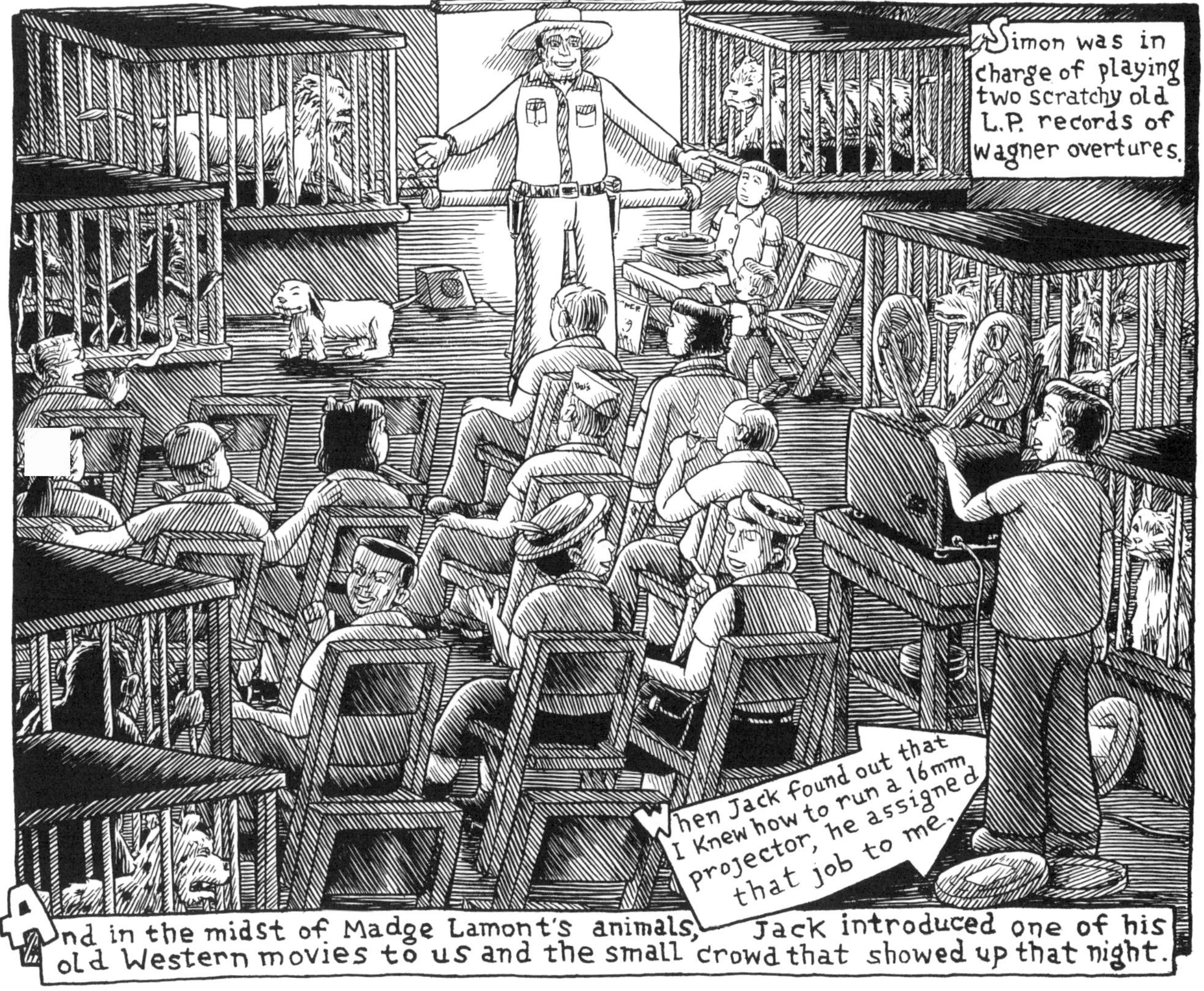
Simon was in charge of playing two scratchy old L.P. records of Wagner overtures.
When Jack found out that I knew how to run a 16mm projector, he assigned that job to me.
And in the midst of Madge Lamont's animals, Jack introduced one of his old Western movies to us and the small crowd that showed up that night.

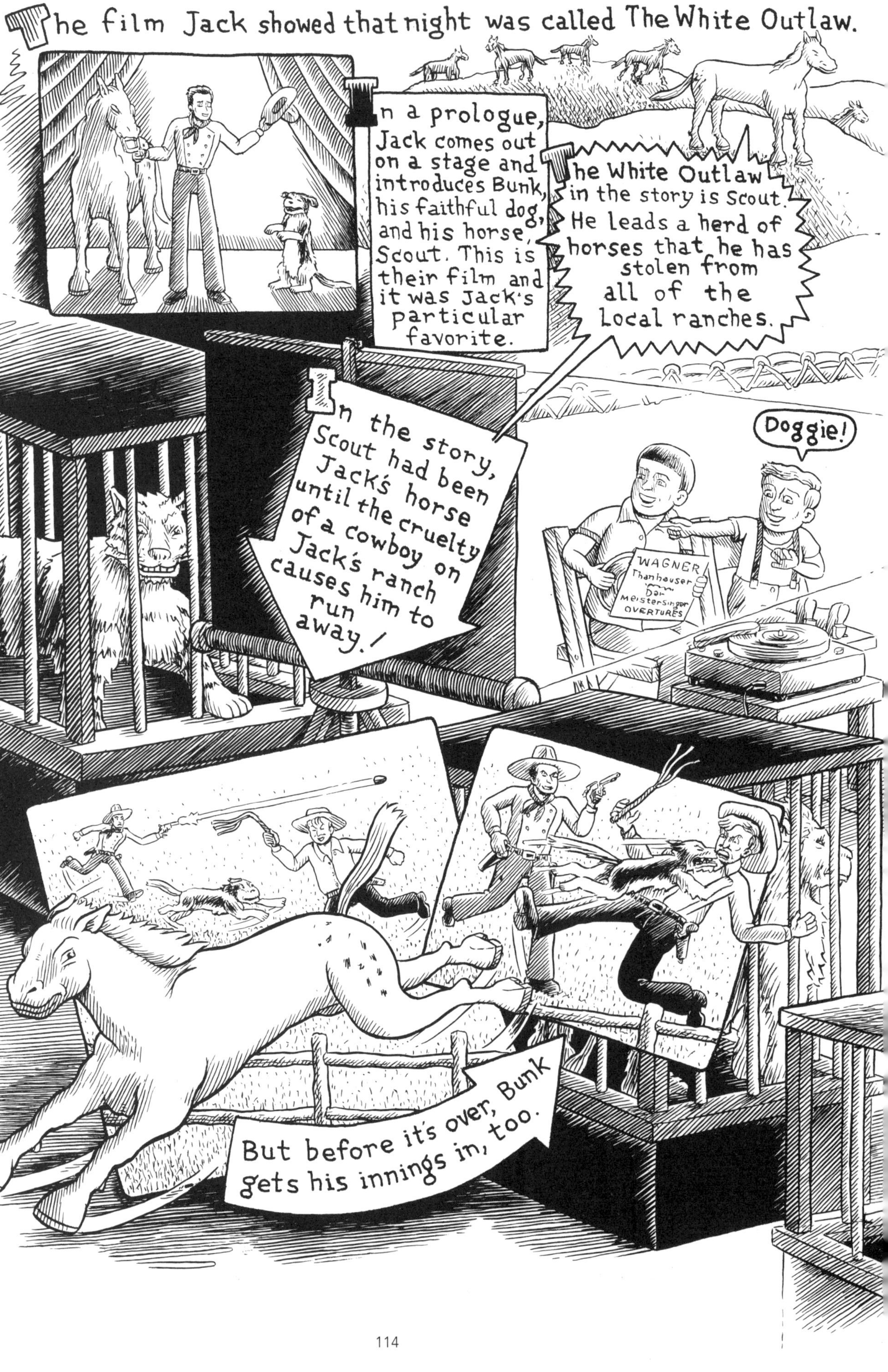
The film Jack showed that night was called The White Outlaw.
In a prologue, Jack comes out on a stage and introduces Bunk, his faithful dog, and his horse, Scout. This is their film and it was Jack's particular favorite.
The White Outlaw in the story is Scout. He leads a herd of horses that he has stolen from all of the local ranches.
In the story, Scout had been Jack's horse until the cruelty of a cowboy on Jack's ranch causes him to run away.!
Doggie!
WAGNER
Thanhauser
Der Meistersinger
OVERTURES
But before it's over, Bunk gets his innings in, too.

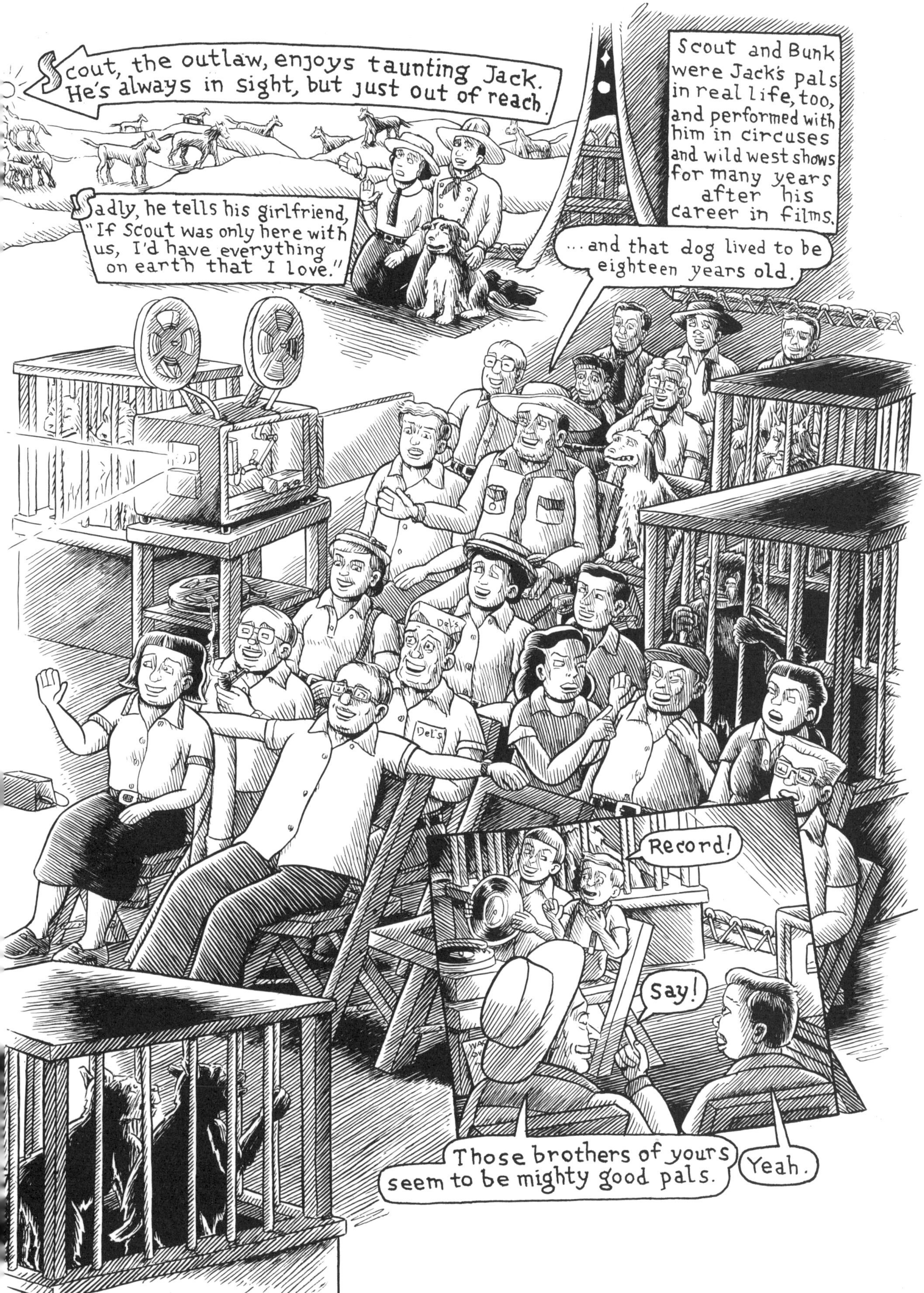
Scout, the outlaw, enjoys taunting Jack. He's always in sight, but just out of reach.
Sadly, he tells his girlfriend, "If Scout was only here with us, I'd have everything on earth that I love."
Scout and Bunk were Jack's pals in real life, too, and performed with him in circuses and wild west shows for many years after his career in films.
...and that dog lived to be eighteen years old.
Del's
Record!
Say!
Those brothers of yours seem to be mighty good pals.
Yeah.

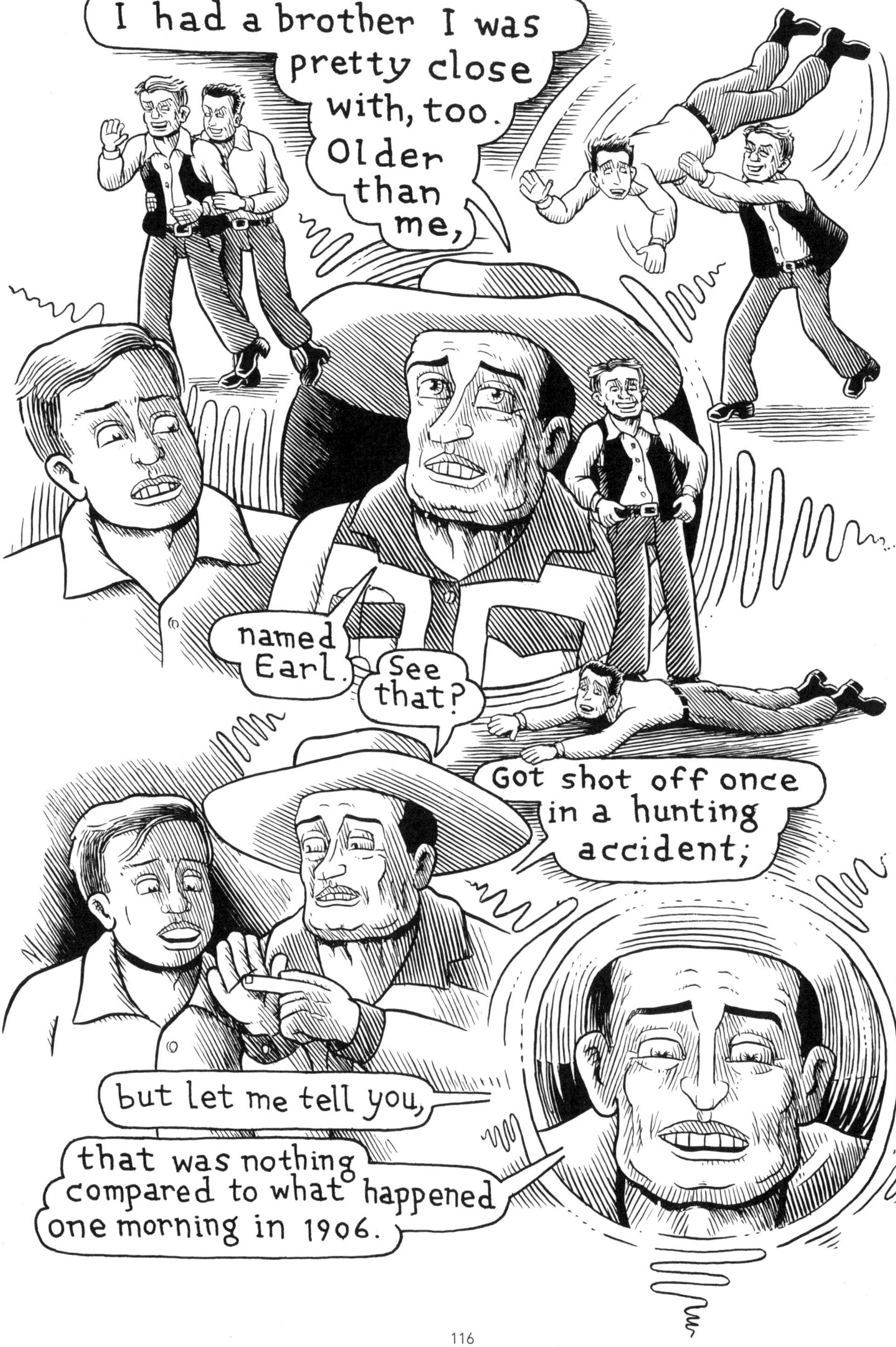
I had a brother I was pretty close with, too. Older than me,
named Earl.
See that?
Got shot off once in a hunting accident;
but let me tell you,
that was nothing compared to what happened one morning in 1906.

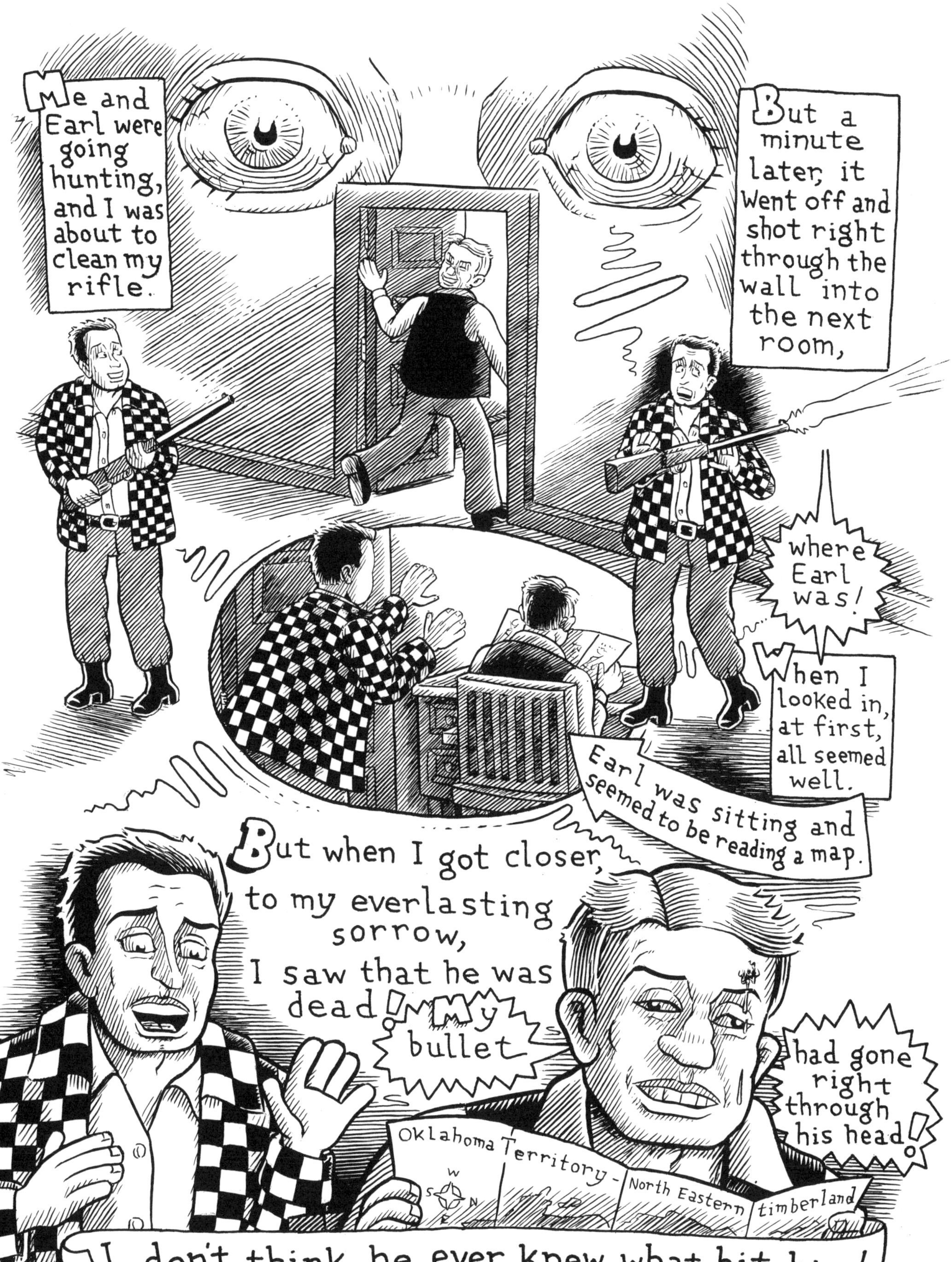
Me and Earl were going hunting, and I was about to clean my rifle.
But a minute later, it went off and shot right through the wall into the next room,
where Earl was!
When I looked in, at first, all seemed well.
Earl was sitting and seemed to be reading a map.
But when I got closer, to my everlasting sorrow, I saw that he was dead!
My bullet
had gone right through his head!
Oklahoma Territory - North Eastern timberland
W
S
N
E
I don't think he ever knew what hit him!

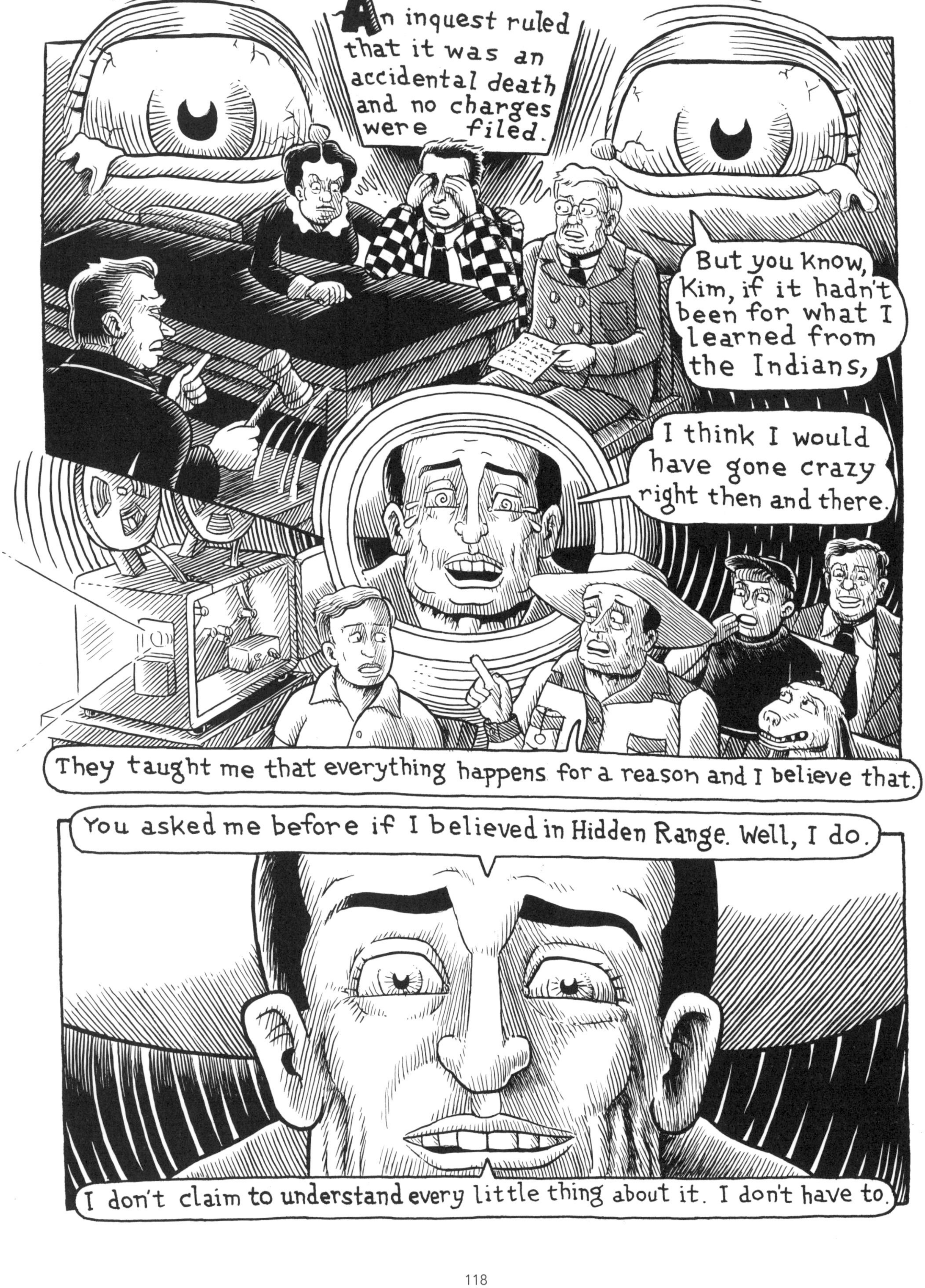
An inquest ruled that it was an accidental death and no charges were filed.
But you know, Kim, if it hadn't been for what I learned from the Indians,
I think I would have gone crazy right then and there.
They taught me that everything happens for a reason and I believe that.
You asked me before if I believed in Hidden Range. Well, I do.
I don't claim to understand every little thing about it. I don't have to.

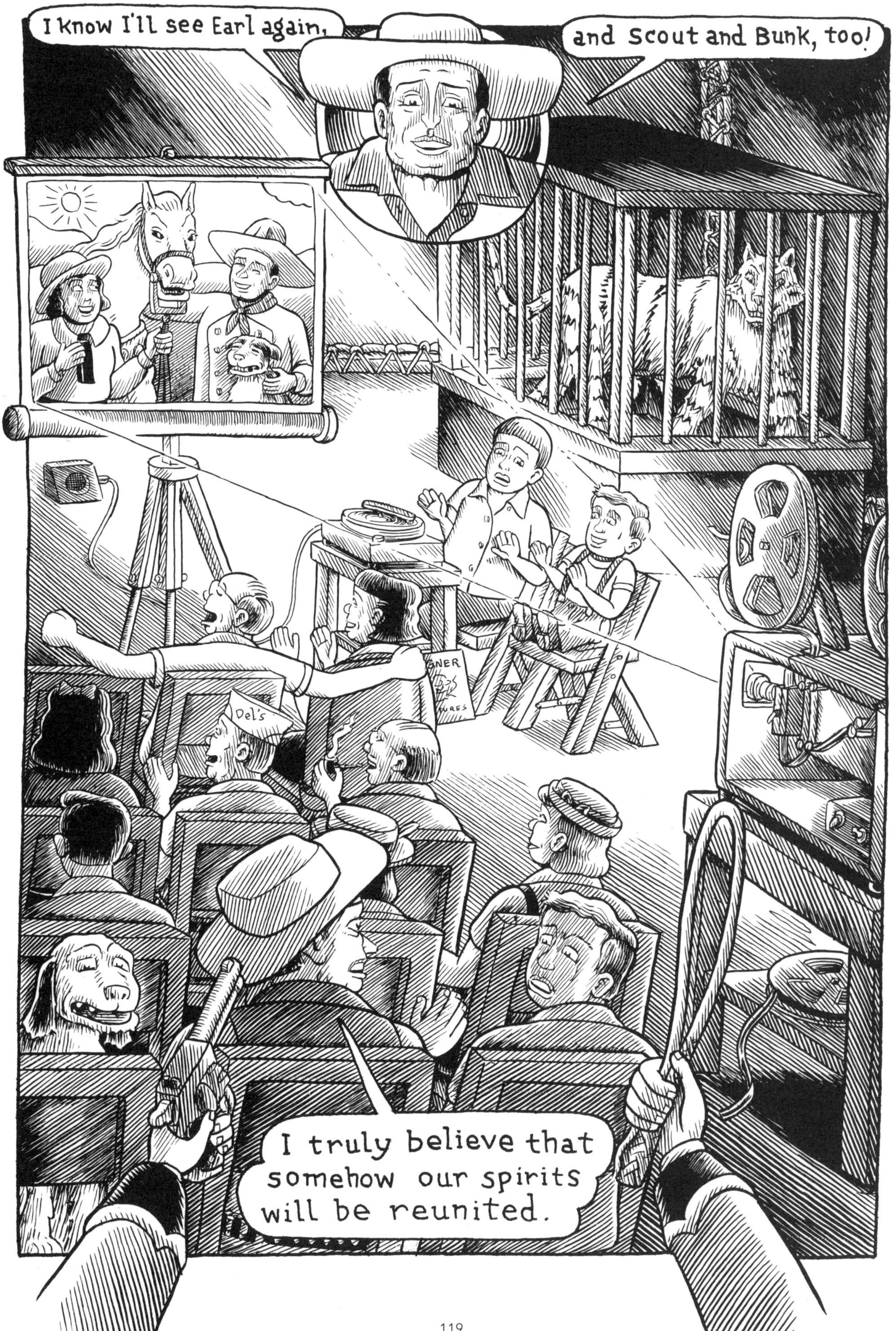
I know I'll see Earl again,
and Scout and Bunk, too!
Del's
I truly believe that somehow our spirits will be reunited.

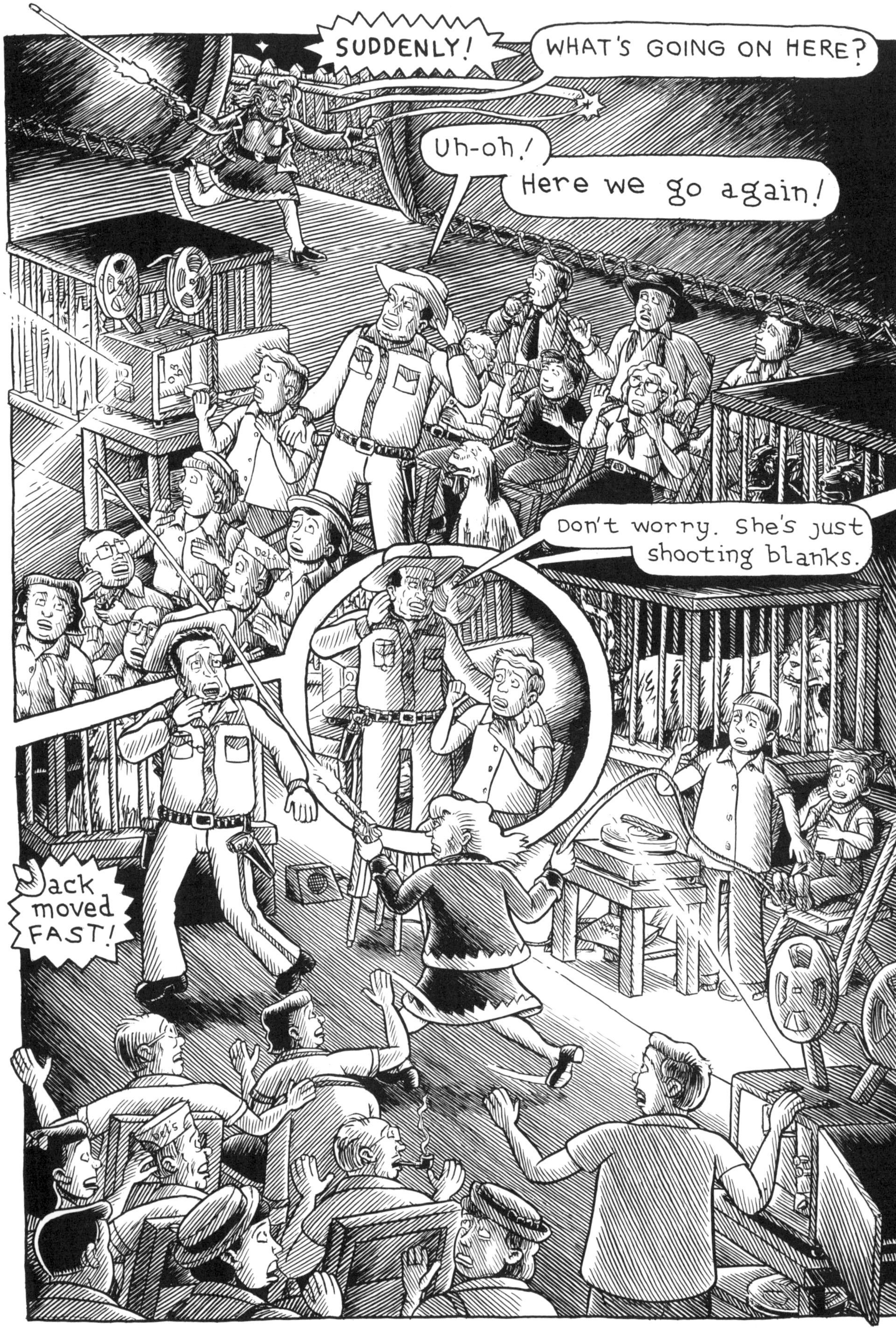
SUDDENLY!
WHAT'S GOING ON HERE?
Uh-oh!
Here we go again!
Don't worry. She's just shooting blanks.
Jack moved FAST!

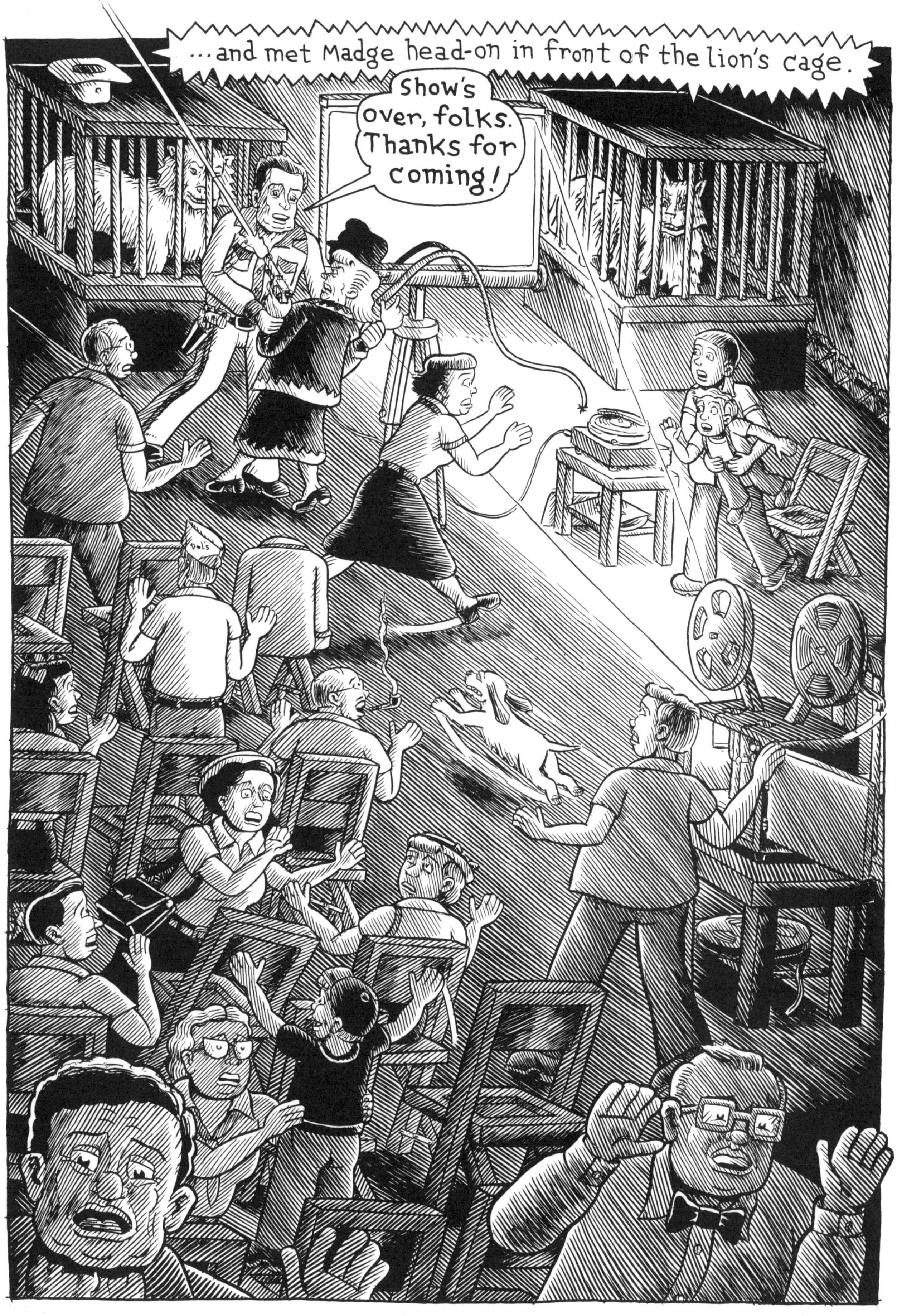
...and met Madge head-on in front of the lion's cage.
Show's over, folks. Thanks for coming!
Dot's

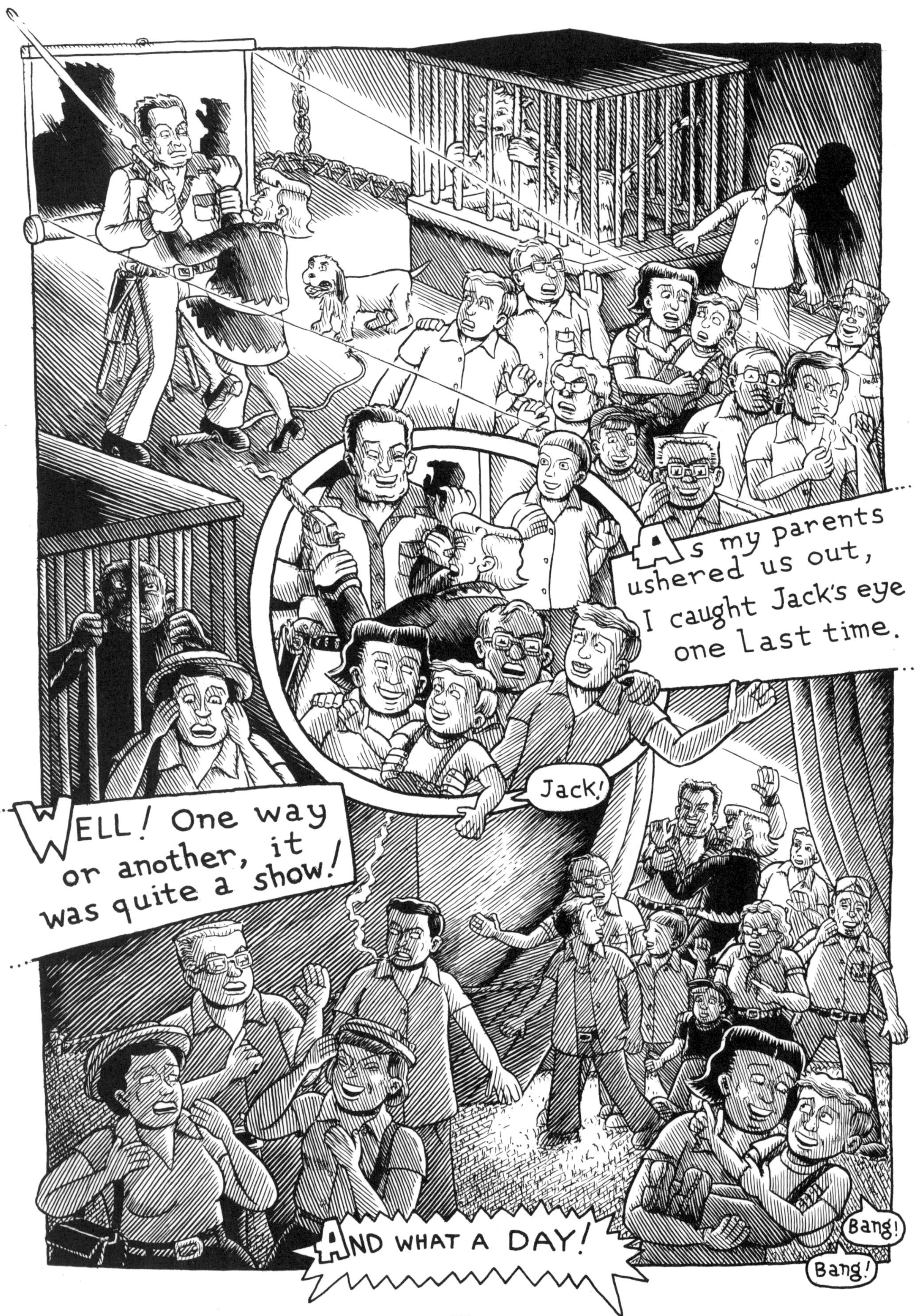
As my parents ushered us out, I caught Jack's eye one last time.
Jack!
WELL! One way or another, it was quite a show!
AND WHAT A DAY!
Bang!
Bang!

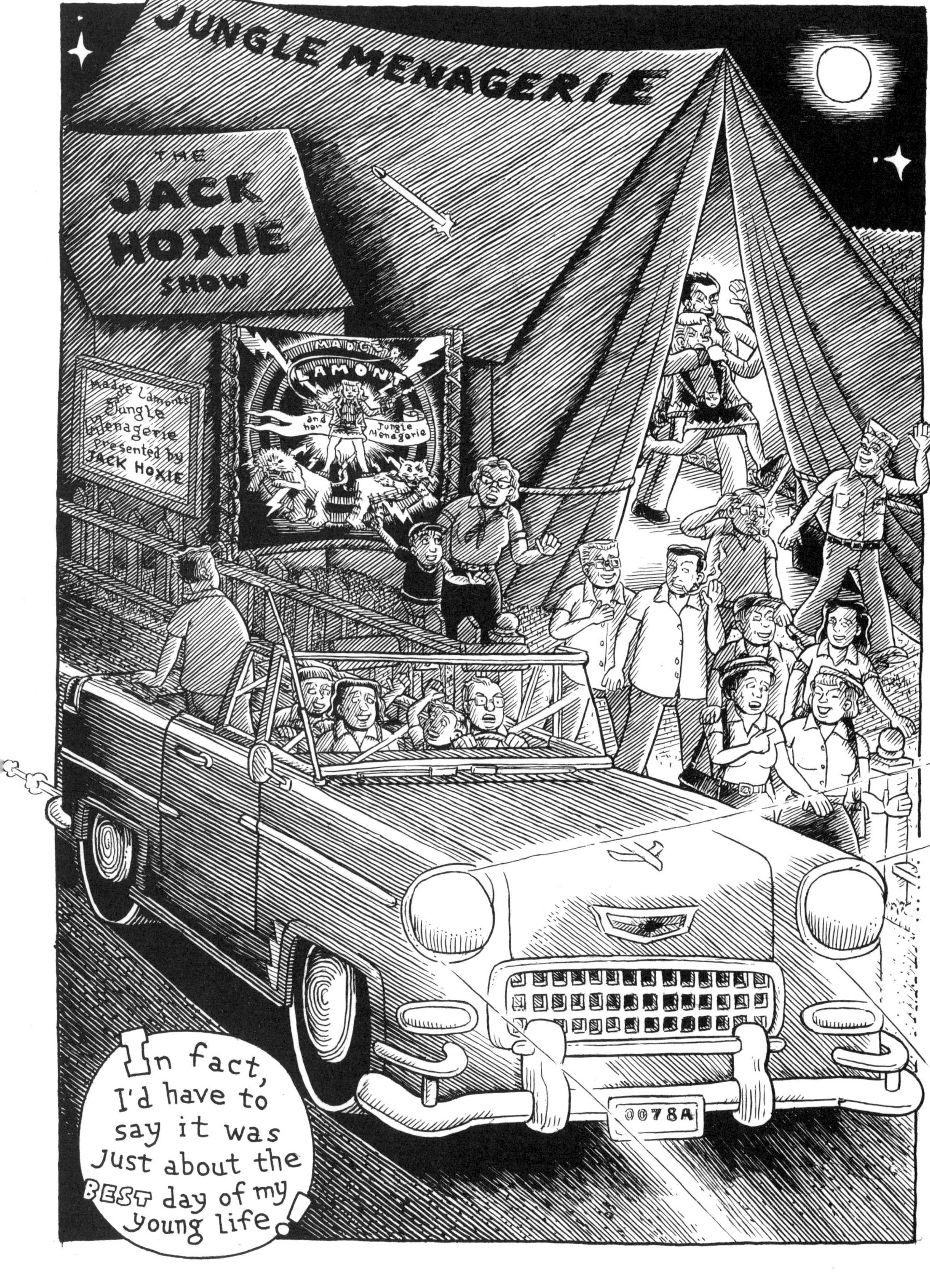
JUNGLE MENAGERIE
THE JACK HOXIE SHOW
MADGE LAMONT and her Jungle Menagerie
Madge Lamont's Jungle Menagerie presented by JACK HOXIE
00 78A
In fact, I'd have to say it was just about the BEST day of my young life!

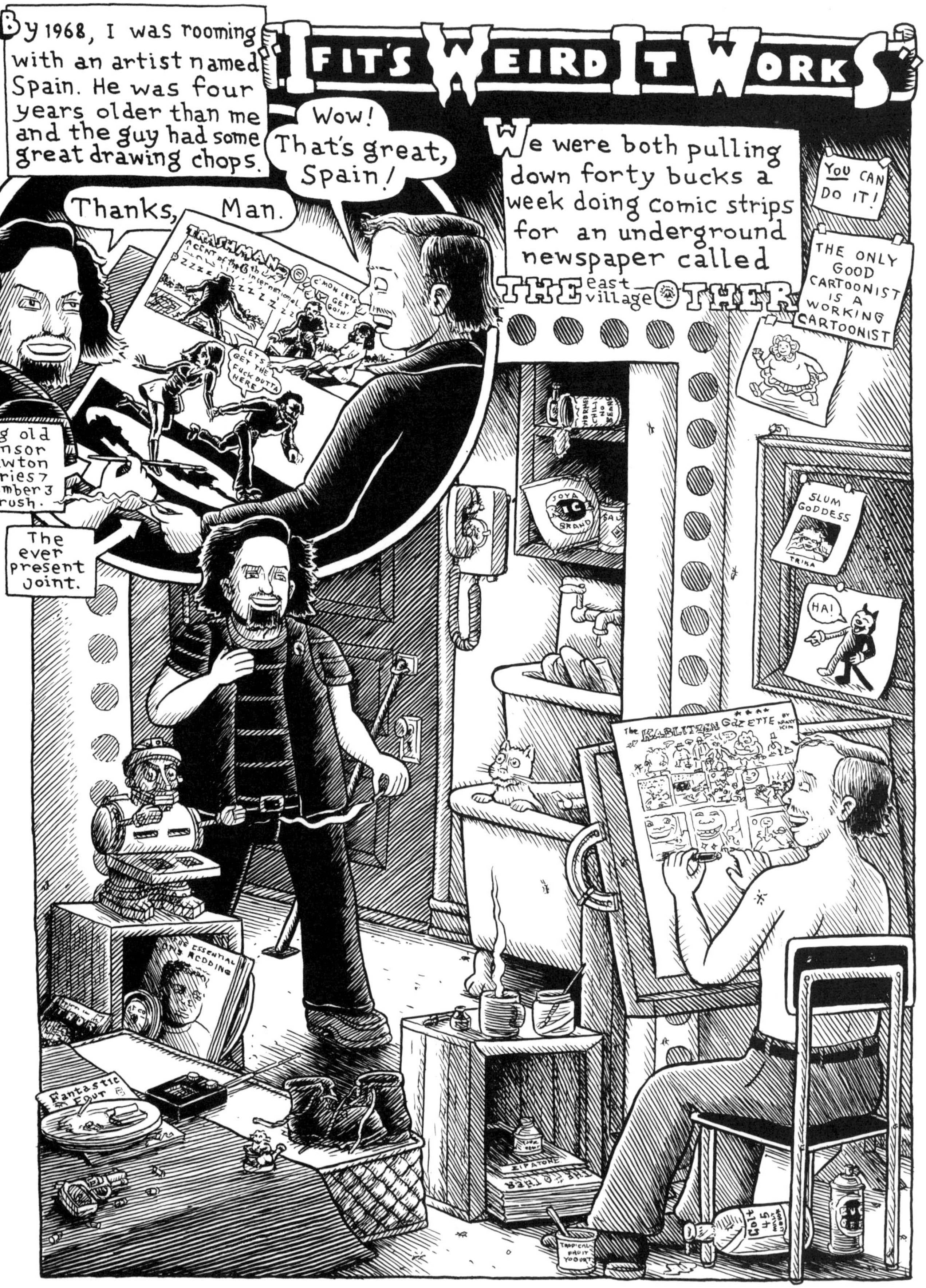

"IF IT'S WEIRD IT WORKS"
By 1968, I was rooming with an artist named Spain. He was four years older than me and the guy had some great drawing chops.
Wow! That's great, Spain!
Thanks, Man.
TRASHMAN
C'MON LETS GET GOIN!
LETS GET THE FUCK OUTTA HERE
Big old Winsor Newton Series 7 number 3 brush.
The ever present joint.
We were both pulling down forty bucks a week doing comic strips for an underground newspaper called
THE east village OTHER
YOU CAN DO IT!
THE ONLY GOOD CARTOONIST IS A WORKING CARTOONIST
SLUM GODDESS
HA!
The KABLITZEN GAZETTE
Fantastic Four
ZIPATONE
TROPICAL FRUIT YOGURT
Colt 45

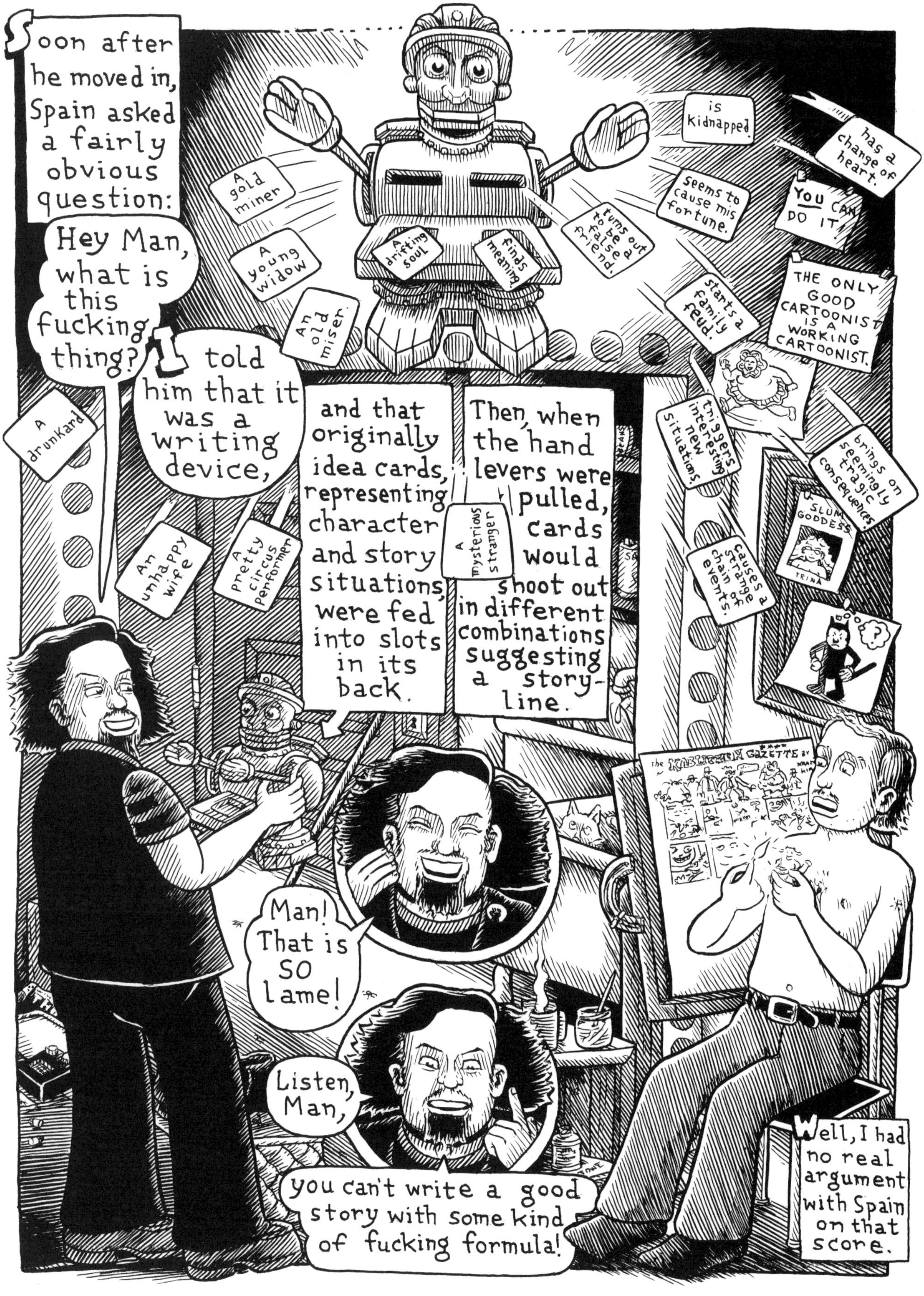
Soon after he moved in, Spain asked a fairly obvious question:
Hey Man, what is this fucking thing?
I told him that it was a writing device,
and that originally idea cards, representing character and story situations, were fed into slots in its back.
Then, when the hand levers were pulled, cards would shoot out in different combinations suggesting a story-line.
A gold miner
A young widow
A drifting soul
finds meaning
An old miser
is kidnapped
has a change of heart.
seems to cause mis fortune.
turns out to be a false friend.
starts a family feud.
YOU CAN DO IT.
THE ONLY GOOD CARTOONIST IS A WORKING CARTOONIST.
A drunkard
An unhappy wife
A pretty circus performer
A mysterious stranger
triggers interesting new situations.
brings on seemingly tragic consequences.
causes a strange chain of events.
SLUM GODDESS
TRINA
The KABLITZEN GAZETTE
Man! That is SO lame!
Listen, Man,
you can't write a good story with some kind of fucking formula!
Well, I had no real argument with Spain on that score.

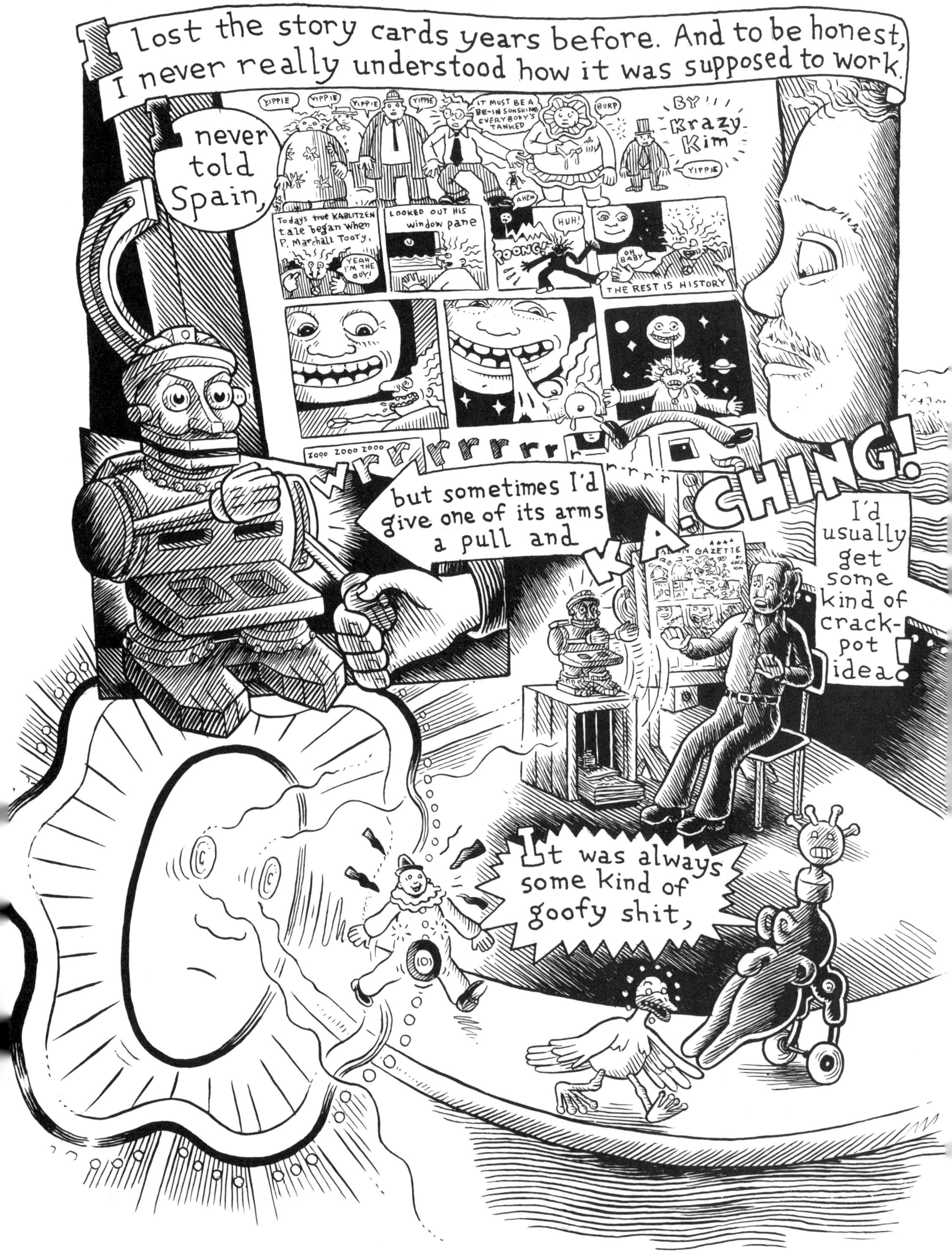
I lost the story cards years before. And to be honest, I never really understood how it was supposed to work.
I never told Spain,
YIPPIE
YIPPIE
YIPPIE
YIPPIE
IT MUST BE A BE-IN SUNSHINE EVERYBODY'S TANKED
BURP
BY Krazy Kim
YIPPIE
Todays true KABLITZEN tale began when P. Marchall Tooty,
YEAH I'M THE GUY!
LOOKED OUT HIS window pane
AHEM
HUH!
POONG!
OH BABY
THE REST IS HISTORY
ZOOO ZOOO ZOOO
wrrrrrrrr
but sometimes I'd give one of its arms a pull and
KA-CHING!
I'd usually get some kind of crack-pot idea!
It was always some kind of goofy shit,

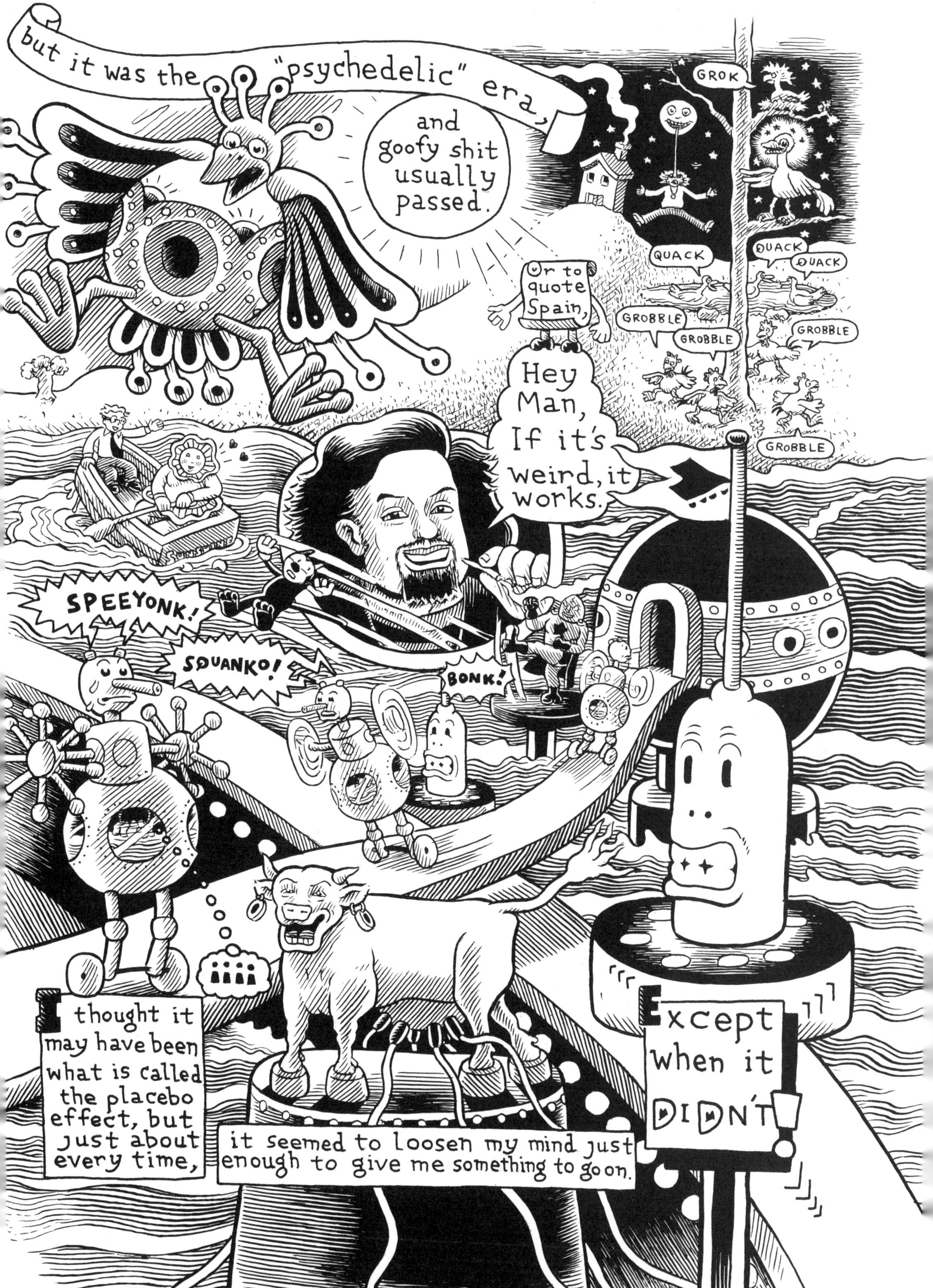

but it was the "psychedelic" era,
and goofy shit usually passed.
GROK
QUACK
QUACK
QUACK
GROBBLE
GROBBLE
GROBBLE
GROBBLE
Or to quote Spain,
Hey Man, If it's weird, it works.
SPEEYONK!
SQUANKO!
BONK!
I thought it may have been what is called the placebo effect, but just about every time,
it seemed to loosen my mind just enough to give me something to go on.
Except when it DIDN'T!

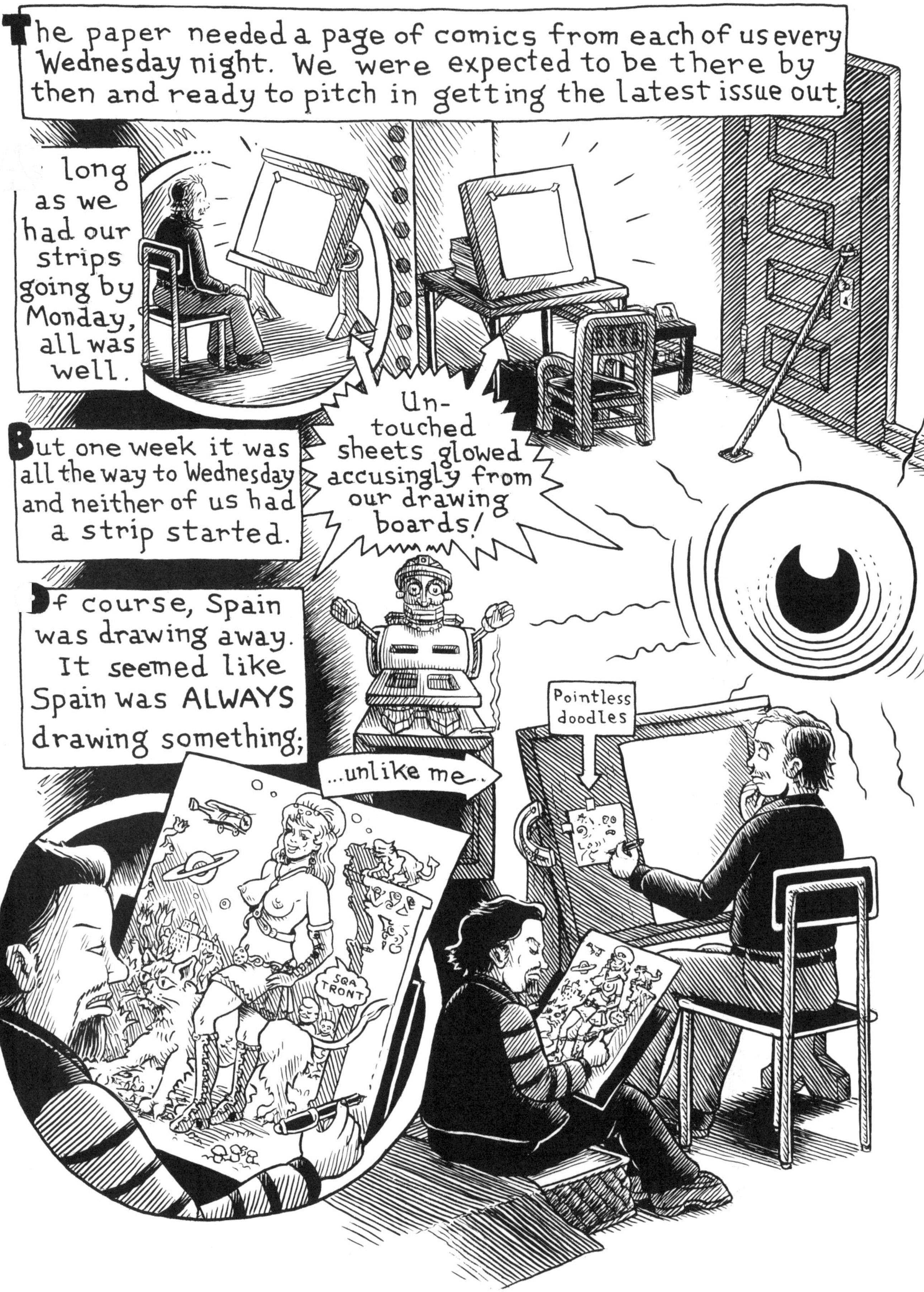
The paper needed a page of comics from each of us every Wednesday night. We were expected to be there by then and ready to pitch in getting the latest issue out.
As long as we had our strips going by Monday, all was well.
But one week it was all the way to Wednesday and neither of us had a strip started.
Un-touched sheets glowed accusingly from our drawing boards!
Of course, Spain was drawing away. It seemed like Spain was ALWAYS drawing something;
...unlike me.
Pointless doodles
SQA TRONT

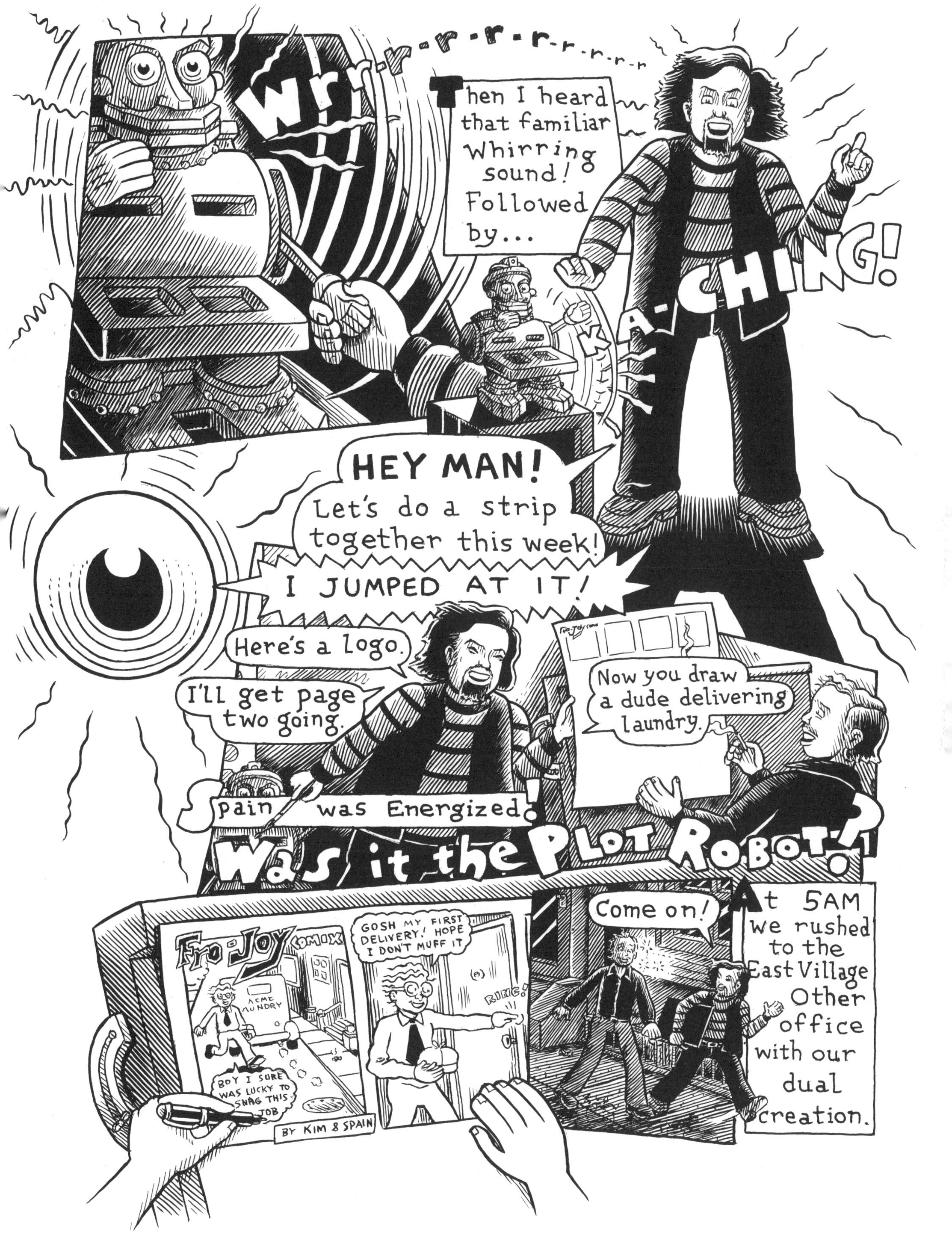

Wrr-r-r-r-r-r-r-r-r-r
Then I heard that familiar Whirring sound! Followed by...
KA-CHING!
HEY MAN! Let's do a strip together this week!
I JUMPED AT IT!
Here's a logo.
I'll get page two going.
Now you draw a dude delivering laundry.
Spain was Energized!
Was it the PLOT ROBOT?![1]
Fro-Joy COMIX
ACME LAUNDRY
BOY I SURE WAS LUCKY TO SNAG THIS JOB
GOSH MY FIRST DELIVERY! HOPE I DON'T MUFF IT
RING!
BY KIM & SPAIN
Come on!
At 5AM we rushed to the East Village Other office with our dual creation.

Exactly as it appeared in 1968; more goofy shit.

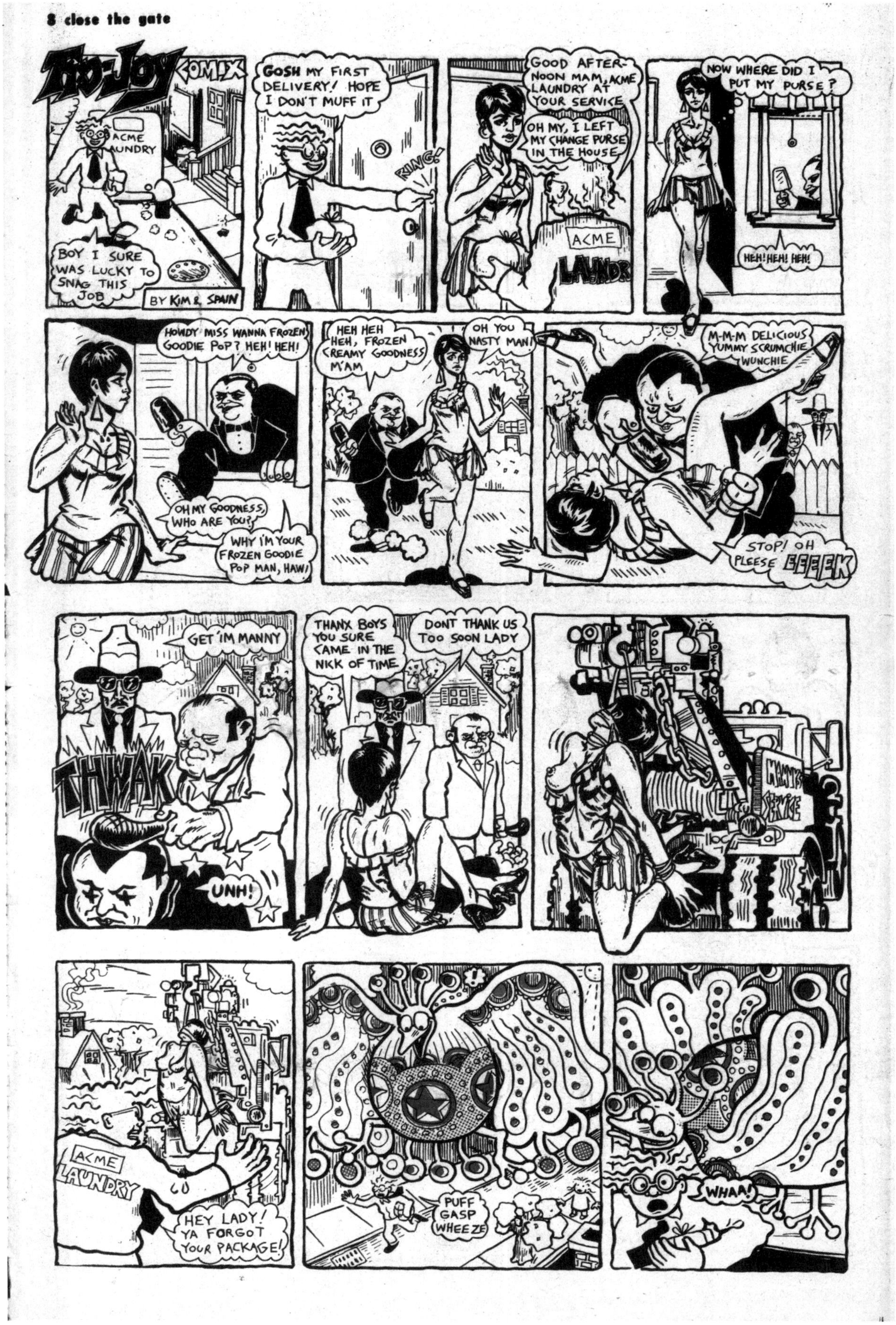

8 close the gate
Tio-Joy COMIX
ACME LAUNDRY
BOY I SURE WAS LUCKY TO SNAG THIS JOB
BY KIM & SPAIN
GOSH MY FIRST DELIVERY! HOPE I DON'T MUFF IT
RING!
GOOD AFTER-NOON MAM, ACME LAUNDRY AT YOUR SERVICE
OH MY, I LEFT MY CHANGE PURSE IN THE HOUSE
ACME LAUNDR
NOW WHERE DID I PUT MY PURSE?
HEH! HEH! HEH!
HOWDY MISS WANNA FROZEN GOODIE POP? HEH! HEH!
OH MY GOODNESS, WHO ARE YOU?
WHY I'M YOUR FROZEN GOODIE POP MAN, HAW!
HEH HEH HEH, FROZEN CREAMY GOODNESS M'AM
OH YOU NASTY MAN!
M-M-M DELICIOUS YUMMY SCRUMCHIE WUNCHIE
STOP! OH PLEESE EEEEK
GET 'IM MANNY
THWAK
UNH!
THANX BOYS YOU SURE CAME IN THE NICK OF TIME
DONT THANK US TOO SOON LADY
MANNY'S SERVICE
ACME LAUNDRY
HEY LADY! YA FORGOT YOUR PACKAGE!
PUFF GASP WHEEZE
WHAA!

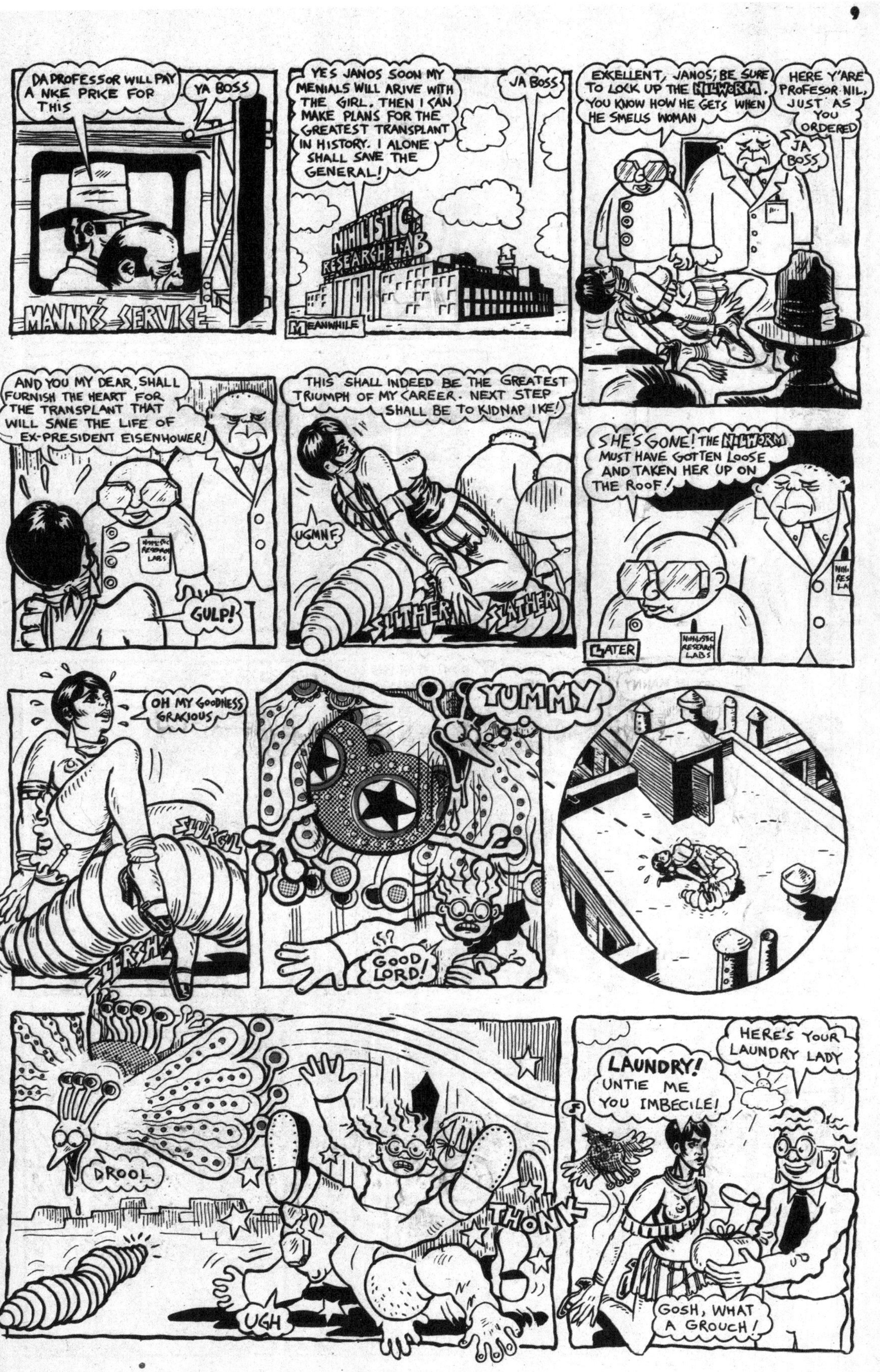
DA PROFESSOR WILL PAY A NICE PRICE FOR THIS
YA BOSS
MANNY'S SERVICE
YES JANOS SOON MY MENIALS WILL ARIVE WITH THE GIRL. THEN I CAN MAKE PLANS FOR THE GREATEST TRANSPLANT IN HISTORY. I ALONE SHALL SAVE THE GENERAL!
JA BOSS
NIHILISTIC RESEARCH LAB
MEANWHILE
EXELLENT, JANOS; BE SURE TO LOCK UP THE NILWORM. YOU KNOW HOW HE GETS WHEN HE SMELLS WOMAN
HERE Y'ARE PROFESOR NIL, JUST AS YOU ORDERED
JA BOSS
AND YOU MY DEAR, SHALL FURNISH THE HEART FOR THE TRANSPLANT THAT WILL SAVE THE LIFE OF EX-PRESIDENT EISENHOWER!
GULP!
THIS SHALL INDEED BE THE GREATEST TRIUMPH OF MY CAREER. NEXT STEP SHALL BE TO KIDNAP IKE!
UGMNF
SLITHER SLATHER
SHE'S GONE! THE NILWORM MUST HAVE GOTTEN LOOSE AND TAKEN HER UP ON THE ROOF!
LATER
OH MY GOODNESS GRACIOUS
SLURGL
YUMMY
GOOD LORD!
DROOL
THONK
UGH
LAUNDRY! UNTIE ME YOU IMBECILE!
HERE'S YOUR LAUNDRY LADY
GOSH, WHAT A GROUCH!

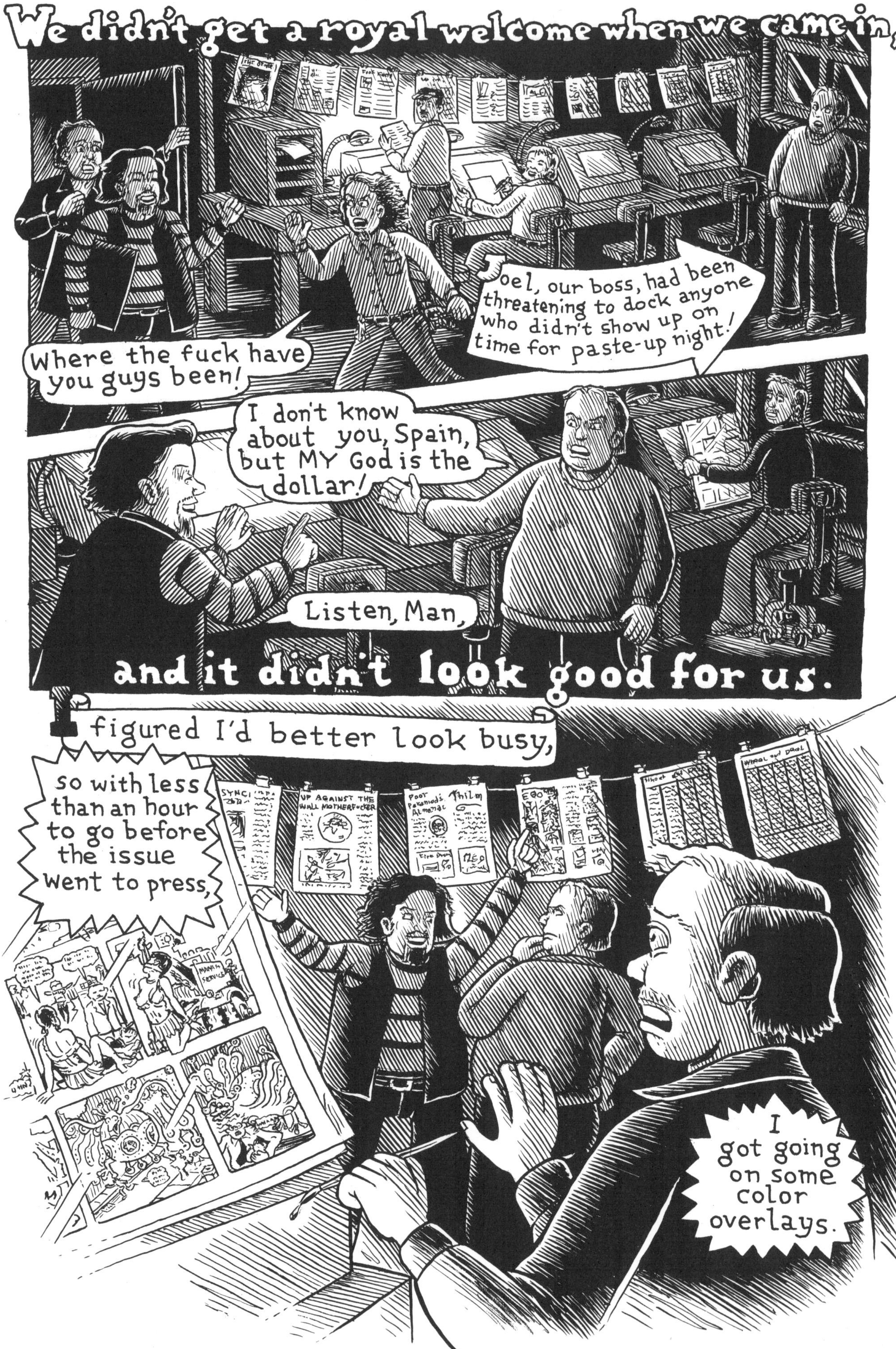
We didn't get a royal welcome when we came in,
Joel, our boss, had been threatening to dock anyone who didn't show up on time for paste-up night!
Where the fuck have you guys been!
I don't know about you, Spain, but MY God is the dollar!
Listen, Man,
and it didn't look good for us.
I figured I'd better look busy,
so with less than an hour to go before the issue went to press,
UP AGAINST THE WALL MOTHERFUCKER
Poor Paranoid's Almanac
I got going on some color overlays.

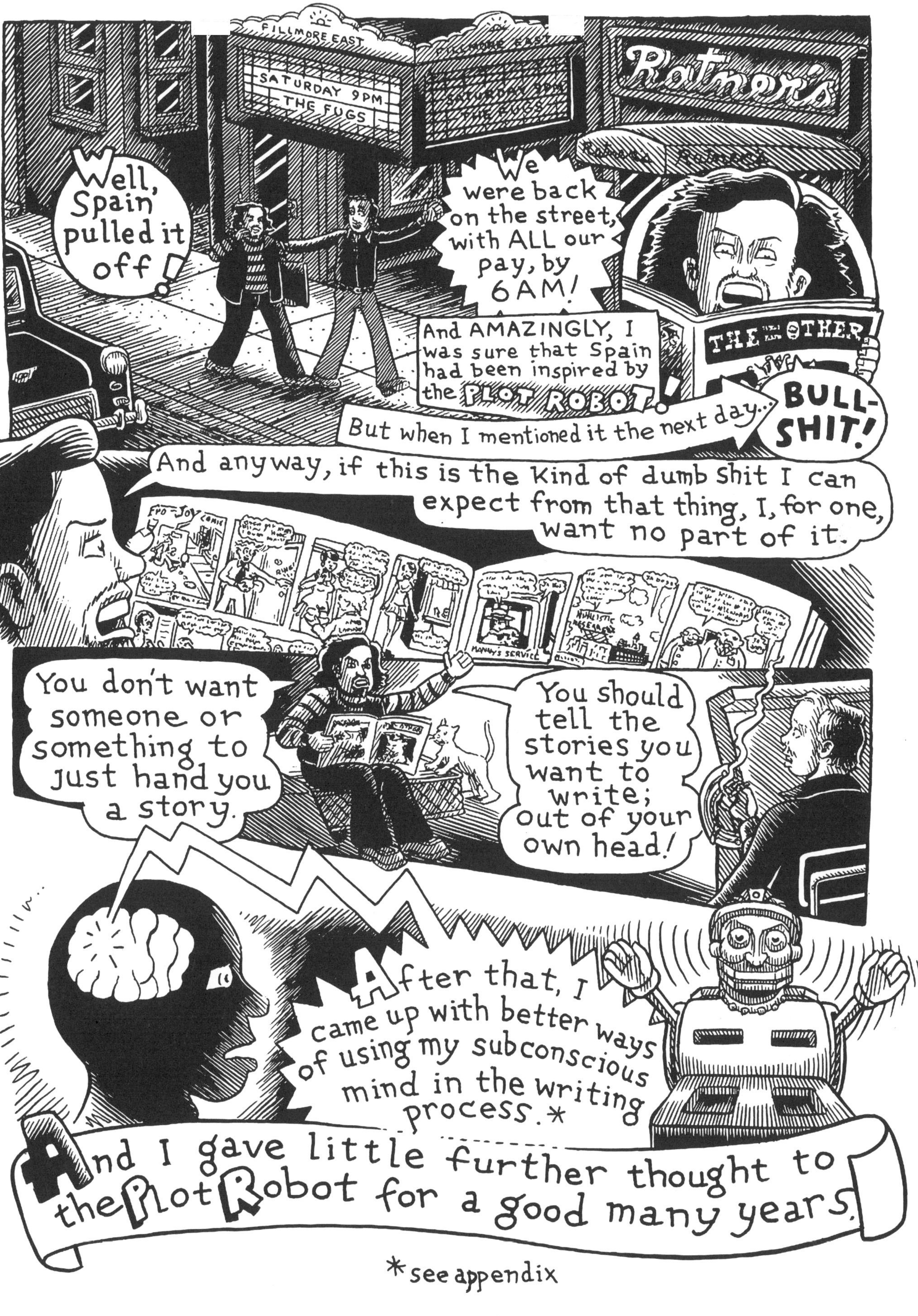
FILLMORE EAST
SATURDAY 9PM
THE FUGS
Ratner's
Well, Spain pulled it off!
We were back on the street, with ALL our pay, by 6AM!
And AMAZINGLY, I was sure that Spain had been inspired by the PLOT ROBOT!
But when I mentioned it the next day...
BULL-SHIT!
THE OTHER
And anyway, if this is the kind of dumb shit I can expect from that thing, I, for one, want no part of it.
You don't want someone or something to just hand you a story.
You should tell the stories you want to write; out of your own head!
After that, I came up with better ways of using my subconscious mind in the writing process.*
And I gave little further thought to the Plot Robot for a good many years.

*see appendix

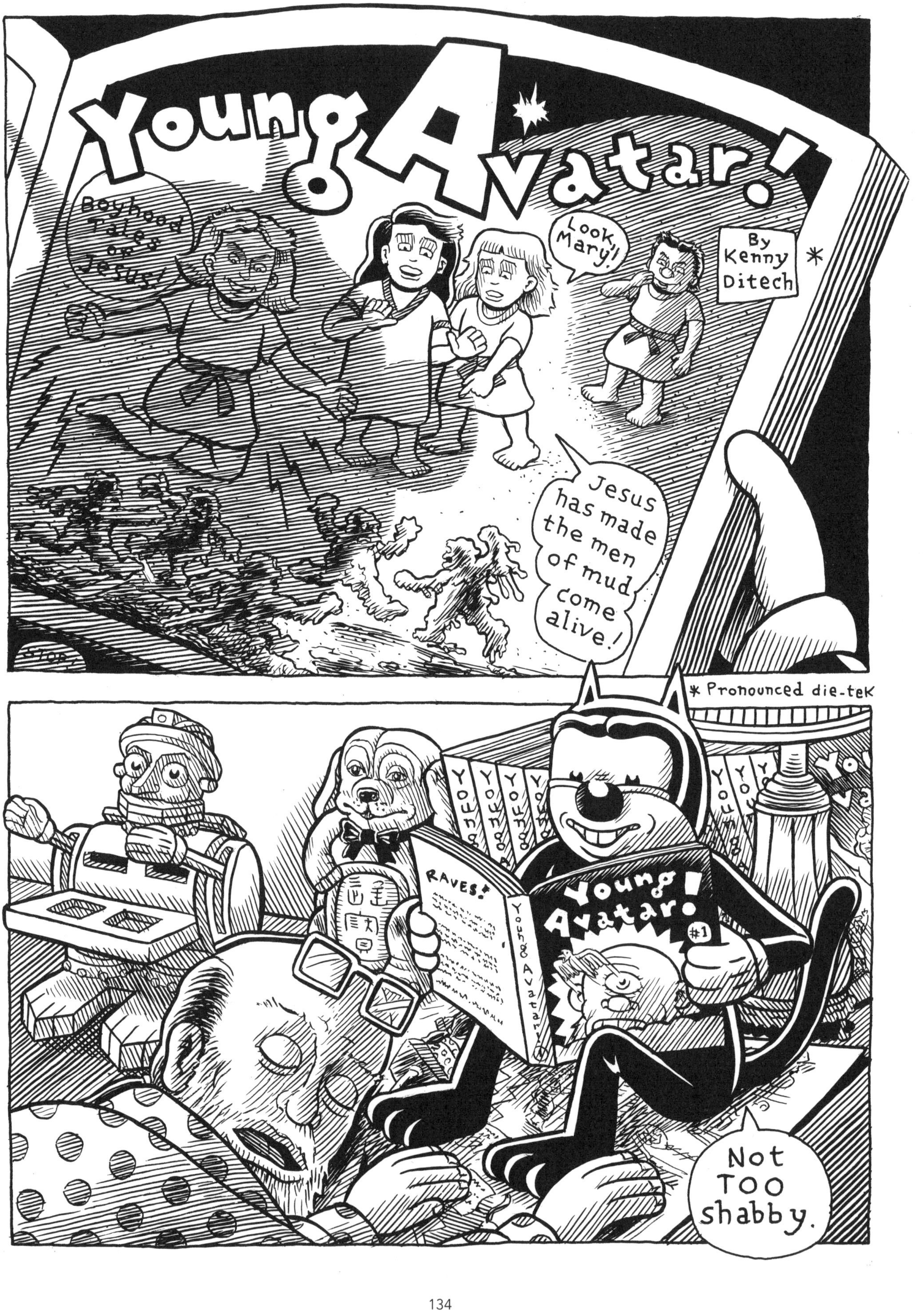
Young Avatar!*
Boyhood Tales of Jesus!
Look, Mary!
By Kenny Ditech *
Jesus has made the men of mud come alive!
* Pronounced die-teK
RAVES!
Young Avatar!
#1
Not TOO shabby.

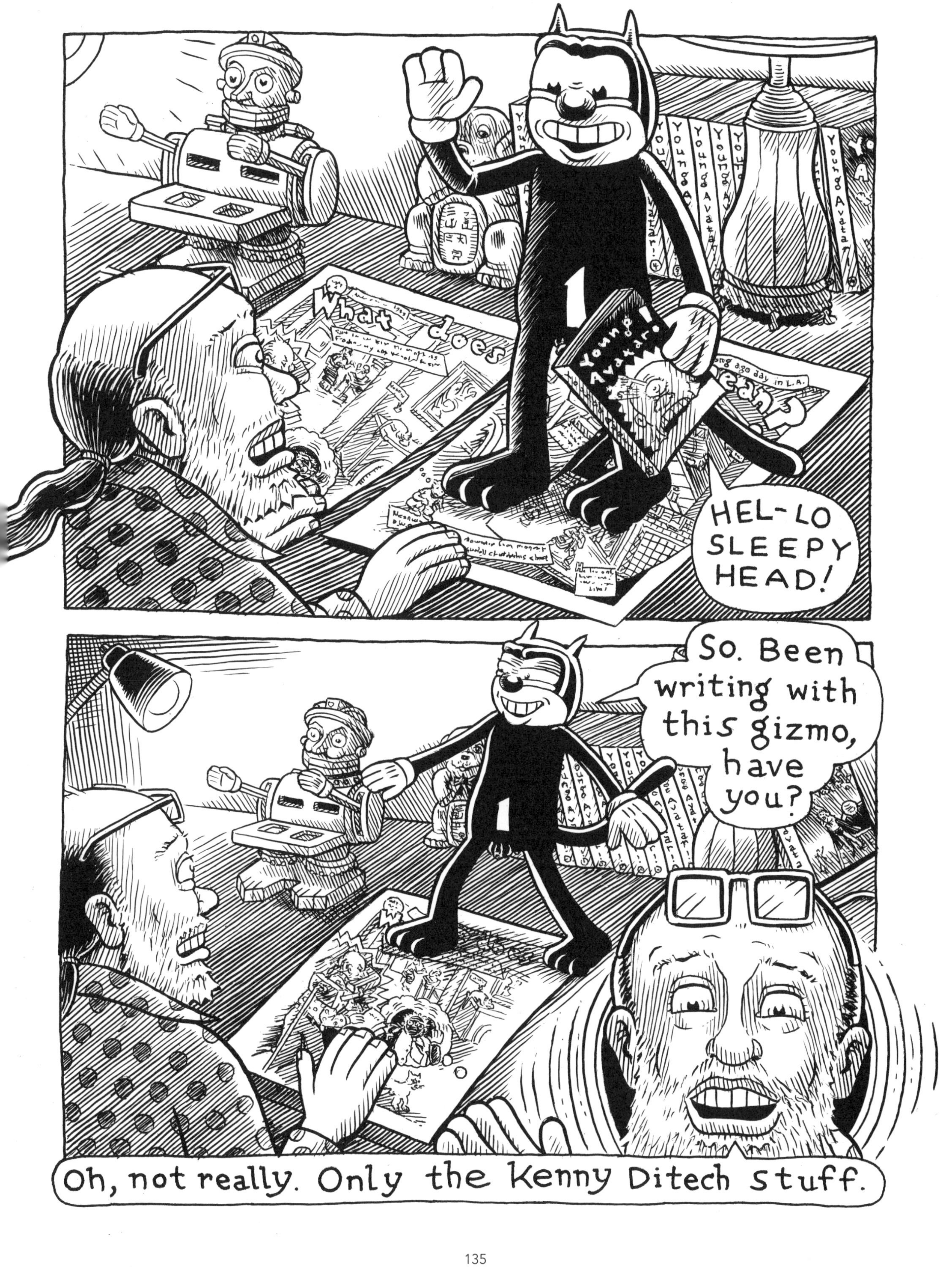
HEL-LO SLEEPY HEAD!
So. Been writing with this gizmo, have you?
Oh, not really. Only the Kenny Ditech stuff.

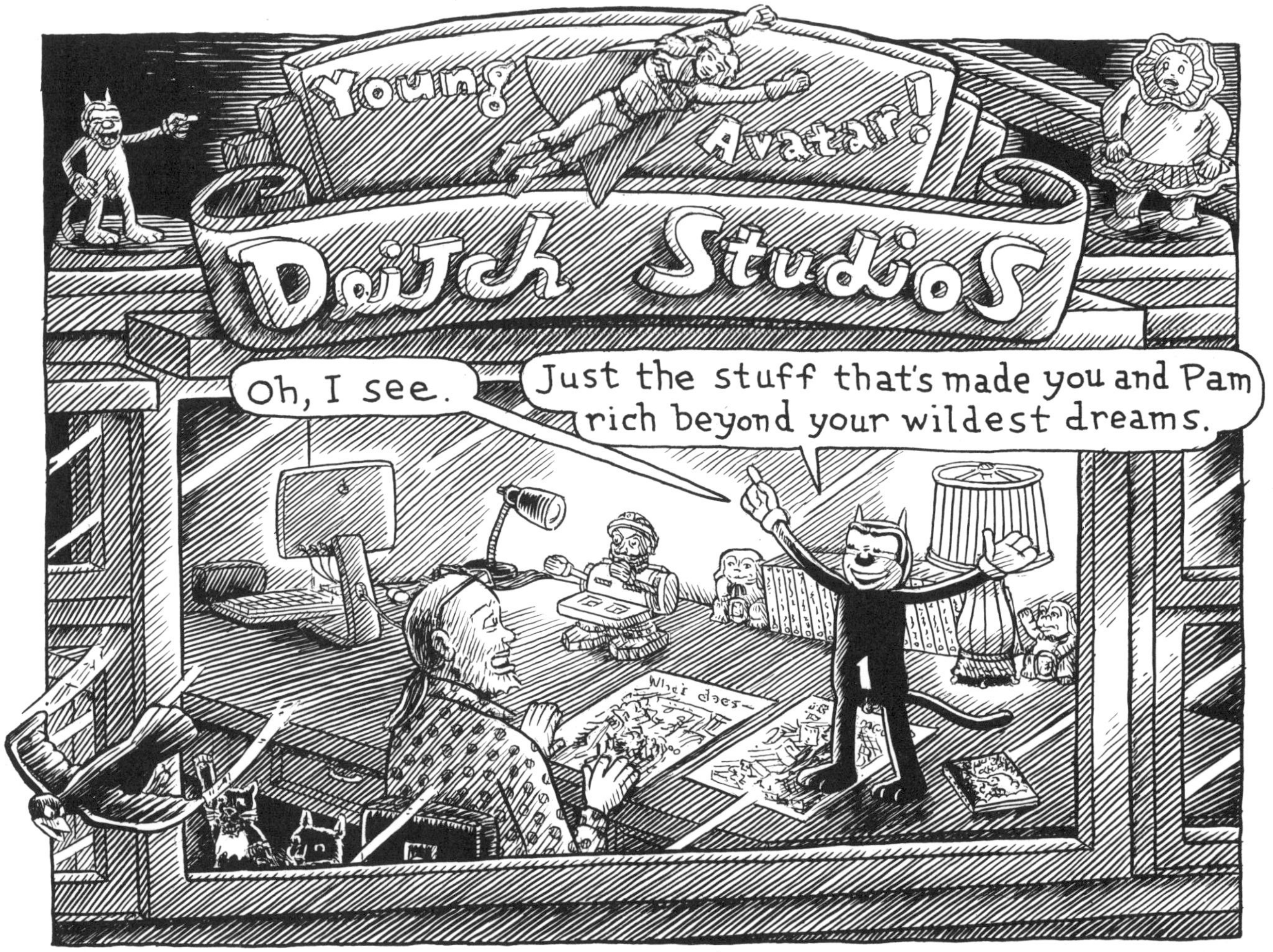
Young Avatar!
Deitch Studios
Oh, I see.
Just the stuff that's made you and Pam rich beyond your wildest dreams.

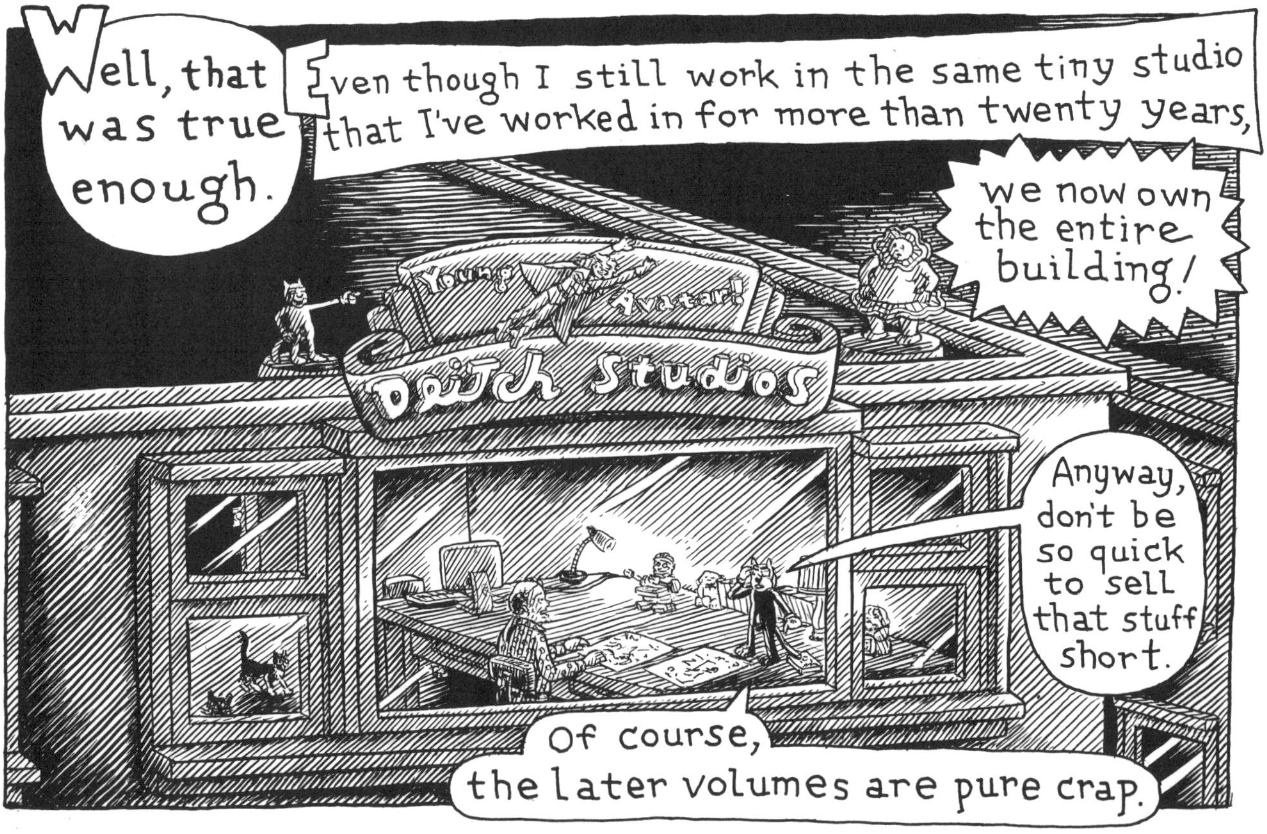
Well, that was true enough.
Even though I still work in the same tiny studio that I've worked in for more than twenty years,
we now own the entire building!
Young Avatar!
Deitch Studios
Anyway, don't be so quick to sell that stuff short.
Of course, the later volumes are pure crap.

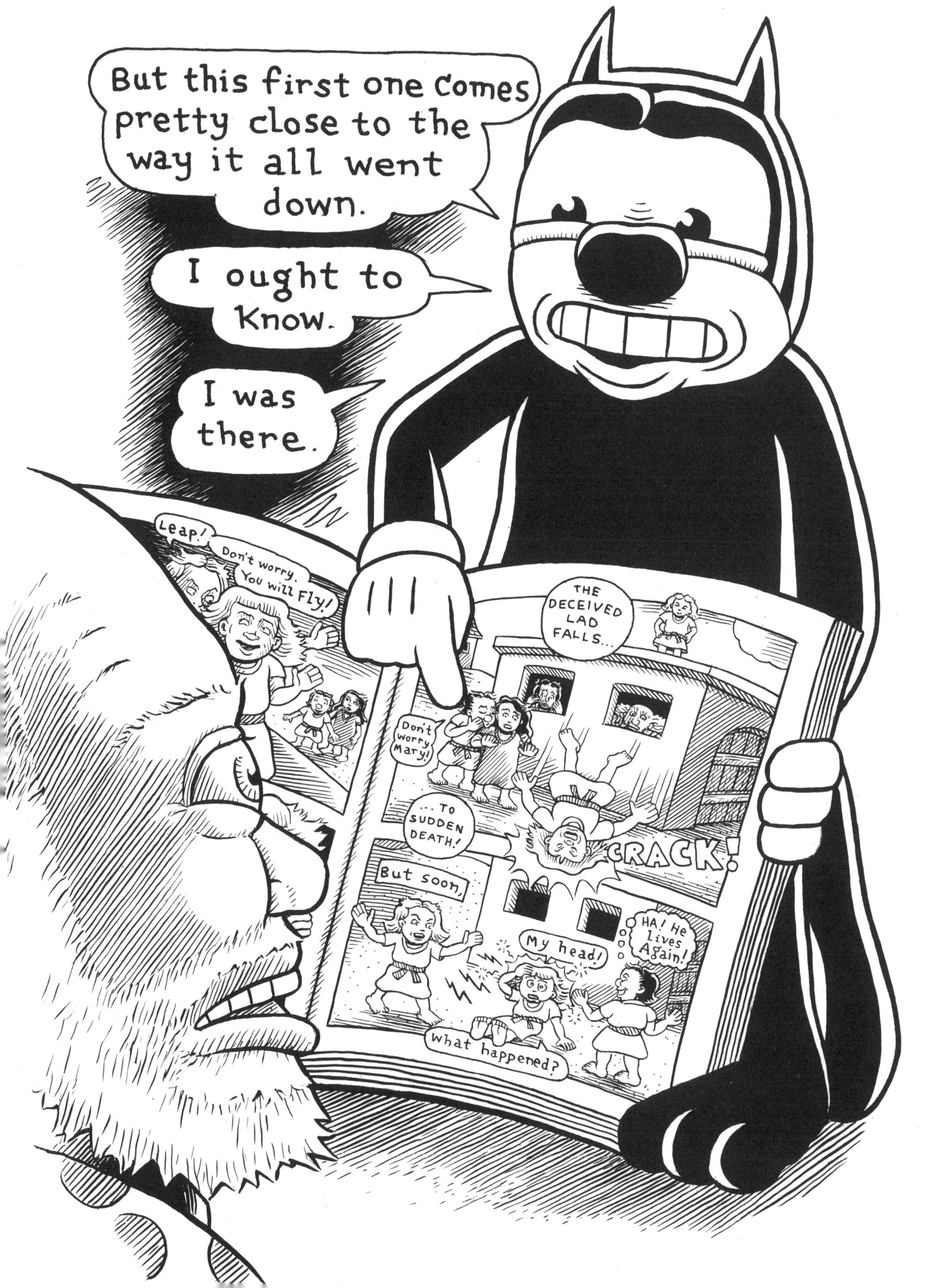
But this first one comes pretty close to the way it all went down.
I ought to Know.
I was there.
Leap!
Don't worry. You will Fly!
THE DECEIVED LAD FALLS...
Don't worry Mary!
...TO SUDDEN DEATH!
CRACK!
But soon,
My head!
HA! He lives Again!
What happened?

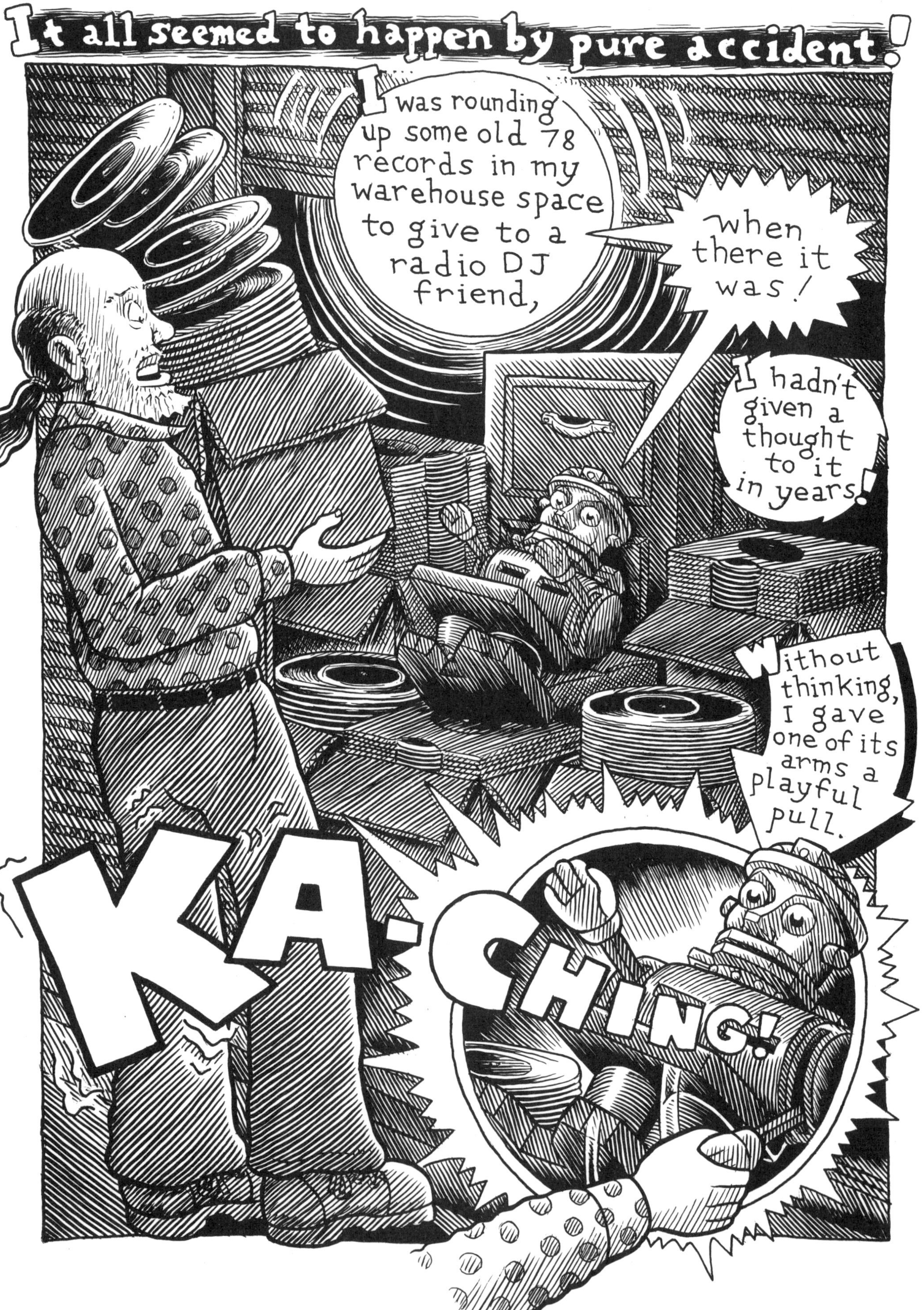

It all seemed to happen by pure accident!
I was rounding up some old 78 records in my warehouse space to give to a radio DJ friend,
when there it was!
I hadn't given a thought to it in years!
Without thinking, I gave one of its arms a playful pull.
KA-CHING!

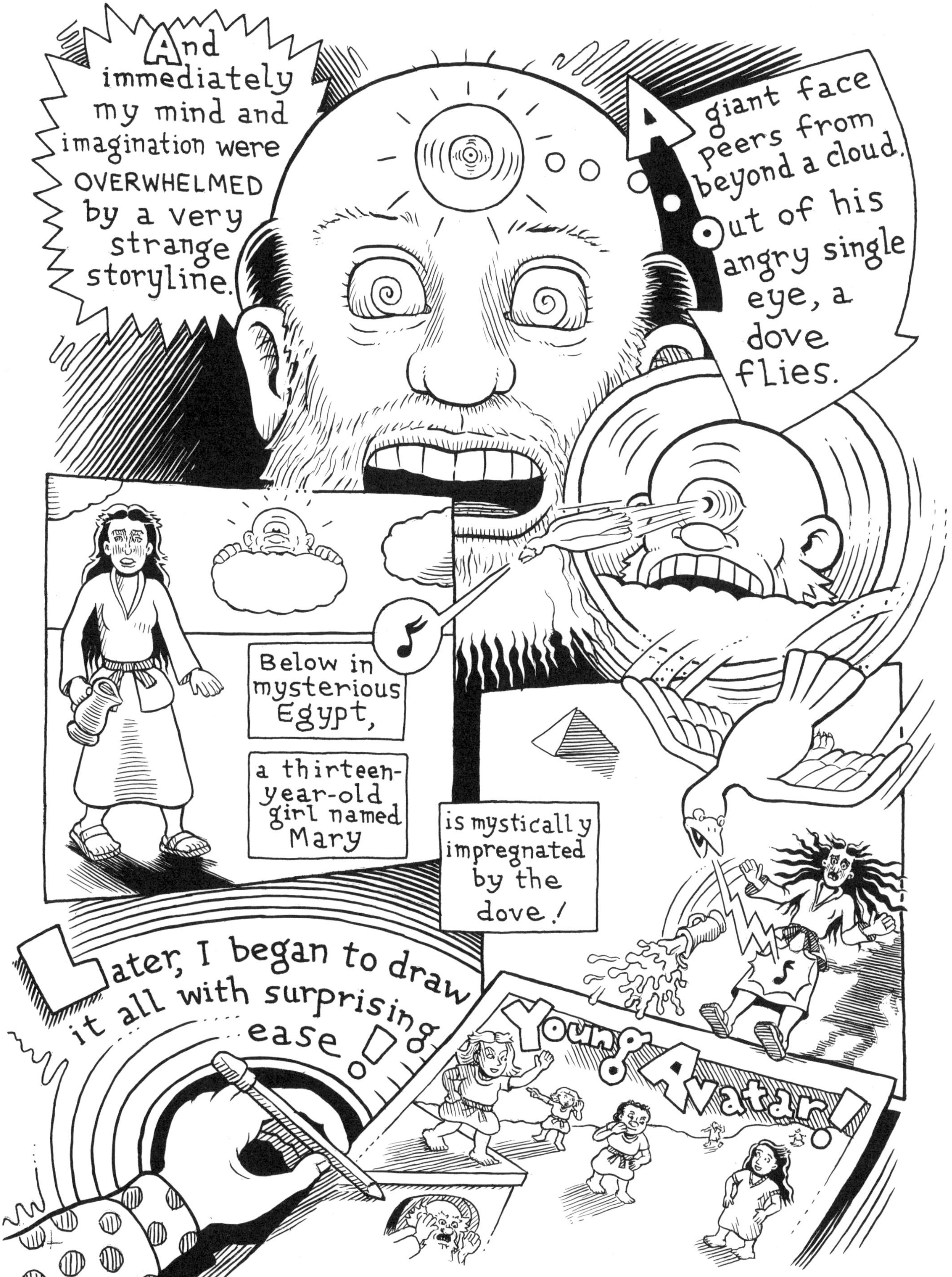
And immediately my mind and imagination were OVERWHELMED by a very strange storyline.
A giant face peers from beyond a cloud.
Out of his angry single eye, a dove flies.
Below in mysterious Egypt,
a thirteen-year-old girl named Mary
is mystically impregnated by the dove!
Later, I began to draw it all with surprising ease!
Young Avatar!

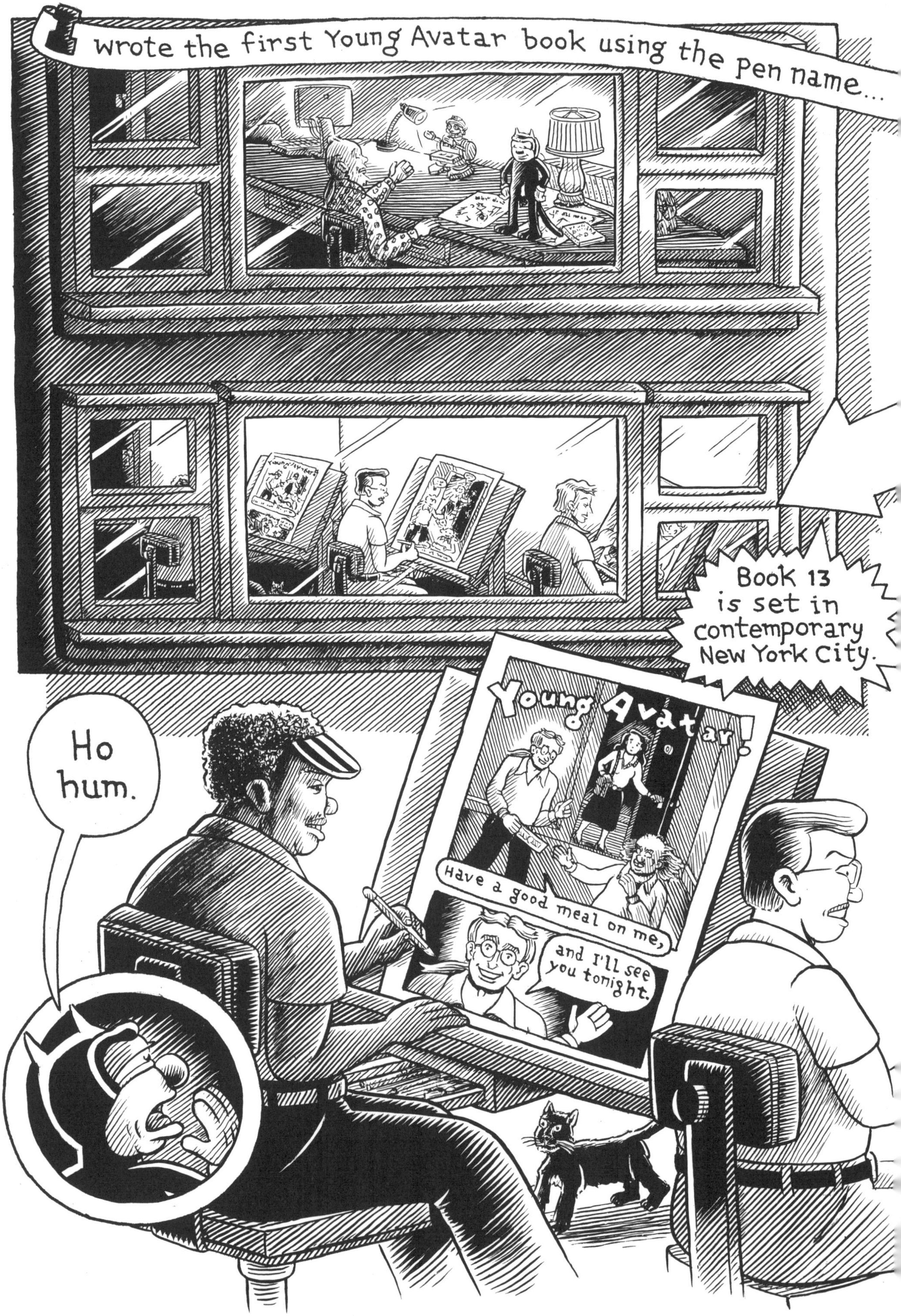
wrote the first Young Avatar book using the pen name...
Book 13 is set in contemporary New York City.
Ho hum.
Young Avatar!
Have a good meal on me,
and I'll see you tonight.

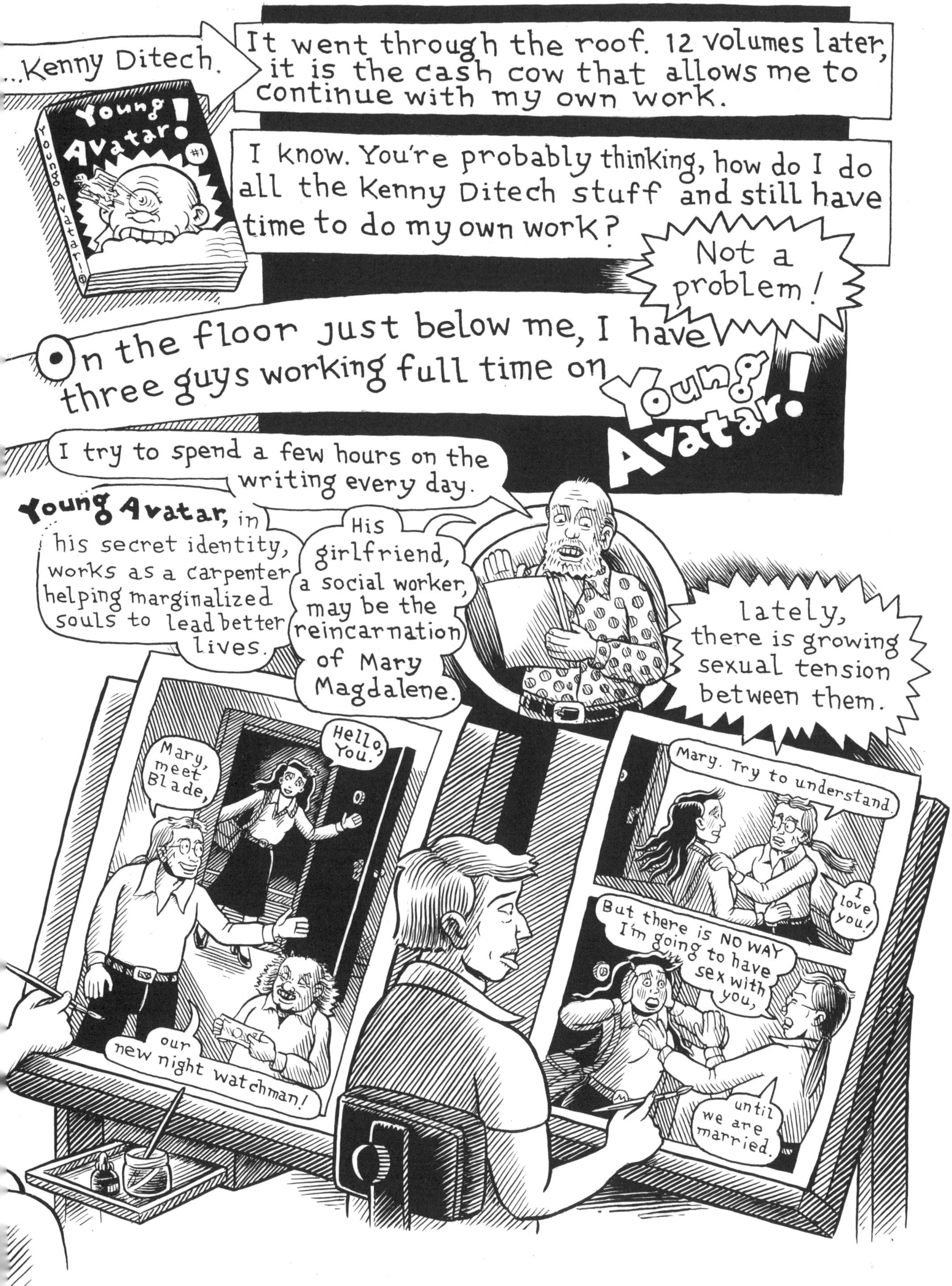
...Kenny Ditech.
It went through the roof. 12 volumes later, it is the cash cow that allows me to continue with my own work.
Young Avatar! #1
I know. You're probably thinking, how do I do all the Kenny Ditech stuff and still have time to do my own work?
Not a problem!
On the floor just below me, I have three guys working full time on Young Avatar!
I try to spend a few hours on the writing every day.
Young Avatar, in his secret identity, works as a carpenter helping marginalized souls to lead better lives.
His girlfriend, a social worker, may be the reincarnation of Mary Magdalene.
Lately, there is growing sexual tension between them.
Mary, meet Blade,
Hello, You.
our new night watchman!
Mary. Try to understand.
I love you!
But there is NO WAY I'm going to have sex with you,
until we are married.

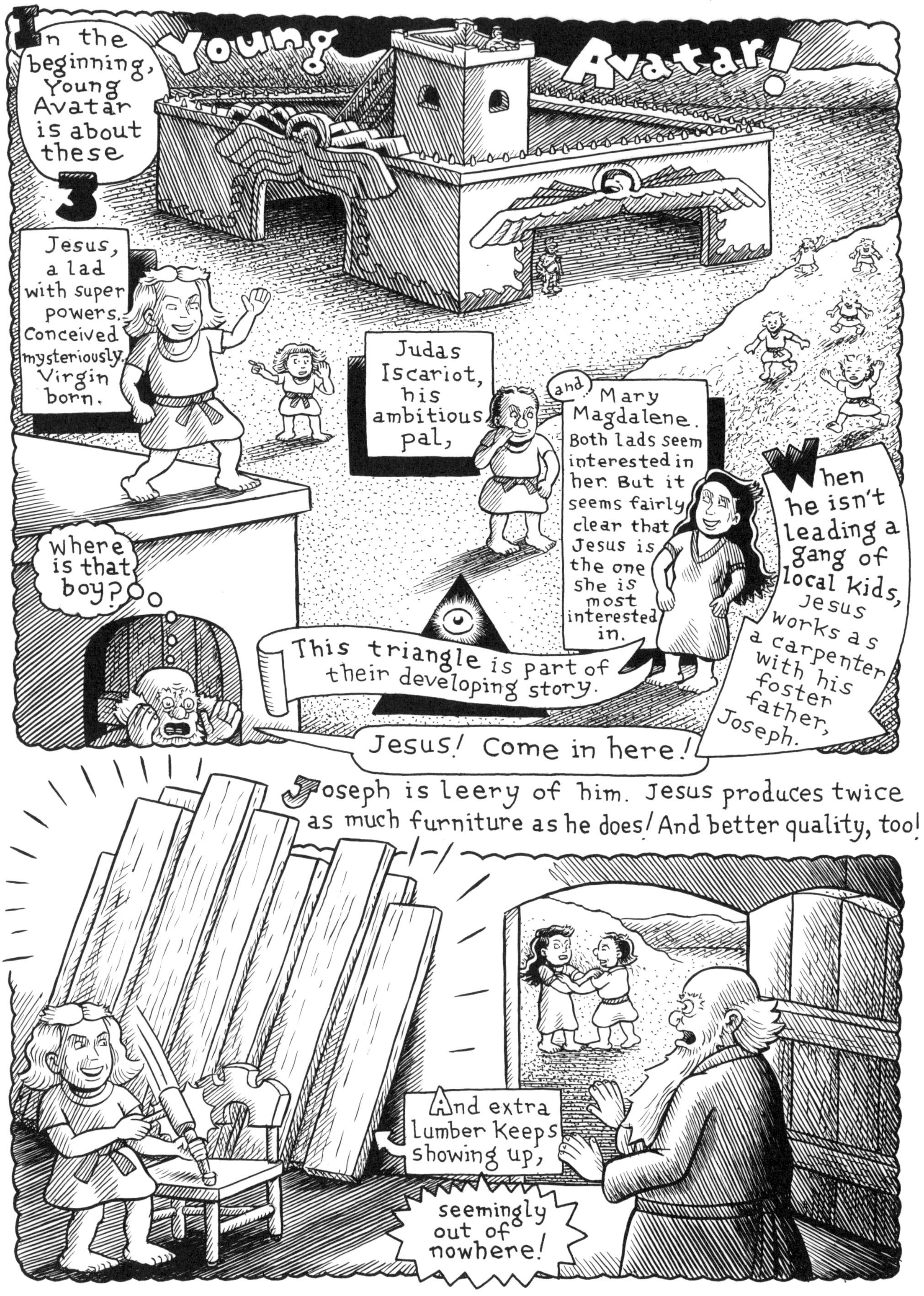
In the beginning, Young Avatar is about these 3
Young Avatar!
Jesus, a lad with super powers. Conceived mysteriously. Virgin born.
Judas Iscariot, his ambitious pal,
and Mary Magdalene. Both lads seem interested in her. But it seems fairly clear that Jesus is the one she is most interested in.
When he isn't leading a gang of local kids, Jesus works as a carpenter with his foster father, Joseph.
This triangle is part of their developing story.
Where is that boy?
Jesus! Come in here!
Joseph is leery of him. Jesus produces twice as much furniture as he does! And better quality, too!
And extra lumber keeps showing up,
seemingly out of nowhere!

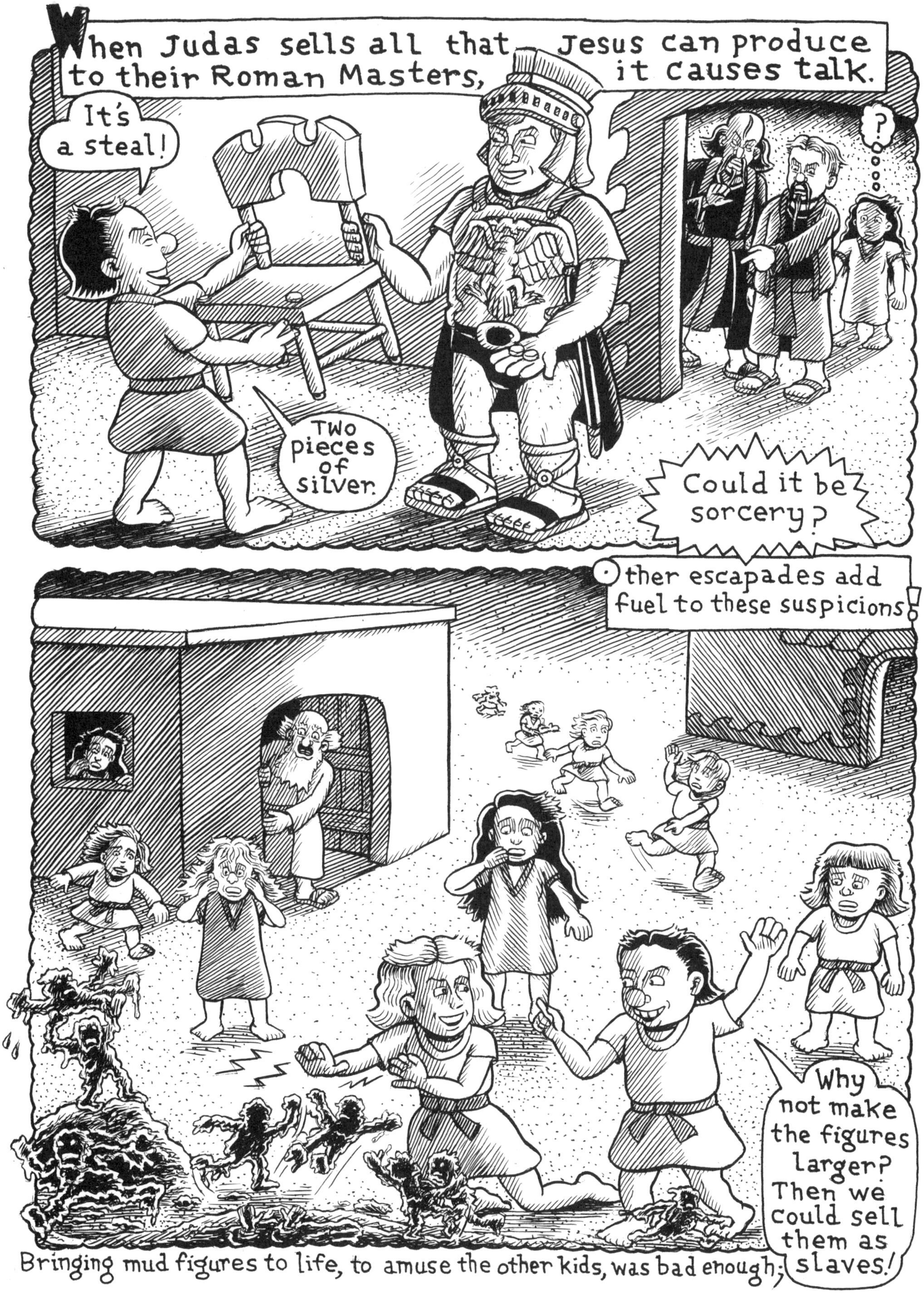
When Judas sells all that Jesus can produce to their Roman Masters, it causes talk.
It's a steal!
Two pieces of silver.
?
Could it be sorcery?
Other escapades add fuel to these suspicions!
Bringing mud figures to life, to amuse the other kids, was bad enough;
Why not make the figures larger? Then we could sell them as slaves!

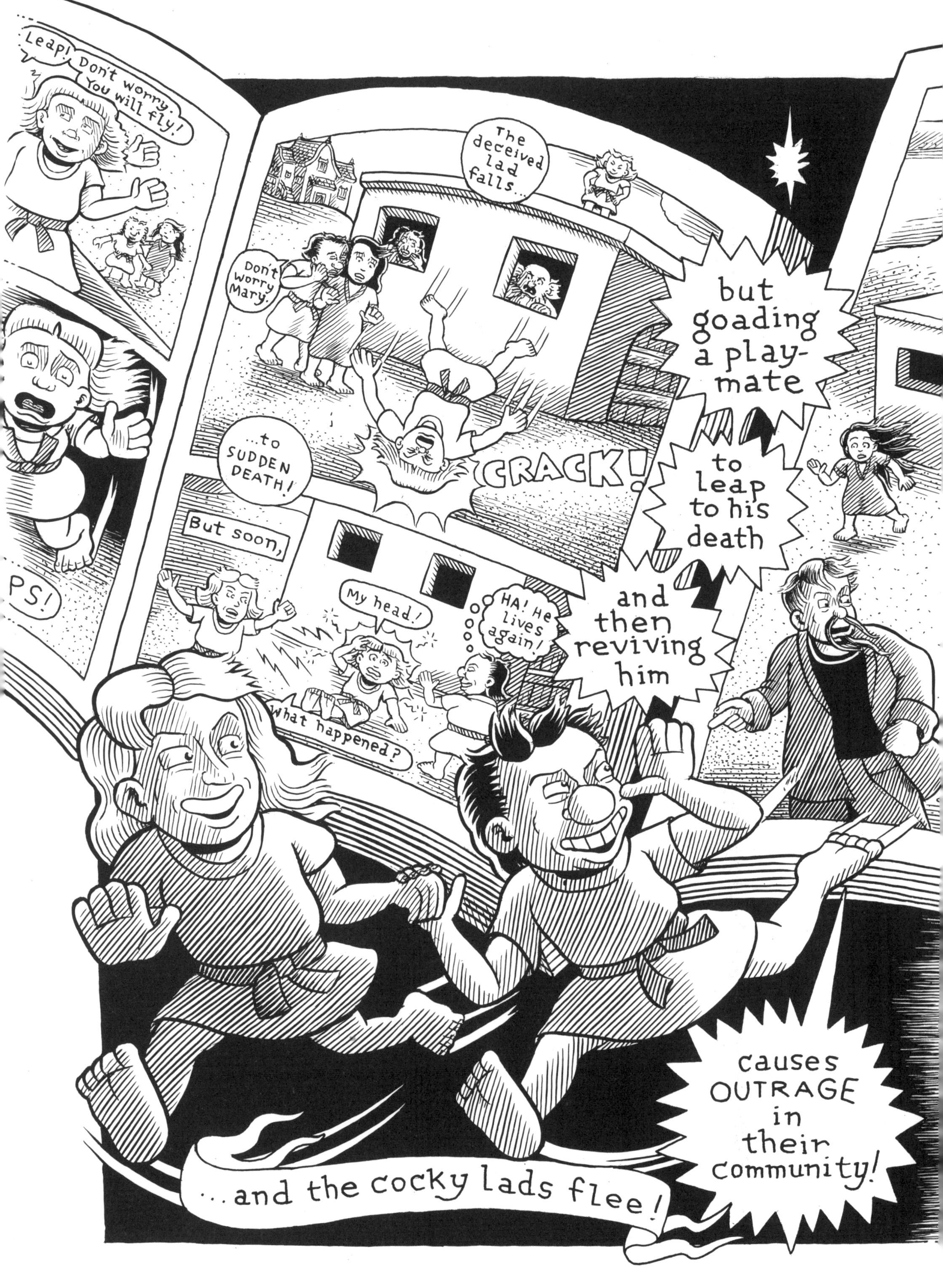

Leap!
Don't worry. You will fly!
PS!
The deceived lad falls...
Don't worry Mary.
...to SUDDEN DEATH!
CRACK!
But soon,
My head!
HA! He lives again!
What happened?
but goading a play-mate
to leap to his death
and then reviving him
causes OUTRAGE in their community!
...and the cocky lads flee!

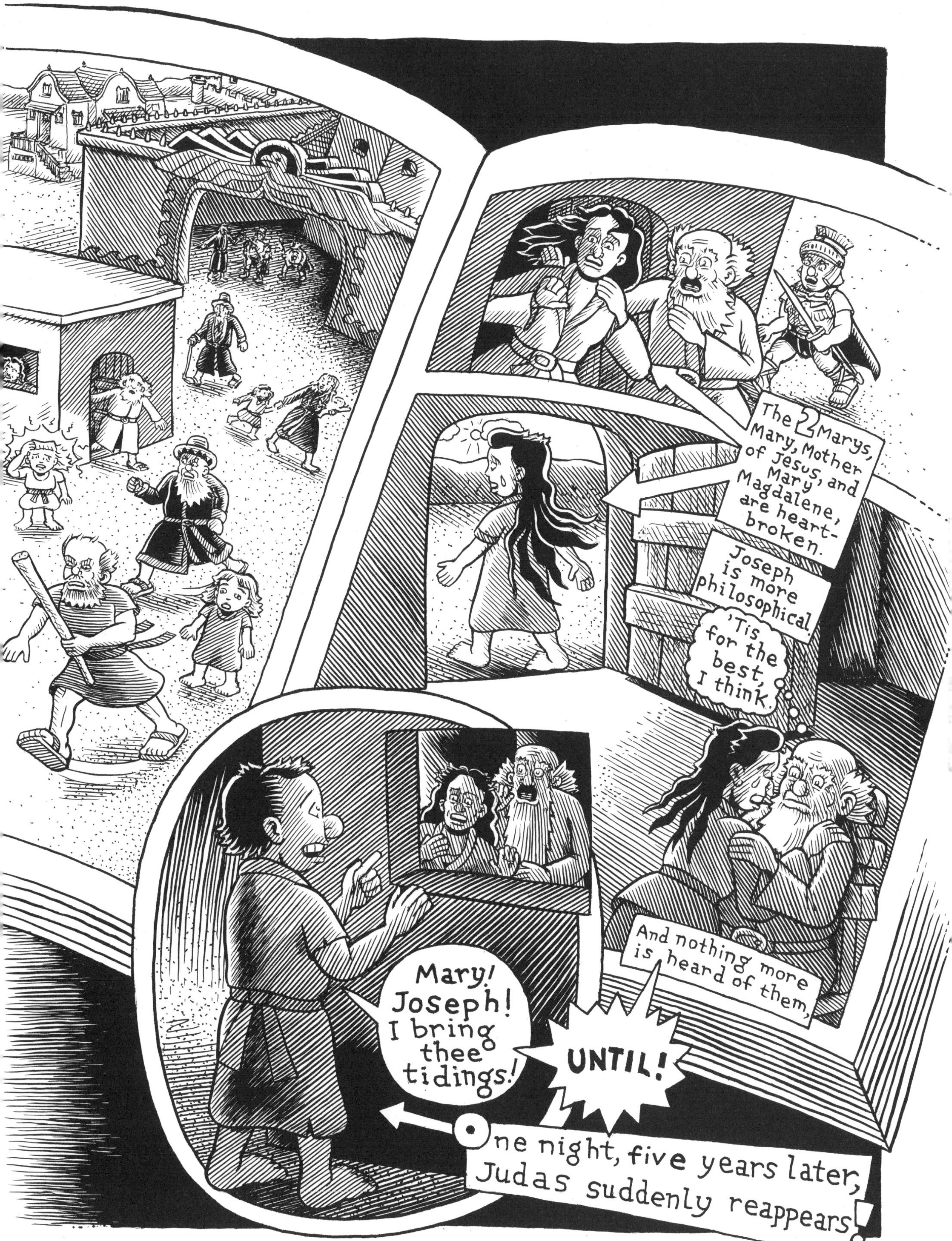
The 2 Marys, Mary, Mother of Jesus, and Mary Magdalene, are heart-broken.
Joseph is more philosophical.
'Tis for the best, I think.
And nothing more is heard of them,
UNTIL!
One night, five years later, Judas suddenly reappears!
Mary! Joseph! I bring thee tidings!

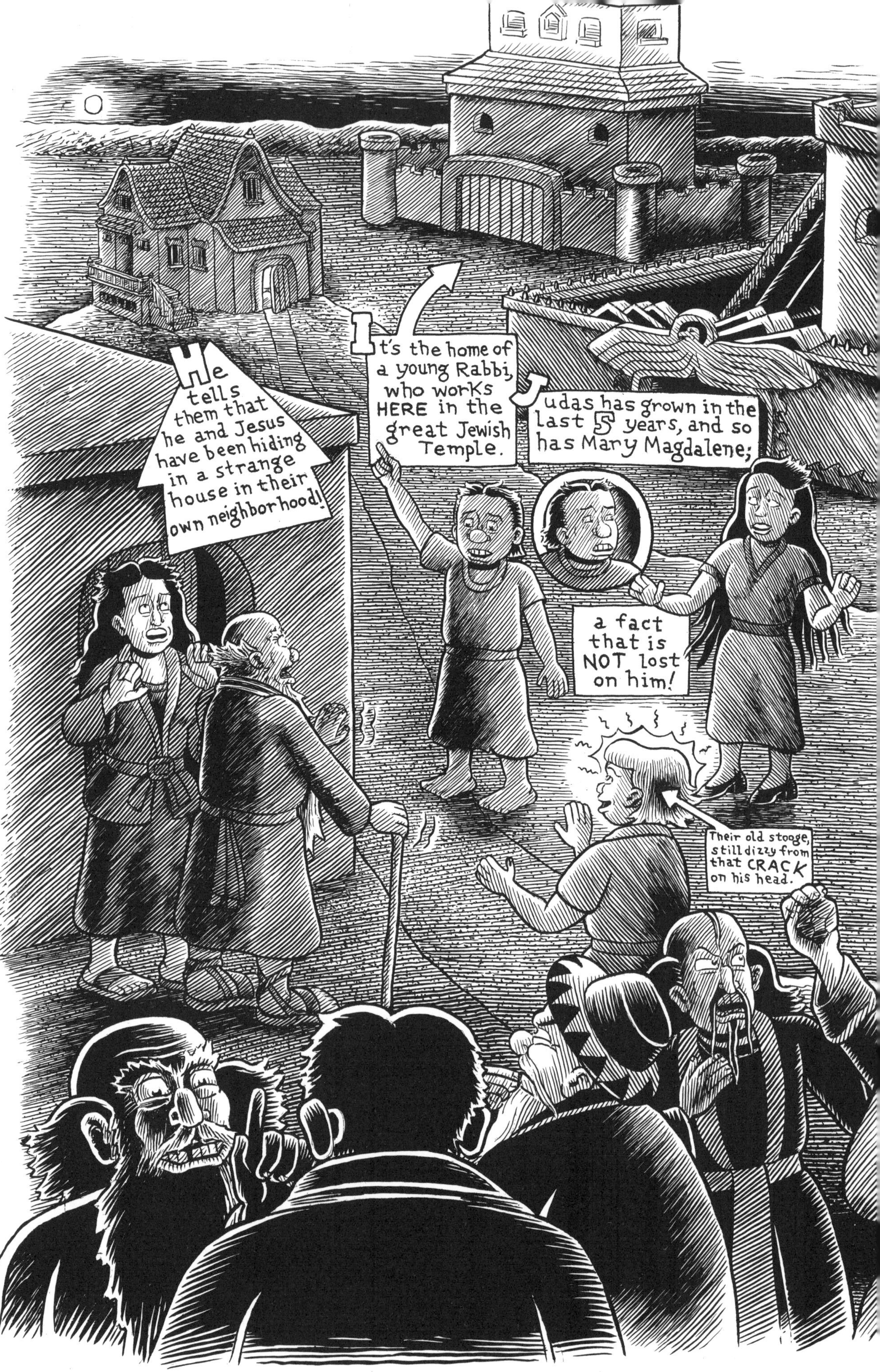
He tells them that he and Jesus have been hiding in a strange house in their own neighborhood!
It's the home of a young Rabbi, who works HERE in the great Jewish Temple.
Judas has grown in the last 5 years, and so has Mary Magdalene;
a fact that is NOT lost on him!
Their old stooge, still dizzy from that CRACK on his head.

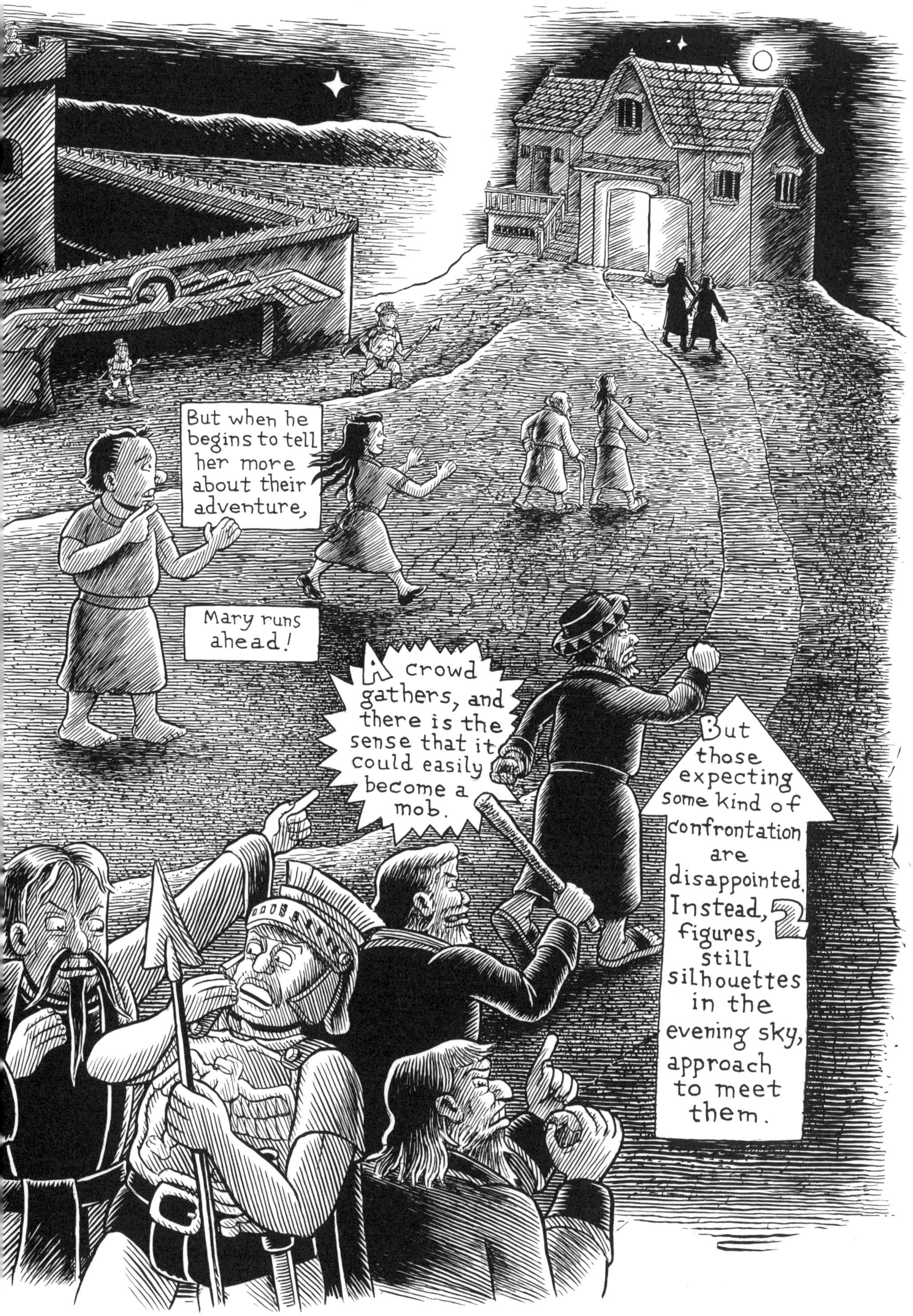
But when he begins to tell her more about their adventure,
Mary runs ahead!
A crowd gathers, and there is the sense that it could easily become a mob.
But those expecting some kind of confrontation are disappointed.
Instead, 2 figures, still silhouettes in the evening sky, approach to meet them.

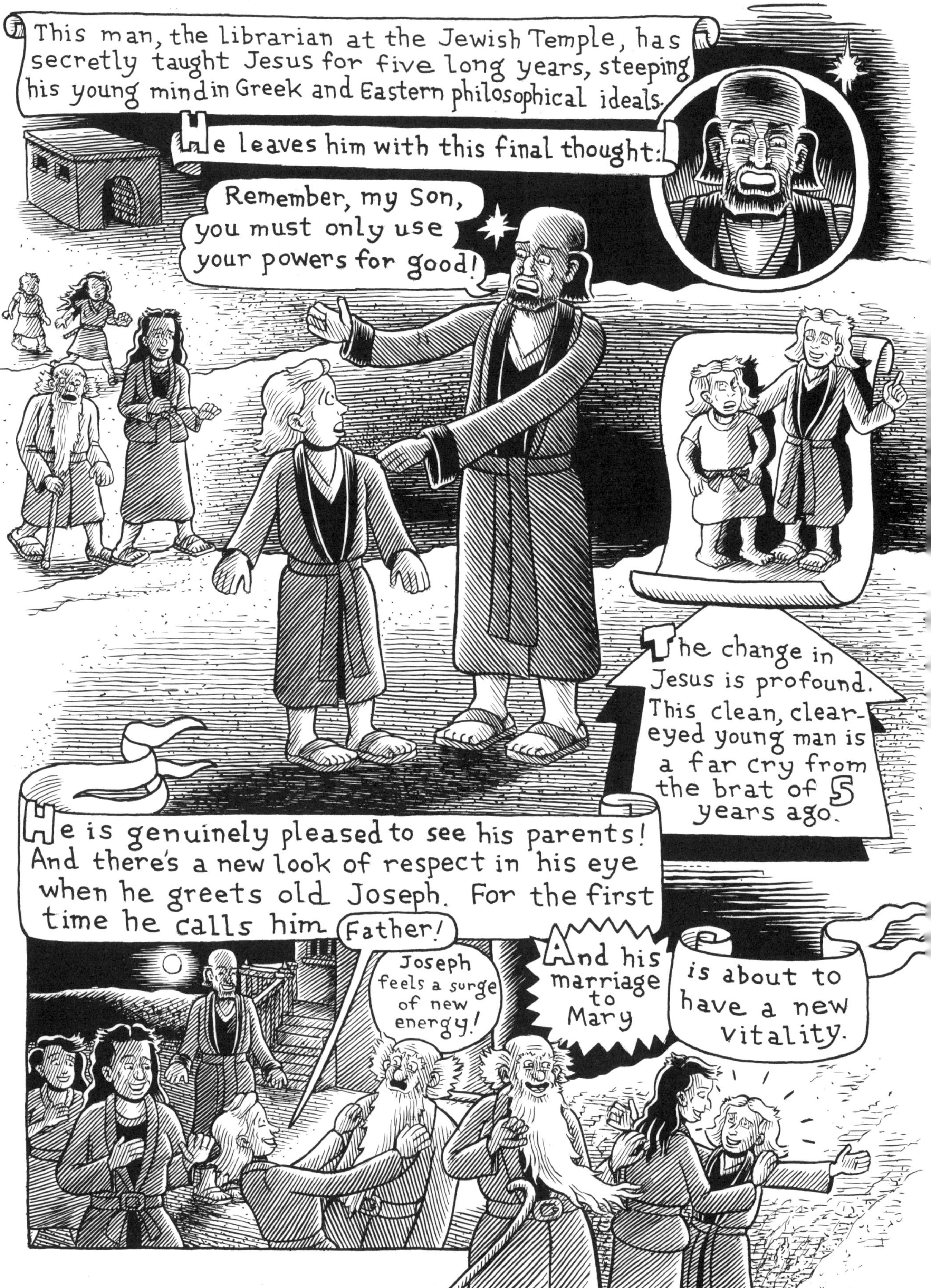
This man, the librarian at the Jewish Temple, has secretly taught Jesus for five long years, steeping his young mind in Greek and Eastern philosophical ideals.
He leaves him with this final thought:
Remember, my Son, you must only use your powers for good!
The change in Jesus is profound. This clean, clear-eyed young man is a far cry from the brat of 5 years ago.
He is genuinely pleased to see his parents! And there's a new look of respect in his eye when he greets old Joseph. For the first time he calls him
Father!
Joseph feels a surge of new energy!
And his marriage to Mary
is about to have a new vitality.

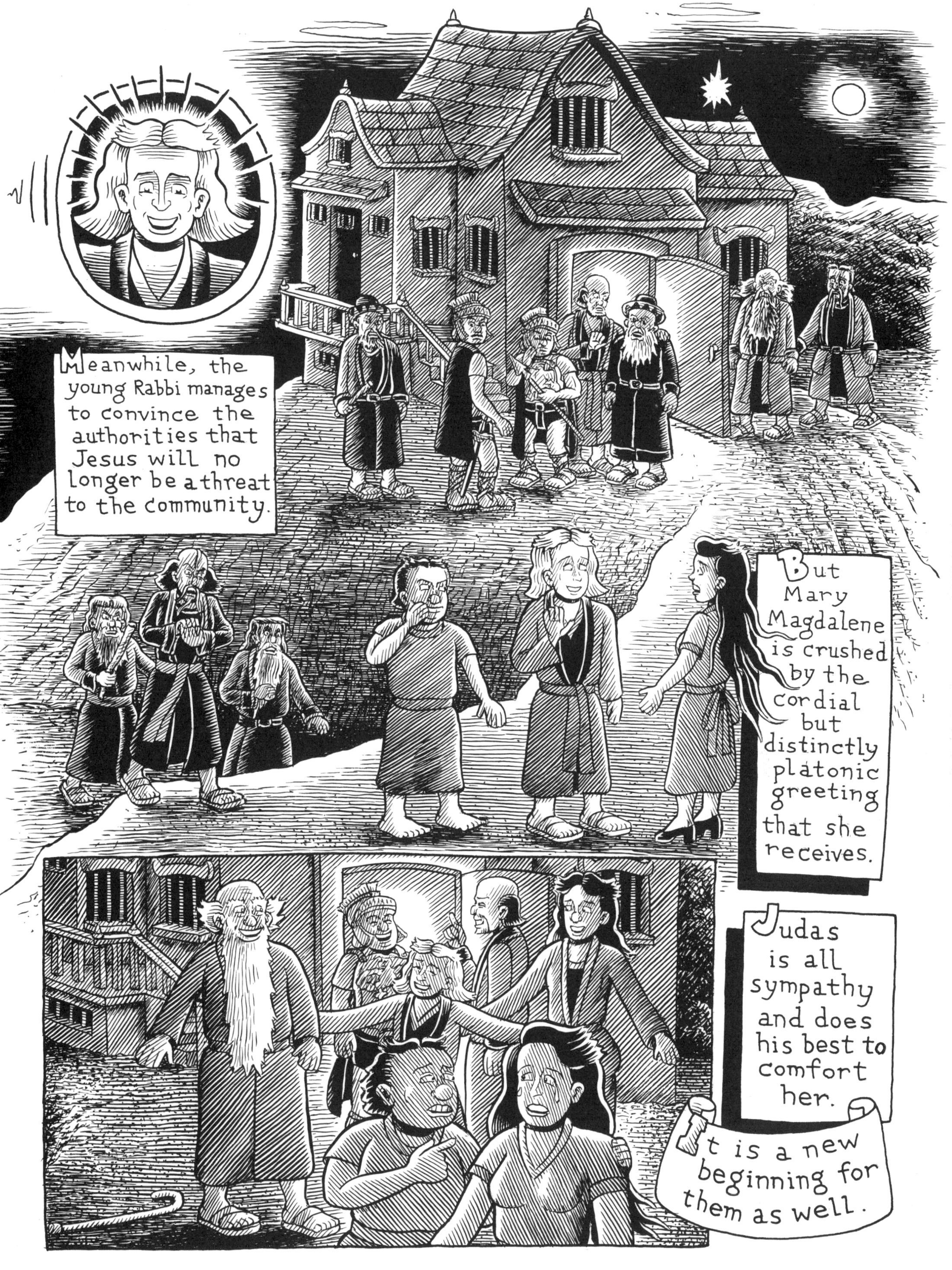
Meanwhile, the young Rabbi manages to convince the authorities that Jesus will no longer be a threat to the community.
But Mary Magdalene is crushed by the cordial but distinctly platonic greeting that she receives.
Judas is all sympathy and does his best to comfort her.
It is a new beginning for them as well.

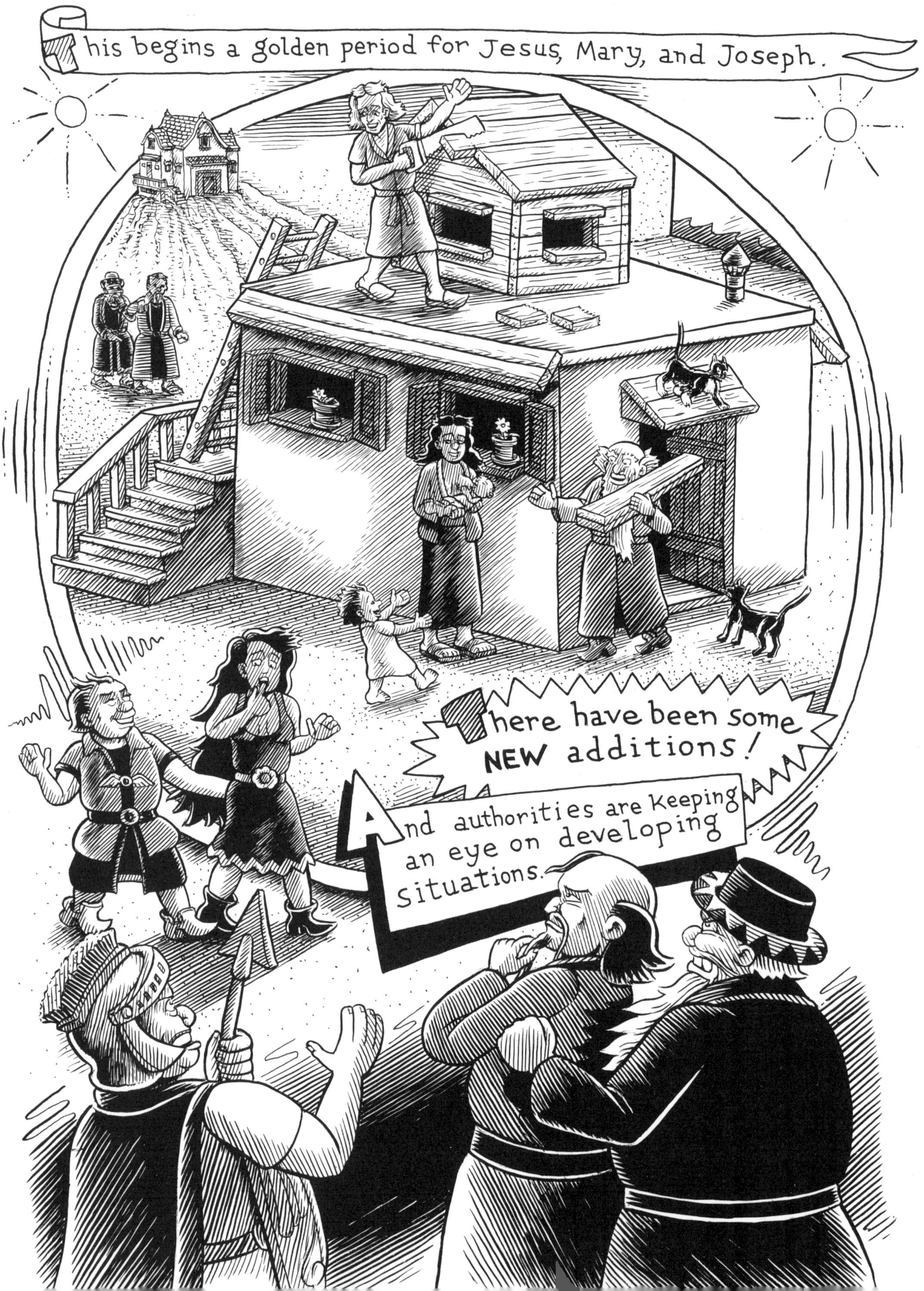
This begins a golden period for Jesus, Mary, and Joseph.
There have been some NEW additions!
And authorities are keeping an eye on developing situations.

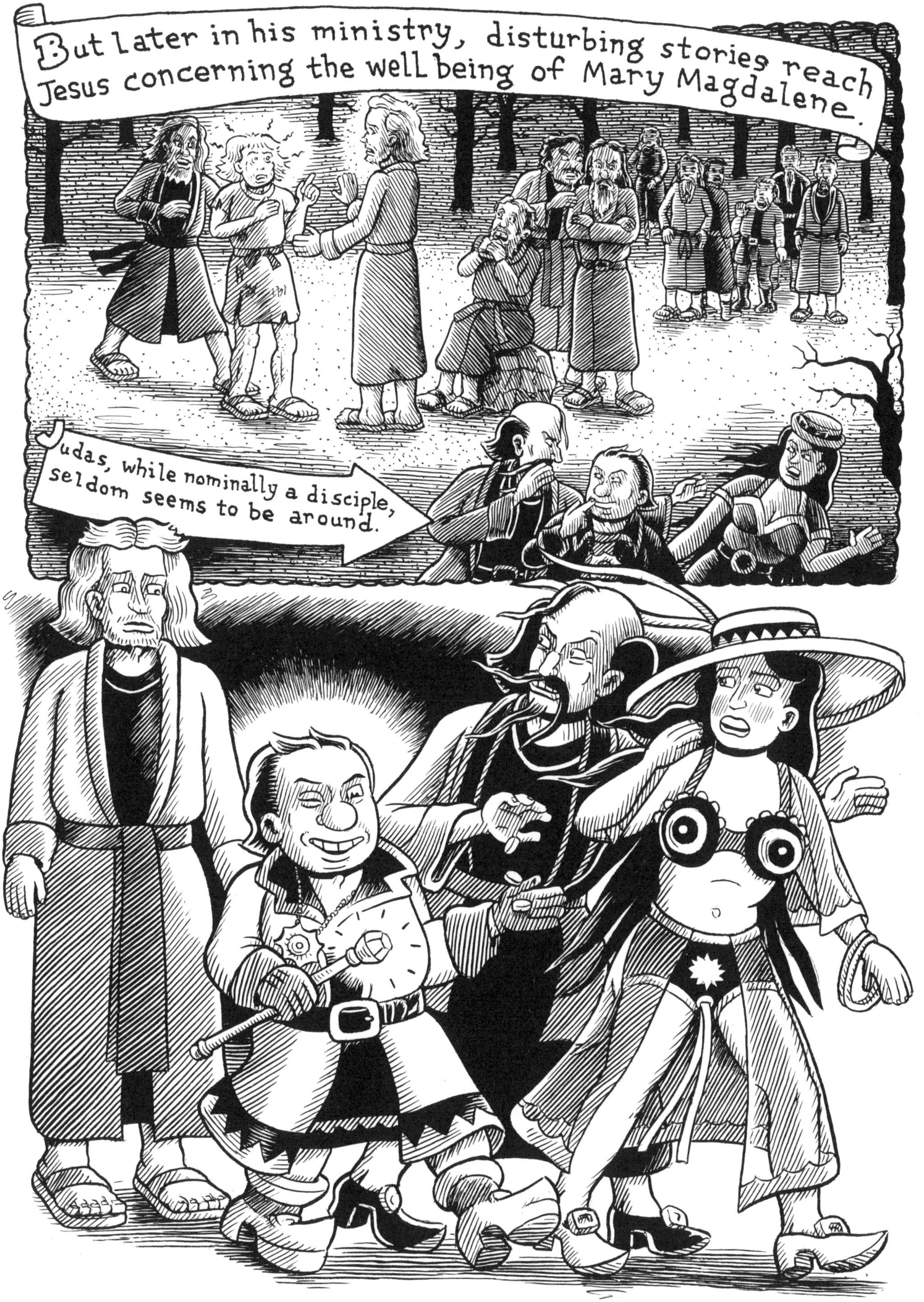

But later in his ministry, disturbing stories reach Jesus concerning the well being of Mary Magdalene.
Judas, while nominally a disciple, seldom seems to be around.

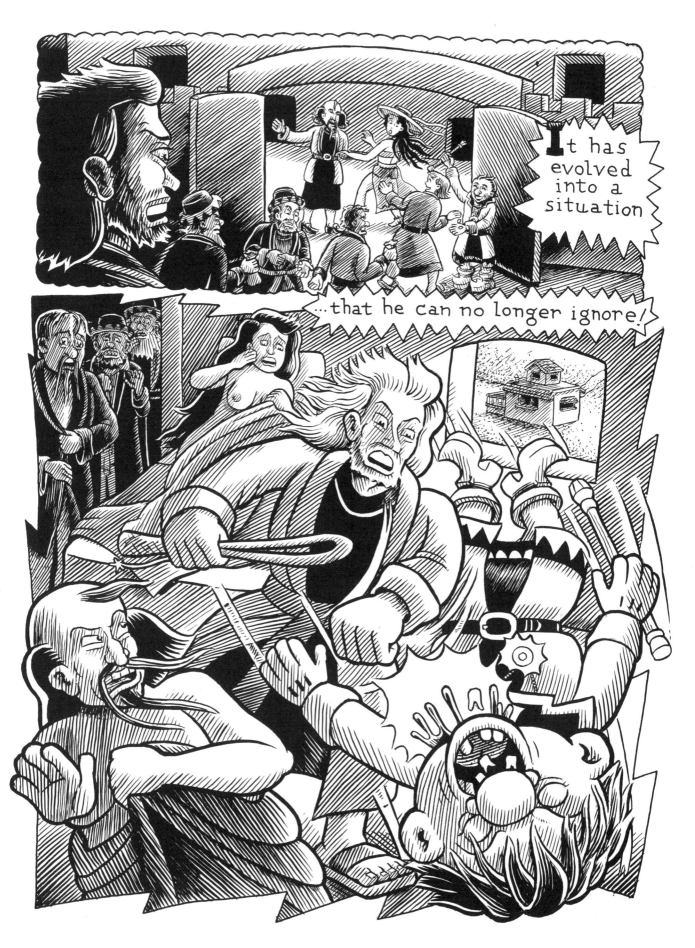

It has evolved into a situation

...that he can no longer ignore!

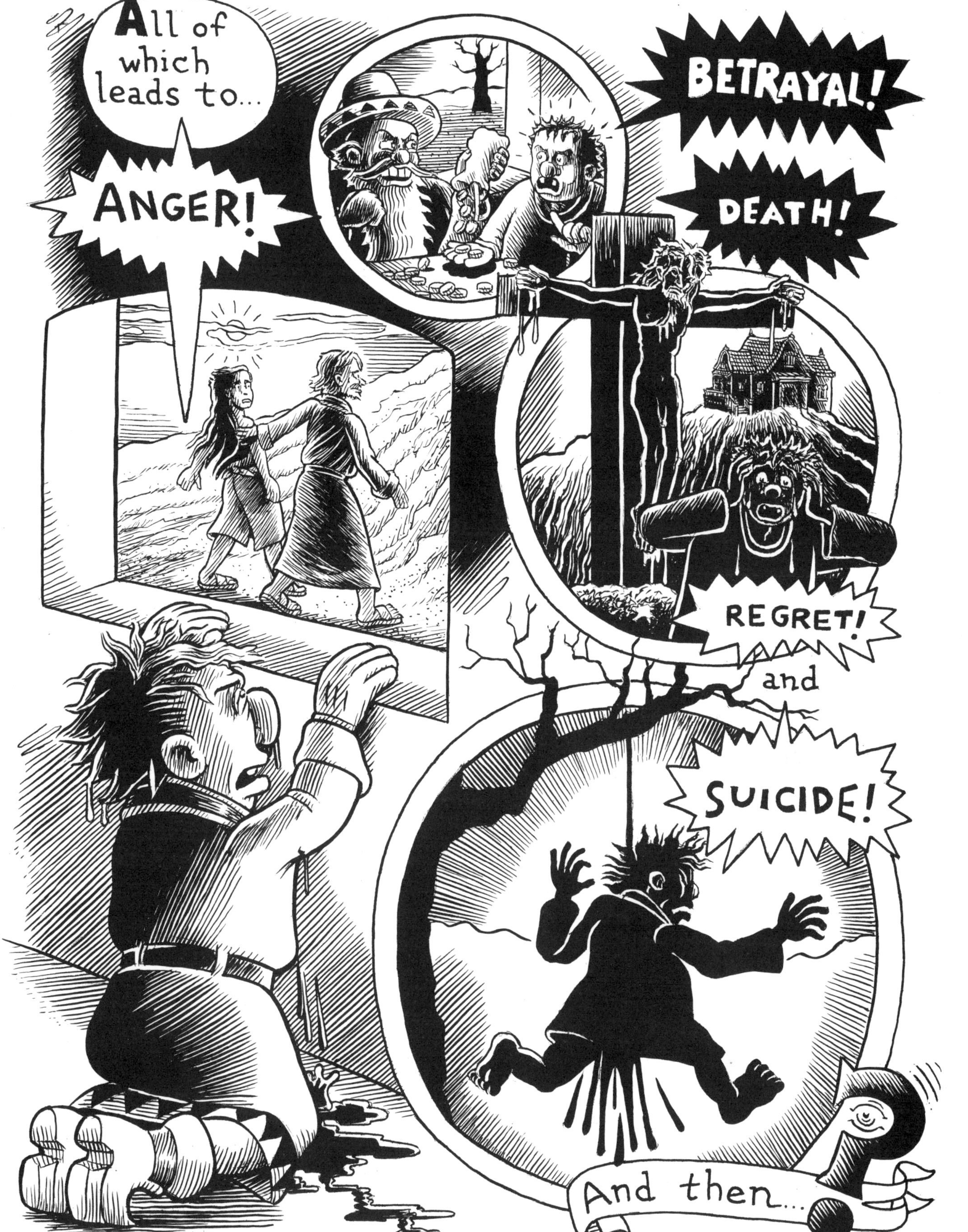
All of which leads to...
ANGER!
BETRAYAL!
DEATH!
REGRET!
and
SUICIDE!
And then...

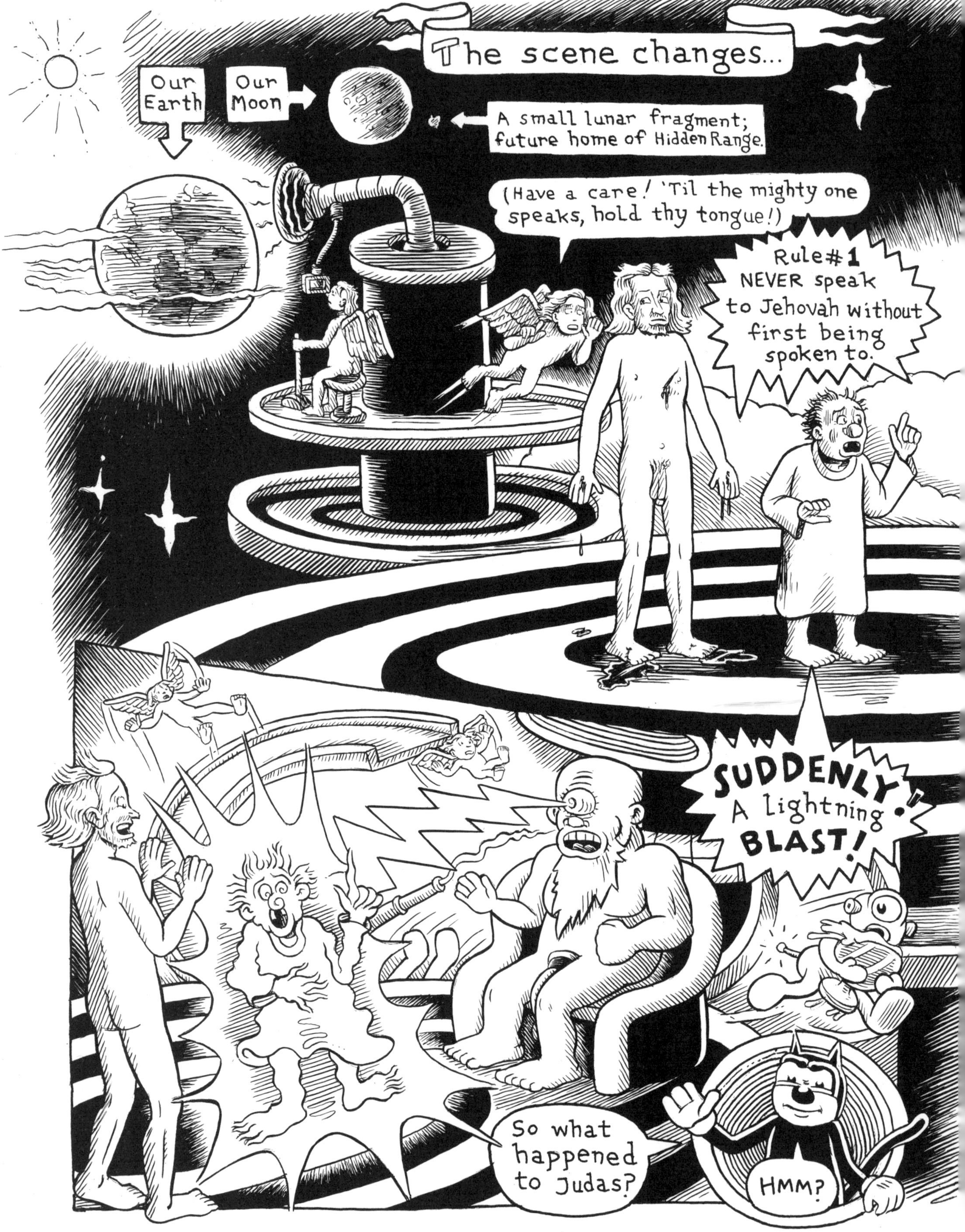
The scene changes...
Our Earth
Our Moon
A small lunar fragment; future home of Hidden Range.
(Have a care! 'Til the mighty one speaks, hold thy tongue!)
Rule #1 NEVER speak to Jehovah without first being spoken to.
SUDDENLY! A lightning BLAST!
So what happened to Judas?
HMM?

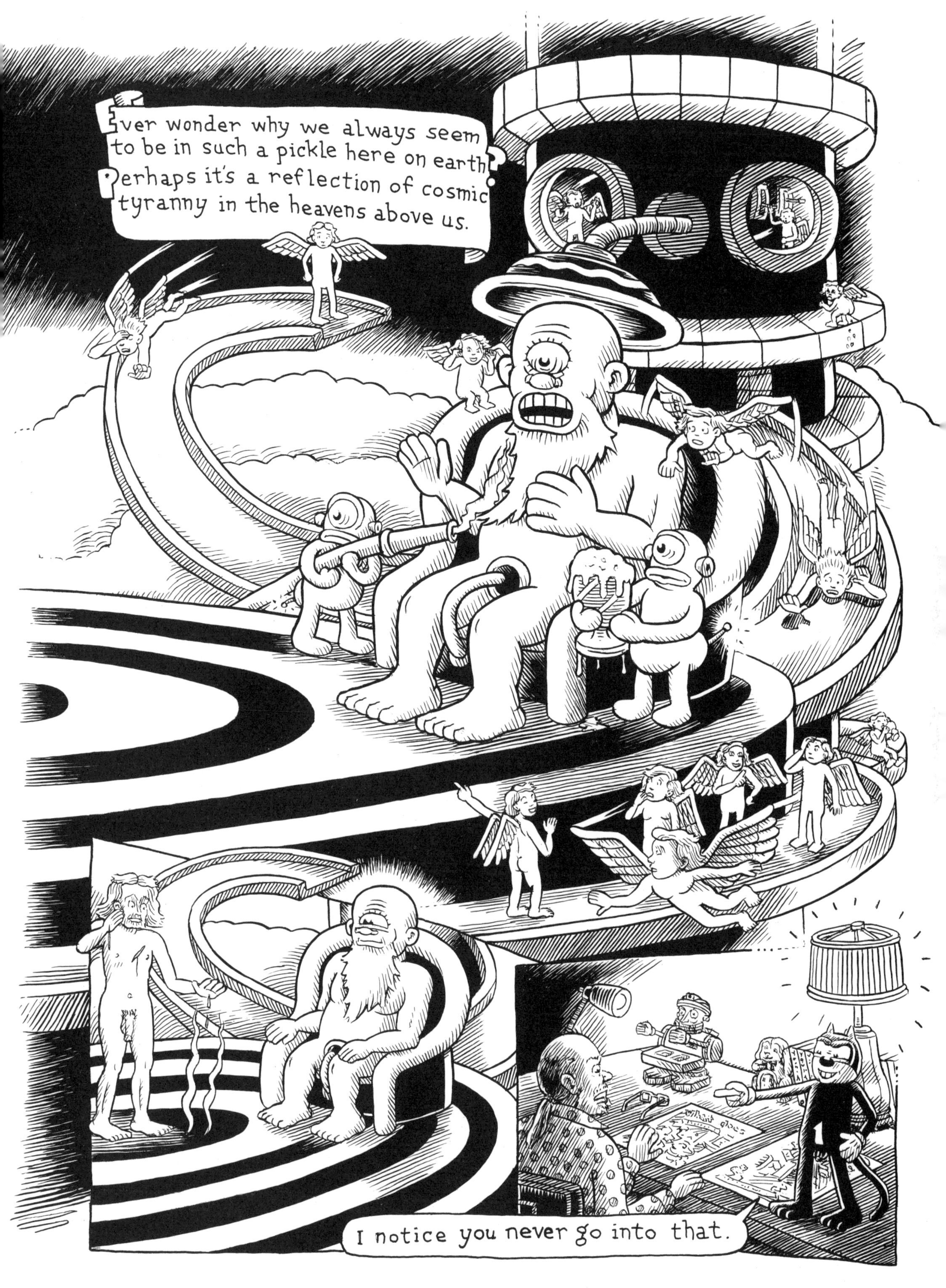
Ever wonder why we always seem to be in such a pickle here on earth? Perhaps it's a reflection of cosmic tyranny in the heavens above us.
I notice you never go into that.

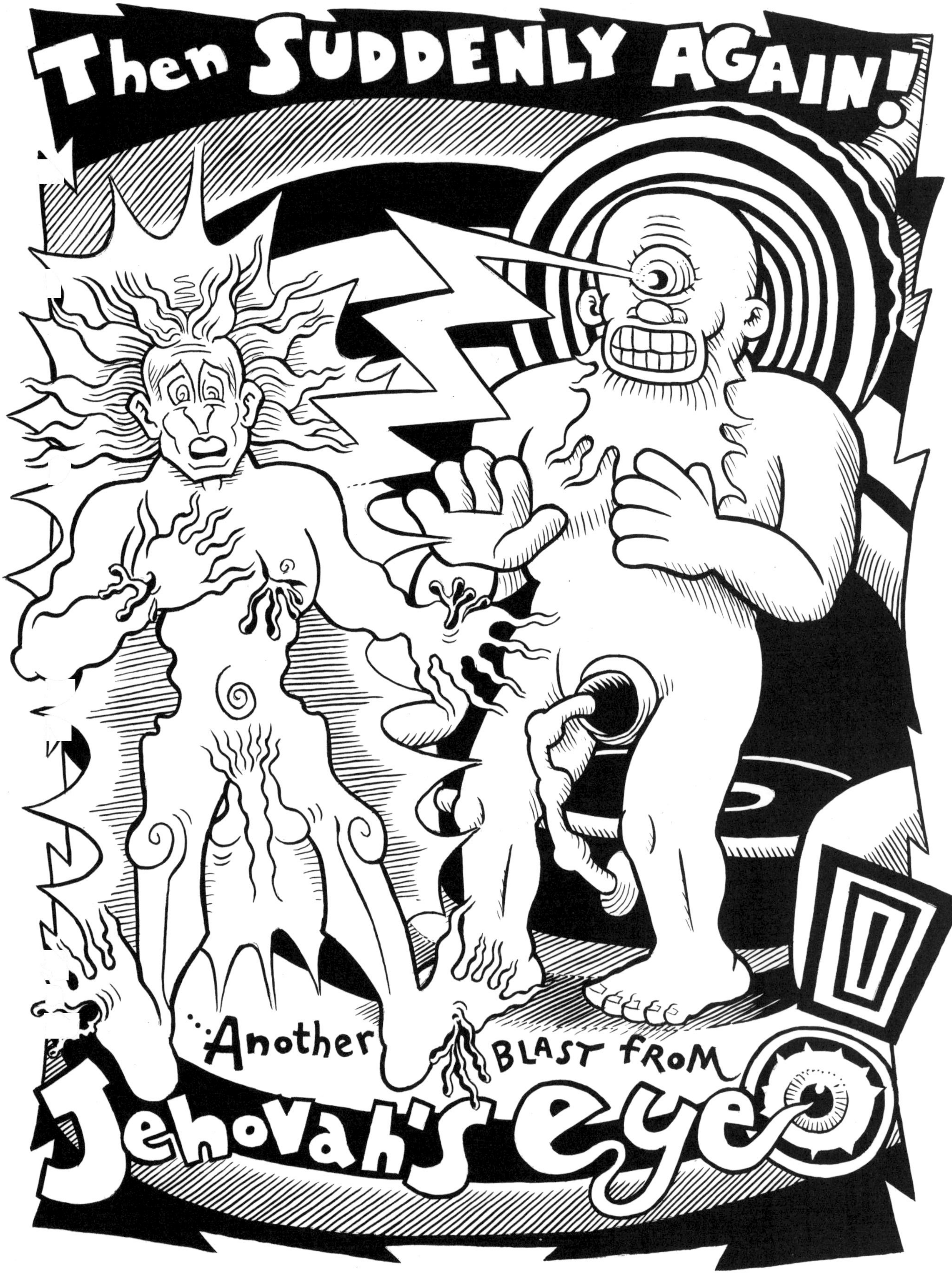
Then SUDDENLY AGAIN!
...Another BLAST FROM
Jehovah's eye

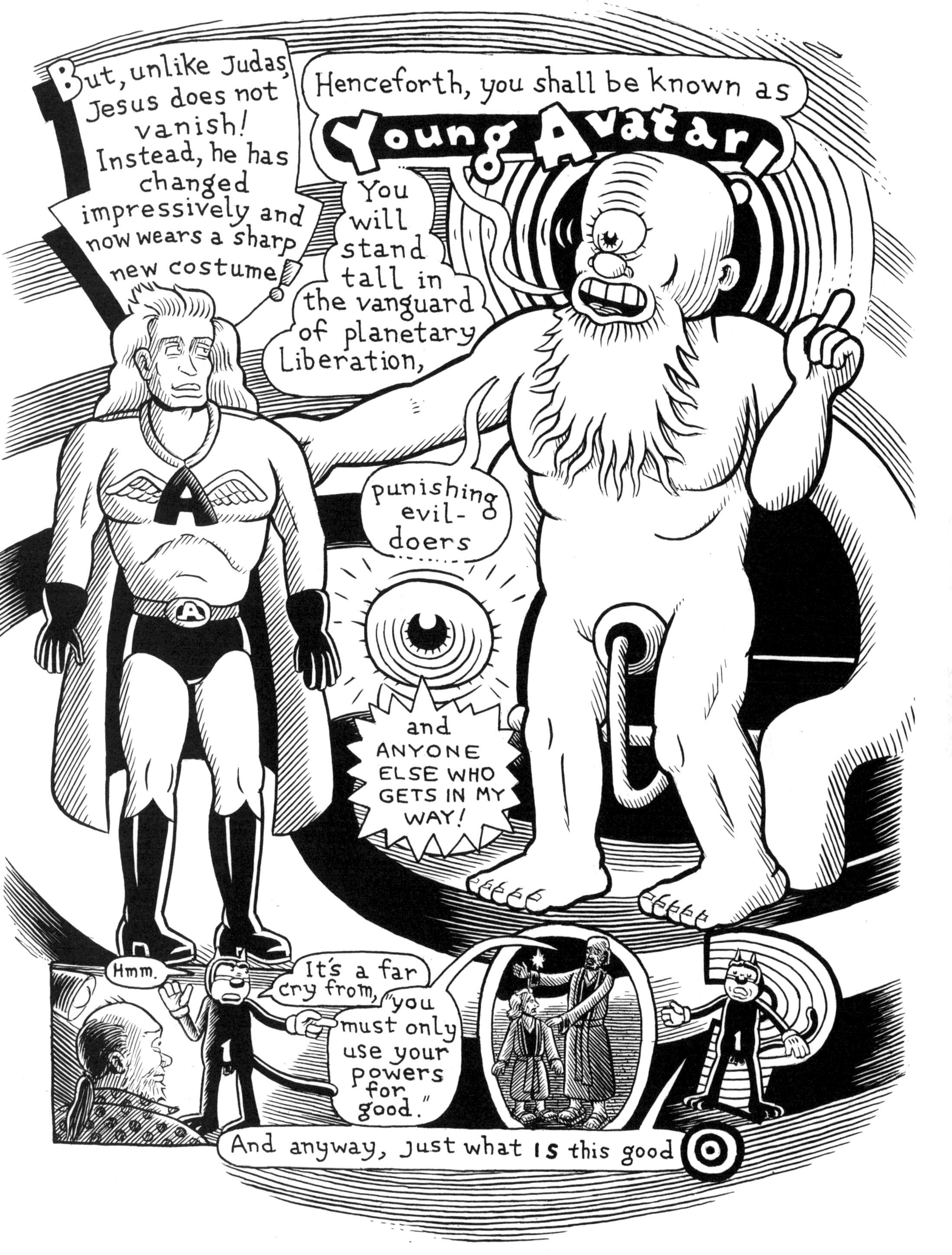
But, unlike Judas, Jesus does not vanish! Instead, he has changed impressively and now wears a sharp new costume!
Henceforth, you shall be known as
Young Avatar!
You will stand tall in the vanguard of planetary Liberation,
punishing evil-doers
and ANYONE ELSE WHO GETS IN MY WAY!
Hmm.
It's a far cry from, "you must only use your powers for good."
And anyway, just what IS this good

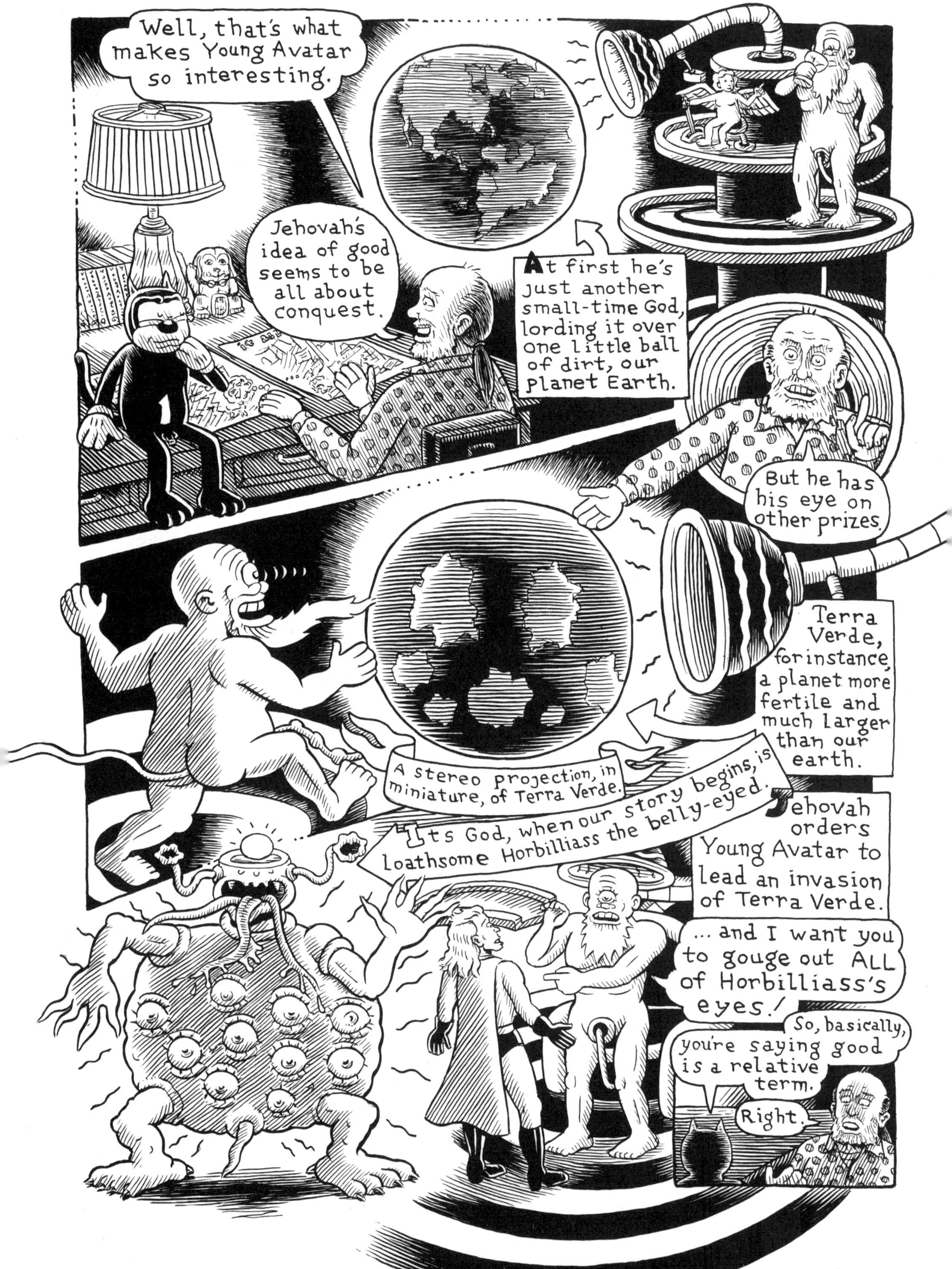

Well, that's what makes Young Avatar so interesting.
Jehovah's idea of good seems to be all about conquest.
At first he's just another small-time God, lording it over one little ball of dirt, our Planet Earth.
But he has his eye on other prizes.
Terra Verde, for instance, a planet more fertile and much larger than our earth.
A stereo projection, in miniature, of Terra Verde.
It's God, when our story begins, is loathsome Horbilliass the belly-eyed.
Jehovah orders Young Avatar to lead an invasion of Terra Verde.
... and I want you to gouge out ALL of Horbilliass's eyes!
So, basically, you're saying good is a relative term.
Right.

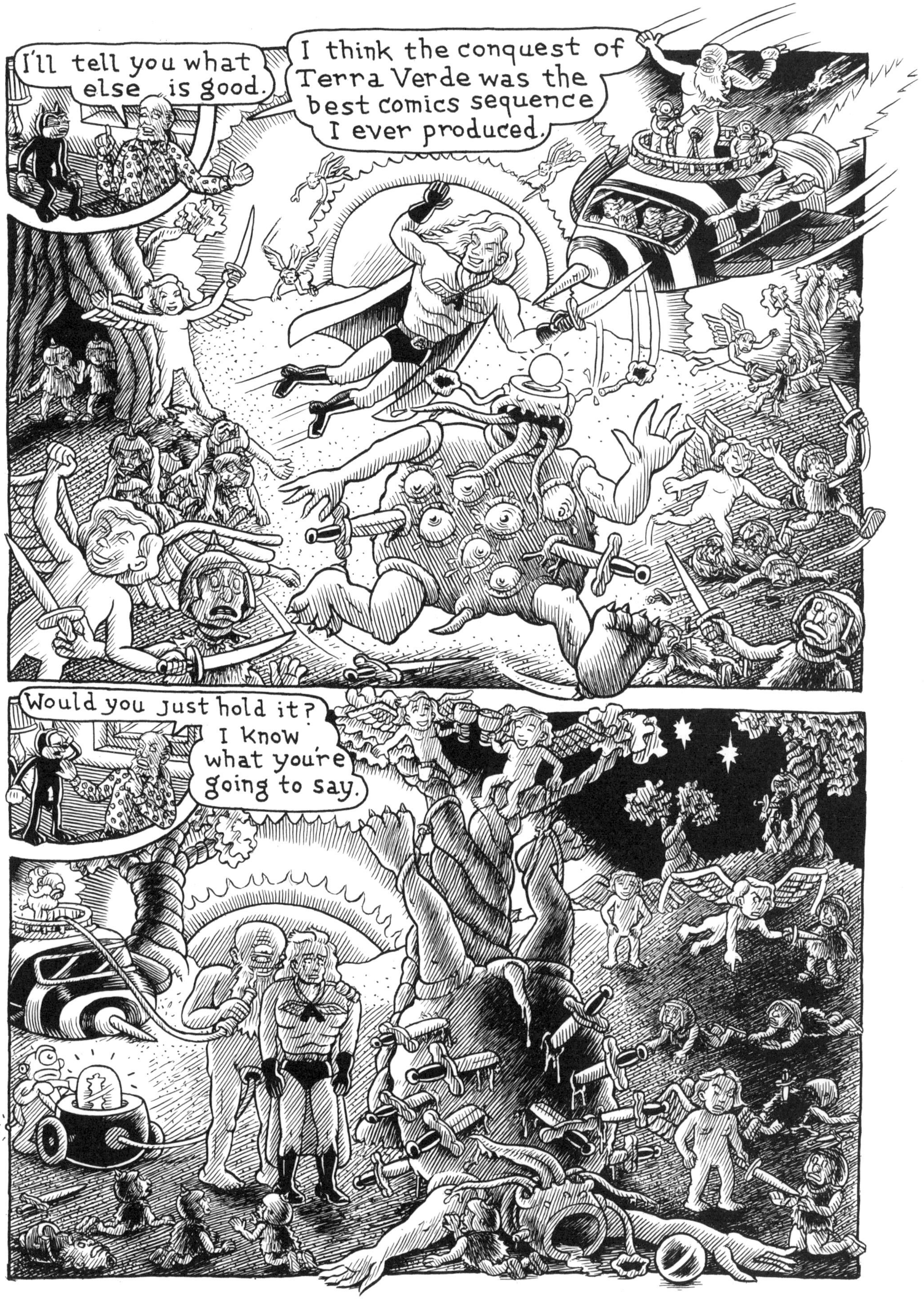
I'll tell you what else is good.
I think the conquest of Terra Verde was the best comics sequence I ever produced.
Would you just hold it? I know what you're going to say.

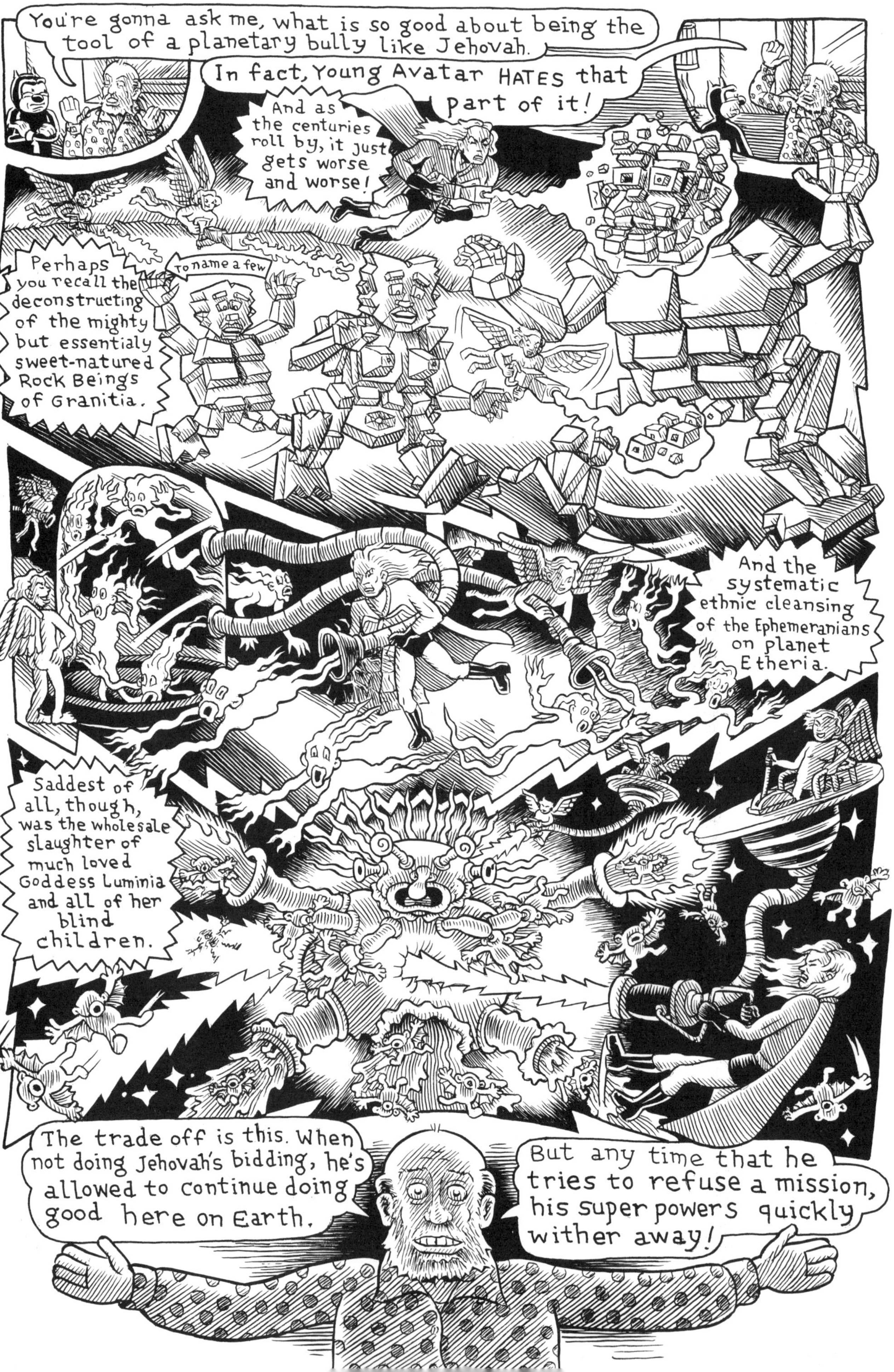
You're gonna ask me, what is so good about being the tool of a planetary bully like Jehovah.
In fact, Young Avatar HATES that part of it!
And as the centuries roll by, it just gets worse and worse!
Perhaps you recall the deconstructing of the mighty but essentialy sweet-natured Rock Beings of Granitia.
To name a few
And the systematic ethnic cleansing of the Ephemeranians on planet Etheria.
Saddest of all, though, was the wholesale slaughter of much loved Goddess Luminia and all of her blind children.
The trade off is this. When not doing Jehovah's bidding, he's allowed to continue doing good here on Earth.
But any time that he tries to refuse a mission, his super powers quickly wither away!

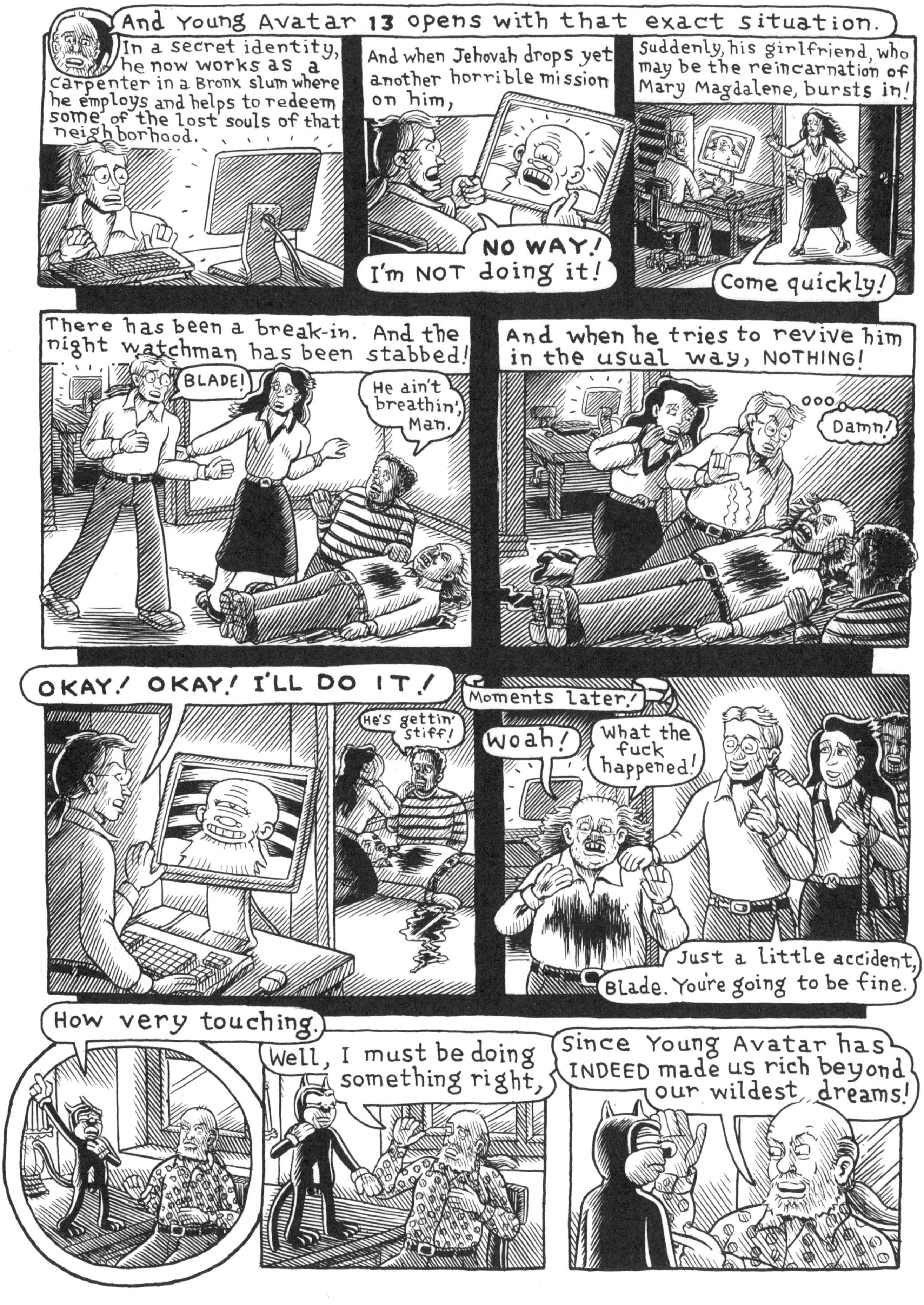

And Young Avatar 13 opens with that exact situation.
In a secret identity, he now works as a carpenter in a Bronx slum where he employs and helps to redeem some of the lost souls of that neighborhood.
And when Jehovah drops yet another horrible mission on him,
NO WAY! I'm NOT doing it!
Suddenly, his girlfriend, who may be the reincarnation of Mary Magdalene, bursts in!
Come quickly!
There has been a break-in. And the night watchman has been stabbed!
BLADE!
He ain't breathin', Man.
And when he tries to revive him in the usual way, NOTHING!
Damn!
OKAY! OKAY! I'LL DO IT!
He's gettin' stiff!
Moments later!
Woah!
What the fuck happened!
Just a little accident, Blade. You're going to be fine.
How very touching.
Well, I must be doing something right,
Since Young Avatar has INDEED made us rich beyond our wildest dreams!

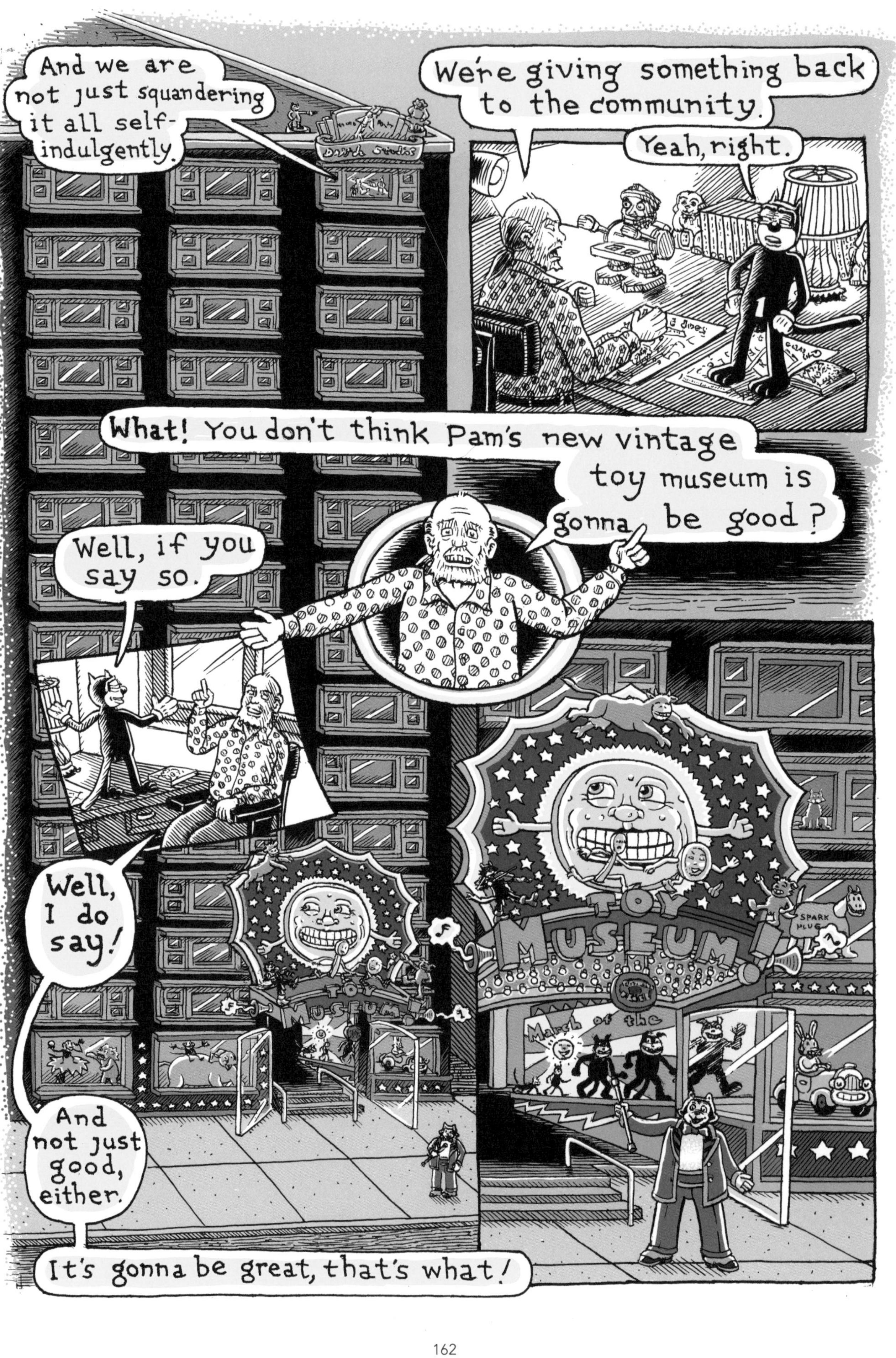
And we are not just squandering it all self-indulgently.
We're giving something back to the community.
Yeah, right.
What! You don't think Pam's new vintage toy museum is gonna be good?
Well, if you say so.
Well, I do say!
And not just good, either.
It's gonna be great, that's what!
TOY MUSEUM!
March of the
SPARK PLUG

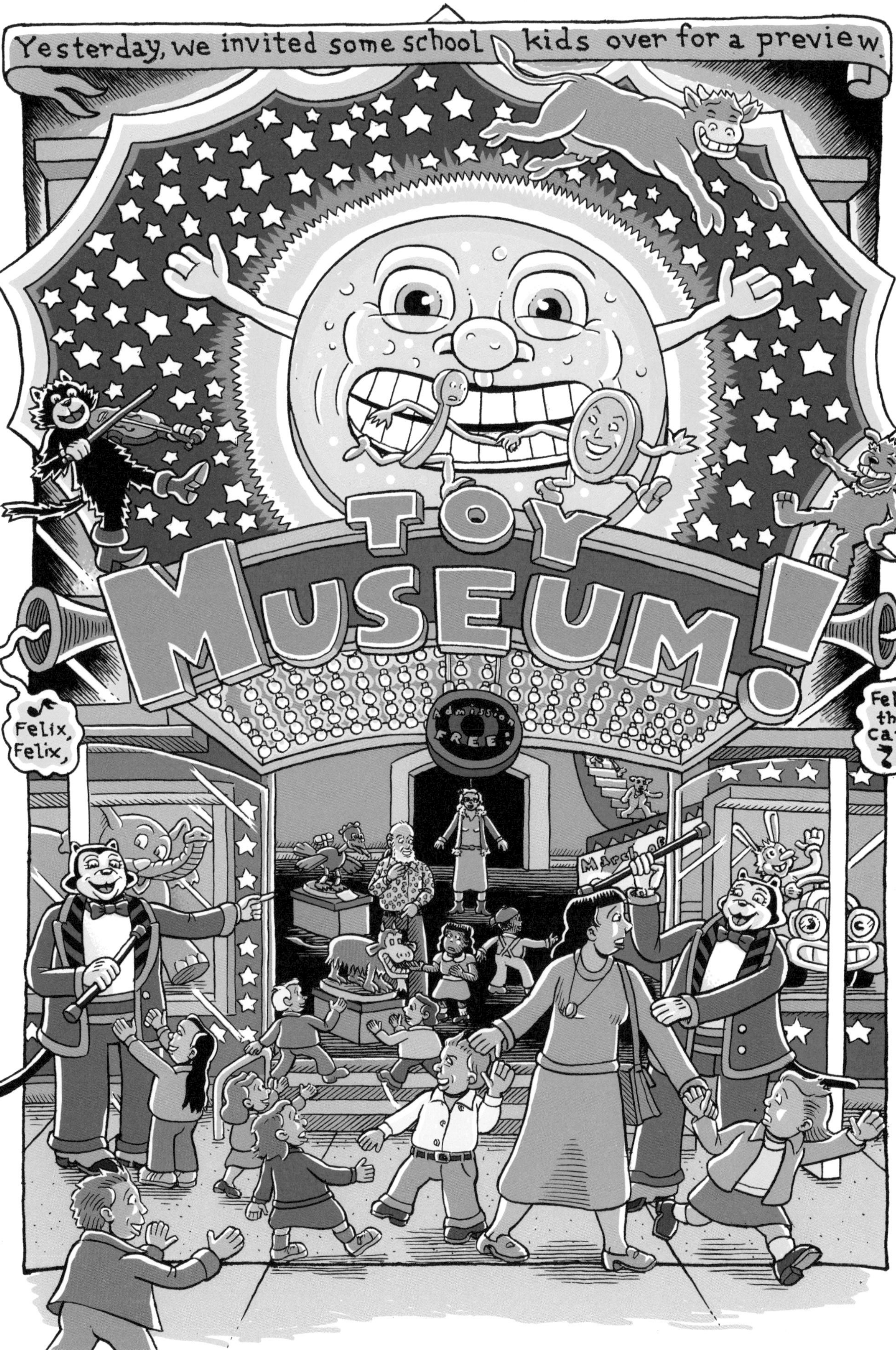
Yesterday, we invited some school kids over for a preview.
TOY MUSEUM!
Admission FREE!
Felix, Felix,
Felix the cat

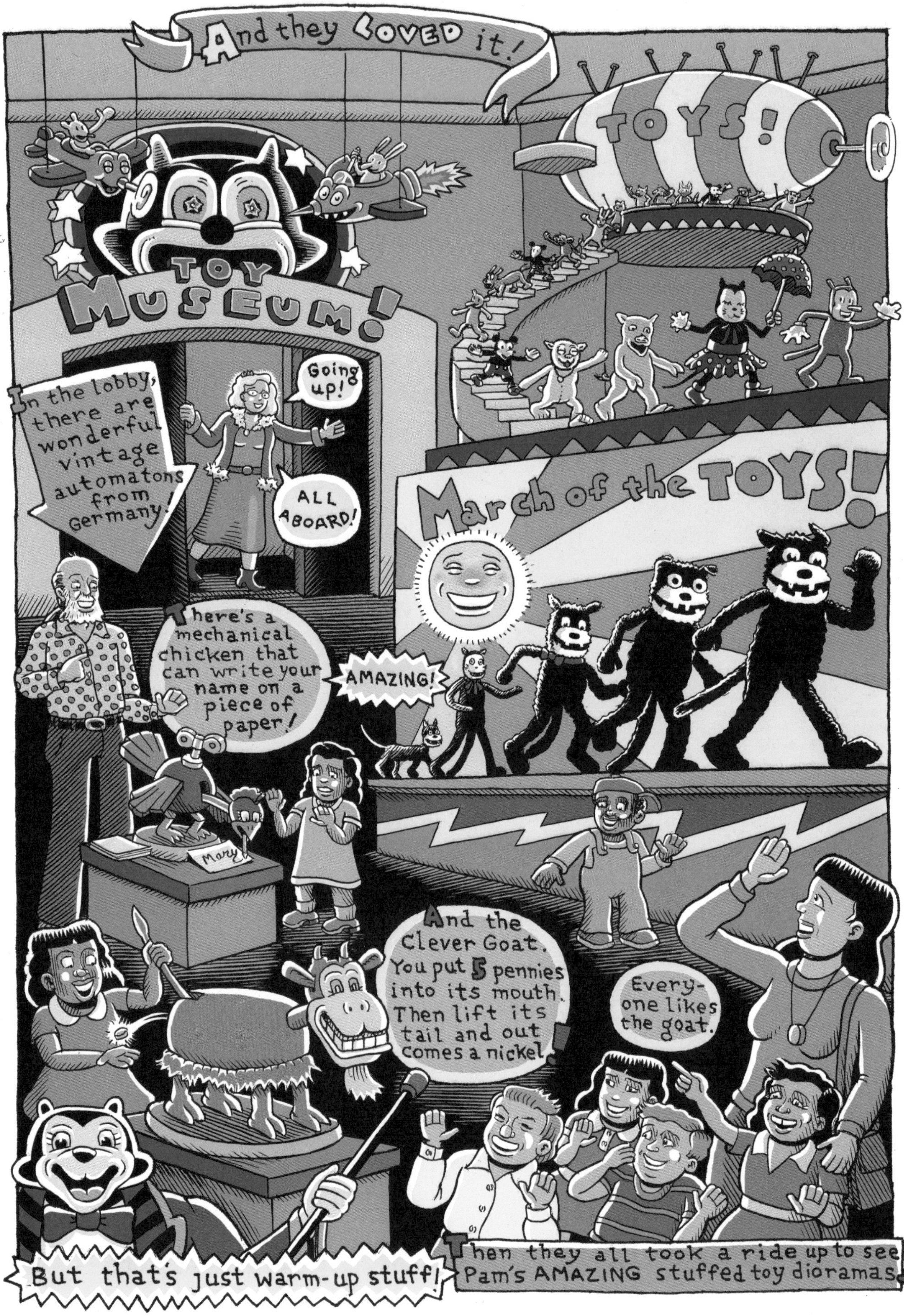

And they LOVED it!
TOY MUSEUM!
TOYS!
In the lobby, there are wonderful vintage automatons from Germany!
Going up!
ALL ABOARD!
March of the TOYS!
There's a mechanical chicken that can write your name on a piece of paper!
AMAZING!
Mary
And the Clever Goat. You put 5 pennies into its mouth. Then lift its tail and out comes a nickel.
Every-one likes the goat.
But that's just warm-up stuff!
Then they all took a ride up to see Pam's AMAZING stuffed toy dioramas!

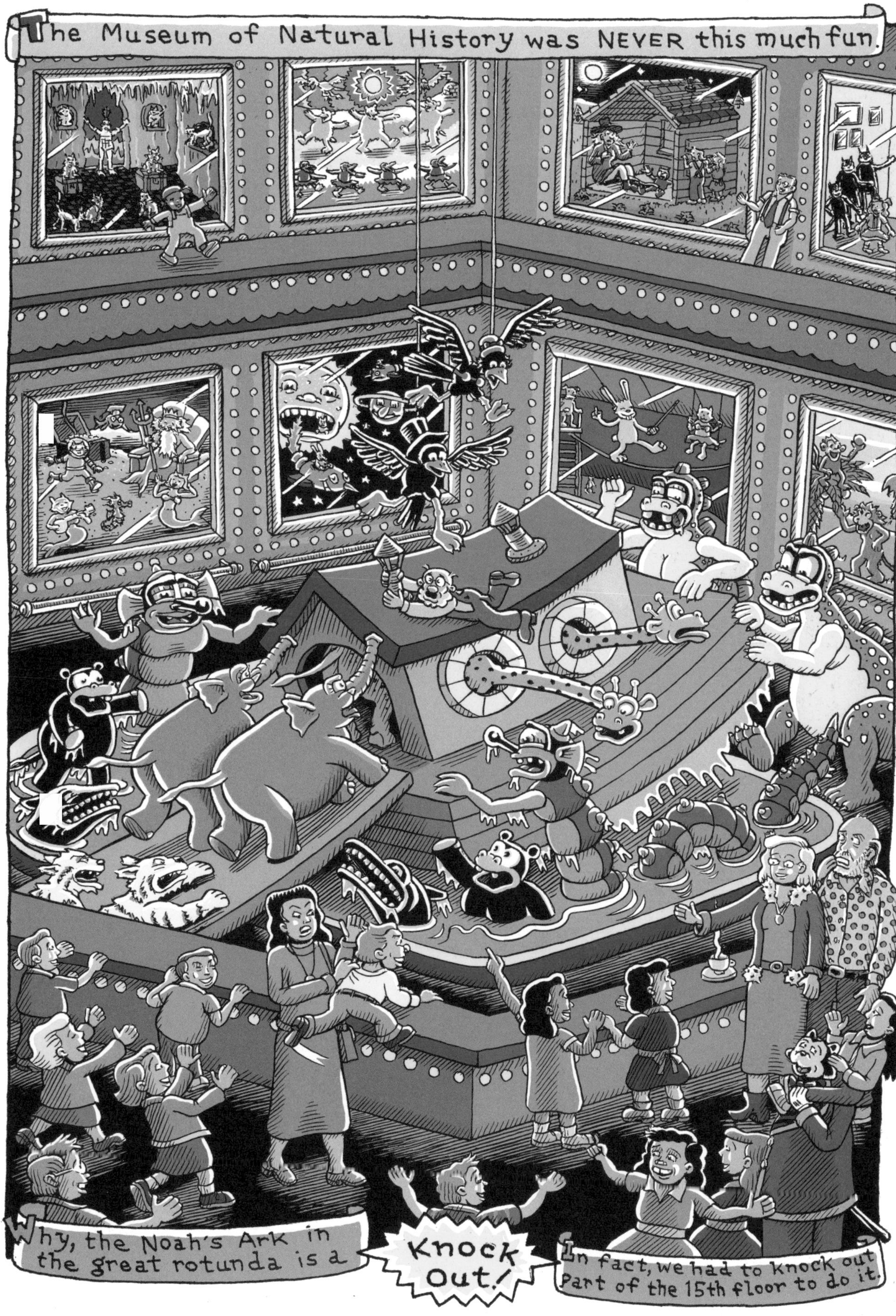
The Museum of Natural History was NEVER this much fun.
Why, the Noah's Ark in the great rotunda is a
Knock Out!
In fact, we had to knock out part of the 15th floor to do it.

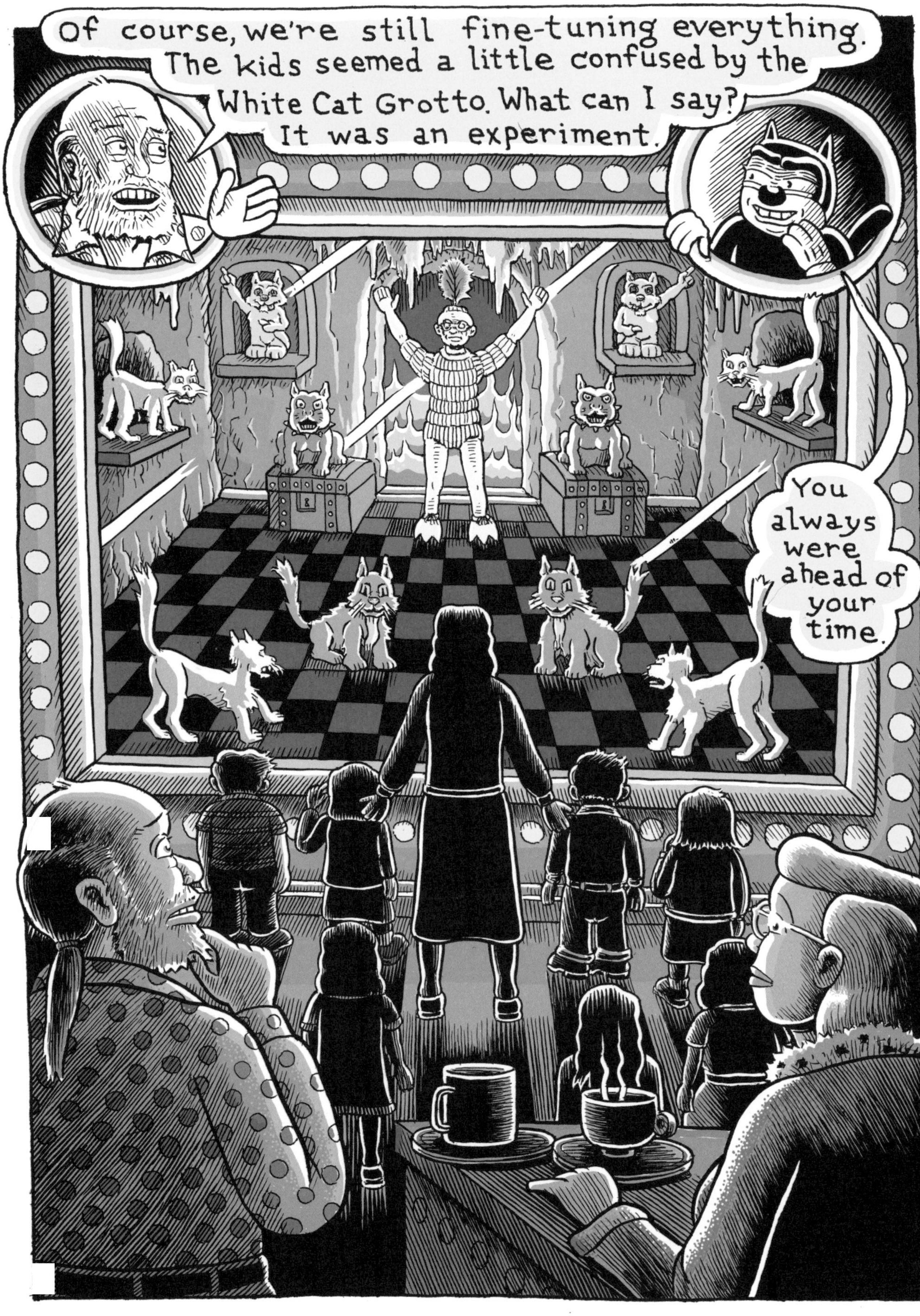
Of course, we're still fine-tuning everything. The kids seemed a little confused by the White Cat Grotto. What can I say? It was an experiment.
You always were ahead of your time.

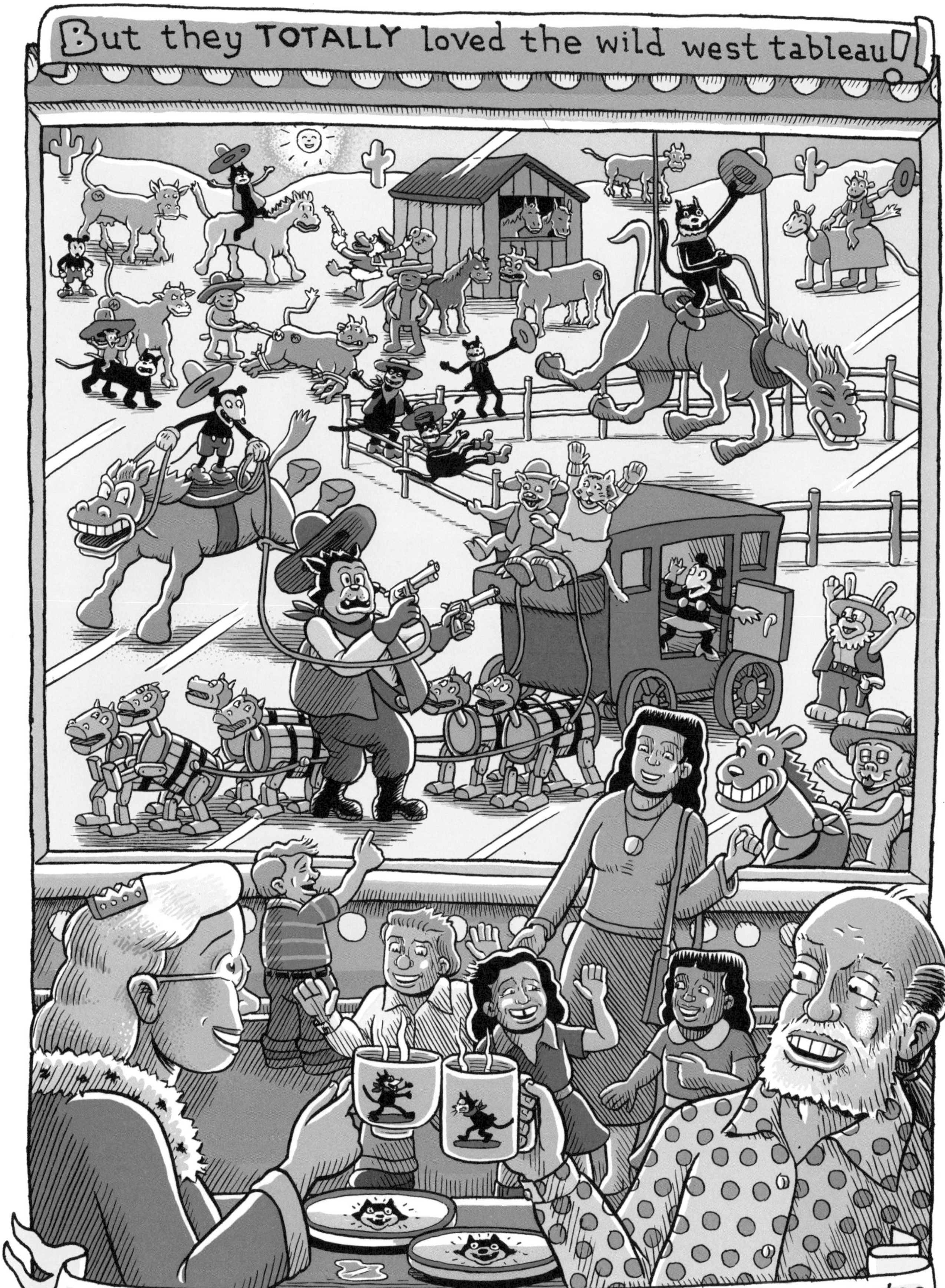
But they TOTALLY loved the wild west tableau!
But, you know, I like some of the simpler ones, too.

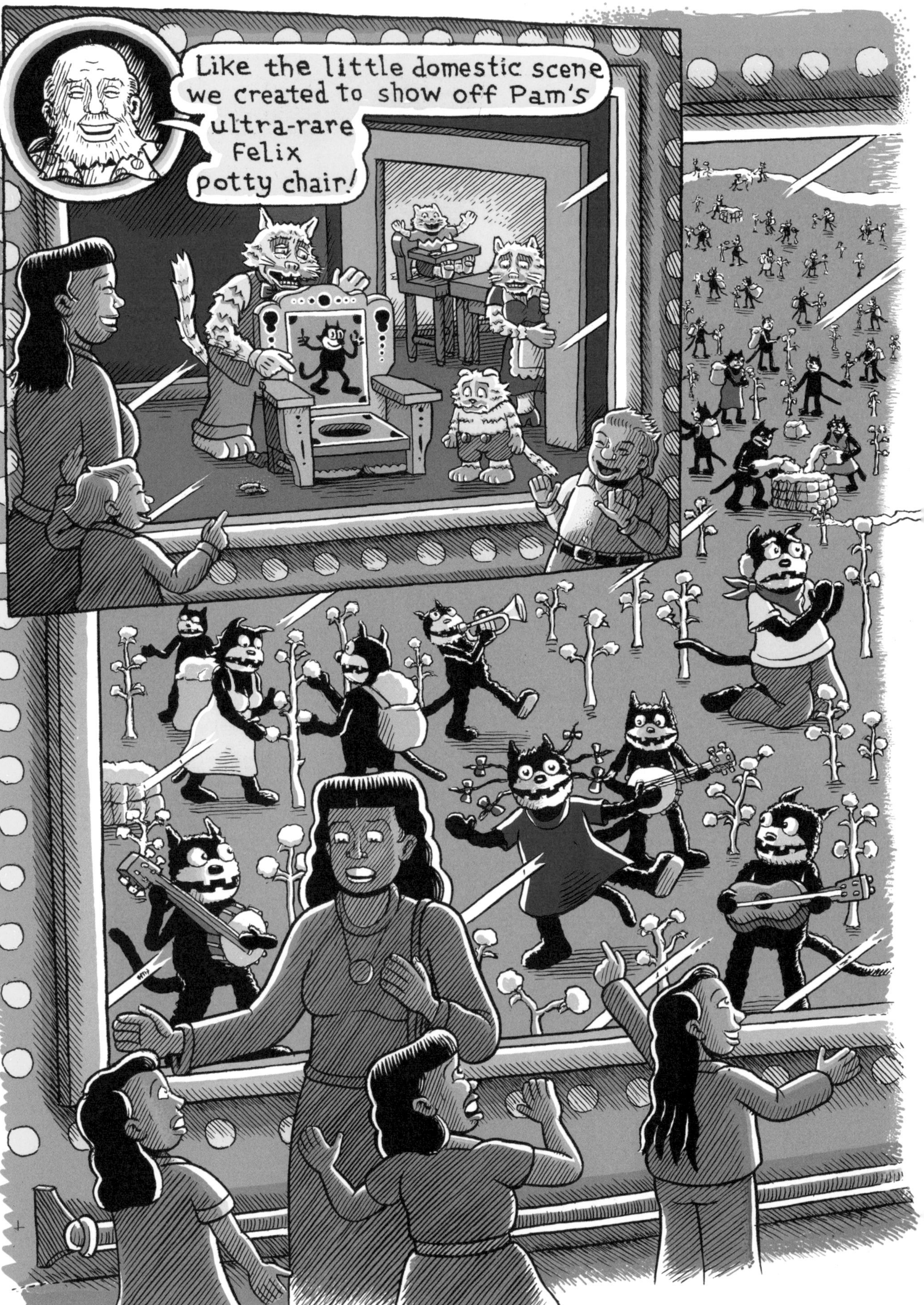
Like the little domestic scene we created to show off Pam's ultra-rare Felix potty chair!

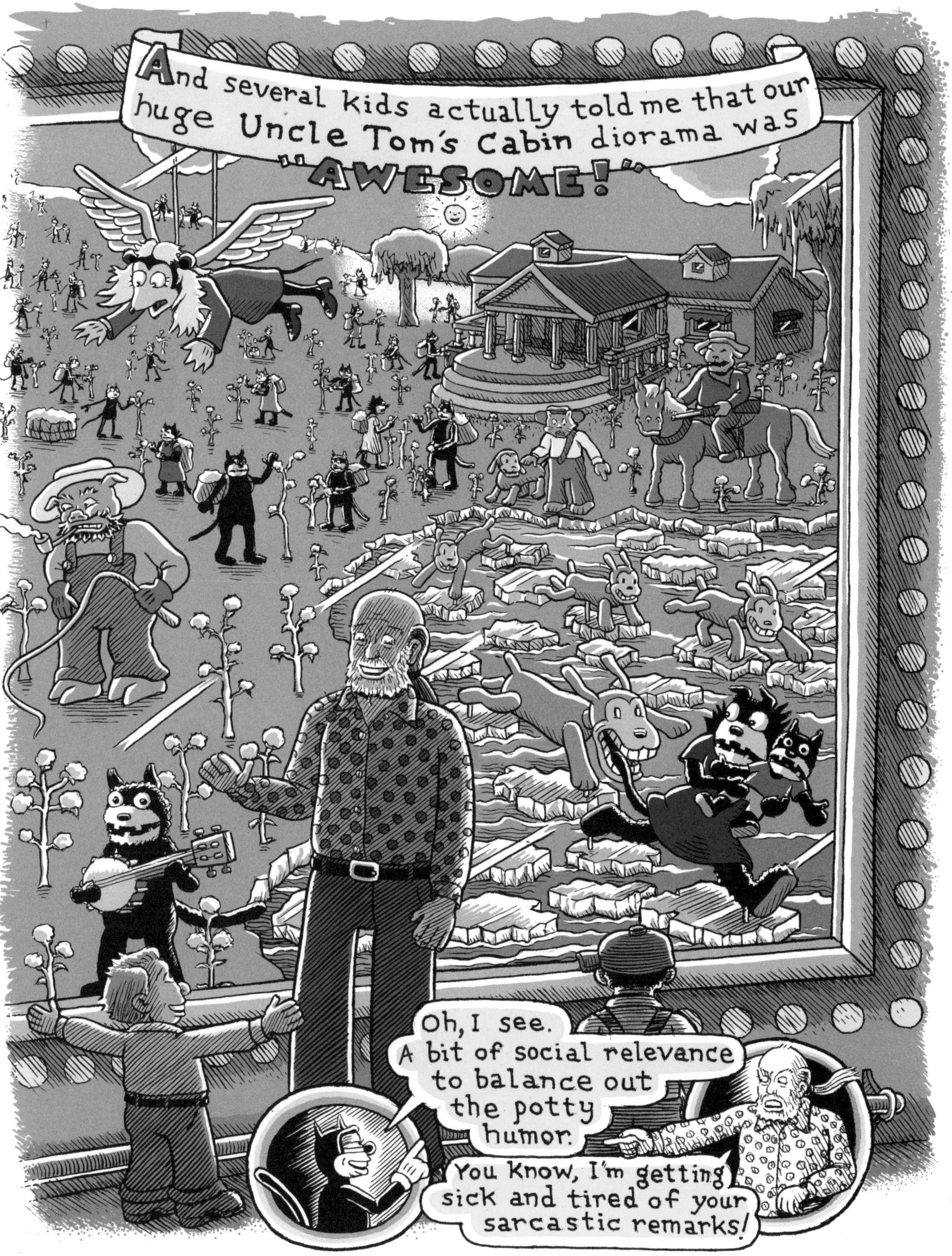
And several kids actually told me that our huge Uncle Tom's Cabin diorama was "AWESOME!"
Oh, I see. A bit of social relevance to balance out the potty humor.
You know, I'm getting sick and tired of your sarcastic remarks!

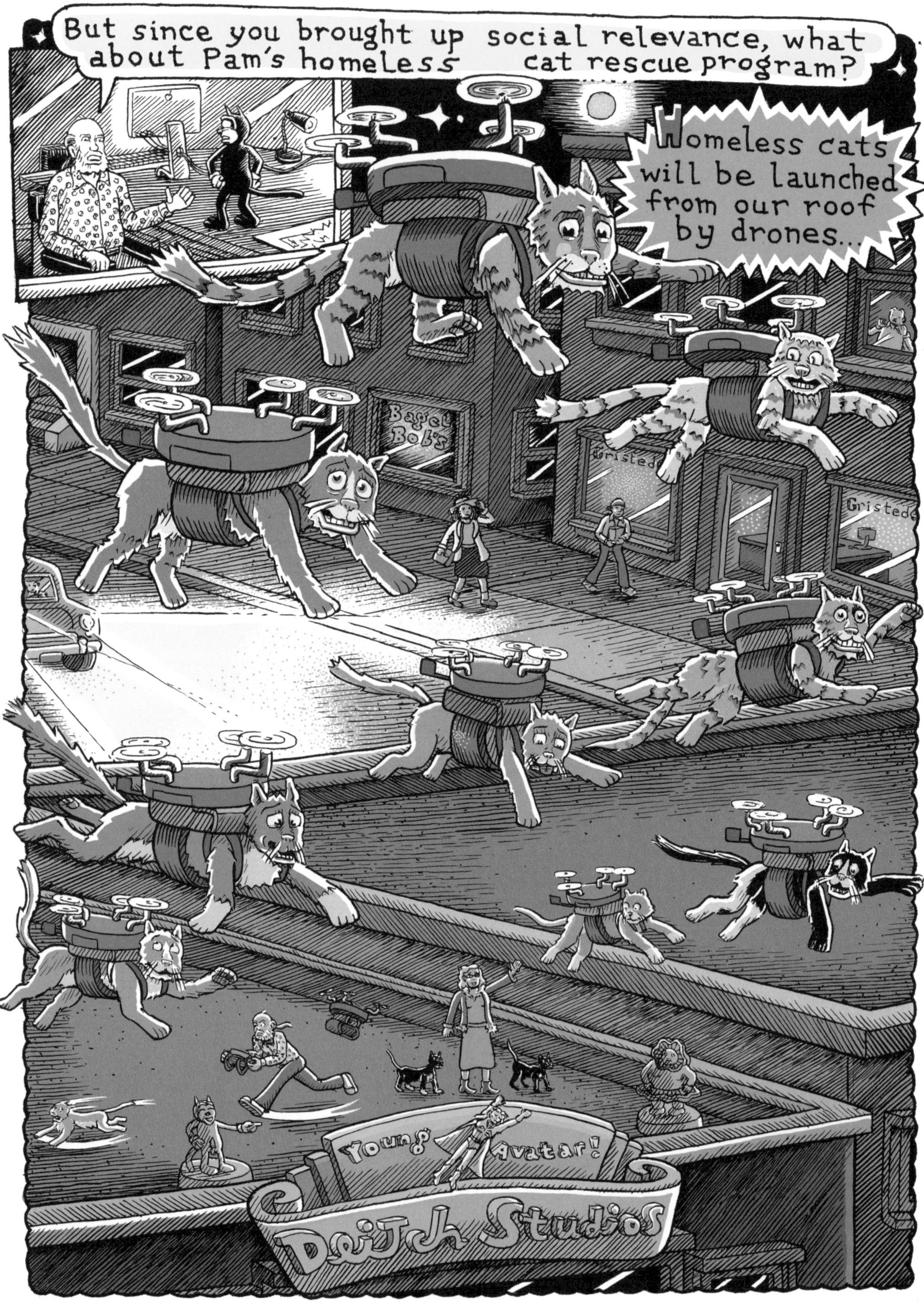
But since you brought up social relevance, what about Pam's homeless cat rescue program?
Homeless cats will be launched from our roof by drones...
Bagel Bob's
Gristede
Gristede
Young Avatar!
Deitch Studios

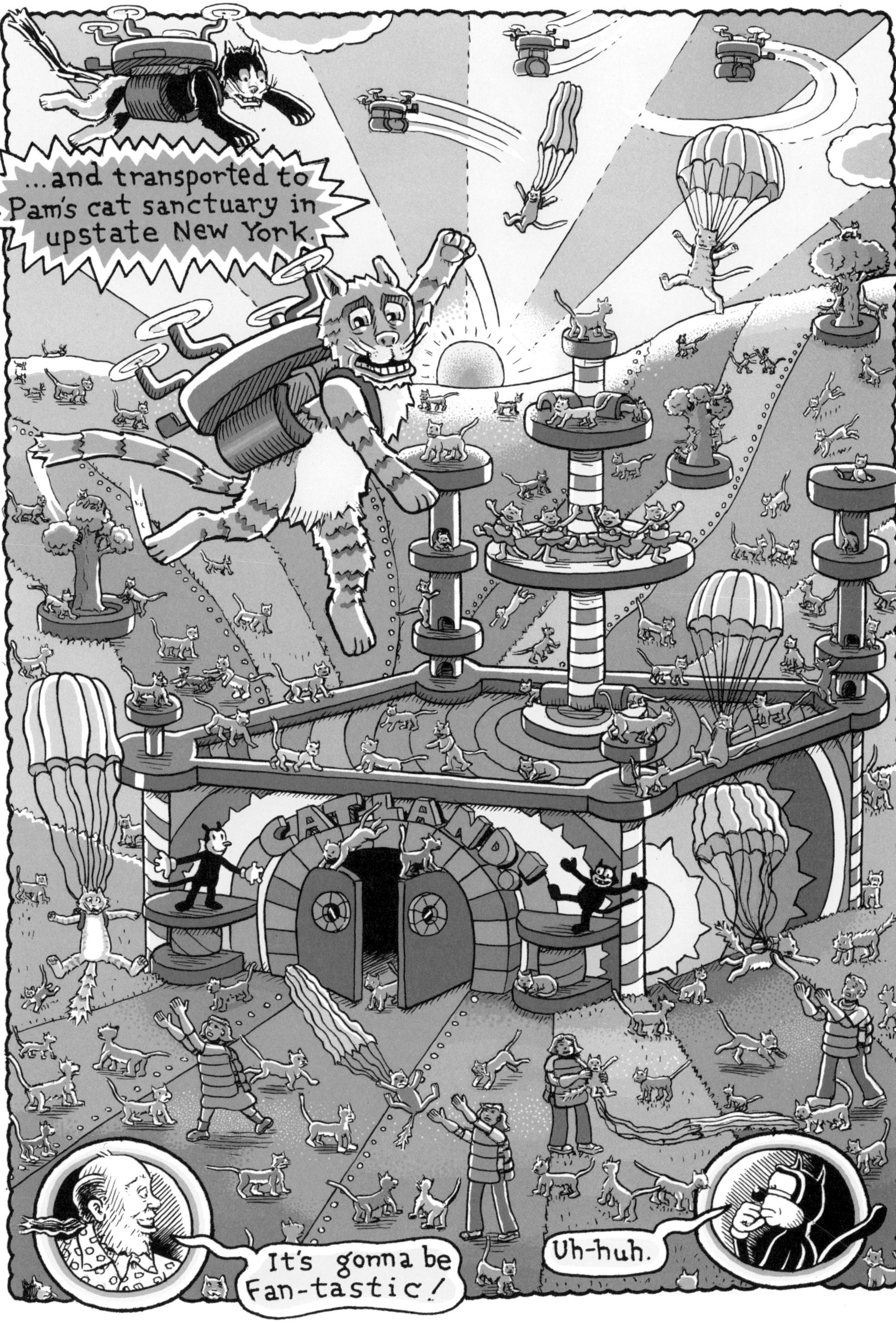
...and transported to Pam's cat sanctuary in upstate New York.
CATLAND
It's gonna be Fan-tastic!
Uh-huh.

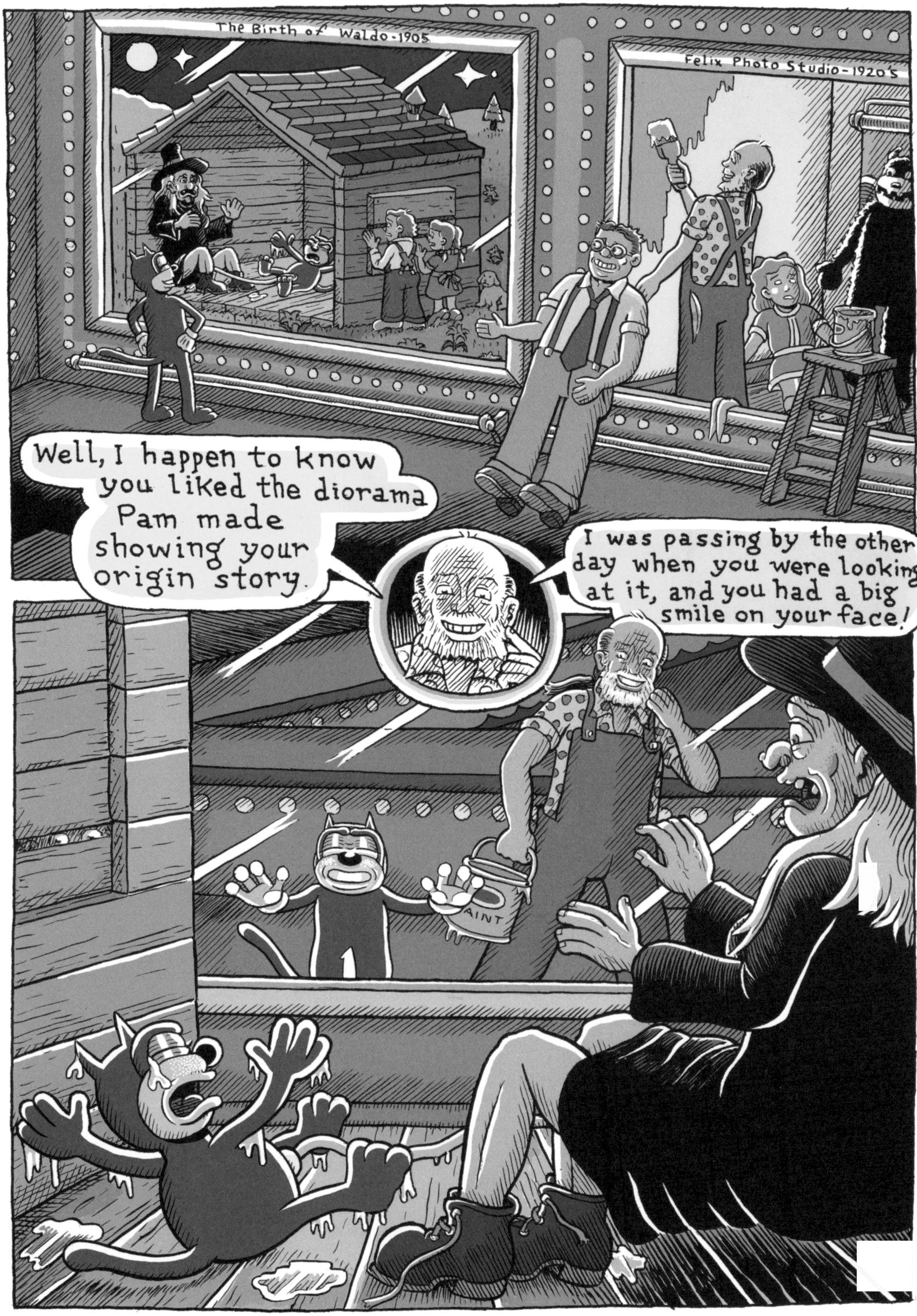
The Birth of Waldo - 1905
Felix Photo Studio - 1920's
Well, I happen to know you liked the diorama Pam made showing your origin story.
I was passing by the other day when you were looking at it, and you had a big smile on your face!
PAINT

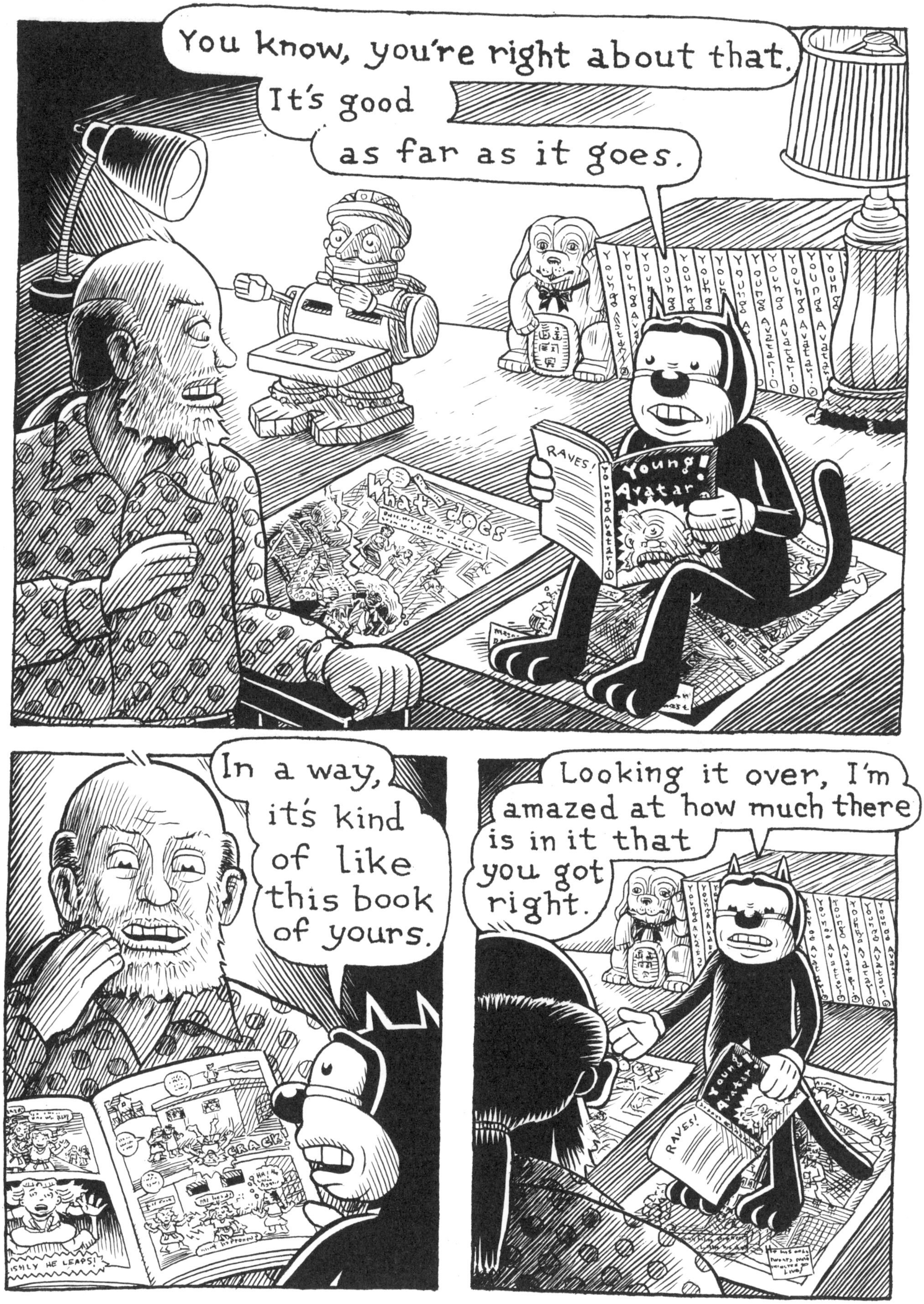
You know, you're right about that.
It's good
as far as it goes.
RAVES!
Young! Avatar
In a way, it's kind of like this book of yours.
CRACK!
Looking it over, I'm amazed at how much there is in it that you got right.
RAVES!

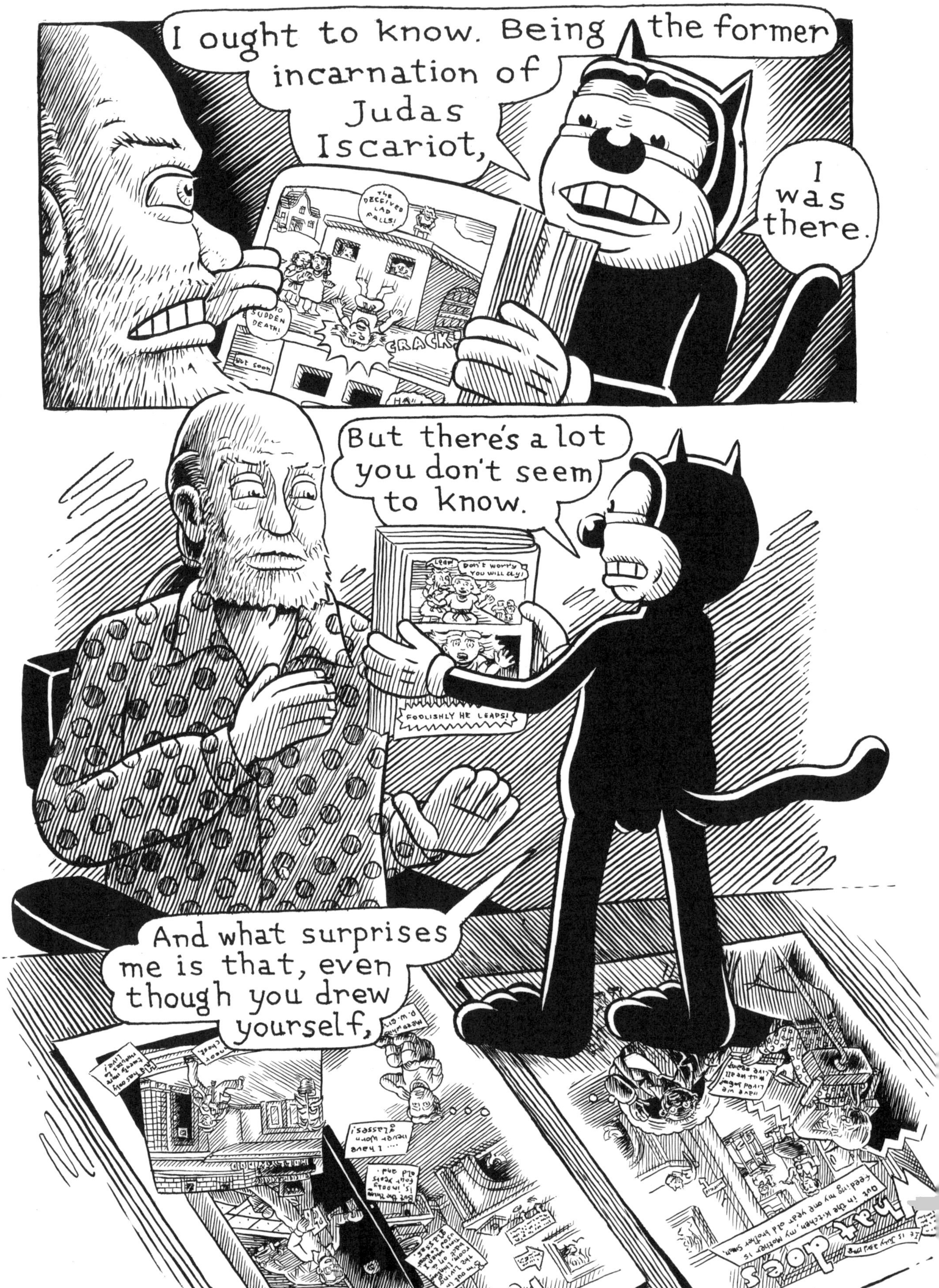

I ought to know. Being the former incarnation of Judas Iscariot,
I was there.
THE DECEIVED LAD FALLS!
TO SUDDEN DEATH!
CRACK
But there's a lot you don't seem to know.
Leap!
Don't worry you will fly!
FOOLISHLY HE LEAPS!
And what surprises me is that, even though you drew yourself,

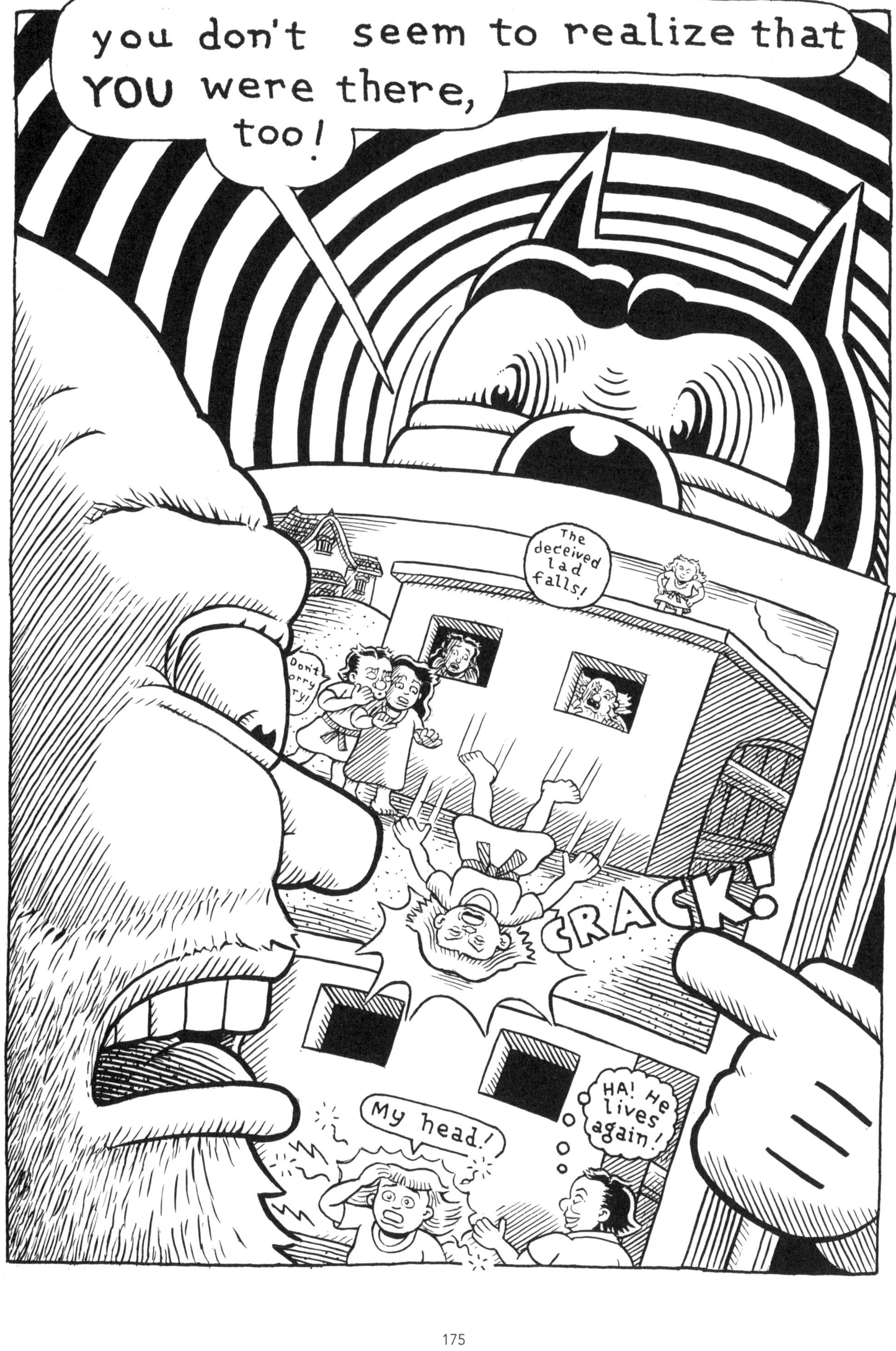
you don't seem to realize that YOU were there, too!
The deceived lad falls!
Don't
CRACK!
My head!
HA! He lives again!

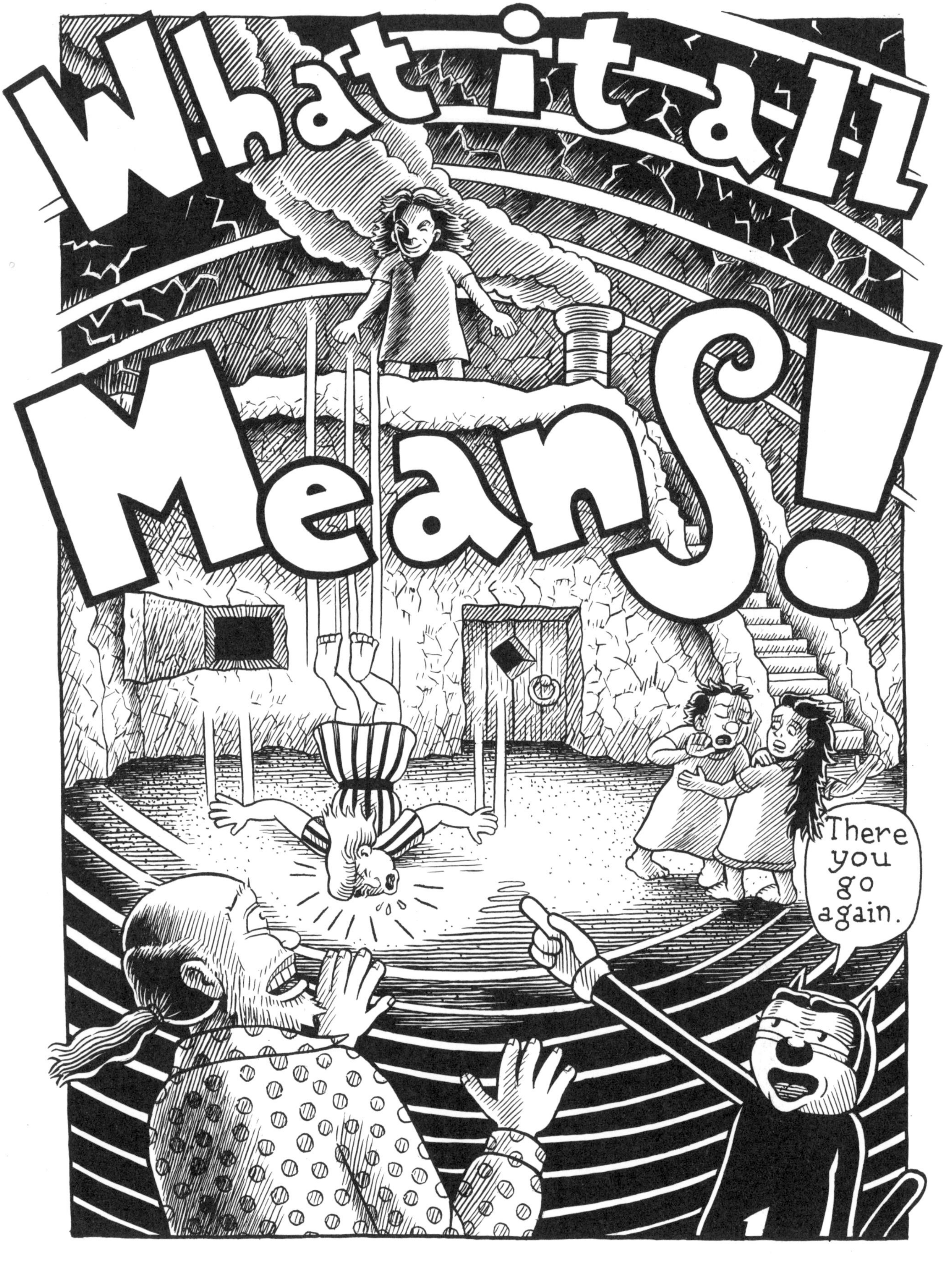
What it all Means!
There you go again.

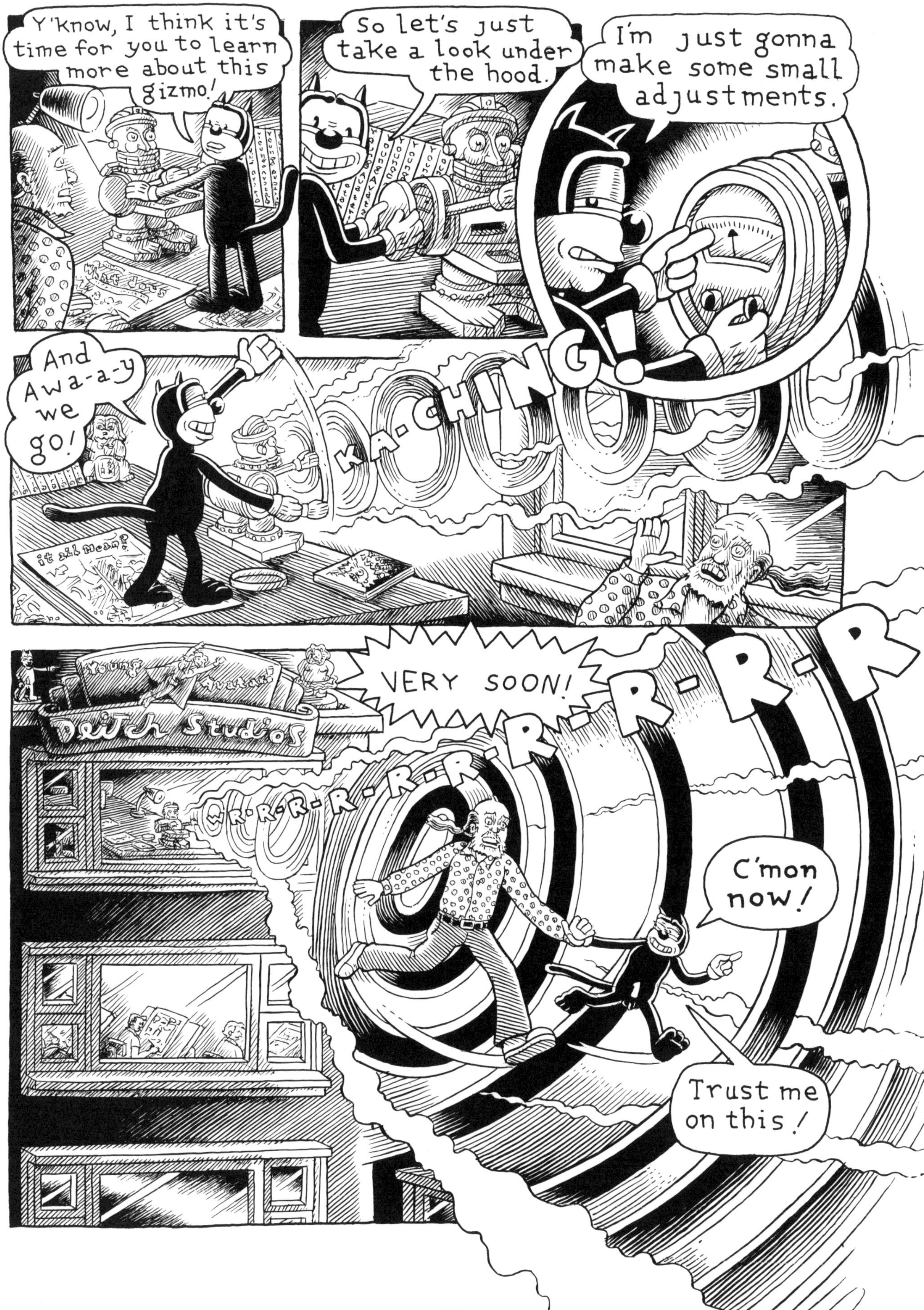

Y'know, I think it's time for you to learn more about this gizmo!
So let's just take a look under the hood.
I'm just gonna make some small adjustments.
KA-CHING!
And Awa-a-y we go!
it all Mean?
Deitch Studios
VERY SOON!
W-R-R-R-R-R-R-R-R-R-R-R-R
C'mon now!
Trust me on this!

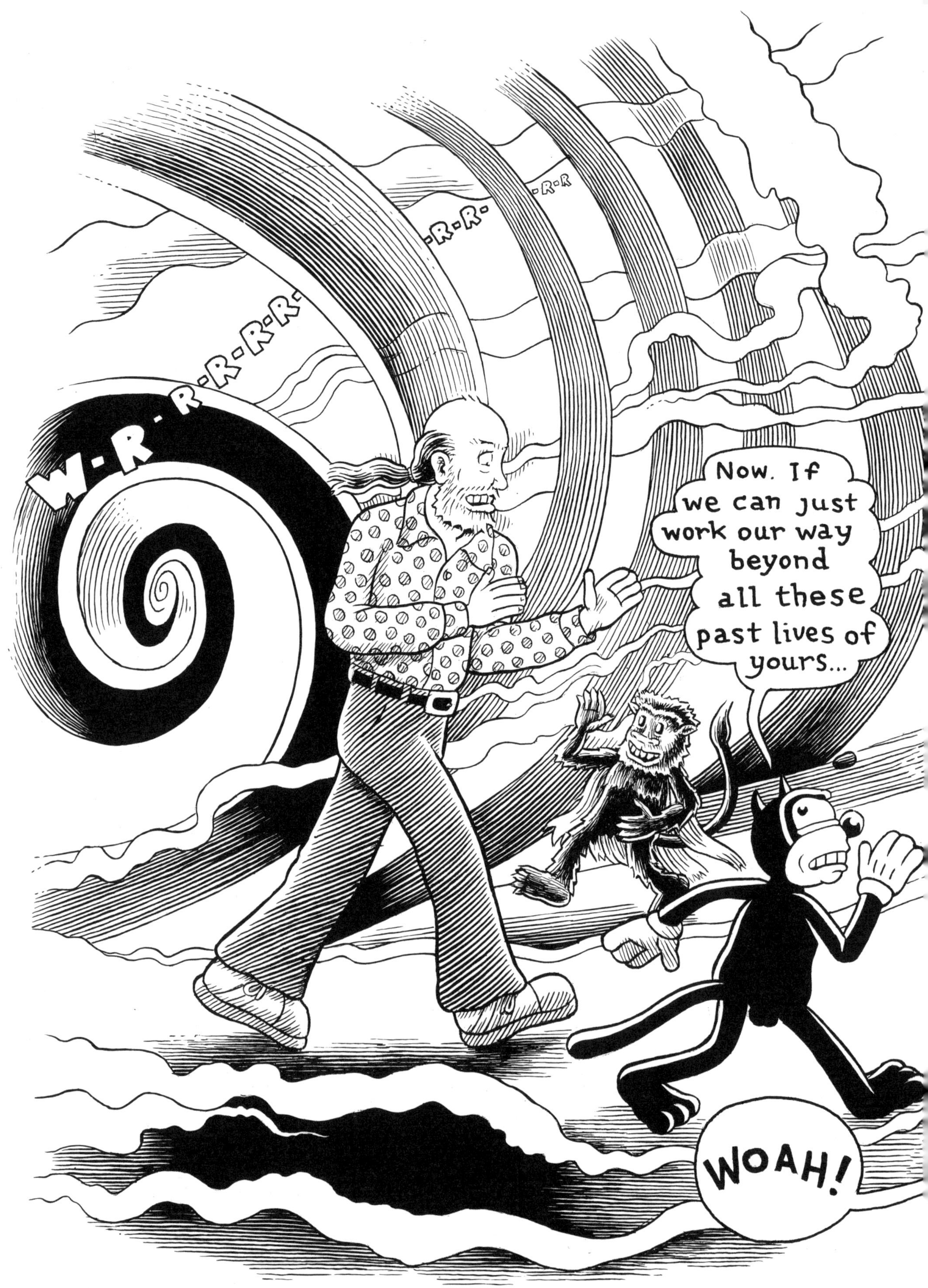
W-R-R-R-R-R-R-R-R-R
Now. If we can just work our way beyond all these past lives of yours...
WOAH!

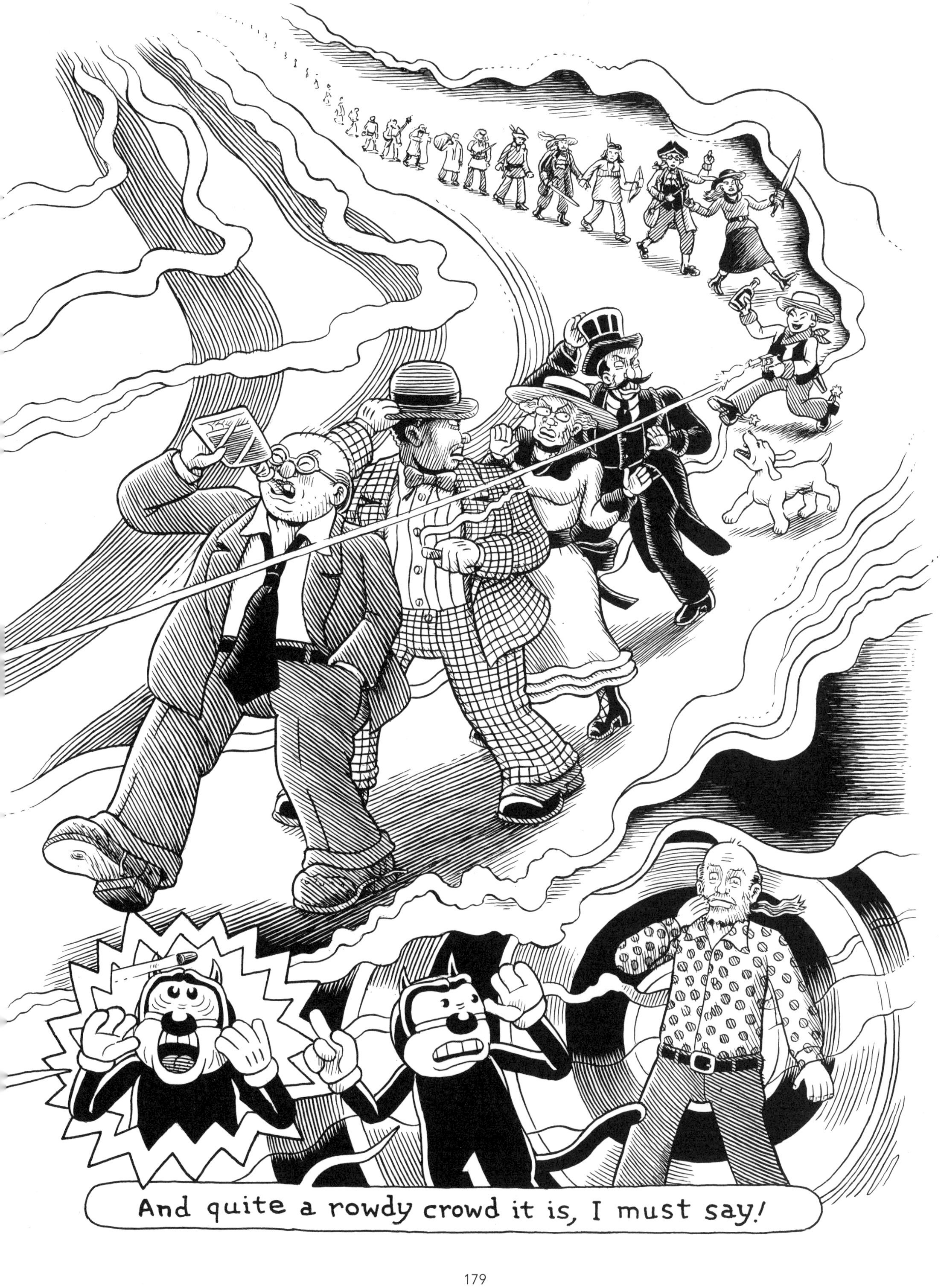
And quite a rowdy crowd it is, I must say!

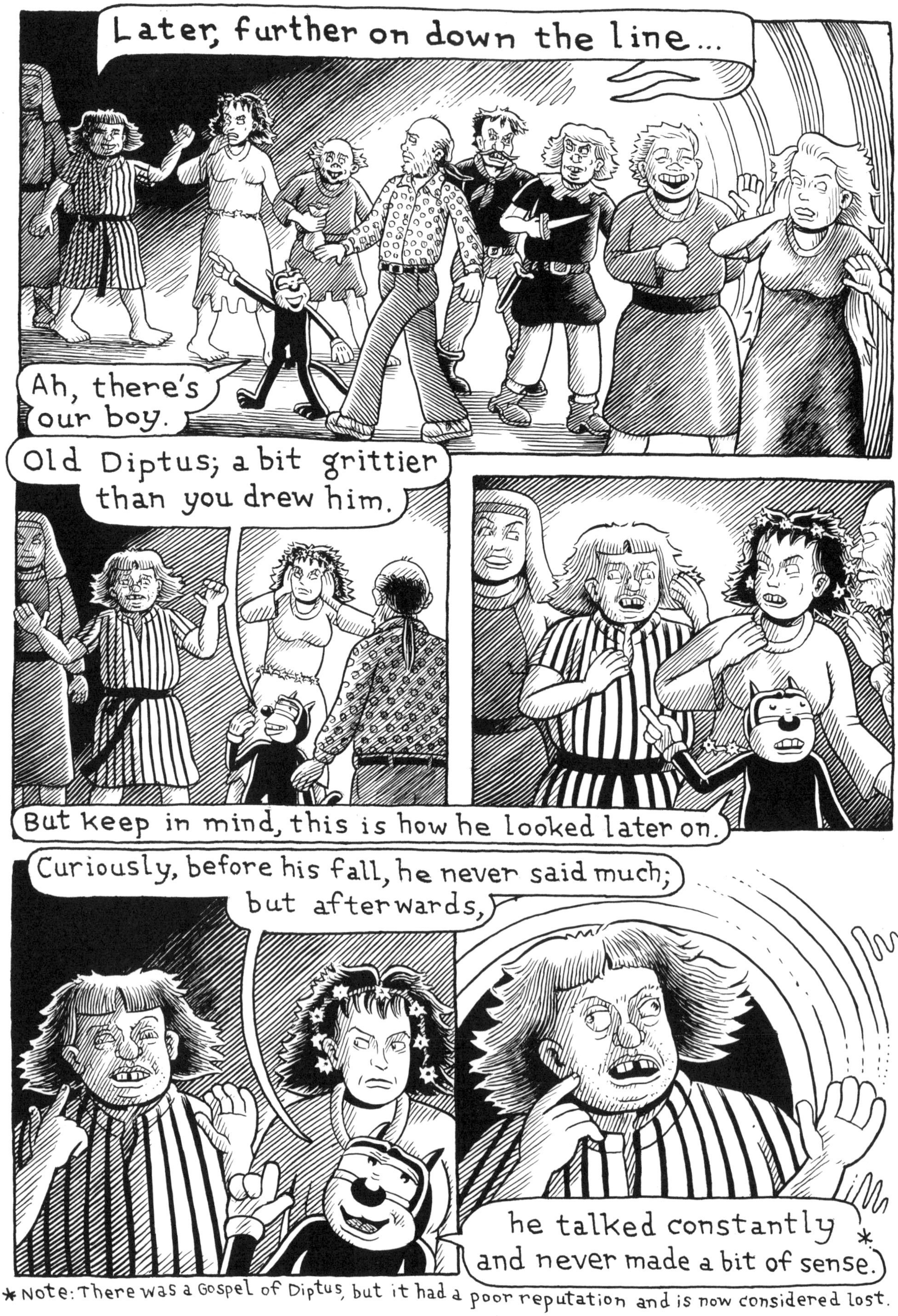
Later, further on down the line...
Ah, there's our boy.
Old Diptus; a bit grittier than you drew him.
But keep in mind, this is how he looked later on.
Curiously, before his fall, he never said much; but afterwards,
he talked constantly and never made a bit of sense.*

* Note: There was a Gospel of Diptus, but it had a poor reputation and is now considered lost.

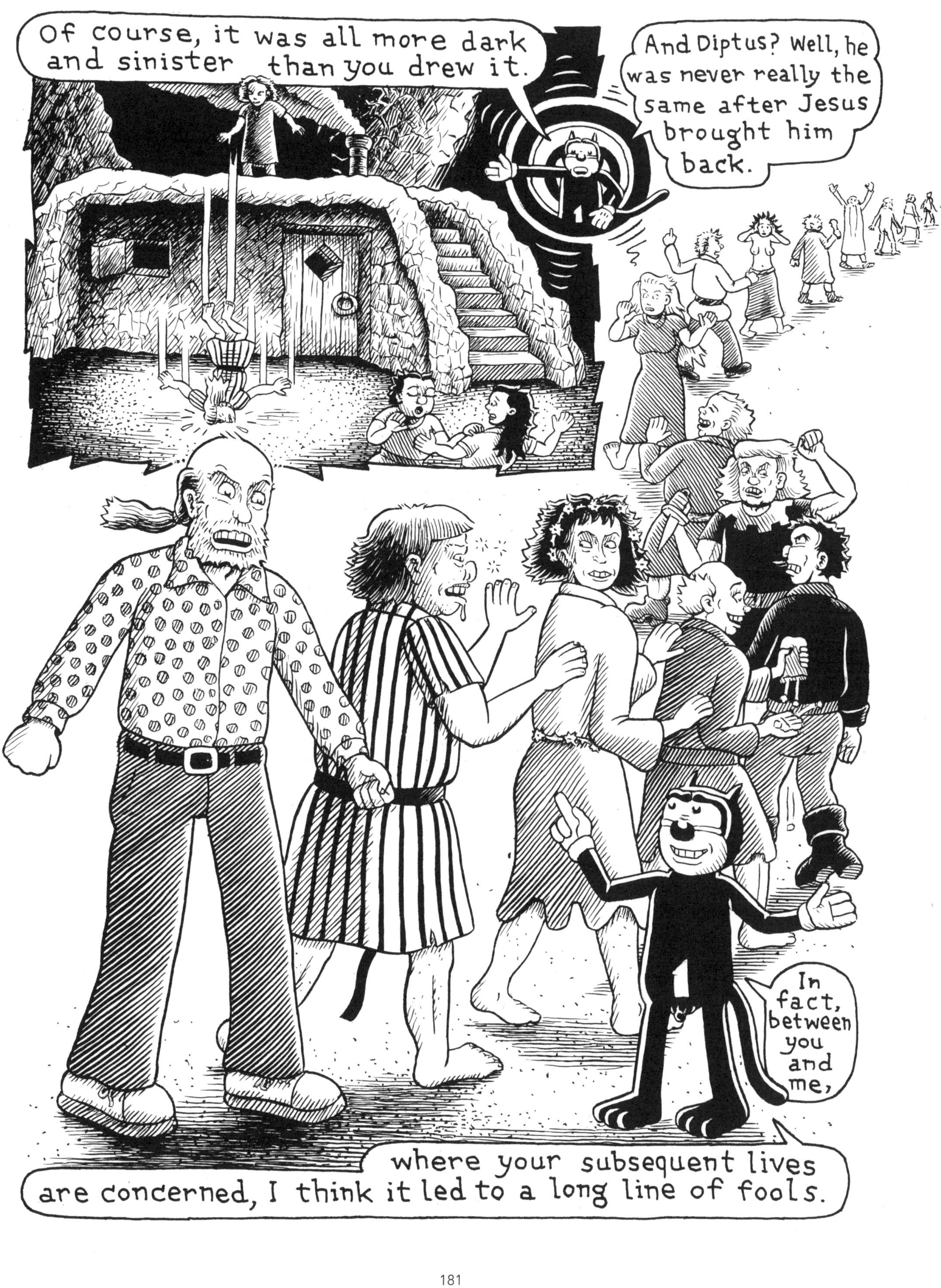
Of course, it was all more dark and sinister than you drew it.
And Diptus? Well, he was never really the same after Jesus brought him back.
In fact, between you and me,
where your subsequent lives are concerned, I think it led to a long line of fools.

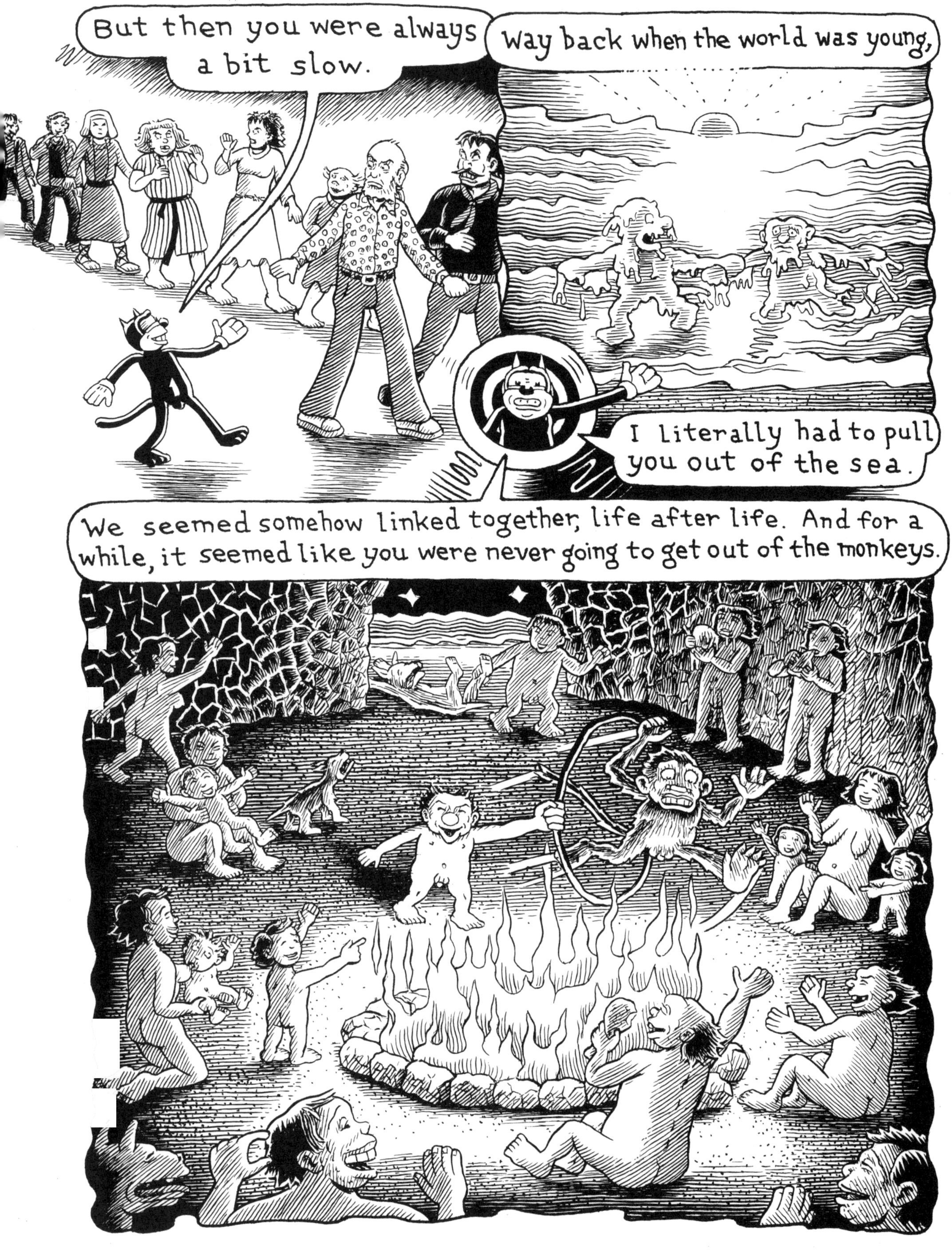
But then you were always a bit slow.
Way back when the world was young,
I literally had to pull you out of the sea.
We seemed somehow linked together, life after life. And for a while, it seemed like you were never going to get out of the monkeys.

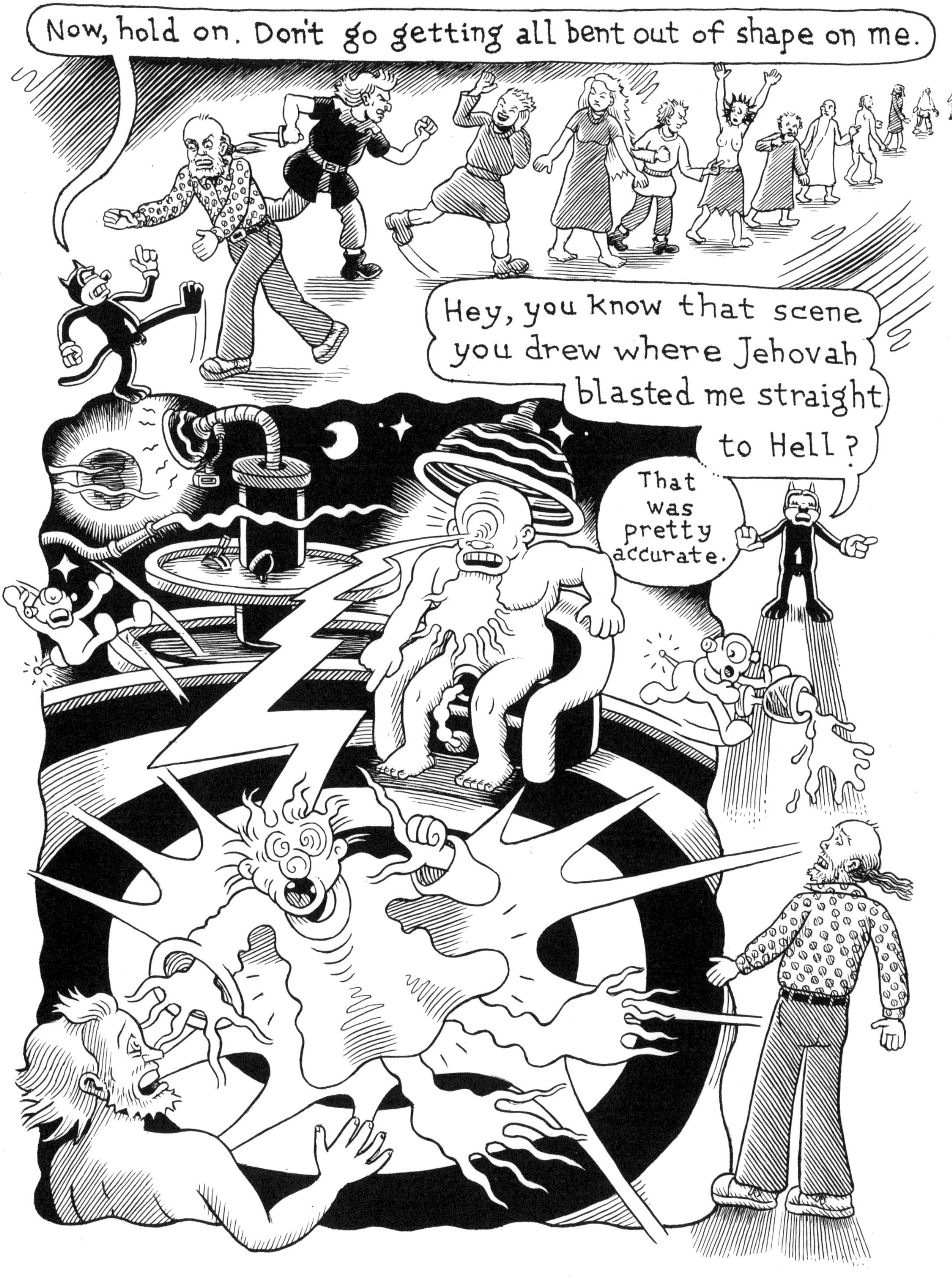
Now, hold on. Don't go getting all bent out of shape on me.
Hey, you know that scene you drew where Jehovah blasted me straight to Hell?
That was pretty accurate.

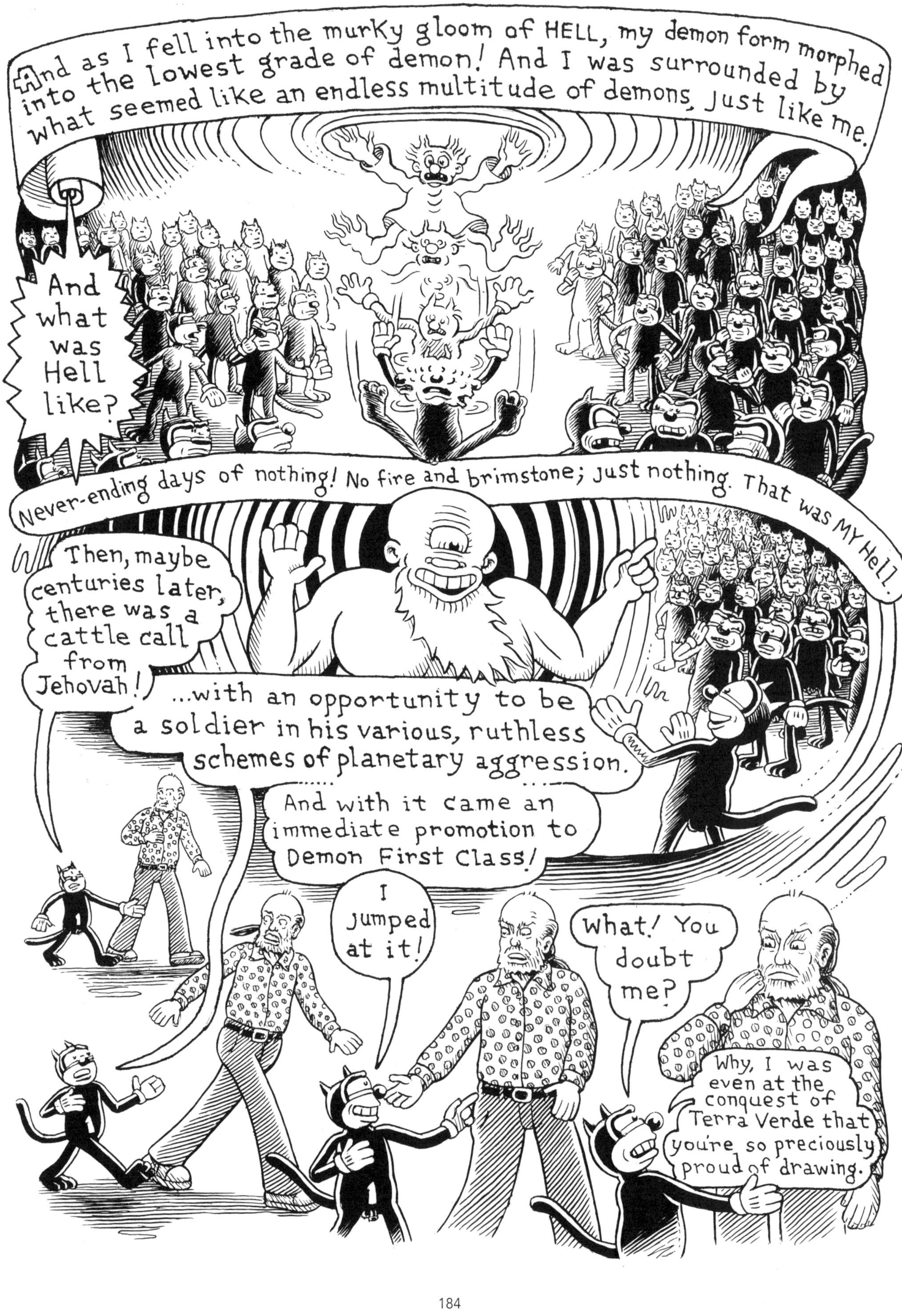
And as I fell into the murky gloom of HELL, my demon form morphed into the lowest grade of demon! And I was surrounded by what seemed like an endless multitude of demons, just like me.
And what was Hell like?
Never-ending days of nothing! No fire and brimstone; just nothing. That was MY Hell.
Then, maybe centuries later, there was a cattle call from Jehovah!
...with an opportunity to be a soldier in his various, ruthless schemes of planetary aggression.
And with it came an immediate promotion to Demon First Class!
I jumped at it!
What! You doubt me?
Why, I was even at the conquest of Terra Verde that you're so preciously proud of drawing.

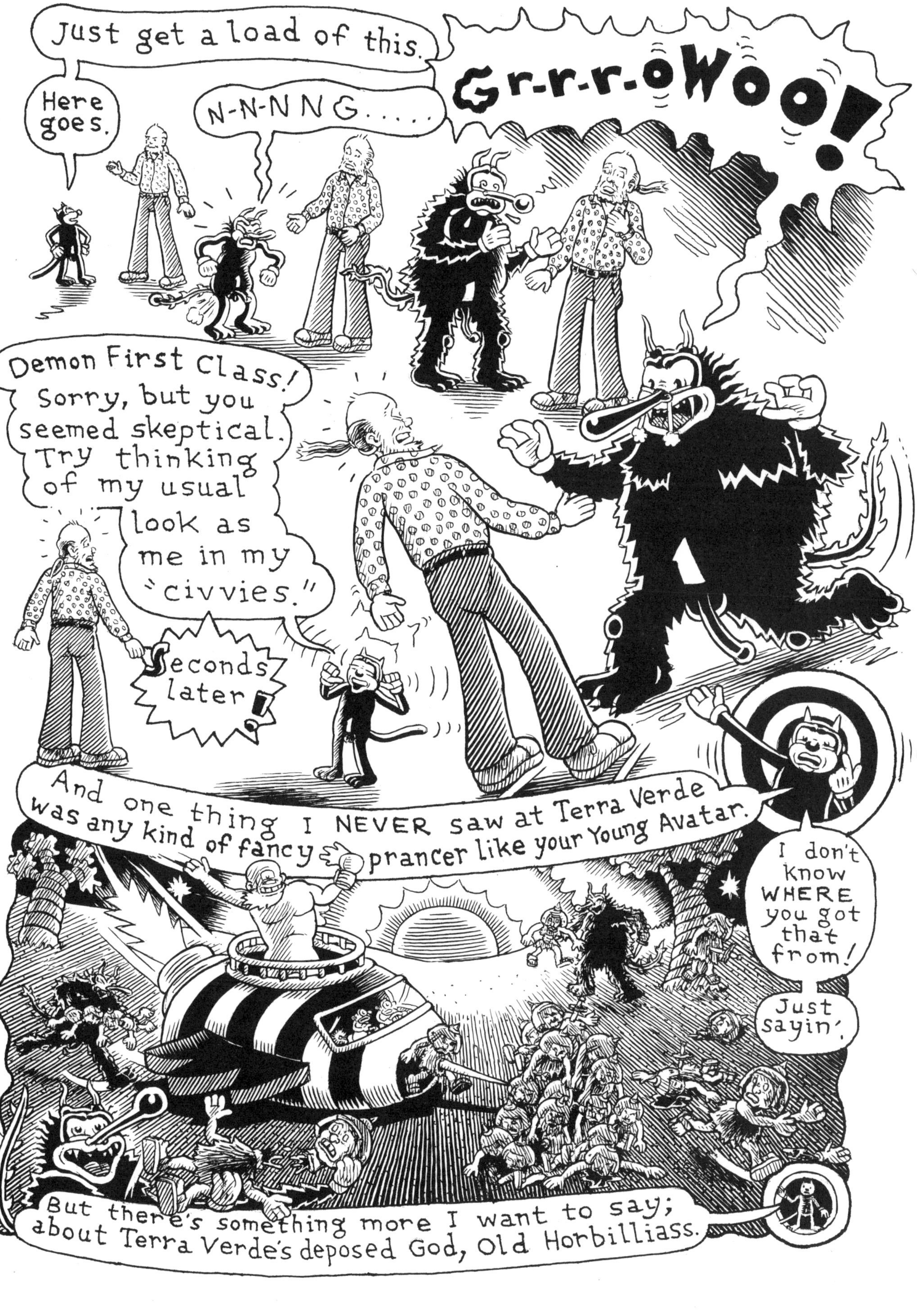
Just get a load of this.
Here goes.
N-N-N N G.....
Gr-r-r-oWOO!
Demon First Class! Sorry, but you seemed skeptical. Try thinking of my usual look as me in my "civvies."
Seconds later!
And one thing I NEVER saw at Terra Verde was any kind of fancy prancer like your Young Avatar.
I don't know WHERE you got that from!
Just sayin'.
But there's something more I want to say; about Terra Verde's deposed God, Old Horbilliass.

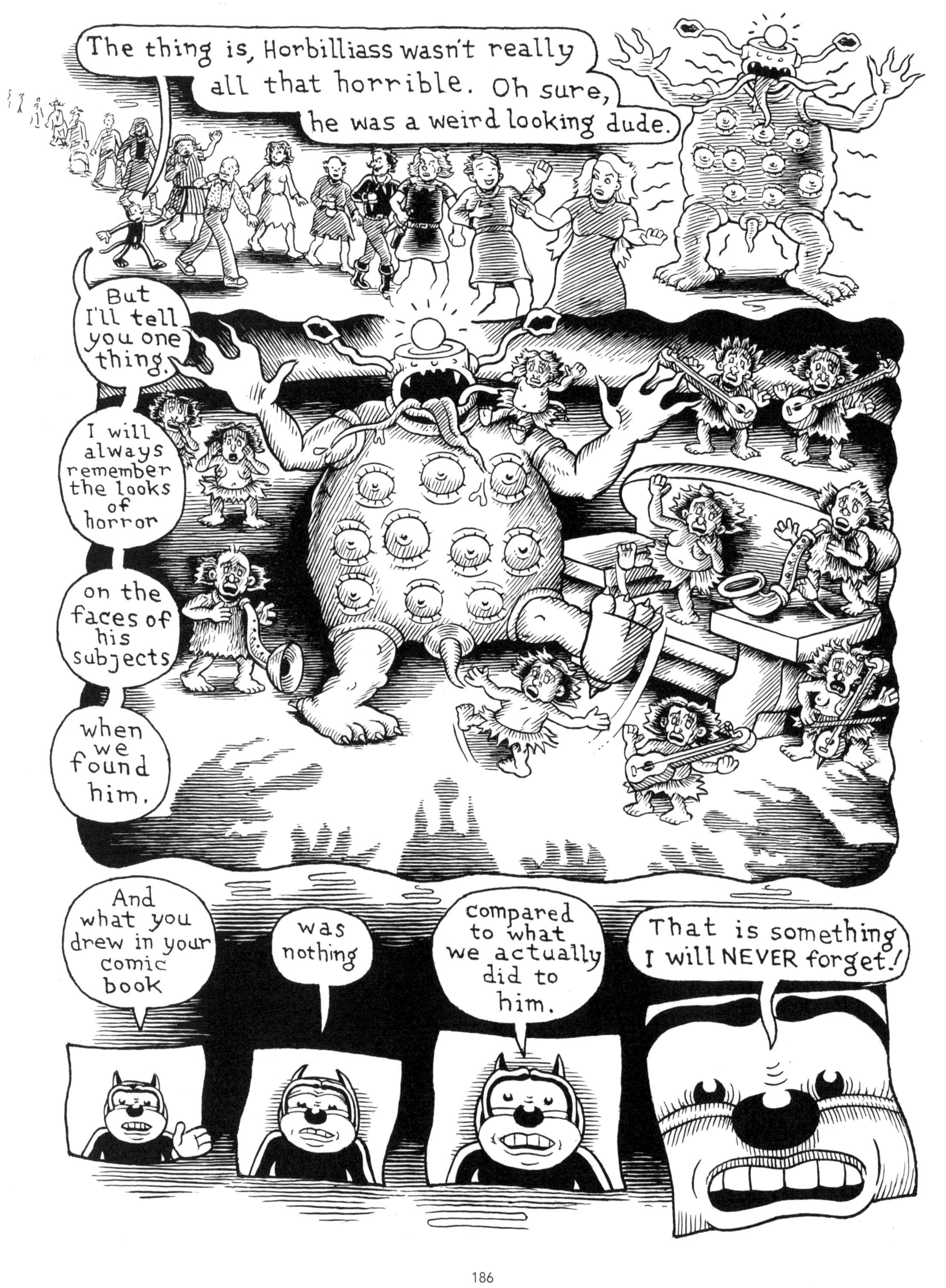

The thing is, Horbilliass wasn't really all that horrible. Oh sure, he was a weird looking dude.
But I'll tell you one thing.
I will always remember the looks of horror
on the faces of his subjects
when we found him.
And what you drew in your comic book
was nothing
compared to what we actually did to him.
That is something I will NEVER forget!

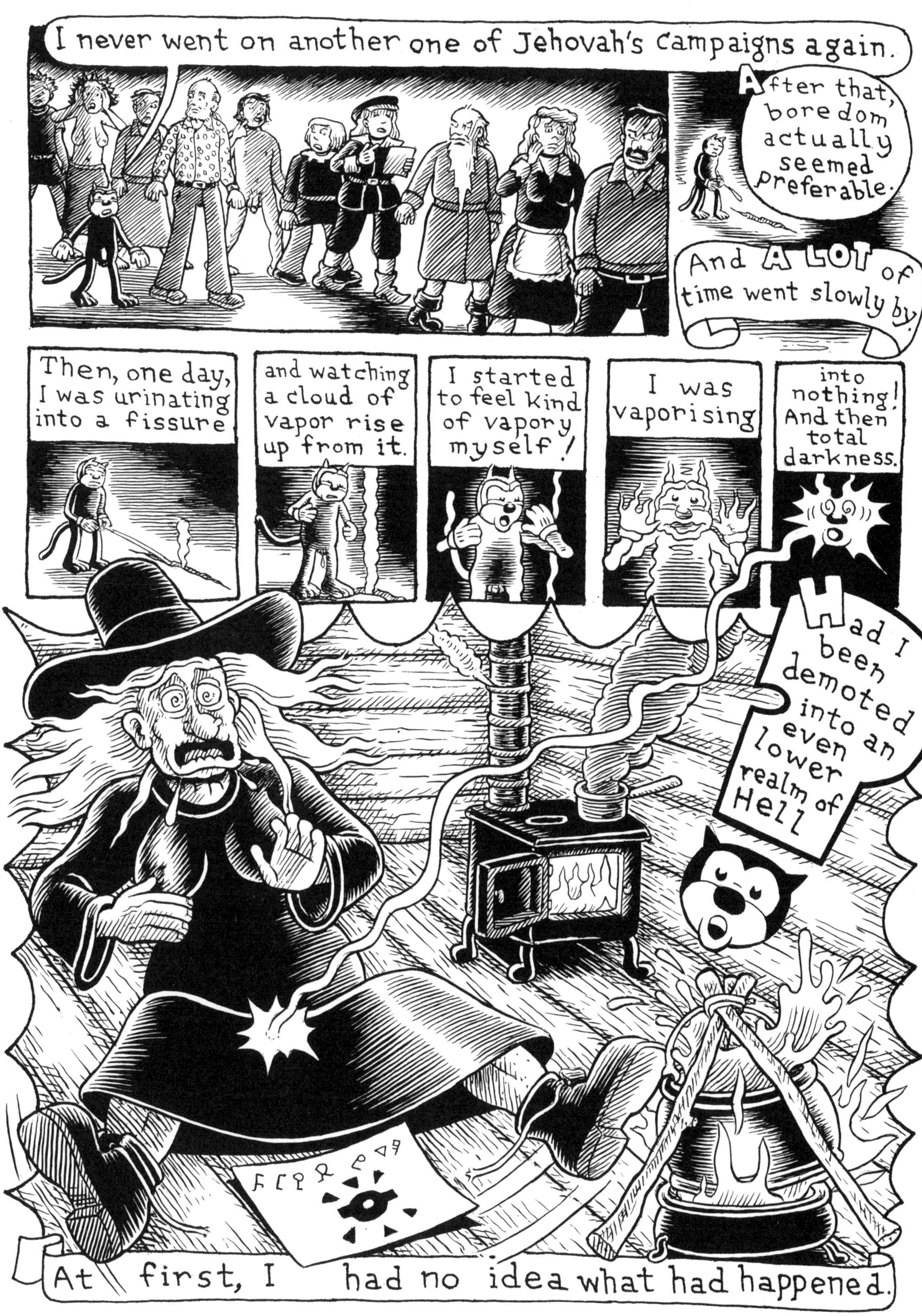

I never went on another one of Jehovah's campaigns again.
After that, boredom actually seemed preferable.
And A LOT of time went slowly by.
Then, one day, I was urinating into a fissure
and watching a cloud of vapor rise up from it.
I started to feel kind of vapory myself!
I was vaporising
into nothing! And then total darkness.
Had I been demoted into an even lower realm of Hell
At first, I had no idea what had happened.

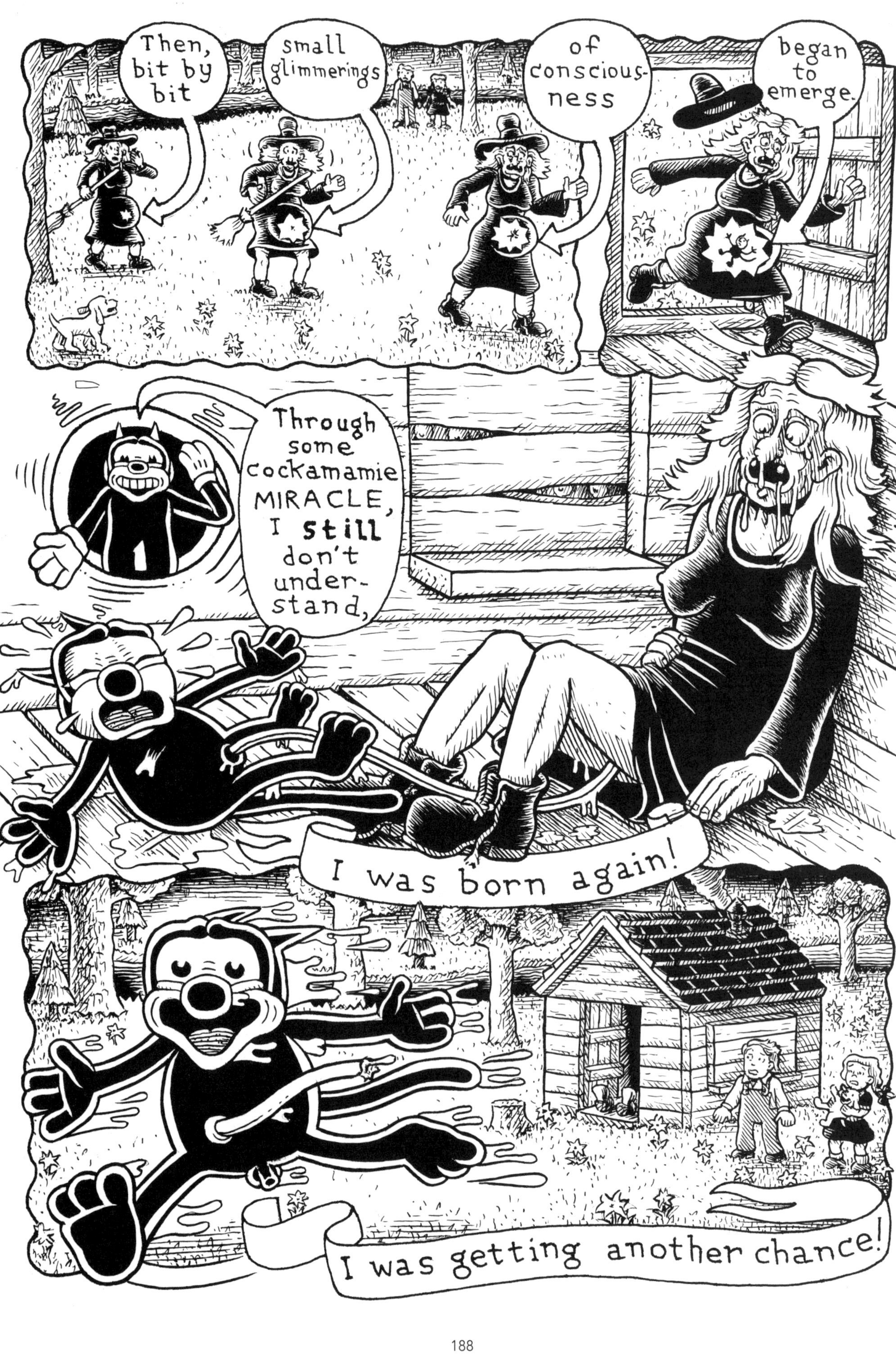
Then, bit by bit
small glimmerings
of consciousness
began to emerge.
Through some cockamamie MIRACLE, I still don't understand,
I was born again!
I was getting another chance!

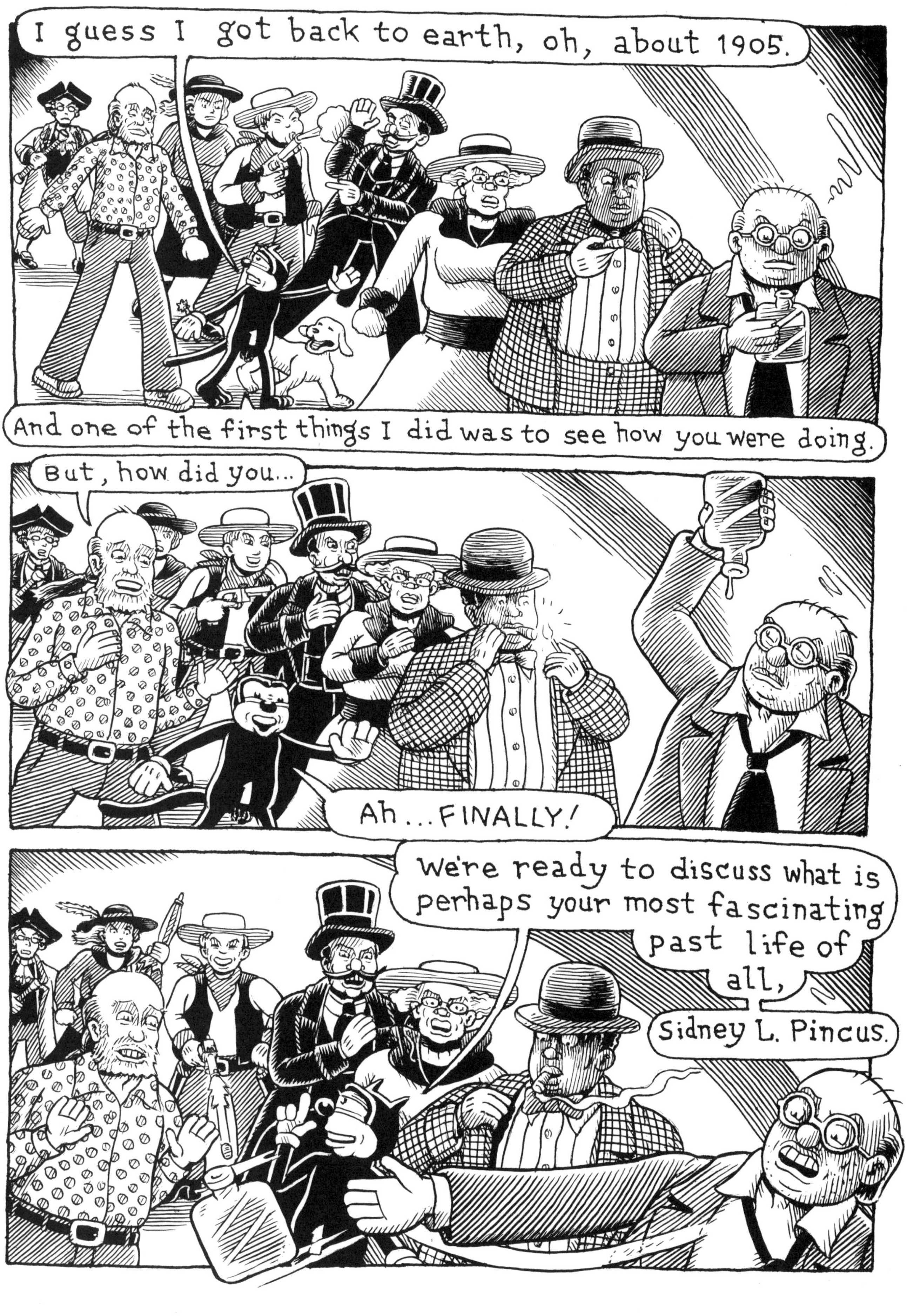

I guess I got back to earth, oh, about 1905.
And one of the first things I did was to see how you were doing.
But, how did you...
Ah... FINALLY!
We're ready to discuss what is perhaps your most fascinating past life of all,
Sidney L. Pincus.

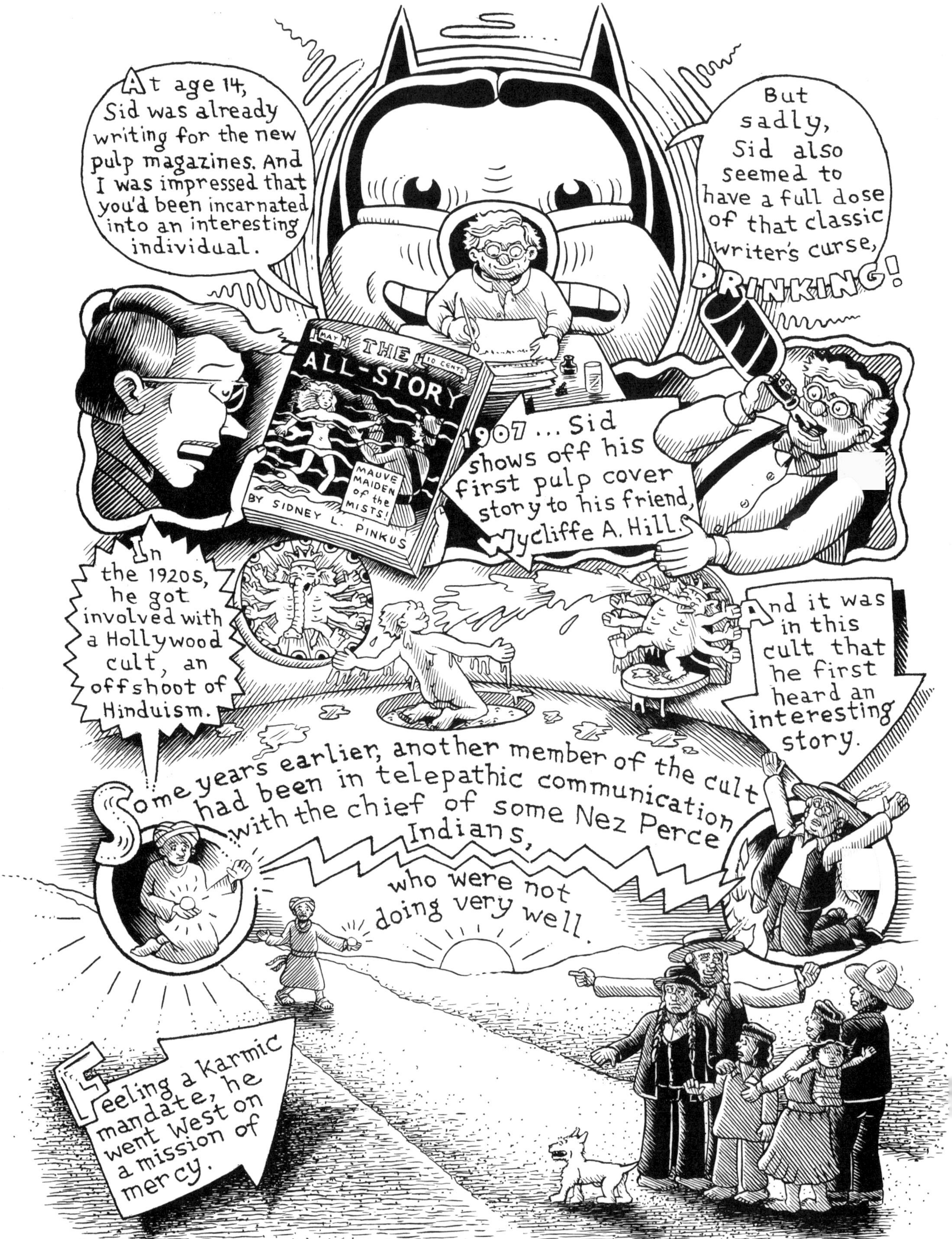
At age 14, Sid was already writing for the new pulp magazines. And I was impressed that you'd been incarnated into an interesting individual.
But sadly, Sid also seemed to have a full dose of that classic writer's curse,
DRINKING!
MAY THE ALL-STORY 10 CENTS
MAUVE MAIDEN of the MISTS!
BY SIDNEY L. PINKUS
1907 ... Sid shows off his first pulp cover story to his friend, Wycliffe A. Hill.
In the 1920s, he got involved with a Hollywood cult, an offshoot of Hinduism.
And it was in this cult that he first heard an interesting story.
Some years earlier, another member of the cult had been in telepathic communication with the chief of some Nez Perce Indians,
who were not doing very well.
Feeling a karmic mandate, he went West on a mission of mercy.

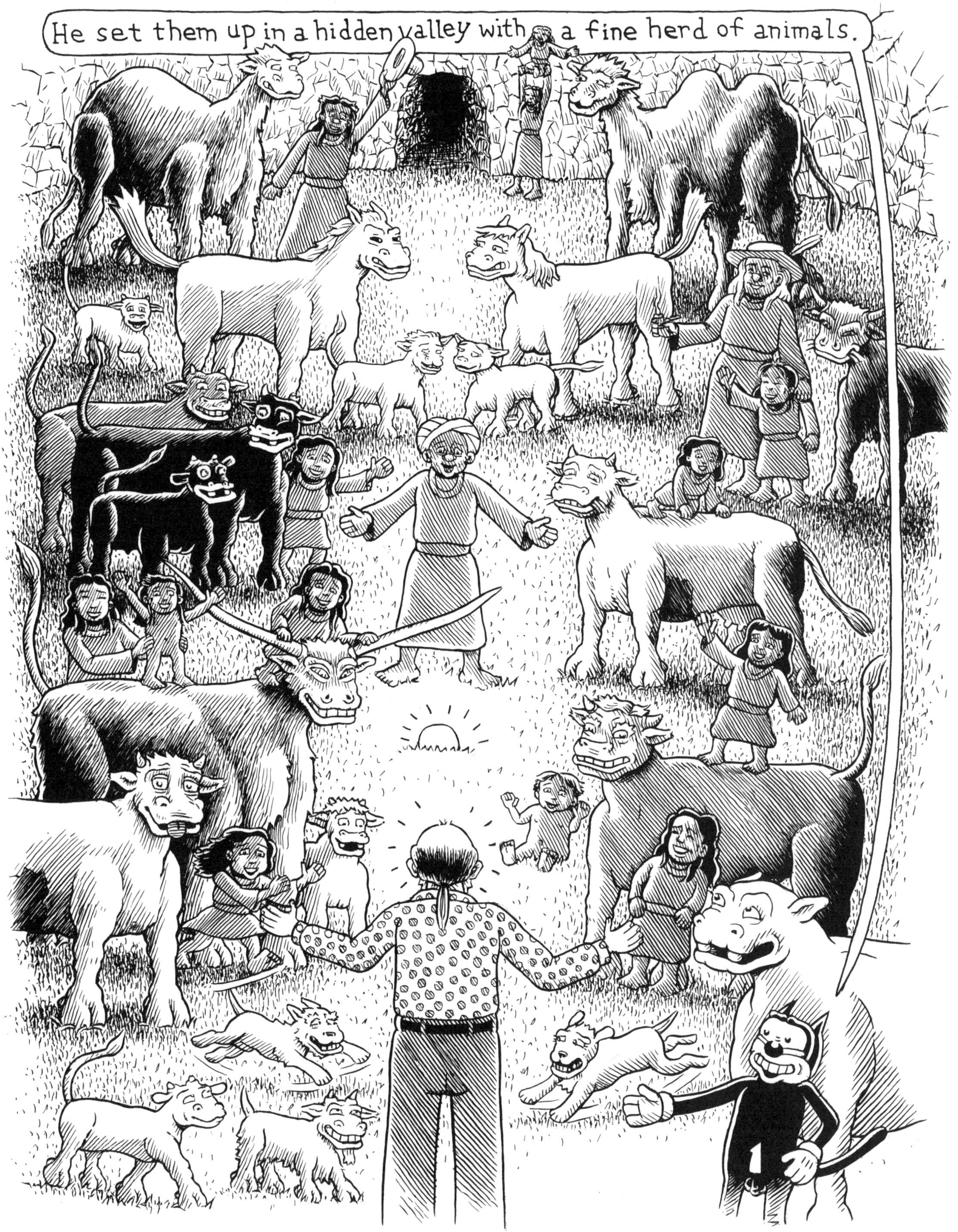
He set them up in a hidden valley with a fine herd of animals.

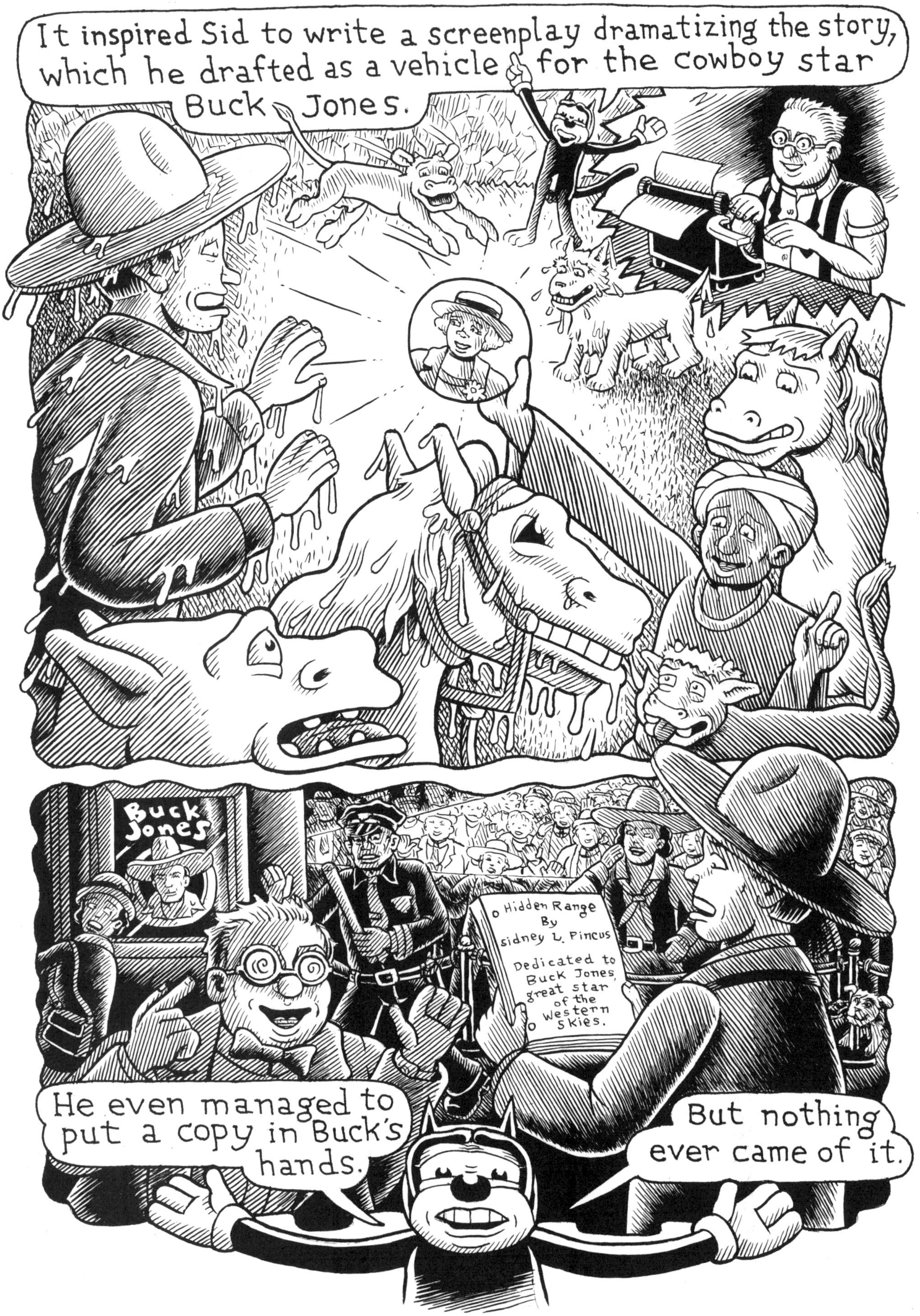
It inspired Sid to write a screenplay dramatizing the story, which he drafted as a vehicle for the cowboy star Buck Jones.
Buck Jones
Hidden Range
By
Sidney L. Pincus
Dedicated to
Buck Jones,
great star
of the
Western
Skies.
He even managed to put a copy in Buck's hands.
But nothing ever came of it.

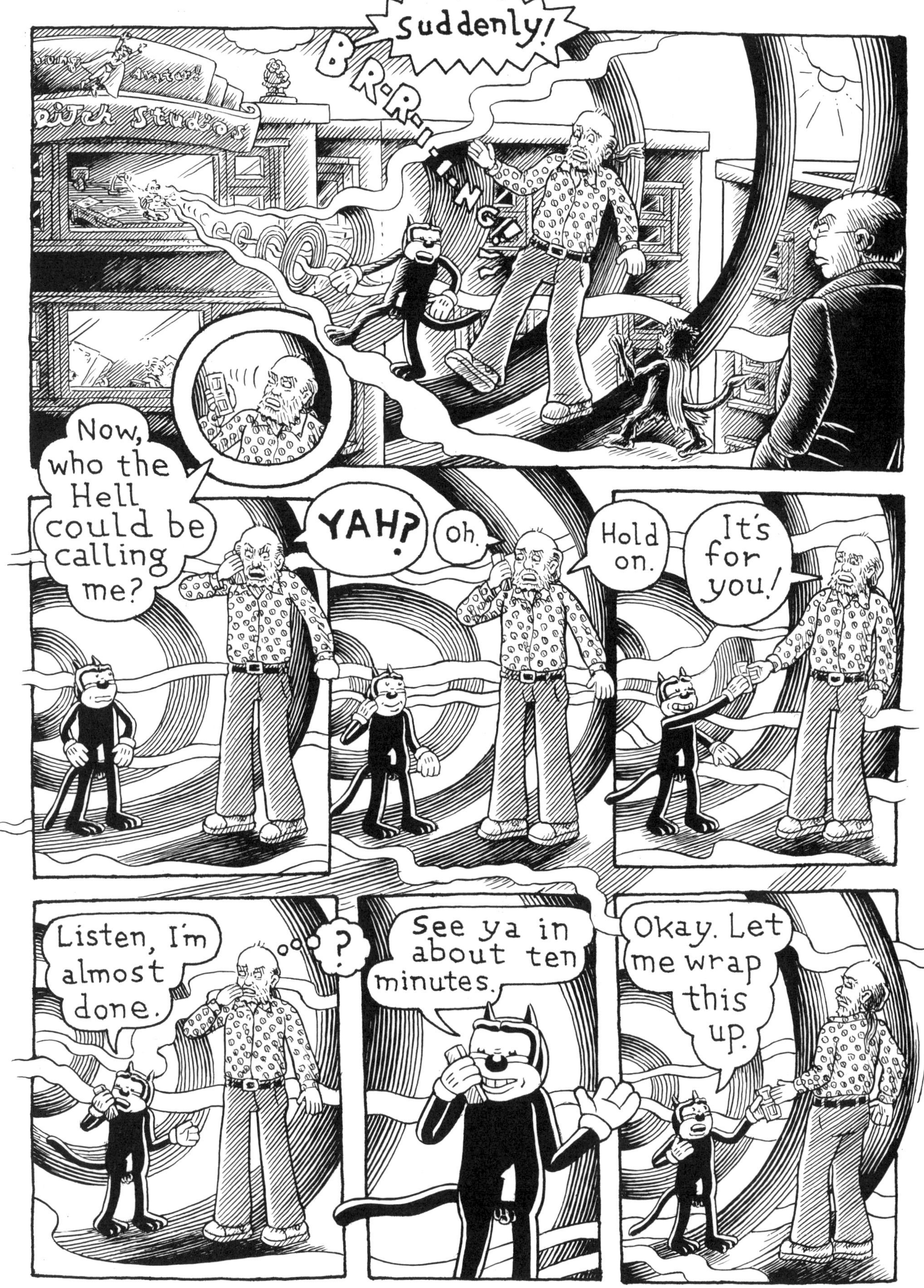
Suddenly!
B-R-R-I-I-N-G!!
Now, who the Hell could be calling me?
YAH?
Oh.
Hold on.
It's for you!
Listen, I'm almost done.
?
See ya in about ten minutes.
Okay. Let me wrap this up.

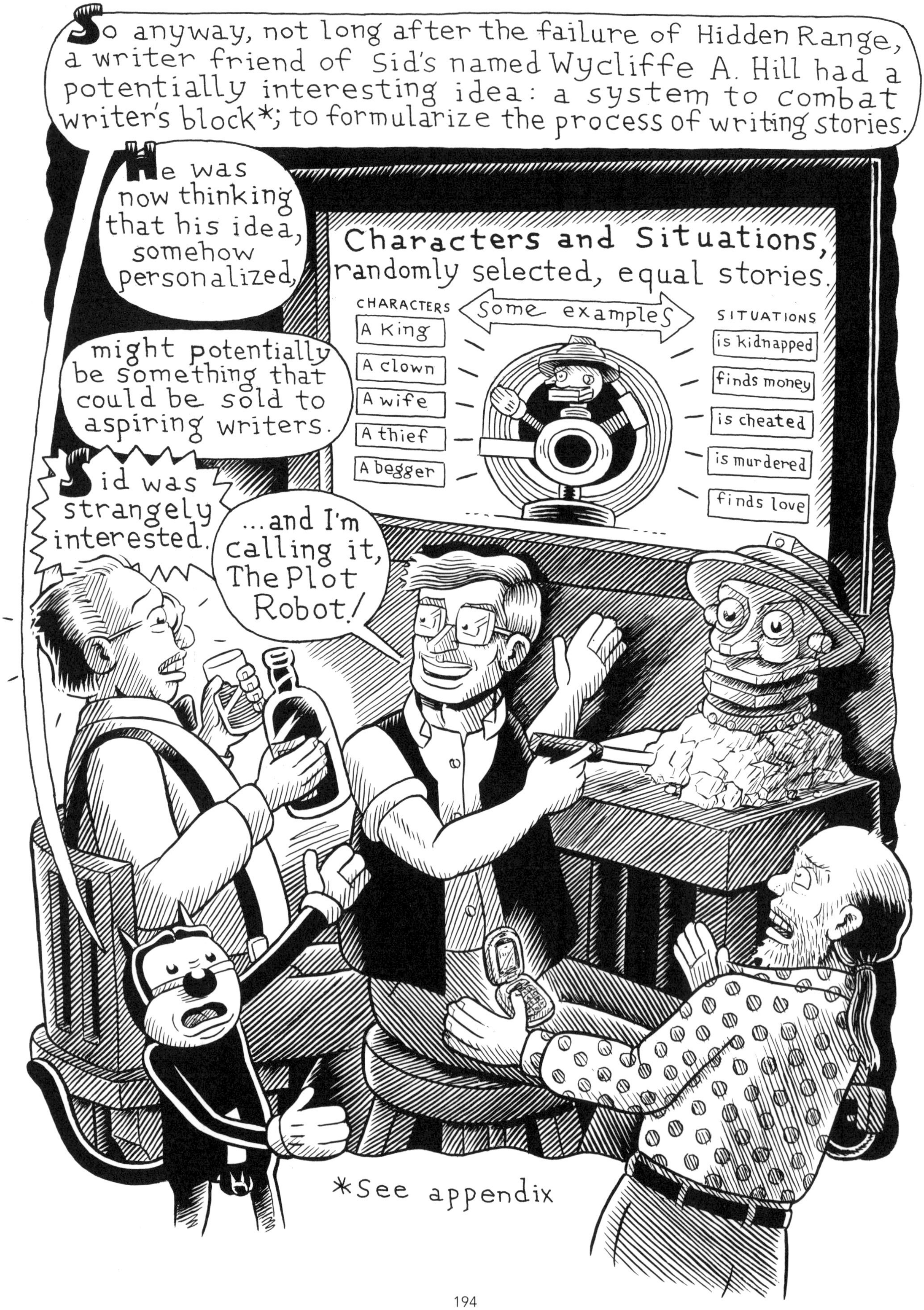

So anyway, not long after the failure of Hidden Range, a writer friend of Sid's named Wycliffe A. Hill had a potentially interesting idea: a system to combat writer's block*; to formularize the process of writing stories.
He was now thinking that his idea, somehow personalized,
might potentially be something that could be sold to aspiring writers.
Characters and Situations, randomly selected, equal stories.
CHARACTERS
Some examples
SITUATIONS
A King
A clown
A wife
A thief
A begger
is kidnapped
finds money
is cheated
is murdered
finds love
Sid was strangely interested.
...and I'm calling it, The Plot Robot!
*See appendix

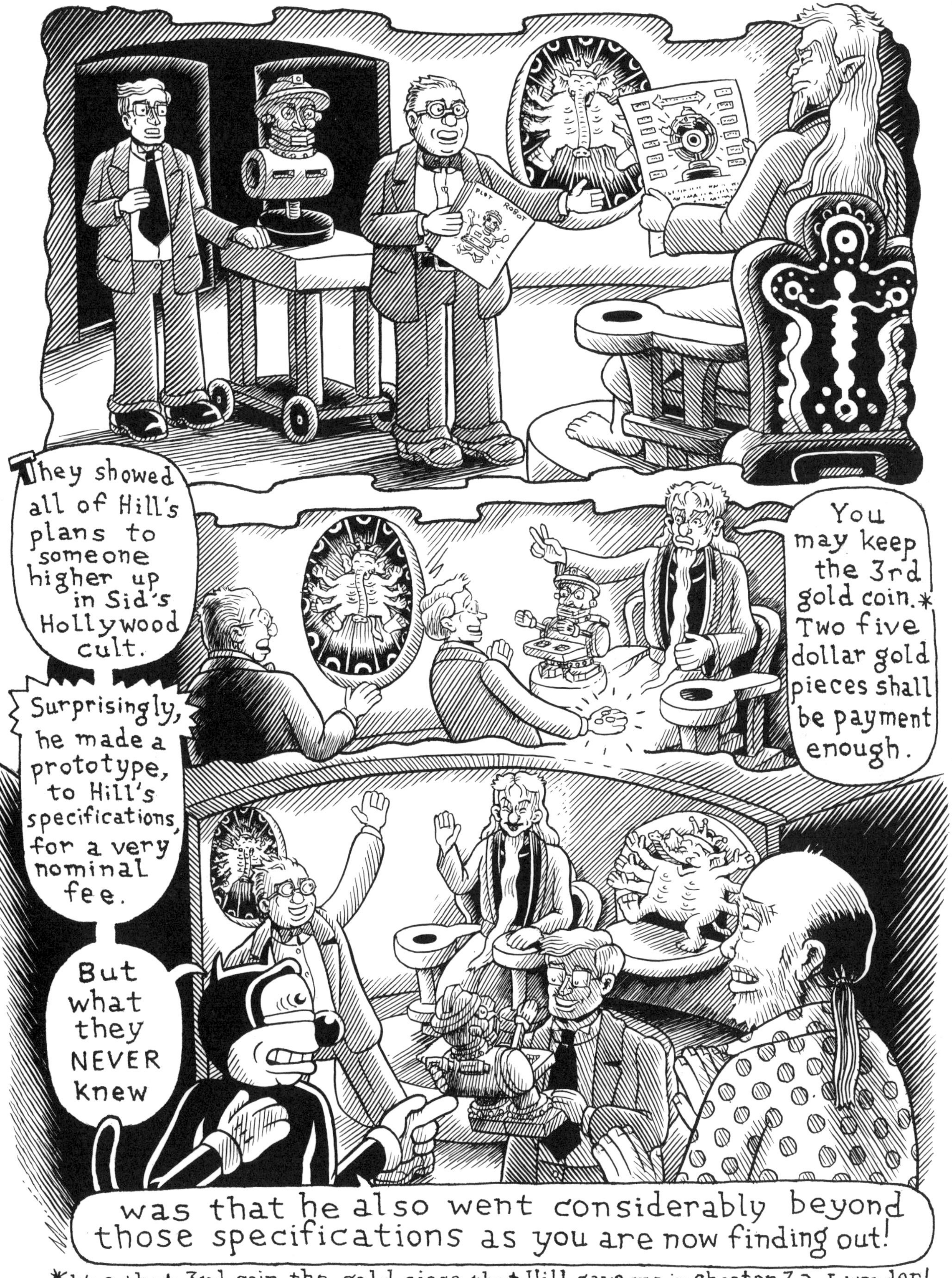

They showed all of Hill's plans to someone higher up in Sid's Hollywood cult.
You may keep the 3rd gold coin.* Two five dollar gold pieces shall be payment enough.
Surprisingly, he made a prototype, to Hill's specifications, for a very nominal fee.
But what they NEVER knew
was that he also went considerably beyond those specifications as you are now finding out!
PLOT ROBOT

*Was that 3rd coin the gold piece that Hill gave me in Chapter 3? I wonder!

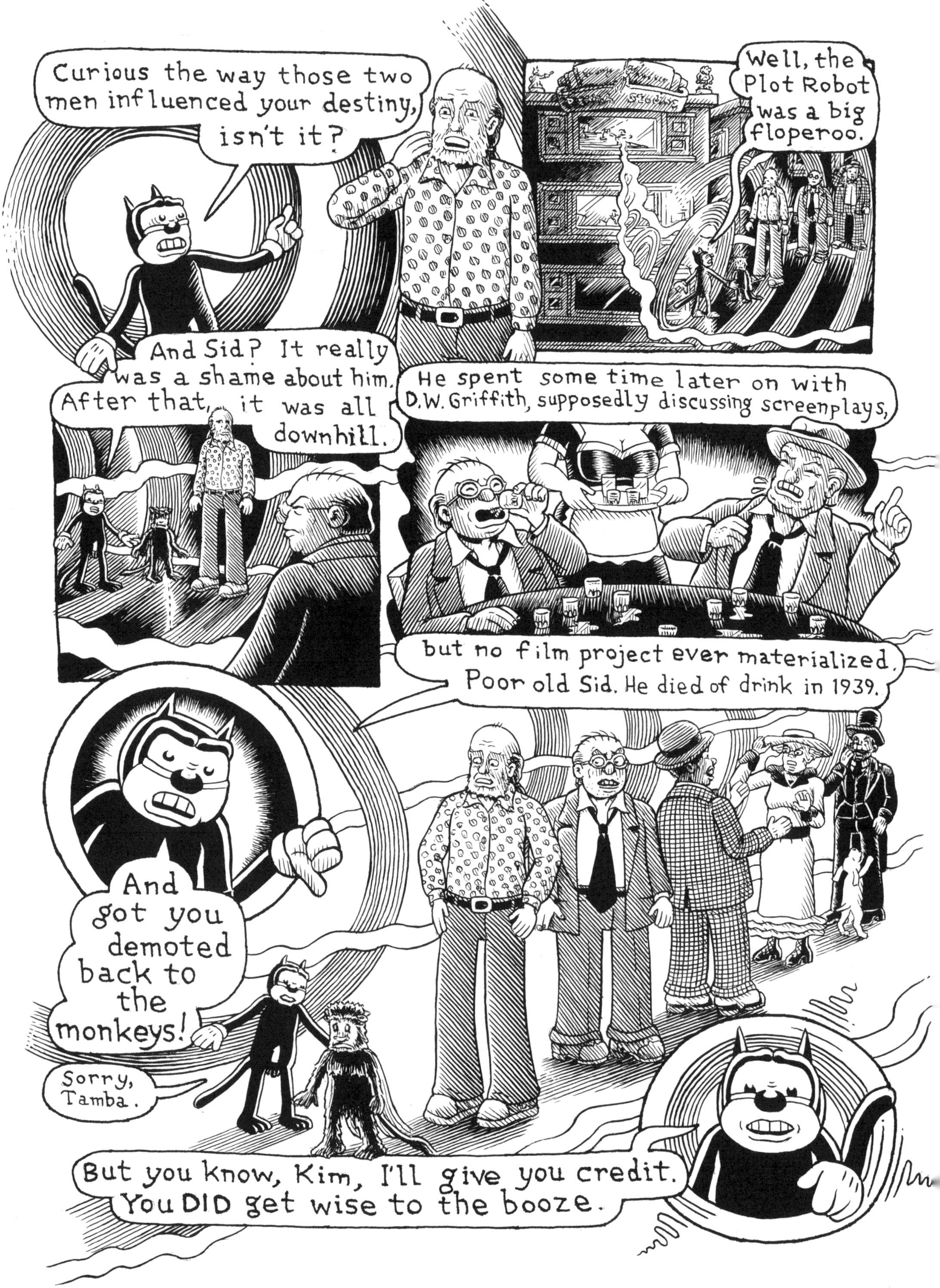
Curious the way those two men influenced your destiny, isn't it?
Well, the Plot Robot was a big floperoo.
And Sid? It really was a shame about him. After that, it was all downhill.
He spent some time later on with D.W. Griffith, supposedly discussing screenplays,
but no film project ever materialized. Poor old Sid. He died of drink in 1939.
And got you demoted back to the monkeys!
Sorry, Tamba.
But you know, Kim, I'll give you credit. You DID get wise to the booze.

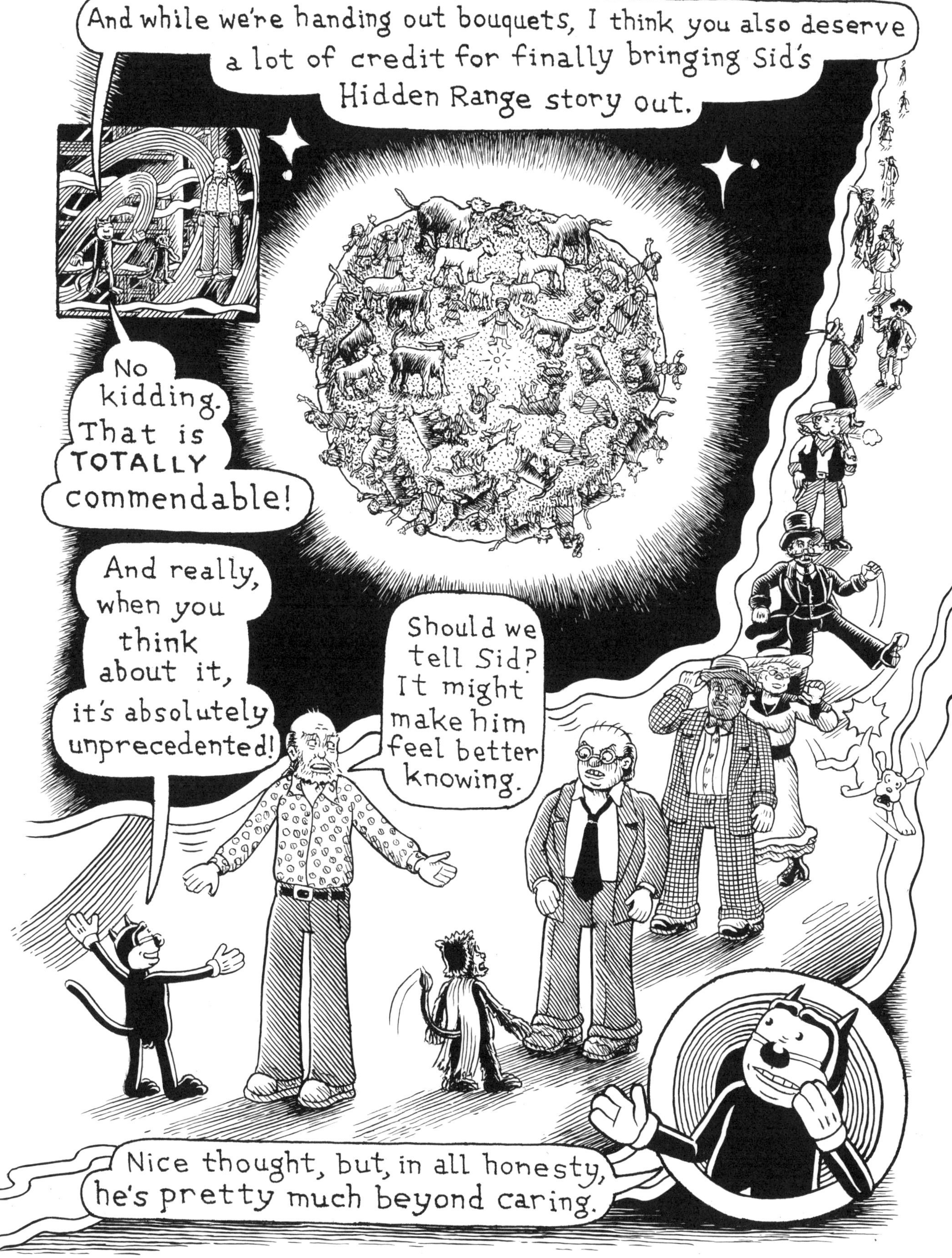

And while we're handing out bouquets, I think you also deserve a lot of credit for finally bringing Sid's Hidden Range story out.
No kidding. That is TOTALLY commendable!
And really, when you think about it, it's absolutely unprecedented!
Should we tell Sid? It might make him feel better knowing.
Nice thought, but, in all honesty, he's pretty much beyond caring.

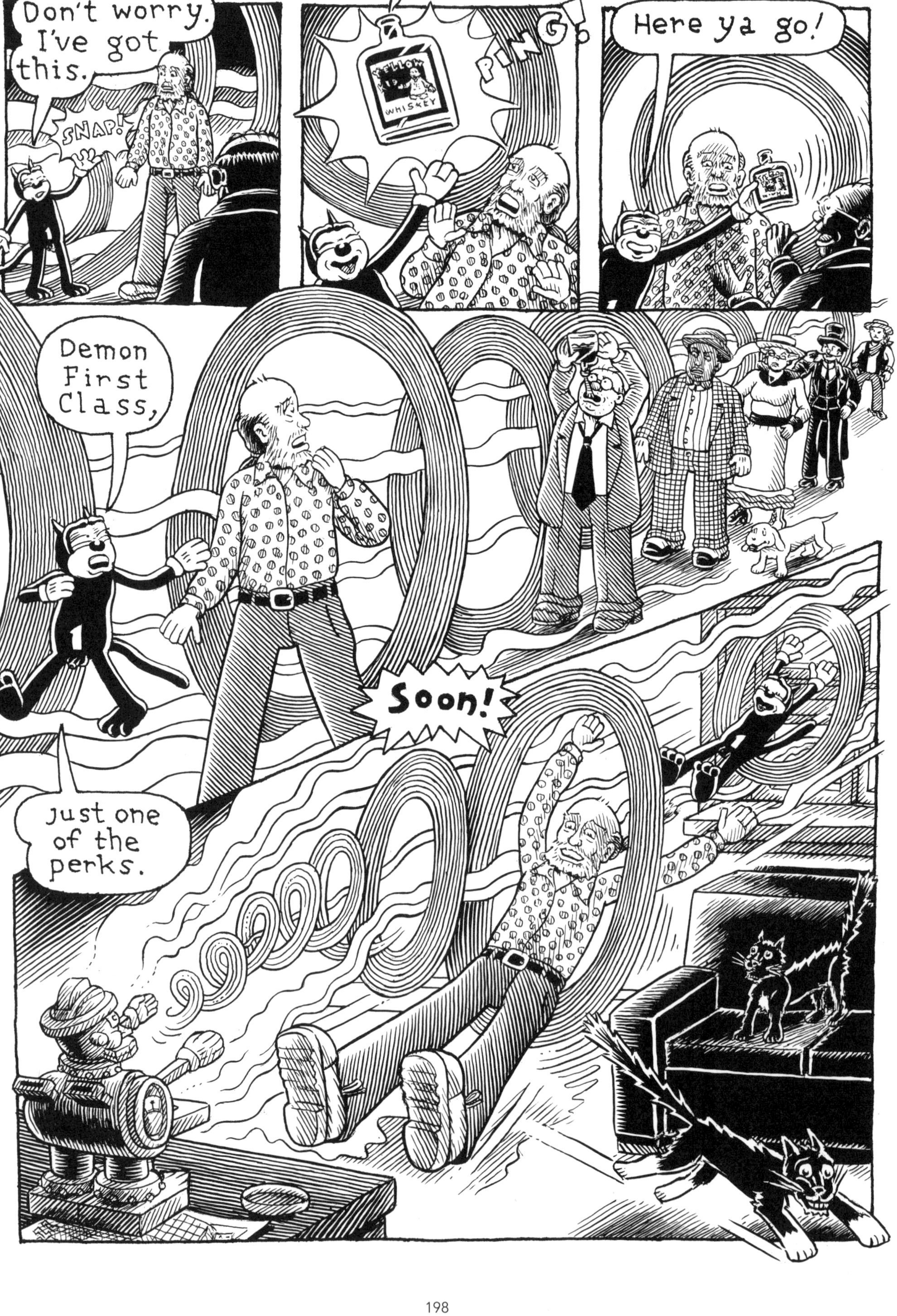
Don't worry. I've got this.
SNAP!
PING!
WHISKEY
Here ya go!
Demon First Class,
Soon!
Just one of the perks.

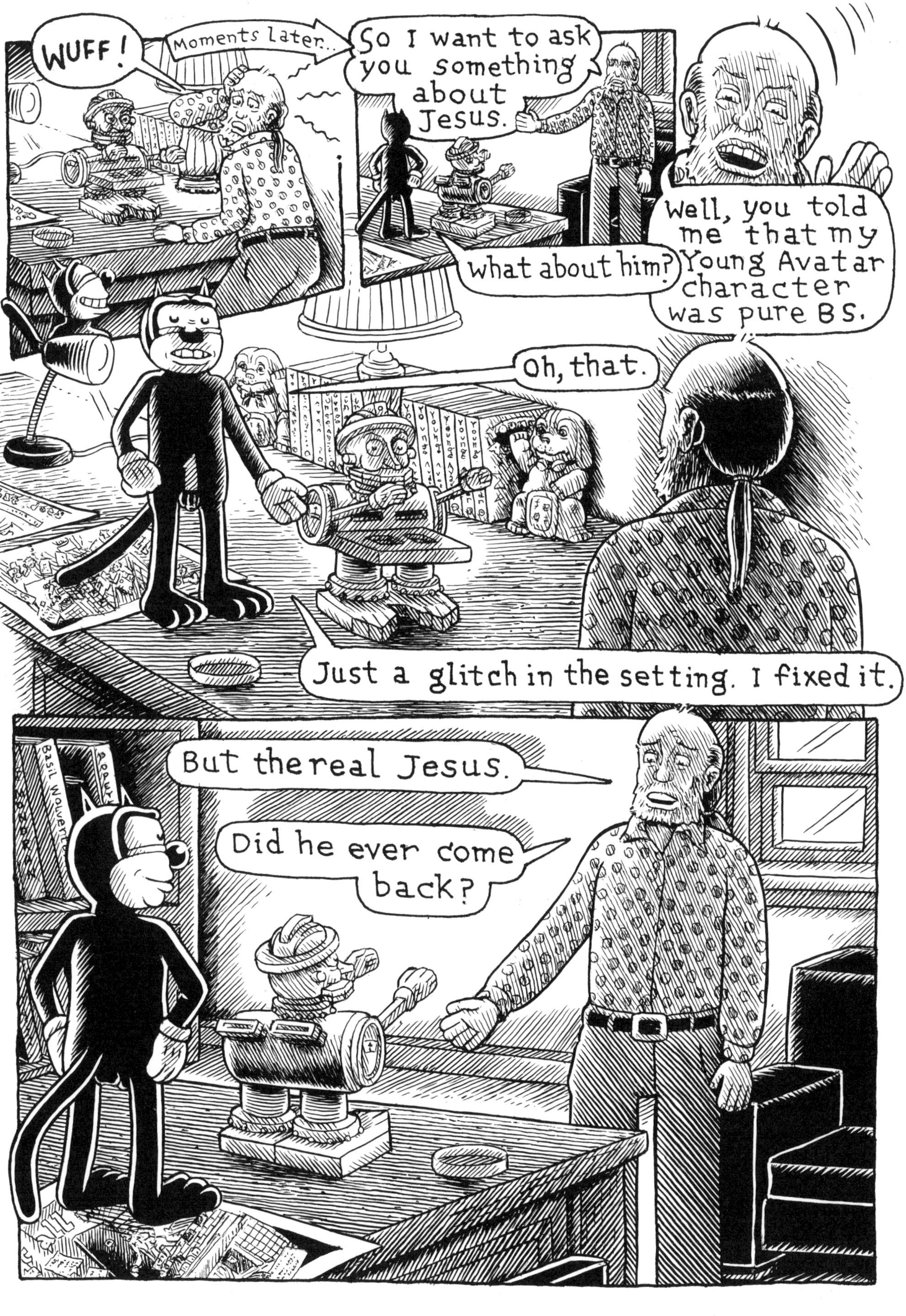
WUFF!
Moments later...
So I want to ask you something about Jesus.
What about him?
Well, you told me that my Young Avatar character was pure BS.
Oh, that.
Just a glitch in the setting. I fixed it.
But the real Jesus.
Did he ever come back?

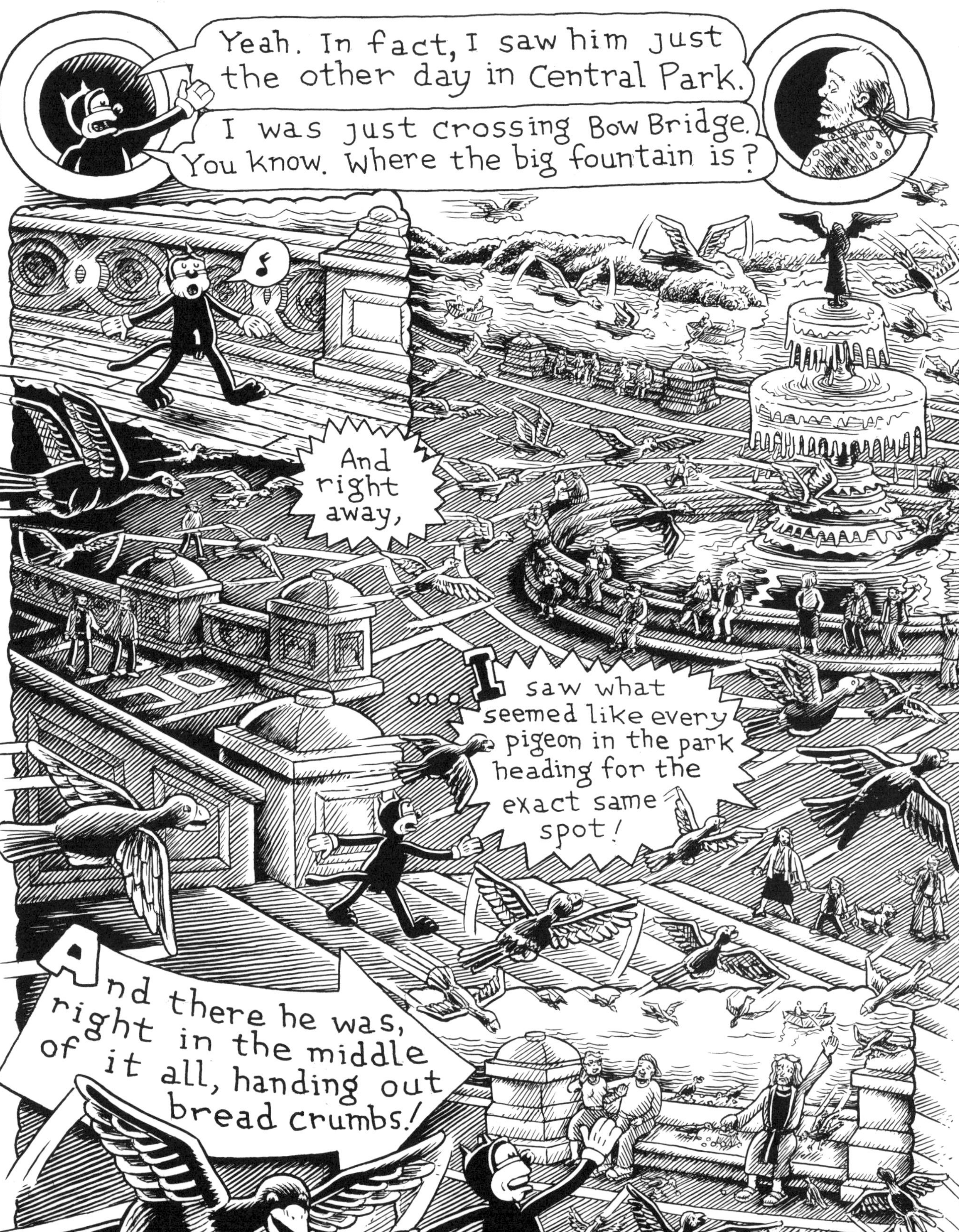

Yeah. In fact, I saw him just the other day in Central Park.
I was just crossing Bow Bridge. You know. Where the big fountain is?
And right away,
...I saw what seemed like every pigeon in the park heading for the exact same spot!
And there he was, right in the middle of it all, handing out bread crumbs!

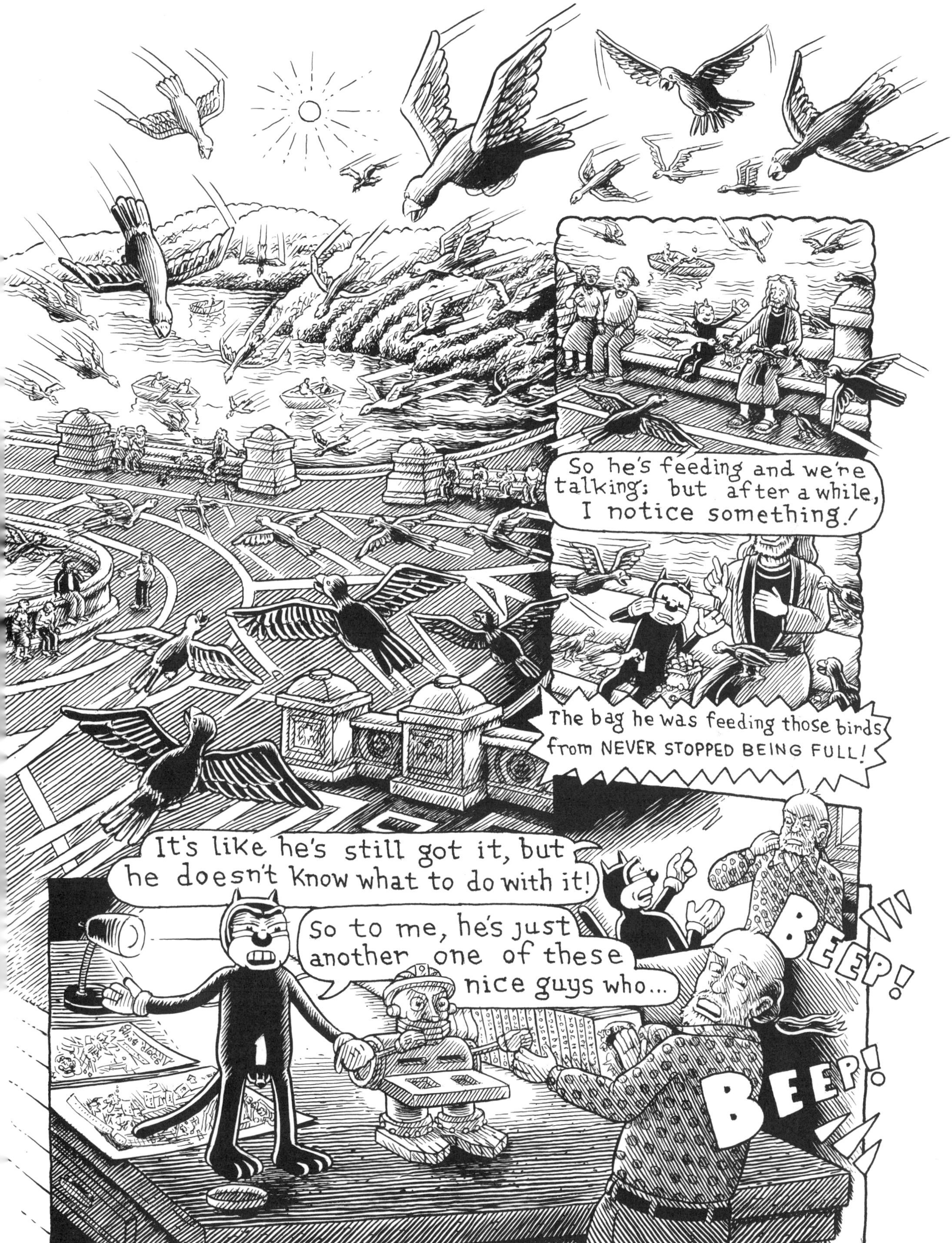

So he's feeding and we're talking; but after a while, I notice something!
The bag he was feeding those birds from NEVER STOPPED BEING FULL!
It's like he's still got it, but he doesn't know what to do with it!
So to me, he's just another one of these nice guys who...
BEEP!
BEEP!

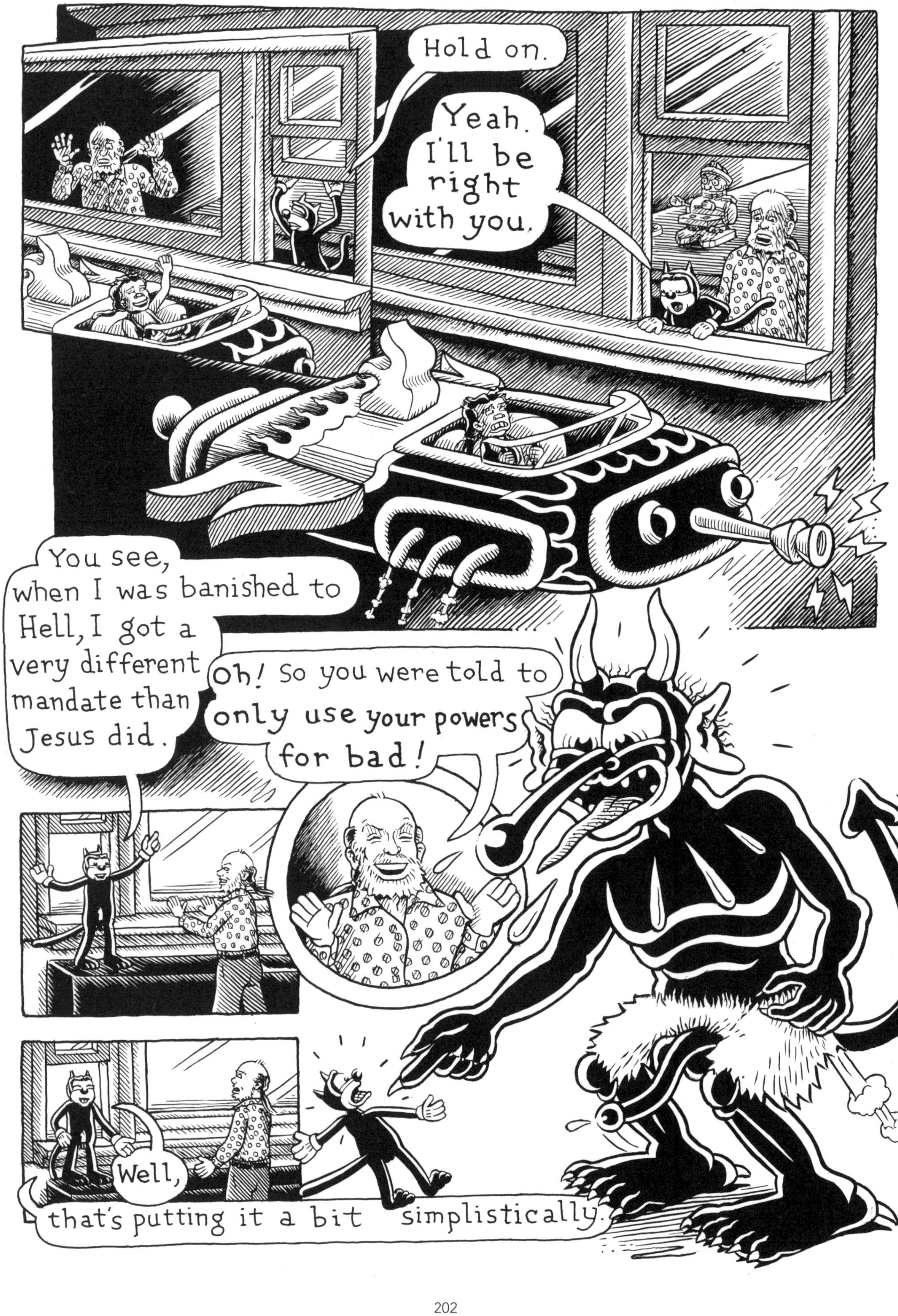
Hold on.
Yeah. I'll be right with you.
You see, when I was banished to Hell, I got a very different mandate than Jesus did.
Oh! So you were told to only use your powers for bad!
Well, that's putting it a bit simplistically.

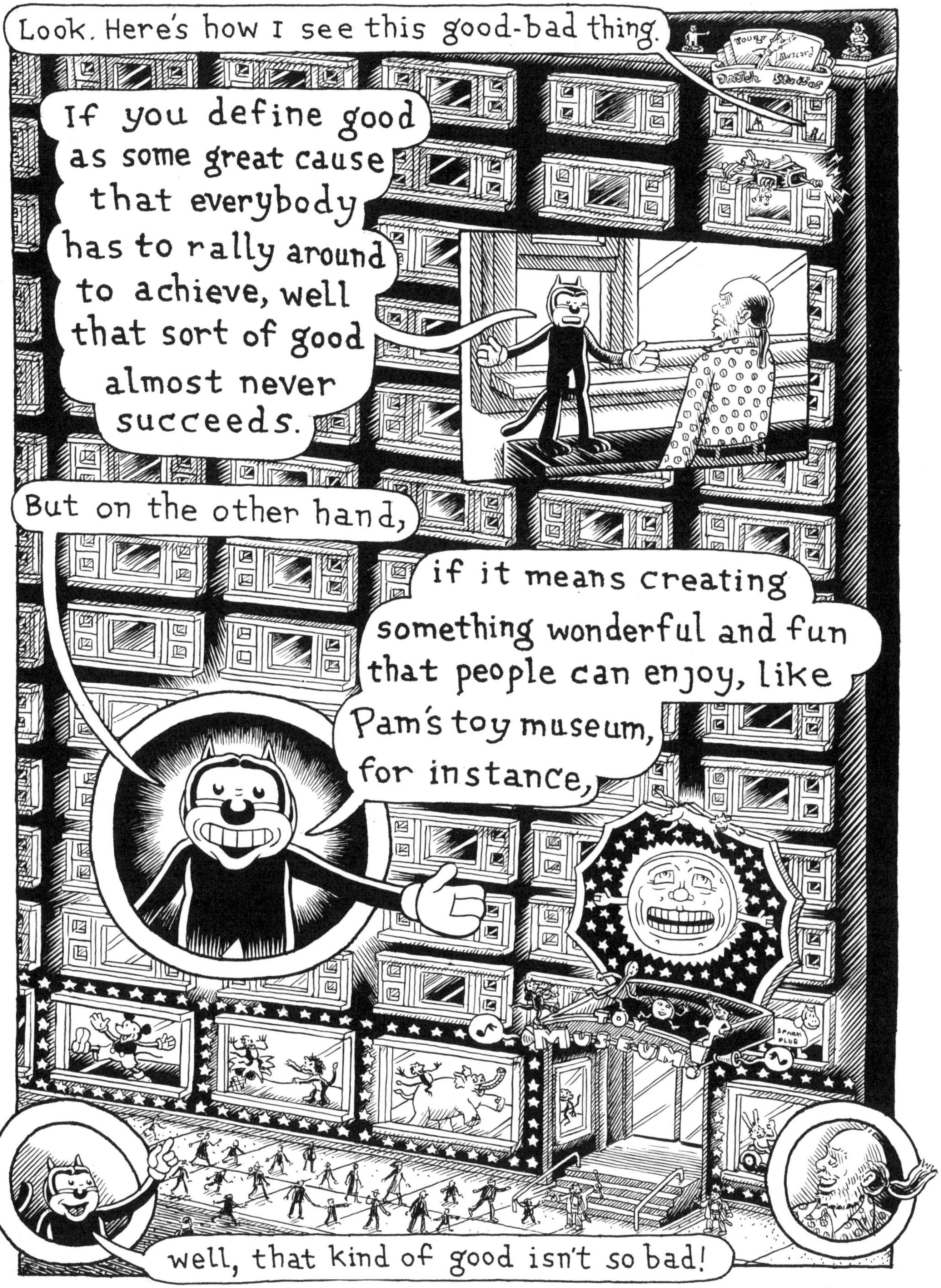
Look. Here's how I see this good-bad thing.
If you define good as some great cause that everybody has to rally around to achieve, well that sort of good almost never succeeds.
But on the other hand,
if it means creating something wonderful and fun that people can enjoy, like Pam's toy museum, for instance,
TOY MUSEUM
well, that kind of good isn't so bad!

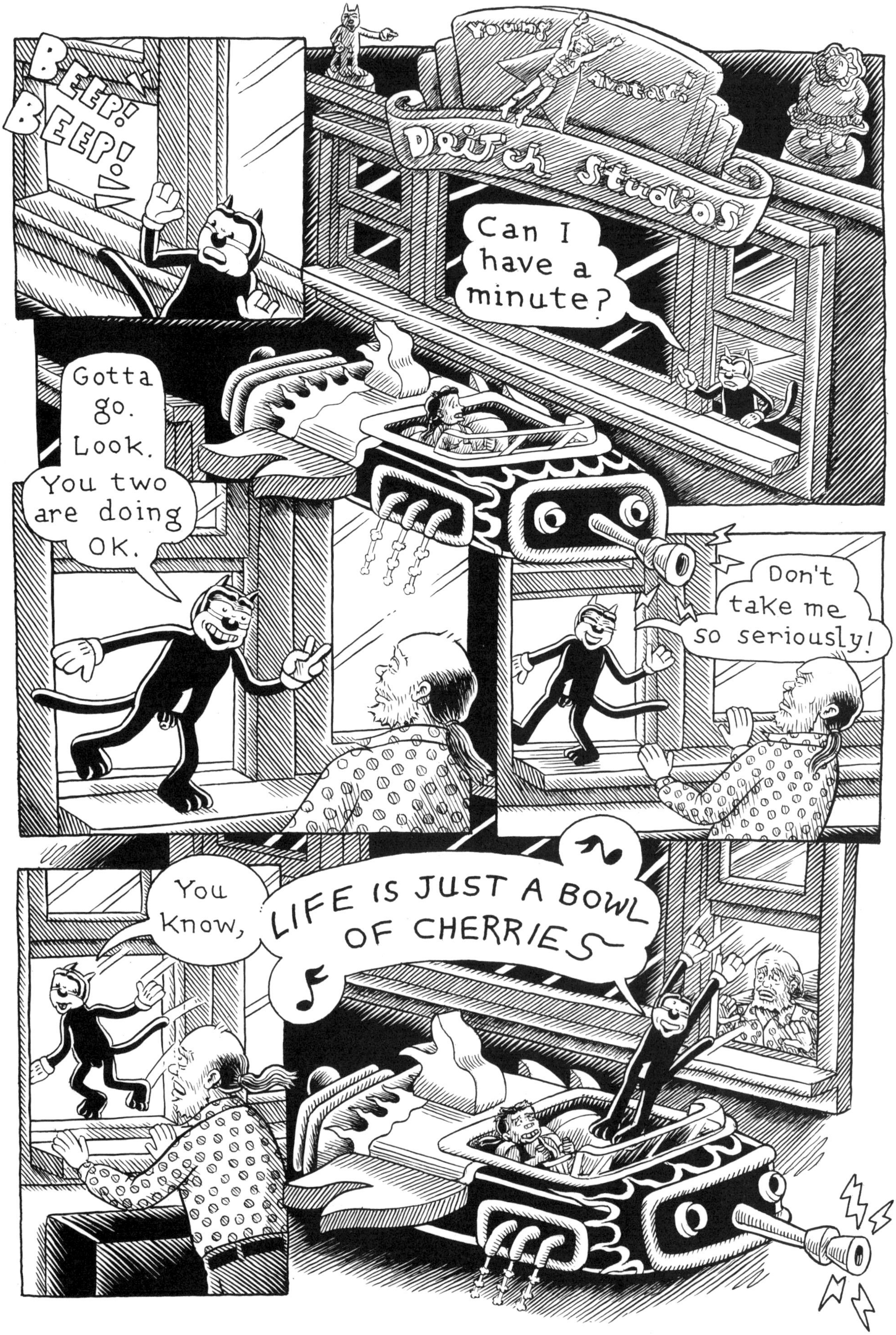
BEEP! BEEP!
Young avatar!
Deitch Studios
Can I have a minute?
Gotta go. Look. You two are doing OK.
Don't take me so seriously!
You know,
LIFE IS JUST A BOWL OF CHERRIES

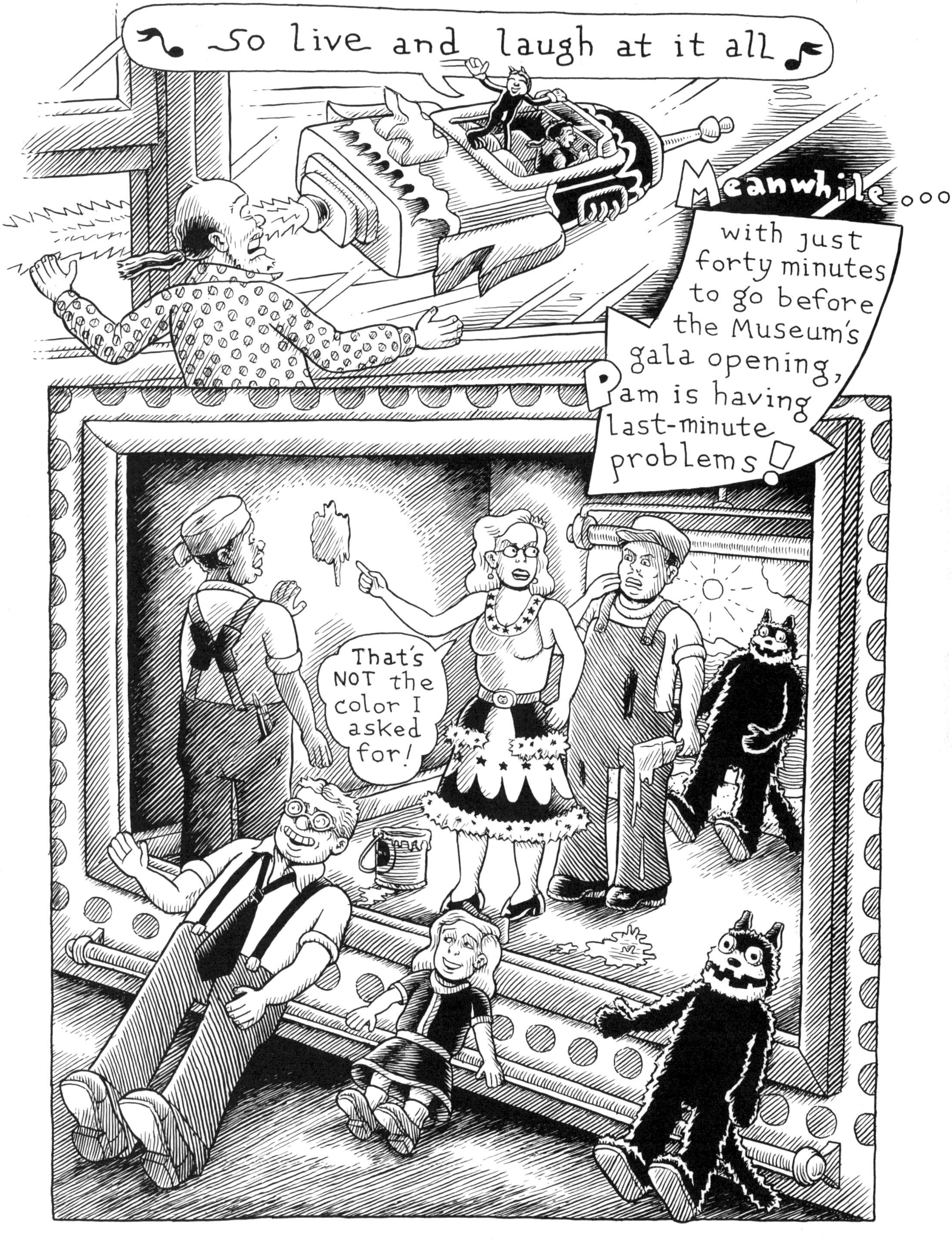
So live and laugh at it all
Meanwhile...
with just forty minutes to go before the Museum's gala opening, Pam is having last-minute problems!
That's NOT the color I asked for!

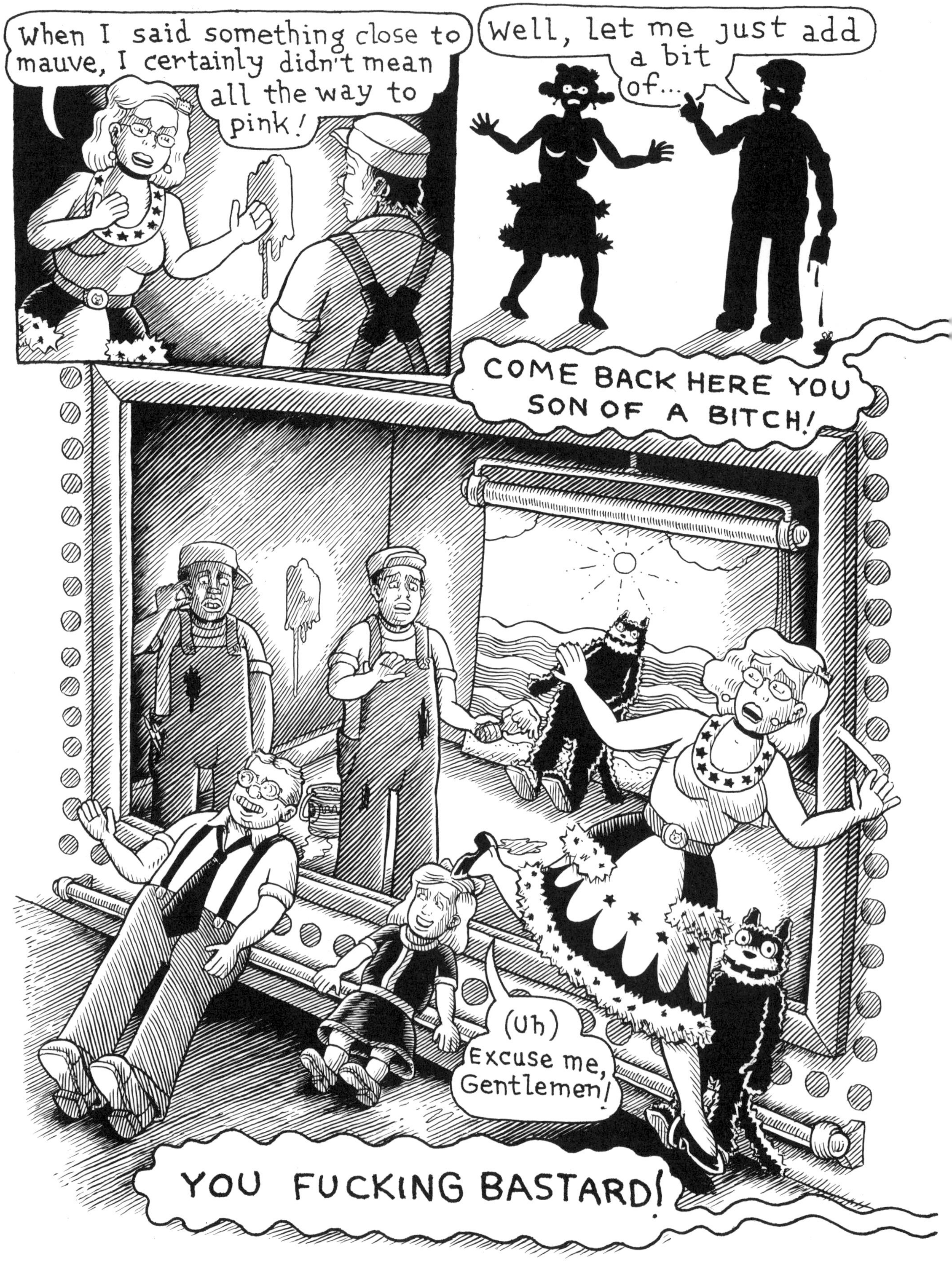
When I said something close to mauve, I certainly didn't mean all the way to pink!
Well, let me just add a bit of...
COME BACK HERE YOU SON OF A BITCH!
(Uh) Excuse me, Gentlemen!
YOU FUCKING BASTARD!

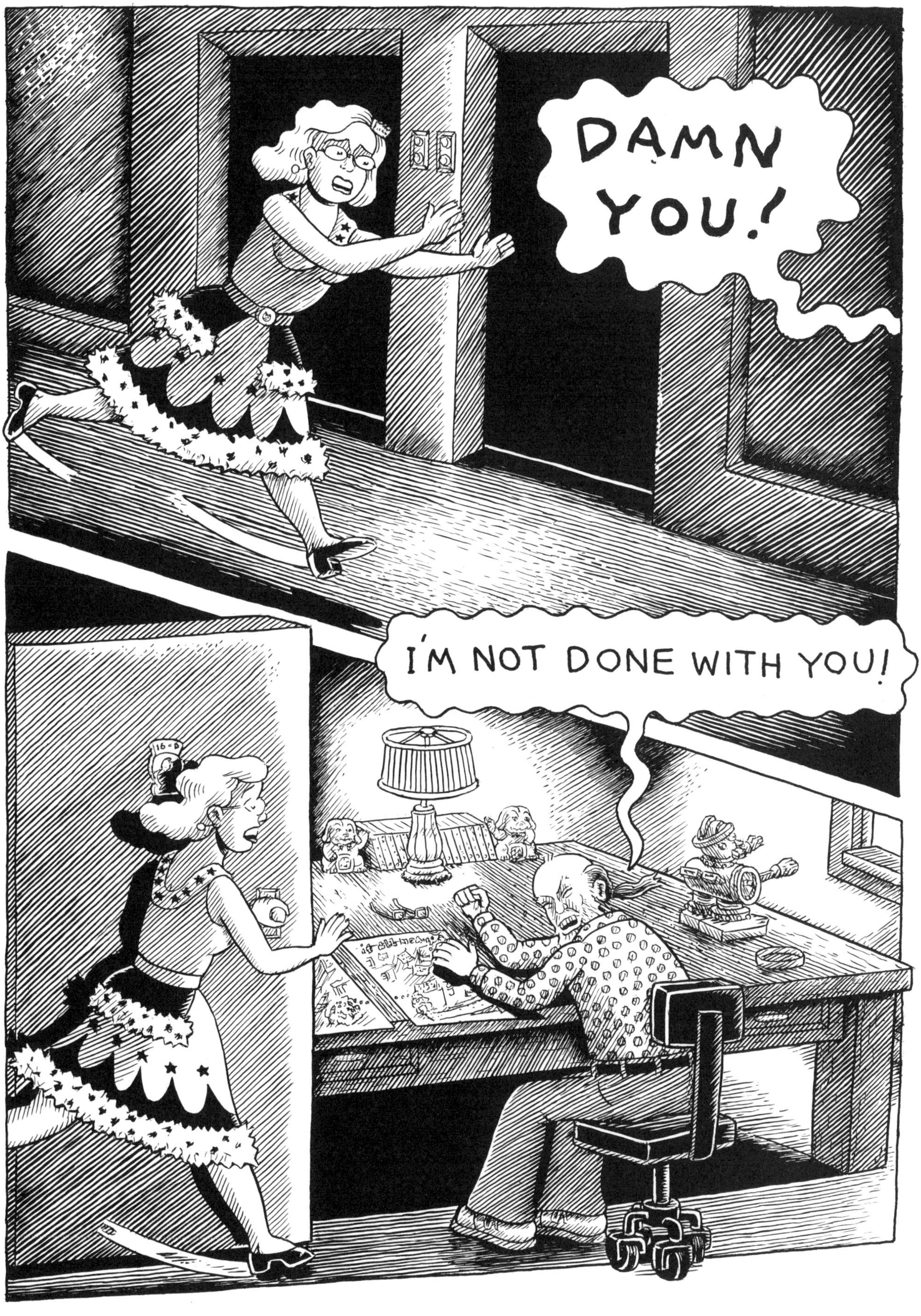
DAMN YOU.!
I'M NOT DONE WITH YOU!

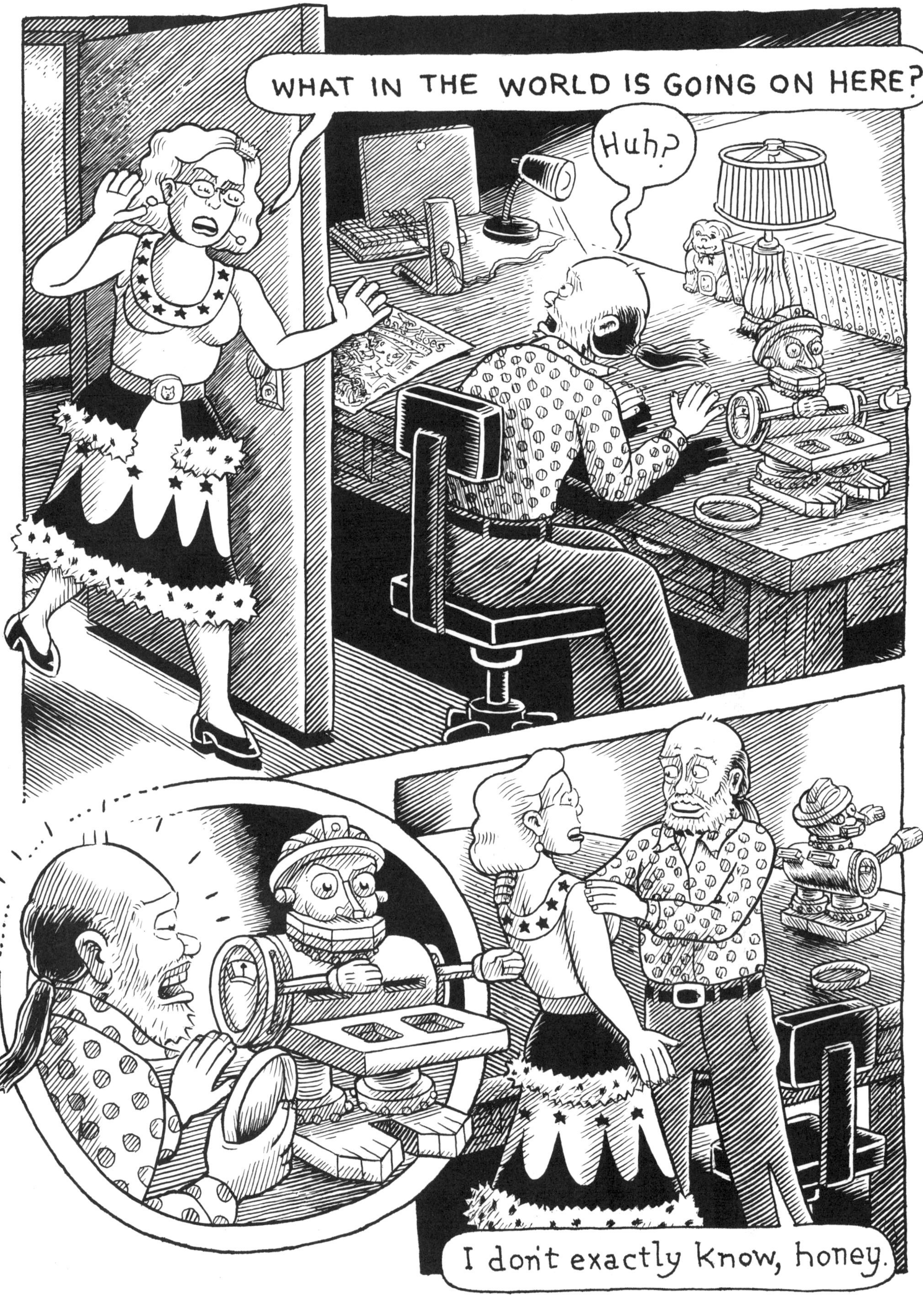
WHAT IN THE WORLD IS GOING ON HERE?
Huh?
I don't exactly know, honey.

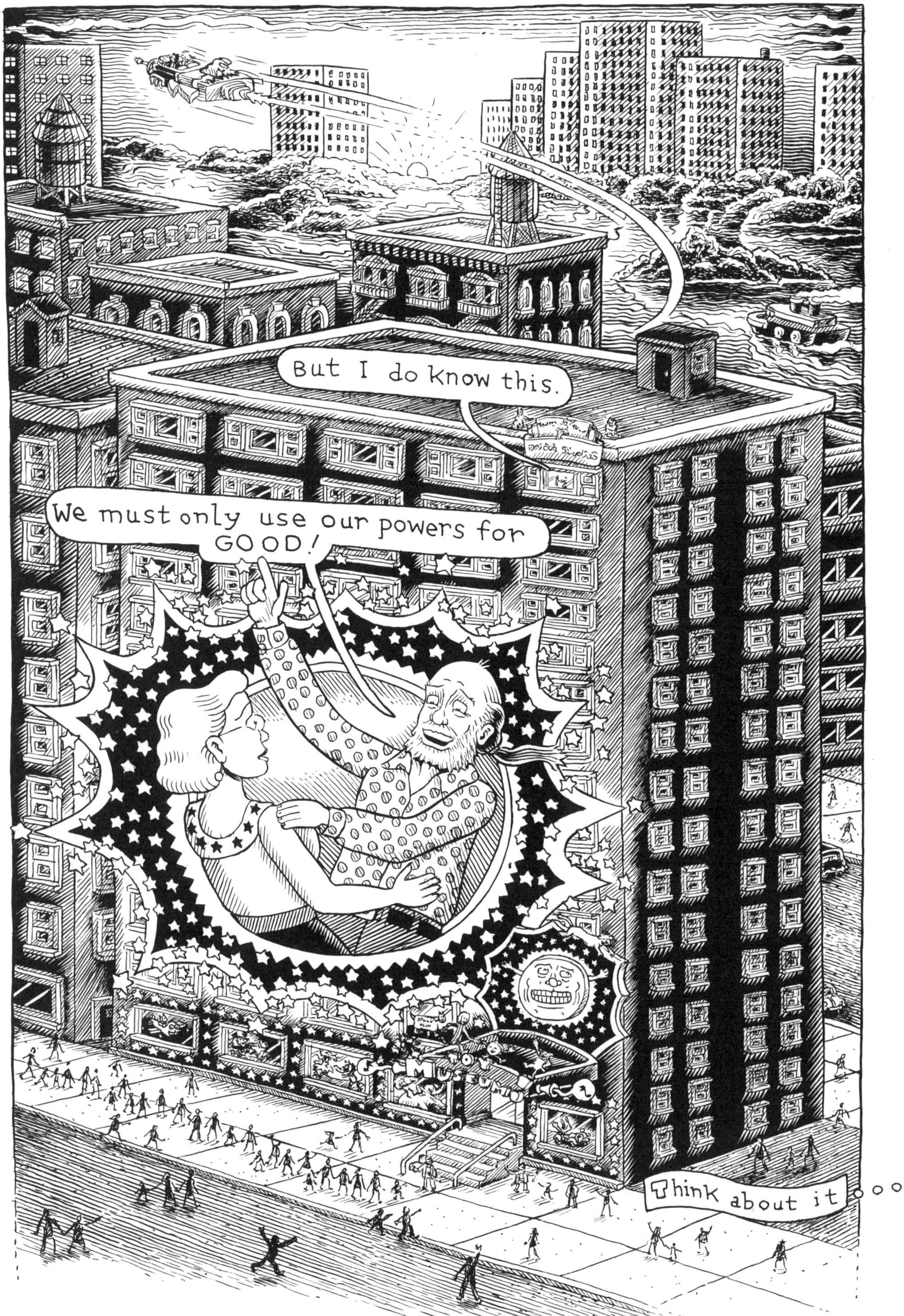
But I do know this.
We must only use our powers for GOOD!
Think about it...

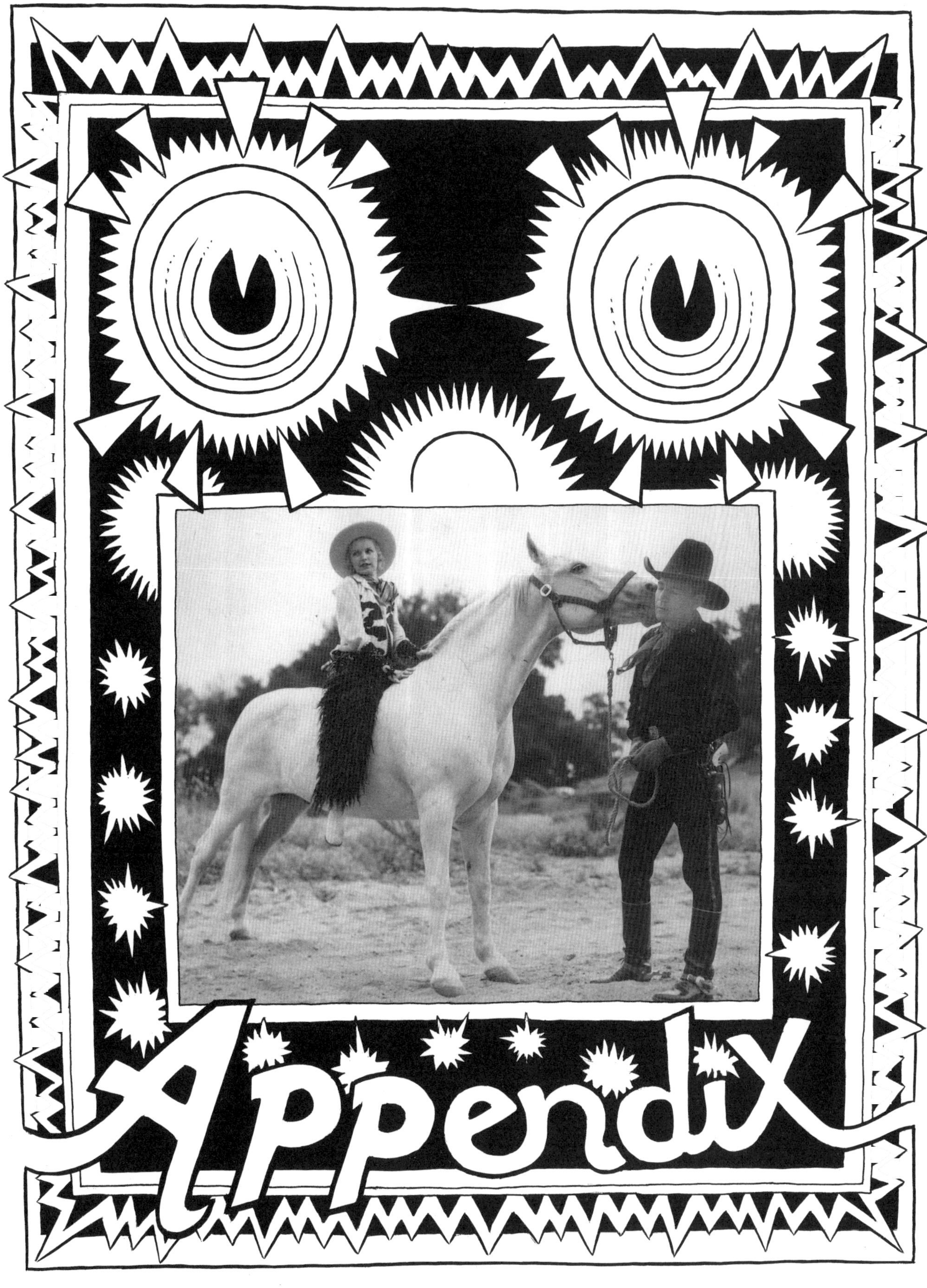
Appendix

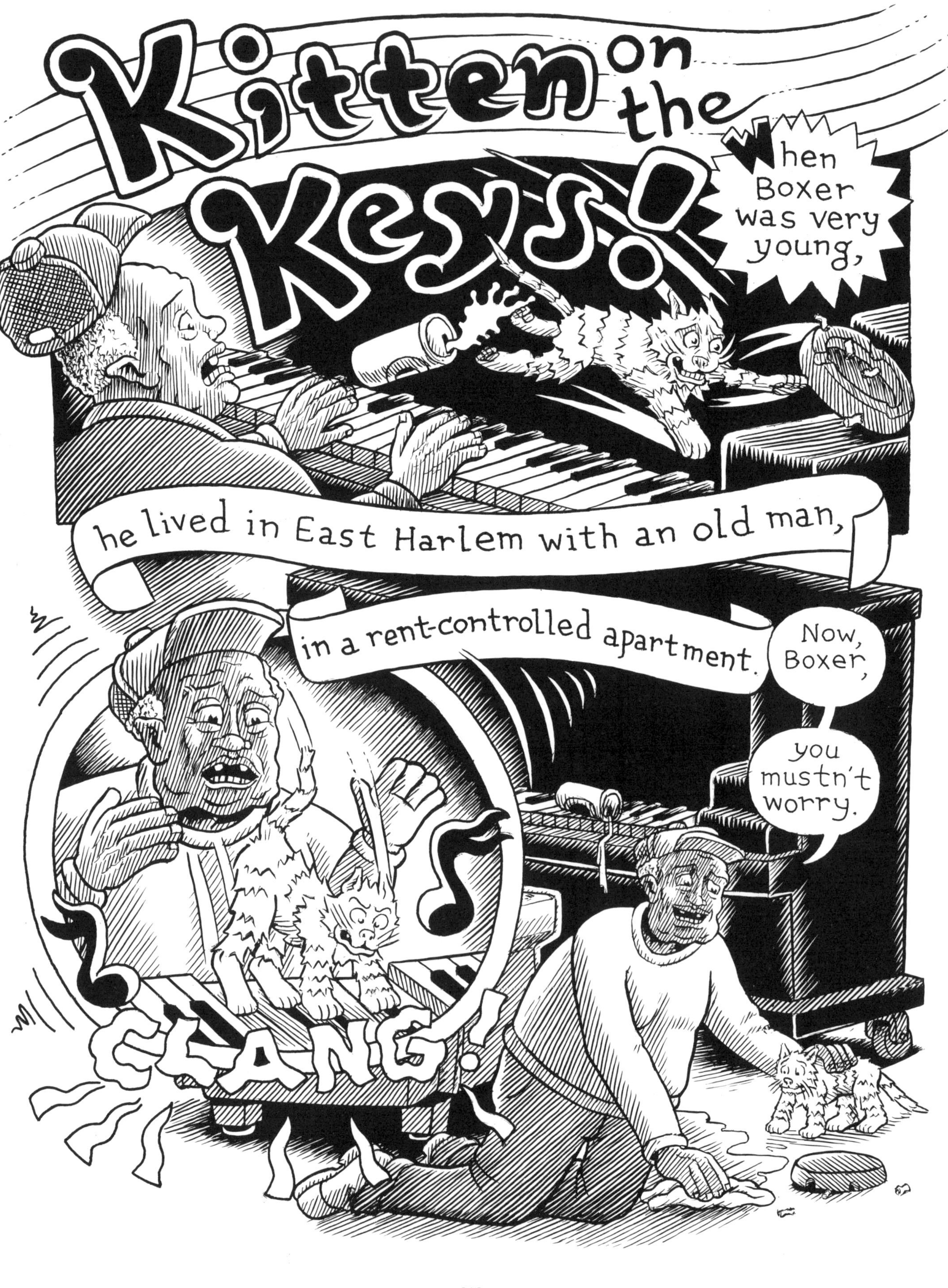
Kitten on the Keys!
When Boxer was very young,
he lived in East Harlem with an old man,
in a rent-controlled apartment.
Now, Boxer,
you mustn't worry.
CLANG!

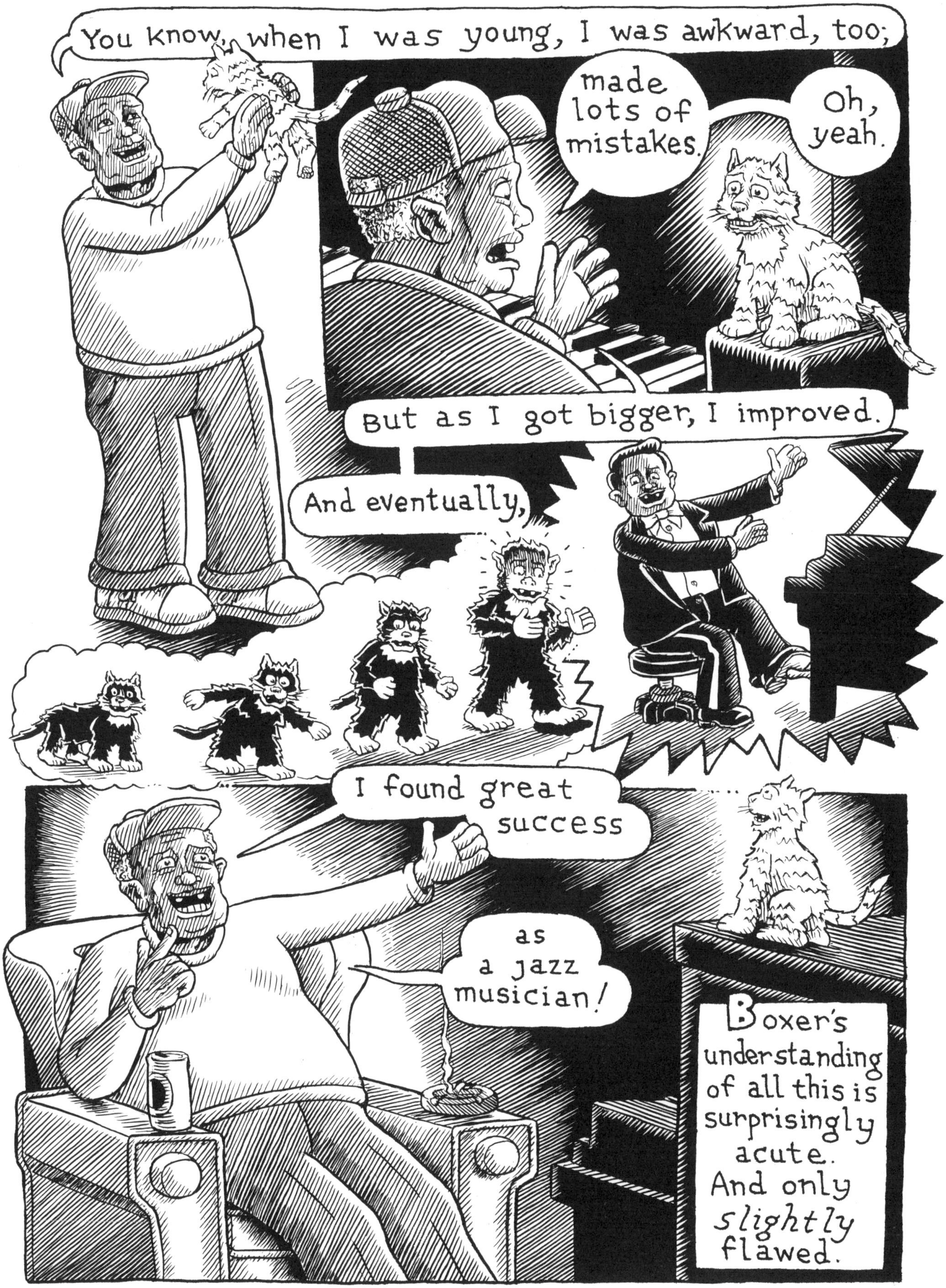
You know, when I was young, I was awkward, too;
made lots of mistakes.
Oh, yeah.
But as I got bigger, I improved.
And eventually,
I found great success
as a jazz musician!
Boxer's understanding of all this is surprisingly acute. And only *slightly* flawed.

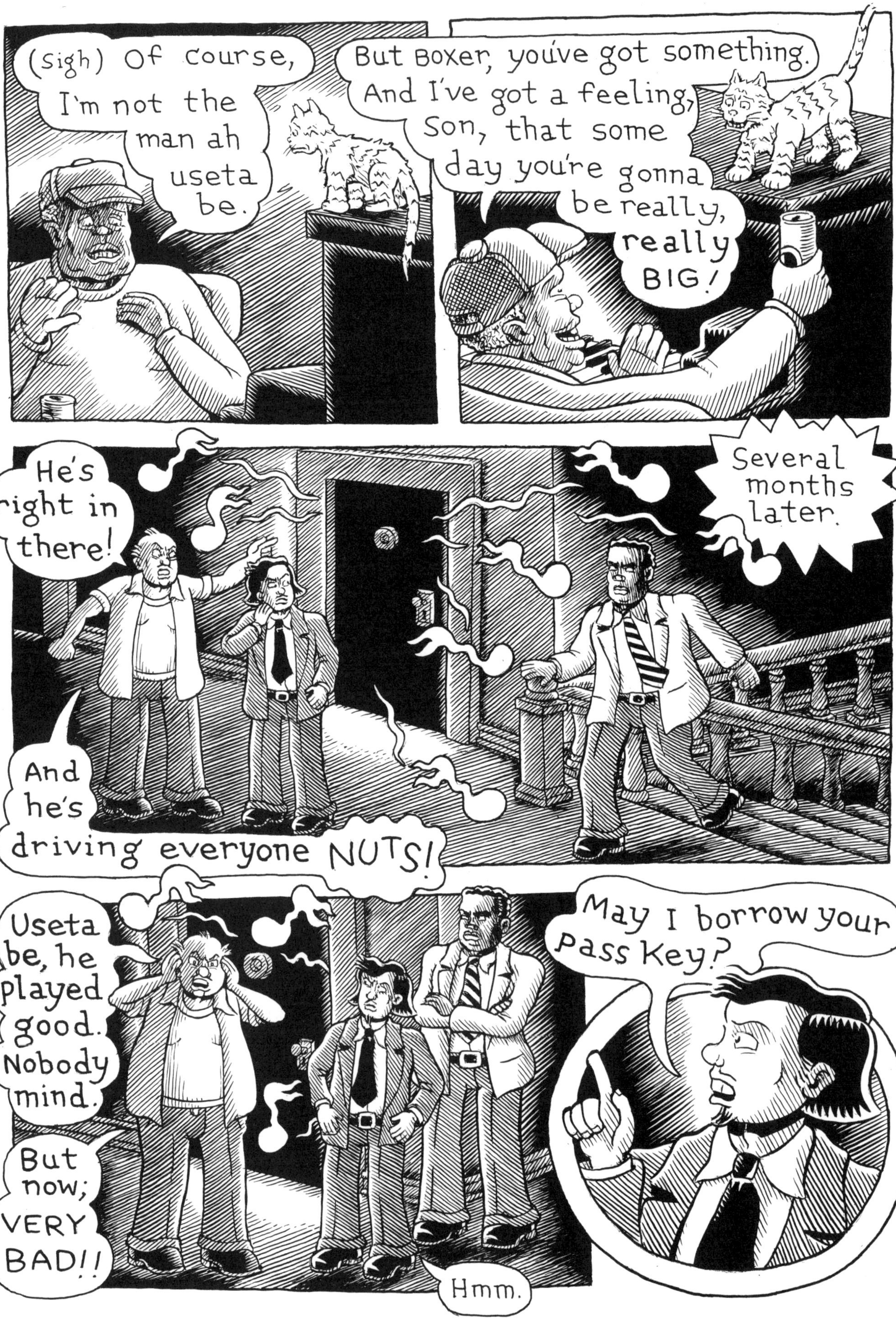
(sigh) Of course, I'm not the man ah useta be.
But Boxer, you've got something. And I've got a feeling, Son, that some day you're gonna be really, really BIG!
Several months later.
He's right in there!
And he's driving everyone NUTS!
Useta be, he played good. Nobody mind.
But now; VERY BAD!!
Hmm.
May I borrow your Pass Key?

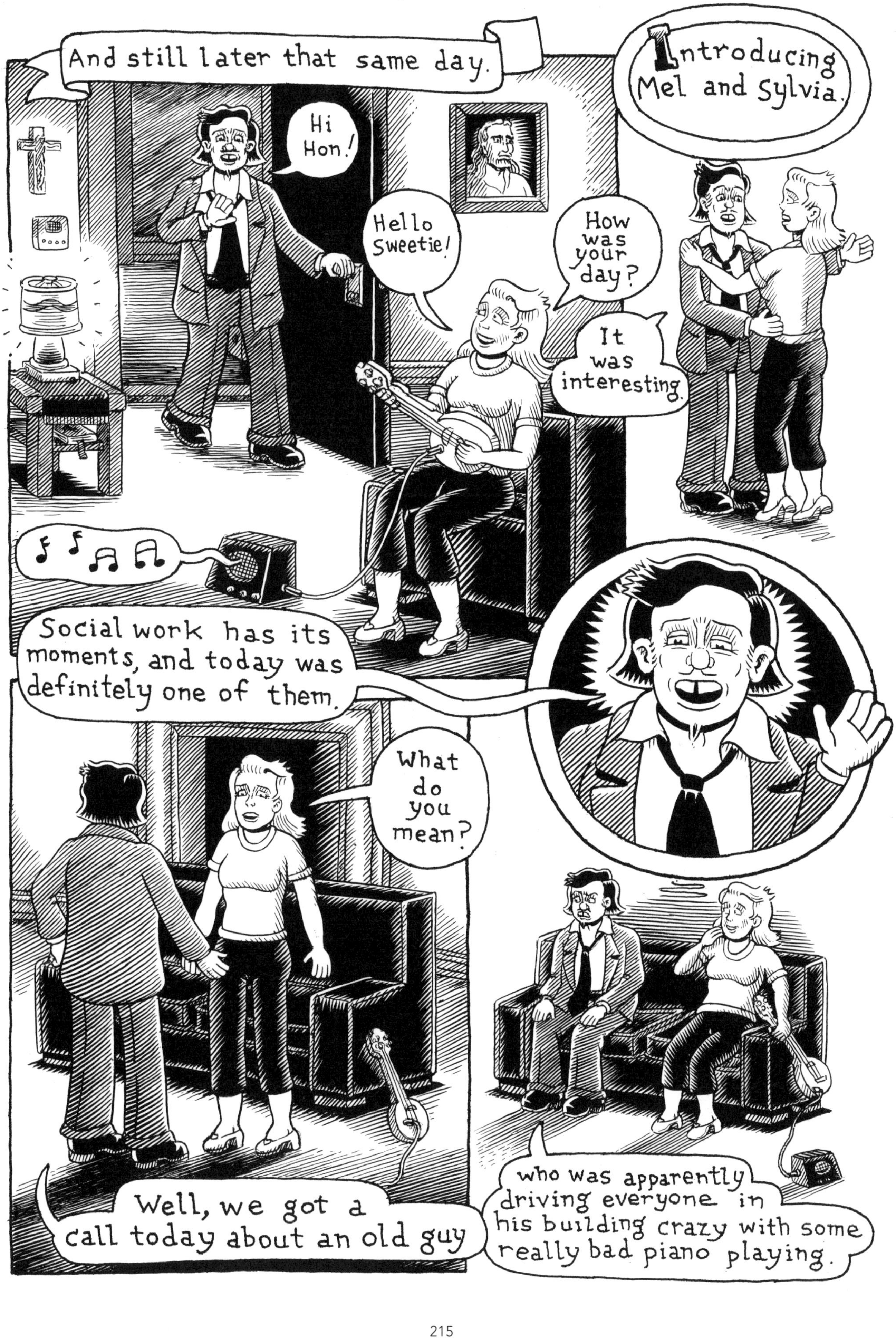

And still later that same day.
Hi Hon!
Hello Sweetie!
How was your day?
It was interesting.
Introducing Mel and Sylvia.
Social work has its moments, and today was definitely one of them.
What do you mean?
Well, we got a call today about an old guy
who was apparently driving everyone in his building crazy with some really bad piano playing.

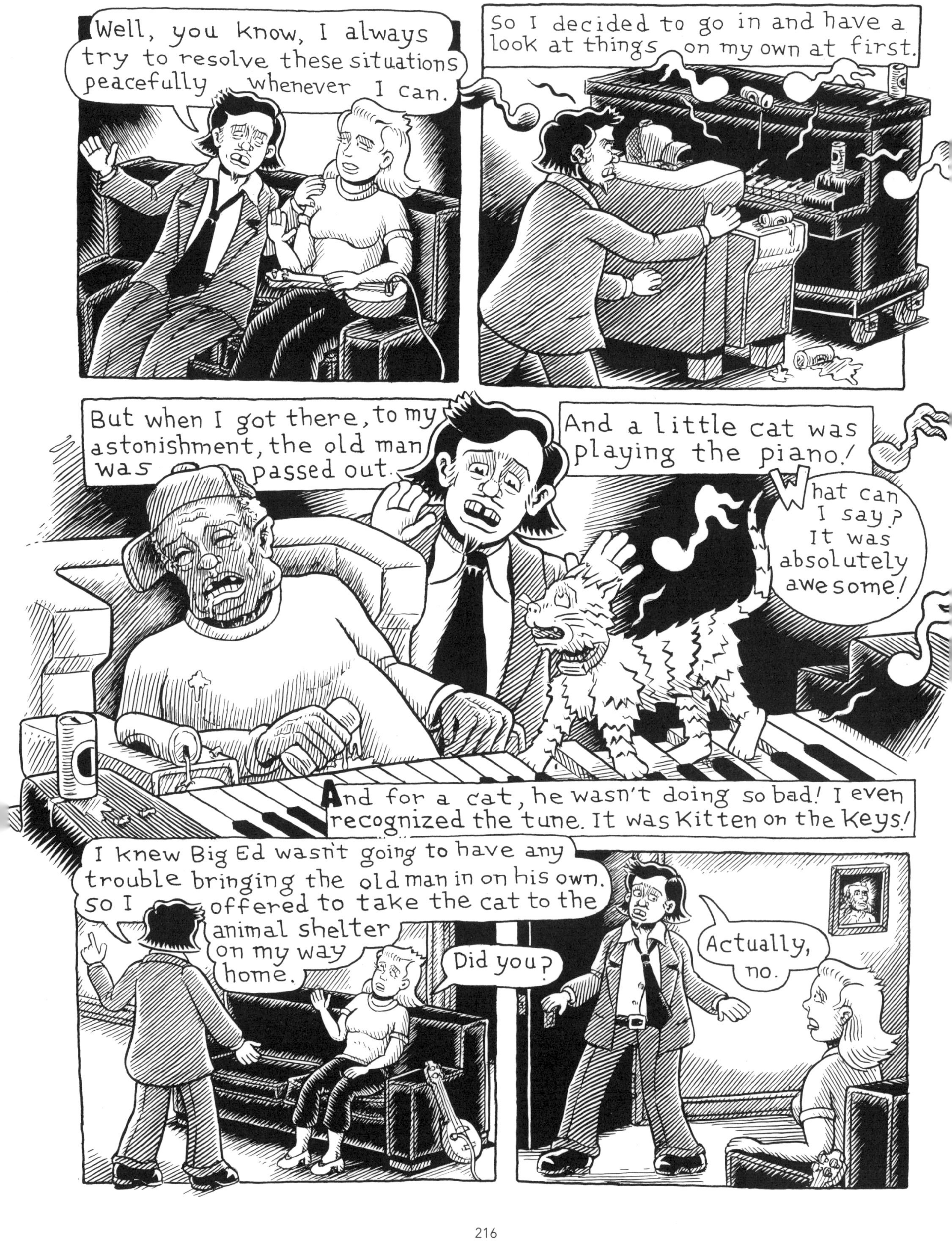
Well, you know, I always try to resolve these situations peacefully whenever I can.
So I decided to go in and have a look at things on my own at first.
But when I got there, to my astonishment, the old man was passed out.
And a little cat was playing the piano!
What can I say? It was absolutely awesome!
And for a cat, he wasn't doing so bad! I even recognized the tune. It was Kitten on the Keys!
I knew Big Ed wasn't going to have any trouble bringing the old man in on his own. So I offered to take the cat to the animal shelter on my way home.
Did you?
Actually, no.

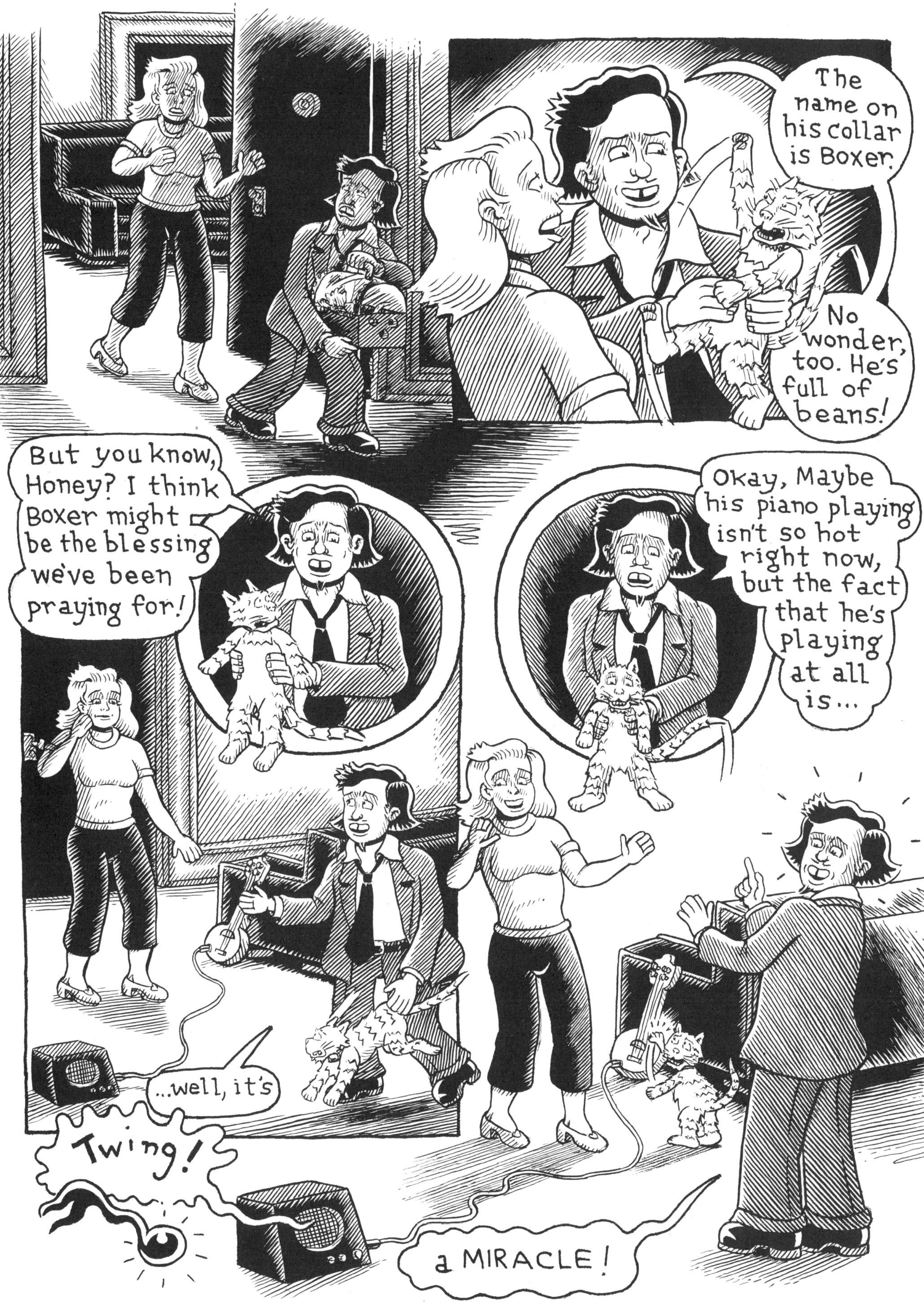
The name on his collar is Boxer.
No wonder, too. He's full of beans!
But you know, Honey? I think Boxer might be the blessing we've been praying for!
Okay, Maybe his piano playing isn't so hot right now, but the fact that he's playing at all is...
...well, it's
Twing!
a MIRACLE!

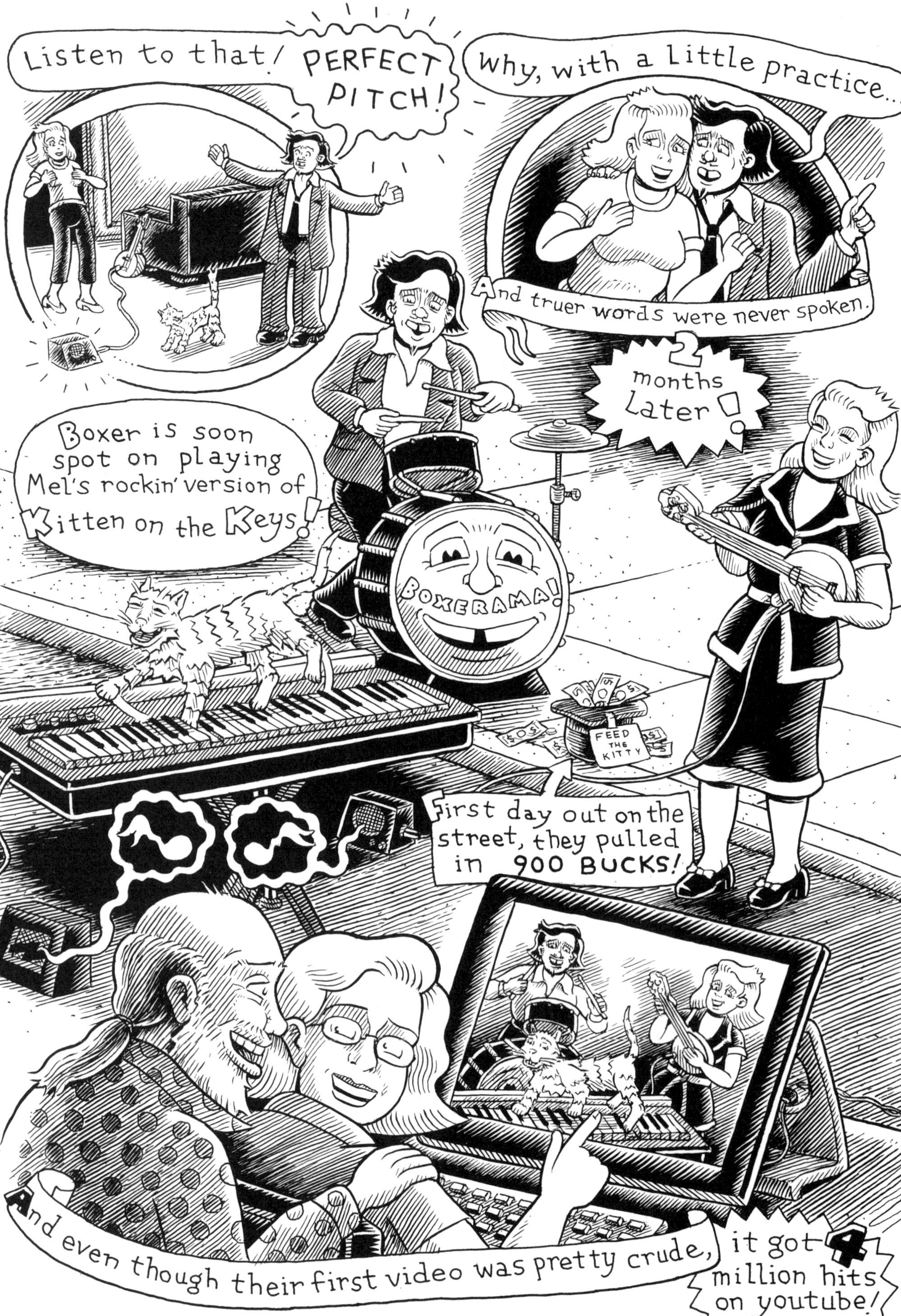
Listen to that! PERFECT PITCH!
Why, with a little practice...
And truer words were never spoken.
2 months Later!
Boxer is soon spot on playing Mel's rockin' version of Kitten on the Keys!
BOXERAMA!
FEED THE KITTY
First day out on the street, they pulled in 900 BUCKS!
And even though their first video was pretty crude,
it got 4 million hits on youtube!

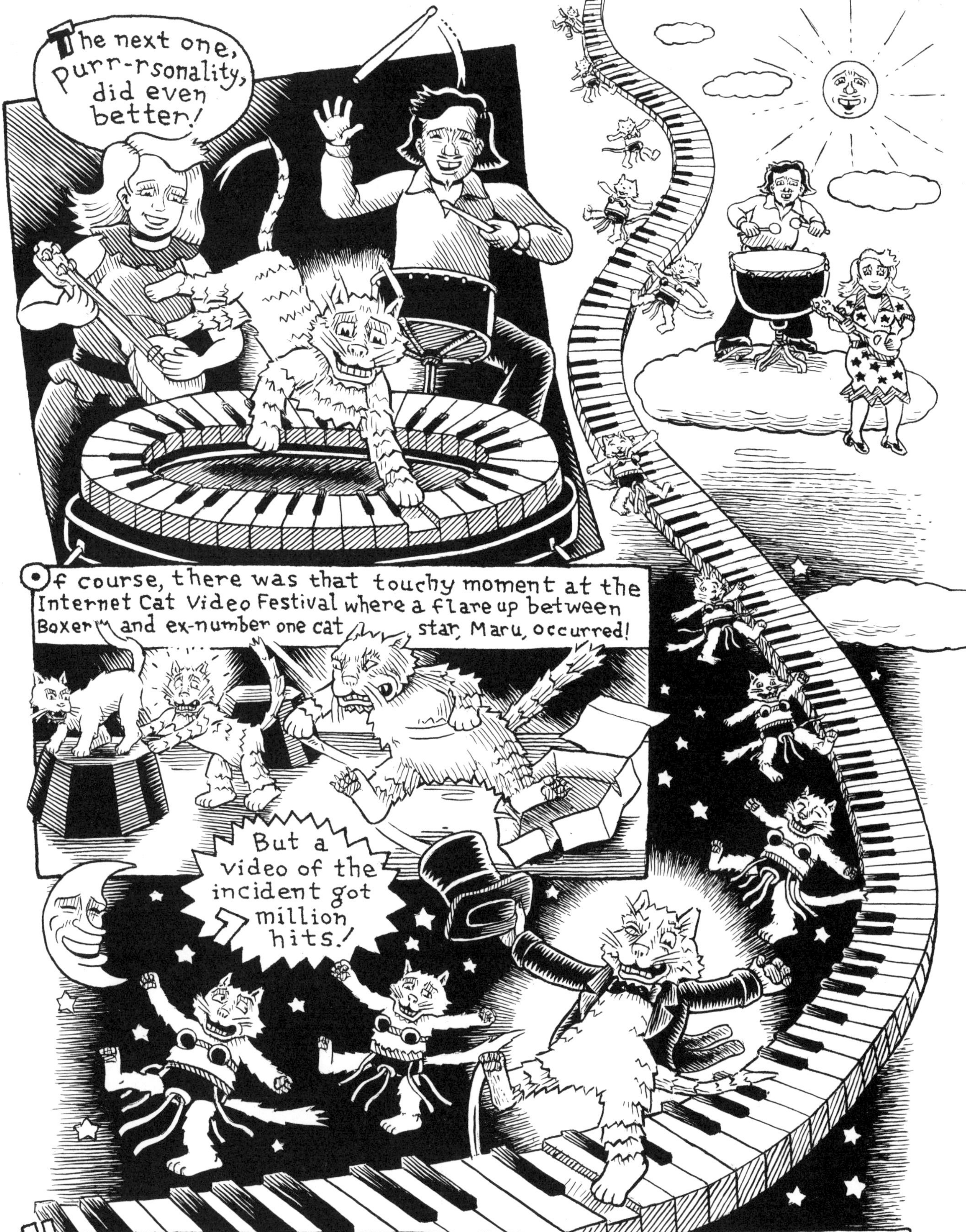
The next one, purr-rsonality, did even better!
Of course, there was that touchy moment at the Internet Cat Video Festival where a flare up between Boxer and ex-number one cat star, Maru, occurred!
But a video of the incident got 7 million hits!
However, Boxer's video triumph was Mel's rockin' arrangement of "Shanghai Shuffle," with its FANTASTIC special effects.

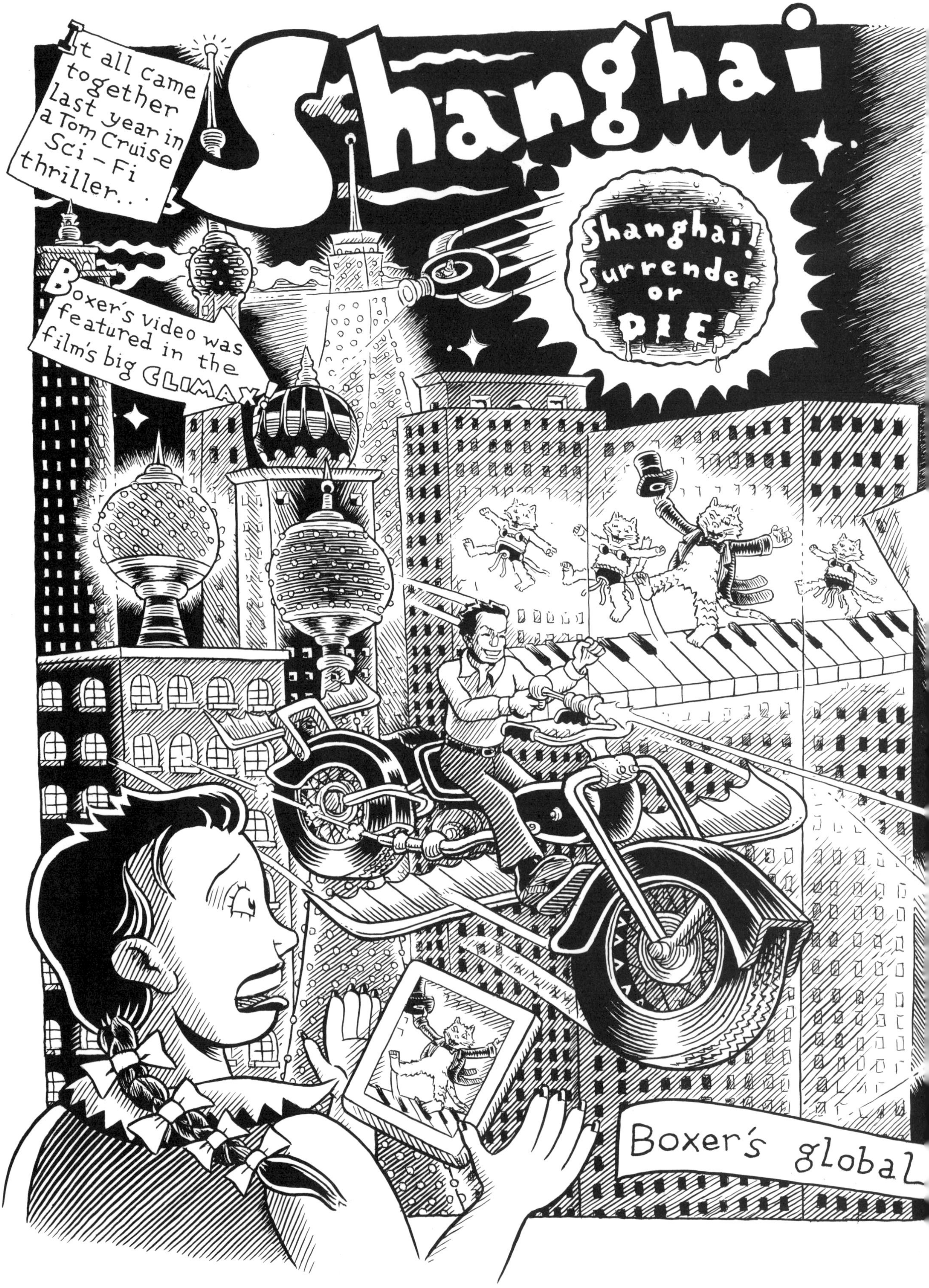
It all came together last year in a Tom Cruise Sci-Fi thriller...
Shanghai
Boxer's video was featured in the film's big CLIMAX!
Shanghai! Surrender or DIE!
Boxer's global

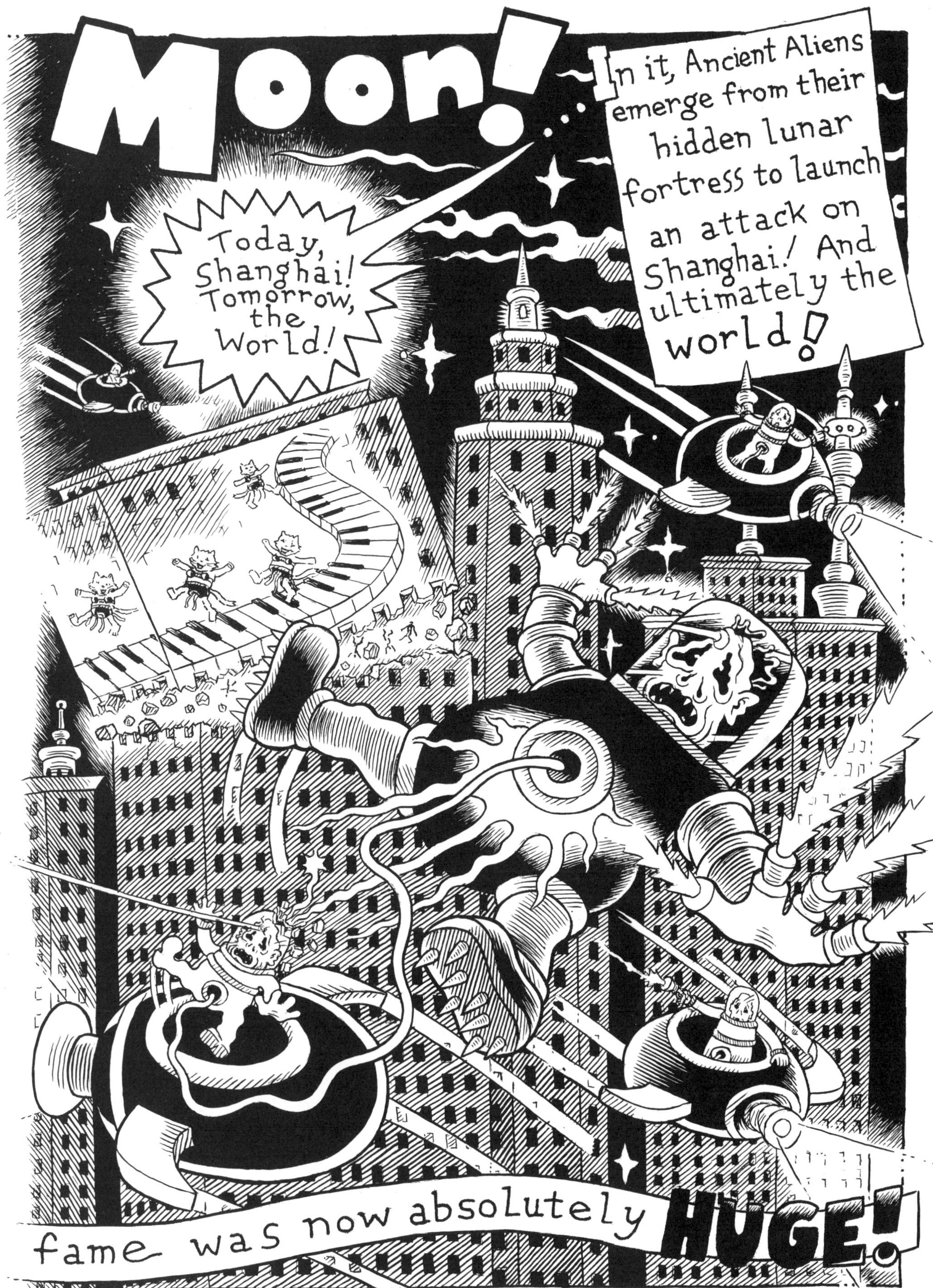

MOON!
In it, Ancient Aliens emerge from their hidden lunar fortress to launch an attack on Shanghai! And ultimately the world!
Today, Shanghai! Tomorrow, the World!
fame was now absolutely HUGE!

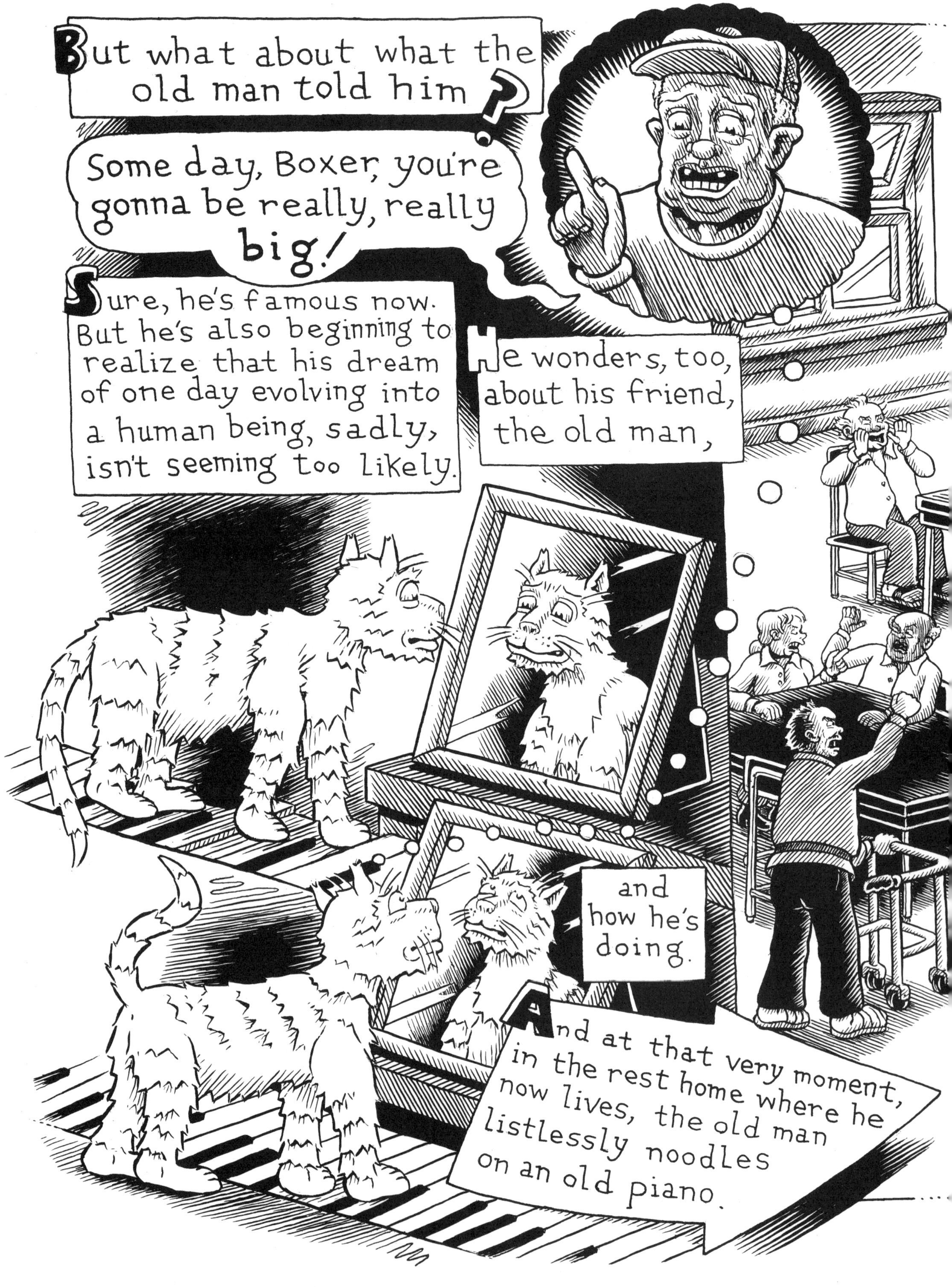

But what about what the old man told him?
Some day, Boxer, you're gonna be really, really big!
Sure, he's famous now. But he's also beginning to realize that his dream of one day evolving into a human being, sadly, isn't seeming too likely.
He wonders, too, about his friend, the old man,
and how he's doing.
And at that very moment, in the rest home where he now lives, the old man listlessly noodles on an old piano.

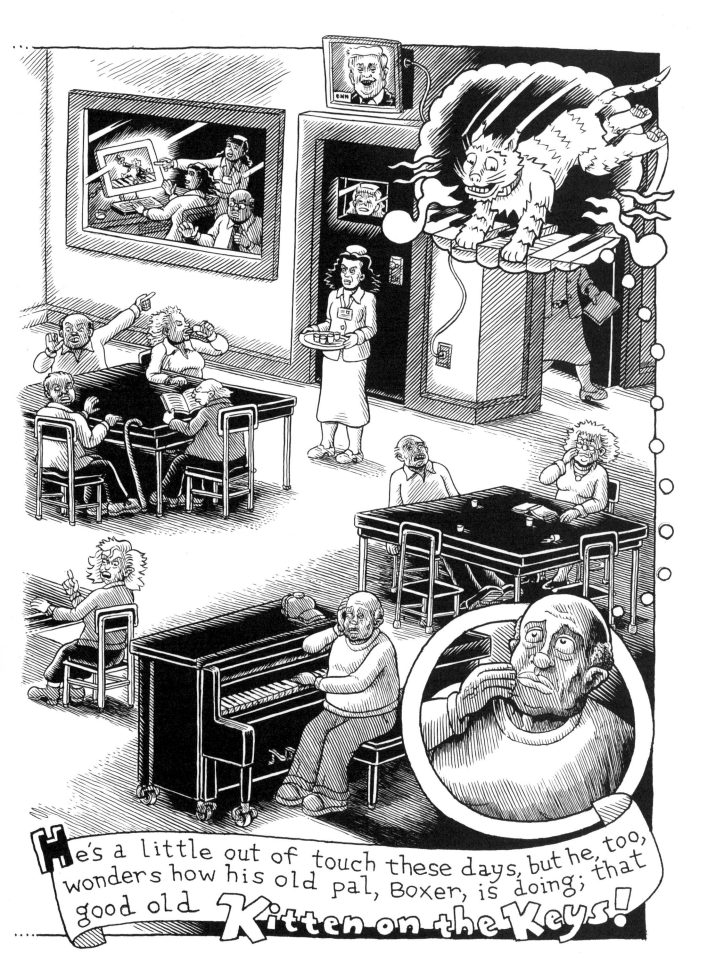

He's a little out of touch these days, but he, too, wonders how his old pal, Boxer, is doing; that good old **Kitten on the Keys!**

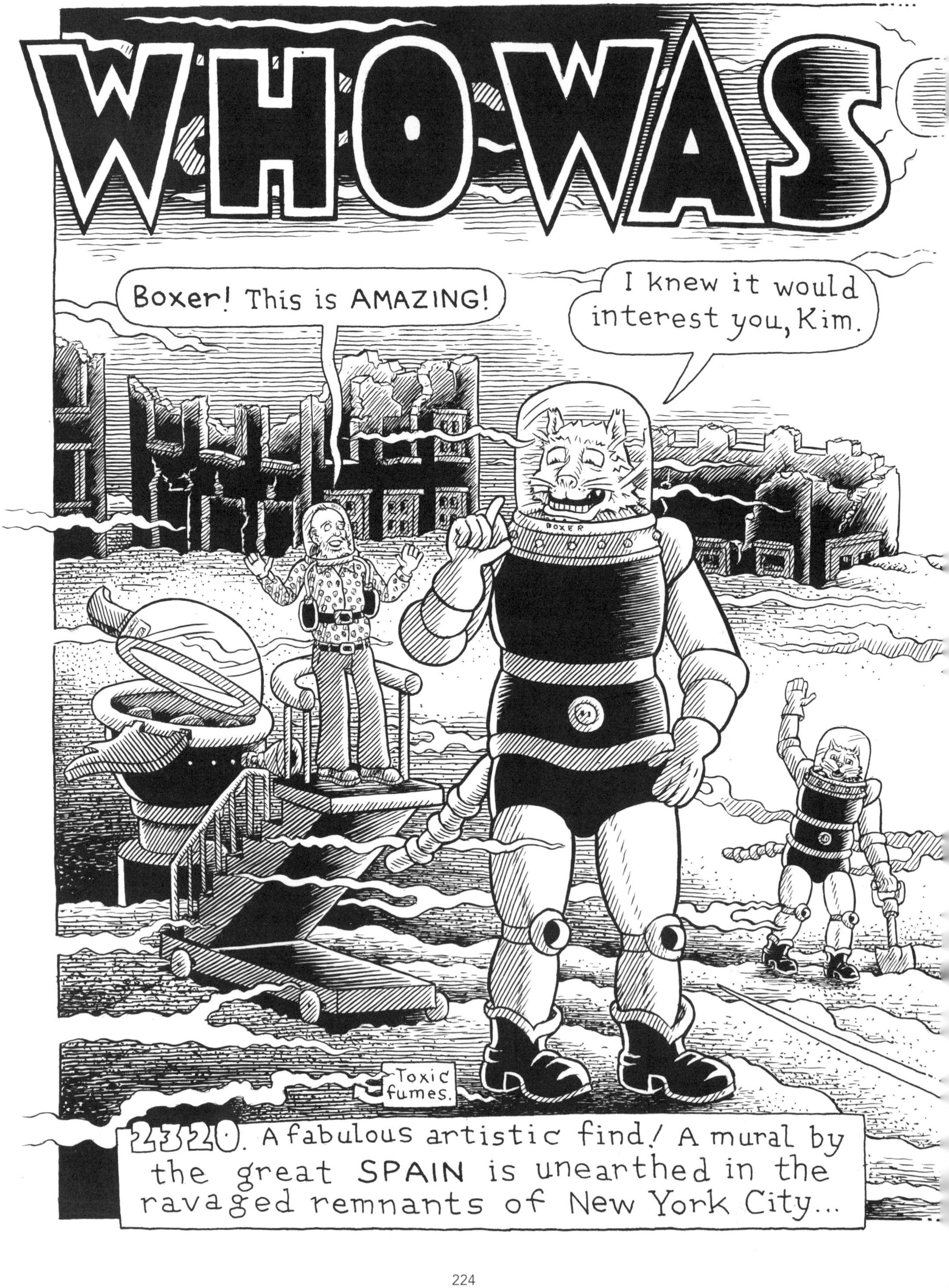
WHO WAS
Boxer! This is AMAZING!
I knew it would interest you, Kim.
BOXER
Toxic fumes.
2320. A fabulous artistic find! A mural by the great SPAIN is unearthed in the ravaged remnants of New York City...

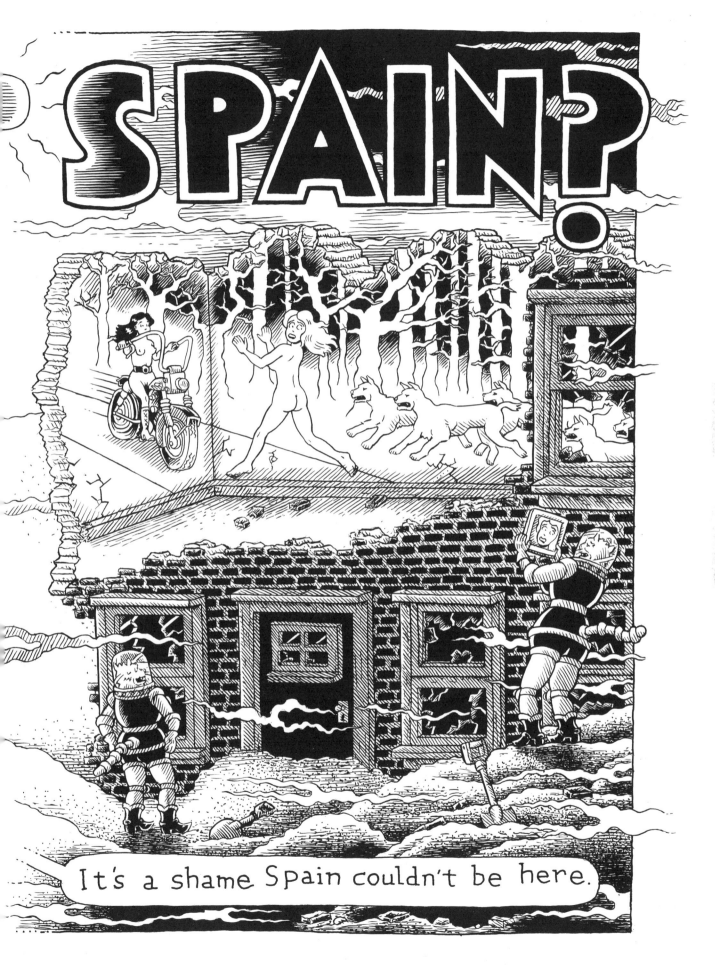

It's a shame Spain couldn't be here.

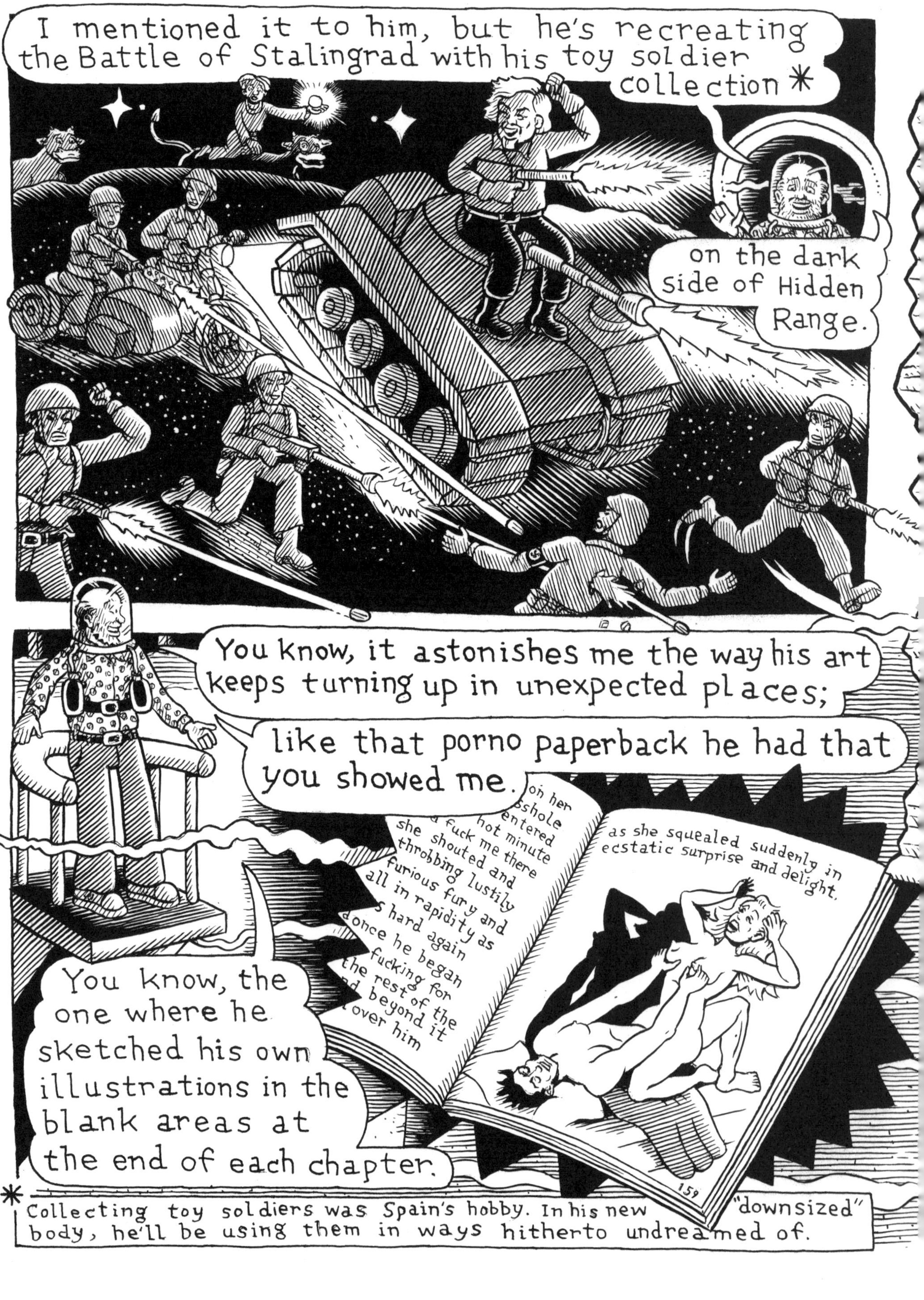
I mentioned it to him, but he's recreating the Battle of Stalingrad with his toy soldier collection *
on the dark side of Hidden Range.
You know, it astonishes me the way his art keeps turning up in unexpected places;
like that porno paperback he had that you showed me.
as she squealed suddenly in ecstatic surprise and delight.
159
You know, the one where he sketched his own illustrations in the blank areas at the end of each chapter.
* Collecting toy soldiers was Spain's hobby. In his new "downsized" body, he'll be using them in ways hitherto undreamed of.

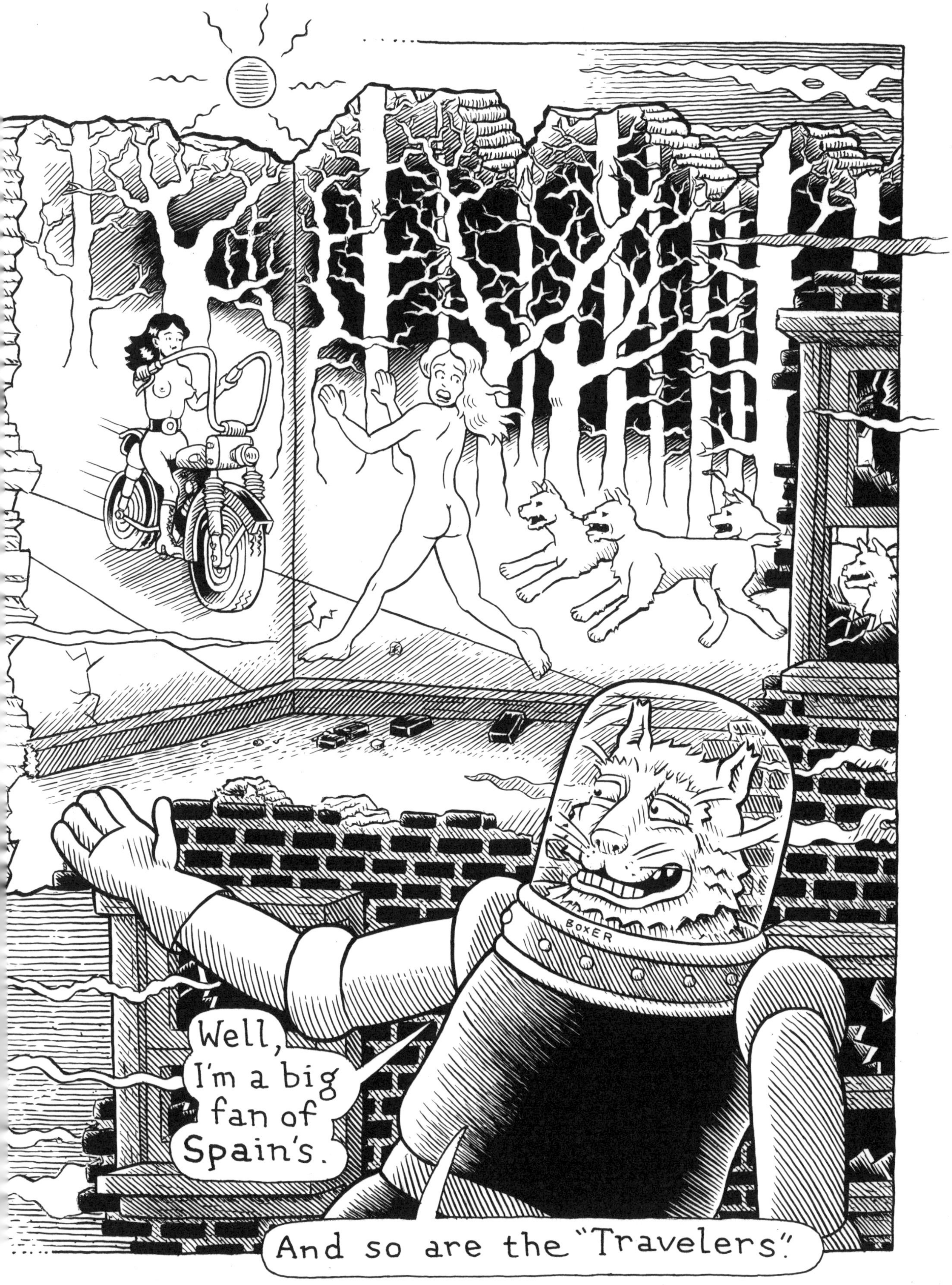

BOXER
Well, I'm a big fan of Spain's.
And so are the "Travelers".

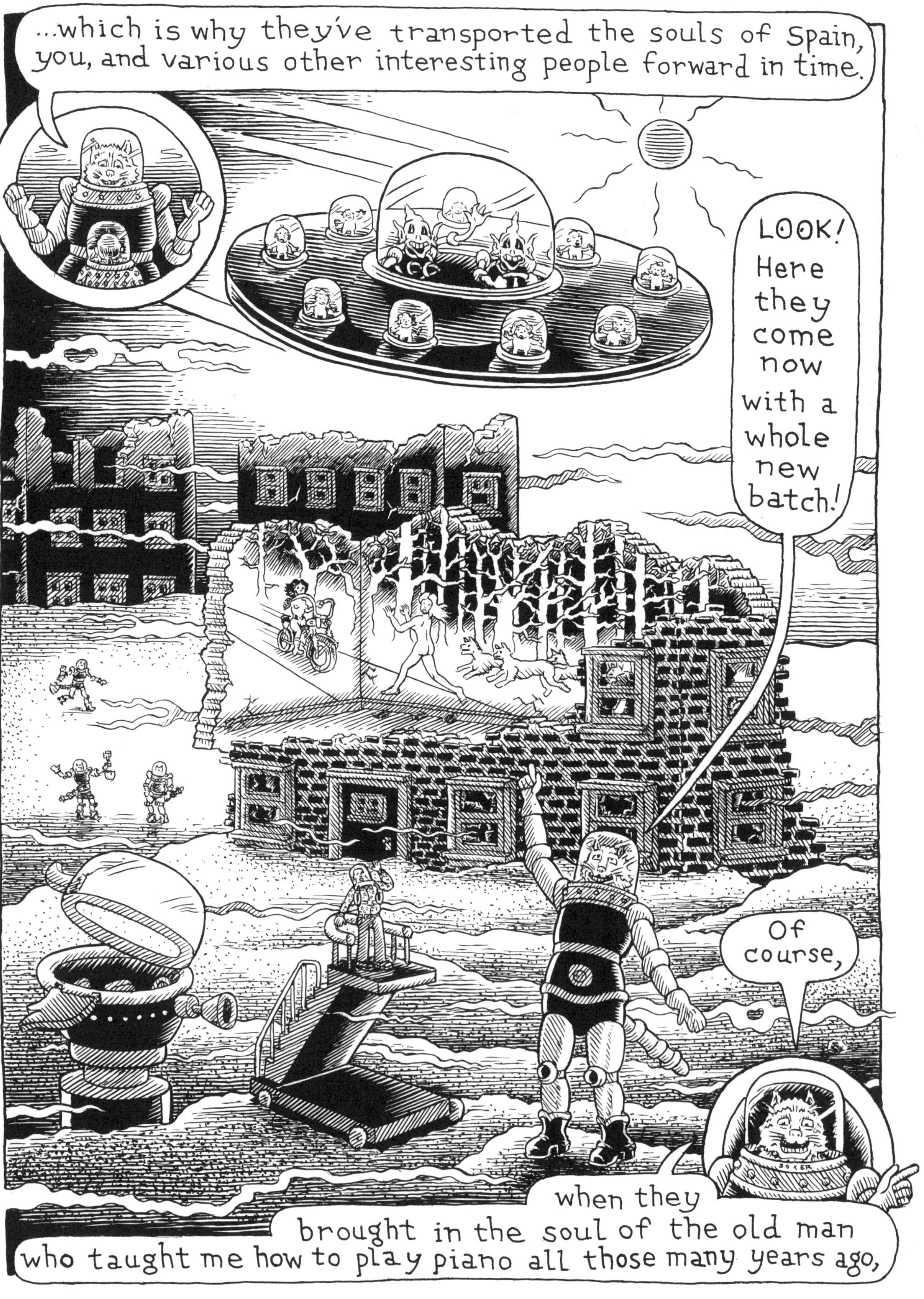
...which is why they've transported the souls of Spain, you, and various other interesting people forward in time.
LOOK! Here they come now with a whole new batch!
Of course,
when they brought in the soul of the old man who taught me how to play piano all those many years ago,

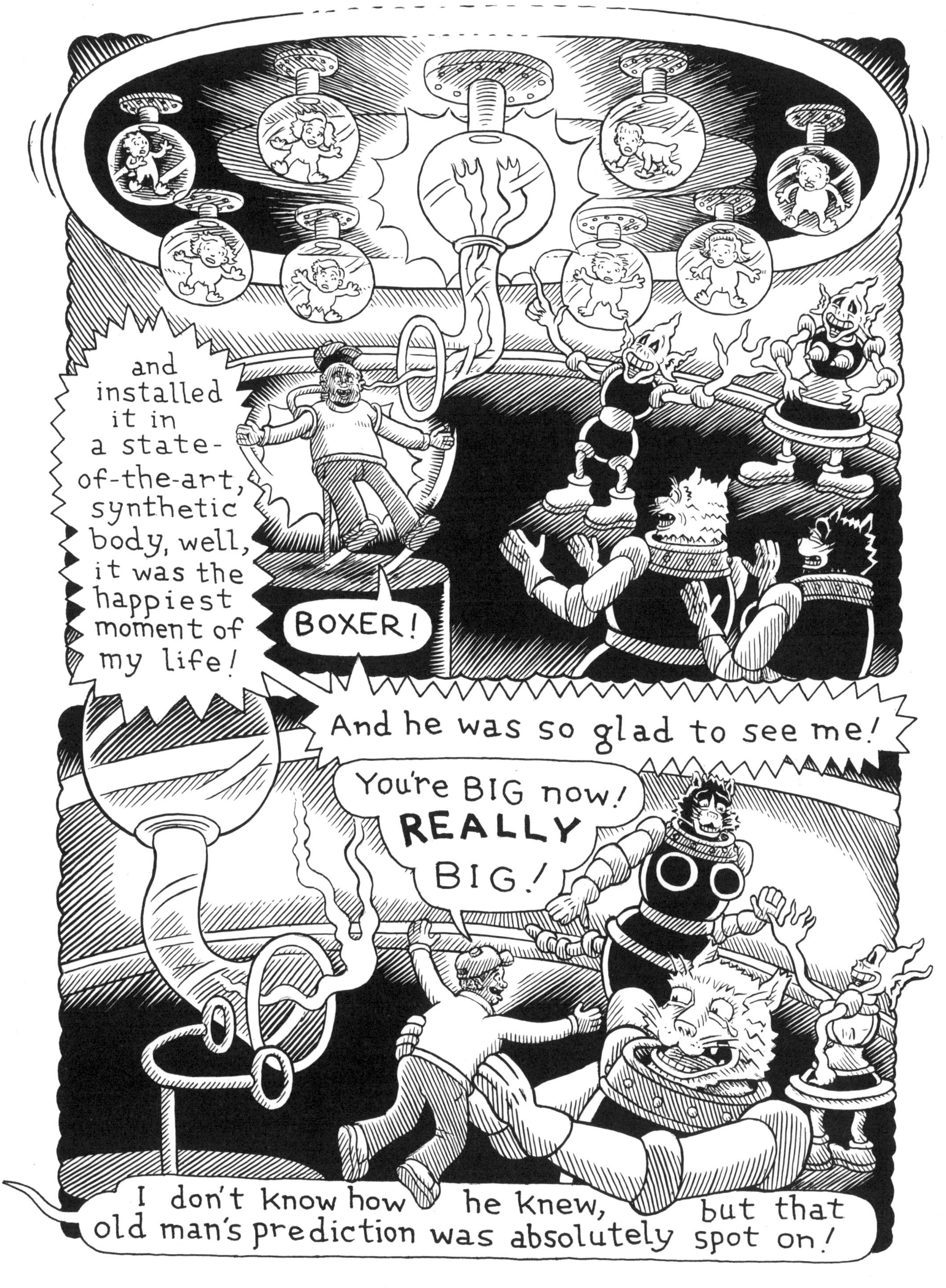
and installed it in a state-of-the-art, synthetic body, well, it was the happiest moment of my life!
BOXER!
And he was so glad to see me!
You're BIG now! REALLY BIG!
I don't know how he knew, but that old man's prediction was absolutely spot on!

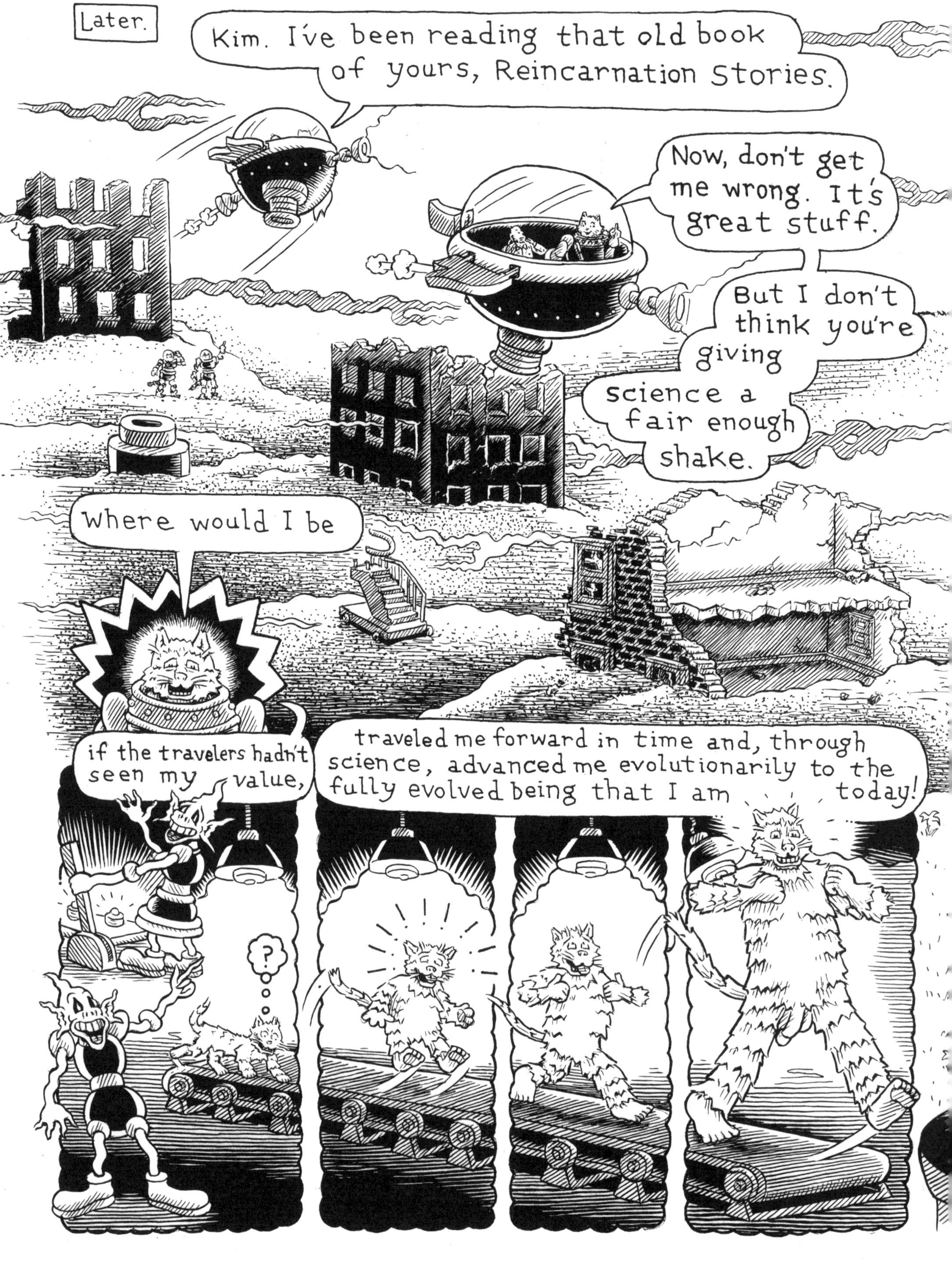
Later.
Kim. I've been reading that old book of yours, Reincarnation Stories.
Now, don't get me wrong. It's great stuff.
But I don't think you're giving science a fair enough shake.
Where would I be
if the travelers hadn't seen my value,
traveled me forward in time and, through science, advanced me evolutionarily to the fully evolved being that I am today!
?

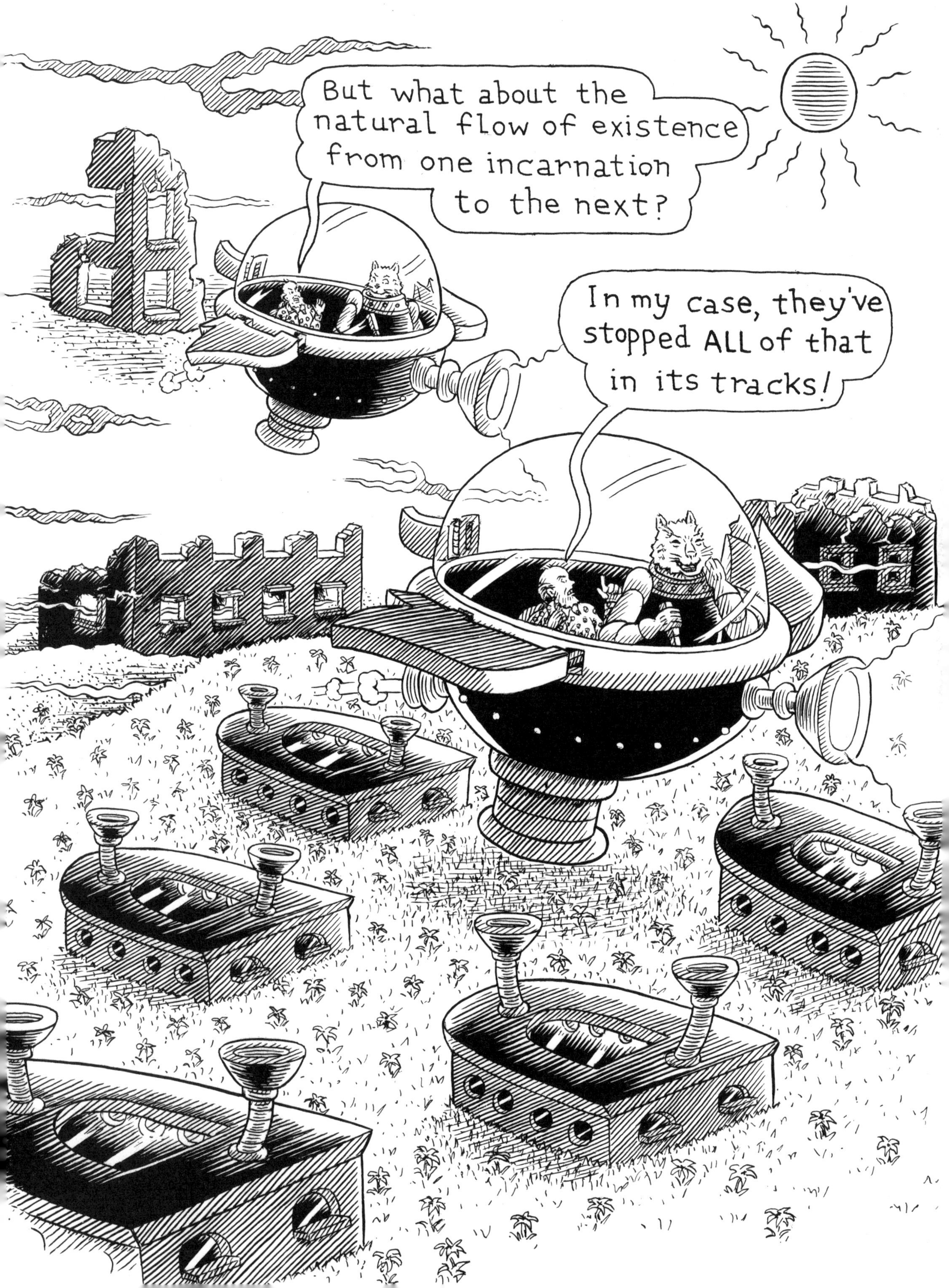
But what about the natural flow of existence from one incarnation to the next?
In my case, they've stopped ALL of that in its tracks!

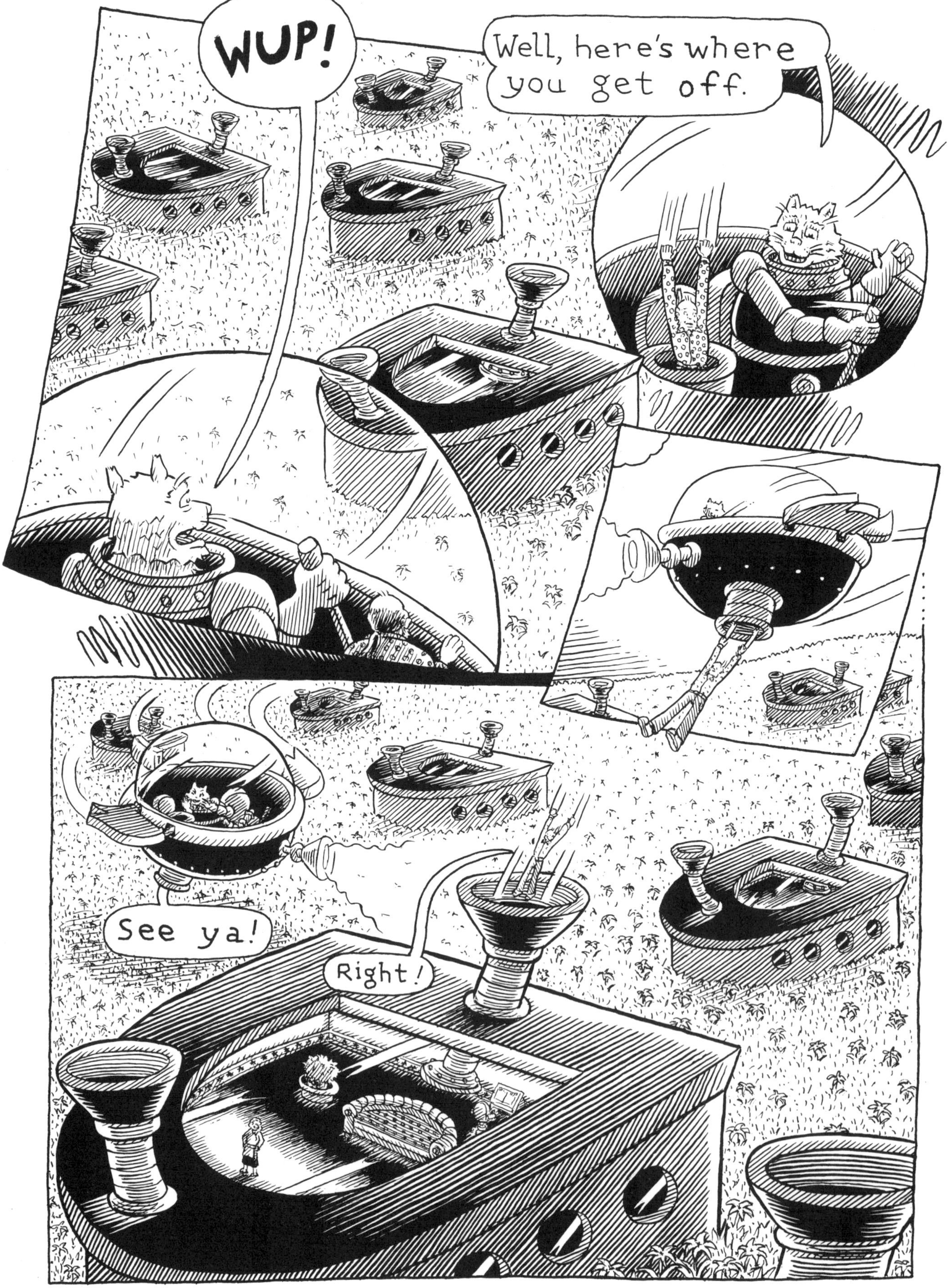
WUP!
Well, here's where you get off.
See ya!
Right!

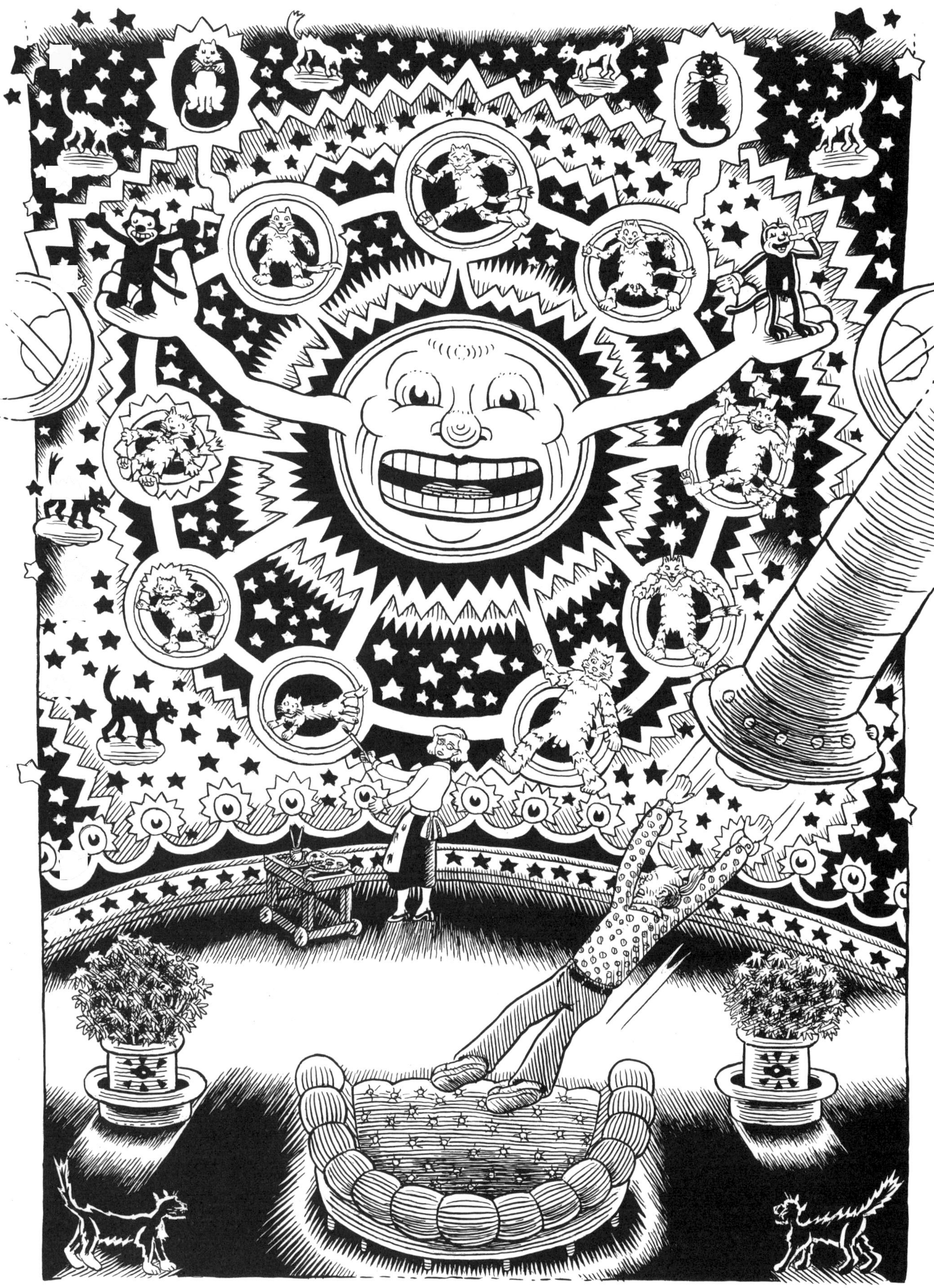

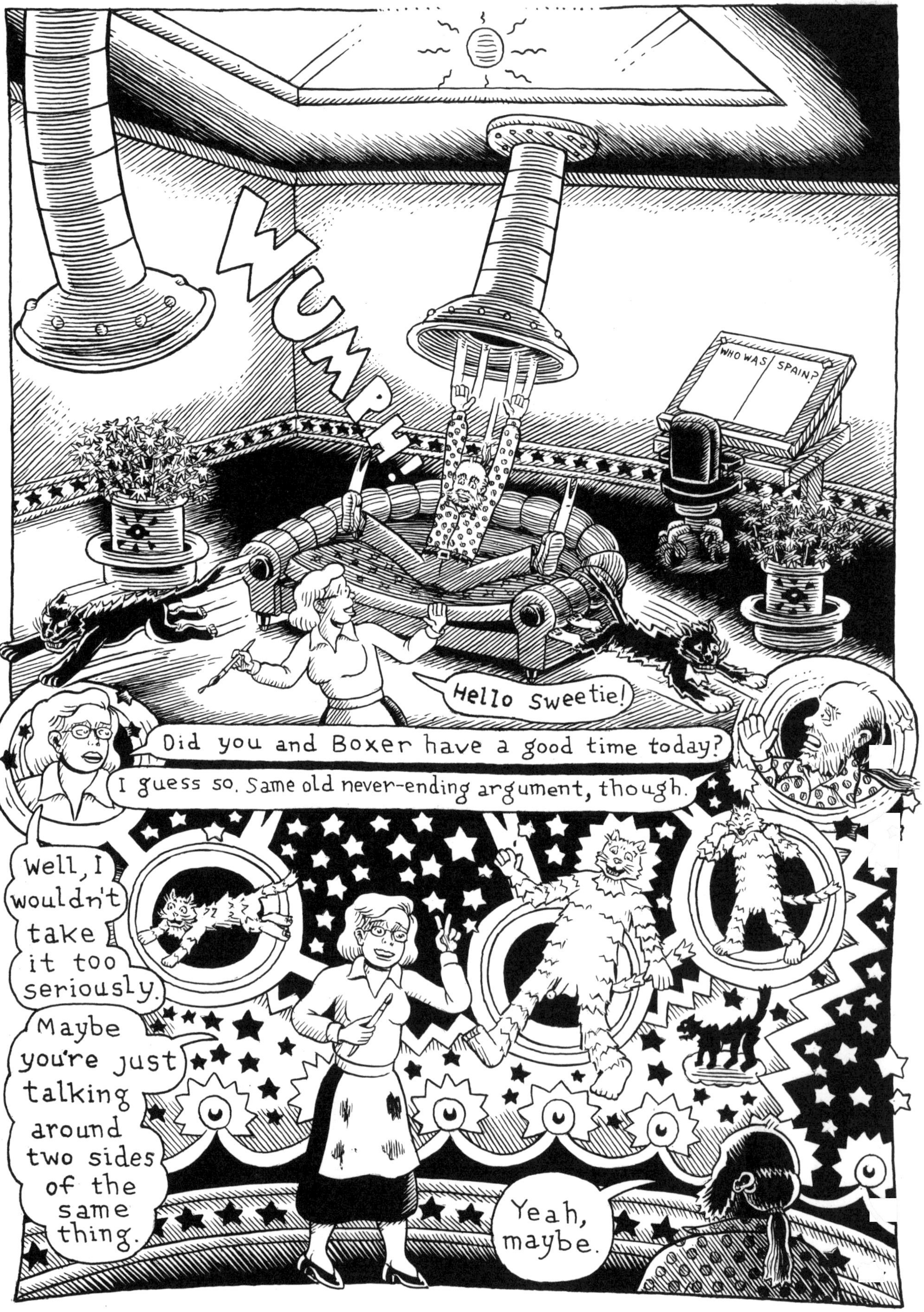
WUMPH!
WHO WAS SPAIN?
Hello Sweetie!
Did you and Boxer have a good time today?
I guess so. Same old never-ending argument, though.
Well, I wouldn't take it too seriously.
Maybe you're just talking around two sides of the same thing.
Yeah, maybe.

Who was Buck Jones?

At age 51, Buck Jones had everything to live for. He looked great and was starring in a well-received new series of westerns. Then came tragedy.

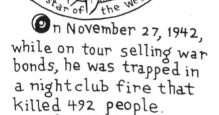

Buck Jones, great star of the Western skies

On November 27, 1942, while on tour selling war bonds, he was trapped in a nightclub fire that killed 492 people.

A cherished legend sprang up at the time of his death. Many people insisted that Buck initially escaped the fire but went back several times to save others before he, too, was killed. Unfortunately, the facts are not there to back this story up; but it does show how very much loved he was by friends and fans.

When bad things happen to good people, sometimes you

Print the Legend!

And what does seem to be quite true is that Buck Jones was indeed a good man.

These pictures are drawn from photos taken on the day just hours before the horrific fire.

Buck visiting a children's hospital in Boston where the fire occurred.

On a local radio show, he promotes the ongoing war effort.

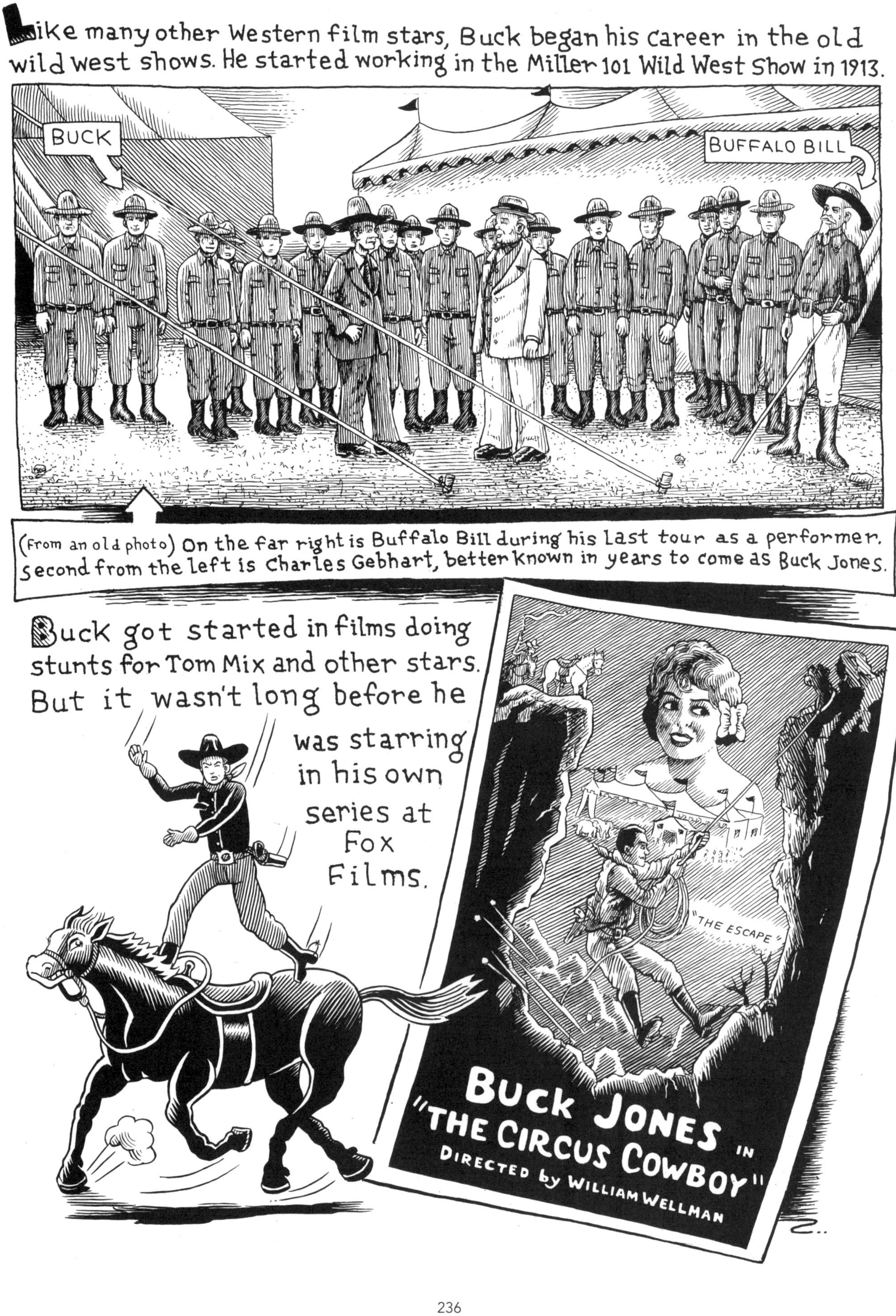
Like many other Western film stars, Buck began his career in the old wild west shows. He started working in the Miller 101 Wild West Show in 1913.
BUCK
BUFFALO BILL
(From an old photo) On the far right is Buffalo Bill during his last tour as a performer. Second from the left is Charles Gebhart, better known in years to come as Buck Jones.
Buck got started in films doing stunts for Tom Mix and other stars. But it wasn't long before he
was starring in his own series at Fox Films.
"THE ESCAPE"
BUCK JONES IN "THE CIRCUS COWBOY"
DIRECTED by WILLIAM WELLMAN

Some of the directors Buck worked with in the silent era were William Wellman, W.S. Van Dyke, and even the great John Ford. Sadly, like so many silent films, most of Buck's 1920s films are now lost or missing. However, in one early film still around, directed by John Ford, Just Pals (1920), an interesting humorous motif about a broken fencegate is introduced. It turns into a running gag that continues through several more of Buck's films.

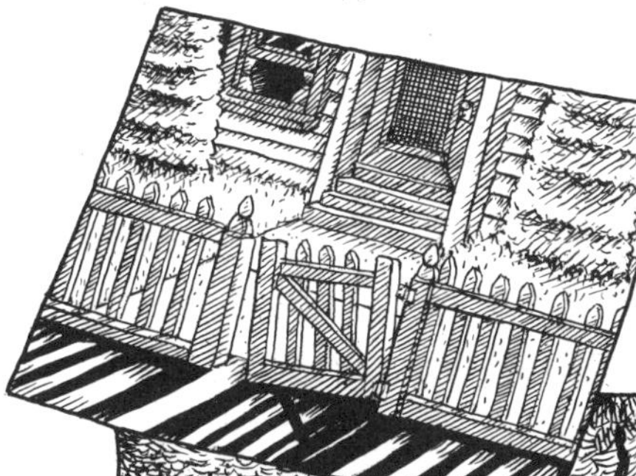

In Lazybones (1925), a non-Western directed by Frank Borzage, the unfixed fencegate

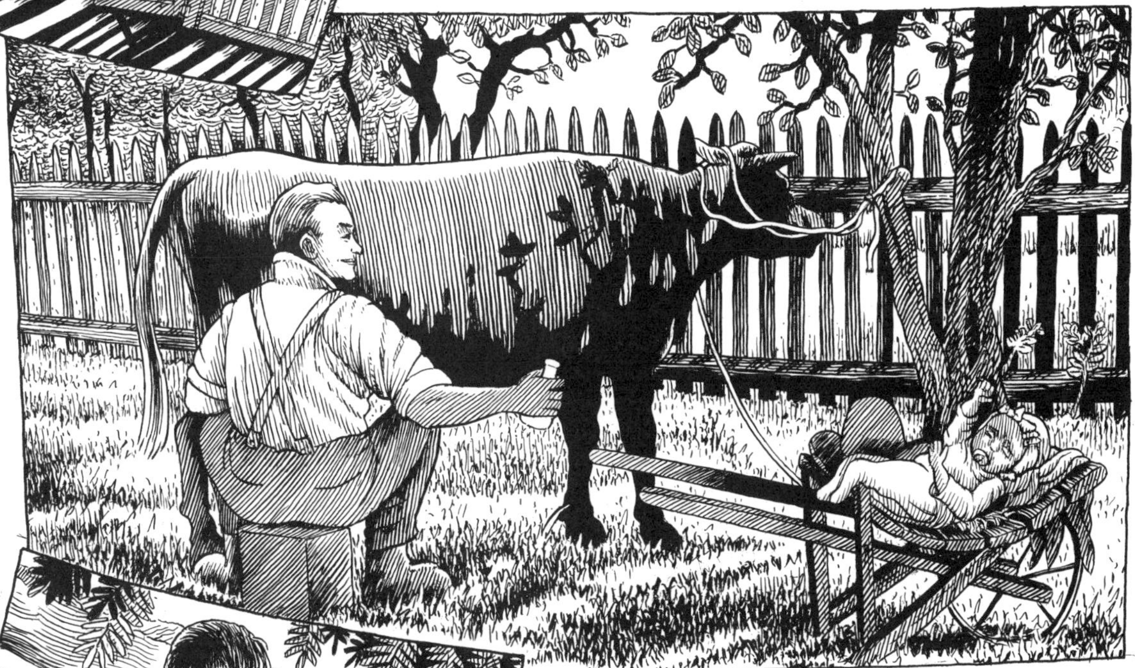

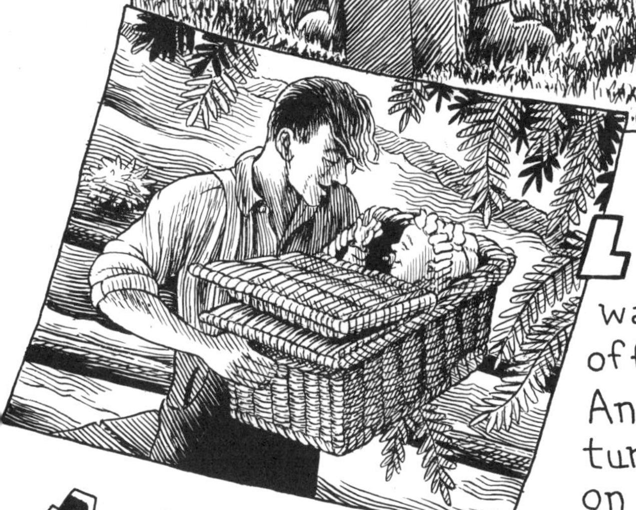

becomes an even bigger part of the storyline.

Lazybones also survives and it is a warm and winning film that shows off Buck's considerable acting chops. And that broken fencegate? It turns up again, still broken, later on in one of Buck's 1930s Westerns.

At the end of the 1920s Buck decided to quit films, take all the money he'd saved, and start a wild west show of his own. It did not pan out and he lost just about every cent he had.

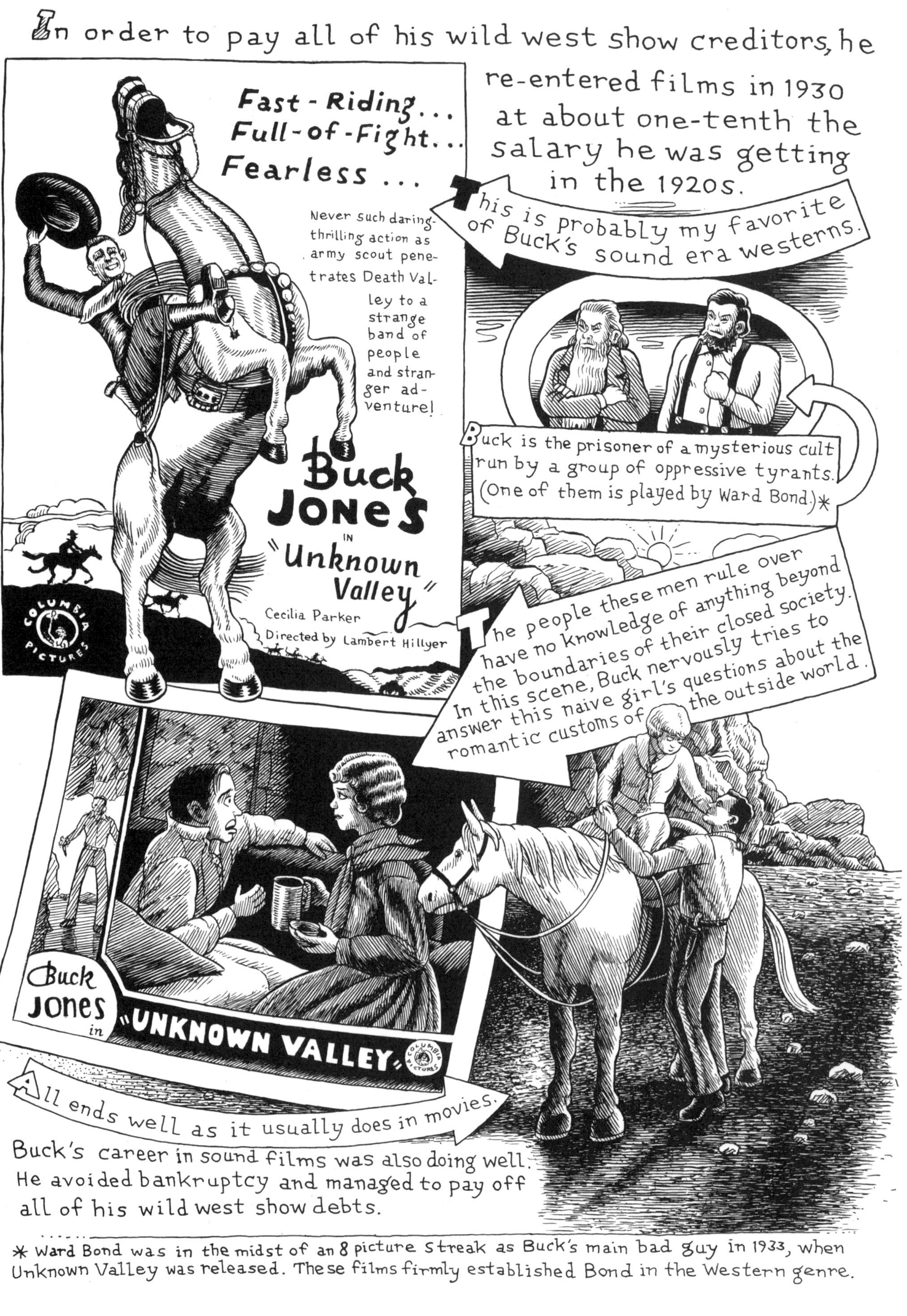
In order to pay all of his wild west show creditors, he re-entered films in 1930 at about one-tenth the salary he was getting in the 1920s.
Fast-Riding... Full-of-Fight... Fearless...
Never such daring-thrilling action as army scout penetrates Death Valley to a strange band of people and stranger adventure!
Buck Jones in "Unknown Valley"
Cecilia Parker
Directed by Lambert Hillyer
Columbia Pictures
This is probably my favorite of Buck's sound era westerns.
Buck is the prisoner of a mysterious cult run by a group of oppressive tyrants. (One of them is played by Ward Bond.)*
The people these men rule over have no knowledge of anything beyond the boundaries of their closed society. In this scene, Buck nervously tries to answer this naive girl's questions about the romantic customs of the outside world.
Buck Jones in "Unknown Valley"
Columbia Pictures
All ends well as it usually does in movies.
Buck's career in sound films was also doing well. He avoided bankruptcy and managed to pay off all of his wild west show debts.
* Ward Bond was in the midst of an 8 picture streak as Buck's main bad guy in 1933, when Unknown Valley was released. These films firmly established Bond in the Western genre.

Around this time, Buck decided to do something that he'd been thinking about for quite awhile. He started a club for boys and girls modeled somewhat on the Boy Scouts, called **The Buck Jones Rangers**.

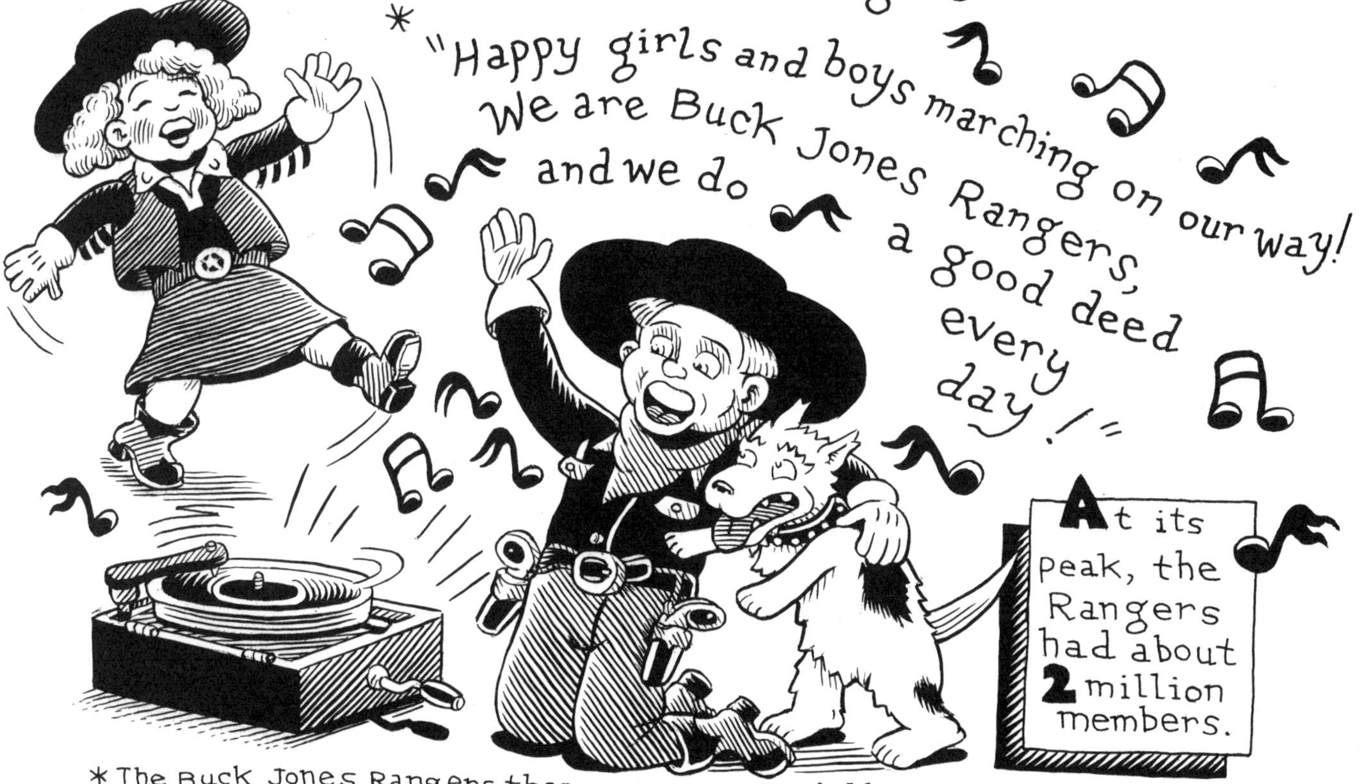

* "Happy girls and boys marching on our way! We are Buck Jones Rangers, and we do a good deed every day!"
At its peak, the Rangers had about 2 million members.

* The Buck Jones Rangers theme song as recorded by Frank Luther in 1935.

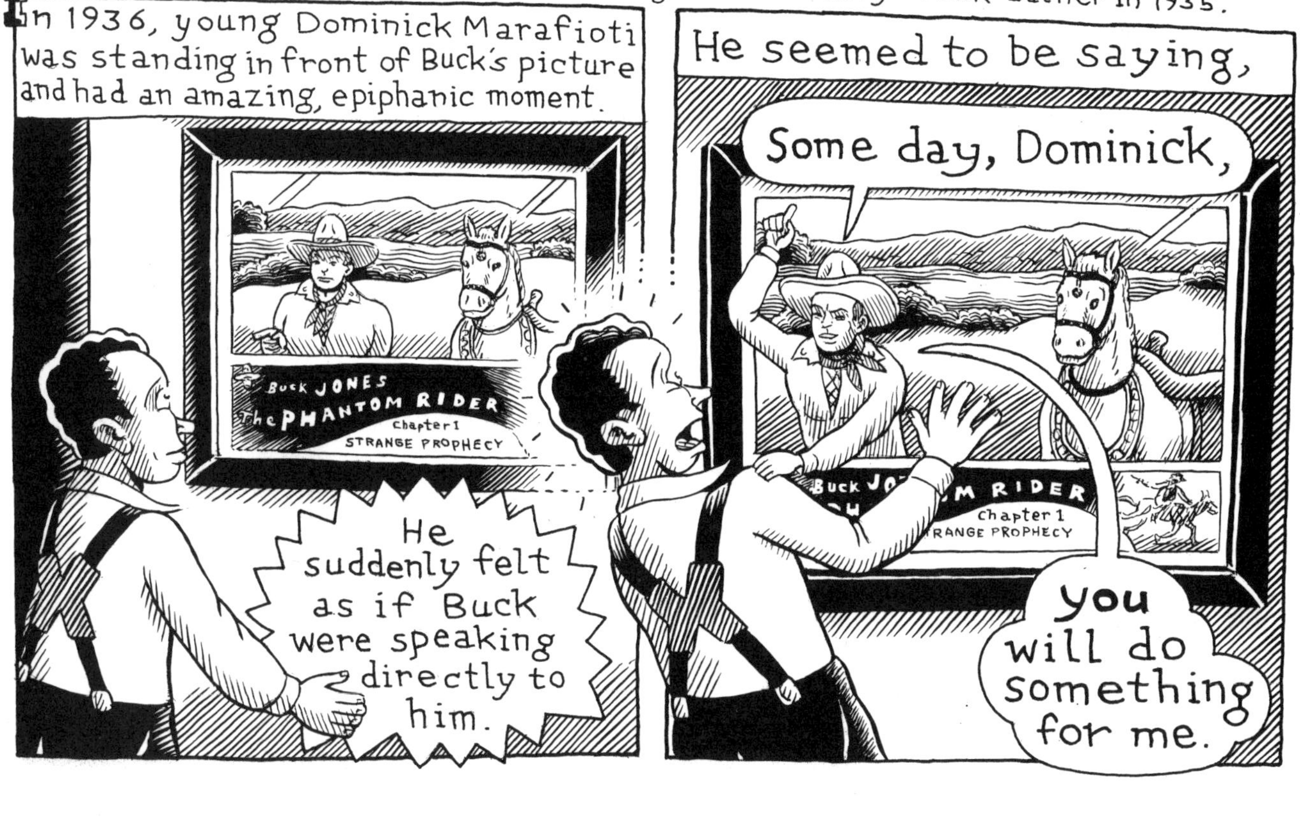

In 1936, young Dominick Marafioti was standing in front of Buck's picture and had an amazing, epiphanic moment.
BUCK JONES
THE PHANTOM RIDER
Chapter 1
STRANGE PROPHECY
He suddenly felt as if Buck were speaking directly to him.
He seemed to be saying,
Some day, Dominick,
you will do something for me.

Well, time went by and the Rangers dwindled away. Dominick grew up, married, and went about establishing his adult life. But he was still haunted by the strange, long ago prophecy that he thought he heard Buck say.

In the 1980s, Dominick decided that the time had finally come for him to fulfill it, and he revived The Buck Jones Rangers.

I joined up in 2004 and Dominick sent me this wonderful photo of himself welcoming me to the Rangers. But there was something rather sad about Dominick. His wife had recently died but he was still signing the communications I was getting from him with both his and his wife's names.

TO KIM DEITCH
Welcome to the
BUCK JONES
TRAIL!
Dominick Marafioti
National Chief
5-13-04

INTRODUCING... DOMINICK MARAFIOTI, FOUNDER AND NATIONAL CHIEF OF THE BUCK JONES RANGERS OF AMERICA. © IN THE U.S. AND EUROPE. SINCE 1979 HAVE PLEDGED THEMSELVES TO BRING LONG OVER DUE HONORS TO THE LATE SUPER WESTERN STAR— BUCK JONES. HE LOST HIS LIFE DUE TO INJURIES SUSTAINED A THE INFAMOUS FIRE AT THE COCONUT GROVE NIGHT CLUB WHILE ON A WAR BOND SELLING TOUR IN 1942, WHILE TRYING TO AID TRAPPED VICTIMS TO SAFETY, HIS LOYALTY TO HIS FELLOW MAN. HE COULD DO NO LESS A HERO ON THE SCREEN; A HERO IN REAL LIFE. AT PRESENT WE HAVE A STAMP PETITION FOR SIGNATURES TO INDUCE THE POSTAL STAMP ADVISORY COMMITTEE TO PLACE BUCK JONES ON A COMMEMORATIVE STAMP. YOU CAN SHOW YOUR SUPPORT. JUST WRITE TO THE ADDRESS LISTED BELOW. THANK YOU AND GOD BLESS!

POSTMASTER GENERAL'S OFFICE, STAMP ADVISORY COMMITTEE, HEADQUARTERS, U.S. POSTAL SERVICE, WASHINGTON, D.C. 20260

He Helped Shape The Youth of America

I should have seen it coming. A month or so after I joined, he sent out a general letter canceling a Buck Jones con he'd planned for later that year because he'd just found out that he had terminal cancer.

I don't think it was even ten days later that I got another form letter. This one had that same striking photo of Dominick wearing that big, white Stetson hat,

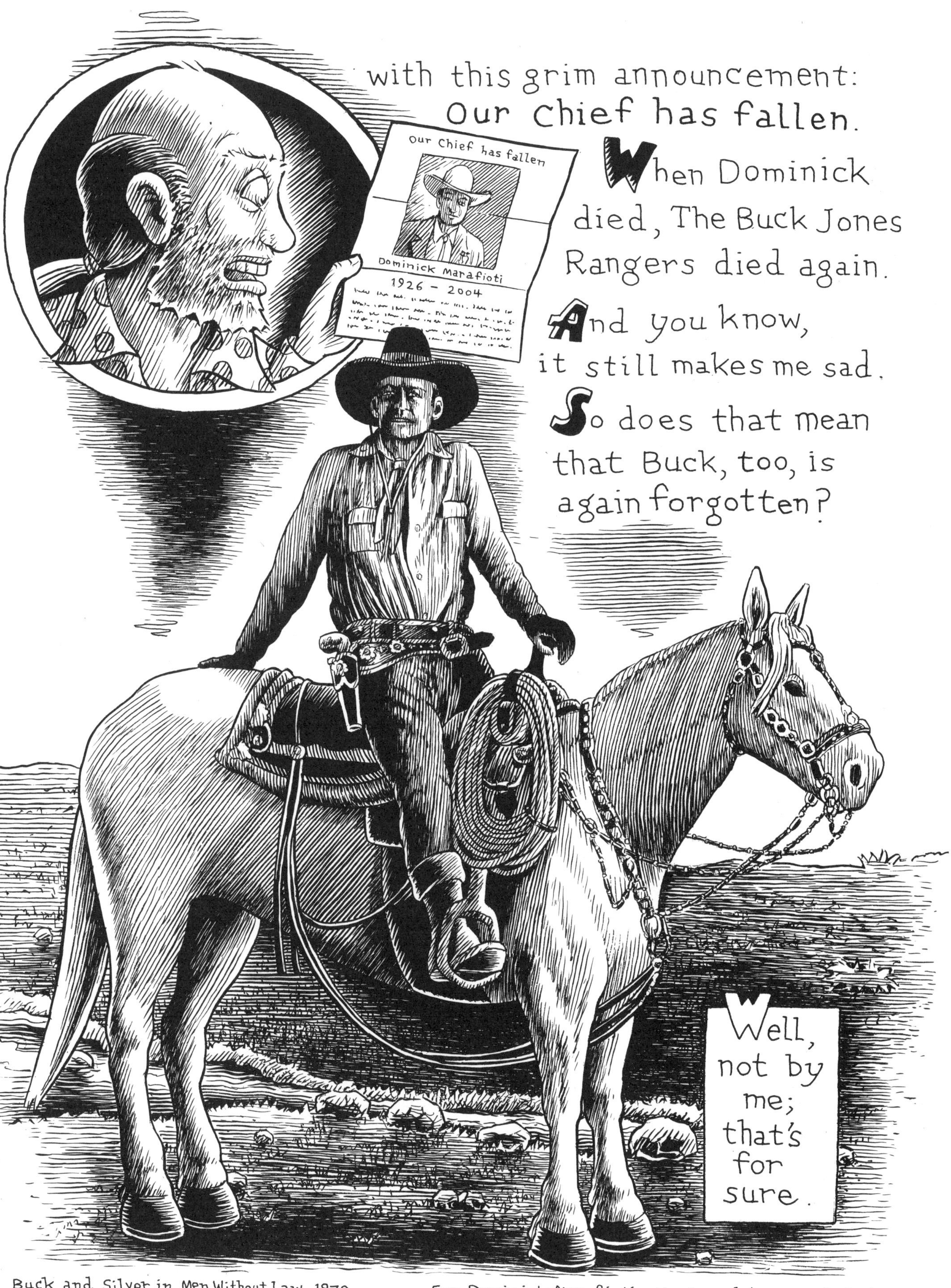
with this grim announcement:
Our Chief has fallen.
Our Chief has fallen
Dominick Marafioti
1926 - 2004
When Dominick died, The Buck Jones Rangers died again.
And you know, it still makes me sad.
So does that mean that Buck, too, is again forgotten?
Well, not by me; that's for sure.

Buck and Silver in Men Without Law, 1930

For Dominick Marafioti. He dared to wear the hat.

WHO WAS Jack HOXIE?

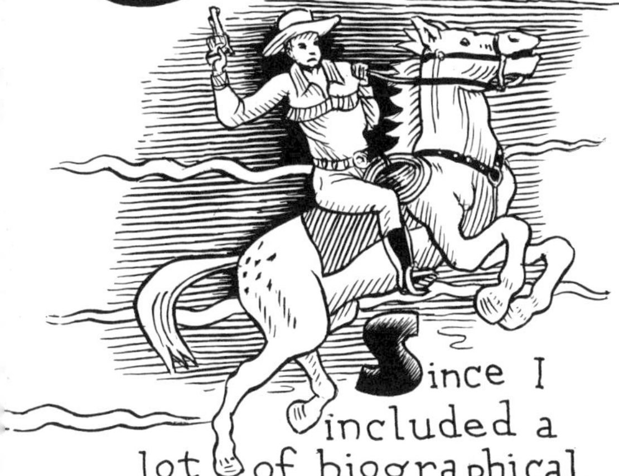

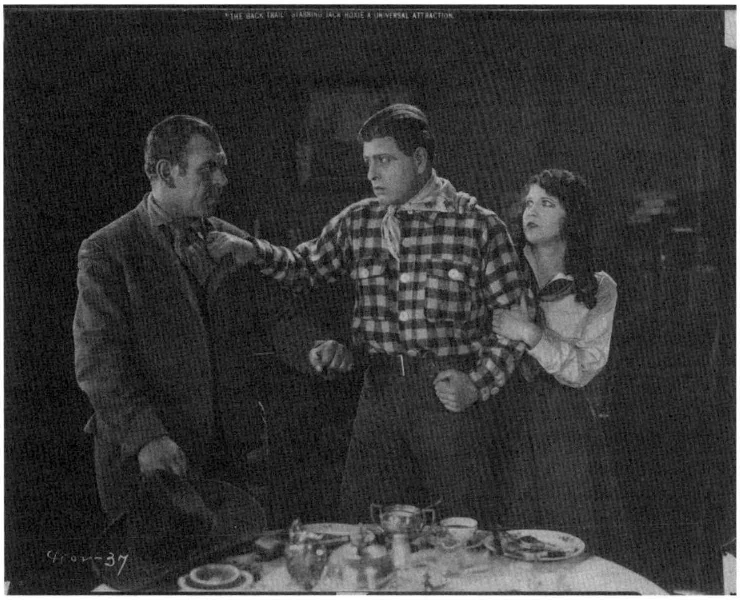
"THE BACK TRAIL" STARRING JACK HOXIE A UNIVERSAL ATTRACTION

Since I included a lot of biographical information in my story about Jack, this will be brief.

One thing that attracted me to Jack, and Buck Jones, too, was the degree of levelheadedness they showed in spite of being big Western film stars.

In Jack's case this may have come from accidentally killing his older brother in 1905. This tragedy seemed to steady him down, and he carried his later fame with a surprising amount of warmth and humanity.

Like Buck Jones, he started his public career in wild west shows. And when fame diminished later on, it was Western-oriented shows that he returned to.

It was a photo of Jack taken in 1958, still looking pretty much like himself, touring out in the boondocks of rural America, that made me think, "Gee, I actually could have met this guy!"

Sometimes a random thought like that makes for the nucleus of a good story.

Jack continued to perform in small shows until around 1960. He died, at age 80, in 1965.

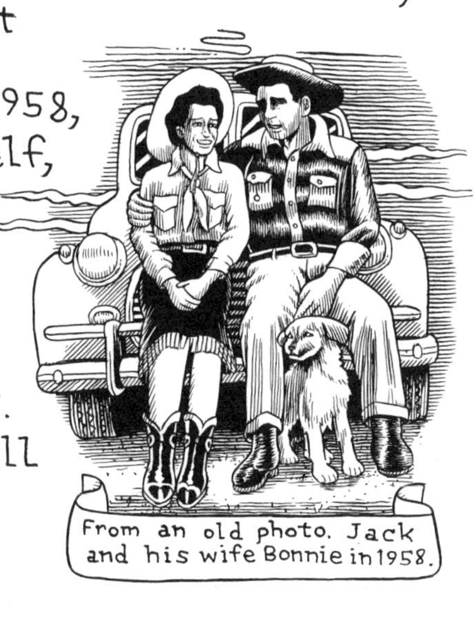

From an old photo. Jack and his wife Bonnie in 1958.

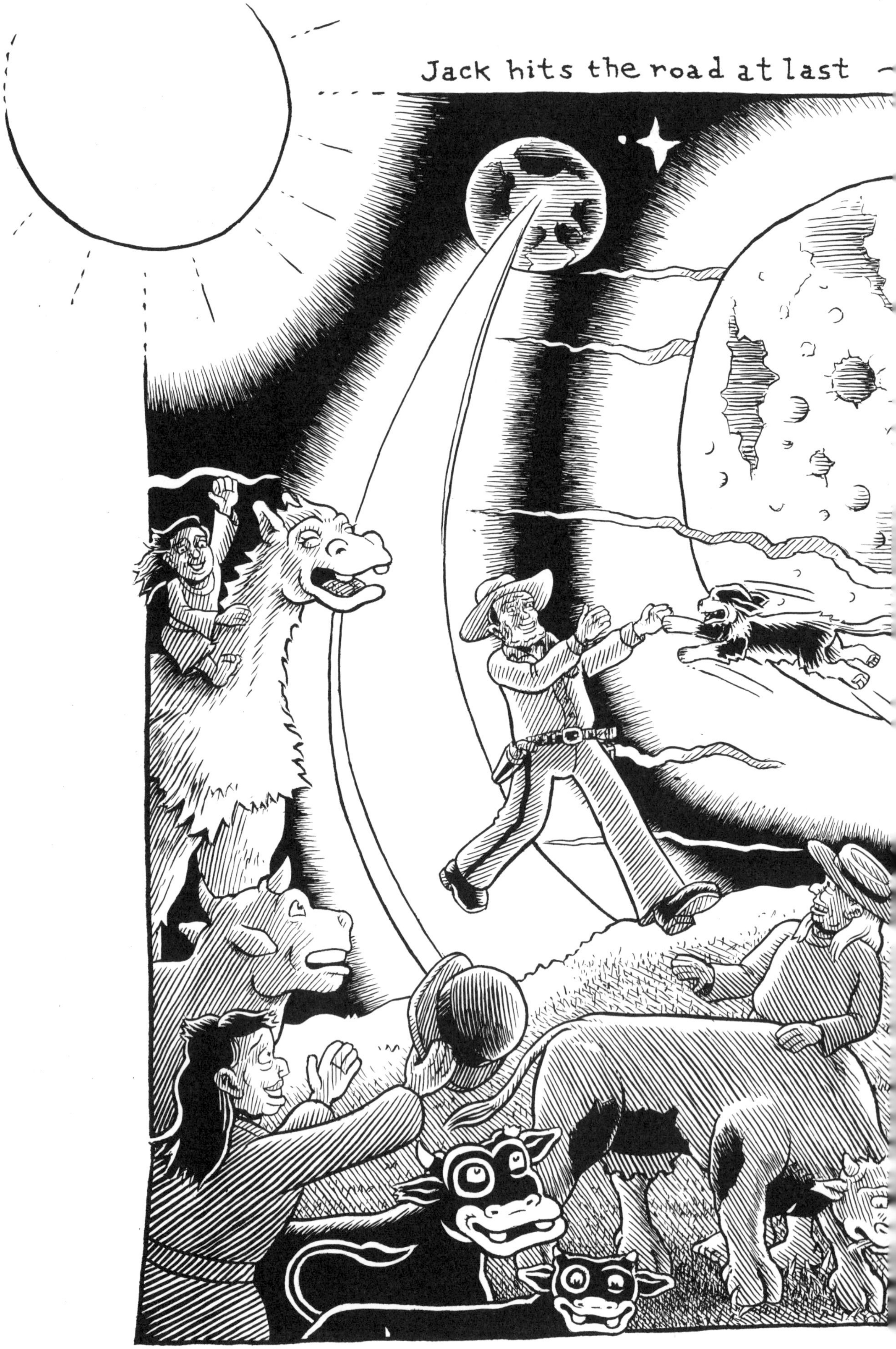
Jack hits the road at last –
1885 –

— for Hidden Range...

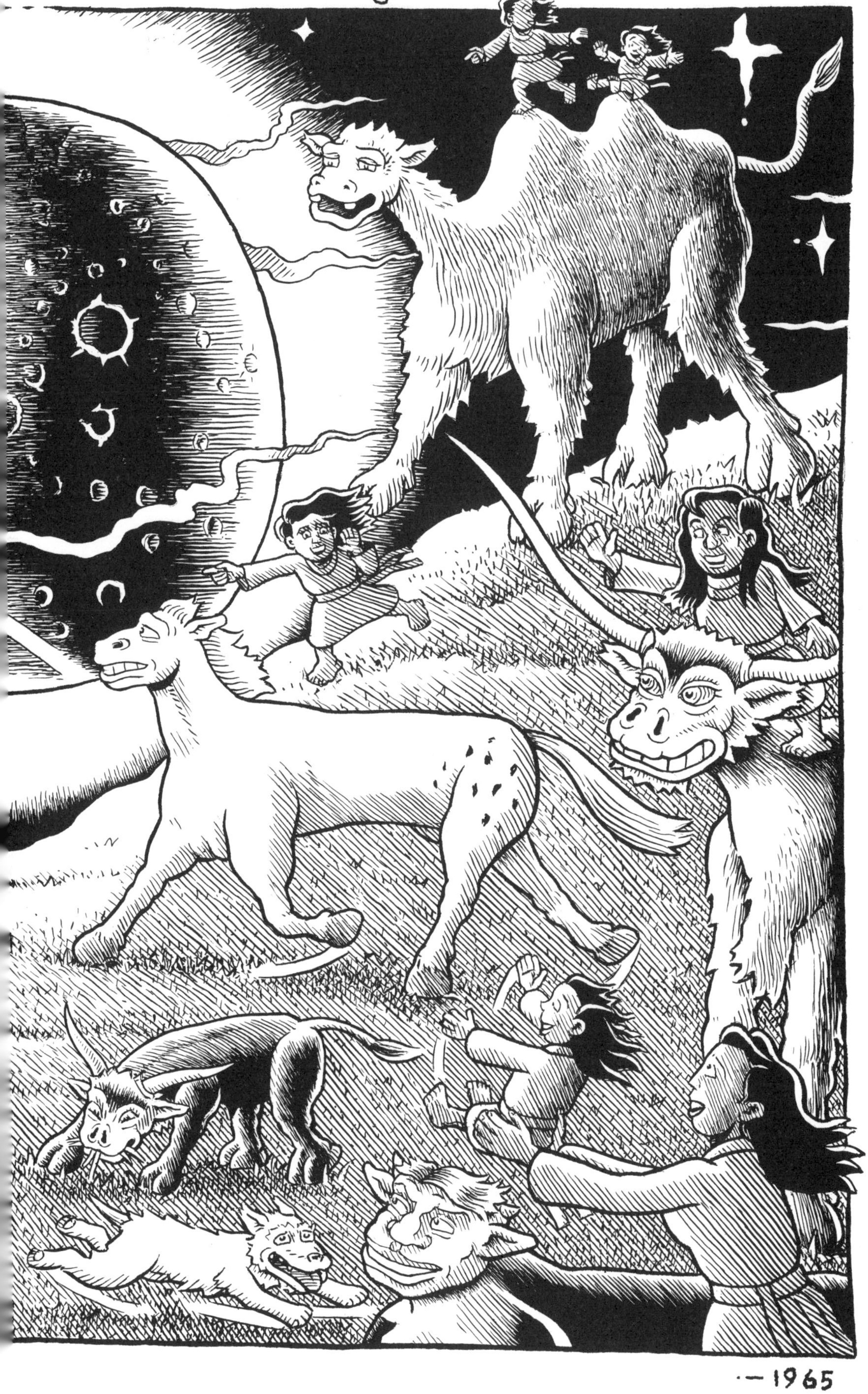

—1965

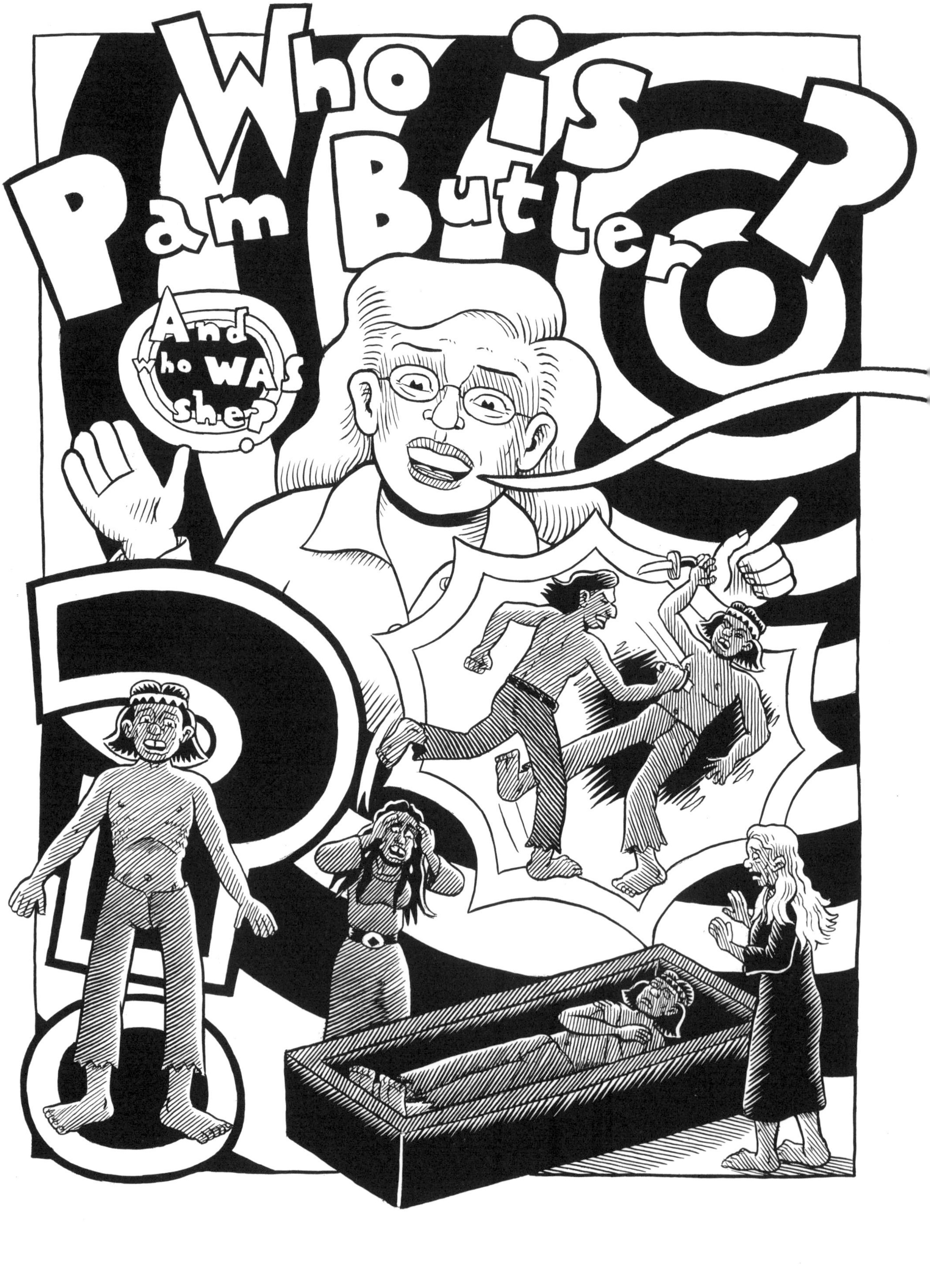
Who is Pam Butler?
And who WAS she?

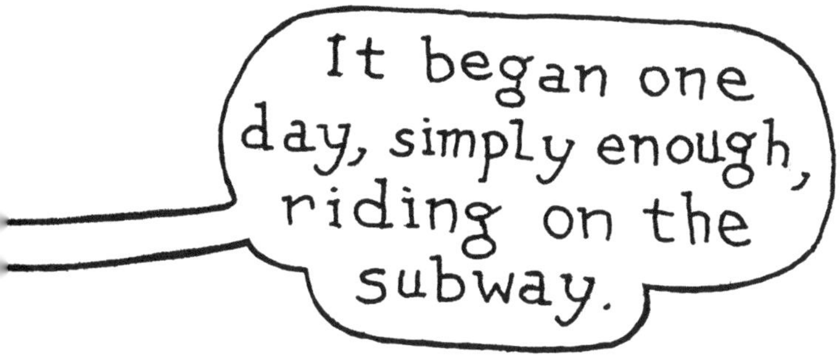
It began one day, simply enough, riding on the subway.

Kim forgot to bring something to read and he picked up a free newsletter for the Learning Annex, cheesy adult "courses" taught by reality TV show stars and people promising you that you, too, can make a killing in NY real estate. (Yep, I think Donald Trump advertised in one of those—who could have guessed?) I looked over his shoulder. Semi-seriously he announced that there was a course in past life regression that he thought he would take—he'd always had a story in mind around reincarnation and maybe it would be a good jumping-off point. So I flippantly said I'd do it, too. And just like that, we decided to phone and make a reservation.

What I didn't tell Kim was that I had been approached about past life regression before and the thought had sort of terrified me. I suffer from a potentially debilitating form of arthritis and more than once it had been suggested to me that I might try to go into my past lives to see what might have caused it. Well, I figured if I had either done something so awful in my past life, or even worse, had some dreadful injury that shook my joints to this day, that I sure as heck didn't want to know about it and relive it. Still, this was the Learning Annex—no need to take it seriously. It would be fun to do with Kim and if he was going to a past-life regression course I sure as heck wasn't going to miss it.

As it happened, the day we were scheduled to attend the evening class was a complicated one for me. It was a sunny and beautiful day as I remember, I want to say spring rather than full on summer. I was working for the Central Park Conservancy at the time, but had taken part of the day off to attend the funeral of Lydia Mananara, a woman I had worked with at the Metropolitan Museum for years. She wasn't much older than me and had died of breast cancer. I had cared for her cat, a lovely, plushy long-haired tabby-stripe, while she was in Italy seeking alternative treatment or perhaps just spending time with family there. After the funeral there was a reception at the Met where I saw former colleagues and met family and friends of hers I had not known. It was a strange moment of displacement having worked there for so long and being back for what may have been the first time since leaving.

That evening after work, Kim and I went down to Union Square to the address of what appeared to be some sort of school. I remember thinking that this was turning into one heck of a long day, and we trudged into a classroom with table desks pushed together to form a large U. There were about ten people in the room and they were as varied as the human content of any subway car on a given morning commute, a few young, some older, generally non-descript. The course instructor entered and he, too, was pretty generic, middle-aged and pale. He started out by telling his story.

Seems that when he was a kid a visiting hypnotist had come to town and he'd gone to see him perform. In what he'd later realize was an unusual vulnerability to hypnosis, he slipped easily into that state and, jarringly, into a past life. Frankly, I can't remember if he was actually the subject of the hypnotist or if he fell into the influence from the audience — the latter seems unlikely. Anyway, he went on to describe, in fairly horrific detail, being a small child running for safety to a root cellar from where he spied his family of prairie settlers terribly murdered by Indians. Of course he had no idea why he experienced it, but a number of years later he took the opportunity to be hypnotized again; this time he was an adult, hidden away on a mountainside witnessing the slaughter of other settlers by Indians once again. This time he understood it to be past lives and devoted future time and energy to developing the skill to hypnotize himself and travel back in time.

He ended his presentation and offered to help us all slip back into our past. He turned the lights down, but traffic thrummed out the window and florescent lights hummed in the hall. At first quieting my mind and focusing seemed unlikely. Still, I had developed some meditation chops and it didn't take very much for me to still my mind into the desired quiet before going to a "safe place" and then rolling back into something else.

He "woke" us up to wherever we had landed in our minds and asked us to look around. I was in the desert, a barefoot and nearly naked young man in my teens. The soil beneath my feet was sandy but hard and reddish. The teacher's voice instructed us to take note of the year (I want to say it was the 1880s, but I have trouble remembering that more precisely now) and things like who was President, to take note of our surroundings. I don't know who was President, and at first I thought I was in Tibet — a place I had been twice and had a great affinity for — but I gradually became aware that I was in the American West instead — and that I was a young Indian man. I was aware of being absolutely dirt poor, hungry, and not educated. I was essentially a dumb young kid.

His voice now guided me to go to the day I died and to take note of how I died. Seems like I died in a stupid fight with another kid — I don't know over what. He told us to take care now to apologize to any-

one I had hurt. I found myself apologizing to the guy who killed me, and then I apologized to my mother and my grandmother. I had left them alone when I died and it had been my responsibility to take care of them. I felt bad about it, but in a dispassionate sort of way. The instructor now guided us out of the past and into the current moment. He turned the lights on and suggested a break before we spoke about our experiences. Kim and I found a water fountain.

Kim: "Man, that was a waste. Nothing!" I looked at him surprised, "Really?" and quickly told him about my experience. We both wondered if somehow the teacher's own experiences related with Indians had influenced my subconscious. I didn't know about that, but I did know I wasn't looking forward to telling him that I had been an Indian!

After the break we sat back down in our seats. Kim and I were about middle. Like Kim, not everyone had experienced anything and only two other stories stood out for me that day which I remember. One was a not especially cogent tale of another planet, and this stayed with me because the instructor didn't seem to find it unusual and said that it happens. The other was quite moving. There was a young, attractive woman in her twenties who had found herself a bench at a bus stop near Union Square, but in the 1940s. It was July and very hot and she was nine months pregnant. She died in childbirth later, I think the same day. I wonder to this day what brought her to the Learning Annex that evening to have that experience.

As for me, I reported in the most straightforward way possible what I had seen and experienced. It certainly isn't the past I would have imagined for myself and yet that is what makes it compelling. As someone who has long been interested in Buddhism I can easily accept the concept of a past life, one in a parade. The idea of even a brief window into a past self that was so different than I: an impoverished Indian teenager who gets himself killed in a fight over something so trivial that it has been lost to time, and all that remains is the knowledge that I had been young and dumb and gotten myself killed when I should have been taking care of my mother and grandmother. I guess the good news is that I got a bit smarter over subsequent lives. The instructor did give me a bit of a fish eye — or maybe I imagined it. But I don't think my former Indian self was doing any of the killing he had witnessed.

I am not sure Kim believes that my experience wasn't entirely one of suggestion placed in my mind by the instructor's own stories. It was a day when I had already had my share of contemplating mortality and it is more than possible. All I can say is that bit of time in another body seemed real and different, and the poignant moment of apology one that had been a long time coming.

On that day I certainly didn't get any insights into the arthritis that troubles me, and it didn't lead to a desire to do it again and learn about other lives, if that is indeed possible. Instead, it left me with a strange sort of shiny spot in my memory. As if out of the dim past one small bit has been brought into high relief. Real or not, I keep it there like a talisman, a lucky penny, dropped from the past into my lap here in the future.

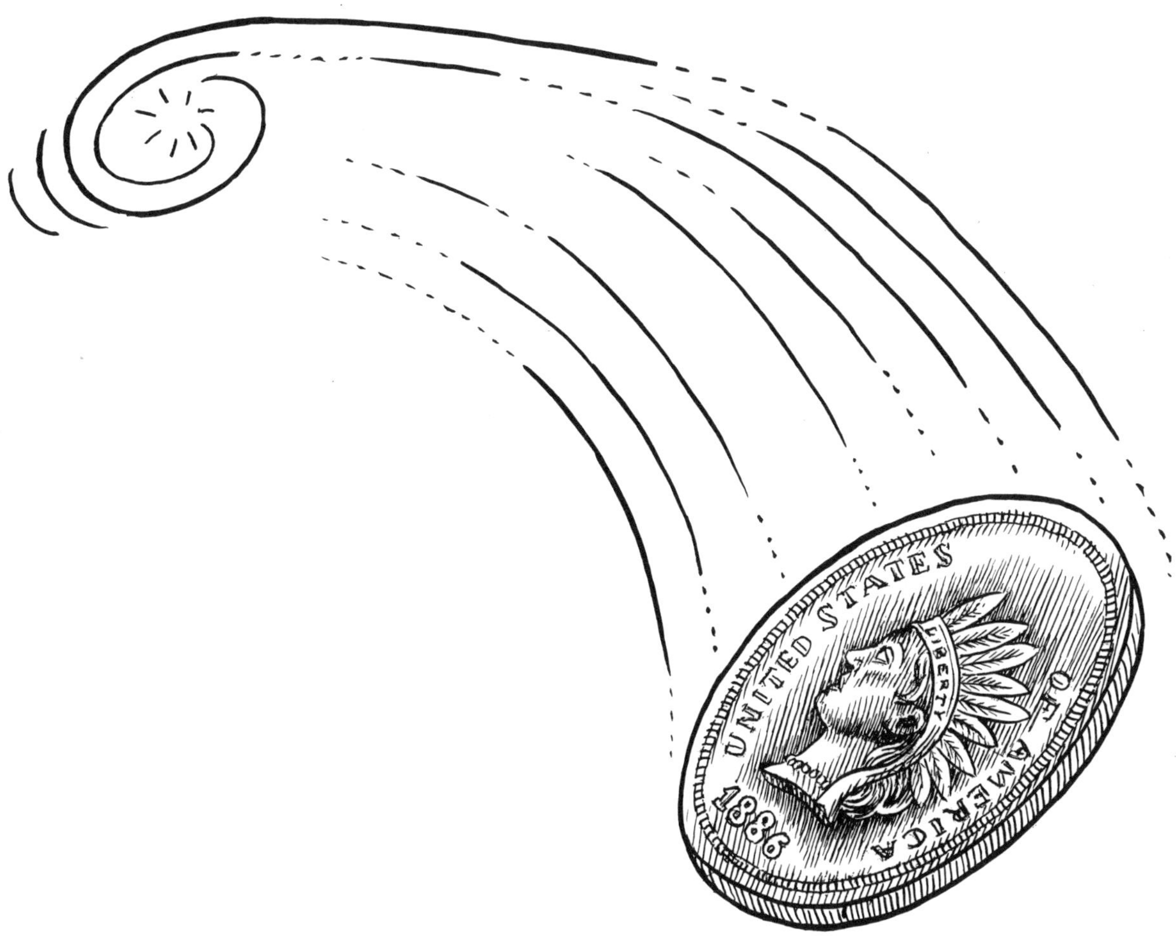
UNITED STATES
OF AMERICA
LIBERTY
1886

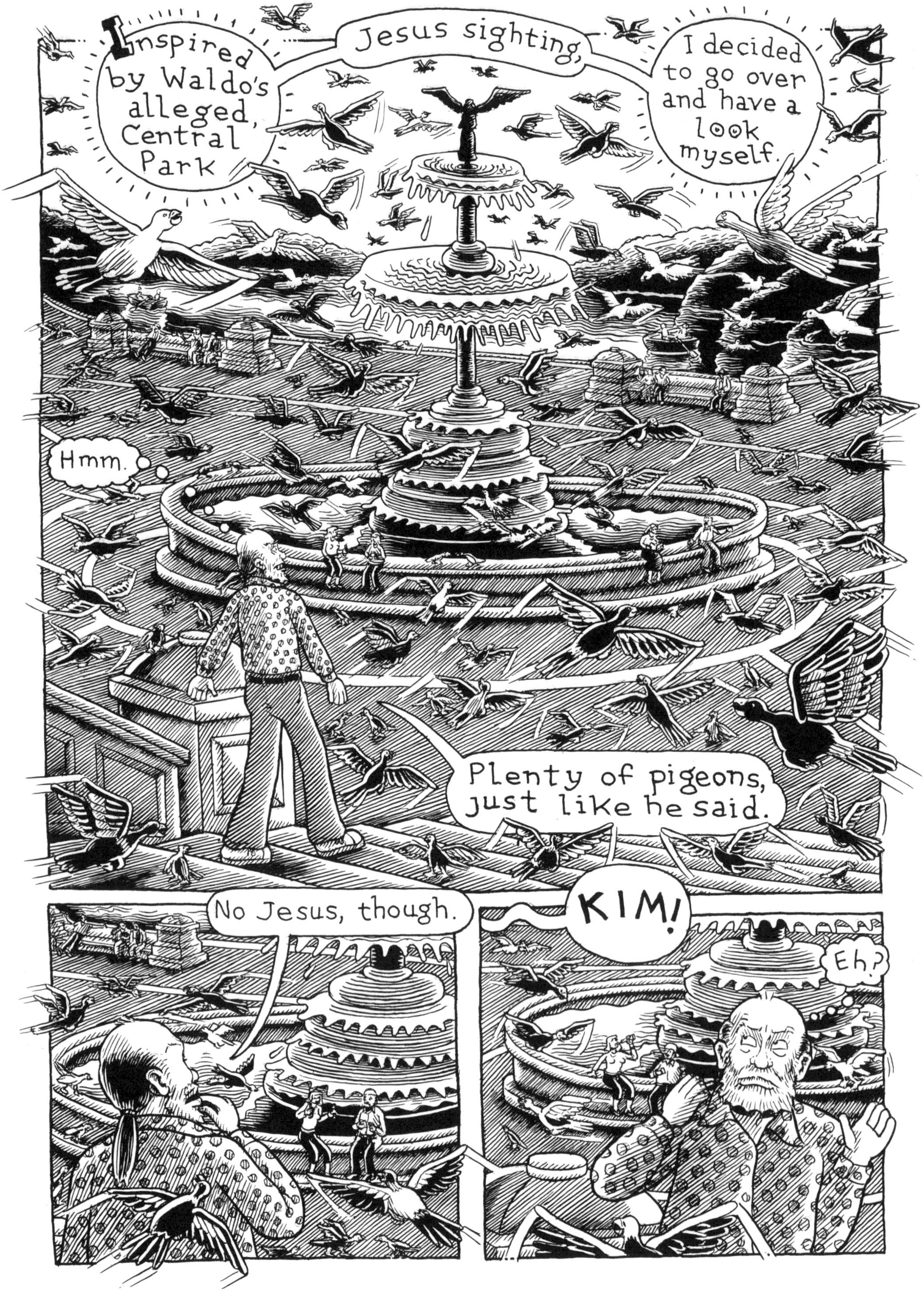
Inspired by Waldo's alleged, Central Park
Jesus sighting,
I decided to go over and have a look myself.
Hmm.
Plenty of pigeons, just like he said.
No Jesus, though.
KIM!
Eh?

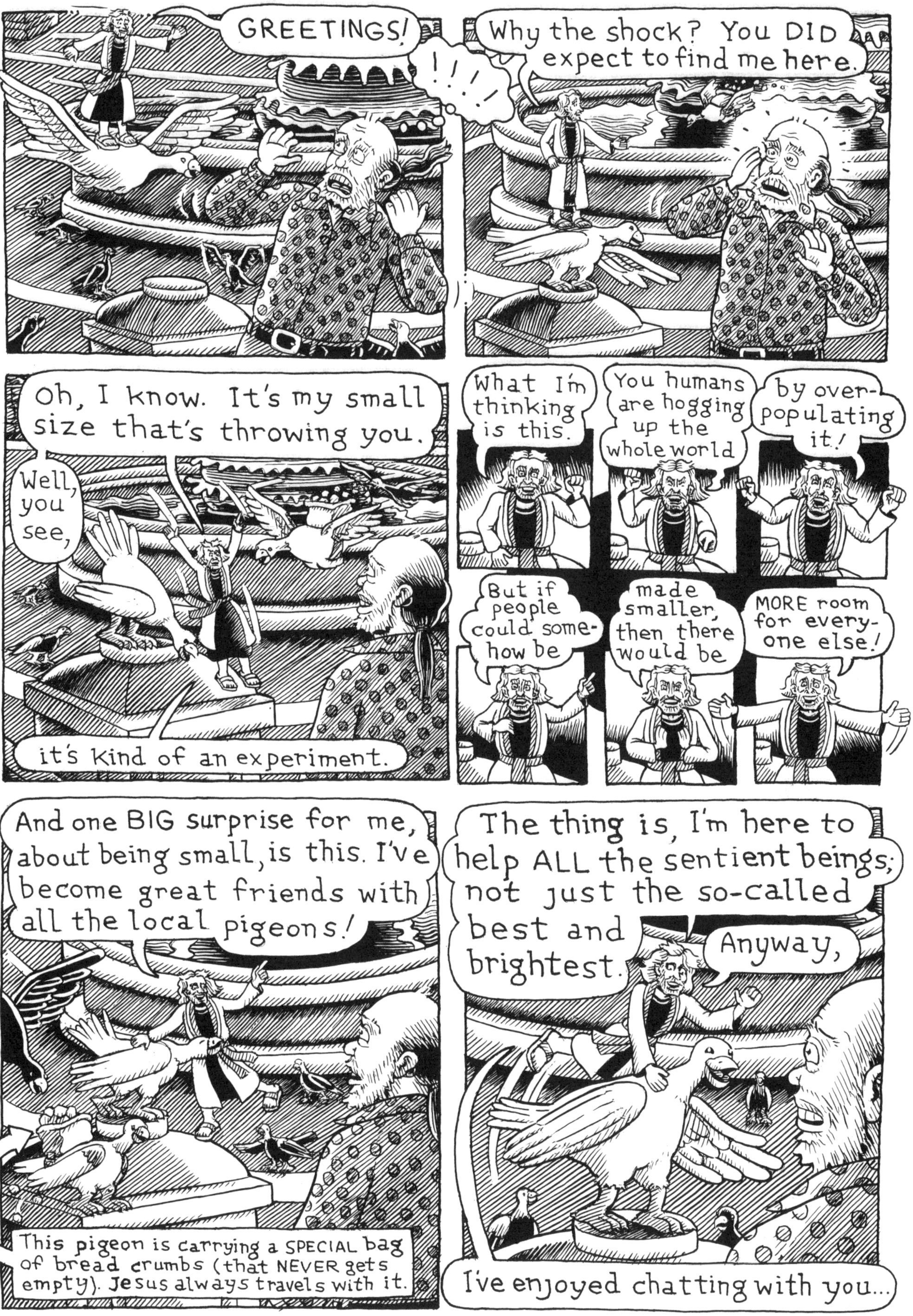
GREETINGS!
!!!!
Why the shock? You DID expect to find me here.
Oh, I know. It's my small size that's throwing you.
Well, you see,
it's kind of an experiment.
What I'm thinking is this.
You humans are hogging up the whole world
by over-populating it!
But if people could some-how be
made smaller, then there would be
MORE room for every-one else!
And one BIG surprise for me, about being small, is this. I've become great friends with all the local pigeons!
This pigeon is carrying a SPECIAL bag of bread crumbs (that NEVER gets empty). Jesus always travels with it.
The thing is, I'm here to help ALL the sentient beings; not just the so-called best and brightest.
Anyway,
I've enjoyed chatting with you...

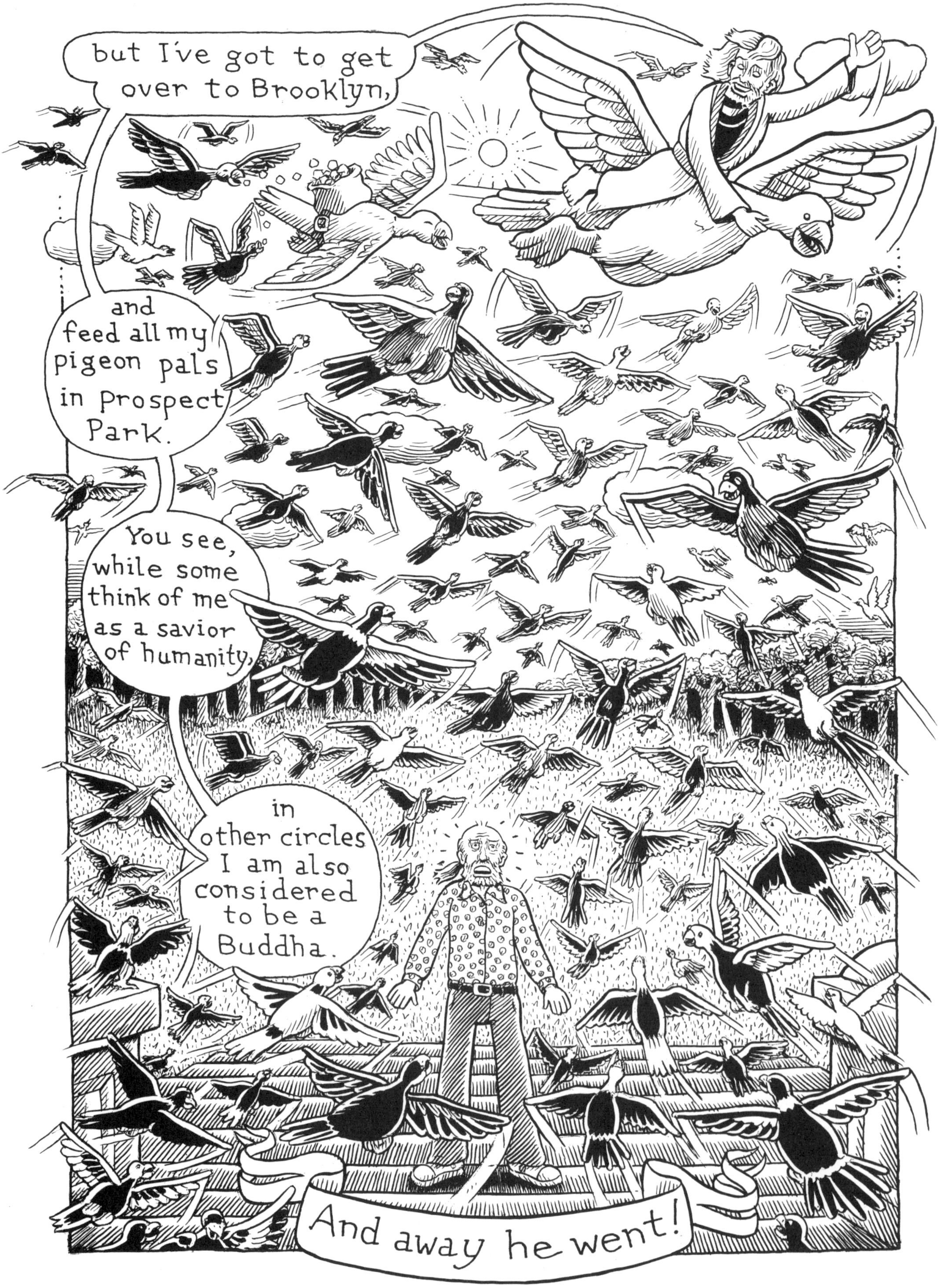
but I've got to get over to Brooklyn,
and feed all my pigeon pals in Prospect Park.
You see, while some think of me as a savior of humanity,
in other circles I am also considered to be a Buddha.
And away he went!

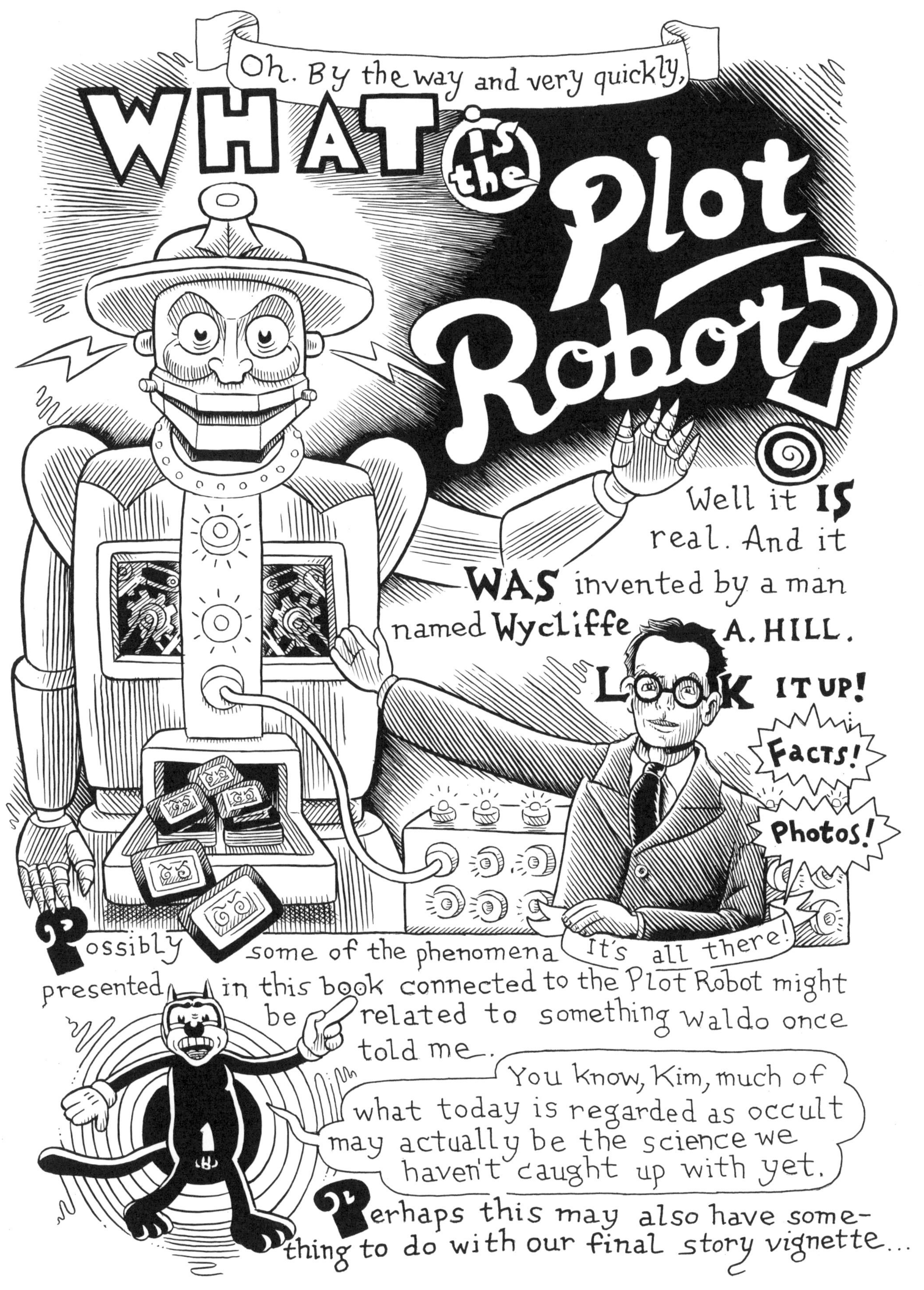

Oh. By the way and very quickly,
WHAT is the Plot Robot?
Well it IS real. And it WAS invented by a man named Wycliffe A. HILL.
LOOK IT UP!
Facts!
Photos!
It's all there!
Possibly some of the phenomena presented in this book connected to the Plot Robot might be related to something Waldo once told me...
You know, Kim, much of what today is regarded as occult may actually be the science we haven't caught up with yet.
Perhaps this may also have something to do with our final story vignette...

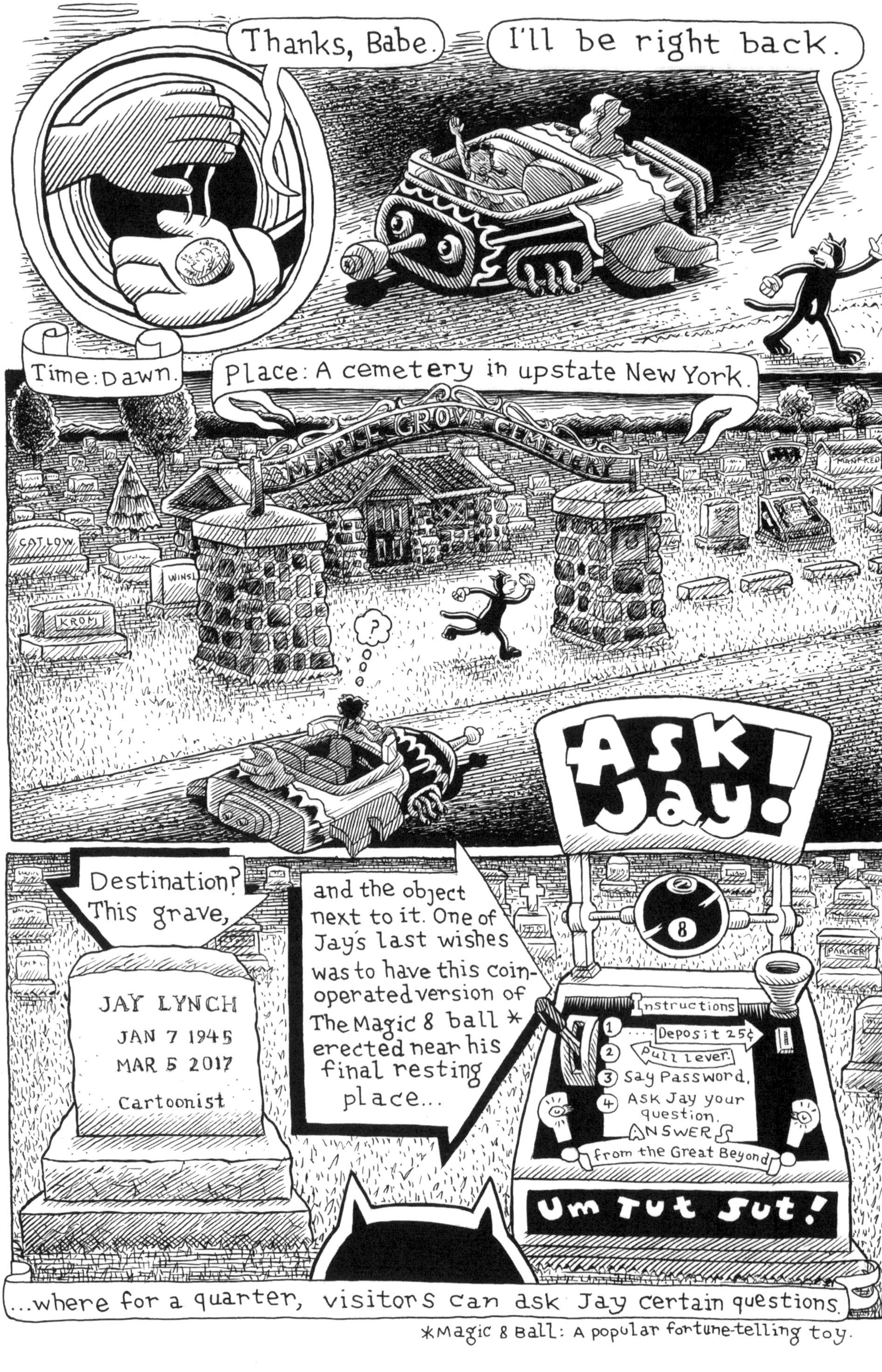
Thanks, Babe.
I'll be right back.
Time: Dawn.
Place: A cemetery in upstate New York.
MAPLE GROVE CEMETERY
CATLOW
WINSL
KROM
MANFRED
ASK Jay!
Destination? This grave,
and the object next to it. One of Jay's last wishes was to have this coin-operated version of The Magic 8 ball * erected near his final resting place...
JAY LYNCH
JAN 7 1945
MAR 5 2017
Cartoonist
PARKER
Instructions
1 Deposit 25¢
2 Pull lever.
3 Say Password.
4 Ask Jay your question.
ANSWERS
from the Great Beyond
Um Tut Sut!
...where for a quarter, visitors can ask Jay certain questions.
*Magic 8 Ball: A popular fortune-telling toy.

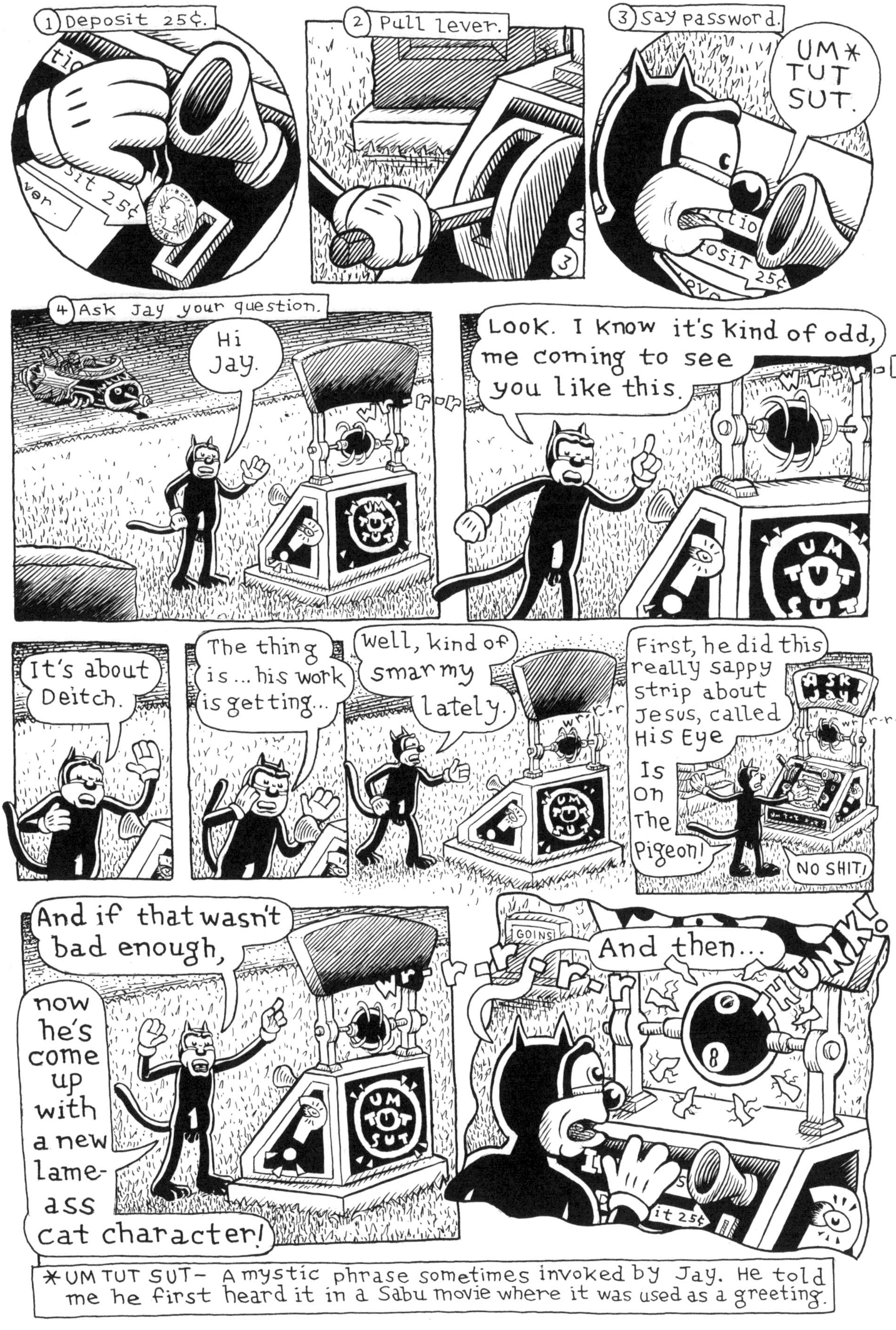

1 Deposit 25¢.
2 Pull lever.
3 Say password.
UM* TUT SUT.
4 Ask Jay your question.
Hi Jay.
wr-r-r-r
Look. I know it's kind of odd, me coming to see you like this.
wr-r-r-r-r
It's about Deitch.
The thing is... his work is getting...
Well, kind of smarmy lately.
First, he did this really sappy strip about Jesus, called His Eye Is On The Pigeon!
NO SHIT!
And if that wasn't bad enough,
now he's come up with a new lame-ass cat character!
wr-r-r-r
And then...
THUNK!
*UM TUT SUT- A mystic phrase sometimes invoked by Jay. He told me he first heard it in a Sabu movie where it was used as a greeting.

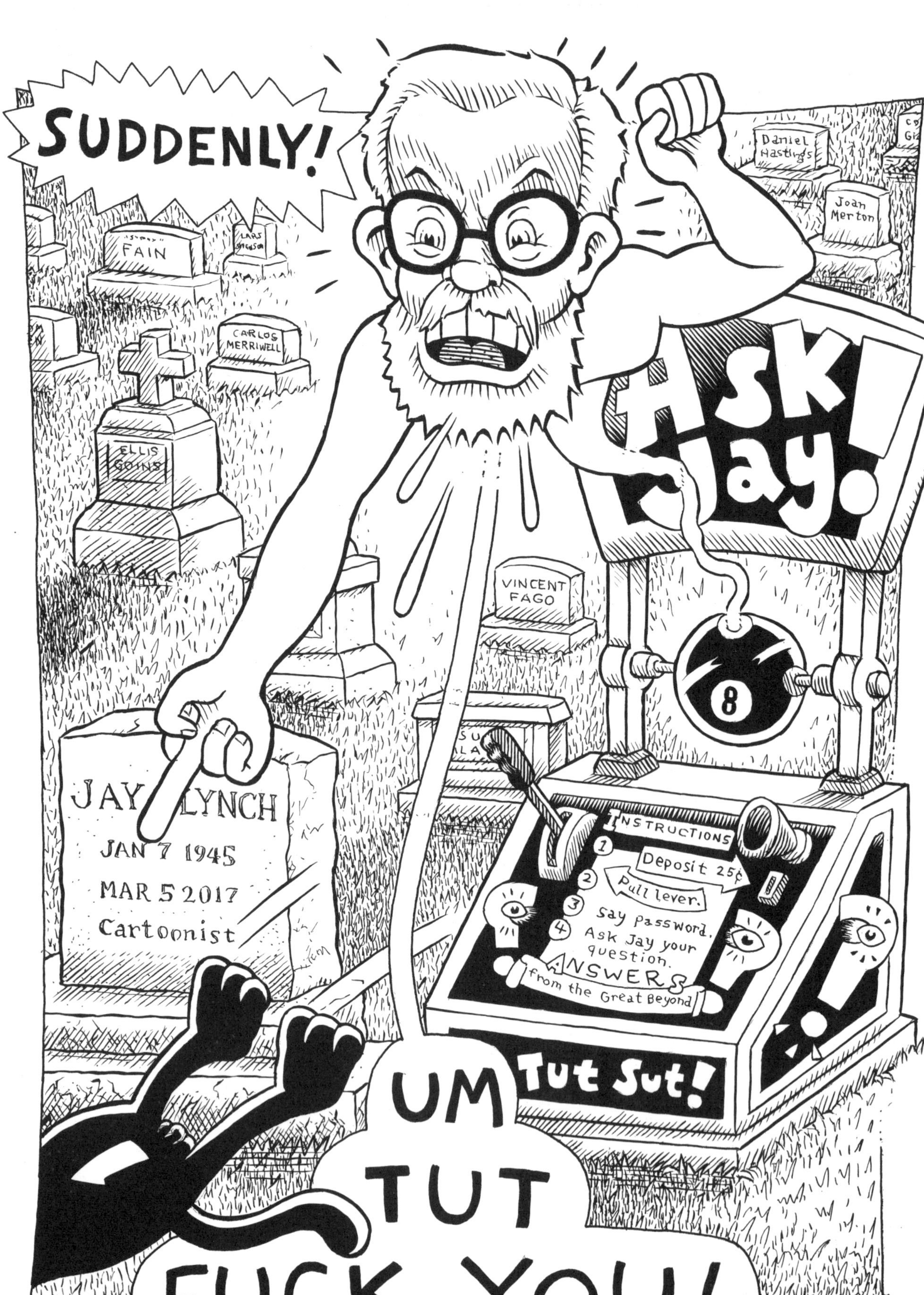
SUDDENLY!
FAIN
CARLOS MERRIWELL
ELLIS GOINS
Daniel Hastings
Joan Merton
VINCENT FAGO
JAY LYNCH
JAN 7 1945
MAR 5 2017
Cartoonist
ASK Jay!
8
INSTRUCTIONS
1 Deposit 25¢
2 Pull lever.
3 Say password.
4 Ask Jay your question.
ANSWERS from the Great Beyond
Tut Sut!
UM TUT FUCK YOU!
That's all Folks!

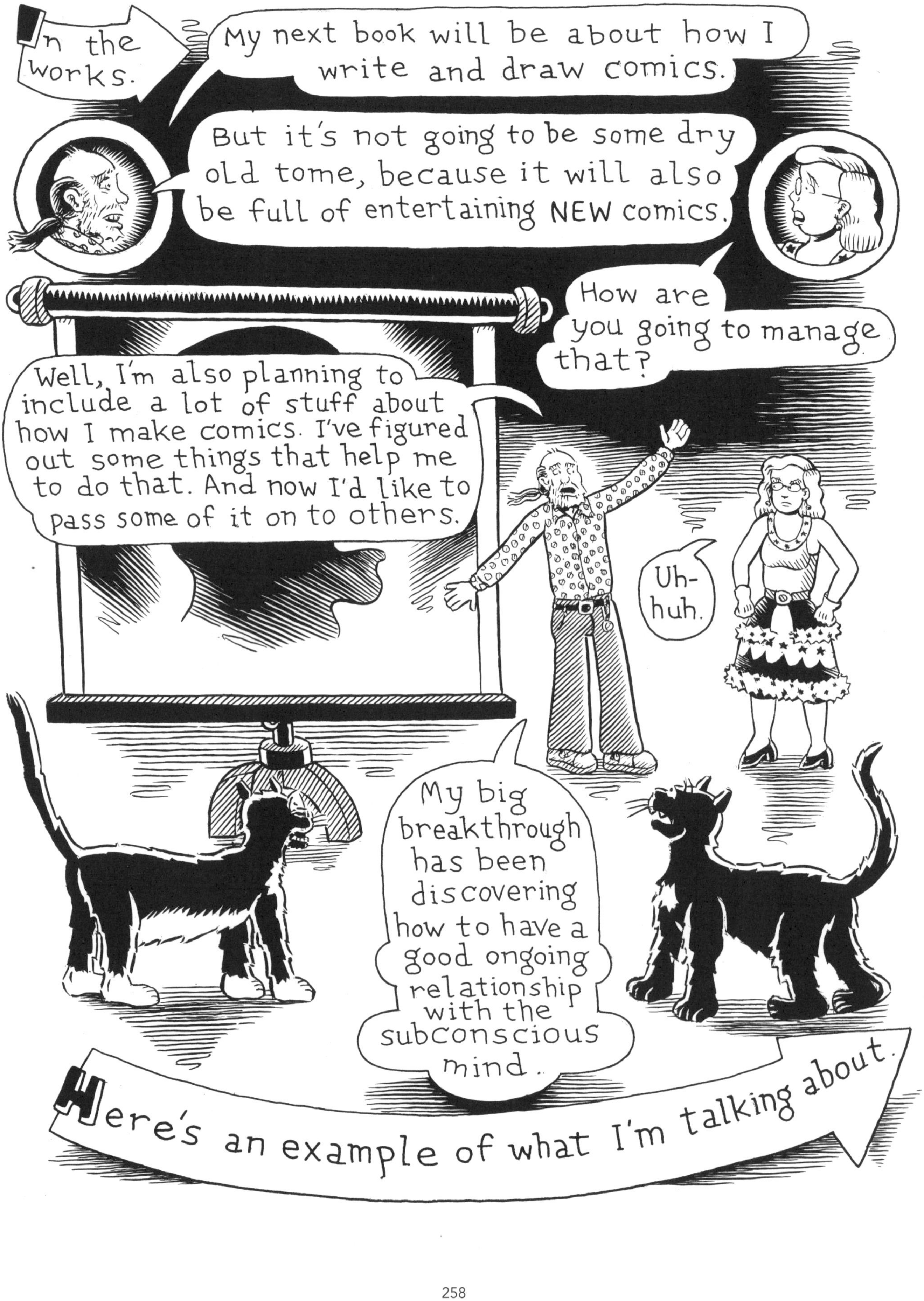
In the works.
My next book will be about how I write and draw comics.
But it's not going to be some dry old tome, because it will also be full of entertaining NEW comics.
How are you going to manage that?
Well, I'm also planning to include a lot of stuff about how I make comics. I've figured out some things that help me to do that. And now I'd like to pass some of it on to others.
Uh-huh.
My big breakthrough has been discovering how to have a good ongoing relationship with the subconscious mind.
Here's an example of what I'm talking about.

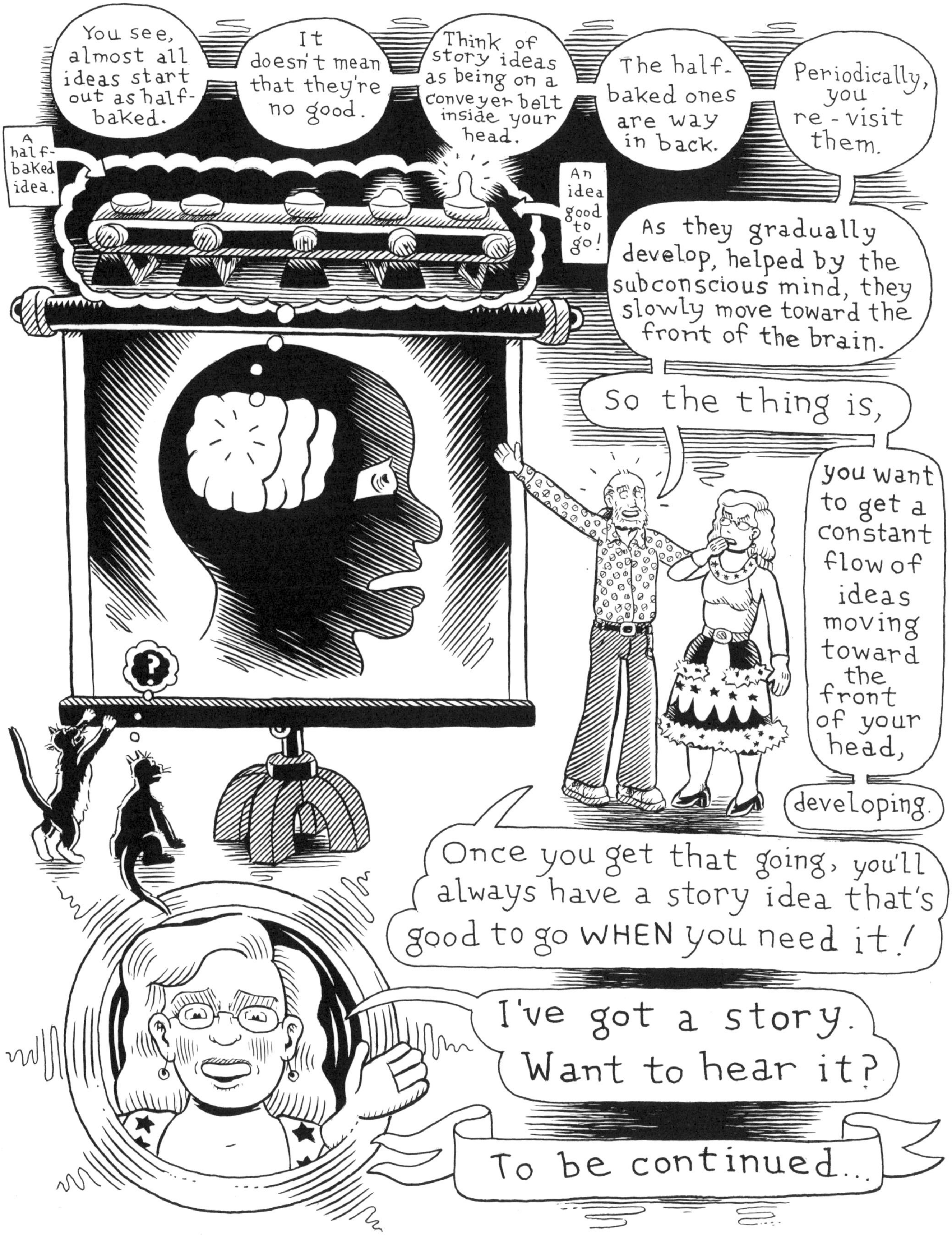

You see, almost all ideas start out as half-baked.
It doesn't mean that they're no good.
Think of story ideas as being on a conveyer belt inside your head.
The half-baked ones are way in back.
Periodically, you re-visit them.
A half-baked idea.
An idea good to go!
As they gradually develop, helped by the subconscious mind, they slowly move toward the front of the brain.
So the thing is,
you want to get a constant flow of ideas moving toward the front of your head,
developing.
Once you get that going, you'll always have a story idea that's good to go WHEN you need it!
I've got a story. Want to hear it?
To be continued...

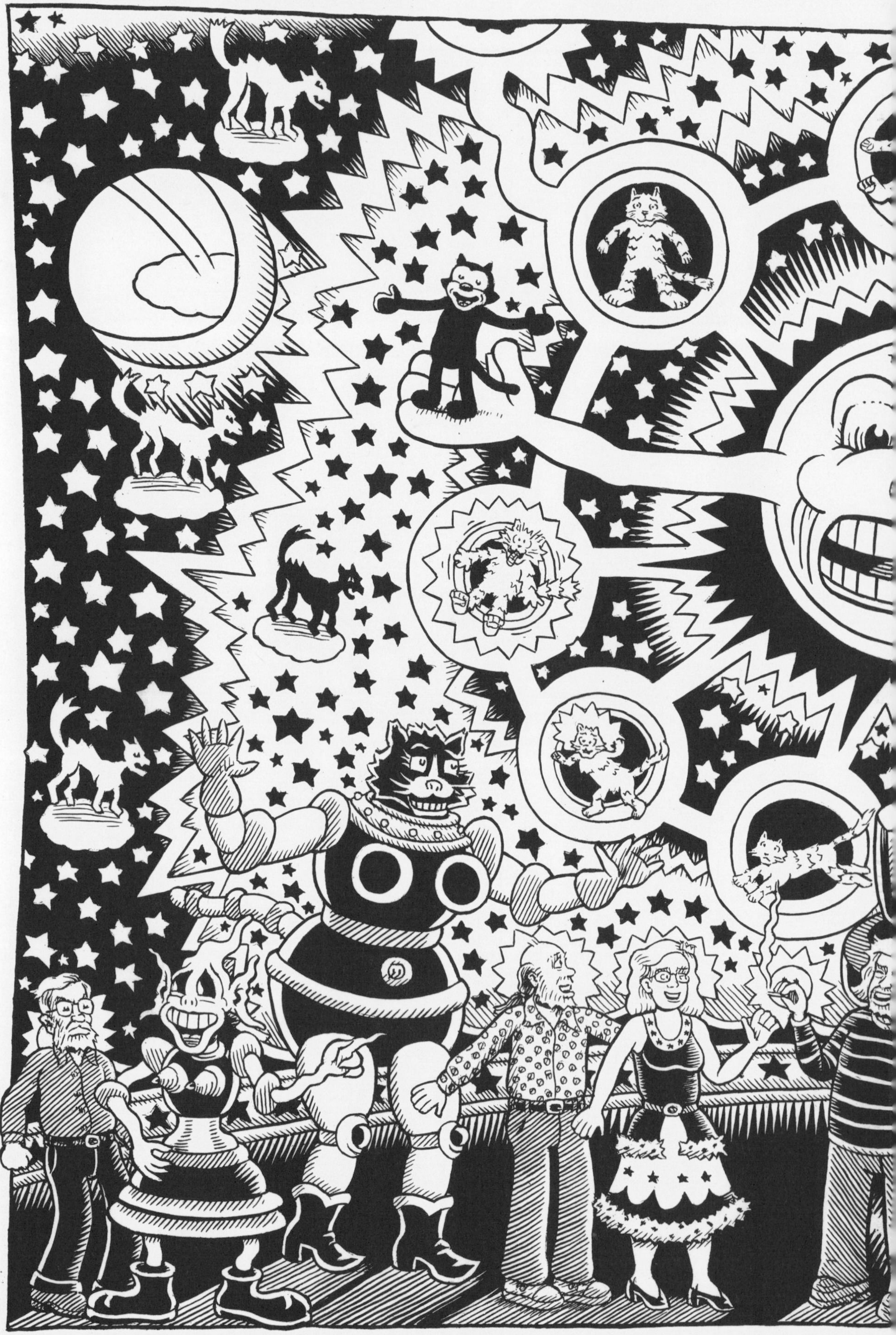